THE EARLY YEARS:

Foundations for Best Practice With Special Children and Their Families

Gail L. Ensher and David A. Clark
with contributing authors

ZERO TO THREE
Early connections last a lifetime

Washington, DC

Published by

ZERO TO THREE
Early connections last a lifetime

ZERO TO THREE
1255 23rd St., NW, Ste. 350
Washington, DC 20037
(202) 638-1144
Toll-free orders (800) 899-4301
Fax: (202) 638-0851
Web: http://www.zerotothree.org

10 9 8 7 6 5 4 3 2 1

ISBN 978-1-938558-55-9

Printed in the United States of America

Suggestion citations:
Book citation: Ensher, G. L., & Clark, D. A. (Eds.). (2016). *The early years: Foundations for best practice with special children and their families.* Washington, DC: ZERO TO THREE.
Chapter citation: Fisher, M. A. (2016). Neurologic development of infants and young children. In G. L. Ensher & D. A. Clark (Eds.). *The early years: Foundations for best practice with special children and their families* (pp. 73–107). Washington, DC: ZERO TO THREE.

Table of Contents

PART 2: SCREENING AND ASSESSMENT OF INFANTS AND YOUNG CHILDREN

CHAPTER 6: Evaluating Infants and Young Children in the First Years. 133
Gail L. Ensher and David A. Clark

PART 3: MEDICAL AND DEVELOPMENTAL PROBLEMS IN INFANTS AND YOUNG CHILDREN 155

CHAPTER 7: Genetic Disorders and Their Impact in Early Infancy 157
Darius Adams and David A. Clark

CHAPTER 8: Hearing: Development and Disorders 183
Joaquim M.B. Pinheiro

CHAPTER 13: Autism and Pervasive Developmental Disorders in Young Children 269
Ellen B. Barnes and Lori Saile

PART 4: COLLABORATIVE CARE, COMMUNITY NETWORKS, AND EARLY INTERVENTION

CHAPTER 14: Families of Young Children in a Contemporary World
Gail L. Ensher and David A. Clark

CHAPTER 15: Mental Health Issues of Children in Military Families
Colleen M. Guthrie, Gail L. Ensher, and David A. Clark

Acknowledgments

Books and their respective chapters bear the names of those primarily responsible for the written word. However, those of us engaged in such efforts know very well that the conception, development, and delivery of these works extend far beyond identified authorship. In recognition of this fact, we are deeply indebted to the following people who have touched our lives and shaped our thinking, and thus made this book possible over the past 3 years:

- Children and grandchildren—those who are no longer with us, those who are growing and thriving, and those yet to be born

- Families and young children whom we have known and worked with across the years

- Students who have challenged us, worked with us, and taught us lessons that we otherwise would not have known

- Special people without whose devoted hours and expertise this manuscript would not have been completed: staff at the Jowonio School in Syracuse, New York; all of our contributing authors; Jeanne Marie Schmidt; Maithreyee Dube; Michelle Mondo; Janis Keehan; and Stefanie Powers and Jennifer Li at ZERO TO THREE, who opened the door for publication of this manuscript, offering invaluable suggestions throughout the process of preparation.

Dedication

The Early Years: Foundations for Best Practice With Special Children and Their Families is dedicated to Dr. Martin "Marty" C. Michaels, who suffered an untimely death in December 2011. Dr. Michaels was a beloved, highly respected pediatrician and "healing advocate," who devoted years of his life to the health care and well-being of families and young children in his community and family practice. He has been sorely missed by all who knew him. We also dedicate this book to the many families, infants, and young children with special health care needs and disabilities with whom we have worked.

INTRODUCTION

Infants and Young Children—Birth to 3

Philosophy and Goals of the Book

Working with infants, young children, and families with special health care needs and disabilities is rewarding, heartwarming, often emotional, usually demanding, complex, and rarely easy! It requires special expertise that crosses multiple fields of training, frequently challenging one beyond comfort levels of knowledge and experience. In addition, this work involves efforts in which social, medical, educational, economic, political, and legal arenas often converge, with no clearly defined answers or solutions. Under the best circumstances, families find it difficult to hear that there may be problems with their baby or young child, because such news inevitably opens a series of unanticipated and unknown experiences. This book is designed to build a foundation of information, strategies, recommendations, and resources for students and professionals who are working, or who intend to work, with infants and children in their earliest months and years of life and their families.

The Early Years: Foundations for Best Practice With Special Children and Their Families is grounded in a strength-based, relationship-centered, ecological perspective of best practices for working in partnership with families and their infants and toddlers with special health care needs and disabilities. The book draws upon the most up-to-date research relating to medical, developmental, clinical, and psycho-educational practices and interventions for developing competence to meet the needs of increasingly diverse groups of families and their young children from birth to 3 years old. The text focuses on ways in which professionals across disciplines can best collaborate with one another and with families to support and enhance the growth and development of infants and toddlers who are challenged with medical and developmental issues. Especially important is the concept of "role release," that is, providers sharing information in professional partnership rather than claiming exclusive ownership of decision making, because professionals commonly work in co-treatment and collaborative situations across disciplines. Finally, the book is rooted in the philosophy that, regardless of the family struggles, there *always* are strengths to draw from that support parents' and caregivers' resilience to move beyond adversity.

For us as authors, medical, educational, and clinical developments in our respective fields have been most significant to our deciding to write this text. First, as educators and professionals, we now know that what happens early in new relationships matters a great deal for both parents or caregivers and newborns. When interactions start well, they form a foundation and set the stage for a lifetime of positive learning, growth, and development. The importance of early relationships is especially important to keep in mind in light of the major technological, economic, and sociocultural changes that have emerged in the United States over the past decade because infants are able to survive when born as early as 23 to 24 weeks' gestation, weighing little more than a pound. These extremely premature infants invariably require prolonged hospital stays that are challenging for families, and they are more likely to later present a range of neurological and developmental problems. Intervening early and partnering with families can be a stabilizing, positive benefit for parents living with such uncertainties, with well-informed professionals affording important touchpoints for building healthy relationships between caregivers and their infants and young children, especially those identified with special health care needs and disabilities.

A second important dynamic in the lives of American families today relates to the hard economic times experienced by increasing numbers of parents. Recent surveys indicate that 1 out of every 5 young children in the United States is part of a family struggling with poverty, experiencing daily worries about putting food on the table (Wight, Chau, & Aratani, 2011). Accordingly, more two-parent families are working, there are more single-parent families, and often infants and young children are in day care for extended hours, most days of the week (Division of Early Childhood & National Association for the Education of Young Children, 2009). As a result, families have less time together as cohesive units. If parents have an infant or toddler

with special health care needs or disabilities, they experience the added stress of finding appropriate caregiving arrangements that can be difficult, if not impossible, to locate. All of these factors have far-reaching ramifications for caregivers raising infants and very young children in an often precariously chaotic and unsympathetic world. Should these youngest consumers qualify for services, all of these factors converge, having a significant impact on the nature of early intervention offered and the building of relationships within the respective families. Moreover, since the turn of the 21st century, these variables have been coupled with an enormous shift toward an increasingly diverse society in terms of culture, ethnicity, family membership, education, and parental age, along with continuing social issues such as teen pregnancies and children from birth to 2 years old being the most rapidly growing group referred to child protective services and the child welfare system (Dicker, 2009). Finally, as noted previously, although technology has enhanced the survival of newborns, the hoped-for improvement in developmental outcomes is yet to be fully realized. Infants with significant special needs continue to be born, and growing numbers of toddlers continue to be identified with behavioral or developmental disabilities, or both.

Audience for the Book

The Early Years: Foundations for Best Practice With Special Children and Their Families is a basic text that offers essential information for working with families, infants, and young children from birth to 3 years old with special health care needs and disabilities. The book focuses on the first 3 years, the period when infants and toddlers with significant health care needs and more severe disabilities often are identified. The text is foundational yet comprehensive in content and is appropriate for students in higher education preparing to work with families and diverse populations of young children and for professionals across multiple disciplines, including early childhood special educators, itinerant early interventionists, clinical professionals (speech, occupational, and physical therapists), psychologists and family therapists, nurses working with newborns and young children, social workers, mental health professionals, and family practice pediatricians. The book also is an important resource for personnel working with infants and toddlers in family and community day care settings and professionals working with infants and young children in the child welfare system. Last, it is hoped that through the inclusion of a wide variety of vignettes by families and of relationship-centered, family-focused strategies, parents of infants and young children with special health care needs and developmental disabilities also will find the book to be an important and informative resource.

Organization of the Book

This book is organized into four major sections and includes features intended to enhance reader learning, understanding, and practical application. Each chapter begins with a set of *Highlights* in order to focus the reader on key elements of the discussion, and concludes with a section on *Implications for Parents and Professionals* that is designed to offer parents and professionals specific strategies for integrating information given in the chapter into child-rearing and best professional practices. Although the target audience of parents and caregivers, students in training, and professionals across disciplines is broad, these are the groups with whom infants and young children primarily interact, who ultimately have a major role in their physical, mental health,

and developmental well-being in the earliest years. Further, although this book is designed to be a professional resource, a major goal of the authors has been to develop a text that is reader-friendly and jargon-free so that it is also accessible to families.

This Introduction focuses on three questions:

- Who are the children?
- Who are the families?
- Who are the service providers?

The remaining sections and chapters of the book then follow a progression, moving from Part 1, typical child development and well-being of infants and toddlers, to Part 2, screening, assessment, and evaluation of newborns, infants, and toddlers when there are concerns, to Part 3, major medical and developmental conditions often seen in infants and toddlers during the first 3 years, to Part 4, strategies and best practices for collaborative care, developing community networks, and early intervention in hospital, home, and community settings. The book concludes with an Afterword that offers a look ahead toward new developments in the medical, clinical, and psycho-educational fields of evidence-based research, service, and best practices. Vignettes, photos, charts, and other practical and illustrative information are infused throughout the text.

Partners in the Process

If there was one word that would best describe *partners in the process* about whom this book is written, it would be *diversity*—in terms of the infants and toddlers, families, and those who offer professional services.

Who Are the Children?

Children from birth to 3 years old who have special health care needs or disabilities represent a quilt of many colors and fabrics. Among others, noteworthy groups of children discussed in this book include the following:

- **Late-preterm infants.** The rate of prematurity in the United States is estimated to be 12.7%, one of the highest rates of preterm births among the industrialized nations (Ensher & Clark, 2011). More than 70% of the premature babies born in the United States are "late-preterm" babies (delivered between 34 [0/7] and 36 [6/7] weeks gestation), who may later manifest behavioral, communication, and feeding challenges or be diagnosed with pervasive developmental disorders, or both (Engle, Tomashek, & Wallman, 2007).

- **Infants born with special health care needs and/or multiple impairments.** Over the past decade, new technologies in the medical fields have resulted in survival rates of infants delivered at increasingly shorter gestational ages (i.e., 23 to 24 weeks being the current limit of viability), that often are paralleled with growing numbers of these newborns having multiple special needs and impairments (Ensher & Clark, 2011; Ensher, Clark, & Songer, 2009).

- **Multiple gestation births.** With the increased use of fertility drugs and other assistive reproductive technologies, multiple gestation births in the United States over the past 10 years have escalated, with "> 1% of US births occurring following use of assisted reproductive technology (ART)" (Reefhuis et al., 2009, p. 360; Squires & Kaplan, 2007). Likely as a result of several factors, studies "suggest that some birth defects occur more often among infants conceived with ART" (Reefhuis et al., 2009, p. 360).

- **Infants and young children diagnosed with pervasive developmental and autism spectrum disorders.** Whether as a result of increased vigilance of parents and pediatricians, earlier diagnosis of symptoms, changes in definitions, or an actual change in incidence, more young children in the United States are being identified as having pervasive developmental and autism spectrum disorders. Typically, a diagnosis of autism has been made between 2 and 3 years old, when toddlers have manifested delays in talking and communication; however, new research is pointing to even earlier diagnoses of symptoms as young as 12 months old (ScienceDaily, 2011). In 2009, the "latest estimate of autism prevalence in the United States, as reported by the Centers for Disease Control, was 1 in 110 children" (Autism Speaks Official Blog, 2010), with more recently released statistics in 2012 suggesting even higher estimates (1 in 88 children with 1 in 54 boys identified; ScienceDaily, 2012).

- **Young children living in poverty.** Recent estimates are that more than 15 million American children live in families that meet federal guidelines for being considered poverty level, which vary by state and the number of family members. From 2000 to 2009, the number of children living in poverty increased by 33% (i.e., 3.8 million more children in 2009 than in 2000; Wight et al., 2011). Moreover, based on a study including more than 2,000 caregivers of low income with young children between 4 and 36 months old at five pediatric clinic/emergency department sites (Arkansas, Maryland, Massachusetts, Minnesota, and Pennsylvania), conducted by the Children's Sentinel Nutritional Assessment Program, 21% of the children lived in food-insecure households, and 14% were developmentally "at risk" (Rose-Jacobs et al., 2008).

- **Infants and young children exposed to "toxic stress."** Toxic stress among infants and toddlers emerges from many sources of adversity including combinations of demographic, family, and environmental factors (Osofsky & Lieberman, 2011). For example,

  — More than 150,000 young children under 6 years old were in foster care in 2003 (Knitzer & Lefkowitz, 2006), and more than 100,000 babies presently are living with families in the child welfare system without a consistent caregiver (Dicker, 2009).

  — More than 300,000 young children have incarcerated parents; at least 50% of these children are infants and toddlers (Knitzer & Lefkowitz, 2006).

  — Largely as a result of the growing incidence of poverty, an estimated 550,000 young children are living in homeless families (Knitzer & Lefkowitz, 2006).

  — Every year more than 175,000 infants and toddlers are victims of substantiated abuse and neglect, with young children under 3 years old having the highest rate of victim investigations, abuse, and neglect, and these incidents are highly likely to reoccur (Knitzer & Lefkowitz, 2006).

The relationship between neurological changes that can develop among infants and young children with chronic exposure to aversive stimuli and conditions has been noted by many scholars (National Research Council & Institute of Medicine, 2000). Although some of the problems created as a result of prolonged stays in neonatal intensive care units have been addressed in recent years with clustered medical care, the use of anesthesia, and protective environments (Ensher et al., 2009), other risks and influences embedded in the social ecology of American culture continue to have a spiraling negative impact, still largely unabated by preventative measures and programs.

Who Are the Families?

When professionals perform early intervention work with young children from birth to 3 years old, they focus as much on families as on their infants and toddlers. Individual Family Service Plans that are written with service providers are developed with families as the cornerstone of goals, objectives, priorities, and strategies on behalf of the respective children. Intervention programs often are carried out within the natural environment of the family home, with siblings and parents or caregivers present. If a child is receiving medical treatment in a hospital, decisions must include the family. Further, more and more medical staffs of neonatal intensive care units across the country are realizing that their environments need to be parent sensitive and caregiver instructive, so that when newborns leave the hospital, families can carry on the essential "work" of parenthood, nurturing and building relationships with their newest family members.

To be sure, family members may have their own unique challenges that warrant specific interventions, mentoring, rehabilitation, or special support and treatment. For instance, some parents are:

- struggling with substance abuse
- living with partners in abusive relationships
- single, separating from spouses, and/or feeling isolated
- struggling financially
- adolescents who are still growing up and maturing

- struggling to heal from histories of child abuse and neglect
- struggling with depression or other mental health concerns

More than one of the foregoing issues may be profoundly affecting their individual lives as well as those of other family members, especially the children.

Accordingly, caregivers and their children come to service providers as a "package," connected by residence and relationship to one another—with all of their individual needs and collective strengths. The task for service providers thus becomes finding and highlighting qualities of resilience in order to maximize the potentials and beneficial outcomes of all members of the family.

Who Are the Service Providers?

Professionals providing services for infants and young children with special health care needs and disabilities must bring to families a wealth of knowledge, experience, and understanding from many diverse backgrounds and disciplines. Among the multiple specialists and service providers who may, at any one time, be involved with infants, toddlers, and their families, the following are likely to play significant roles if a young child has special health care needs, disabilities, or both: pediatricians, neonatologists, neurologists, orthopedists, or physicians in other areas of specialty; nurses; early childhood educators; family service coordinators; child life specialists; physical, speech, and occupational therapists; social workers; nutritionists; psychologists; marriage and family therapists; and professionals within the judicial system. Each of these has a specific body of knowledge, skills, training, and expertise. However, professionals across all disciplines also require a unique set of proficiencies and

dispositions that facilitate best practices with families, infants, and their young children who have special needs. At a minimum, these abilities are:

- to listen to all members of the family, including parents, siblings, and the child with special needs
- to have an understanding of all developmental domains no matter their own discipline, in light of the extensive interactions among developmental areas across the birth-to-3 age range
- to value the priorities and goals expressed by family members
- to use a strength-based, solution-oriented perspective in working with parents and colleagues regarding challenges (medical, developmental, collaborative, or interactive)
- to communicate information to families in clear and jargon-free language
- to allow families "wait" time (as circumstances permit) so that they can process hard-to-hear information
- to support families who are grieving the death of a child
- to value and respect the diversity of families, including their cultures, ethnicities, languages, educational backgrounds, family membership, and economic circumstances, which may vary from those of the respective service provider
- to discern and highlight diverse family strengths
- to include families as equal partners in the decision-making processes of caring for, treating, and educating their infants and toddlers, to the extent possible
- to set aside personal agendas in the team process with families and professional colleagues

- to learn from professional experiences with families and colleagues, without self-judgment
- to be flexible in accommodating the needs and schedules of families and other professional colleagues
- to be able to network across agencies and professional systems of service
- to make inevitably difficult decisions with families, while at the same time suspending judgment

In the full scope and process of working with infants, young children, and their families, professionals with abilities and skills, or in disciplines other than those mentioned here may be needed; however, from our perspective, the skills noted above are the most paramount, as well as the most common across disciplines.

References

Autism Speaks Official Blog. (2010, October 22). *What is causing the increase in autism prevalence?* Retrieved from http://blog.autismspeaks.org/2010/10/22got-questions-answers-to-your-questions

Dicker, S. (2009). *Reversing the odds: Improving outcomes for babies in the child welfare system.* Baltimore, MD: Brookes.

Division for Early Childhood & National Association for the Education of Young Children. (2009). *Early childhood inclusion: A joint position statement of the Division for Early Childhood (DEC) and the National Association for the Education of Young Children (NAEYC).* Chapel Hill: The University of North Carolina, FPG Child Development Institute. Retrieved from http://npdci.fpg.unc.edu/resources/articles/Early_Childhood_Inclusion

Engle, W. A., Tomashek, K. M., & Wallman, C. (2007). "Late-preterm" infants: A population at risk. *Pediatrics, 120*(6), 1390–1401.

Ensher, G. L., & Clark, D. A. (2011). *Relationship-centered practices in early childhood: Working with families, infants, and young children at risk.* Baltimore, MD: Brookes.

Ensher, G. L., Clark, D. A., & Songer, N. (Eds.). (2009). *Families, infants, and young children at risk: Pathways to best practice* (pp. 211–234). Baltimore, MD: Brookes

Knitzer, J., & Lefkowitz, J. (2006, January). *Helping the most vulnerable infants, toddlers, and their families.* National Center for Children in Poverty. Retrieved from www.nccp.org/publications/pub_669.html

National Research Council & Institute of Medicine. (2000). *From neurons to neighborhoods: The science of early childhood development.* J. P. Shonkoff & D. A. Phillips (Eds.). Washington, DC: National Academy Press.

Osofsky, J. D., & Lieberman, A. F. (2011). A call for integrating a mental health perspective into systems of care for abused and neglected infants and young children. *American Psychologist, 66*(2), 120–128.

Reefhuis, J., Honein, M. A. Schieve, L. A., Correa, A., Hobbs, C. A., Rasmussen, S. A., & the National Birth Defects Prevention Study. (2009). Assisted reproductive technology and major structural birth defects in the United States. *Human Reproduction, 24*(2), 360–366.

Rose-Jacobs, R., Black, M. M., Casey, P. H., Cook, J. T., Cutts, D. B., Chilton, M., . . . Frank, D.A. (2008). Household food insecurity: Associations with at-risk infant and toddler development. *Pediatrics, 121*(1), 65–72.

ScienceDaily. (2011, October 11). *Earlier autism diagnosis could mean earlier interventions.* Retrieved from www.sciencedaily.com/releases/2011/10/111013154000.htm?+Brain+News+--+Autism

ScienceDaily. (2012, March 29). *Autism more common than previously thought: CDC report shows one in 54 boys identified.* Retrieved from www.sciencedaily.com/releases/2012/03/120329142630.htm

Squires, J., & Kaplan, P. (2007). Developmental outcomes of children born after assisted reproductive technologies. *Infants & Young Children, 20*(1), 2–10.

Wight, V. R., Chau, M., & Aratani, Y. (2011). *Who are America's poor children?* National Center for Children in Poverty (NCCP). Retrieved from www.nccp.org/publications/pub_1001.html

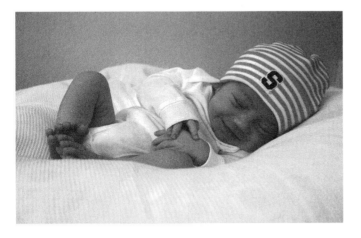

PART 1

Development and Well-Being of Infants and Young Children

CHAPTER 1

Development in the First 3 Years

Gail L. Ensher and David A. Clark

Highlights of the Chapter

At the conclusion of the chapter, the reader will:

- understand continuity and change in the development of infants, toddlers, and preschoolers

- understand typical variations in the emergence of developmental skills and behavior of infants and young children

- understand diverse styles of learning among infants and toddlers

- acquire a foundational knowledge of key developmental domains (i.e., neuromotor, sensorimotor, cognitive, language and communication, social-emotional, and adaptive behavior)

The Unfolding of Development in the First 3 Years

Typical child development is a miraculous process of change. For those who work with infants, toddlers, and their families, understanding typical trajectories of child development is an essential knowledge base to be acquired by students in training programs, families, and professionals. First and foremost, it is important to be aware that development in young children from birth to 3 years old follows relatively predictable progressions of ability, skill acquisition, and mastery, with certain basic responses present at birth. For example, many neonates at delivery have several inborn reflexes that, over the first few months of life, gradually are integrated into more mature functional behaviors and skills. As described in chapter 10 (Cummings & Fisher, 2016), these reflexes are evident at birth, regardless of culture or country of origin, and their absence can signal the presence of major neurological impairments (e.g., absence of the rooting response—the infant's head turning toward the soft stroking of the cheek or side of the mouth in search for the nipple or breast). In addition, physical growth and development in infants and toddlers is predictably directional in at least three ways (i.e., large or gross motor to fine motor, head to toe or top to bottom, and inside to outside or proximal to distal; Condon & Neville, 2011).

At the same time, there are normal, expectable variations that characterize typical child development processes, and these are noteworthy in the following ways:

- The emergence of skills and abilities across developmental domains is sequential but also reflects an uneven, scaffolding process, and there are different rates of skill and behavioral maturation and acquisition across developmental domains (gross motor, sensorimotor, cognitive, language and communication, social-emotional, and adaptive behavior).

- Within developmental domains, the emergence and mastery of skills vary, with certain abilities serving as underlying functions for the attainment of others. Such patterns typically can be seen, for instance, in observations that receptive language abilities of toddlers (or the understanding of language) precede their expressive language abilities. This is not always the case; for example, some toddlers never crawl, but simply begin to take steps—appearing to skip this important developmental milestone stage.

- Infants and toddlers display differential growth spurts in their development. During periods of rapid skill acquisition in one developmental domain, young children may seem to plateau or regress in other areas of development. For instance, parents often comment that when their toddlers are experiencing rapid growth in their gross motor development, they stop talking or appear to lose words previously attained.

- Individual trajectories of development and the acquisition of skills are influenced by experiences and environment, as well as by genetic factors. For example, some caregivers are reluctant to place their infants in prone position because their babies tend to become fussy. As a result, such babies may initially be slower to develop weight-bearing skills, slower in being able to move into 4-point positions, and slower in beginning to crawl. Infants and young children need opportunities to practice for learning; play and exploration are the primary means toward that end!

- Researchers are learning more about the interconnectedness or interdependence of different developmental domains, in particular, the significant ways in which social–emotional development, temperament, and attention affect the acquisition of cognitive skills (e.g., a child's motivation to explore his environment; Greenspan & Wieder, 1998; Landy, 2009).

- Finally, as discussed in later chapters of this book, special health care needs and disabilities can have a major impact on the ways in which infants and young children develop and acquire new skills and behavior. In particular, Osofsky and Lieberman (2011) wrote that in order to optimize infant and toddler development:

> *Babies' emotional, social, and cognitive competencies unfold in the context of their caregiving relationships, with the corollary that both the infant and primary caregiver need support in order to optimize the child's functioning. For young children, the caregivers' emotional well-being and life circumstances profoundly affect the quality of infant-caregiver relationships.* (p. 120)

Stated in another way, learning and growing from birth to 3 years are reciprocal processes.

Ages, Stages, and Milestones of Development

Throughout decades of research, developmental domains of infants and young children have been defined and measured in multiple ways, using a variety of approaches, assessment tools, and evaluation strategies (Bagnato, Neisworth, & Pretti-Frontczak, 2010; Linder, 2008; McLean, Wolery, & Bailey, 2004; Salvia, Ysseldyke, & Bolt, 2007). Moreover, formats for evaluation of children birth to 3 years old have changed dramatically over time, shifting from a heavy reliance on norm-referenced instruments toward more authentic experiences carried out within natural environments of home or familiar surroundings (Bagnato et al., 2010). Related to that changing context, however, most measures continue to include items that can offer snapshots of development and behavior across neuromotor, sensory–perceptual, language and communication, cognitive, social–emotional, and adaptive behavior domains—typically constituting the basis of eligibility for early intervention (EI) and preschool services. In the earliest months of the first year, there is a particularly heavy focus on both norm-referenced (i.e., conventional, standardized materials developed through psychometric procedures; Bagnato, Neisworth, & Munson, 1997, p. 3) and criterion-referenced (i.e., measurement of performance relative to a stated standard; Bagnato et al., 1997, p. 8) measures on neuromotor and sensory–perceptual abilities, whereas later-month items reflect the emerging, increasingly sophisticated contributions of language and communication, social–emotional and adaptive behavior, and cognitive abilities. Thus as development unfolds, the totally dependent newborn—functioning almost entirely on a reflexive level—grows and matures over the course of the first 3 years into an amazingly vibrant toddler and preschooler, competent to meet her ever-widening world of interactions and experiences, prepared to conquer new challenges.

For further information on developmental checklists and criterion-referenced instruments, see Appendix A of this chapter and chapter 6 (Ensher & Clark, 2016) of this text.

The First 12 Months

Birth to 3 months

At the time of delivery, newborns are primed to respond with their own unique temperaments as they begin to interact with family members and the immediate world around them. Typically, infants sleep 20 to 22 hours a day, focusing on the faces of their caregivers (a distance of approximately 8 to 10 inches) as they nurse or bottle-feed, cooing and crying and occasionally appearing to smile in response to soft talking and rocking. Their movements are arrhythmic, and their bodies are asymmetrical, often seen in a "fencing" position, with the arm and leg on one side flexed and the opposite arm and leg extended (i.e., asymmetrical tonic neck reflex). The Moro or startle response is prominent when the infant is allowed to drop backward, as are other newborn reflexes such as the rooting response, the grasp reflex (when an object or finger is placed in the infant's palm), the plantar reflex (contraction of the baby's toes with irritation of the sole of the foot), and the stepping response (the infant makes reflexive stepping motions when held upright under the arms). In addition, from 1 to 3 months old, infants begin to lift and rotate their heads, kick reciprocally when on their backs, and demonstrate a coordinated suck-swallow response when a nipple or bottle is placed in their mouths. Weight bearing is limited in

1-to-3-month-olds, with heads raised to no more than a 30- to 45-degree angle so as to move from side to side. When pulled to a sitting position from a supine position, infants can momentarily hold their heads erect, in an upright-supported-sitting position. Between 1 and 3 months, babies occasionally roll from their stomachs to their backs, often by accident, then gaze in wonderment about what has just happened.

In addition to these common behaviors, infants also present their own individual needs, temperaments, and unique patterns of interaction. As many parents will confirm, no two babies born into a single family are the same. Some are more active, seeming to be in constant motion; alert and displaying more wakeful periods throughout the day; cooing, vocalizing, and quieting more in response to caregivers; and seeming to be more observant of their environments. Others are more laid back, easygoing, able to self-calm more readily with longer periods of self-contentment, seeming to be more responsive to cuddling and holding, appearing to require less attention, and sleeping longer periods throughout the night with less frequent periods of nursing and feeding.

4 to 6 months

By 4 months, infants are becoming more differentiated little persons, increasingly aware of their environments and immediate surroundings. Most babies within this period are propping forward and side to side, with many infants able to support their weight and sit independently for brief periods of time, especially with attractive toys placed within reach. While in supine and in supported or unsupported sitting, they are able to bring their hands to midline, reach in anticipation of a toy, and grasp for brief periods of 10 to 15 seconds, still dropping objects without awareness. At this point in their development, voluntary

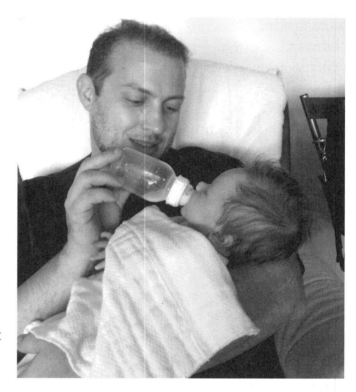

movements are beginning to take over, with many of the basic reflexes having been integrated. When pulled to a sitting position, they are able to hold their heads in line with their bodies, maintaining an erect position throughout a pull-to-sit. Weight-bearing in prone position with flexed or extended arms and occasional rocking back and forth in place are emerging, in preparation for the later stages of creeping, crawling, and greater mobility; and movement has become graded and smooth. By 6 months, most babies can roll from stomach to back and from back to stomach. In terms of feeding, many babies are starting to take pureed food and are able to move their tongues in and out of their mouths while cleaning an infant-size spoon. Many babies at this stage are beginning to hold their bottles with hands in midline.

Between 4 and 6 months, babies are experiencing more wakeful periods but still may require two to three naps per day. They become increasingly more interactive, capable of playing simple games such as peek-a-boo, and by 6 months will look for a partially covered object or desired toy, the sign of developing object permanence.

Concurrent with infants becoming increasingly aware of their environment, their vocalizations become more differentiated, and babies communicate varying needs with different cries. Vocal play becomes the harbinger of reduplicated and variegated babbling which emerges within 2 to 3 months, and depending upon individual temperament, babies manifest longer periods of contentment, smiling and laughing at engaging routines.

7 to 9 months

By 7 months old, babies are becoming much more active, self-expressive little beings, with ever-increasing mobility and schemes of interaction. They participate in repetitive play, dropping objects from high chairs and, especially in the presence of an attentive adult, will continue that activity over and over and over again with great delight! Depending on the temperament, a child may display a "sense of humor" with his caregiver. Babies at this stage are capable of gaining and maintaining attention of the caregiver and vocalizing across two or more turns. They respond playfully to games such as pat-a-cake and use play to practice familiar or known skills and routines such as banging objects together. In addition, they are

becoming increasingly adept at communicating their various needs, such as being tired, hungry, or fearful of strangers (evidence of stranger anxiety) or situations. Reduplicated and variegated babbling is observed, along with various vowel sounds, and early consonants such as *p*, *b*, *t*, *d*, *m*, and *n* (Ensher et al., 2007; Linder, 2008). Babies at this stage are able to imitate sounds and a variety of gestures such as wrinkling of the nose, puckering lips, hiccupping, or simulating coughing. Turn-taking skills continue to develop, and babies between 7 and 9 months old sitting on the floor, greatly enjoy rolling an infant-size ball back and forth to a familiar family member for several turns.

For the 7–9-month-old, the world has become a place for active exploration. Babies can easily transition in and out of sitting, are crawling forward and backward, and are beginning to pull to stand with the support of a person or furniture. Some precocious 9-month-olds are even starting to stand independently, taking a few tentative steps before collapsing to the floor. Meanwhile, increasingly mature fine motor abilities, in particular arm and hand use, facilitate the acquisition of new play and feeding skills. Babies now can voluntarily release objects with awareness, transfer toys from hand to hand, poke, and grasp small items between the thumb and lateral side of the index finger in preparation for finger feeding.

10 to 12 months

By 10 to 12 months old, babies have developed mobility skills that allow them to move to almost everywhere they desire, and they are acquiring multiple foundation skills that will serve them well in their later toddler and preschool years. They can cruise around furniture, are gaining trunk and lower extremity strength to walk with one hand held, can transition easily in and out of a variety of positions, and have even developed backward protective

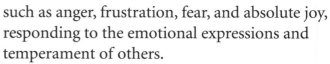

such as anger, frustration, fear, and absolute joy, responding to the emotional expressions and temperament of others.

The increasing independence of the 10–12-month-old also is reflected in more sustained periods of attention, play, exploration, and experimentation in terms of means–ends and problem-solving. They repeat actions that evoke responses of laughter and delight from caregivers, engage in simple reciprocal games of give-and-take and chase, and seek clues and cues for approval from others in their ever-widening circles of communication and social cognitive abilities.

By 12 months old, the agile and competent young child is on the verge of toddlerhood. He can imitate actions and behaviors of others in play scenarios without models present. Pretend play is more goal-directed and may simulate related sequences of activities such as feeding a baby doll and putting "baby" to bed, at the same time reflecting greater possibilities for experimentation with the more inclusive fine and gross motor skills available for exploring the immediate environment.

Both receptive and expressive language abilities increase dramatically during this period, with the child understanding up to 50 to 60 familiar words and labeling simple concrete objects and people (Ensher et al., 2007; Linder, 2008). However, because expressive language yet lags behind comprehension, jargon and gibberish still are very much in evidence and remain a primary means for communication and expression of emotions. Given a book, the 12-month-old is starting to point to individual pictures named by the caregiver, particularly photos of familiar persons in the family. As part of emergent literacy, very young children will hold a large toddler-size crayon with a gross pincer grasp and will make scribbling marks on paper or imitate scribbling demonstrated by an adult.

responses and balance reactions. The more agile 10–12-month-old is self-feeding with finger foods, drinking from sippy cups, pulling off her own socks, poking with fingers, clapping hands as a sign of great delight, and walking independently.

Modes and means of communication likewise become increasingly versatile and complex. Very young children at this age begin to use single words, although many times overgeneralizing when referring to specific objects or people. Their gestural repertoire has expanded and developed to meet a number of diverse needs such as gaining adult attention, pointing to objects, waving for greetings of "hi" and "bye," and giving objects to others in simple requests for help. Nonverbally as well, the pre-toddler is able to signal a range of emotions

Finally, in terms of emotional and behavioral regulation, the adept 1-year-old can respond appropriately to simple one-step requests and directions and understands (but may not always comply with) behavioral limitations when told "no."

The Middle Months: 13 to 24 Months

As she moves into the middle months, the now-emergent, increasingly more independent toddler truly reflects her own individual and unique personhood. Two-year-olds are known for their "noncompliant" behavior and a desire to express their own wishes and desires of the moment, which often do not coincide with adult or caregiver requests. They are a unique combination of "warm-and-fuzzy" affection directed toward toys, animals, and other persons with a clear perception of autonomy and a desire to do-on-her-own without help. On the other hand, in the event of another person's hurt or sad feelings, most of the time the toddler is a great sympathizer, quick to shower affection with hugs and kisses to comfort a friend. Parallel play is still paramount, but the 15–18-month-old also can be a willing participant, interacting with a familiar playmate in some activities of mutual interest. The toddler is capable of turn taking and sharing, while clearly defining her own turf of "mine"!

With increasing independence, the toddler develops a greater sense of self as separate from others. He can recall events and situations past without having persons or objects immediately visible or present; attends to stories read for brief periods of time; differentiates himself from others; refers to self with " I," "me," and his own name; and displays a greater sense of emotional and behavioral regulation, for example, attempting to gain praise for tasks accomplished. For most toddlers at this stage, there also is a growing sense of empowerment, with his greater ability to affect his environment due to greater access of expressive language and communication. Expressive language may still be less than 50% intelligible until the child is 2 years old, but by means of nonverbal as well as verbal communication, the child's desires and needs most of the time can be clearly understood by familiar adults. By 18 months, the toddler may have up to 20 words in his expressive vocabulary and by 2 years a minimum of 50 words, intelligible to a familiar adult (Linder, 2008). He understands simple questions and can answer "yes" or "no," although the latter is likely the dominant response as the toddler approaches his second birthday. In addition, he can anticipate the positive or negative responses and consequences from caregivers as a result of his behavior.

Finally, the 2-year-old's growing independence is also evident in more developed

adaptive and sensorimotor abilities, that is, helping with dressing, eating a variety of food textures, indicating needs for toileting, drinking from a cup with no loss of fluid, and using a spoon with little spillage.

The Second Year: 25 to 36 Months

Between 25 and 36 months, the 2-year-old begins to emerge from a focus on self and "me" into a more social, readily compliant, and interactive toddler. She is more willing to share, cooperate, respond positively to requests, and join in associative play with peers. Many toddlers at this stage of development know their own age and sex and display a greater understanding of their own feelings and emotions and those of others such as happy, sad, afraid, and angry. At 30–36 months old, the toddler still demonstrates impulsive behavior but gradually gains greater control over the regulation of her emotions, is able to calm more readily from periods of upset, and displays a growing ability to talk about feelings. At the same time, with maturation, the toddler is able to attend to and persist in problem-solving tasks without losing interest or becoming frustrated. Feelings and emotions also often are reflected in the pretend play scenarios of young children at this age, for example, with dolls, stuffed animals, or even real pets.

Greater access with developing speech, language, and communication skills facilitates both the understanding of emotions and behavior of self and others and, likewise, the expression of these feelings. The young child between 25 and 36 months is able to initiate a topic, converse across two or more turns, and respond with new information and discourse. He has an expressive vocabulary of 200+ words, approaching the third birthday, and is intelligible more than 50% of the time by unfamiliar persons, and more so (approximately 70 to 80% of the time) by those familiar with his speech, language, and communication patterns. By the time that the toddler/preschooler reaches 36 months, he should have between 300 and 1,000 words in his expressive vocabulary; should verbalize at least three prepositions; upon request should be able to give his full name; use nouns, verbs, and pronouns; and ask questions of "what," "where," and "when." The growing complexity of language expressions is evident in two- to three-word sentences at 24 to 30 months, and those extend to five-word sentences by 36 months (Linder, 2008).

Finally, between 24 and 36 months, neuromotor skills (both gross and fine motor) escalate. The fisted hand grasp of 23 to 24 months by 36 months for most toddlers/preschoolers is replaced by the tripod grasp of a crayon or writing utensil, using thumb, index, and middle fingers. At 24 months, the toddler can snip with scissors and turn pages of a book one at a time, and by 36 months can actually cut along a straight line and string ½-inch beads. By the child's third birthday, one side of the body is differentiated from the opposite side, allowing for navigating stairs and pedaling a tricycle with alternating feet.

The accomplishment of self-help and adaptive skills often is extremely diverse with 2–3-year-olds. Toilet training frequently is adult-initiated around 2½ years old or shortly before that time, but the child still may require adult assistance and may experience frequent accidents following her third birthday. Other skills often achieved between 30 and 36 months include the young child's ability to blow his/her own nose, place belongings in appropriate places such as cubbies in nursery school, use a fork, pour liquid from a small container, unwrap small packages of food, button large buttons, dress semi-independently with some adult supervision and assistance, and understand common risks and dangers, for example, staying away from a hot stove.

Thus, as preschoolers approach their third birthdays, they typically have grown into vibrant, inquisitive, more affectionate and caring, and interactive little persons, increasingly capable of understanding the world about them and more adept at communicating with the significant others who fill their lives and relationships.

Trajectories of Development: Contributing Links and Essential Connections

Many contributing factors, links, and essential connections affect the trajectories of development in infants, toddlers, and young children throughout the first 3 years of life. Such variables do not impact development and behavior in isolation. Always there is interaction and interfacing among child, family, and environmental-social influences that shape the infant's individual characteristics and qualities and the person he eventually becomes. That interaction is complex. For families and those in the medical, mental health, educational, policy making, and clinical fields, the challenge is to continually search for opportunities and ways to positively influence the trajectories of growth and development, hopefully to facilitate and maximize the potential of each infant and young child.

Beginnings and Origins: What Do Children Bring?

There are child characteristics that emerge from the time of conception, such as the genetic and neurological make-up of the child (Gervai, 2009; Saudino, 2005) and/or the early onset of unique predispositions such as variables of temperament (Tremblay et al., 2004) that influence the direction and rate of development. Some of these qualities that are indigenous to the child are amenable to change, but they also often are present for a lifetime. Moreover, as will be discussed in later chapters of this book, other events sometimes develop that place an infant or young child at risk, for example, prematurity (Chyi, Lee, Hintz, Gould, & Sutcliffe, 2008; de Kieviet, Piek, Aarnoudse-Moens, & Oosterlaan, 2009; Ensher & Clark, 2011; Ensher, Clark, & Songer, 2009;

Limperopoulos et al. 2008; Manley et al., 2010; Petrini et al., 2009; Taylor et al., 2011), gestational age (Hemming, Colver, Hutton, Kurinczuk, & Pharoah, 2008), and birth weight (Vohr et al., 2009). Recent studies have suggested, for instance, that attention-deficit/hyperactive disorders, behavioral disorders, and other later school-related problems, likely the result of multiple factors, have been found to be more prevalent among young children who were "late preterm" infants (Engle, Tomashek, & Wallman, 2007; Morse, Zheng, Tang, & Roth, 2009).

Finally, in addition to the variables noted previously, there are numerous other prenatal, perinatal, and postnatal factors and events that place newborns, infants, and young children at risk, including the teratologic effects of maternal substance abuse (Singer et al., 2008; Stroud et al., 2009), infections, the effects of medications (Clark, 2012), malformations, and other neurologic insults. Moreover, future research on the impact of the environment on genetics will surely yield new, unprecedented information, with enormous implications for newborns and their families in terms of possibilities for prevention of illness and other untoward conditions (Clark, 2012). In this regard, a burgeoning area of research on "fetal programming" in the field of medicine holds much promise for the prevention of health-related and developmental defects/delays in later life, as well as for reversing the adverse effects of toxic stress, among other environmental influences (Davis & Thompson, 2014; Drake & Walker, 2004; Gicquel, El-Osta, & LeBouc, 2007).

Families and Environment: What Do They Bring?

Although contemporary studies vary in their emphasis, most acknowledge the essential contributions of both "nature" and "nurture" to the trajectories of growth and development of infants and young children. More than a decade ago, Shonkoff and Phillips (National Research Council & Institute of Medicine, 2000) wrote about this complex, miraculous interplay among genetic matter, brain development, and the impact of environments:

The past 20 years have seen unprecedented progress in understanding how the brain develops and, in particular, the phenomenal changes in both its circuitry and neurochemistry that occur during prenatal and early postnatal development. . . . Knowledge of the ways in which genes and the environment interact to affect the maturation of the brain has expanded by leaps and bounds. The years ahead will bring even more breathtaking progress as, for example, knowledge of the human genome is increasingly transformed into knowledge about how genes are expressed in the brain. This promises a dramatic expansion in the ability to understand the interweaving of genetic and environmental influences as they affect both the brain and behavioral development. (pp. 182–183)

Illustrating this point, professionals know that infants can have extremely challenging medical courses in neonatal intensive care units. However, with the passage of time, those medical factors may have increasingly less influence, as exposure to family interaction, relationships, and other environmental factors prevail and reflect more dominant effects (Ensher & Clark, 1994). Ulrich (2010), writing about the opportunities for early intervention based on theory, basic neuroscience, and clinical science, highlighted the "importance of frequent bouts of functionally relevant activity on the self-organization of behavioral patterns [and the] impact that should be expected from the use of rigorous interventions on underlying subsystems . . . that support these outcomes" (p. 1868). She further concluded that "more new, creative approaches that can be adapted for home-based, parent-administered, activity-based interventions" (p. 1877) are within reach with the pursuit of evidence-based research.

In the end, opportunities abound for nurturing and enhancing the trajectories of growth, development, and behavior of infants and young children. Always, these processes take place within the ecological contexts of relationships that include parents, siblings, extended family members, and eventually peers, friends, and professionals in communities with whom young children interact (Ensher & Clark, 2011). The mental health and well-being of infants, toddlers, and young children are firmly rooted in such relationships that largely determine the directions, pathways, and fulfillment of developmental courses during the first 3 years of life. As Osofsky and Lieberman (2010) so artfully wrote in quoting from Irving B. Harris,

"There is no excuse for our society's not putting scientific knowledge into practical use…. We must remember—the first few months of life are not a rehearsal. This is the real show." (p. 120)

It is an awesome responsibility that is laid at the feet of parents and professionals who spend time and work with infants and young children. Without exception, all professionals need to seize every opportunity to support them with all of the compassion, knowledge, understanding, strength, affection, and care within their grasp!

Chapter Summary

This chapter has described ages, stages, and developmental milestones over the first 3 years of life; discussed variations that typically occur across six primary developmental domains including cognitive, language, sensorimotor, social-emotional, gross motor, and adaptive skills and behavior; and considered some

essential biological and environmental links and connections that affect the trajectories of development in infants and young children and that offer opportunities for families in nurturing their young children and for professionals carrying out early intervention.

Key Points to Remember

- Typical development occurs in a predictable sequence and timetable, but there are normal variations in development.

- Although development takes place in predictable ways, early interactions and intervention affect the trajectories of that development in significant ways and offer important opportunities for enhancing the potentials of infants and young children.

- Future research on "fetal programming" and epigenetics likely will yield new information that will have enormous implications for newborns and their families in terms of possibilities for the prevention of illness and other untoward condtions and developmental outcomes.

Implications for Families and Professionals

As parents play with their babies and toddlers during the first 3 years, it is helpful for them to have a basic understanding of what infants and toddlers usually do at various developmental stages (especially if their babies are the first born in their families). As we have emphasized in this chapter, there is a great deal of variability and a range within which particular skills and behaviors emerge. On the other hand, professionals historically have noted that, typically, parents know and understand their children best. More often than not, they are aware of "the red flags" that may signal medical or developmental problems, or both, that need to be examined further.

The simple *Developmental Checklists—Birth to Five* (see Appendix A) developed by Menapace and the Central New York Early Childhood Direction Center (2012) has been used and found to be helpful for more than a decade by numerous families, as they have followed the development of their babies and young children in the face of concerns. It is a basic measure that professionals and parents can use in the natural environment of homes over a period of time, the observations of which can then be shared with EI professionals and pediatricians for more in-depth follow-up, as needed. The checklist is not a standardized measure; however, it has been field-tested by students and professionals in EI and in child care, preschool, and clinical settings across 15 states in the United States, in addition to programs and settings in Australia, Ecuador, Kenya, Tanzania, Rwanda, Manitoba, and New Mexico (with a database of more than 4,600 infants and young children). Accordingly, the Early Childhood Development Center Checklist (see Appendix A) offers developmental benchmarks across the first 5 years that can easily be noted during the course of observation of infants and young children at play, interacting with family members and peers, in everyday life and natural environments to validate developmental patterns of concern as well as highlight domains of noteworthy strength.

Finally, during the course of working with families, certain basic questions and needs within the daily routines of caring for their infants and toddlers surface repeatedly. Whether a baby or toddler has special needs, the Caregiver Interview Form (Ensher et al., 1998; see Appendix B) is a simple form that can be used by pediatricians, early intervention teams, and other clinical and health care professionals in determining the immediate and sometimes

critical needs of parents, and their strengths, in caring for their infants and young children during the first 3 years.

References

Bagnato, S. J., Neisworth, J. T., & Munson, S. M. (1997). *LINKing assessment and early intervention: An authentic curriculum-based approach.* Baltimore, MD: Brookes.

Bagnato, S. J., Neisworth, J. T., & Pretti-Frontczak, K. (2010). *LINKing authentic assessment & early childhood intervention: Best measures for best practices* (2nd ed.). Baltimore, MD: Brookes.

Chyi, L., Lee, H., Hintz, S., Gould, J., & Sutcliffe, T. (2008). School outcomes of late preterm infants: Special needs and challenges for infants born at 32 to 36 weeks gestation. *Journal of Pediatrics, 153*(1), 25–31.

Clark, D. A. (2012, February). *Non-genetic causes of hearing loss.* Paper presented at the Academy of Pediatrics Conference on Hearing Impairment, Syracuse, NY.

Condon, M., & Neville, L. (2011). *Physical development in the young child.* Unpublished manuscript.

Cummings, J. J., & Fisher, M. A. (2016). Major physical, motor, and neurologic impairments. In G. L. Ensher & D. A. Clark (Eds.), *The early years: Foundations for best practice with special children and their families* (pp. 209–228). Washington, DC: ZERO TO THREE.

Davis, E. P., & Thompson, R. A. (2014). Prenatal foundations: Fetal programming of health and development. *Zero to Three, 34*(4), 6–11.

Drake, A. J., & Walker, B. R. (2004). The intergenerational effects of fetal programming: Non-genomic mechanisms for the inheritance of low birth weight and cardiovascular risk. *Journal of Endocrinology, 180*, 1–16.

de Kieviet, J. F., Piek, J. P., Aarnoudse-Moens, C. S., & Oosterlaan, J. (2009) Motor development of very low-birth-weight children from birth to adolescence: A meta-analysis. *Journal of the American Medical Association, 302*(20), 2235–2242.

Engle, W. A., Tomashek, K. M., & Wallman, C. (2007). "Late-preterm" infants: A population at risk. *Pediatrics, 120*(6), 1390–1401.

Ensher, G. L., Bobish, T. P., Gardner, E. F., Michaels, C. A., Butler, K. G., Foertsch, D. J., & Cooper, C. (1998). *Syracuse Dynamic Assessment for Birth to Three.* Chicago, IL: Applied Symbolix.

Ensher, G. L., Bobish, T. P., Gardner, E. F., Reinson, C. L., Byden, D. A., & Foertsch, D. J. (2007). *Partners in play: Assessing infants and toddlers in natural contexts.* Clifton Park, NY: Thomson-Delmar Learning.

Ensher, G. L., & Clark, D. A. (1994). *The high risk infant: Medical treatment and psycho-educational intervention* (2nd ed.). Gaithersburg, MD: Aspen Publishers.

Ensher, G. L., & Clark, D. A. (2011). *Relationship-centered practices in early childhood: Working with families, infants, and young children at risk.* Baltimore, MD: Brookes.

Ensher, G. L., & Clark, D. A. (2016). Evaluating infants and young children in the first years. In G. L. Ensher & D. A. Clark (Eds.), *The early years: Foundations for best practice with special children and their families* (pp. 133–153). Washington, DC: ZERO TO THREE.

Ensher, G. L., Clark, D. A., & Songer, N. S. (2009). *Families, infants, and young children at risk: Pathways to best practice.* Baltimore, MD: Brookes.

Gervai, J. (2009). Environmental and genetic influences on early attachment. *Child and Adolescent Psychiatry and Mental Health, 3*, 25. Retrieved from www.capmh.com/content/3/1/25

Gicquel, C., El-Osta, A., & LeBouc, Y. (2007). Epigenetic regulation and fetal programming. *Best Practice & Research: Clinical Endocrinology & Metabolism, 22*(1), 1–16.

Greenspan, S. I., & Wieder, S. (1998). *The child with special needs: Encouraging intellectual and emotional growth.* Reading, MA: Addison Wesley.

Hemming, K., Colver, A., Hutton, J. L., Kurinczuk, J. J., & Pharoah, P. O. D. (2008). The influence of gestational age on severity of impairment in spastic cerebral palsy. *The Journal of Pediatrics, 153*(2), 203–208.

Landy, S. (2009). *Pathways to competence: Encouraging healthy social and emotional development in young children* (2nd ed.). Baltimore, MD: Brookes.

Limperopoulos, C., Bassan, H., Sullivan, N. R., Soul, J. S., Robertson, Jr., R. L., Moore, M., . . . du Plessis, A. J. (2008). Positive screening for autism for ex-preterm infants: Prevalence and risk factors. *Pediatrics, 121*(4), 758–765.

Linder, T. (2008). *Transdisciplinary play-based assessment* (2nd ed.). Baltimore, MD: Brookes.

Manley, B. J., Dawson, J. A., Kamlin, C. O. F., Donath, S. M., Morley, C. J., & Davis, P. G.(2010). Clinical assessment of extremely premature infants in the delivery room is a poor predictor of survival. *Pediatrics, 125*, e559–e564.

McLean, M., Wolery, M., & Bailey, D. B., Jr. (2004). *Assessing infants and preschoolers with special needs* (3rd ed.). Upper Saddle River, NJ: Pearson.

Menapace, T., & Early Childhood Direction Center. (2012). *Developmental checklists; Birth to five.* Syracuse, NY: Early Childhood Direction Center.

Morse, S. B., Zheng, H., Tang, Y., & Roth, J. (2009). Early school-age outcomes of late preterm infants. *Pediatrics, 123*(4), e622–e629.

National Research Council & Institute of Medicine. (2000). *From neurons to neighborhoods: The science of early childhood development.* J. P. Shonkoff, & D. A. Phillips (Eds.). Washington, DC: National Academy Press.

Osofsky, J. D., & Lieberman, A. F. (2011). A call for integrating a mental health perspective into systems of care for abused and neglected infants and young children. *American Psychologist, 66*(2), 120–128.

Petrini, J. R., Dias, T., McCormick, M. C., Massolo, M. L., Green, N. S., & Escobar, G. J. (2009). Increased risk of adverse neurological development for late preterm infants. *The Journal of Pediatrics, 154*(2), 169–176.

Salvia, J., Ysseldyke, J. E., & Bolt, S. (2007). *Assessment in special and inclusive education* (10th ed.). Boston, MA: Houghton Mifflin.

Saudino, K. J. (2005). Behavioral genetics and child temperament. *Journal of Developmental & Behavioral Pediatrics, 26*(3), 214–223.

Singer, L. T., Nelson, S., Short, E., Min, M. O., Lewis, B., Russ, S., & Minnes, S. (2008). Prenatal cocaine exposure: Drug and environmental effects at 9 years. *The Journal of Pediatrics, 153*(1), 105–110.

Stroud, L. R., Paster, R. L., Papandonatos, G. D., Niaura, R., Salisbury, A.L., Battle, C., . . . Lester, B. (2009). Maternal smoking during pregnancy and newborn neurobehavior: Effects at 10 to 27 days. *The Journal of Pediatrics, 154*(1), 10–16.

Taylor, H. G., Klein, N., Anselmo, M. G., Minich, N., Espy, K. A., & Hack, M. (2011). Learning problems in kindergarten students with extremely preterm birth. *Archives of Pediatric and Adolescent Medicine, 165*(9), 819–825.

Tremblay, R. E., Nagin, D. S., Seguin, J. R., Zoccolillo, M., Zelazo, P. D., Boivin, M., . . .Japel, C., (2004). Physical aggression during early childhood: Trajectories and predictors. *Pediatrics, 114*(1), e43–e50.

Ulrich, B. D. (2010). Opportunities for early intervention based on theory, basic neuroscience, and clinical science. *Physical Therapy, 90*(12), 1868–1880.

Vohr, B. R., Tyson, J. E., Wright, L. L., Perritt, R. L., Li, L., Poole, W. K., & NICHD Neonatal Network. (2009). Maternal age, multiple birth, and extremely low birth weight infants. *The Journal of Pediatrics, 154*(4), 498–503.

Appendix A

Developmental Checklists, Birth to 5

the early childhood direction center

**If you are concerned about your child's development,
contact the Mid-State ECDC for information on screening, evaluation, and assessment.**
Mid-State Early Childhood Direction Center
Syracuse University, 805 S. Crouse Avenue, Syracuse, NY 13244-2280
Phone: 315-443-4444 Toll-free: 1-800-962-5488 Fax: 315-443-4338
E-mail: ecdc@syr.edu website: http://ecdc.syr.edu

Adapted by the Mid-State Early Childhood Direction Center from:

The American Academy of Pediatrics: Caring for Your Baby and Young Child Birth to Age 5: The Complete and Authoritative Guide. Shelov, S. P., & Hannemann, R. E. (1994). New York, NY: Bantam Doubleday Dell Pub.

Hawaii Early Learning Profile (HELP)- Vort Corporation, P.O. Box 60132, Palo Alto, CA 94306 .Revised Checklist 2004

IDA- Infant Toddler Developmental Assessment- : Provence, Sally M.D., Erikson, Joanna, M.P.H., Vater , Susan, Ed. M, Palmeri, Saro, M.D. Riverside Publishing Company, 8420 Bryn Mawr Avenue, Chicago, IL 60631, 1995

ASQ and ASQ-SE-Paul H. Brookes Publishing Company, P.O. Box10624, Baltimore, Maryland, www.brookespublishing.com, May 2010

Revised 2012

Developmental Checklist (1 to 3 Months)

CHILD'S NAME: _____

DATE OF BIRTH: _____

PARENT OR GUARDIAN: _____

MILESTONES   **DATE OBSERVED**

MOTOR

✓ Retains hold of object/rattle (1-2mos.)   _____

✓ Brings hands towards center of body when lying on back (1-2 mos.) _____

✓ Raises head and cheek when lying on stomach (3 mos.)   _____

✓ Supports upper body with arms when lying on stomach (3 mos.)   _____

✓ Stretches legs out when lying on stomach or back (2-3 mos.)   _____

✓ Opens and shuts hands (2-3 mos.)   _____

✓ Pushes down on his legs when his feet are placed on firm surface (3 mos.) _____

✓ Occasionally rolls from stomach to back   _____

COGNITIVE

✓ Responds to voice i.e. turn to, wiggle, reacts (0-1 mos.)   _____

✓ Watches face intently (2-3 mos.)   _____

✓ Follows moving objects (2 mos.)   _____

✓ Recognizes familiar objects and people at a distance (3 mos.)   _____

✓ Starts using hands and eyes in coordination (3 mos.)   _____

LANGUAGE   _____

✓ Makes sucking sounds (1-2 mos.)   _____

✓ Smiles at the sound of voice (2-3 mos.)   _____

✓ Coos; vocal play (begins at 3 mos.)   _____

✓ Attends to sound (1-3 mos.)   _____

✓ Startles to loud noise (1-3 mos.)   _____

SOCIAL/EMOTIONAL

✓ Makes eye contact (0-1 mos.)   _____

✓ Begins to develop a social smile (1-3 mos.)   _____

✓ Enjoys playing with other people and may cry when playing stops (2-3 mos.) _____

✓ Becomes more communicative and expressive with face and body (2-3 mos.) _____

✓ Imitates some movements and facial expressions   _____

Developmental Red Flags (1 to 3 Months)

- ❑ Doesn't seem to respond to loud noises
- ❑ Doesn't follow moving objects with eyes by 2 to 3 months
- ❑ Doesn't smile at the sound of your voice by 2 months
- ❑ Doesn't grasp and hold objects by 3 months
- ❑ Doesn't smile at people by 3 months
- ❑ Cannot support head well at 3 months
- ❑ Doesn't reach for and grasp toys by 3 to 4 months
- ❑ Doesn't bring objects to mouth by 4 months
- ❑ Doesn't push down with legs when feet are placed on a firm surface by 4 months
- ❑ Has trouble moving one or both eyes in all directions
- ❑ Crosses eyes most of the time (occasional crossing of the eyes is normal in these first months)

COMMENTS: _____

_____

_____

_____

_____

_____

_____

_____

_____

_____

_____

_____

_____

_____

_____

_____

_____

_____

Developmental Checklist (4 to 7 Months)

CHILD'S NAME: _____

DATE OF BIRTH: _____

PARENT OR GUARDIAN: _____

MILESTONES   **DATE OBSERVED**

MOTOR

✓ Pushes up on extended arms (5 mos.)   _____

✓ Pulls to sitting with no head lag (5 mos.)   _____

✓ Sits with support of his hands (5-6 mos.)   _____

✓ Sits unsupported for short periods (6-8 mos.)   _____

✓ Supports whole weight on legs (6-7 mos.)   _____

✓ Grasps feet (6 mos.)   _____

✓ Transfers objects from hand to hand (6-7 mos.)   _____

✓ Uses raking grasp (not pincer) (6 mos.)   _____

✓ Routinely rolls from stomach to back and back to stomach   _____

COGNITIVE

✓ Plays peek-a-boo (4-7 mos.)   _____

✓ Looks for a family member or pet when named (4-7 mos.)   _____

✓ Explores with hands and mouth (4-7 mos.)   _____

✓ Tracks moving objects with ease (4-7 mos.)   _____

✓ Finds partially hidden objects (6-7 mos.)   _____

✓ Grasps objects dangling in front of him or her (5-6 mos.)   _____

✓ Looks for fallen toys (5-7 mos.)   _____

LANGUAGE

✓ Laughs and squeals out loud (4-7 mos.)   _____

✓ Distinguishes emotions by tone of voice (4-7 mos.)   _____

✓ Responds to sound by making sounds (4-6 mos.)   _____

✓ Responds to spoken "bye-bye" by waving (4-7 mos.)   _____

✓ Uses voice to express joy and displeasure (4-6 mos.)   _____

✓ Syllable repetition begins (5-7 mos.)   _____

✓ Localizes or turns toward sounds   _____

SOCIAL/EMOTIONAL

✓ Enjoys social play (4-7 mos.)   _____

✓ Interested in mirror images (5-7 mos.)   _____

✓ Can calm down within ½ hour when upset (6 mos.)   _____

✓ Responds to other people's expression of emotion (4-7 mos.)   _____

Developmental Red Flags (4 to 7 Months)

- ❑ Seems very stiff, tight muscles
- ❑ Seems very floppy, like a rag doll
- ❑ Head still flops back when body is pulled to sitting position (by 5 months still exhibits head lag)
- ❑ Shows little or no affection for the person who cares for them
- ❑ Doesn't seem to enjoy being around people
- ❑ One or both eyes consistently turn in or out
- ❑ Persistent tearing, eye drainage, or sensitivity to light
- ❑ Does not respond to sounds around them
- ❑ Has difficulty getting objects to mouth
- ❑ Does not turn head to locate sounds by 4 months
- ❑ Doesn't roll over (stomach to back) by 6 months
- ❑ Cannot sit with help by 6 months (not by themselves)
- ❑ Does not laugh or make squealing sounds by 5 months
- ❑ Does not actively reach for objects by 6 months
- ❑ Does not follow objects with both eyes
- ❑ Does not bear some weight on legs by 5 months
- ❑ Has difficulty calming self, cries for long periods of time

COMMENTS: _____

_____

_____

_____

_____

_____

_____

_____

_____

_____

_____

_____

Developmental Checklist (8 to 12 Months)

CHILD'S NAME: _____

DATE OF BIRTH: _____

PARENT OR GUARDIAN: _____

MILESTONES 　　　　　　　　　　　　　　　　　　　　　　　　　　　　　　　**DATE OBSERVED**

GROSS MOTOR

✓ Moves to sitting position without assistance (8-10 mos.)　　　_____

✓ Crawls forward on belly　　　_____

✓ Assumes hand and knee position　　　_____

✓ Creeps on hands and knees　　　_____

✓ Gets from sitting to crawling or prone (lying on stomach) position (10-12 mos.)　　　_____

✓ Pulls up self to standing position　　　_____

✓ Walks holding on to furniture or person　　　_____

✓ Stands momentarily without support　　　_____

✓ May walk two or three steps without support　　　_____

FINE MOTOR

✓ Uses pincer grasp (grasp using thumb and index finger) (7-10 mos.)　　　_____

✓ Bangs two small toys together　　　_____

✓ Puts objects into container (10-12 mos.)　　　_____

✓ Takes objects out of container (10-12 mos.)　　　_____

✓ Pokes with index finger　　　_____

✓ Tries to imitate scribbling　　　_____

✓ Finger feeds self　　　_____

COGNITIVE

✓ Explores objects in many different ways (shaking, banging, throwing, dropping) (8-10 mos.)　　　_____

✓ Finds hidden objects easily (10-12 mos.)　　　_____

✓ Looks at correct picture when image is named　　　_____

✓ Enjoys looking at pictures in books (9-12 mos.)　　　_____

✓ Imitates gestures (9-12 mos.)　　　_____

✓ Engages in simple games of Peek-a-Boo, Pat-a-Cake, or rolling ball back and forth　　　_____

LANGUAGE

✓ Responds to simple verbal requests such as "Give me."　　　_____

✓ Responds to "no" by briefly stopping activity and noticing adult　　　_____

✓ Makes simple gestures such as shaking head for no　　　_____

LANGUAGE (continued)

✓ Babbles "dada" and "mama" (8-10 mos.) _____

✓ Says "dada" and "mama" for specific person (11-12 mos.) _____

✓ Uses exclamations such as "oh-oh" _____

✓ Babbles with inflection (8-10 mos.) _____

SELF-HELP

✓ Finger-feeds himself (8-12 mos.) _____

✓ Extends arm or leg to help when being dressed (9-12 mos.) _____

✓ May hold spoon when feeding (9-12 mos.) _____

SOCIAL/EMOTIONAL

✓ Shy or anxious with strangers (8-12 mos.) _____

✓ Cries when mother or father leaves (8-12 mos.) _____

✓ Enjoys imitating people in his play (10-12 mos.) _____

✓ Shows specific preferences for certain people and toys (8-12 mos.) _____

✓ Prefers mother and/or regular care provider over all others (8-12 mos.) _____

✓ Repeats sounds or gestures for attention (10-12 mos.) _____

✓ May test parents at bed time (9-12 mos.) _____

✓ Displays contented temperament for the majority of the time _____

Developmental Red Flags (8 to 12 Months)

❑ Does not crawl

❑ Drags one side of body while crawling (for over one month)

❑ Cannot stand when supported

❑ Does not search for objects that are hidden (10-12 mos.)

❑ Says no single words ("mama" or "dada")

❑ Does not learn to use gestures such as waving or shaking head

❑ Does not sit steadily by 10 months

❑ Does not react to new environments and people

❑ Does not seek out caregiver when stressed

❑ Does not show interest in Peek-a-Boo or Pat-a Cake by 8 mos.

❑ Does not babble by 8 mos. ("dada," "baba," "mama")

❑ Is upset by loud noises, being touched, and other environmental stimuli

❑ Responds negatively to certain types of clothing or textures, foods, taking a bath, having dirty hands

COMMENTS: _____

_____

_____

_____

_____

_____

_____

_____

_____

_____

_____

_____

_____

_____

_____

_____

Developmental Checklist (12 to 24 Months)

CHILD'S NAME: _____

DATE OF BIRTH:_____

PARENT OR GUARDIAN:_____

MILESTONES   **DATE OBSERVED**

GROSS MOTOR

✔ Walks alone (12-16 mos.)   _____

✔ Pulls toys behind him/her while walking (13-16 mos.)   _____

✔ Carries large toy or several toys while walking (12-15 mos.)   _____

✔ Begins to run stiffly (16-18 mos.)   _____

✔ Walks into ball that is tossed toward him or her (18-24 mos.)   _____

✔ Climbs onto and down from furniture unsupported (16-24 mos.)   _____

✔ Walks up and down stairs holding on to support (18-24 mos.)   _____

FINE MOTOR

✔ Scribbles spontaneously (14-16 mos.)   _____

✔ Turns over container to pour out contents (12-18 mos.)   _____

✔ Builds tower of four blocks or more (20-24 mos.)   _____

✔ Completes simple knobbed wooden puzzles of 3 to 4 pieces   _____

LANGUAGE

✔ Says "no" with meaning (13-15 mos.)   _____

✔ Follows simple, one-step instructions (14-18 mos.)   _____

✔ Says several single words (15-18 mos.)   _____

✔ Recognizes names of familiar people, objects, and body parts (18-24 mos.)   _____

✔ Points to object or picture when it's named for them (18-24 mos.)   _____

✔ Repeats words overheard in conversations (16-18 mos.)   _____

✔ Uses two-word sentences (18-24 mos.)   _____

COGNITIVE

✔ Finds objects, hidden under 2 or 3 covers   _____

✔ Identifies one body part (15-24 mos.)   _____

✔ Begins to sort shapes and colors (20-24 mos.)   _____

✔ Begins make-believe play (20-24 mos.)   _____

✔ Will listen to short story book with pictures   _____

DATE OBSERVED

SELF-HELP

✓ Likes to play with food when eating (18-24 mos.) _____

✓ Can put on shoes with help (20-24 mos.) _____

✓ Can open doors by turning knobs (18-24 mos.) _____

✓ Can drink from open cup, with some spilling (18-24 mos.) _____

✓ Starts to feed self with spoon, with some spilling _____

SOCIAL/EMOTIONAL

✓ Imitates behavior of others, especially adults and older children (18-24 mos.) _____

✓ Increasingly enthusiastic about company or other children (20-24 mos.) _____

✓ Demonstrates increasing independence (18-24 mos.) _____

✓ Begins to show "defiant" behavior (18-24 mos.) _____

✓ Episodes of separation anxiety increase toward midyear, then fade _____

Developmental Red Flags (12 to 24 Months)

- ❏ Cannot walk by 18 months
- ❏ Does not demonstrate a mature heel-toe walking pattern after several months of walking, or walks exclusively on toes
- ❏ Does not speak at least 15 words by 18 months
- ❏ Does not use unique two-word phrases by age 2 (more milk, big dog, mommy help)
- ❏ By 15 months does not seem to know the function of common household objects (brush, telephone, cup, fork, spoon)
- ❏ Does not imitate actions or words by 24 mos.
- ❏ Does not follow simple 1-step instructions by 24 mos.
- ❏ Cannot identify self
- ❏ Cannot hold and use a spoon or cup for eating and drinking
- ❏ Does not display a wide array of emotions (anger, fear, happy, excited, frustrated)
- ❏ Has extreme difficulty calming self after becoming upset
- ❏ Has difficulty transitioning from one activity to another
- ❏ Is frequently discontented throughout the day
- ❏ Seems very distractible

COMMENTS: _____

_____

_____

_____

_____

_____

_____

_____

_____

_____

_____

_____

_____

_____

_____

Developmental Checklist (24 to 36 Months)

CHILD'S NAME: _____

DATE OF BIRTH: _____

PARENT OR GUARDIAN: _____

MILESTONES   **DATE OBSERVED**

GROSS MOTOR

✓ Climbs well (24-30 mos.)   _____

✓ Walks down stairs alone, placing both feet on each step (26-28 mos.)   _____

✓ Walks up stairs alternating feet with support (24-30 mos.)   _____

✓ Swings leg to kick ball (24-30 mos.)   _____

✓ Runs easily (24-26 mos.)   _____

✓ Pedals tricycle (30-36 mos.)   _____

✓ Bends over easily without falling (24-30 mos.)   _____

FINE MOTOR

✓ Makes vertical, horizontal, circular strokes with pencil or crayon (30-36 mos.)   _____

✓ Turns book pages one at a time (24-30 mos.)   _____

✓ Builds a tower of more than 6 blocks (24-30 mos.)   _____

✓ Holds a pencil in writing position (30-36 mos.)   _____

✓ Screws and unscrews jar lids, nuts, and bolts (24-30 mos.)   _____

✓ Turns rotating handles (door knob) (24-30 mos.)   _____

LANGUAGE

✓ Uses pronouns (I, you, me, we, they) (24-30 mos.)   _____

✓ Understands most sentences (24-40 mos.)   _____

✓ Recognizes and identifies almost all common objects and pictures (26-32 mos.)   _____

✓ Shows frustration when not understood by others (28-36 mos.)   _____

✓ Understands physical relationships (on, in, under) (30-36 mos.)   _____

✓ Can say name, age, and sex (30-36 mos.)   _____

✓ Uses words to communicate wants and needs (30-36 mos.)   _____

✓ Knows simple rhymes and songs (30-36 mos.)   _____

✓ Strangers can understand most of words (30-36 mos.)   _____

DATE OBSERVED

COGNITIVE

✓ Makes mechanical toys work (30-36 mos.) _____

✓ Matches an object in hand or room to a picture in a book (24-30 mos.) _____

✓ Plays make-believe with dolls, animals, and people (24-36 mos.) _____

✓ Sorts objects by color (30-36 mos.) _____

✓ Completes puzzles with 3 or 4 pieces (24-36 mos.) _____

✓ Understands concept of "two" (26-32 mos.) _____

✓ Listens to stories (24-36 mos.) _____

✓ Knows several body parts (24-36 mos.) _____

SELF-HELP

✓ Can pull pants down with help (24-36 mos.) _____

✓ Helps put things away (24-36 mos.) _____

✓ Serves self at table with some spilling (30-36 mos.) _____

SOCIAL/EMOTIONAL

✓ Uses the word "mine" often (24-36 mos.)

✓ Says "no" but will still do what is asked (24-36 mos.)

✓ Expresses a wide range of emotions (24-36 mos.)

✓ Objects to major changes in routine, but is becoming more compliant (30-36 mos.)

✓ Begins to follow simple rules (30-36 mos.)

✓ Begins to separate more easily from parents (by 36 mos.)

Developmental Red Flags (24 to 36 Months)

- ❑ Frequently fall and has difficulty with stairs
- ❑ Persistently drools
- ❑ Verbal expressions are understood by unfamiliar persons less than 50% of the time
- ❑ Inability to build a tower of more than 4 blocks
- ❑ Has difficulty manipulating small objects
- ❑ Is unable to copy a circle by 3 years old
- ❑ Is unable to communicate in short phrases
- ❑ Does not participate in pretend play
- ❑ Cannot feed self with spoon or drink from cup independently
- ❑ Does not understand simple instructions
- ❑ Shows little interest in other children
- ❑ Extreme difficulty separating from primary caregiver
- ❑ Has difficulty with changes in routines and transitions
- ❑ Is bothered by certain types of clothing, textures, foods, and/or other environmental stimuli such as sounds

COMMENTS: _____

_____

_____

_____

_____

_____

_____

_____

_____

_____

_____

_____

_____

Developmental Checklist (3 to 4 Years)

PART 1

CHILD'S NAME: _____

DATE OF BIRTH:_____

PARENT OR GUARDIAN:_____

MILESTONES	DATE OBSERVED

GROSS MOTOR

✓ Hops and stands on one foot up to 5 seconds _____

✓ Goes upstairs and downstairs without support _____

✓ Kicks ball forward _____

✓ Throws ball overhand _____

✓ Catches bounced ball most of the time _____

✓ Moves forward and backward _____

✓ Uses riding toys _____

FINE MOTOR

✓ Copies square shapes _____

✓ Draws a person with 2-4 body parts _____

✓ Uses scissors _____

✓ Draws circles and squares _____

✓ Begins to copy some capital letters _____

✓ Can feed self with spoon without spilling _____

LANGUAGE

✓ Understands the concepts of "same" and "different" _____

✓ Has mastered some basic rules of grammar _____

✓ Speaks in sentences of 5-6 words _____

✓ Asks questions _____

✓ Speaks clearly enough for strangers to understand _____

✓ Tells stories _____

COGNITIVE

✓ Correctly names some colors _____

✓ Understands the concept of counting and may know a few numbers _____

✓ Begins to have a clearer sense of time _____

✓ Follows 3-part commands _____

✓ Recalls parts of a story _____

✓ Engages in fantasy play _____

✓ Understands causality ("I can make things happen") _____

DATE OBSERVED

SELF-HELP

✓ Washes and dries hands and face _____

✓ Can do simple household tasks (help set the table) _____

✓ Can put on simple clothing items, with help for button, zipper,
shoelace (jacket, pants, shoes) _____

✓ Can run a brush or comb through own hair _____

SOCIAL/EMOTIONAL

✓ Interested in new experiences _____

✓ Cooperates/plays with other children _____

✓ Plays "mom "or "dad" _____

✓ More inventive in fantasy play _____

✓ Can stay on topic during conversations _____

✓ More independent _____

✓ Plays simple games with simple rules _____

✓ Begins to share toys with other children _____

✓ Often cannot distinguish between fantasy and reality _____

✓ May have imaginary friends or see monsters _____

Developmental Red Flags (3 to 4 Years)

❑ Cannot jump in place
❑ Cannot ride a trike
❑ Cannot grasp a crayon between thumb and fingers
❑ Has difficulty scribbling
❑ Cannot copy a circle
❑ Cannot stack 4 blocks
❑ Still clings or cries when parents leave him
❑ Shows no interest in interactive games
❑ Ignores other children
❑ Doesn't respond to people outside the family
❑ Doesn't engage in fantasy play
❑ Resists dressing, sleeping, using the toilet
❑ Lashes out without any self-control when angry or upset
❑ Doesn't use sentences of more than three words
❑ Doesn't use "me" or "you" appropriately

COMMENTS: _____

_____

_____

_____

_____

_____

_____

_____

_____

_____

_____

_____

_____

_____

Developmental Checklist (4 to 5 Years)

CHILD'S NAME: _____

DATE OF BIRTH:_____

PARENT OR GUARDIAN:_____

MILESTONES   **DATE OBSERVED**

GROSS MOTOR

✓ Stands on one foot for 10 seconds or longer   _____

✓ Hops, somersaults   _____

✓ Swings, climbs   _____

✓ May be able to skip   _____

FINE MOTOR

✓ Copies triangle and other geometric patterns   _____

✓ Draws person with body   _____

✓ Prints some letters   _____

✓ Uses fork, spoon   _____

✓ Usually cares for own toilet needs   _____

LANGUAGE

✓ Recalls parts of a story   _____

✓ Speaks sentences of more than 5 words   _____

✓ Uses future tense   _____

✓ Tells longer stories   _____

✓ Says name and address   _____

COGNITIVE

✓ Can count 10 or more objects   _____

✓ Correctly names at least 4 colors   _____

✓ Works in small groups for 5-10 minutes   _____

✓ Better understands the concept of time   _____

✓ Knows about things used every day in the home (money, food, etc.)   _____

SELF-HELP

✓ Can chew with lips closed   _____

✓ Goes to the bathroom independently, with reminders   _____

✓ Undresses and dresses independently, may be able to unbutton and unzip   _____

SOCIAL/EMOTIONAL
- ✓ Wants to please   _____
- ✓ Prefers to be with friends   _____
- ✓ More likely to agree to rules   _____
- ✓ Likes to sing, dance, and act   _____
- ✓ Shows more independence   _____

Developmental Red Flags (4 to 5 Years)

❑ Exhibits extremely aggressive, fearful, or timid behavior

❑ Is unable to separate from parents

❑ Is easily distracted and unable to concentrate on any single activity for more than 5 minutes

❑ Shows little interest in playing with other children

❑ Refuses to respond to people in general

❑ Rarely uses fantasy or imitation in play

❑ Seems unhappy or sad much of the time

❑ Avoids or seems aloof with other children and adults

❑ Does not express a wide range of emotions

❑ Has trouble eating, sleeping, or using the toilet

❑ Cannot differentiate between fantasy and reality

❑ Seems unusually passive

❑ Does not understand prepositions ("put the cup on the table"; "get the ball under the couch")

❑ Does not follow 2-part commands ("pick up the toy and put it on the shelf")

❑ Does not give his/her first and last name

❑ Does not use plurals or past tense

❑ Does not build a tower of 6 to 8 blocks

❑ Holds crayon with fisted grasp

❑ Has trouble taking off clothing

❑ Unable to brush teeth or wash and dry hands

COMMENTS: _____

_____

_____

_____

_____

_____

_____

_____

_____

_____

Appendix B

Syracuse Dynamic Assessment for Birth to Three*

Gail L. Ensher, Tasia P. Bobish, Eric F. Gardner, Cynthia A. Michaels, Katharine G. Butler, Daniel J. Foertsch, and Christine Cooper

*Modified from version published with Applied Symbolix, Inc.

Caregiver Interview Form*

Instructions to Interviewer: The Caregiver Interview Form can be used by professionals to identify caregiver/ family needs and strengths.

NA – Does not apply to our family

1 – I need help with this immediately

2 – I need help with this, but it is not my highest priority

3 – I am interested in learning more about this, but it is not an immediate concern

4 – I feel comfortable with this—I do not need help in this area

5 – This is an area of strength for me (and my family)

PART 1: HOME AND FAMILY

1. Feeding my child . . . . _____

2. Knowing how to play with my child . . . . _____

3. Getting my child to sleep . . . . _____

4. Understanding my child's health and physical needs . . . . _____

5. Understanding my child's behavior . . . . _____

6. Communicating with my child. . . . . _____

7. Managing my family at mealtimes. . . . . _____

8. Getting enough rest . . . . _____

9. Taking time for myself . . . . _____

10. Finding day care, respite care, or babysitting . . . . _____

*Modified from Syracuse Dynamic Assessment (Ensher, Bobish, Gardner, Michaels, Butler, et al., Applied Symbolix, 2007).

CAREGIVER REPORT (continued)

11. Knowing how to touch and hold my child. . . . . _____

12. Finding helpful doctors . . . . _____

13. Finding helpful dentists. . . . . _____

14. Dealing with my child's behavior. . . . . _____

15. Dealing with the other children in our family . . . . _____

16. Finding support for our family . . . . _____

17. Knowing how to make our home safe for my child . . . . _____

18. Coordinating all of my child's appointments and services . . . . _____

Do you have any special needs or priorities that are not listed above? _____

_____

_____

_____

Do you have special abilities, skills, and strengths not listed above? _____

_____

_____

_____

_____

CHAPTER 2

Social-Emotional Development, Families, and Mental Health Needs in the Earliest Years

Gail L. Ensher and David A. Clark

Highlights of the Chapter

At the conclusion of the chapter, the reader will:

- have a basic understanding of the social and emotional development of infants and young children in the first 3 years of life

- understand important aspects of nurturing family relationships that lead to healthy attachment, self-regulation, and optimal emotional development of young children throughout the first 3 years of life

- have knowledge of the risk factors and family dynamics that can adversely affect the social and emotional development of infants and young children

- understand ways in which accessible family supports can tip the balance of developmental outcomes of infants and young children toward greater resilience and healthier mental health patterns

- understand ways in which early childhood intervention and medical professionals can develop positive supports, alliances, and partnerships with families to facilitate healthy social and emotional development in infants and young children during the first 3 years of life

Healthy Social and Emotional Development of Infants and Young Children

For decades, scholars and researchers have acknowledged the essential roles of parents and caregivers in determining the trajectories of social and emotional development of their infants and young children (Bowlby, 1969; Brazelton & Sparrow, 2006; Cooper, Masi, & Vick, 2009; Coyle, 2011; Onunaku, 2005). However, it is only within recent years that child development specialists, educators, physicians, family counselors, psychologists, and other

professionals serving our youngest populations have recognized the mental health issues of such populations within their respective "systems of care" (Osofsky & Lieberman, 2011, p. 120; Poulsen, 2013; Summers & Chazan-Cohen, 2012; Van Ornum, 2011). At least three often-related influences have been paramount in drawing attention to this pressing need:

1. The large numbers of infants and young children under 5 years old that are reported to child protective services as a result of abuse and neglect by their caregivers, parents, or others who may or may not be known to family members;

2. Communities and local neighborhoods plagued with violence and poverty; and

3. The growing numbers of family members with infants and young children who themselves are struggling with depression, anxiety, substance abuse, and other mental health disorders.

The fact that certain populations of infants and young children are more likely targets of child abuse and neglect within their families is also well documented. These groups include babies born prematurely, children born with impairments and disabilities, infants born to adolescent caregivers, young children under 5 years old who have been placed in the child welfare system, young children born into families of poverty with limited resources and education, infants and young children chronically exposed to violence and trauma, and families where parents have been deployed into the armed services (Ensher & Clark, 2011; Knitzer & Lefkowitz, 2006; Lieberman, 2010; National Research Council & Institute of Medicine, 2000; Nelson & Mann, 2011; Tronick & Beeghly, 2011).

In her presentation "Repairing the Effects of Trauma on Early Attachment," sponsored by The National Child Traumatic Stress Network, Alicia Lieberman (2010) defined *infant mental health* as:

- The capacity to grow well and to love well,

- The ability to express and regulate emotions and recover from dysregulation,

- The ability to establish trusting relationships and repair conflict, and

- The ability to explore and learn within the society's cultural values.

Given the normal course of variation in rates of development and individual differences in temperament, how does Lieberman's definition translate into typical patterns of social and emotional behavior and "healthy" mental well-being of infants, toddlers, and young children throughout the first 3 years of life?

Attachment, Security, and an Emotional Home

Most of the time, infants start life with all of the bio-neurological-sensory resources and social/emotional readiness to begin their journey toward learning how to relate to their closest family members and, eventually, people in their wider world. Attachment, bonding, security, and an emotional home with significant, consistent caregivers are the basic, requisite foundation for launching them onto this life-long pathway. Moreover, in many ways, healthy social and emotional development is the scaffolding for all other aspects of development. Echoing this point, Onunaku (2005) has written:

Babies are hardwired to develop strong, emotional connections, or attachment, *with their primary caregivers. The ability to attach to a significant adult allows young children to become trusting, confident, and capable of regulating stress and distress. The most important part of attachment is the quality of attachment formed, as it predicts later development. Ideally, children develop secure attachment (a healthy emotional bond) with caregivers. Infants who develop secure attachment with a primary caregiver during the early years of life are more likely to have positive relationships with peers, be liked by their teachers, perform better in school, and respond with resilience in the face of adversity as preschoolers and older children. Attachment is integral to the emotional development of the young child; . . . babies need to become attached to at least one close, trusting adult.* (p. 4)

Everyday Care and Healthy Interactions

Nurturing between infant and caregiver during the early months after birth takes place within many biological, social, and emotional contexts that ultimately form the building blocks for trusting, caring relationships. During normal times of feeding and nursing, infants are able to hold their moms' and dads' faces in mutual, visual regard. Newborns are the parents' best teachers—of when they have had enough to eat, when they need to be picked up and comforted, when they are tired, when they have had too much stimulation, when they require quiet time, and when they have other unmet needs. Behavior—on the part of babies and the caregivers—is communication! Most important, caregivers soon discover that their newborns are unique, with different styles and patterns of emotional expression, with different temperaments, and with different levels of intensity and activity. All of these characteristics fall within the continuum and synchrony of "typical social and emotional behavior." Moreover, for caregivers and parents, "touching, holding, rocking, and talking are as important as getting the baby fed" (Brazelton & Sparrow, 2006, p. 57).

The First Year: Beginnings

The first 6 months of an infant's life is a period of great social and emotional learning, responsiveness, predictability, and growing exploration, as babies interact with the significant caregivers of their emotional homes. They very quickly develop different cries to signal different needs such as comfort for being hurt, food, sleep, or a diaper change. In turn, parents usually are able to "read" these cues, and without much hesitation, comply to meet these needs. Although infants vary regarding when they first smile in response to another person (usually a consistent caregiver), this milestone typically occurs within the first 6 to 8 weeks and is welcomed with great joy by the recipients! The emotional response from others becomes the catalyst for future smiles and vocal expressions by the infant that initiates the vitally important "circles of communication" (Greenspan & Wieder, 1998) that increase in complexity with further development of speech and language throughout the first 12 months.

That said, even within the first 3 months, infants become little social beings, differentiating their caregivers or parents from other adults and responding with increased vocalizations, smiling, and activity; beginning to self-regulate and self-calm; and developing somewhat predictable patterns of sleeping and waking—all signs of an emerging trusting relationship between parent and child.

By 4 to 6 months, the baby has become vigilant, increasingly aware of his environment and people in the immediate surroundings—localizing sounds and processing stimuli within visual range. With this growing ability to respond and attend, he is now able to engage in newly discovered and pleasurable reciprocal play and communication such as peek-a-boo with screams of delight, laughing, smiling, and anticipation of parent responses. Moreover,

from 7 to 9 months, the baby—approaching his first birthday—has learned to distinguish himself from less familiar people, often becoming distressed when handed to extended family members such as grandparents—a behavior which clearly highlights the emotional bond between parent and child. Between 10 and 12 months, grounded in the security of parent–child attachment, the baby is now ready to extend relationships to others in the outside world, at the same time not venturing far from the assurance of parent comfort nearby.

The Second Year: Growing Independence and Autonomy

As the baby begins the second year of life, the normal course of social and emotional development typically becomes manifest in very different patterns of behavior. With the benefit of emerging motor, cognitive, and language abilities, the child grows increasingly adept at communicating needs, wants, and preferences. "No," "me," and "mine" become familiar toddler responses, and parents experience their first introduction to the need for establishing warm, loving, but firm and developmentally appropriate social-emotional limits. This is an age that can be particularly challenging for parents and caregivers, wondering when to give and pull back, when to hold on to expectations set, and how to be consistent with establishing socializing boundaries. The emergent toddler is likely to test limits repeatedly with outcomes of frequent child temper tantrums. Throughout this period, parents need to be especially mindful of creating a balance between discipline and praise. In the absence of caregiver consistency, confrontations and emotional "battles" can quickly escalate and get out of hand. Setting limits is a particularly important dimension of positive parent-child relationships at this point, in light of increasing dangers that present themselves for the agile and mobile toddler and the child's testing of caregiver love and affection. On the other hand, it is clear that within the context of the child's behavior the parent or caregiver remains the "emotional home base" and security "touch-point" for the child.

From Toddlerhood to Preschool: Trusting the World to Explore, Play, and Express Feelings

Parent-child "survival" of the "terrible twos" is an important door and pathway to social-emotional well-being, competence, and positive mental health outcomes for toddlers and young children. Coupled with the dramatic shifts and swings in mood, temperament, and emotions, as toddlers move from 2 to 3 years old, they become ever more capable of displaying a range of emotions and feelings, demonstrating these in play scenarios and from person to person. Although they are still limited mainly to concrete expressions, they can show sympathy for others who are sad, happiness and joy when praised for accomplishments, anger when frustrated, guilt when they know that they have done something "wrong," as well as a variety of other feelings. They can be funny and excitable, willing to share and cooperate, but still tied to routines and resistant to change. Their playtime is equally divided, parallel to that of peers and reflective of emerging associative interactions. They can be demanding of attention, particularly in the presence of another sibling. As all caregivers and professionals who work with infants and toddlers know, every child is unique, with some remaining at certain stages longer than others. How parents "negotiate" these typical, changeable, sometimes volatile, selectively independent, and joyous moments continues to cement the building blocks toward positive mental health for the toddler, young child, and

thereafter—an enormous task, especially for first-time mothers and fathers. Most important, parents and caregivers need to remember that "discipline is not the same as punishment. Discipline means teaching and it is a long-term process" (Brazelton & Sparrow, 2006, p.167).

What Happens in the First 3 Years Really Matters: Trauma, Risk, and Toxic Stress

Those who have raised children likely would agree that being a parent or caregiver probably is the most challenging responsibility that they have ever had, with all of the uncertainties and ups and downs and few "hard and fast" rules and guidelines to follow. It is also evident that, in the 21st century, this responsibility is becoming ever more difficult with the fast pace of life; multiple roles that parents assume; increasing demands; and the growing hazards, pressures, and economics of day-to-day living. These mounting challenges are evident in the increasing numbers of families who struggle with mental health issues, as well as the growing numbers of children referred to child welfare and child protective systems because of suspected abuse and neglect. Further, it is well documented that the overwhelming numbers of children living in these often toxic situations are infants or young children less than 5 years old (Dicker, 2009; Ensher & Clark, 2009; Finello, Hampton, & Poulsen, 2011; Knitzer & Lefkowitz, 2006; Landy & Menna, 2006; Poulsen, 2013).

Adversity Within the Environment and Its Consequences

More than a decade ago, Shonkoff and Phillips (National Research Council & Institute of Medicine, 2000) emphasized the consequences of environmental/family adversity and stress for infants and young children that can and do take place as a result of early emotional impairments. These issues are as true today, perhaps even more so, as they were in 2000:

> *Early child development can be seriously compromised by social, regulatory, and emotional impairments. The causes of such impairments are multiple but often revolve around disturbances in close relationships. Indeed, young children are capable of deep and lasting sadness, grief, and disorganization in response to trauma, loss, and early personal rejection. Given the substantial short- and long-term risks that accompany early mental health impairments, the incapacity of many early childhood programs to address these concerns and the severe shortage of early childhood professionals with mental health expertise are urgent problems.* (p. 387)

It is safe to say that the ecology of the world, local communities, and neighborhoods where parents and caregivers live and raise their infants and young children, have changed dramatically since Urie Bronfenbrenner's publication of *The Ecology of Human Development* in 1979. Safety in cities, in towns, on the streets, in public schools, in movie theaters, and on college campuses has become a serious concern in the United States, as seen in the tragically horrific events of Aurora, Colorado; Newtown, Connecticut; and more recently, Boston, Massachusetts. To be sure, violence in large cities, plagued with pockets of poverty, used to be the most frequent settings for such violence. In the early 21st century, however, this is no longer the case. Further, regardless of the position of people in terms of policies and regulations for gun control, families, legislators, educators, physicians, and professionals are now more aware than ever of the undetected mental health issues of adolescents and adults that have gone untreated, later to surface

in unforeseen catastrophes such as those in Colorado and Connecticut. And even if families physically reside distances away from locations of tragedies, the realities are brought into their homes, over and over again, via the internet, cell phones, television, and other forms of technology that are within arms' length. The impact is significant for families, no longer comfortable and confident that they and their children are protected from harm's way.

The first of these major incidents took place on September 11, 2001, when families across the United States experienced terrorism, loss, and devastation on American soil, unparalleled in the history of this country. The severe psychological and mental health effects on parents and their children who witnessed these unimaginable events, either in person or via the media, have been the subject of much study for more than a decade (Chemtob et al., 2010; Gershoff, Aber, Ware, & Kotler, 2010; Melnyk et al., 2002; ScienceDaily, 2010).

On a smaller scale than 9/11 in terms of the loss of life and devastation, families continue to be ridden with anxiety around the acts of violence carried out in local communities and neighborhoods and schools, because they are happening in places assumed to be safe and protected from such atrocities. These events have dramatically changed the lives of families and young children forever! It is no surprise that the numbers of parents struggling with depression in the United States (emerging from multiple sources) is on the rise (now cited to be 1 in 10 adults; Centers for Disease Control and Prevention, 2010), mental health issues that are subsequently revisited upon their infants and young children.

Discussion about adversity within the environment would not be complete without addressing growing concerns about the effects of electronic media on infants, toddlers, and young children, referenced above. In addition to the exposure of children at very early ages to violence through news broadcasts and other technological venues on a daily basis, the widespread production and marketing of often developmentally inappropriate media materials for infants and very young children, from birth to 6 years old, have infiltrated almost every aspect of American family life. Schmidt et al. (2005), summarizing the findings of seminal studies on the effects of electronic media on young children, cautioned:

Media influences on young children are not only strong and pervasive, but also potentially controllable—especially in the early years when parents determine the majority of their children's media exposure. In order to ensure healthy media diets among children, it is important to understand how parents make decisions about their children's media use, so that effective interventions can be designed where appropriate. Anticipatory guidance and child-healthy advice about media use provided by pediatricians at "well-baby" visits can function as a "tipping point" to encourage parents to think carefully about the media their children consume. (p. 11)

Families at Risk

There is a wealth of research that highlights the adverse consequences of toxic family and environmental stress on infants and young children, emanating from discord and violence within home settings and beyond. In addition, multiple social, economic, and educational risk factors (Golden, McDaniel, Loprest, & Stanczyk, 2013), including the following, contribute to such problems:

- Poverty/poor economic resources including poor nutrition and unemployment
- Parental histories of child abuse and neglect
- Poor family supports and social isolation

- Teen pregnancy and adolescent caregiving
- Substance abuse
- Low levels of caregiver education
- Lack of information about positive approaches for guiding challenging behavior
- Unrealistic expectations of children by caregivers
- Single-parent families
- Parental depression and other mental health issues

Moreover, numerous studies on child abuse, neglect, and family violence have found that risk factors frequently coexist (Tronick & Beeghly, 2011), one or more hardships and stressors leading to additional situations, events, and challenges (Ensher & Clark, 2011), that perpetuate cycles of vulnerability (Tronick & Beeghly, 2011). Finally, underlying these findings is the fact that infants and young children from birth to 3 years old who are chronically exposed to toxic stress and adversity may experience neurological and social-emotional changes that have serious, negative consequences for later developmental and mental health outcomes. For instance, Shonkoff, Garner, and colleagues of the Committee on Psychosocial Aspects of Child and Family Health, Committee on Early Childhood, Adoption, and Dependent Care, and Section on Developmental and Behavioral Pediatrics (2012) wrote:

Advances in fields of inquiry as diverse as neuroscience, molecular biology, genomics, developmental psychology, epidemiology, sociology, and economics are catalyzing an important paradigm shift in our understanding of health and disease across the lifespan. This converging multidisciplinary science of human development has profound implications for our ability to enhance the life prospects of children and to strengthen the social and economic fabric of society. Drawing on these multiple streams of investigation, this report presents an ecobiodevelopmental framework that illustrates how early experiences and environmental influences can leave a lasting signature on the genetic predispositions that affect emerging brain architecture and long-term health. The report also examines extensive evidence of the disruptive impacts of toxic stress, offering intriguing insights and causal mechanisms that link early adversity to later impairments in learning, behavior, and both physical and mental well-being. . . .[The implications] suggest that many adult diseases should be viewed as developmental disorders that begin early in life and that persistent health disparities associated with poverty, discrimination, or maltreatment could be reduced by alleviation of toxic stress in childhood. (p. e232)

Children at Risk

The promising evidence noted previously, coupled with the identification of certain populations of infants and young children who often are more prominent targets of neglect, abuse, and toxic stress, holds much potential for early intervention and more positive developmental and mental health outcomes.

Researchers know, for instance, that the incidence of child abuse and neglect is considerably higher among:

- Infants and young children, 3 years old and under (Dicker, 2009; Wu et al., 2004)

- Infants born prematurely where bonding and attachment may have been compromised because of extended hospital stays (Summers & Chazan-Cohen, 2012)

- Young children in the child welfare system and foster care (Dicker, 2009)

- Infants and young children with learning, temperament, and behavioral challenges (DePanfilis, 2006; Goldman, Salus, Wolcott, & Kennedy, 2003).

The reasons for these noteworthy findings are many. Ultimately, these factors reflect multiple familial, cultural, racial, and environmental contributors, in the absence of sufficient caregiving and parenting supports to counterbalance negative agents, antecedents, and effects. Immaturities of parents, inadequate knowledge about positive approaches for guiding challenging child behavior, lack of knowledge and understanding of appropriate developmental milestones and abilities, poor choices of partners living in homes of infants and young children, parent overload of responsibilities with few community resources, caregiver inabilities to manage normal stressful periods of discontent of infants and young children, and growing problems of substance abuse all add to the mix of possible unsafe and/or adverse family situations. Moreover, in many instances, reaching families with *coordinated preventative efforts* across child advocacy and early intervention agencies has been a challenging, elusive task in the United States. Early intervention service providers, pre-k teachers, pediatricians, and medical and social services personnel in hospitals (should infants be admitted to pediatric or neonatal intensive care units) are frontline professionals who must be vigilant with regard to symptoms of family stress and adversity, as well as other obvious "red flags" related to child behavior and injuries (Ensher & Clark, 2009).

The "Tipping Point" for Developmental Outcomes

Despite the overwhelming "weight" of risk indicators that may lead to future mental health problems, there are infants and young children who somehow are "protected" from these influences, survive, and fare better than do other children. Indeed, as Hanson (2013) has noted, in the face of such adversity, "it is tempting to focus attention in education, health care, and the social services on what can and does go wrong; however, many things also go right in human development and within families" (p. 61). Identifying and strengthening these protective factors proactively can set a very different course and much more positive pathway for both caregivers and their young children.

Addressing the questions and issues about "resilience" and the variations among infants and young children, Ensher and Clark (2009) have written:

Some of the differences reside in the severity of exposure to violence, the presence of a significant other who can serve to "protect" the child, the age of exposure to maltreatment, the length of time during which the child was subjected to abuse and/or neglect, relief or removal from the violence, and child-specific characteristics. Most likely, resilience or an ability to adapt beyond adversity for more favorable outcomes ultimately will reside with the benefit of a combination of factors influencing any given child within the context of his or her family. Also, how professionals determine and who identifies positive outcomes and when in the lives of children those questions are examined may vary across agencies, teachers, or those making such judgment calls. Children change. They may "look" adjusted at one point in their lives; yet, given a different set of circumstances, they may need support and intervention at another time. Thus, on the continuum of living from day to day, these are indeed difficult determinations to make. However, there are children who, in reality, do better than others, and it is imperative to examine why and how that can be and then to translate that evidence into practice whenever possible. (p. 281)

Reversing the Odds of Risk

In his insightful chapter "Resilience Reconsidered", Rutter (2000) wrote that family events and situations are fluid and dynamic. Just as multiple influences leading to "new morbidities" and later mental health problems for infants and young children likely coexist, it is equally probable that "multiple levels of influence" (Shonkoff et al., 2012, p. e234) can facilitate and promote healthier behavioral, social, and emotional outcomes for young children.

Essential foundations

Most scholars, researchers, policymakers, and professionals across multiple disciplines including early childhood education, special education, pediatrics, and clinical practice agree that reversing the odds of risk is a formidable task that will require a shift in paradigms, community resources, training and teaching, cooperation and collaboration across the respective fields of endeavor, and the family-centered interventions and practices. However, the focus will need to move from a deficit orientation to the adoption of a strength-based implementation, grounded in a commitment and ability to carry out policies and strategies of prevention. Professionals know, for instance, that:

- Secure, healthy, nurturing family relationships are essential to the well-being and development of young children.

- As indicated in chapter 4 (Clark & Clark, 2016), good nutrition is critical to a positive course of physical, social-emotional, and cognitive/language progress. This needs to start prenatally and continue throughout a mother's pregnancy.

- Families under stress need to be reached before crises lead to child abuse and neglect. Many families in distress are isolated, without other family members and friends to assist, counsel, or support. Under the best of circumstances, raising and nurturing infants and young children is challenging.

- Accessible, affordable, and available pediatric care is essential to infants and young children throughout the first 3 years of life and beyond. These services need to be culturally and ethnically sensitive, as well as responsive to populations of caregivers who are diverse in terms of age, educational backgrounds, economic status, race, languages spoken within the home, family membership, locations of residence, and any special needs of their children.

- Addressing maternal mental health issues such as depression has the potential of greatly enhancing parent-child relationships, during the first 3 years and beyond, when the focus of effective intervention is the mother-child dyad (Shonkoff et al., 2012). With the documented growing numbers of caregivers struggling with such concerns, this area of adult and child health constitutes a major opportunity for intervention with mothers prenatally, throughout pregnancy, into the earliest months and years of life (National Scientific Council on the Developing Child, 2010).

- In the face of mild to moderate to severe disabilities, early intervention offered to infants and young children can change the trajectories of developmental outcomes, thus slowing and/or reducing the impact of disabilities (Goode, Diefendorf, & Colgan, 2011). This finding has important implications for infants and young children (birth to 3 years old) in the child welfare system (who are supposed to be afforded early intervention, as mandated by the Infants and Toddlers with Disabilities Program, Part C).

- Transition and implementation plans—from hospital to home, from foster care to parent homes, from early intervention to preschool programs and services—need to be developed and monitored. These important activities can be accomplished with the assistance of professionals such as EI teachers, social workers connected to the child welfare system, and pediatricians in medical home and community pediatric health care facilities who are likely to see and visit with families, their infants, and young children (Committee on Psychosocial Aspects of Child and Family Health, 2001).

Windows of Opportunity at Home: Using the "Touchpoints" of Social-Emotional Development

Without a doubt, it is much easier to talk about problems and concerns related to the mental health issues of families, infants, and their young children than to effect real differences in real lives. On the other hand, there are some "windows of opportunity" for healthy social-emotional development of young children that are common to families representing very diverse cultures, racial and ethnic groups, levels of income and education, ages of caregivers, and styles of parenting. Pursuant to this assumption, as authors, we do not intend to minimize the challenges of changing the course of adverse or potentially toxic situations within families. On the other hand, it is possible that with utilizing a framework of relationship-based interventions, the following "touchpoints" can be helpful to professionals (partnering with families) toward fostering positive outcomes between parents and their children.

- *Using daily routines for developing nurturing, consistent, and quality caregiving/parenting practices with infants and young children.* These routines include a number of predictable tasks and activities that parents and their young children engage in as they communicate and interact. These "touchpoints" include feeding and mealtimes; changing, bathing, dressing, and eventually toilet-training; bedtime; and comforting and soothing during periods of child frustration and discontent.

Lieberman, Padron, Van Horn, and Harris (2005) discussed "moments of particular connectedness, intense shared affect, and heightened intimacy between the parent and child" (p. 509) "as growth-promoting" and moments that are an "integral part of the child's identity" (p. 509). As authors, we are suggesting that as parents and their children participate in the daily routines of living together, such tasks, activities, and times offer essential opportunities for bonding, attachment, and growing together across the age span of the first 3 years. They are "teachable" moments for relationship building, learning, and "falling in love" that can serve as a springboard for professionals to enhance parenting and caregiving abilities.

- *Engaging in child's play.* Just as play is the child's most powerful way of learning, play is one of the most powerful means for relationship building between a parent and child. This reality is true for every stage of development throughout the first 3 years of life and beyond, regardless of a child's temperament, abilities, or learning or behavioral challenges. Play opens windows of opportunity for communication that can be shaped and adapted to a child's individual interests, preferences, and styles of learning. Play can take place within numerous settings and according to

multiple formats. It can be spontaneous or initiated, it can be unstructured or structured, play can take place between caregiver and child or among several children, it can take place with toys and concrete materials or within imaginary or pretend contexts. Play can happen using gestures or prompts or with much verbal expression. In sum, the possibilities are endless! And perhaps most important, play can be a time for learning about one another through interaction, give and take, listening, self-regulation, developing social competence (National Association for the Education of Young Children, 2007), and giving of and expressing oneself—for child and caregiver alike. Emphasizing the importance of play in promoting healthy child development and maintaining strong parent-child bonds, Ginsburg (2007) wrote,

Play allows children to use their creativity while developing their imagination, dexterity, and physical, cognitive, and emotional strength. Play is important to healthy brain development. It is through play that children at a very early age engage and interact in the world around them. Play allows children to create and explore a world they can master, conquering their fears while practicing adult roles, sometimes in conjunction with other children or adult caregivers. As they master their work, play helps children develop new competencies that lead to enhanced confidence and the resiliency they will need to face future challenges. (p. 183)

In sum, play is the essential right of every infant and young child.

- *Supporting appropriate child behavior.* Children learn what they live, and these "lessons" are transparent and transcending! A warm and developmentally supportive emotional home is the foundation of strong parent-child relationships. The effects of negative, violent, or traumatic home environments on infants are well documented (Ensher & Clark, 2011), as is the fact that "how parents respond when encouraging a particular developmental capacity in their child—such as self-esteem, attachment, or communication—is critically important" (Landy, 2009, p.xxi).

- *Creating and maintaining a healthy and growth-promoting environment for the child.* In large part, the foundation of relationship-centered interactions between parents and their young children that are safe and growth-promoting are grounded in parents' basic understanding of child health and development In particular, parents must be able to create a safe physical environment at home; parents need to have age-appropriate, reasonable expectations of their children; and parents must raise their children with a common-sense awareness of age-appropriate nutritional needs and health-related concerns. Such guidelines and principles are vital to the well-being of all children, but especially so within the first 3 years of life when safeguards are paramount. Moreover, these needs and parenting practices necessarily change over time, as children grow; indeed, meeting these goals often becomes even more complex when a child has special needs and/or disabilities.

There are no easy answers to such dilemmas. Ultimately, parents and caregivers are most effective if they are supported by professionals as partners, rather than as the recipients of knowledge that they do not own or understand. Weston (2005) wrote:

It is humbling to come to the understanding that we do not have truth, that our professional, technical knowledge is best considered hypothesis in its relevance to this particular family and baby. When we understand that those with whom we work have "all the information we need . . . then our attitude conveys this" and the parent (and the child) can sense themselves as sources, partners, rather than as assessed and judged recipients. (p. 346)

Accessible and Effective Mental Health Resources and Interventions

For the past 10 years, there has been a dominant emphasis in the field of early childhood special education on providing medical, educational, and clinical services to families and their young children within their natural environments (McWilliam, 2010) and within routines-based contexts (McWilliam & Casey, 2008) at home and in the community. In so doing, delivering services within the ecology of where families live, work, and interact with their friends and other family members affords families more opportunities for accessing and utilizing ongoing mental health resources and interventions, as needed. "Touchpoints" discussed previously reinforce this important concept, as does the discussion following.

Gateways to Intervention

Although it is clear that special education and medical services for infants and young children (and their families) are dependent upon the children meeting specified criteria or conditions for eligibility, the focus of services always needs to include prevention, as well as treatment and remediation. This requirement is especially true relative to the provision of mental health services that can go unnoticed or undetected for extended periods of time, that later lead to cumulative, long-term serious consequences for all family members. It is also clear that when mental health conditions are at issue, often comprehensive, collaborative, integrated efforts (Osofsky & Lieberman, 2011), in tandem with strengths of a family, are necessary. Osofsky and Lieberman (2011) have stated the premise in this way:

For young children, the caregivers' emotional well-being and life circumstances profoundly affect the quality of infant-caregiver relationships. Public policy plays an integral role in the conceptualization of infant mental health interventions because society has a pivotal role in promoting consistent, protective, and nurturing parent-child relationships as an essential vehicle for raising developmentally competent children. (p. 120)

Accessing educational services through Early Intervention

As discussed in chapters 6 (Ensher & Clark, 2016) and 17 (Beckstrand, Pienkowski, Powers, & Scanlon, 2016), early intervention (EI) is one of the primary "gateways" for the provision of educational, clinical, and therapeutic services that are specifically designed for infants, toddlers, and young children from birth to 3 years old. They are the parent's option and opportunity, but are not required. Should children meet state-specified criteria for eligibility, such services usually are carried out in home, day care, or otherwise natural community settings that are easily accessible to professional providers and family members. EI practiced in home and other natural settings incorporates the ecology of the entire family–child environment and ideally comprises a meaningful and realistic delivery of services for all members of the family and friends involved.

Ideally, family members are present during the delivery of services in order to facilitate possibilities for carry-over throughout the routines of daily parent caregiving, although this does not always take place given family work schedules. In addition, although eligibility for EI is contingent upon the child's qualifying for services, the context for the delivery of services is the *family*. This fundamental difference between the provision of services for younger versus older children is important because it takes into consideration family priorities and goals for their children, available resources, the home setting, and multiple other factors that influence the ways in which interventions can be effectively provided. For example, family members themselves can and should be directly involved in home visits by professionals, asking questions about child responses and behavior, as well as using toys and materials that are available in the home setting. If siblings are present during sessions, they likewise can participate with professionals—thus having opportunities to observe family interactions and dynamics. Finally, with caregivers and parents available in home settings, the needs of other family members are more likely to surface and assistance can be secured.

Accessing medical, dental, and mental health services through the medical home

When infants and young children are referred for EI, their special health care needs and/or disabilities are often relatively apparent, manifesting multiple medical and/or developmental needs that require follow-up with specialists across multiple disciplines. In the best interests of coordinating accessible medical and clinical services for families and their young children (Cooley, 2004; Council on Children With Disabilities/Section on Developmental Behavioral Pediatrics, Bright Futures Steering Committee, & Medical Home Initiatives for Children With Special Needs Project Advisory Committee, 2006; Dorros, Kurtzer-White, Ahlgren, Simon, & Vohr, 2007; Medical Home Initiatives for Children With Special Needs

Project Advisory Committee, 2002; National Institute for Health Care Management [NIHCM] Foundation, 2009; Palfrey et al., 2004), the medical home was "born."

The concept of the *medical home* was proposed and defined in a 1992 policy statement by the American Academy of Pediatrics. In particular, the original intent of the medical home was to offer families, children, and adolescents medical care that was "accessible, continuous, comprehensive, family-centered, coordinated, compassionate, and culturally effective" (Medical Home Initiatives for Children With Special Needs Project Advisory Committee, 2002, p. 184). Moreover, medical home initiatives are specifically designed to enable primary care providers to "address the myriad needs of their patients and families in one setting" (NIHCM Foundation, 2009, p. 17), with special emphasis on pediatric, developmental surveillance, early identification of special needs of young children in the first 3 years, and facilitation of access to mental health services through primary care practices. In a 2009 report, the NIHCM stated:

Originally developed to address the complex set of services needed by children with special health care needs, the medical home is now recognized as the standard of care for all children as well as for adults. Building medical homes often incorporates the use of technology, such as electronic health records, implementation of care coordination strategies, and linkages with other resources in the community. As defined, medical homes provide a strong basis for integrating mental health into primary care practice. Complex issues of implementation and reimbursement aside, the concept of the medical home ideally offers a promising vehicle for reaching underserved and some of the most vulnerable populations of infants and young children within a comprehensive context of family-centered, integrated, community-based

pediatric health care practices through "consultation, co-location, and collaborative care models" (NIHCM Foundation, 2009, pp. 18–20).

Such issues are especially relevant to one of the most vulnerable groups of infants and young children within the child welfare system, who continue to lack medical, dental, mental health, and EI services (Dicker, 2009).

Two key elements of offering "triple A" (appropriate, accessible, and available) medical and mental health services to families, infants, and young children across all income, educational, and cultural groups are:

- Developing collaborative partnerships across service, protective, and intervention programs; and

- Reaching families and children in need preventatively.

Neither one of these two challenges is easy to address. On the other hand, using an ecological approach that increases linkages among community-based resources and services could, in large part, benefit a significant number of families in locations where they reside and carry out the activities of their daily lives and routines.

Establishing family networks through community resources

Networks for families include both formal and informal supports, and in times of need and crisis, informal resources and friends are often the most critical and readily available. Bailey, Nelson, Hebbeler, and Spiker (2007) noted:

The outcomes experienced by young children with disabilities and their families will be influenced by a complex interplay of child, family, program, and community variables. Specialized services (e.g., those provided by pediatricians, therapists, or special educators) constitute only one aspect of support, and the benefits of early intervention could be enhanced or reduced depending on other resources and the extent to which they are integrated and coordinated. . . . Research consistently shows that families with strong support systems are able to handle challenges more effectively than families with low supports. (p. e993)

Such networks are incredibly beneficial to families in times of crisis, when they need a break from daily caregiving responsibilities, when parents need a friend to talk to or need advice, when they need an extra hand to help, and for countless other considerations. These networks can be developed from parent-to-parent connections, specific support groups for families with children who have special health care needs or disabilities, through religious groups, through contacts with day care providers, and myriad other community-based organizations that are readily available to family members. Indeed, our many years of experience with families of infants and young children with special needs have led us to the absolute conclusion that when individual family members find themselves isolated, with no resources or relationships to which they can turn, they find themselves in serious difficulty! And thus, these are the times when crises are more likely to surface.

Relationship-based interventions

Relationships are the foundation and framework of best practices in working with families, infants, and young children in the earliest years. This principle is true across all professional disciplines, family compositions, cultural and ethnic groups, levels and types of ability and disability of young children, and educational and economic family backgrounds. They are the key dimensions and extensions that determine the well-being of infants, young children, and individual family members that "tip" the balance of developmental outcomes—for worse or for the better!

More than a decade ago, there was a major shift in early childhood paradigms from an exclusive focus on the child toward a more ecological perspective of seeing the child within the context of the family. This new perspective accordingly acknowledged realities always recognized by EI, clinical, medical, and other professionals that the social and emotional well-being of the child was primarily determined by the nature of relationships and interactions between parents/caregivers and the child (Edelman, 2004).

Ushered in with this new perspective was a new understanding that the roles of professionals also needed to change. Rather than being primary decision makers, professionals needed to "give over" to parents their rightful and appropriate responsibilities as the genuine caregivers and teachers in the nurturing, relationship-based processes. In so doing, parents and families have become and now are recognized as full partners in decision-making roles, rather than merely recipients of information and "expert advice" in help-giving services for children.

Strengthening this new agenda of facilitating relationships in natural, family-centered contexts has challenged traditional ways of working with families and young children with special needs across all venues and professional disciplines. In particular, the new agenda of working with families in natural contexts means that professionals will need to:

- Suspend judgment and start with family goals and priorities

- Recognize individual family member needs as well as those of the child

- Reduce family stress and depression (if evident)

- Listen and wait before responding

- Be willing to release roles and control

- Identify and emphasize family strengths

- Help families to recognize and draw upon their own strengths

- Utilize the talents of all family members in the life of the child

- Be flexible and value perspectives other than self-owned viewpoints

- Draw upon respective family resources that are available within the context of the communities in which they live (including giving family members a break)

In the long term, day after day, year after year, parents are the constants in the lives of their children. To the extent possible, professionals need to "empower" families and help them to help themselves, rather than assume responsibilities that ultimately "disable" parents of infants and young children with special needs. Such is not to minimize the often overwhelming challenges that families face or to deny them justifiable support required at certain times in their lives and those of their children. However, in the end, effective relationship-based, family-centered interventions with parents and their young children need to leave families better able, more confident, and more resilient to carry on when professionals are no longer service providers in their lives.

Home visiting

Home visiting is a well-known strategy that is used widely for developing relationships with families in their own natural home environments. This approach is especially important for parents and caregivers who are isolated, who are less advantaged and have less access to community resources, and/or who themselves may be dealing with mental health concerns. Such approaches hold much promise when they are combined with resources of the pediatric medical home, offering high-quality well-child care, as well as services by specialists and other clinical professionals (Council on Community Pediatrics, 2009).

Home visiting is not a new concept. It was adopted years ago in several countries in addition to the United States. However within the last 30 years, there has been renewed interest in this country in using this approach to deliver EI services to pregnant mothers and to infants and young children. In particular, home visiting has been used extensively in efforts toward enhancing prenatal care and the prevention of child abuse and neglect, although the effectiveness of such services is yet to be clearly demonstrated because of the heterogeneity of contexts and situations where they have been practiced (Council on Community Pediatrics, 2009).

David Olds is a researcher best known for his pioneering work in developing and evaluating a variety of models for delivering services through home visiting, nurse–family partnerships (Dawley, Loch, & Bindrich, 2007; Kitzman et al., 1997; Olds, 2006; Olds et al., 1998; Olds, et al., 2004; Olds et al., 2007), and home visiting by paraprofessionals (Olds, Robinson, et al., 2002, 2004). There have been numerous short- and long-term follow-up studies of the effects of these interventions. While researchers are still learning about the respective benefits, successful home visiting efforts that have important implications for EI with families and their young children seem to indicate that:

- Socially disadvantaged mothers show the greatest benefits from home visiting.

- Professional or nurse-based home visiting is generally advantageous for clients. The role of paraprofessional home visitors is less known.

- Home visits may be useful for children born preterm or with low birth weight and may result in positive effects on child development. . .which may fade without sustained support.

- Services of longer duration and greater intensity correlate with higher degrees of effectiveness.

- Generally, the more risk factors present in a child's life, the more likely that developmental outcomes will be affected. However, those families with the poorest functioning are often unresponsive to engagement and intervention. (Council on Community Pediatrics, 2009, p. 600)

In sum, availability, accessibility, and advocacy play a large part in whatever professionals do on behalf of families and their infants and young children. As always, how to reach the most vulnerable individuals and keep them engaged in programs is a challenge that likely will pervade whatever efforts professionals pursue.

Influencing Resilience by Strengthening Family Resources: A Continuing Agenda

The greatest gift that professionals can give families with infants and young children with and without special care needs and disabilities is the realization of their own self-owned, self-discovered resilience, their abilities to grow and adapt, in the face of adversity. As several authors (Benzies & Mychasuik, 2009; Black & Lobo, 2008; Coyle, 2011) have pointed out, resilience is not a static concept. It is a dynamic and fluid process that changes over time, given different individuals who enter and exit from people's lives, given new challenges and circumstances

confronting family members, given the resources available at any given time for family members, and given the context of risk and protective factors encountered by family members. In the long term, resilience is a quality that strengthens family members as they face life challenges. Some researchers have pointed out that the quality of family resilience can emerge even stronger than it was before the family faced difficult circumstances (Black & Lobo, 2008).

The question then becomes what are those *protective factors* or entry points that lead to enhancing the abilities of families to manage and solve life problems? Some of these protective factors are short term; others are more systematic and long term. For some families, circumstances do not change over time, but individuals' perceptions and perspectives do change (e.g., family responses to the birth of a child with serious medical problems or disabilities). For other families, their situation may call for the modification or altering of individual family behavior (e.g., dealing with problems of substance abuse). Finally, as professionals engage in developing relationships with family members, listening to their stories, needs, and perceptions, they gain an understanding of where and how they can support families in problem-solving and reflective practice processes. Ultimately, however, family members themselves will need to do the hard work of changing their circumstances, self-owned perspectives, or both. Toward this end, the following have been cited by Black and Lobo (2008) as having potential for strengthening "resilient family prominent protective and recovery factor characteristics" (p. 38):

- positive outlook (i.e., confidence and optimism; repertoire of approaches; sense of humor)

- spirituality (i.e., an internal value system that gives meaning to stressors)

- family members accord (i.e., family member ability to nurture; cohesion; absence of hostility and violence)

- stability with flexibility (i.e., stable family roles with situational and developmental flexibility)

- family communication (i.e., collaborative problem solving and a willingness to talk through concerns and differences in perspectives)

- financial stability and adequate housing (i.e., sufficient and stable financial income; family warmth despite periodic financial challenges)

- family time for leisure and recreation (i.e., family time for shared daily tasks and relaxing together)

- routines and rituals (i.e., embedded activities that facilitate close family relationships and shared family time or nonworking hours)

- support networks (i.e., individual, family-related, and community networks as resources, especially for families with limited financial resources) (p. 38)

- willingness of family members to seek assistance, as needed, and access to quality health care (i.e., counseling for specific mental health concerns, addictions, anger issues, and other adverse risk-taking behaviors; abilities of family members to recognize the need for additional professional help)

- adequate and safe housing

- recognition by individual family members that they have the self-owned potential to change!

Resilience is a fluid, dynamic quality that is ever changing for families, and it always needs to be assessed within the ecological context of family membership, tasks, circumstances, perspectives, and the problem-solving strategies and approaches that family members bring to new encounters. Professionals need to take care that they do not deny family members important opportunities to resolve their own issues and concerns so that, in the end, when professionals are no longer present, family members can continue to live meaningful, stronger, and more healthy lives. This is a key continuing agenda!

Chapter Summary

This chapter discusses important dimensions of nurturing family relationships that lead to healthy attachment, self-regulation, and optimal emotional development of young children throughout the first 3 years of life. The chapter describes some of the most prominent risk factors and adverse family-community dynamics that can adversely affect the healthy social and emotional well-being of infants and young children. On the other hand, the authors discuss accessible family supports and strategies that can tip the balance of developmental outcomes of infants and young children and their families toward greater resilience and healthier mental health outcomes.

Key Points to Remember

- Although a preponderance of infants and young children from birth to 5 years old are referred to the child welfare system because of child abuse and neglect, few mental health resources and services exist for this age group.

- The social, emotional, and developmental well-being of infants and young children depend on healthy family relationships.

- To develop meaningful solutions and interventions for both children and adults, professionals working with families that struggle with adverse and challenging events need to discern the strengths that family members bring to those situations. The parent–professional partnerships that emerge will allow families to continue on their own when they stop receiving services.

- Infants and young children can survive adverse and dysfunctional family situations if protective factors are established to foster and contribute to family strength and resilience.

- As persons, events, and combinations of situations within families are constantly changing, protective interventions will need to account for new challenges and responsibilities.

- Services for families, infants, and young children need to be affordable, accessible, and available within the ecology of their own home and community environments.

Implications for Families and Professionals

Proactively addressing the mental health needs of families, and infants and young children leads to better and less costly outcomes. Based on recent studies, many later-onset child maladies can be prevented if addressed in the early years.

To accomplish this preventative goal, parents and professionals need to work together as partners. Too often, families and providers wait until violence or crises erupt, and tragedies result. After such events, officials often ask, Were there ongoing "warning signs"? In most instances, the answer is "yes."

All families raising young children will encounter risky and difficult situations. To effectively address these challenges, professionals must develop comprehensive, integrated "preventative interventions" that can support and strengthen families in the face of adversity. Inherent in current federal and state legislation for EI is the mandate for collaboration across agencies and multiple disciplines—a system of care, education, and public policy that necessarily varies in terms of implementation and effectiveness. When services are integrated well, families and young children benefit. When they are fragmented, they fall short of the potential for effective mental health solutions. The latter is particularly troubling in light of the growing needs for mental health services for families and children in their earliest years. However, the efforts of today's professionals—including EI educators, pediatricians, social workers, those in the legal fields, and other professionals serving families and young children—will significantly contribute to achieving a comprehensive system of mental health services from which parents and caregivers can benefit.

Recommendations for professionals

- Seek to establish meaningful and equal partnerships with parents and caregivers, valuing what families bring to situations.

- Discover and strengthen the potentials of families, setting aside preconceived perceptions.

- Seek to understand children within the context of their families.

- In the absence of a consistent, nurturing adult, seek alternative family relatives and friends as supports for children.

- Problem solve immediate adverse situations and issues along with families, and search for positive alternatives.

- Examine their own lenses of bias as they interact with families and colleagues across disciplines and agencies different from their own; refrain from judging difference and celebrate diversity.

- Seek to engage families in preventative solutions, widening supportive networks and knowledge of accessible community resources.

- Develop a family-specific plan for service coordination.

Recommendations for parents

- View challenging situations as opportunities for learning.

- Seek to create stable and safe home environments for themselves and their children.

- Seek strategies for strengthening and nurturing their relationships with their child/children.

- Understand their child's behavior as communication.

- As needed, develop age-appropriate functional behavior plans with professionals to guide children's challenging behaviors.

- As needed, learn how to appropriately play with their infants and young children.

- Acknowledge and value their own strengths and self-owned resilience.

- Be willing to adapt to challenging situations.

- Be willing to ask for help and assistance, but also assume the appropriate responsibilities of parenting their own child/children.

- Finally, despite the multiple challenges of parenting, recognize and reaffirm the many gifts and opportunities that raising their child/children brings to their lives.

References

Bailey, D. B., Jr., Nelson, L., Hebbeler, K, & Spiker, D. (2007). Modeling the impact of formal and informal supports for young children with disabilities and their families. *Pediatrics, 120*(4), e992–e1001.

Beckstrand, K., Pienkowski, T., Powers, S., & Scanlon, J. (2016). Early intervention at home: When, why, and how? In G. L. Ensher & D. A. Clark, *The early years: Foundations for best practice with special children and their families* (pp. 353–365). Washington, DC: ZERO TO THREE.

Benzies, K., & Mychasiuk, R. (2009). Fostering family resilience: A review of the key protective factors. *Child and Family Social Work, 14*, 103–114.

Black, K., & Lobo, M. (2008). A conceptual review of family resilience factors. *Journal of Family Nursing, 14*(1), 33–55.

Bowlby, J. (1969). *Attachment* (Vol. 1). New York: Basic Books.

Brazelton, T. B., & Sparrow, J. D. (2006). *Touchpoints: Birth to three—Your child's emotional and behavioral development* (2nd ed.). Cambridge, MA: Da Capo Press.

Bronfenbrenner, U. (1979). *The ecology of human development: Experiments by nature and design.* Cambridge, MA: Harvard University Press.

Centers for Disease Control and Prevention. (2010). Current depression among adults—United States, 2006 and 2008. *Morbidity and Mortality Weekly Report (MMWR), 59*(38). Retrieved from www.cdc.gov/mmwr/preview/mmwrhtml/mm5938a2.htm

Chemtob, C. M., Nomura, Y., Rajendran, K., Yehuda, R., Schwartz, D., & Abramovitz, R. (2010). Impact of maternal posttraumatic stress disorder and depression following exposure to the September 11 attacks on preschool children's behavior. *Child Development, 81*(4), 1129–1141.

Clark, M., & Clark, D. A. (2016). Nutrition and oral health of infants and toddlers. In G. L. Ensher & D. A. Clark (Eds.), *The early years: Foundations for best practice with special children and their families* (pp. 109–117). Washington, DC: ZERO TO THREE.

Committee on Psychosocial Aspects of Child and Family Health. (2001). The new morbidity revisited: A renewed commitment to the psychosocial aspects of pediatric care. *Pediatrics, 108*(5), 1227–1230.

Cooley, W. C. (2004). Providing a primary care medical home for children and youth with cerebral palsy. *Pediatrics, 114*(4), 1106–1113.

Cooper, J. L., Masi, R., & Vick, J. (2009). *Social-emotional development in early childhood: What every policymaker should know.* New York, NY: National Center for Children in Poverty, Mailman School of Public Health, Columbia University.

Council on Children With Disabilities, Section on Developmental Behavioral Pediatrics, Bright Futures Steering Committee, & Medical Home Initiatives for Children With Special Needs Project Advisory Committee. (2006). Identifying infants and young children with developmental disorders in the medical home: An algorithm for developmental surveillance and screening. *Pediatrics, 118*(1), 405–420.

Council on Community Pediatrics. (2009). The role of preschool home-visiting programs in improving children's developmental and health outcomes. *Pediatrics, 123*(2), 598–603.

Coyle, J. P. (2011). Resilient families help make resilient children. *Journal of Family Strengths, 11*(1). Retrieved from http://digitalcommons.library.tme.edu/jfs/vol11/iss1/5

Dawley, K., Loch, J., & Bindrich, I. (2007). The nurse-family partnership. *American Journal of Nursing, 107*(11), 60–67.

DePanfilis, D. (2006). *Child neglect: A guide for prevention, assessment, and intervention.* Washington, DC, Office of Child Abuse and Neglect, Children's Bureau. Retrieved on 4/15/13 from www.childwelfare.gov/pubs/usermanuals/neglect

Dicker, S. (2009). *Reversing the odds: Improving outcomes for babies in the child welfare system.* Baltimore, MD: Brookes.

Dorros, C., Kurtzer-White, E., Ahlgren, M., Simon, P., & Vohr, B., (2007). Medical home for children with hearing loss: Physician perspectives and practices. *Pediatrics, 120*(2), 288–294.

Edelman, L. (2004). The relationship-based approach to early intervention. *Resources and Connections, 3*(2). Retrieved from www.cde.sstate.co.us/earlychildhoodconnections/Technical.htm

Ensher, G. L., & Clark, D. A. (2009). The web of family abuse, neglect, and violence. In G. L. Ensher, D. A. Clark, & N. S. Songer, *Families, infants, and young children at risk: Pathways to best practice* (pp. 273–286). Baltimore, MD: Brookes.

Ensher, G. L., & Clark, D. A. (2011). *Relationship-centered practices in early childhood: Working with families, infants, and young children at risk.* Baltimore, MD: Brookes.

Ensher, G. L., & Clark, D. A. (2016). Evaluating infants and young children in the first years. In G. L. Ensher & D. A. Clark (Eds.), *The early years: Foundations for best practice with special children and their families* (pp. 133–153). Washington, DC: ZERO TO THREE.

Finello, K. M., Hampton, P., & Poulsen, M. K. (2011). *Challenges in the implementation of evidence-based mental health practices for birth-to-five year olds and their families* (Issue brief based on National Think Tank on Evidence-Based Practices in Early Childhood). Sacramento, CA: California Center for Infant-Family and Early Childhood Mental Health, WestEd Center for Prevention & Early Intervention.

Gershoff, E. T., Aber, J. L., Ware, A., & Kotler, J. A. (2010). Exposure to 9/11 among youth and their mothers in New York City: Enduring associations with mental health and sociopolitical attitudes. *Child Development, 81*(1), 1142–1160.

Ginsburg, K. R. (2007). The importance of play in promoting health child development and maintaining strong parent-child bonds. *Pediatrics, 119*(1), 182–191.

Golden, O., McDaniel, M., Loprest, P., & Stanczyk, A. (2013). *Disconnected mothers and the well-being of children: A research report.* The Urban Institute. Retrieved from www.urban.org/UploadedPDF/412815-Disconnected-Mothers-and-the-Well-Being-of-Children.pdf

Goldman, J., Salus, M. K., Wolcott, D., & Kennedy, K. Y. (2003). *What factors contribute to child abuse and neglect?* Administration for Children and Families, Office on Child Abuse & Neglect, Children's Bureau. Retrieved from www.childwelfare.gov/pubs/user manuals/foundation/foundations.cfm

Goode, S., Diefendorf, M., & Colgan, S. (2011, July). *The importance of early intervention for infants and toddlers with disabilities and their families.* Chapel Hill: The University of North Carolina, FPG Child Development Institute, National Early Childhood Technical Assistance Center.

Greenspan, S. I., & Wieder, S. (1998). *The child with special needs: Encouraging intellectual and emotional growth.* Boston, MA: Addison-Wesley.

Hanson, M. J. (2013). Families in context. In M. J. Hanson & E. W. Lynch, *Understanding families: Supportive approaches to diversity, disability, and risk* (2nd ed.; pp. 43–71). Baltimore, MD: Brookes.

Kitzman, H., Olds, D. L., Henderson, C. R. Jr., Hanks, C., Cole, R., Tatelbaum, R., . . . Barnard, K. (1997). Effect of prenatal and infancy home visitation by nurses on pregnancy outcomes, childhood injuries, and repeated childbearing—a randomized controlled trial. *Journal of the American Medical Association, 278*(8), 644–652.

Knitzer, J., & Lefkowitz, J. (2006). *Pathways to early school success: Helping the most vulnerable infants, toddlers, and their families.* New York, NY: National Center for Children in Poverty, Mailman School of Public Health, Columbia University.

Landy, S. (2009). *Pathways to competence: Encouraging healthy social and emotional development in young children* (2nd ed.). Baltimore, MD: Brookes.

Landy, S., & Menna, R. (2006). *Early intervention with multi-risk families: An integrative approach.* Baltimore, MD: Brookes.

Lieberman, A. F. (2010, May 12). *Repairing the effects of trauma on early attachment.* Presentation sponsored by the National Child Trauma Stress Network (NCTSN).

Lieberman, A. F., Padron, E., Van Horn, P., & Harris, W. W. (2005). Angels in the nursery: The intergenerational transmission of benevolent parental influences. *Infant Mental Health Journal, 26*(6), 504–520.

McWilliam, R. A. (Ed.). (2010). *Working with families of young children with special needs.* New York, NY: Guilford.

McWilliam, R. A., & Casey, A. M. (2008). *Engagement of every child in the preschool classroom.* Baltimore, MD: Brookes.

Medical Home Initiatives for Children With Special Needs Project Advisory Committee. (2002). The medical home. *Pediatrics, 120*(5), 1153–1158.

Melnyk, B. M., Feinstein, N. F., Tuttle, J., Moldenhauer, Z., Herendeen, P. Veenema, T. H., . . . Small, L. (2002). Mental health worries, communication, and needs in the year of the U.S. terrorist attack: National KySS survey findings. *Journal of Pediatric Health Care, 16*, 222–234.

National Association for the Education of Young Children. (2007). *References to play in NAEYC position statements.* Retrieved from www.naeyc.org/positionstatements/dap

National Institute for Health Care Management (NIHCM) Foundation. (2009). *Strategies to support the integration of mental health into pediatric primary care.* Washington, DC: Author. Retrieved from www.nihcm.org/pdf/PediatricMF-Final.pdf

National Research Council & Institute of Medicine. (2000). J. P. Shonkoff & D. A. Phillips (Eds.), *From neurons to neighborhoods: The science of early childhood development.* Washington, DC: National Academy Press.

National Scientific Council on the Developing Child/National Forum on Early Childhood Policy and Programs. (2010). *The foundations of lifelong health are built in early childhood.* Retrieved from www.developingchild.harvard.edu/resources/the-foundations-of-lifelong-health-are-built-in-early-childhood

Nelson, F., & Mann, T. (2011). Opportunities in public policy to support infant and early childhood mental health. *American Psychologist, 66*(2), 129–139.

Olds, D. L. (2006). The nurse-family partnership: An evidence-based preventive intervention. *Infant Mental Health Journal, 27*(1), 5–25.

Olds, D. L., Henderson, C. R. Jr., Cole, R., Eckenrode, J., Kitzman, H., Luckey, D., . . . Powers, J. (1998). Long-term effects of nurse home visitation on children's criminal and antisocial behavior: 15-year follow-up of a randomized controlled trial. *Journal of the American Medical Association, 280*(14), 1238–1244.

Olds, D. L., Kitzman, H., Cole, R., Robinson, J., Sidora, K., Luckey, D. W., . . . Holmberg, J. (2004). Effects of nurse home-visiting on maternal life course and child development: Age 6 follow-up results of a randomized trial. *Pediatrics, 114*(6), 1550–1559.

Olds, D. L., Kitzman, H., Hanks, C., Cole, R., Anson, E., Sidora-Arcoleo, K., . . . Bondy, J. (2007). Effects of nurse home visiting on maternal and child functioning: Age 9 follow-up of a randomized trial. *Pediatrics, 120*(4), e832–e845.

Olds, D. L., Robinson, J., O'Brien, E., Luckey, D. W., Pettitt, L. M., Henderson, C. R., . . . Talmi, A. (2002). Home visiting by paraprofessionals and by nurses: A randomized, controlled trial. *Pediatrics, 110*(3), 486–496.

Olds, D. L., Robinson, J., Pettitt, L., Luckey, D. W., Holmberg., J., Ng, R. K., . . . Henderson, C. R. Jr. (2004). Effects of home visits by paraprofessionals and by nurses: Age 4 follow-up results of a randomized trial. *Pediatrics, 114*(6), 1560–1568.

Onunaku, N. (2005). *Improving maternal and infant mental health: Focus on maternal depression.* Los Angeles, CA: National Center for Infant and Early Childhood Health at UCLA.

Osofsky, J. D., & Lieberman, A. F. (2011) A call for integrating a mental health perspective into systems of care for abused and neglected infants and young children. *American Psychologist, 66*(2), 120–128.

Palfrey, J. S., Sofis, L. A., Davidson, E. J., Liu, J., Freeman, L., & Ganz, M. L. (2004). The pediatric alliance for coordinated care: Evaluation of a medical home model. *Pediatrics, 113*, 1507–1516.

Poulsen, M. K. (2013). Infant/family and early childhood mental health. In M. J. Hanson & E. W. Lynch (Eds.), *Understanding families: Supportive approaches to diversity, disability, and risk* (2nd ed., pp. 171–199). Baltimore, MD: Brookes.

Rutter, M. (2000). Resilience reconsidered: Conceptual considerations, empirical findings, and policy implications. In J. P. Shonkoff & S. J. Meisels (Eds.), *Handbook of early childhood interventions* (2nd ed., pp. 651–682). New York, NY: Cambridge University Press.

Schmidt, M. E., Bickham, D., King, B., Slaby, R., Branner, A. C., & Rich, M. (2005). *The effects of electronic media on children ages zero to six: A history of research* (Issue brief). Menlo Park, CA: The Henry J. Kaiser Family Foundation.

ScienceDaily. (2010). *Young children especially vulnerable to effects of 9/11.* Retrieved from www.sciencedaily.com/releases/2010/07/100715090645.htm

Shonkoff, J. P., Garner, A. S., & the Committee on Psychosocial Aspects of Child and Family Health, Committee on Early Childhood, Adoption, and Dependent Care, & Section on Developmental and Behavioral Pediatrics (2012). The lifelong effects of early childhood adversity and toxic stress. *Pediatrics, 129*, e232–e246.

Summers, S. J., & Chazan-Cohen, R. (Eds.). (2012). *Understanding early childhood mental health: A practical guide for professionals.* Baltimore, MD: Brookes.

Tronick, E., & Beeghly, M. (2011). Infants' meaning-making and the development of mental health problems, *American Psychologist, 66*(2), 107–119.

Van Ornum, W. (2011). *Infants, toddlers, and mental health treatment.* American Mental Health Foundation. Retrieved from http://americanmentalhealthfoundation.org/entry.php?id-227

Weston, D. R. (2005). Training in infant mental health: Educating the reflective practitioner. *Infants and Young Children, 18*(4), 337–348.

Wu, S. S., Ma, C. X., Carter, R. L., Ariet, M., Feaver, F. A., Resnick, M. B., & Roth, J. (2004). Risk factors for infant maltreatment: A population-based study. *Child Abuse & Neglect, 28*(12), 1253–1264.

CHAPTER 3

Neurologic Development of Infants and Young Children

Marilyn A. Fisher

Highlights of the Chapter

After reading this chapter, the reader will:

- understand typical prenatal and early postnatal neurologic development
- recognize atypical *formation* of the nervous system and selected etiologies
- understand atypical *function* of the nervous system and selected etiologies
- be familiar with the management of various types of malformation/dysfunction of the neonatal neurologic system

The vignette that follows presents two different scenarios that illustrate the positive effect of responsive, informed caregiving practices with regard to parents' involvement in the care of their vulnerable newborn.

The Birth of Nevaeh: Two Scenarios

Aisha and Damien had anxiously anticipated the birth of their first baby. Little Nevaeh had been moving and growing well in utero; the fetal ultrasounds were all normal, and Aisha's doctors had had no particular concerns. When Aisha finally went into labor, she was already a week late. Nevaeh did not tolerate the labor very well, having worrisome fetal heart rate decelerations. When the bag of water was ruptured, instead of being clear, the amniotic fluid was stained green with meconium. Due to fetal distress, Nevaeh had had a bowel movement before her delivery, causing the normally clear amniotic fluid to be contaminated with particles of Nevaeh's stool. Further drops in Nevaeh's heart rate prompted Aisha's doctors to perform an emergency caesarean section. During the caesarean section, Aisha was put to sleep and Damien was not allowed to be in the operating room. The pediatrician was called in to help stabilize Nevaeh at the time of delivery. When Nevaeh was born by caesarean section, she had a very low heart rate and did not try to breathe on her own. Knowing that she might have gasped meconium into her windpipe before delivery, the pediatrician placed a breathing tube into Nevaeh's windpipe several times to suction meconium out of her airway. After her airway was as clear as possible, and no spontaneous breathing occurred, Nevaeh had another breathing tube inserted into her windpipe so that the ventilator machine could breathe for her. She was whisked away to the neonatal intensive care unit (NICU), without Aisha or Damien having had a chance to see her.

Aisha and Damien were not allowed to see Nevaeh in the NICU during the first 2 hours of her life because the NICU staff was placing special IVs into her umbilical cord blood vessels and was otherwise working to stabilize her. Aisha had not yet recovered from her general anesthesia and caesarean section; Damien stayed at Aisha's bedside.

In the NICU, Nevaeh was diagnosed with meconium aspiration syndrome, which caused her lungs to be very sick for about 2 weeks. She also had persistent pulmonary hypertension; the blood vessels leading to the lungs had constricted so much that it was difficult for blood to get to the lungs to get oxygen. Due to the difficulties she had before, during, and after delivery, Nevaeh had asphyxia of her organs, including hypoxic-ischemic encephalopathy (HIE) of her brain. She was comatose for more than a week. During the first several days of her life, she had seizures. When she finally started to move, she had abnormal behavior, a poor level of alertness, weak muscle tone, jitteriness, and absent neonatal reflexes (e.g., suck reflex, gag reflex, Moro reflex, corneal reflex). She had kidney failure that lasted about a week, as well as a temporary disorder in clotting, called disseminated vascular coagulation, which was treated with transfusions of clotting factors. For 3 days, Nevaeh's HIE of the brain was treated with a bonnet that cools the head. During this time, Nevaeh's parents and doctors had to watch and wait to see how much brain function Nevaeh would regain. After the cooling cap was removed from her head, ultrasounds and magnetic resonance imaging (MRIs) of her brain

showed evidence of cortical atrophy (shrinking of the brain due to loss of cells) as well as a stroke in one region of the brain. Her seizures were difficult to control and required the use of five different antiseizure medications.

Aisha and Damien are clearly facing a complicated and uncertain future for their baby. The manner in which the medical staff provides resources, support, and parental education can have a dramatic impact on the way that Aisha and Damien interact with Nevaeh. This, in turn, will have a dramatic impact on Nevaeh's health and developmental potential. Consider the following scenarios, which paint two very different pictures of family involvement, quality of caregiving, and developmental outcomes.

Scenario 1

The doctors and nurses in the NICU let Aisha and Damien know that Nevaeh was brain damaged. They told them that Nevaeh would never be able to breathe on her own or be able to come off the ventilator. They told them that Nevaeh was so brain damaged that she would never be able to recognize her parents and that she would need to live her life in an institution. Aisha and Damien grieved the loss of their daughter profoundly. Their visits to the NICU to see Nevaeh became rare. They were not there the day that Nevaeh was actually able to breathe regularly enough to come off the mechanical ventilator. Nevaeh's intestines eventually were able to tolerate formula, and her IVs could be removed. When Nevaeh was unable to feed by mouth, Aisha and Damien gave permission for the surgeons to place a feeding gastrostomy tube (g-tube) through her abdominal wall into her stomach, so that formula could be infused continuously and provide her with nutrition. Eventually, breathing independently and tolerating formula feedings through her g-tube, Nevaeh was ready to leave the NICU. Aisha and Damien had not been involved in her care, because she had been declared hopelessly brain damaged, and did not feel comfortable taking her home, so Nevaeh was placed into an institution located 3 hours away from Aisha and Damien's home. There, Nevaeh's parents were only rarely able to come to visit her.

Scenario 2

The doctors and nurses in the NICU let Aisha and Damien know that Nevaeh had incurred significant damage to her brain. The health care professionals also let Aisha and Damien know that some limited recovery might be possible. They told them that appropriate medical management to maximize her brain function included ensuring that her breathing was supported as much as necessary; that her blood levels of sugar, salts, and so forth were kept normal; and that her seizures were kept under the best control possible. They told them that an appropriate amount of stimulation and occupational and physical therapy might also help Nevaeh to develop her brain function to her best potential. Even while Nevaeh was still on the ventilator and the cooling bonnet, the doctors and nurses encouraged Aisha and Damien to talk gently to her and read books to her, because Nevaeh had heard their voice tones throughout Aisha's pregnancy, so she might find those familiar. The nurses also helped Aisha and Damien to provide gentle and appropriate tactile stimulation to Nevaeh. At first, they leaned into her incubator, cupping her in their hands, and gently stroking her skin. Later, when Nevaeh was more stable, the nurses stretched the ventilator tubing over to the easy chair in which Aisha or Damien sat and helped them to hold Nevaeh skin-to-skin. The nurses showed them how to gently flex and extend Nevaeh's joints so as to avoid joint contractures. When Nevaeh started to breathe spontaneously, Aisha and Damien were present at her bedside on the day of her much-anticipated scheduled extubation (removal

from the breathing machine). They were there to cheer her on as she adapted to breathing on her own. The nurses encouraged Aisha to pump her breast milk and save it for Nevaeh, so that Nevaeh could receive the benefits of breast milk (enhanced ability to fight off infection and better feeding tolerance than with formula) and Aisha could contribute in this way to her baby's care. After Nevaeh was able to come off the ventilator and breathe independently, she did not have the ability to locate Aisha's nipple (root reflex), or to suck and swallow, so the nurses helped Aisha to express droplets of breast milk and put them onto Nevaeh's tongue while Nevaeh was at her breast. Because Nevaeh was unable to successfully breast feed at first, she received feedings through a nasogastric tube that entered her nose with its tip in her stomach, while at Aisha's breast. In this way, Nevaeh was able to smell Aisha and to taste her breast milk while associating those sensations with the filling up of her stomach with warm milk. Over time, Nevaeh slowly began to take small amounts of Aisha's milk by mouth. When Nevaeh was ready to go home, she could not take all of her nutrition by mouth, and Aisha and Damien gave the surgeons permission to place a feeding g-tube. They understood that Nevaeh might need the feeding g-tube permanently, but if she continued to improve with her feeding skills, it might one day be able to be removed.

Aisha and Damien spent countless hours in the NICU at Nevaeh's bedside, working with the nurses in caring for her, working with the physical therapists in preventing joint contractures, working with the speech and occupational therapists in promoting improved feeding skills, working with the lactation specialists in improving breastfeeding skills, working with the neuro-developmental specialists toward improving her level of alertness and social interactions. Aisha and Damien learned how to feed Nevaeh through the feeding tube, and how to properly cleanse the surgical site. They continued to work with her on her skills of *feeding by mouth, both from the breast as well as taking pumped breast milk from a bottle, and she made some slow progress. When Nevaeh was ready to leave the NICU, Aisha and Damien were already well versed in every aspect of her care and exuberant about finally bringing her home. At home, they were able to provide appropriate interventions to meet Nevaeh's special needs and were able to help her develop to her best potential.*

The two scenarios described above would have led to two very different developmental outcomes for this newborn, who was clearly neurologically impaired. However, in Scenario 2, the infant was given the benefit of best practices, with NICU staff working closely in collaboration with the parents in preparation for discharge from hospital to home and, likely, a direct and immediate referral to early intervention services. In the end, Nevaeh's impairments most certainly remained significant, requiring life-long, multiple special education services. On the other hand, chances were that the quality of life for both the family and this child following Scenario 2 would be greatly improved over that following Scenario 1 and would lead to a healthier parent–child relationship.

Normal Prenatal Brain Development

Development of the fetal brain may be appreciated on the basis of its anatomic maturation or on the basis of its functional maturation.

Prenatal Anatomic Development of the Brain

As is evident from our following discussion, normal neurologic development throughout the first 3 years of life is a miraculous process. It first begins with prenatal development, which is divided into two stages: embryonic and fetal.

Embryonic period

The embryonic stage occurs during Weeks 3–8. Organogenesis (formation of the organs) occurs during embryonic life. After fertilization of the 23-chromosome ovum by the 23-chromosome spermatozoa, a 46-chromosome, single-cell, living zygote develops, which then repeatedly divides by mitosis and, by 4 days after fertilization, has matured into a blastocyst. The blastocyst implants into the uterine wall 6 days after fertilization and continues its development into a two-layer, then three-layer, embryo. The term *embryo* is not generally used until the developing human reaches the two-layer phase, around 2 weeks after the first missed menstrual period. During embryonic life, the embryo transforms from a flat, two-layer disk to a three-layer disk to a curved cylinder. The embryonic notochord, the structure around which the vertebral column will form, induces ectodermal tissue above it to form the neural plate, which, in turn, gives rise to the brain and spinal cord (see Figure 3.1). The neural plate invaginates into the neural groove, then into the neural tube, which separates from the surface ectoderm. The neural tube closes (neurulation) at the cranial end on Day 25 after fertilization and on Day 27 after fertilization at the posterior end.

The neural tube should be completely closed by the 28th day of embryonic life. Complete failure of closure of the most anterior portion of the neural tube gives rise to anencephaly (see Figure 3.2). Failure to close caudally gives rise to myelomeningocele (see chapter 9, Munshi & Clark, 2016 and chapter 10, Cummings & Fisher, 2016).

The neural cells give rise to the autonomic nervous system, the spinal ganglia, and the ganglia of certain cranial nerves (V, VII, IX, and X). The forebrain folds down toward the heart, making the head more rounded, beginning to resemble a human. Microscopically, during the embryonic period, the neural cells within the forebrain

FIGURE 3.1 The neural plate folds into the neural groove beginning on Day 18 (Figures 3.1B, C, D). The neural groove closes to form the neural tube (Figure 3.1E). The neural tube will ultimately form the brain and spinal cord.

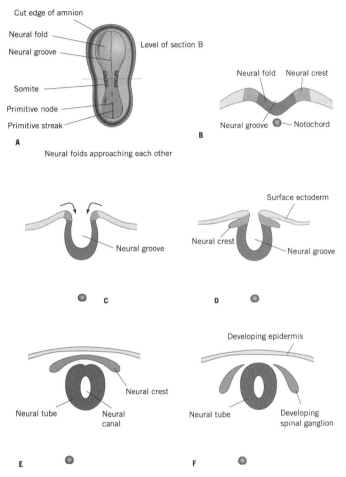

From Moore, et al. (2013). *The Developing Human: Clinically Oriented Embryology* (9th ed., pp. 63). Chapter 4: The Third Week of Human Development. Saunders/Elsevier, Philadelphia, Pennsylvania. Reprinted with permission.

differentiate, collect, and migrate, forming the cells of the brain, spinal cord, and motor and sensory nerves, including the sensory cells of the eyes, ears, and nose. The prosencephalon (early forebrain) begins its development late in embryonic life, continuing into early fetal life. During this time, the forebrain, face, eyes, ears, cerebral hemispheres, thalamus, hypothalamus, corpus callosum, septum pellucidum, and optic nerves all form.

FIGURE 3.2 Anencephaly

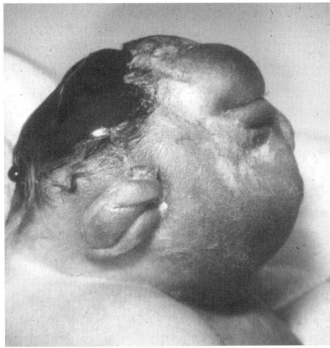

Fetal period

The fetal period occurs between Weeks 9 and 38 of gestation. During the fetal period, organs already formed during the embryonic period complete their development. Although most tissues, including the heart and limbs, are fully formed during embryonic life and only need to grow in size during the fetal period, the brain is still undergoing important developmental changes during the fetal period, and it will continue to differentiate and develop for many years after birth as well. Therefore, the brain is most susceptible to damage not only during the embryonic period, but also during the fetal period, as well as during early childhood.

The first important developmental stage of the brain occurring during fetal life is *neuronal proliferation*. During this stage, the number of brain cells increases, with its peak time at 3–4 months of gestation. Neuronal proliferation occurs when brain cells replicate their DNA, migrating, dividing, and migrating again to spread out within the structure of the brain. Another method of neuronal proliferation involves glial cell multiplication (from 5 months gestation until beyond a year after full-term birth). During the period of neuronal proliferation, the arteries and veins supplying the brain are also formed.

The second important developmental stage of the brain, which occurs during fetal life, is glial cell migration (3–5 months gestation). During this stage, millions of glial brain cells migrate from sites adjacent to the brain's ventricles (collections of cerebral spinal fluid) to more distant locations within the central nervous system, including the cerebral cortex (the location of higher thought processes). Once the cells reach their final destinations, they will remain there for life.

The third important developmental stage of the brain occurring during fetal life is organization of brain cells (5 months gestation until many years after birth). During this time, brain cells are established, differentiated, and oriented with respect to each other. Connections (synapses) are established between cells, and unnecessary synapses and unnecessary nerve tissue are eliminated.

The fourth and final stage of development of the brain is myelination. A sheath of myelin deposited, by oligodendroglial cells, onto neural tissue is essential for mature transmission of afferent and efferent impulses along nerve pathways. The oligodendroglial cells first appear in the brain during the 20th week of gestation. Myelination continues from this time until adulthood. Availability of fatty acids is essential for proper myelination. The omega-3 fatty acid docosahexaenoic acid (DHA) is found in high concentrations in the cerebral cortex and retina. DHA is crucial in the synthesis of brain tissue, metabolism of neurotransmitters, cellular differentiation, and synaptogenesis (Sabel, Lundqvist-Persson, Bona, Petzold, & Strandvik, 2009). The placenta actively transports DHA from the pregnant woman's circulation into the fetal circulation for brain growth during

gestation, with the bulk of accrual of fetal DHA occurring during the last trimester. Placental transfer of DHA is dependent on levels of DHA in the maternal serum. Supplementation of the pregnant woman's diet with DHA has been shown to result in higher DHA levels of the baby and improved problem-solving skills in infants at 9 months of age (Judge, Harel, & Lammi-Keefe, 2007) and improved memory function in school-age children (Boucher et al., 2011). Disorders in myelination can be seen in the presence of primary cerebral white matter hypoplasia, cerebral white matter injury of the premature infant (periventricular leukomalacia), amino acid and organic acid disturbances, hypothyroidism, deletion 18q syndrome (deficient gene for myelin basic protein, a key structural protein for myelin), perinatal/early infantile neurologic insults, and iron deficiency.

The developing human is extremely vulnerable to injury. Significant insult occuring during the first 2 weeks after fertilization most likely results in spontaneous termination of the pregnancy, due to direct toxicity to the embryo or because it causes the uterine environment to be hostile to the implantation of the blastocyst. Severe malformations of the brain often get their start in the first 8 weeks after fertilization. Because the face, eyes, and ears all form at the same time, and from the same prosencephalic structures as the forebrain, significant facial anomalies may herald the diagnosis of severe brain malformations. Insults after the third week following fertilization, during organogenesis, are likely to result in fetal malformations or death. Factors that adversely affect the developing fetus are called teratogens. Teratogens that may cause brain malformations include toxins, such as certain drugs, alcohol, radiation exposure, infections with certain viruses, and nutritional deficiencies, including deficiencies of folic acid, iron, protein, and DHA. Chromosomal abnormalities may also cause brain malformations. Even without an actual chromosomal abnormality, a genetic predisposition or multifactorial factors favoring development of a particular malformation, when combined with other undetermined factors, may result in a fetal brain malformation.

Functional Development of the Brain Before Full Term

Even before birth, a fetus increases its level of alertness and motor strength, develops its senses, and is capable of experiencing pain.

Alertness

The level of alertness, or vigilance, is one of the most sensitive indicators of neurologic function. Prenatal ultrasound studies and the observation of premature neonates over 28 weeks gestation have demonstrated states of sleep and wakefulness, and an increased level of alertness with increasing gestational age. After 28 weeks gestation, fetuses and premature neonates have spontaneous episodes of wakefulness as well as the ability to be roused from sleep for several minutes by tactile stimulation. By 32 weeks gestation, fetuses and premature neonates demonstrate sleep, alternating with wakefulness manifested by opening of the eyes for several minutes with spontaneous eye-roving movements. By 36 weeks after conception, fetuses and premature neonates demonstrate vigorous crying movements while awake and responses to visual and auditory stimuli, in addition to the more primitive response to tactile stimuli (Volpe, 2001a).

Motor function

Muscle tone/posture. With the passage of time, a premature infant demonstrates increasing muscle resistance to passive manipulation. Whereas at 28 weeks there is very little muscle tone, by 32 weeks, flexor tone appears in the lower extremities only, and, by 36 weeks, flexor tone is significant in the lower extremities and present in

the upper extremities. By 40 weeks, strong flexor tone is present in all four extremities.

Movement and power. Fetuses, premature neonates, and full-term neonates in the first 4 weeks of life tend to exhibit spontaneous "writhing" types of movement. This progresses to "fidgety" movements from 4–12 weeks after full term, and large "swipe" movements after about 8–12 weeks after full term (Volpe, 2001b). Premature infants, when stimulated, will often flex their hips and knees simultaneously. With maturity, a full-term neonate, when stimulated, will flex her legs in an alternating rhythm. Muscle tone also improves with increasing maturity. A 32-week neonate has complete head lag (poor neck flexion strength) when pulled to a sitting position. By 36 weeks, a neonate exhibits some strength of the neck extensor muscles, and by 40 weeks, he demonstrates some strength of the neck flexor muscles as well.

Feeding skills. Cranial Nerve V (Trigeminal) mediates facial sensation and also masticatory (chewing) power. With maturity of Cranial Nerve V, a fetus or neonate is able to suck and chew with greater strength. The vital skills of sucking and swallowing are important for the fetus/premature neonate as well as the full-term baby. Swallowing has been observed in utero as early as 11 weeks gestation (Miller, 1982). Sucking can be seen as early as 28 weeks gestation. However, the delicate balance of sucking, swallowing, and breathing is not sufficiently mature until at least 32 to 34 weeks gestation. A premature infant without suck-swallow-breathing coordination who is fed by mouth is at risk of aspirating milk into his lungs. The eventual development of the gag reflex as the baby approaches full term can help him to keep milk out of his airway and lungs, thus preventing aspiration pneumonitis.

Senses

Olfaction (sense of smell). Studies on premature neonates have shown that, with increasing gestation, the baby can increasingly perceive, and respond to, olfactory stimuli (Sarnat, 1978). This skill has functional significance, because premature neonates become increasingly able to turn their faces and attention toward the smell of their own mothers' milk, thus seeking nutrition from the correct lactating mother.

Vision. By 26 weeks gestation, premature neonates are able to blink and squint in response to a bright light (Saint-Anne Dargassies, 1977). Fetuses and premature neonates above 30 weeks gestation demonstrate an increasing ability to constrict the pupils in response to bright light (Robinson & Fielder, 1990). This sensitivity to light, and the degree of pupillary constriction in response to light, increases with increasing gestation. Pupillary constriction in response to light is also mediated via a reflex arc that does not require cerebral function. When no pupillary response to light is noted in a full-term neonate, the pupils being fixed and dilated rather than normally reactive to light, following HIE, it implies that there is brain-stem failure in addition to failure of the cerebral cortex.

By 32 weeks, premature babies will exhibit the dazzle reflex of Peiper, keeping their eyes closed for as long as the light persists (Peiper, 1963). The eyelids of premature infants are thin and will, even when closed, allow light to enter the eyes. Therefore, parents and health care providers should take precautions to protect preterm babies from excessive light levels. Also, beginning at 32 weeks, premature babies demonstrate an increasing ability to fixate on a large object placed a short distance from their eyes (Hack, Mostow, & Miranda, 1976). Although preterm infants of 30 to 32 weeks may be able to fixate on a visual stimulus (such as high-contrast black-and-white patterns), due to their immature visual systems, they may be unable to regulate such intense incoming information, become disorganized and distressed by it, and become unable to break their gaze away from it (Glass, 1999). The combination

of exposure to early visual stimulation, DHA insufficiency, and/or brain injury may predispose to visual impairment in preterm infants (Molloy, Doyle, Makrides, & Anderson, 2012). By 34 weeks, not only should preterm babies be able to visually fixate on an object, but they will track (follow) a large moving object with their eyes (Palmer, Dubowitz, Verghote, & Dubowitz, 1982). By 37 weeks, 90% of infants will turn their eyes to seek the source of a soft light (Saint-Anne Dargassies, 1977). Because visual fixating and tracking can be appreciated in babies with brain malformations (such as holoprosencephaly) and brain damage (due to HIE) who do not have a functioning occipital cerebral cortex, these developing visual skills are thought to be due to a maturing subcortical neurologic system involving the retina, optic nerves, optic tract, pulvinar, and superior colliculus (Aylward, Lazzara, & Meyer, 1978; Cocker, Moseley, Stirling, & Fielder, 1998; Dubowitz, DeVries, Mushin, & Arden, 1986; Jan, Wong, Groenveld, Flodmark, & Hoyt, 1986; Snyder, Hata, Brann, & Mills, 1990) rather than to maturing of the cerebral cortex. Therefore, the presence of these abilities is essentially primitive and reflexive, and not related to intellect nor ability to perform visual discrimination.

The presence of the *doll's eye reflex* (eyes tend to fixate on an object even though the head is being turned) beginning at 25 weeks gestation, the positive cold caloric stimulation test (eyes deviate toward the ear being infused with cold water), and spontaneous eye roving beginning at 32 weeks gestation demonstrate the progressive maturing of the cranial nerves. The development of these findings does not necessarily indicate that there is any purposefulness to them.

Hearing. With the maturing of the auditory cranial nerve, the fetus/premature neonate is able to startle or blink in response to auditory stimuli beginning at 28 weeks. With maturity, the neonate is able to exhibit a more sophisticated response to sound, such as stopping her spontaneous motor activity, opening her mouth and/or eyes, and changing her respiratory pattern (Pieper, 1963; Saint-Anne Dargassies 1977). It is clear that fetuses are able to perceive sound that filters through to them.

Taste. The fetus/preterm neonate clearly has a developing sense of taste, which is mediated by Cranial Nerves VII (Facial), IX (Glossopharyngeal), and X (Vagus). Oral administration of a 25% glucose solution is associated with a decrease in external manifestations of pain to heel lancing (crying, facial grimacing) when compared to breast milk administration, as assessed by the Premature Infant Pain Profile (PIPP) score (Bueno et al., 2012).

Because neonates appear to have an attenuated pain response during painful procedures, such as obtaining a blood sample via heel lancing, when given oral glucose, health care professionals routinely administer oral glucose to babies as analgesia for selected painful procedures (Chermont, Falcao, de Souza Silva, de Cassia Zavier Balda, & Guinsburg, 2009). The composition, and, thus, the taste of amniotic fluid change, based on the mother's food choices (Mennella, Johnson, & Beauchamp, 1995). The mother's dietary flavors make their way into the amniotic fluid, affecting the fetus by leading to heightened neonatal preference for those flavors (Beauchamp & Mennella, 2009). The existence of fetal taste sensation is responsible for the ontogeny of flavor learning of any given individual. Substances in the pregnant woman's diet routinely cross into the amniotic fluid, rendering a unique taste and odor to the amniotic fluid (Mennella et al., 1995) to which the fetus is exposed. Repeated exposures to specific tastes cause a gustatory imprinting, affecting the child's future dietary preferences.

Prenatal exposure to high salt levels may predispose fetuses to seek salty foods as children. Pregnant women with frequent vomiting may develop significant and chronic dehydration with concentrated levels of serum sodium. Their fetuses are, therefore, exposed to elevated sodium levels in the amniotic fluid. After birth, these babies show a preference to salty solutions compared to control infants, measured by quantities of salty fluid consumed and facial reactions to solutions consumed (Crystal & Bernstein, 1998).

Pain. Decades ago, physicians believed that neonates were incapable of experiencing pain due to the fact that their nervous systems were not yet fully developed. At that time, painful procedures were performed on neonates without adequate analgesia. Professionals currently recognize that neonates do, in fact, experience pain. A neonate attempts to *withdraw* from a painful stimulus by pulling the affected extremity away from the source of pain, making a facial grimace, crying, or turning the face away from the pain source. A recent literature review (Bellieni & Buonocore, 2012) revealed that the majority of health care professionals appreciate that fetuses in the third trimester can perceive pain as well. Premature neonates born in the third trimester may be too weak to cry aloud or to withdraw from a painful stimulus, but they can show evidence of pain by grimacing, clenching their fists, curling or extending their toes, grimacing, frowning, squeezing their eyes shut, dropping their circulating oxygen levels, or increasing their heart rate or blood pressure. Because the spino-thalamic pathways of pain fibers (developed at the 20th week of gestation) and the connections of the thalamus with the sub-plate (developed at the 23rd week) are being formed in the second trimester, some scientists believe that even second-trimester fetuses are capable of experiencing pain. Others believe that, even though reflex pain fibers may transmit painful impulses in this fetal population, the second trimester cerebral cortex is too immature to allow the fetus to be aware of pain, being virtually unable to be roused from an almost continuous state of sleep.

Normal Postnatal Brain Development

Just as the rapidly developing fetal brain is vulnerable to adverse effects, so is the immature, postnatal brain susceptible to injury.

Development of the Central Nervous System

During childhood, environmental factors, including the nutritional milieu in which the brain is growing, may affect the brain. Surges in thyroid hormone at the time of birth lead to increased alertness, improving a neonate's ability to suckle at the breast and to thrive. Neonates' ability to recognize pain and then to respond to it specifically continues to develop after birth.

The first 12 months of life

Animal studies have demonstrated that alterations in dietary nutrients can affect the morphology and biochemical functioning of the brain. There are less data about the effect of early childhood nutrition on the developing human brain.

Protein. Deprivation of protein during early childhood can adversely affect the brain, as evidenced by poor brain growth, impaired chemical neurotransmitter function, changes in protein phosphorylation, and altered formation of the hippocampus. Undernourishment (generally involving protein deprivation) of children under 3 years old has been associated with lower levels of achievement in school, lower developmental scores, and poorer behavior (Bonatto et al., 2006). Protein, energy, and micronutrient supplementation has been shown to ameliorate these effects (Grantham-McGregor & Baker-Henningham, 2005).

Insulin-like growth factor (IGF-1) affects brain development. An appropriate amount of IGF-1 provides neuro-protection after neuronal damage (Gluckman et al., 1998), enhances neurogenesis, myelination (Carlson, Behringer, Brinster, & McMorris, 1993), synaptogenesis, and branching of the dendrites (Anjos et al., 2013; Niblock, Brunso-Bechtold, & Riddle, 2000). Overexpression and underexpression of the IGF-1 gene cause increased and decreased brain size, respectively (Beck, Powell-Braxton, Widmer, Valverde, & Hefti, 1995). Breastfed infants have both a lower protein intake and lower levels of IGF-1 than do formula-fed infants (Chellakooty et al., 2006). However, children who are breastfed during the first weeks of life ultimately have higher IQs than do formula-fed infants (Lucas, Morley, Cole, Lister, & Leeson-Payne, 1992). This suggests that factors other than absolute IGF-1 levels also have an impact on brain development.

The two most abundant long-chain polyunsaturated fatty acids in the brain are DHA and arachidonic acid (ARA). The presence of these substances has been correlated with improved short-term memory and vision. These substances are considered essential because they cannot be synthesized by the human body and must come from the diet. During fetal life, DHA is deposited in the prefrontal cortex and retina, especially during the third trimester. Therefore, babies born before the third trimester are predisposed to a deficiency of DHA, putting them at increased neurodevelopmental risk. After birth, brain and retinal deposition of DHA continues. DHA is present in breast milk, and breastfed babies have higher levels of DHA in their red blood cells and cerebral cortices than non-DHA /non-ARA-supplemented formula-fed infants. Children of lactating mothers whose diet is rich in DHA have been shown to have an improved IQ at 4 years old. In one study, supplementation of formula with DHA and ARA was shown to result in infant neurodevelopment that is similar to that of breastfed infants (Agostoni, 2008). In another study of 4-year-olds, DHA-supplemented formula did not result in verbal IQ scores any higher than those of babies fed non-supplemented formula (Birch et al., 2007). In addition, it is possible that some measured differences in children's intelligence, based on the type of milk fed, may be due to confounding factors associated with breastfeeding unrelated to protein, DHA, ARA intake, or IGF-1 levels, such as maternal–infant attachment, environment, and nurturing.

Alertness. At the time of birth, perhaps due to the drop in core body temperature, neonates experience a surge in levels of thyroid stimulating hormone (TSH), which persists for 6 to 24 hours. In response, circulating levels of triiodothyroxine (T3), tetraiodothyroxine (T4), and free T4 rise and peak at 48 hours after birth. Gestational age lowers the ability of the thyroid to respond to increased TSH levels induced by the birth process. Nevertheless, even preterm infants experience a sudden rise in TSH at the time of birth, with a less-intense rise in the iodothyronines than is seen in full-term babies. This rise in levels of circulating thyroid hormones occurring at birth may improve the level of alertness of the newborn and may promote more vigorous feeding at the breast.

Sensation. As noted previously, in past years, physicians believed that infants were incapable of feeling pain because their nervous systems were too immature. As a result, painful procedures were routinely performed on infants without any attempt to control pain. It is now recognized that even extremely immature infants are capable of differentiating between touch and pain. When touched, infants may become more alert and make spontaneous movements; when exposed to painful stimuli, they may attempt to cry and even attempt to pull away from the source of the pain (Bartocci, Berquist, Lagercrantz, & Anand, 2006). In neonatal intensive care units today, health care professionals are sensitive to findings that might indicate pain in the neonate: withdrawal from pain, crying aloud, grimacing, fist clenching, curling or extension of the toes, or elevation of the

blood pressure and/or heart rate. Even though a very sick or very premature infant may be too weak to pull an extremity away from the source of a painful stimulus or to emit a loud cry, if other more subtle findings are detected, then the infant is treated for pain.

Developmental milestones during the first 3 years of life are covered elsewhere in this book (chapter 1, Ensher & Clark, 2016).

Variations in Neurologic Development

Circumstances arising during the embryonic, fetal, or postnatal periods may cause neurologic development to be atypical.

Fetal Period

Abnormal development may be caused by such factors as disorders in proliferation of the neurons, abnormal migration of the glial cells, poor organization or myelination of the brain cells, and exposure to exogenous or endogenous teratogens.

Disorders of neuronal proliferation

These disorders constitute one type of developmental brain abnormality.

Primary micrencephaly (small brain) refers to that type of brain malformation that is due to disordered, inadequate neuronal proliferation. In this condition, the brain is small and has simplified gyri. Clinically, the central nervous system may be expected to be profoundly adversely affected. One type of primary micrencephaly, micrencephaly vera, is often inherited in an autosomal recessive mode. Other etiologies for micrencephaly may include familial factors, which warrant familial genetic counseling. Syndromic and sporadic etiologies also exist. It is important to note that micrencephaly may also be caused by teratogenic factors, such as exposure of the fetus during the first 18 weeks of gestation to radiation (as seen in Nagasaki and Hiroshima, Japan, in the aftermath of the August 1945 nuclear bombings), cocaine, alcohol, and high levels of phenylalanine in poorly controlled maternal phenylketonuria [PKU] (Volpe, 2001b).

Macrencephaly. Another disorder of neuronal proliferation involves excessive neuronal proliferation. This results in a large brain (macrencephaly). Because the skull forms based on the volume of brain inside it, the head will also be large, causing macrencephaly. Macrencephaly may also be due to diminished *apoptosis* (programmed cell death). Macrencephaly can be seen in achondroplasia, fragile X syndrome, and the neurocutaneous syndromes (such as neurofibromatosis). Clinically, it may cause no neurologic deficit, or it may cause severe intellectual deficiency and seizures. Familial, isolated macrencephaly is the most common variety of macrencephaly. Familial macrencephaly may be of the autosomal dominant variety. In this condition, the head circumference is greater than the 90th percentile, and normal intelligence is usual. Diagnosis is often made when the health care providers realize that at least one of the parents, like the child, has a head circumference of greater than the 90th percentile. In contrast, autosomal recessive macrencephaly is more likely to be associated with seizures, and intellectual and motor deficits. Unilateral (one-sided) macrencephaly may occur due to a localized disorder of proliferation on only one side of the brain. It is often associated with severely disturbed neurodevelopment as well as seizures that are recalcitrant to anti-epileptic therapy. It may be associated with certain syndromes including epidermal nevus syndrome, and other disorders of skin and tissue growth.

Epidermal nevus syndrome. This syndrome is manifested by growth disorders including epidermal nevi (often of the face or scalp), eye abnormalities (nevi, coloboma, corneal opacity, nystagmus), skeletal abnormalities (vertebral abnormalities, short limbs, hemihypertrophy), disorders of the central nervous system (seizures, intellectual disability, hemiparesis), and a higher incidence of malignant tumors.

Tuberous sclerosis. This systemic disorder characterized by intracerebral tumors, seizures, depigmented skin lesions (ash-leaf spots), collagenomas (shagreen patches) and cardiac tumors (rhabdomyomas), is associated with abnormalities of both neuronal and glial proliferation as well as abnormal differentiation. The disorder is caused by abnormal genes carried by chromosome 9 and/or 16, which encode for the hamartin and tuberin proteins, which signal for cell growth.

Disorders of neuronal migration

These disorders are most often manifested by seizures. Neuronal/glial migration disorders may also be recognized by abnormalities of the gyri (folding of the brain in response to the rapid increase in cerebral cortex surface area).

Lissencephaly. In lissencephaly, the brain remains relatively smooth (with few gyri) due to poor neuronal migration in both the inner and outer layers of the cerebral cortex (Volpe, 2008a).

Polymicrogyria. In polymicrogyria, the surface of the brain has excess gyri because the outer layer of the brain has more robust neuronal migration and growth, creating a greater surface area, compared to the poor neuronal migration in the inner layer of the brain.

Schizencephaly. Schizencephaly (cleft brain) represents a severe, localized abnormality of primitive neuronal migration (Barkovich & Norman, 1988).

Agenesis of corpus callosum, absent septum pellucidum. Neuronal migration abnormalities may also be responsible for the relatively common agenesis of the corpus callosum and absence of the septum pellucidum.

Zellweger cerebrohepatorenal syndrome. Zellweger cerebrohepatorenal syndrome is an autosomal recessive metabolic disorder of neuronal migration (as well as myelination) manifested by polymicrogyria and pachygyria of the brain. It is due to deficiency of peroxisomes and multiple peroxisomal enzymes. Enzymes produced in the cell are not imported into the peroxisome, so proteins are degraded within the cytosol, perhaps leading to the neuronal migrational disorder for which Zellweger syndrome is best known. Neonates afflicted with Zellweger syndrome have a characteristic dysmorphic craniofacial appearance, cataracts, retinopathy, visual and auditory impairment, enlarged liver, glomerulocystic kidney disease, calcific stippling of the bones, hypotonia, areflexia, seizures, and death by 6 months old. Because this syndrome causes marked abnormality of brain development before 20 weeks gestation, postnatal therapies are unlikely to confer significant benefit. Neonatal adrenoleukodystrophy, another autosomal, recessive, metabolically mediated peroxisomal disorder, causes less severe deficiencies of neuronal migration, but more severe disturbance in myelination, than does Zellweger syndrome.

Disorders of brain cell organization

These disorders can cause seizures and mental retardation. Brain cell disorganization can be seen in patients with Rett syndrome, Angelman syndrome, fragile X syndrome, Duchenne muscular dystrophy, autism, and Down syndrome (trisomy 21). Even in patients without a genetic predisposition to brain cell disorganization, disorganization of brain cells may occur due to adverse perinatal events during the vulnerable perinatal period, such as HIE in the full-term baby, poor brain perfusion leading to periventricular leukomalacia in the preterm (Volpe, 2005), postnatal treatment with dexamethasone (Thebaud, Lacaze-Masmonteil, & Watterberg, 2001), transient hypothyroidism of prematurity (Vulsma & Kok, 1996), nutritional deficiency of long-chain polyunsaturated fatty acids (which

are present in breast milk; Bouwstra et al., 2005), lack of appropriate environmental stimulation (Als et al., 2004), excess environmental stimulation (Whiteus, Freitas, & Grutzendler, 2013), repeated exposure to inhaled anesthetics (Zuo, 2013), infection, acidosis, intracranial hemorrhage, cerebral infarction, seizures (Shinnar et al., 2012), and presence of congenital cardiac defects (Miller et al., 2007). When babies are born small-for-gestational age (SGA), the brain, as well as the body, may be small due to an adverse intrauterine environment. MRI studies of these babies reveal abnormal brain organization at both global and regional levels. These SGA babies without sparing of the head circumference have been found to have decreased volume of both grey and white matter in the cerebral cortex and cerebellum, smaller volumes of subcortical structures, and reduced surface of the cerebral cortex. These abnormalities of intra-uterine brain organization may translate into decreased intelligence and cognitive impairments in SGA children without head-sparing of growth (De Bie et al., 2011). Because brain organization occurs from the fetal period through many years after birth, brain organization can also be affected by the learning environment very early in childhood. Children reared in an intellectually deprived environment are significantly more likely to have deficits in language production and comprehension, deficits in cognitive function, a higher incidence of attention-deficit/hyperactivity disorder, and a higher incidence of psychopathology in general. Corresponding to these clinical findings, MRIs performed on children who have grown up in an institution revealed smaller white and grey matter volume and smaller corpora callosa. During early childhood, there is hypothesized to be an overproduction of neuronal synapses (Changeux & Danchin, 1976). Elimination of certain synapses, and the maintenance of others, during a type of fine-tuning begins to occur at the time of puberty. The child's environment may affect this brain reorganization process, which may represent a critical time window of plasticity during which a deprived or damaged brain may still exhibit a positive response to intervention (Khundrakpam et al., 2013). Clinically, children "rescued" by foster care from institutionalization show some ability to "catch up" developmentally; their brains' white matter also demonstrates catch-up growth and improved brain organization following rescue from the adverse environment of institutionalization (Sheridan, Fox, Zeanah, McLaughlin, & Nelson, 2012).

Disorders in brain myelination

Undermyelination of neurons, with its associated cerebral palsy and neurocognitive and behavioral disorders, has been found to be associated with intrauterine growth restriction (IUGR; Reid, Murray, Marsh, Golden, Simmons, & Grinspan, 2012). People with Down syndrome (trisomy 21) generally have delayed and decreased myelination of the hippocampus and dentate gyrus areas of the brain, which has been postulated to contribute to the intellectual deficiency seen in persons with Down syndrome (Abraham et al., 2012). Premature babies, with their immature, poorly myelinated brains, are at risk of damage to the white matter (periventricular leukomalacia) from episodes of poor brain oxygenation. Brain immaturity can also be seen in certain full-term babies with specific neurologic risk factors, including complex congenital cardiac malformations (especially transposition of the great vessels and hypoplastic left heart syndrome), genetic syndromes, and polymorphisms of the gene for apolipoprotein E (APOE). Like premature babies, they have only small numbers of highly vulnerable premyelinating oligodendrocyte precursor cells and are subject to episodes of poor brain oxygenation. Their oligodendrocyte precursor cells, not yet present in adequate amounts, have not yet made adequate quantities of myelin so that the exposed white matter is

also at increased risk to hypoxia-ischemia. This immature brain, even though present in full-term babies, is highly susceptible to injury, and the development of periventricular leukomalacia, from low levels of oxygenation. This brain vulnerability places these select full-term babies (as well as normal premature babies) at significant risk for the clinical findings of poor tone, difficulty with feeding, and seizures (Licht et al., 2009).

An adrenal corticosteroid, betamethasone, is often administered to pregnant women at risk of delivering their babies prematurely. It helps the fetus's lungs to mature more rapidly. Another adrenal corticosteroid, dexamethasone, is used to treat neonates who are unable to wean down from high settings on the mechanical ventilator due to their severe inflammation of the lungs. In addition to causing brain cell disorganization, there is some evidence that antenatal administration of corticosteroids may also delay myelination of the brain (Antonow-Schlorke et al., 2009; Raschke, Schmidt, Schwab, & Jirikowski, 2008). Postnatal administration of corticosteroids to extremely premature infants is associated with an increased incidence of periventricular leukomalacia, neuromotor abnormalities, and cerebral palsy (Thebaud et al., 2001).

Zellweger syndrome, discussed above under disorders of neuronal migration, is also responsible for disordered neuronal myelination. In Zellweger syndrome, the peroxisomal enzymes needed to break down very-long-chain (26 carbon) fatty acids to 22 carbon fatty acids known as plasmalogens are absent within the peroxisome. Plasmalogens compose an integral part of the brain and the myelin sheath of nerve tissue. Their absence contributes to the brain abnormalities seen in this syndrome. The autosomal recessive metabolic disorder, neonatal adrenoleukodystrophy, is marked by more severe deficiency in myelination than that of Zellweger syndrome. Like Zellweger syndrome, patients with neonatal adrenoleukodystrophy have elevation of very-long-chain fatty acids as well as a deficiency of plasmalogens. There is a deficiency of peroxisomes in number as well as quantity of peroxisomal enzymes. Afflicted patients have a dysmorphic craniofacial appearance, hypotonia, poor ability to feed, optic and adrenal atrophy, macrocephaly, visual and auditory impairment, seizures, and death by approximately 3 years old. Because the metabolic defect causing neonatal adrenoleukodystrophy profoundly affects the developing brain in utero, it is not likely that any therapy after birth can reverse the process. However, some research is being done on dietary manipulation (limiting intake of very-long-chain fatty acids and increasing intake of mono-unsaturated fatty acids) in the less severe X-linked adrenoleukodystrophy, before the onset of symptoms, or providing dietary supplementation of DHA or sodium 4-phenylbutyrate for peroxisomal disorders in general.

Thyroid hormone affects all stages of development of the brain, especially myelination (Bernal, 2007). During the first few weeks of gestation (before the fetus begins to make thyroid hormone), maternal thyroid hormone crosses the placenta from the mother to the fetus. This likely helps the fetal brain to begin its development in a proper manner. Later in gestation, however, the fetus must depend on its own thyroid hormone production to prevent it from becoming hypothyroid. When a fetus is not capable of producing enough thyroid hormone, that stage of proper brain development does not occur. In the United States, congenital hypothyroidism is diagnosed by the mandatory neonatal state metabolic screening tests, whereupon affected babies are immediately started on thyroid hormone replacement. The goal of this treatment is to allow the brain to develop normally. However, during in utero life, when there was no thyroid hormone supplementation, the brain may have already sustained a developmental insult. A diagnosis of congenital

hypothyroidism, even when diagnosed and treated immediately after birth, places affected babies at significant neurodevelopmental risk.

Teratogens

During the periods of embryonic, fetal, and early childhood brain development, the nervous system is vulnerable to adverse factors.

Infections

Exposure to certain infections during periods of rapid brain development may cause malformations and dysfunction of the brain.

Cytomegalovirus (CMV). About 50% of women have attained immunity to CMV during their childhood because they had an infection with this virus. Nonimmune pregnant women are at risk of acquiring the viral infection if they are exposed to children who may be asymptomatically shedding the virus in their urine and secretions. Day care providers and mothers of toddlers may be at increased risk of exposure. Maternal infection can be asymptomatic or may present as a systemic illness with fever, malaise, rash, or other signs. When CMV enters the developing fetal central nervous system, it causes inflammation, tissue destruction, neuronal migration disorders, and microcephaly (small head) due to decreased number of brain cells. The earlier in gestation the infection occurs, the more severe the neurologic deficit. Cerebral calcifications, progressive hearing loss, chorioretinitis of the eye, and hydrocephalus may occur. In addition, pneumonia, abnormal blood clotting function, and liver disease may occur. For fetuses infected with CMV who have obvious neurological abnormalities, nearly 95% have intellectual deficits, cerebral palsy, deafness, seizures, and/or death. The mean IQ for neurologically affected survivors is 50–70%. Medical treatment for CMV is relatively ineffective. Long-term infusion of the antiviral medication gancyclovir has been associated with slight improvement in some of the systemic findings of the infection (hypotonia, liver dysfunction), and may slow the progression of the sensorineural hearing loss. Use of CMV immune globulin intravenous in nonimmune pregnant women infected with CMV during pregnancy may decrease viral transmission to the fetus (Buxmann et al., 2012).

Toxoplasmosis. Toxoplasmosis is the disease caused by the protozoa *Toxoplasma gondii*, a parasite that may be ingested by a pregnant woman in undercooked meat (especially pork) or that may reach the pregnant woman via the feces of a house cat that consumes raw meat. Concern about toxoplasmosis is what prompts obstetricians to caution their pregnant patients to not touch their house cat's litter box. Once the pregnant woman ingests the organism, it proliferates within her blood stream, infects the placenta, and crosses the placenta to enter the fetal circulation. It causes tissue inflammation and destruction of the immature fetal nervous system, especially in the region of the aqueduct of Sylvius, which often leads to aqueductal stenosis and consequent hydrocephalus. Porencephalic cysts, multifocal encephalomalacia, and hydranencephaly may also be caused by toxoplasmosis. If toxoplasmosis is diagnosed during pregnancy, treatment of the maternal-fetal dyad with spiramycin, pyrimethamine, sulfadiazine, and folinic acid may lessen the severity of the fetal infection. After birth, treatment of the infected newborn has prevented progressive injury of the central nervous system and may allow for some reversal of injury. Affected babies are at high risk for poor brain (and head) growth, vision impairment, seizures, and deafness. Mean IQ for survivors of congenital toxoplasmosis is 89.

Varicella. Congenital varicella ("chicken pox"), a member of the herpes family, may be transmitted to the fetus if its nonimmune mother becomes infected during pregnancy. If infected during the first 20 weeks of gestation, the fetus may develop a variety of brain, eye, and other malformations, as well as intellectual deficiencies.

Rubella. When a nonimmune pregnant woman contracts rubella ("3-day measles") during the first 8 weeks of gestation, there exists a 90% likelihood that the disease may be transmitted to the fetus. Manifestations of congenital rubella include small brain, intellectual disabilities, cataracts and other eye abnormalities, hearing loss, and congenital cardiac defects.

Herpes simplex. This virus is teratogenic if it crosses across the placenta from the mother's circulation to that of the fetus. It may cause the fetus to be poorly grown and to have microcephaly (small brain), calcifications within the brain, damage to the eye, seizures, and necrosis of brain tissue with reabsorption of the dead brain tissue, leading to porencephalic cysts, multicystic encephalomalacia, or hydranencephaly. Transplacentally acquired herpes simplex infection is relatively rare and usually occurs as a result of a first-time infection of a nonimmune pregnant woman.

Metabolic defects

Pregnant women with poorly controlled PKU have extremely high serum levels of phenylalanine, a naturally occurring chemical found in only small quantities in people without this metabolic defect. When an embryo or fetus is exposed to high levels of phenylalanine via its mother, it is at high risk of dying in utero, or for the development of microcephaly, intellectual disability, intrauterine growth restriction, and congenital cardiac abnormalities. Thus, an embryo or fetus may be severely and permanently affected by exposure to high phenylalanine levels due to maternal PKU without actually having the metabolic defect itself.

Adverse environmental factors

Certain environmental factors may have adverse effects on the developing embryonic or fetal brain. Maternal hyperthermia (elevated body temperature) due either to fever or to hot tub use during the first trimester of fetal brain formation is associated with neural tube defects, small brain, and small eyes. Maternal exposure to lead, a heavy metal, is associated with intellectual disability and attention-deficit/hyperactivity disorder. Exposure of a pregnant woman to mercury, another heavy metal, is associated with intellectual disabilities, small brain, vision problems, and cerebral palsy.

Radiation is another teratogen. Exposure of an embryo to radiation less than 2 weeks after conception will either cause its death or no effect at all. Between 2 and 18 weeks gestation, exposure of an embryo or fetus to increasing doses of ionizing radiation is associated with increasingly poor brain growth and intellectual disability (Yamazaki & Schull, 1990). Fetuses from 8 to 15 weeks gestation exposed to 1 Gy (100 rads) have a 50% chance of intellectual deficiency. Fetuses from 16 to 25 weeks gestation exposed to 1 Gy (100 rads) have a 20% chance of intellectual deficiency (Otake, Hoshimaru, & Schull, 1989). Throughout gestation, the greater the amount of ionizing radiation to which an embryo or fetus is exposed, the greater the chance of in utero death, multiple malformations, intellectual disability, intrauterine growth restriction, hydrocephalus, eye abnormalities, and childhood cancer. Even exposure to 5 rads can have some adverse effect on fetal brain growth and intellect. An average routine chest x-ray, however, exposes the patient to only approximately 0.02 rads. The fetus is also somewhat protected from ionizing radiation by the maternal tissues and amniotic fluid that surround it, so it is not likely to be exposed to as many rads as is its mother. A pregnant woman would need 250 chest x-rays during her pregnancy to potentially expose her fetus to a cumulative dose of about 5 rads. Abdominal and pelvic x-rays involve exposure to greater amounts of radiation (~0.9 rads). Fluoroscopic studies expose patients to about 0.02 rads per minute. Caution must be taken when prescribing computerized axial tomography (CT scans) for pregnant women because a CT scan of the maternal pelvis may expose a fetus to up to 4 to 5 rads.

Teratogenic drugs

The greatest risk to a fetus from exposure to teratogens occurs during the first trimester, during the period of organogenesis (formation of organs).

Alcohol. Whether it occurs prenatally or postnatally, when the developing brain is exposed to alcohol, brain quantities of DHA and phosphatidylserine decrease, causing apoptosis (premature death) of brain cells. This is believed to be the mechanism for development of fetal alcohol syndrome (FAS). In FAS, abnormalities in every stage of brain development may be seen. There may be prenatal and postnatal somatic growth failure, microcephaly, intellectual disabilities, hyperactivity, and other behavioral disturbances. These disabilities do not tend to improve significantly, even if the home environment is optimal. Infants with FAS may have characteristic faces including a thin, curvy upper lip, a long philtrum in the midline between the nose and upper lip, and small eyes. They may have cardiac malformations, especially ventriculoseptal defects.

Cocaine. Cocaine may be responsible for brain malformations such as microcephaly and brain and eye malformations due to disordered neuronal migration and abnormal neuronal proliferation and differentiation. The development of neuronal circuitry may be disordered as well. In addition, cocaine is a potent vasoconstrictor of blood vessels. When blood vessels in the brain constrict, the brain tissue downstream does not receive enough oxygen or perfusion, and downstream cells may die and become reabsorbed, leaving porencephalic cysts, multifocal encephalomalacia, or hydranencephaly. When cocaine causes constriction of placental blood vessels, the entire fetus may experience extremely low amounts of perfusion of oxygenated blood from the placenta. This can cause poor blood flow to the fetus's brain. Sudden increases in blood pressure due to stress (or the effect of cocaine) may precipitate an intracranial hemorrhage, further exposing the fetal brain to compromise. Cocaine-exposed infants have a higher chance of having tremor, irritability, and a high-pitched cry. Some infants exposed to cocaine prenatally may have normal neurodevelopment; others have neurobehavioral and motor (movement) abnormalities.

Anticonvulsants. Several anticonvulsants used to control seizures may have adverse effects on the fetus. Although it is important for the pregnant woman to have her seizure disorder controlled, it is also important to try to avoid any teratogenic effects of anticonvulsants on the fetus. Hydantoin (phenytoin), phenobarbital, primidone, and carbamazepine have all been associated with multiple fetal malformations, including atypical facial appearance, nail defects, microcephaly, and intellectual disability. Trimethadione and paramethadione are associated with intellectual disabilities, microcephaly, atypical facial appearance, and malformations of the heart, genitourinary tract, trachea, and esophagus. Valproic acid has been associated with minor abnormalities of the face, bony defects of the arms and legs, myelomeningocele, encephalocele (see Figure 3.3), and cardiac malformations. Carbamazepine has been associated with encephalocele. These drugs exert their teratogenic effects when used during organogenesis; they may be used relatively safely in infancy and childhood to control seizures. When a woman who uses anticonvulsant medications is considering becoming pregnant, she and her physicians should select her anticonvulsants carefully.

Isotretinoin. Isotretinoin (a vitamin A analogue) is used orally and topically to treat severe acne. Approximately one third of isotretinoin users are women 13 to 19 years old, who may be at risk for an unplanned pregnancy. Isotretinoin

FIGURE 3.3 Encephalocele

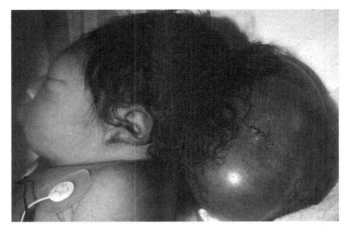

causes fetuses to have malformed or absent ears, small brains, hydrocephalus, intellectual disabilities, and severe cardiac malformations. Fetuses exposed to isotretinoin have a 25% chance of miscarriage; 36% of fetuses exposed to isotretinoin during the 1st trimester have serious malformations or fetal death. Because isotretinoin is such a potent teratogen, the prescribing physician and the drug manufacturer usually require that a woman about to receive the drug sign a contract promising that she will not become pregnant while she is being treated with the drug.

Disorders of Brain Development: Embryonic, Fetal, or Postnatal Periods

An assortment of brain malformations, hemorrhage, or infections occurring any time during embryonic, fetal, or postnatal life may be associated with hydrocephalus.

Hydrocephalus

Progressive enlargement of the ventricles with its onset during fetal life may be due to a variety of causes and may have its onset in the embryonic, fetal, or postnatal period (see Figure 3.4). Forty-five percent of neonates with congenital hydrocephalus have the brain developmental disorder, with holoprosencephaly as its etiology.

FIGURE 3.4 Hydrochephalus

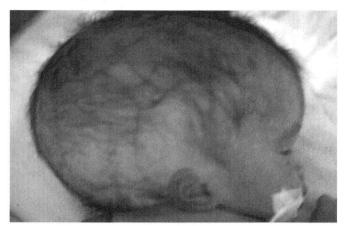

Twenty-five percent of neonates with congenital hydrocephalus have isolated meningomyelocele as its etiology. Ten percent each have Dandy-Walker malformation and X-linked aqueductal stenosis as their etiologies.

Holoprosencephaly

Holoprosencephaly is the most severe disorder of prosencephalic (forebrain) development. With holoprosencephaly, early embryonic development of the left and right cerebral hemispheres is faulty and incomplete. The cerebral cortex may have one single large anterior ventricle, sometimes considered a type of hydrocephalus *ex vacuo* (caused by insufficient brain volume to occupy the skull) and absence of the inter-hemispheric fissure. Holoprosencephaly may be associated with the lethal chromosomal defect Trisomy 13. It may also occur in the absence of a genetic abnormality. Midline-facial defects, such as hypotelorism (eyes extremely close together), cyclopia (a single, midline eye), cleft lip or palate, and a single midline nostril are often associated with holoprosencephaly. Surviving patients with holoprosencephaly exhibit severe intellectual disabilities, motor deficits, and are at high risk for seizures. Seizures in the presence of a brain malformation are difficult to control with anti-convulsant medications because the underlying problem, the brain malformation, cannot be corrected. The pituitary and hypothalamus are endocrine glands located in the midline of the brain. Their hormones control numerous bodily functions, including quantities of urine produced and thermoregulation. Patients with holopros-encephaly frequently have dehydration due to diabetes insipidus and problems with body temperature control.

Dandy-Walker malformation

Patients with Dandy-Walker malformation have complete or partial agenesis of the cerebellar vermis, a severely dilated fourth ventricle, and consequent enlargement of the posterior fossa of the skull with the tentorium pushed upward. Seventy percent of patients with Dandy-Walker malformation have associated abnormalities of the central nervous system, especially agenesis of the corpus callosum and defective neuronal migration. This defect occurs during the 2nd to 3rd month of gestation. Dandy-Walker malformation occurs when the cells of the newly closed neural tube do not differentiate properly. Therefore, the foramen of Magendie does not form in the roof of the fourth ventricle. Consequently, cerebrospinal fluid (CSF) accumulates in large quantities within the fourth ventricle. Dandy-Walker malformation may be related to identifiable chromosomal abnormalities or to various syndromes. In addition to having a strong association with other brain malformations, patients with Dandy-Walker malformation have a 30%–40% chance of having other, systemic, malformations, such as cardiac and urinary tract malformations. Outcome for fetuses/neonates diagnosed with Dandy-Walker malformation is unfavorable, with a nearly 40% chance of death; survivors have a 75% chance of having cognitive deficits. Survivors have an IQ score of only 45 (Volpe, 2008c). Surgical treatment for the ventricular distension of Dandy-Walker malformation is challenging. Neurosurgeons will typically place a Y-shaped ventriculoperitoneal shunt with one tip in the cystic fourth ventricle, one tip in a lateral ventricle, and the third tip in the peritoneal space.

Aqueductal stenosis

Hydrocephalus caused by narrowing of the aqueduct of Sylvius may be due to (a) non-familial reasons; (b) an X-linked condition caused by a mutation in a neural cell adhesion molecule also associated with agenesis of the corpus callosum, intellectual delay, and adducted thumbs; and (c) autosomal recessive inheritance.

Vein of Galen malformation

Malformation of the vein of Galen may also cause hydrocephalus. With this condition, cerebral arteries deliver blood into a normally transient fetal brain blood vessel that supplies the vein of Galen. The blood vessel swells with cerebral blood like an aneurysm would. The blood accumulating within this blood vessel prevents delivery of normally oxygenated blood to the other areas of the brain. This may result in cerebral infarctions, hemorrhages, and the development of a mass effect of the massive aneurysmal dilation. If the dilated blood vessel compresses the aqueduct of Sylvius, hydrocephalus may ensue. On physical exam, in addition to an abnormal neurologic exam, a cerebral bruit (murmur) may be heard over the back of the patient's head. In addition, high output congestive heart failure may occur because the heart does not have access to enough blood to efficiently perfuse the body. This causes a high heart rate, low stroke volume, and low blood pressure. This condition was previously lethal in more than 80% of cases, but current invasive management involving embolization of the arteries feeding the dilated vein or embolization of the dilated vein itself has led to the survival of two thirds of afflicted infants. Nearly half of survivors may now demonstrate normal neurodevelopment.

Intrauterine infection

Intrauterine infection, especially with cytomegalovirus and the protozoa *Toxoplasma gondii*, can be a cause of congenital hydrocephalus.

Hydranencephaly

Babies born with hydranencephaly may be initially thought to be normal. They may appear normal, and even exhibit sleep–wake cycles, blink in response to light and sound, have normal pupillary responses to light, and have reflex extraocular movements. They may have apparently normal movement of their facial muscles, normal movement of their limbs, and normal deep tendon reflexes. Their primitive neonatal reflexes are present, and they have the ability to root, suck, and gag. However, there are subtle abnormal findings on their neurological exams. Their primitive neonatal reflexes can be elicited repeatedly in short periods of time without any habituation. Therefore, repeated exposure in short intervals to sudden light, sound, or pinprick results in the same extreme response each time.

Hydranencephaly usually develops as the result of bilateral infarction of the previously normally formed brain involving the cerebral cortex in the distribution of the internal carotid arteries anteriorly and, occasionally, the posterior cerebral circulation. Hydrocephalus occurring with hydranencephaly due to brain infarction is different from the other types of hydrocephalus discussed in this chapter. Even though the skull is filled principally with CSF, there is generally no increased pressure because CSF simply fills in the empty space that brain tissue previously occupied. This may not require placement of a ventriculoperitoneal shunt. However, hydraencephaly may also develop as the result of severe intrauterine infection that destroys cerebral tissue and causes tissue inflammation/scarring. Congenital toxoplasmosis and herpes simplex may be associated with severe brain destruction resulting in (in order of increasing severity) porencephalic cysts, multicystic encephalomalacia, and hydranencephaly. In this situation, inflammation of the ventriclar walls and scarring of the aqueduct of Sylvius may lead to excess pressure within the skull, warranting surgical placement of a ventricular peritoneal shunt.

Posthemorrhagic hydrocephalus

There is a risk for hydrocephalus to occur following an intraventricular hemorrhage. The more severe the hemorrhage, the higher the chance of the development of hydrocephalus. Blood within the ventricles of the brain acts as an irritant, causing excess production of CSF. In addition, if any blood clot or fibrous scar tissue that forms after the hemorrhage is in a location to obstruct the normal flow of CSF, there is an overaccumulation of fluid within the ventricles. When posthemorrhagic hydrocephalus occurs, serial measurements of the volume of fluid within the ventricles is accomplished by neurodiagnostic imaging (ultrasounds, MRIs, CT scans). Sometimes, posthemorrhagic ventricular dilation is temporary and resolves. Other times, posthemorrhagic hydrocephalus does not resolve and requires neurosurgical management.

Seizures

Seizures in the neonate may present in a variety of ways and may have a wide variety of etiologies.

Clinical presentations

Neonatal seizures are a result of abnormal electrical activity emanating from the brain. Neonatal seizures may be manifested by rhythmic, slow, relatively intense jerking movements of the extremities or by movements that are much more subtle. Seizures may involve rowing movements of the arms, bicycling movements of the legs, prolonged extension or stretching of one or more extremities, neck extension and turning of

the head in one direction, lip-smacking, tongue-thrusting (which may be misinterpreted as signs that the baby is hungry), eyelid twitching or fluttering, horizontal jerking of the eyes to one side, nonsynchronized twitching of body parts, cessation of breathing (apnea), or subtle autonomic changes (e.g., an abnormal drop in or rise of heart rate or blood pressure).

An important distinguishing feature between seizures and other neonatal behaviors is that seizures cannot be stopped or extinguished by other people. For instance, during a seizure, touching, cradling, or rubbing a baby will not cause the seizure to cease. If a neonate who is having some unusual behaviors is touched and the behaviors stop, those behaviors likely were not the result of seizures. Similarly, seizures cannot be elicited by other people. Startling a baby with a sudden loud noise or sudden touch may cause him or her to exhibit a Moro startle reflex, to alter level of arousal, or even to show some temporary jittery movements; however, being startled cannot cause a neonate to have a seizure.

When a neonate is suspected of having seizures, an electroencephalogram (EEG) is typically performed to verify this suspicion. An EEG measures brain wave activity by utilizing electrodes and wires that are temporarily glued to the baby's scalp. However, an EEG can actually miss detecting the seizure if the seizure does not occur during the period of time that the EEG is being performed. An EEG may also miss a seizure that occurs during performance of the EEG if the abnormal brain waves occur in the center of the brain but do not move all the way to the periphery of the brain where the EEG electrodes are positioned. Even if electrical seizure activity is not seen on an EEG in a baby who has seizures, the EEG may still be useful. In cases where the seizure's electrical activity does not reach the peripherally placed EEG electrodes or when the seizure occurred before the EEG was begun, some localized evidence of cerebral irritability may still be evident in the electrical waveforms. Also, the baseline brainwave activity may be abnormal, which indicates some cerebral disturbance (e.g., HIE) that can make a baby vulnerable to seizures.

When a baby is suspected of having seizures, the brain is often imaged using ultrasound, CT scan, or MRI. The purpose of the imaging study is to help to determine the reason for the seizures. Likewise, when a baby is suspected of having a seizure, various blood tests are drawn to help to determine the etiology of the seizure.

Etiologies of seizures

Neonatal seizures have many potential etiologies and, as noted previously, the medical work-up is performed to determine the reason for the seizure. Once the reason for the seizure is known, health care professionals have a better chance of successfully stopping the seizures. Unlike more mature pediatric patients, neonates do not have seizures due to fever (febrile seizures), and the etiology of their seizures rarely is determined to be idiopathic epilepsy. Most commonly, the etiology of their seizures is an acute insult to the central nervous system, such as HIE or infection.

HIE

Approximately 50%–60% of neonatal seizures are caused by HIE, which is usually secondary to perinatal asphyxia. Typically, the seizures occur within the first 24 hours after birth. Frequently, the neonate will appear extremely irritable or lethargic before the onset of HIE-associated seizures. Approximately one fifth of neonates with seizures due to HIE will have cerebral infarction recognized on brain imaging studies. Asphyxia is the damage that occurs in the tissues as a result of low levels of oxygen, high levels of carbon dioxide, poor perfusion (blood flow), and/or abnormally low pH (acidosis) in the blood of the fetus or newborn. Perinatal asphyxia may cause temporary or permanent dysfunction of the fetal or newborn brain. Often, as asphyxia is occurring, the body will attempt to send adequate amounts of blood to the brain at the expense of blood flow to less vital organs. Therefore, an asphyxiated baby with brain dysfunction may also be expected to have at least temporary dysfunction of the intestines, kidneys, bone marrow, liver, or all of these.

Timing of asphyxia/HIE

Although it is sometimes assumed that all neonatal asphyxia occurs during the delivery process, this is not true. Asphyxia can occur while the fetus is still within the uterus before any labor begins. If the mother herself suffers from low oxygen levels in the blood as a result of cardiac or lung problems or if she has severe anemia, she will not be able to send enough oxygen to her fetus. Red blood cells carry oxygen to the tissues; if there are not enough red blood cells in the mother's circulation, not enough oxygen will be delivered to her fetus. If there is a problem with the placenta, such as abruption placenta (premature separation of the placenta from the uterine wall) or placenta previa (placenta growing over the cervical opening), which causes inadequate fetal carbon dioxide elimination and/or inadequate fetal oxygenation, then the fetus will be at risk. If the mother is unable to send enough blood to her side of the placenta due to low maternal blood pressure, severe maternal hypertension with blood vessel constriction, or excessively strong and prolonged uterine contractions, then the fetus will not get enough oxygen and will have inadequate carbon dioxide elimination. If this problem goes on in a relatively mild manner for several weeks, it may manifest only by poor fetal growth without acute asphyxia. If the poor fetal growth is reflected in poor growth of the head and brain, there is an increased neurodevelopmental risk to that infant. The fetus will also not get enough oxygen or gas-exchanging ability if the umbilical cord circulation is impaired by the cord being compressed between the baby's head and a maternal pelvic bone, twisted around the baby's body parts, or prolapsed through an open cervix with the baby's head compressing it, or by having a true tight knot in the cord. If the fetus itself has poor oxygen delivery to its organs due to severe fetal anemia, then the fetus is at risk for asphyxia. Furthermore, if the fetus has extremely low blood pressure because of infection or bleeding, then it will not have adequate perfusion to its organs and will also be at risk for asphyxia. After birth, if the baby has severe cardiac or pulmonary problems or cannot adjust to the extrauterine environment, he may experience poor oxygen delivery or suboptimal blood flow to the organs, increasing the risk for asphyxia. Both the seriousness of the perfusion and oxygenation abnormalities, as well as the length of time the fetus is exposed to poor perfusion and/or low oxygen levels, may be correlated with the degree of severity of the neonate's asphyxia.

Historical points regarding asphyxia/HIE

Physicians previously did not recognize that cerebral palsy might be associated with asphyxia occurring before labor or after delivery. Therefore, they often blamed the delivery process as the sole etiology of cerebral palsy. However, they observed that cerebral palsy would occur despite intermittent auscultation of (listening to) the fetal heart rate by physicians. In the 1960s, development of Doppler (ultrasound) technology to continuously monitor the fetal heart rate and of fetal scalp blood sampling to detect fetal pH were expected to significantly decrease the incidence of cerebral palsy, birth asphyxia, HIE, and fetal and/or neonatal death. However, the use of fetal Doppler technology has not been shown to significantly decrease the incidence of cerebral palsy. Cerebral palsy still occurs in 1 to 2 babies of 1,000 live births (Naeye, Peters, Bartholomew, & Landis, 1989). Cerebral palsy linked to fetal

asphyxia occurs only 1 to 2 times in 10,000 live births. Only 9% of cases of cerebral palsy have been linked to intrapartum events (MacDonald, 1997), and more than 80% of children with cerebral palsy had no evidence of intrapartum nor perinatal asphyxia (Blair & Stanley, 1988). This is because most asphyxia occurs independent of the labor process. In most cases, the factor responsible for the cerebral palsy or brain injury cannot be identified (Kuban & Leviton, 1994). Doppler assessment of umbilical cord arterial blood flow velocity has the potential to identify those fetuses at increased risk for cerebral palsy, asphyxia, HIE, and in utero death due to rising blood pressure in the placenta due to placental pathology. Doppler technology cannot be expected to identify brain damage. Once risk factors are identified, the pregnant woman and her physicians must balance the risks of premature elective delivery with the risks of continuing poor intrauterine blood flow.

Severity of HIE

Full-term babies with asphyxia have a higher survival rate than do premature babies with asphyxia. Researchers have divided HIE into three categories. Mild HIE may show up initially as brain dysfunction (e.g., excessive irritability; uncoordinated suck, swallow, or breathing; excessive sleepiness), which is sometimes not recognized by the neonate's caregivers. A mildly asphyxiated neonate's initial hyperirritability may be misinterpreted by caregivers as indicating that the baby is just hungry. It may be the baby's inability to take in substantial amounts of milk that draws attention to the fact that something is not right with the baby. Babies with mild HIE do not have seizures as a result of their insult. An EEG to measure brain wave activity will not show seizure activity for these mildly asphyxiated brains but may show some abnormalities of baseline brainwave activity. These abnormalities of the EEG may be temporary; in the case of mild HIE, they last fewer than 14 days. Clinically, by 14 days old, the mildly asphyxiated baby has a completely normal neurologic examination and EEG. Babies with mild HIE have a good likelihood of ultimately becoming neurodevelopmentally normal.

Babies with severe HIE typically have poor Apgar scores, which are assessed at birth in order to record neonatal health. It has been noted that full-term babies with Apgar scores that are persistently low (0–3 out of a possible 10) at 20 minutes after birth have a 59% chance of dying in the first year of life; survivors have a 57% incidence of cerebral palsy (Volpe, 2008a). No full-term babies with severe neonatal neurologic syndrome of HIE (stuporous, flaccid, and absent primitive reflexes) have a normal neurologic outcome, and 80% of them die (Robertson & Finer, 1985). Severe HIE often presents with coma or initial hyperirritability (due to brain swelling), which subsides into lethargy and coma when the brain swelling subsides. Babies with severe HIE may have seizures, and they may lack the normal primitive neonatal reflexes. Seizures may be apparent on EEG. Abnormalities of the baseline brain waves, including the ominous burst-suppression pattern, may also be apparent on EEG. Persistence of these electrographic findings is worrisome, as they are both poor prognostic indicators. The most severely abnormal EEG would be isoelectric, with no brainwaves whatsoever. Such an isoelectric EEG may be used to help the physicians confirm their clinical suspicions of brain death. If, over the course of many hours, a severely asphyxiated infant exhibits no self-preserving reflexes (e.g., no eye blinking, no withdrawal from painful stimuli), no spontaneous movements, no attempt to breathe even when his serum carbon dioxide level is elevated, physicians may entertain the diagnosis of brain death. In the unfortunate situation in which brain death is confirmed, the physicians would discuss the diagnosis with the baby's family. After brain death occurs, the brain's role in regulating heart rate and blood

pressure is lacking. Such a patient's heart rate and blood pressure would slowly drop to zero, even if the patient remained on mechanical ventilation. Therefore, after a diagnosis of brain death is made and the family is notified, plans are made to remove the patient from the ventilator because further efforts to make the baby survive or to have a typical life would be futile. Many families choose to be present to hold their babies when they are removed from the ventilator. The hospital staff is available to assist families through this difficult time.

Moderate HIE represents a middle ground between mild and severe HIE. These infants often initially present with decreased spontaneous movements and hypotonia or with hyperirritability. Some of these babies will have seizures; some will not. Many will have some improvement in their initially abnormal neurologic exam, but still will be left with some permanent disabilities.

Treatment of HIE

HIE may be treated in several ways. It is important to support the baby's breathing. If the baby is not breathing well enough on her own, mechanical ventilation is indicated. Keeping an asphyxiated baby's blood sugar in the normal range is important so that the brain will have adequate energy for its healing activities. Controlled brain cooling using a cooling blanket or cooling bonnet has been shown to reduce the metabolic rate of the asphyxiated brain and allow more opportunity for brain recovery.

Clinical features of HIE

Immediately following HIE, a baby may have hypertonia and hyperirritability, or hypotonia, stupor, and coma. He may have seizures and/or inability to breathe regularly on his own. During the next day or two, some of the abnormal findings may worsen, as brain swelling occurs. The brain swelling (cerebral edema) may last several days then start to resolve spontaneously. Whether the baby's neurological exam eventually becomes normal depends on the severity of the hypoxic-ischemic insult the brain has sustained. In the neonatal period, they may exhibit stupor and coma, seizures, hypotonia, oculomotor disturbances, and abnormal sucking, swallowing, and tongue movements. Over the long term, they may have cognitive deficiency (especially with injury to the basal ganglia and thalamus), spastic quadriparesis-stiffness (cerebral palsy), choreo-athetosis (involuntary writhing movements), seizure disorder, and ataxia (difficulty walking; Volpe, 2008a). When infants with severe HIE survive, they may require daily medications to help prevent seizures. If they have inability to suck and swallow, they may require nutrition (pumped breast milk or formula) to be fed to them via feeding tubes. Initially, a small, flexible plastic tube can be inserted through the nose or mouth into the stomach through which the infant may be fed. If the infant demonstrates continued inability to feed by mouth, a feeding g-tube can be inserted by the surgeons into the stomach through a nick placed in the abdominal wall. The surgically placed g-tube has the advantage that it does not often fall out (but if it does fall out, it requires a health care professional to replace it), and it is hidden under clothing. In addition to having feeding difficulties, babies with severe HIE may have difficulty swallowing their own oral secretions, as well as difficulty with gastroesophageal reflux, when stomach contents are regurgitated up into the mouth. Medications and another surgical procedure called a fundoplication, to tighten up the connection between the esophagus (swallowing tube) and the stomach, can help with this problem. However, despite these procedures, infants with severe HIE are at increased risk of having recurring aspiration pneumonias due to the breathing of secretions or milk/formula into their lungs. Aspiration pneumonia is a significant cause of shortened life span in these babies (Fisher, 2009).

As illustrated in Scenario 2 at the beginning of this chapter, gentle and appropriate intervention in providing parental education; lactation, occupational, speech, and physical therapy; seizure control; and neurodevelopmental intervention may help babies who survive with the sequela of HIE to develop to their best potential.

Meningoencephalitis

A neonate with seizures may have a fever, or more commonly, a low body temperature as a result of meningoencephalitis (infection and inflammation of the brain and surrounding membranes). In this situation, meningoencephalitis causes both the seizures and the abnormal body temperature; the abnormal temperature is not the cause of the seizures. Meningoencephalitis can also be a cause of seizures or abnormal neurologic activity without an abnormal body temperature. Meningoencephalitis can be due to a variety of bacteria or viruses. When a baby comes to medical attention due to seizures, it is important to obtain a sample of CSF by means of a lumbar puncture to test for bacterial or viral (especially herpes simplex) meningitis. Prompt institution of broad-spectrum antibiotics is important, with consideration of starting an antiherpes medication (acyclovir) as well (Fisher, 2009).

Hypoglycemia

Hypoglycemia (low blood sugar) can cause the brain to have a deficit of sugar or energy, which can lead to seizures. Before developing seizures, a hypoglycemic baby may be jittery (shaky movements while conscious), sweaty, limp, or unresponsive. It is ironic that seizure activity further depletes the brain of its energy stores and may precipitate more seizures. Treatment of hypoglycemic seizures with anticonvulsant medications is ineffective. Instead, correction of the low blood sugar will cause the seizures to stop.

Low blood sugar may be seen in infants of diabetic women. In this situation, if the mother had chronically high blood sugar levels, the fetus, throughout gestation, would have been exposed to high sugar levels crossing from the mother via the placenta. The fetus responds by making a large amount of insulin in an attempt to bring its blood sugar down toward normal. This high amount of insulin causes energy derived from sugar to be stored in the fetus's body in the form of fat. Once birth occurs, however, the newborn cannot suddenly turn off insulin production, so the blood sugar levels drop dangerously low. Physicians generally consider a blood sugar level lower than 40 milligrams per deciliter to be risky in a full-term neonate; levels below 35 milligrams per deciliter are considered too low for premature neonates. Treatment for neonatal hypoglycemia involves getting additional glucose (sugar) into the baby. This may be accomplished through oral or tube feedings, intravenous (IV) fluids containing a moderate concentration of glucose through a peripheral IV, and/or intravenous fluids containing a high glucose concentration through an umbilical venous catheter or other central line (Fisher, 2009).

Hyponatremia

Hyponatremia (low sodium levels in the blood, below approximately 130 milliequivalents per liter) can lead to seizures. Similar to the case with low glucose levels, treatment of seizures due to hyponatremia with anticonvulsant medications is ineffective in stopping seizures. Instead, treatment of the low blood sodium will stop the seizures. Babies may develop severely low sodium levels for a few reasons. If the baby consumes too much water compared to the amount of sodium she ingests, her serum sodium level will become diluted by free water, causing the sodium level in the serum to drop. This most commonly occurs when the baby's infant formula is mixed with water in the wrong

concentration, which can cause water intoxication. A baby may also have a condition known as syndrome of inappropriate antidiuretic hormone, causing his or her body to conserve water inappropriately. In this situation, a baby becomes edematous (puffy), and his blood sodium level drops as he becomes overwhelmed with too much water. In congenital adrenal hyperplasia, a baby may waste excess sodium in the urine while retaining excess potassium. The high blood potassium may cause abnormal rhythms of the heart, and the low blood sodium may cause seizures. Congenital adrenal hyperplasia may also be associated with incomplete differentiation of the genitalia (Fisher, 2009).

Hypocalcemia

Hypocalcemia (low calcium levels in the serum, generally below 8 milligrams per deciliter) can cause seizures. Before they actually develop seizures from low calcium levels, babies may have jitteriness, twitching of the muscles, and abnormal heart rhythms. Treatment of seizures due to low calcium levels with anticonvulsants is likely to be ineffective. Instead, treatment should be directed at correcting the low calcium level in the bloodstream. Low calcium levels may occur in babies who have high phosphorus levels (due to kidney disease or consumption of cow milk too early in life), in infants of diabetic mothers, in babies that are small for gestational age, and in babies with a poorly functioning parathyroid gland. Babies with hypoparathyroidism may also have a poorly functioning thymus gland and abnormalities of the heart and of the great vessels emanating from the heart found in DiGeorge syndrome, which is caused by a gene deletion of the 22nd chromosome (Fisher, 2009).

Hypomagnesemia

Rarely, low magnesium levels may be associated with seizures. Magnesium levels may be low due to either the mother or the neonate wasting large amounts of magnesium in the urine (Fisher, 2009).

Narcotic withdrawal

When a pregnant woman chronically receives narcotics, both she and her fetus become physiologically dependent on these medications. When the baby is born, it is suddenly removed from the narcotic source. Within 24 to 72 hours after birth, infants may show signs of narcotic withdrawal syndrome. They may have frantic sucking, excessive feeding, excess irritability, prolonged crying, fevers, sweating, fast heart rate, vomiting, diarrhea, and seizures. Treatment for neonatal narcotic withdrawal syndrome includes providing a dark, quiet environment with minimal external stimuli, and swaddling the infant to make her feel enveloped. Some physicians treat seizures due to narcotic withdrawal with anticonvulsants, but such seizures and other clinical signs of narcotic withdrawal respond well to a regimen of slowly decreasing doses of narcotic (Fisher, 2009).

Strokes (cerebral infarctions)

Strokes may cause seizures in a neonate, or they may cause a more subtle focal neurologic deficit, such as weakness of one hand. If the neurologic deficit is minor, the fact that the infant had a stroke may not be immediately recognized. Strokes are relatively rare in the neonate. When they do occur, they may be associated with poor cerebral blood flow occurring during an event that also caused HIE. Strokes may occur as a consequence of cerebral arterial occlusion that is caused by an embolus (blood clot) that breaks loose from another location, such as the placenta, or a thrombus that forms in the cerebral blood vessel. When such an event occurs, physicians may decide to do laboratory studies to determine whether the baby has excessive and inappropriate clotting of the blood. This diagnosis is important to make in order to prevent future strokes or clotting within blood vessels that supply blood to important organs. Because the excess clotting

disorder (hypercoagulability) may run in families and may have health implications with regard to other family members, doctors may need permission from parents to do genetic studies on the baby. If a genetically mediated hypercoagulability is identified, the family may be invited to discuss this with a genetic counselor or doctor.

Strokes also may occur because the blood that was supposed to perfuse a particular region of the brain never reaches that area due to hemorrhaging of one of the blood vessels leading to that area. This is called a hemorrhagic infarction or hemorrhagic stroke.

Treatment for stroke includes supporting the neonate's cardiorespiratory status, supporting blood volume and blood pressure, controlling any seizures that may occur, and working to prevent further strokes by diagnosing the cause of the stroke, anticoagulating the blood (in the case of hypercoagulability), or correcting any deficient clotting factors in the case of a hemorrhagic stroke (Fisher, 2009).

Intracranial hemorrhage

Bleeding within the skull can have many different causes. It may or may not lead to seizures, and it may or may not lead to permanent or temporary neurological disability. Outcome may depend on which area of the brain is affected by the bleeding, the extent of the bleeding, and how much of the adjacent brain has been poorly perfused during the hemorrhagic event. Whenever any type of intracranial bleeding occurs, attention must be directed to whether the baby has the expected ability to clot their blood. If the infant's blood does not clot correctly, he may have one of various types of bleeding disorders, such as low platelet count, hemophilia, or disseminated intravascular coagulation (blood clots forming within the blood vessels, using up circulating clotting factors). Transfusion of clotting factors may help to bring the hemorrhaging under control.

Furthermore, all forms of hemorrhage may be increased in infants who have vitamin K–deficient hemorrhagic disease of the newborn. In this case, the baby's prothrombin activity in the blood is decreased, setting it up for bleeding. Vitamin K levels in the newborn are generally low, especially from the 2nd to 7th day of life. Hemorrhagic disease of the newborn occurs most frequently on these days in infants who do not receive a vitamin K1 injection into the muscle around the time of delivery. Oral vitamin K3, when attempted to be used as an alternative, is potentially dangerous because it causes hemolytic anemia, which could lead to jaundice, kernicterus, and brain damage. Therefore, the safe and effective injectable vitamin K1 is administered to neonates shortly after birth.

Subarachnoid hemorrhage may be related to a traumatic delivery, a hypoxic-ischemic event, or a premature delivery. Some subarachnoid hemorrhages are minor and present with only minimal signs or are asymptomatic. Some present with seizures in an otherwise healthy-appearing baby, usually on the second day of life. Rarely, a subarachnoid hemorrhage will present with massive intracranial blood loss shortly after birth with a catastrophic progression to death. Diagnosis of subarachnoid is best performed with a CT scan or MRI. Outcome varies with the severity of the hemorrhage. Patients with minimal neurologic signs generally do very well. Even those with seizures as a complication of subarachnoid hemorrhage ultimately have a normal neurodevelopmental follow-up 90% of the time (Volpe, 2008b). Those with catastrophic subarachnoid hemorrhage either die or are left with serious permanent neurologic deficits.

Subdural hemorrhage is the least common of the neonatal varieties of intracranial hemorrhage. It occurs most commonly after traumatic deliveries in both full-term and premature neonates. Therefore, subdural hemorrhage is most likely to occur if: the baby is large in comparison to the birth canal, the maternal pelvis is rigid (first-time or older mother), labor is not long enough to allow the pelvis to dilate maximally, labor is too long (subjecting the fetal head to prolonged repetitive compressions), or mal-presentation of the fetus occurs, the fetal skull is very compliant (as with premature fetuses), or extraction of the fetus requires forceps, vacuum, or rotational procedures. Similar to other types of intracranial hemorrhage, subdural hemorrhages may have no clinical signs, minimal signs (hyperalertness, apneas, irritability), moderate signs (focal neurologic signs, seizures), or severe or lethal signs (hypotension, seizures, obtundation, coma, death). Diagnosis is best made with CT scan or MRI. Posthemorrhagic hydrocephalus may occur, and some patients may need a ventriculoperitoneal shunt to be inserted. Outcomes are variable.

Intraventricular hemorrhage (IVH) is most common in the premature infant. The more premature the infant, the more frequent and the more severe the IVH that may occur. The fetal brain has a rich supply of immature and fragile blood vessels that course along its surface and dive down into the brain tissue. These blood vessels are vulnerable to asphyxia and to fluctuations in blood pressure. They are prone to leaking and bleeding, which usually start in the region of the subependymal germinal matrix. IVHs have been grouped into four categories. Grade 1 IVH refers to hemorrhaging that has occurred only along the surface of the brain in the area of the subependymal germinal matrix. Grade 2 IVH refers to hemorrhaging that has broken through the subependymal germinal matrix into the spinal fluid-filled lakes within the brain (the lateral ventricles). Grade 3 IVH refers to hemorrhaging that has not only entered the lateral ventricles but has filled the ventricles with blood and, therefore, distended them. Grade 4 IVH occurs when the hemorrhaging has also invaded and destroyed the brain tissue. This is believed to be the result of a hemorrhagic infarction (i.e., hemorrhagic stroke), caused by the lower-grade hemorrhaging. When blood is not being delivered to brain tissue downstream from a lower grade IVH, a hemorrhagic stroke can occur in the poorly perfused brain tissue.

Outcomes following IVH are generally more favorable with the lower grades (Grades 1 and 2) than with the higher grades (Grades 3 and 4) IVH. However, any baby with IVH may be at risk for neurodevelopmental complications. There are a few reasons for this. Hemorrhage in the subependymal germinal matrix can lead to destruction of glial precursor cells whose job is to migrate into the still-developing brain tissue and provide further brain development. Loss of blood from important brain blood vessels means that the vulnerable brain is not getting appropriate amounts of blood supply in downstream regions. Therefore, localized regions of poorly perfused, poorly oxygenated brain tissue may develop. Blood clots within the ventricles may both stimulate the production of excessive amounts of CSF and block the reabsorption of CSF. Over time, the irritating effect of the blood clot may cause permanent scarring that obstructs CSF flow and absorption. Ultimately, too much CSF may accumulate, causing post-hemorrhagic hydrocephalus. The skull bones of a baby will eventually fuse and cause the skull to become, essentially, a closed box. If the swelling of the ventricles within the skull is sufficient to cause concern that there will be excessive pressure within the closed skull and pressure on the brain that impairs its blood flow, the baby may require placement of a ventriculoperitoneal shunt.

Development of IVH in a full-term baby is relatively uncommon. When a full-term baby does develop an IVH, a history of a traumatic delivery or asphyxia should be sought. However, 25% of full-term babies with IVH have no history of trauma or asphyxia. As described previously, full-term babies with intracranial hemorrhaging should generally have an investigation of their ability to clot because clotting disorders may predispose toward intracranial hemorrhage. The lack of IVH in premature babies and in full-term babies does not necessarily mean that the babies' brains will function normally.

An abnormal connection of cerebral arteries to cerebral veins, known as an arteriovenous malformation, may result in hemorrhage (a bleeding arteriovenous malformation) within the brain. Although intracranial hemorrhage is the most common way that these blood vessel malformations present, even without hemorrhage, these patients may have seizures, signs of high-output congestive heart failure due to inefficient delivery of blood to the brain, hydrocephalus, and neurologic dysfunction. The physician may hear a bruit (i.e., murmur), when listening over the scalp with a stethoscope. Treatment is surgical (Fisher, 2009).

Developmental brain defects

When an error during embryonic or fetal brain development results in a brain with abnormal anatomy and/or function, it places the affected baby at high risk for seizures. Unfortunately, such seizures are not easily controlled with anticonvulsant medications, and physicians cannot correct the underlying condition. In addition to seizures, these patients will not have typical neurodevelopmental outcome because the brain is not formed properly (Fisher, 2009).

Inborn errors of metabolism

When a baby with a congenital inability to metabolize nutrients is in utero, the placenta allows the mother to eliminate the toxic metabolites from the fetal circulation. The newborn will, therefore, appear asymptomatic at birth. However, within the first several days of life, as the infant ingests milk that she is unable to properly metabolize, the toxic metabolites will build up in her circulation. These toxic metabolites may include ammonia and excessive quantities of certain amino acids from the improper metabolism of proteins in her diet; organic acids due to improper metabolism of carbohydrates or proteins in the diet; or organic acids, fatty acids, and/or ammonia due to improper metabolism of fatty acids in the mitochondria or peroxisomes of the cells. Excessive quantities of certain amino acids, organic acids, or ammonia can lead to neurodevelopmental abnormalities, including seizures, acidosis, and death. Treatment for these conditions is complicated and incomplete. It involves restriction of whatever component of milk is unable to be metabolized, occasionally dialysis to remove the offending toxins, and a variety of partially effective medications. Even breastfeeding may need to be curtailed. These infants are at extremely high risk for long-term neurodevelopmental complications and death due to their metabolic disorder. After diagnosis of an inborn error of metabolism, genetic counseling for the family is indicated.

Hyperbilirubinemia

Bilirubin arises from the breaking down of red blood cells. High bilirubin levels in the blood may occur as a result of blood group incompatibility between the mother and her fetus, or because of the formation of abnormal red blood cells in the baby, with excessive breakdown of these cells. High bilirubin levels can also occur because of poor feeding or poor stooling, dehydration, prematurity, and breakdown of red blood cells in the baby's skin (bruising), or within a body compartment. Excess bilirubin causes jaundice, a yellow coloring of the skin and eyes. Severe jaundice can cause bilirubin to pass from the bloodstream into the brain, causing seizures, neurodevelopmental delay, and deafness. Neurologic effects of the hyperbilirubinemia can be temporary (acute bilirubin encephalopathy) or permanent (kernicterus). Seizures due to hyperbilirubinemia may be managed by anticonvulsant medications as well as by double volume exchange transfusion and phototherapy to decrease the level of the

bilirubin. If seizures persist after the bilirubin has been controlled, chronic treatment with anticonvulsants may be necessary (Fisher, 2009).

Fifth day fits (benign idiopathic neonatal seizures)

Some infants develop a flurry of seizure activity on approximately the fifth day of life. Between seizures, their neurologic exam seems normal. The fact that the seizures have occurred is generally surprising because there is no medical history of asphyxia or other common causes of neonatal seizures. The EEG confirms seizure activity; however, the medical work-up for its etiology yields no results. The seizures generally disappear before 15 days of age and never recur. Providing their respiratory function is supported during the seizures, these infants generally grow up to be neurologically typical (Clancy, 1997; Fisher, 2009).

Benign neonatal familial seizures

As with fifth day fits, benign neonatal familial seizures are considered benign because the seizures are generally mild, easily controlled, do not limit the quality of life nor shorten the length of life, and are not associated with neurologic disability. EEG confirms seizure activity. Benign neonatal familial seizures are genetically transmitted in an autosomal dominant fashion that is linked to either the long arm of the 20th or the 8th chromosome. The affected gene causes an abnormal production of an acetylcholine receptor in the maturing brain. Usually, this seizure disorder disappears with maturity; however, such babies may be at increased risk for febrile seizures of childhood and for epilepsy later in life (Clancy, 1997; Fisher, 2009).

Pyridoxine dependency

When one of the B vitamins (vitamin B6), pyridoxine, does not bind to the glutamic acid decarboxylase apoprotein properly, not enough gamma-aminobutyric acid (GABA) and too much glutamate are present in the CSF. GABA's role is to inhibit excitatory neurotransmitters such as glutamate. Without enough GABA and with too much glutamate, seizures can occur that are refractory to standard anticonvulsant medications. Supplementing pyridoxine levels should help to stop the seizures as well as to arrest the brain abnormalities that may occur due to exposure to excess glutamate levels. Maternal placental function does not help to correct this problem, unlike many of the other metabolic problems that can cause neonatal seizures. Therefore, babies with pyridoxine dependency may have seizures within the first hours after birth or even while in utero (Fisher, 2009).

Benign neonatal sleep myoclonus

Some babies may have repetitive and usually symmetric jerking of the extremities that occurs only during sleep. These myoclonic jerks are not associated with an abnormal EEG and resolve spontaneously within a couple of months. Although they appear to be similar to a seizure, these movements are actually not seizures. These babies are expected to be neurologically typical (Fisher, 2009).

Treatment of seizures

Treatment for neonatal seizures is supportive (i.e., maintenance of adequate respiratory, cardiologic, and metabolic function) and includes the correction of any underlying abnormality, if possible, and the consideration of treatment with a variety of anticonvulsants. The choices of anticonvulsant medications are more limited in treatment of neonatal seizures than for treatment of adult seizures because there are fewer scientific data available on the use of these drugs in neonates (Fisher, 2009).

Chapter Summary

The birth of a baby with normal neurodevelopmental potential is a remarkable event. There are many points in the embryonic and fetal development of the brain and nervous system at which variations from typical may occur. Intrinsic developmental malformations of the brain or malformations caused by teratogens may occur. Abnormal brain function due to inherited factors may take place. Insult to the brain during pregnancy or the labor and delivery processes may also leave a neonate with neurodevelopmental challenges. Damage to the peripheral nerves can occur, generally during labor and delivery.

Key Points to Remember

- A neonate who survives with neurodevelopmental compromise is best served by a multidisciplinary team approach to the care.

- Involving the parents in the baby's care is crucial.

- Regular contributions to the infant's care by the neurologist, neurodevelopmental specialist, various therapists (occupational, speech, physical, and lactation), geneticist, orthopedic surgeon, urologist, and others as appropriate ensure that the baby is able to face challenges with the most support possible, as well as providing the parents with the resources that they need to raise their child.

Implications for Familes and Professionals

In the NICU, infants can receive care that promotes relationship-based, developmentally appropriate support (Als & Gilkerson, 1995). Within this framework, infant care is provided in a manner that is least disruptive to the infant's state. For instance, a routine phlebotomy can be postponed until the infant is more awake and ready to be handled. During such a painful procedure, the parent can offer comfort to the baby and help it to control its state by establishing physical boundaries using warmed, cupped hands, speaking calmly and softly to the baby, and perhaps offering a sucrose-soaked pacifier. Such relationship-based care supports the infant's natural sleep–wake cycle, neurologic development, and social reciprocity. Health care providers in the NICU can help parents learn to interpret their baby's cues, involve parents in the care of their infant, and promote parental feelings of competence in caring for their baby. Strategies to accomplish these goals include:

- providing privacy at the bedside and in consultation rooms

- facilitating parental participation in medical rounds

- including siblings in bedside discussions

- providing primary nurses to offer consistent care

- affirming the parent's role as the ultimate decision maker

- encouraging parental touching, holding, and participation in the infant's routine care

- personalizing the infant's space

- promoting breastfeeding

- encouraging parent participation in their infant's pain care

- supporting parental efforts in the routines of care for the baby

- encouraging interaction of reluctant or absent parents (McGrath, Samra, & Kenner, 2011)

- health care providers within the NICU can help to provide a positive emotional experience for the infant and parent unit, which may help to compensate for the medical risks

References

Abraham, H., Vincze, A., Veszpremi, B., Kraviak, A., Gomori, E., Kovacs, G. G., & Seress, L. (2012). Impaired myelination of the human hippocampal formation in Down syndrome. *International Journal of Development and Neuroscience, 30*(2), 147–158.

Agostoni, C. (2008). Role of long-chain polyunsaturated fatty acids in the first year of life. *Journal of Pediatric Gastroenterology Nutrition, 47*(Supp. 2), S41–S44.

Als, H., Duffy, F. H., McAnulty, G. B., Rivkin, M. J., Vajapeyam, S., Mulkern, R. V., . . . Eichenwald, E. C. (2004). Early experience alters brain function and structure. *Pediatrics, 113*, 846–857.

Als, H., & Gilkerson, L. (1995). Developmentally supportive care in the neonatal intensive care unit. *Zero to Three, 15*(6), 2–10.

Anjos, T., Altmäe, S., Emmett, P., Tiemeier, H., Closa-Monasterolo, R., Luque, V., ...NUTRIMENTHE Research Group. (2013). Nutrition and neurodevelopment in children: Focus on NUTRIMENTHE project., *European Journal of Nutrition, 52*(8), 1825–1842. doi: 10.1007/s00394-013-0560-4. PMID:23884402.

Antonow-Schlorke, I., Helgert, A., Gey, C., Coksaygan, T., Schubert, H., Nathanielsz, P. W.,... Schwab, M. (2009). Adverse effects of antenatal glucocorticoids on cerebral myelination in sheep. *Obstetrics & Gynecology, 113*(1), 142–152.

Aylward, G. P., Lazzara, A., & Meyer, J. (1978). Behavioral and neurological characteristics of a hydranencephalic infant. *Developmental Medicine & Child Neurology, 20*, 211–217.

Barkovich, A. J., & Norman, D. (1988). MR imaging of schizencephaly. *American Journal of Roentgenology, 150*(6), 1391–1396. PMID:3259384

Bartocci, M., Berquist, K. K., Lagercrantz, H., & Anand, K. J. (2006). Pain activates cortical areas in the preterm newborn brain. *Pain, 122*(1–2), 109–117.

Beauchamp, G. K., & Mennella, J. A. (2009). Early flavor learning and its impact on later feeding behavior. *Journal of Pediatric Gastroenterology and Nutrition, 48*, 525–530.

Beck, K. D., Powell-Braxton, L., Widmer, H. R., Valverde, J., & Hefti, F. (1995). Igf1 gene disruption result in reduced brain size, CNS hypomyelination, and loss of hippocampal granule and striatal parvalbumin-containing neurons. *Neuron. 14*, 717–730.

Bellieni, C. V., & Buonocore, G. (2012). Is fetal pain a real evidence? *Journal of Maternal Fetal Neonatal Medicine, 25*(8), 1203–1208.

Bernal, J. (2007).Thyroid hormone receptors in brain development and function. *Nature Reviews Endocrinology, 3*, 249–259. doi:10.1038/ncpendmet0424

Birch, E. E., Garfield, S., Castenada, Y., Hughbanks-Wheaton, D., Uauy, R., & Hoffman. D. (2007). Visual and cognitive outcomes at 4 years of age in a double-blind, randomized trial of long-chain polyunsaturated fatty acid-supplemented infant formula. *Early Human Development, 83*(5), 279–284.

Blair, E., & Stanley, F. (1988). Intrapartum asphyxia: A rare cause of cerebral palsy. *Paediatrics, 112*, 515–519.

Bonatto, F., Polydoro, M., Andrades, M.E., Conte de Frota, M. L. Jr., Dal-Pizzol, F., Rotta, L. N., . . . Fonseca Moreira, J. C. (2006). Effects of maternal protein malnutrition on oxidative markers in the young rat cortex and cerebellum. *Neuroscience Letters, 406*, 281–284.

Boucher, O., Burden, M. J., Muckle, G., Saint-Amour, D., Ayotte, P., Dewailly, E., . . . Jacobson, J. L (2011). Neurophysiologic and neurobehavioral evidence of beneficial effects of prenatal omega-3 fatty acid intake on memory function at school age. *American Journal of Clinical Nutrition, 93*(5), 1025–1037.

Bouwstra, H., Dijck-Brouwer, D. A. J., Boehm, G., Boersma, E. R., Muskiet, F. A., & Hadders-Algra, M. (2005). Long-chain polyunsaturated fatty acids and neurological developmental outcome at 18 months in healthy term infants. *Acta Paediatrica, 94*, 26–32.

Bueno, M., Stevens, B., de Camargo, P. P., Toma, E., Krebs, V. L., & Kimura, A. F. (2012). Breast milk and glucose for pain relief in preterm infants: A noninferiority randomized controlled trial. *Pediatrics, 129*(4), 664–670. doi: 10.1542/peds.2011-2024.

Buxmann H., Stackelberg O. M., Schlösser, R. L., Enders, G., Gonser, M., Meyer-Wittkopf, M., Hamprecht, K., & Enders, M. (2012). Use of cytomegalovirus hyperimmunoglobulin for prevention of congenital cytomegalovirus disease: A retrospective analysis. *Journal of Perinatal Medicine, 40*(4), 439–446. doi: 10.1515/jpm-2011-0257.

Carlson, J. M., Behringer, R. R., Brinster, R. L., & McMorris, F. A. (1993). Insulin-like growth factor I increases brain growth and central nervous system myelination in transgenic mice. *Neuron*, 729–740.

Changeux, J. P., & Danchin, A. (1976). Selective stabilization of developing synapses as a mechanism for the specification of neuronal networks. *Nature, 264*, 705–712.

Chellakooty, M., Juul, A., Boisen, K. A., Damgaard, I. N., Kai, C. M., Schmidt, I. M., . . . Main, K. M. (2006). A prospective study of serum insulin-like growth factor I (IGF-1) and IGF-binding protein-3 in 942 healthy infants: Associations with birth weight, gender, growth velocity, and breastfeeding. *Journal of Clinical Endocrinology Metabolism, 91*, 820–826.

Chermont, A. G., Falcao, L. F., de Souza Silva, E. H., de Cassia Zavier Balda, R.., & Guinsburg, R. (2009). Skin-to-skin contact and/or oral 25% dextrose for procedural pain relief for term newborn infants. *Pediatrics, 124*(6), e1101–e1107.

Clancy, R. R. (1997). The management of neonatal seizures. In D. K. Stevenson & P. Sunshine (Eds.), *Fetal and neonatal brain injury: Mechanisms, management, and the risks of practice* (2nd ed., p. 432–461). New York, NY: Oxford University Press.

Cocker, K. D., Mosele, M. J., Stirling, H. F., & Fielder, A. R. (1998). Delayed visual maturation: Pupillary responses implicate subcortical and cortical visual systems. *Developmental Medicine & Child Neurology, 40*, 160–162.

Cummings, J. J., & Fisher, M. A. (2016). Major physical, motor, and neurologic impairments. In G. L. Ensher & D. A. Clark (Eds.), *The early years: Foundations for best practice with special children and their families* (pp. 209–228). Washington, DC: ZERO TO THREE.

Crystal, S. R., & Bernstein, I. L. (1998). Infant salt preference and mother's morning sickness. *Appetite, 30*(3), 297–307.

De Bie, H. M., Oostrom, K. J., Boersma, M., Veltman, D. J., Barkhof, F., Delemarre-van de Waal, H. A., & van den Heuvel, M. P. (2001). Global and regional differences in brain anatomy of young children born small for gestational age. *PLoS One, 6*(9), e24116.

Dubowitz, L. M., De Vries, L., Mushin, J., & Arden, G. B. (1986). Visual function in the newborn infant: Is it cortically mediated? *Lancet, 327*(8490), 1139–1141.

Ensher, G. L., & Clark, D. A. (2016). Development in the first 3 years. In G. L. Ensher & D. A. Clark (Eds.), *The early years: Foundations for best practice with special children and their families* (pp. 11–47). Washington, DC: ZERO TO THREE.

Fisher M. (2009). Neonatal neurology. In G. L Ensher, D. A Clark, & N. S. Songer (Eds.), *Families, infants, & young children at risk. Pathways to best practice* (pp. 74–83). Baltimore, MD: Brookes.

Glass, P. (1999). The vulnerable neonate and the neonatal intensive care environment. In G. B. Avery, M. A. Fletcher, & M. G. MacDonald (Eds.), *Neonatology: Pathophysiology and management of the newborn* (5th ed., pp. 242–246). Philadelphia, PA: Lipppincott, Williams, & Wilkins.

Gluckman, P. D., Guan, J., Williams, C., Scheepens, A., Zhang, R., Bennet, L., & Gunn, A. (1998). Asphyxial brain injury: The role of the IGF system. *Molecular Cell Endocrinology, 140*, 95–99.

Grantham-McGregor. S., & Baker-Henningham, H. (2005). Review of the evidence linking protein and energy to mental development. *Public Health Nutrition, 8*, 1191–1201.

Hack, M., Mostow, A., & Miranda, S. B. (1976). Development of attention in preterm infants. *Pediatrics, 58*, 669–674.

Jan, J. F., Wong, P. F., Groenveld, M., Flodmark, O., & Hoyt, C. S. (1986). Travel vision: "Collicular visual system?" *Pediatric Neurology, 2*, 359–363.

Judge, M. P., Harel, O., & Lammi-Keefe, C. J. (2007). Maternal consumption of a docosahexaenoic acid-containing functional food during pregnancy: Benefit for infant performance on problem-solving but not on recognition memory tasks at age 9 mo. *American Journal of Clinical Nutrition, 85*(6), 1572–1577.

Khundrakpam, B. S., Reid, A., Brauer, J., Carbonell, F., Lewis, Ameis S., . . . Brain Development Cooperative Group. (2013). Developmental changes in organization of structural brain networks. *Cerebral Cortex, 23*(9), 272–275. doi:10.1093/cercor/bhs187.

Kuban, K. C. K., & Leviton, A. (1994). The epidemiology of cerebral palsy. *The New England Journal of Medicine, 330*, 188–195.

Licht, D. J., Shera, D. M., Clancy, R. R., Wernovsky, G., Montenegro, L. M., Nicolson, S. C.,. . .Vossough, A. (2009). Brain maturation is delayed in infants with complex congenital heart defects. *Journal of Thoracic and Cardiovascular Surgery, 137*(3), 529–537.

Lucas, A., Morley, R., Cole, T. J., Lister, G., & Leeson-Payne, C. (1992). Breast milk and subsequent intelligence quotients in children born preterm. *Lancet, 339*, 261–264.

MacDonald, D. (1997). The use of intrapartum fetal heart rate monitoring to reduce perinatal asphyxia in the term infant. In D. K. Stevenson & P. Sunshine (Eds.), *Fetal and neonatal brain injury: Mechanisms, management, and the risks of practice* (2nd ed., pp. 167–180). New York, NY: Oxford University Press.

McGrath, J. M., Samra, H. A., & Kenner, C. (2011). Family-centered developmental care practices and research: what will the next century bring? *Journal of Perinatal & Neonatal Nursing, 25*(2), 165–170. doi: 10.1097/JPN.0b013e31821a6706. PMID:21540694

Mennella, J. A., Johnson, A., & Beauchamp, G. K. (1995). Garlic ingestion by pregnant women alters the odor of amniotic fluid. *Chemical Senses, 20*(2), 207–209.

Miller, A. J. (1982). Deglutition. *Physiological Reviews, 62*, 129–184.

Miller, S. P., McQuillen, P. S., Hamrick, S., Xu, D., Glidden, D. V., Charlton, N., . . . Vigneron, D. B. (2007). Abnormal brain development in newborns with congenital heart disease. *The New England Journal of Medicine, 357*(19), 1928–1938.

Molloy, C., Doyle, L. W., Makrides, M., & Anderson, P. J. (2012). Docosahexaenoic acid and visual functioning in preterm infants: A review. *Neuropsychological Reviews, 22*, 425–437.

Munshi, U. K., & Clark, D. A. (2016). Respiratory distress in newborns and young children. In G. L. Ensher & D. A. Clark (Eds.), *The early years: Foundations for best practice with special children and their families* (pp. 197–208). Washington, DC: ZERO TO THREE.

Naeye, R. L., Peters, E. C., Bartholomew, M., & Landis, J. R. (1989). Origins of cerebral palsy. *American Journal of Diseases of Children, 143*(10), 1154–1161. PMID:2486190

Niblock, M. M., Brunso-Bechtold, J. K., & Riddle, D. R. (2000). Insulin-like growth factor I stimulates dendritic growth in primary somatosensory cortex. *Journal of Neuroscience, 20*, 4165–4172.

Otake, M., Hoshimaru, H., & Schull, W. J. (1989). Prenatal exposure to atomic radiation and brain damage. *Congenital Abnormalities, 29*, 309–320.

Palmer, P. G., Dubowitz, L. M., Verghote, M., & Dubowitz, V. (1982). Neurological and neurobehavioral differences between preterm infants at term and full-term newborn infants. *Neuropediatrics 13*, 183–189.

Peiper, A. (1963). *Cerebral function in infancy and childhood.* New York, NY: Consultants Bureau.

Raschke, C., Schmidt, S., Schwab, M., & Jirikowski, G. (2008). Effects of betamethasone treatment on central myelination in fetal sheep: An electron microscopical study. *Anatomy, Histology, & Embryology, 37*(2), 95–100.

Reid, M. V., Murray, K. A., Marsh, E. D., Golden, J. A., Simmons, R. A., & Grinspan, J. B. (2012). Delayed myelination in an intrauterine growth retardation model is mediated by oxidative stress up-regulating bone morphogenetic protein 4. *Journal of*

Neuropathology & Experimental Neurology, 71(7), 640–653.

Robertson, C., & Finer, N. (1985). Term infants with hypoxic-ischemic encephalopathy: Outcome at 3.5 years. *Developmental Medicine & Child Neurology, 27,* 473–484.

Robinson, J., & Fielder, A. R. (1990). Pupillary diameter and reaction to light in preterm neonates. *Archives of Disease in Children, 65,* 35–38.

Sabel, K-G., Lundqvist-Persson, C., Bona, E., Petzold, M., & Strandvik, B. (2009). Fatty acid patterns early after premature birth, simultaneously analyzed in mothers' food, breast milk and serum phospholipids of mothers and infants. *Lipids in Health and Disease, 8,* 20.

Saint-Anne Dargassies, S. (1977). *Neurological development in the full-term and premature neonate.* New York, NY: Excerpta Medica.

Sarnat, H. B. (1978). Olfactory reflexes in the newborn infant. *Journal of Pediatrics, 92,* 624–626.

Sheridan, M. A., Fox, N. A., Zeanah, C. H., McLaughlin, K. A. &, Nelson III, C. A. (2012). Variation in neural development as a result of exposure to institutionalization early in childhood. *Proceedings of the National Academy of Sciences, 109*(32), 12927–12932.

Shinnar, S., Bello, J. A., Chan, S., Hesdorffer, D. C., Lewis, D. V., Macfall, J., . . . FEBSTAT Study Team (2012). *Neurology, 79*(9), 871–877.

Snyder, R. D., Hata, S. K., Brann, B. S., & Mills, R. M. (1990). Subcortical visual function in the newborn. *Pediatric Neurology, 6,* 333–336.

Thebaud, B., Lacaze-Masmonteil, T., & Watterberg, K. (2001). Postnatal glucocorticoids in very preterm infants: "The good, the bad, and the ugly?" *Pediatrics, 107,* 413–415.

Volpe, J. J. (2001a). Intracranial hemorrhage: Germinal matrix—intraventricular hemorrhage of the premature infant. In J. J. Volpe (Ed.), *Neurology of the newborn* (4th ed; pp. 428–493). Philadelphia, PA: W. B. Saunders.

Volpe, J. J. (2001b). Neurological examination: Normal and abnormal features. In J. J. Volpe (Ed.), *Neurology of the newborn* (4th ed; pp. 103–133). Philadelphia, PA: W. B. Saunders.

Volpe, J. J. (2001c). Neuronal proliferation, migration, organization, and myelination. In J. J. Volpe (Ed.), *Neurology of the newborn* (4th ed; pp. 45–49). Philadelphia, PA: W. B. Saunders.

Volpe, J. J. (2005). Encephalopathy of prematurity includes neuronal abnormalities. *Pediatrics 116,* 221–225.

Volpe, J. J. (2008a). Hypoxic-ischemic encephalopathy: Clinical aspects. In J. J. Volpe (Ed.), *Neurology of the newborn* (5th ed., pp. 400–480). Philadelphia, PA: W. B. Saunders.

Volpe, J. J. (2008b). Intracranial hemorrhage: Subdural, primary subarachnoid, cerebellar, intraventricular (term infant), and miscellaneous. In J. J. Volpe (Ed.), *Neurology of the newborn* (5th ed., pp. 483–516). Philadelphia, PA: W. B. Saunders.

Volpe, J. J. (2008c). Neural tube formation and prosencephalic development. In J. J. Volpe (Ed.), *Neurology of the newborn* (5th ed., pp. 3–50). Philadelphia, PA: W. B. Saunders.

Vulsma, T., & Kok, J. H. (1996). Prematurity-associated neurologic and developmental abnormalities and neonatal thyroid function. *New England Journal of Medicine, 334,* 856–857.

Whiteus, C., Freitas, C., & Grutzendler, J. (2013). Perturbed neural activity disrupts cerebral angiogenesis during a postnatal critical period. *Nature, 505,* 407–411. doi:10.1038/nature 12821.

Yamazaki, J. N., & Schull, W. J. (1990). Perinatal loss and neurological abnormalities among children of the atomic bomb. *Journal of the American Medical Association, 264,* 605–609.

Zuo, Z. (2013). Postoperative cognitive effects in newborns: The role of inflammatory processes. *Anesthesiology, 18,* 481–483.

CHAPTER 4

Nutrition and Oral Health of Infants and Toddlers

Melinda Clark and David A. Clark

Highlights of the Chapter

At the conclusion of the chapter, the reader will:

- understand that proper nutrition is important for all children and may be especially challenging for families caring for young children with special health care needs, who are at increased risk both for failure to gain appropriate weight and for becoming overweight.

- understand that early childhood caries are a preventable disease caused by bacteria vertically transmitted from mothers or caregivers to infants

- recognize the consequences of and risk factors for development of early childhood caries (tooth decay) and their adverse impact on overall health

- recognize the appropriate age for oral health risk assessment and timing for referral of children with special health care needs for establishment of a dental home

- recognize that dental care is the most common unmet health care need within special needs populations in the united states

- be aware of the importance of access to regular dental care and other proven methods of preventing dental caries

Meeting Everyday Nutritional Needs in the First 3 Years of Life

Families often identify healthy eating and ensuring good nutrition as challenging. This concern may be amplified with young children and those who have special health care needs. Dietary choices of children are influenced by a number of factors, including health and medical issues, family preferences, cultural norms, texture, taste, availability, and financial considerations. In the first year of life, infants rely heavily on breast milk or formula to meet calorie and nutritional needs, with introduction

of solid foods encouraged at 6 months old (American Academy of Pediatrics Section on Breastfeeding [AAP], 2012). Pediatricians recognize breast milk as ideal for the majority of babies, because there are few contraindications to breastfeeding. Professionals and family members play an important role in supporting mothers who experience breastfeeding challenges. The AAP recommends breastfeeding exclusively for 6 months and continuing "until 1 year or older as mutually desired by mother and infant" (AAP, 2012, p. e827). The benefits of breast milk for mothers, babies, and society are well documented and include lowering the risk of viral infections in children (upper respiratory and gastrointestinal), ear infections, asthma, eczema, obesity, several autoimmune conditions (celiac disease, diabetes, inflammatory bowel disease) and conferring many positive health benefits to mothers. In addition, there are known financial and socioeconomic benefits (AAP, 2012). Babies who are formula fed commonly begin with a cow's-milk-based

formula that is modified and fortified to resemble human milk as closely as current technology allows. Formula changes should be made in consultation with a medical professional, such as the primary care clinician. Many babies with special health care needs require specialty formula to promote optimal growth and development. The trajectory for tolerating solid foods is often delayed in children with special health care needs due to oral aversion, difficulty with texture, delayed swallowing, aspiration risk, or receipt of calories through a supplemental feeding tube. Many of these concerns can be identified and addressed by a qualified speech pathologist. Speech therapists, who are available through state early intervention (EI) programs, are an excellent resource to support and educate families on oral feeding techniques in the home.

Children with special health care needs are at increased risk for failure to gain appropriate weight or for becoming overweight. Failure to gain appropriate weight can be caused by inability to tolerate adequate nutrition by mouth, excessive losses, foods refusal, texture sensitivity or avoidance, and an inability to access appropriate foods. Children with special health care needs can also be at risk for becoming overweight. Obesity is increasing in prevalence across all populations in the United States (Ogden, Carroll, Kit, & Flegal, 2012). In addition to commonly known risks, factors contributing to excess weight gain unique to children with special health care needs include low activity levels and medications that promote weight gain (especially medications for seizure and behavioral/mood management).

Recommendations for appropriate caloric intake for proper growth as well as the food sources (e.g., dairy, meats, grains, fruits) are frequently updated by the U.S. Department of Agriculture, the Food and Drug Administration, and various professional groups such as the AAP and the American College of Nutrition.

The Importance of Good Oral Health for the Young Child

Because the mouth is the entryway to the gastrointestinal tract, nutrition and oral health are closely intertwined. Pain and tooth loss from tooth decay can interfere with chewing and impair weight gain. Frequent ingestion of simple sugars contributes to obesity and dental caries (tooth decay), whereas fruits, vegetables, and whole grains are less cariogenic (cavity-causing) and less likely to cause obesity.

The remainder of this chapter will focus on the importance of good oral health and its relationship to general health, because good "oral health is integral to general health" (U.S. Department of Health and Human Services, 2000, p. 2). Dental disease is largely preventable; "safe and effective disease prevention measures exist that everyone can adopt to improve oral health and prevent disease" (U.S. Department of Health and Human Services, 2000, p. 3). Dental care is the most common unmet need among children with special health care needs in the United States, according to the 2006 National Survey of Children With Special Health Care Needs (Lewis, 2009). Failure to prevent can have significant and lasting negative health effects.

Dental caries is the most common chronic condition of childhood in the Unites States (U.S. Department of Health and Human Services, 2000). Focusing only on the primary dentition, 42.2% of children 2–11 years old have had tooth decay, and 22.9% have untreated dental disease. Among 2–5-year-olds, 27.9% have had some tooth decay and 20.5% have untreated dental caries (Institute of Medicine [IOM], 2011). Early childhood caries (the process of tooth cavitation in children younger than 5 years old) affect 25% of all the nation's children but disproportionately affect poor, young, and minority children (Tomar & Reeves, 2009; U.S. Department of Health and Human Services, 2000).

Consequences of early childhood caries (American Academy of Pediatric Dentistry [AAPD], 2011a; U.S. Department of Health and Human Services, 2000) includes:

- Pain—Tooth pain occurs when the enamel is destroyed and the pulp becomes infected. Pain can cause loss of sleep, difficulty concentrating, and interrupted learning.

- Dental abscesses—These are painful and can also spread to the skin (cellulitis) and cause other infections.

- Impaired chewing and nutrition.

- Difficulty with speech.

- School/work absences—Early childhood caries are responsible for 51 million lost school hours per year in the United States, which also means lost work hours for the adult caregivers (Blumenshine, Vann, Gizlice, & Lee, 2008; U.S. Department of Health and Human Services, 2000).

- Destruction and loss of teeth leading to decreased self-esteem and impaired socialization (Gift, Reisine, & Larach, 1992).

- Dental work completed under general anesthesia that may incur increased risks and costs (Kanellis, Damiano, & Monamy, 2000).

- Damage to permanent teeth, because early childhood caries increase the risk of caries development in permanent teeth (Al-Shalan, Erickson, & Hardie, 1997).

Tooth decay begins with the presence of bacteria, which metabolize dietary carbohydrates and produce acid as a by-product. The acid dissolves the surface of the enamel that, if left unchecked, causes the enamel to become weaker, and ultimately a hole develops in the enamel called a *cavity*.

Dental Caries Process

Teeth, bacteria, fermentable carbohydrates, and time are all necessary elements in the caries process (Featherstone, 2004).

1. Teeth–Enamel serves as a physical barrier to bacterial invasion of the root. Some populations are at increased risk for congenital enamel defects, especially babies born prematurely and some children with genetic and metabolic disorders (e.g., ectodermal dysplasia). These children should be prioritized for early establishment of a dental home, as the enamel strength can be modified with proper hygiene, appropriate nutrition, and regular dental care (Hale & American Academy of Pediatrics Section on Pediatric Dentistry and Oral Health, 2003).

2. Bacteria–Oral bacteria metabolize the sugars from dietary carbohydrates into acid, which demineralizes the tooth enamel. *Streptococcus mutans* are the best understood bacteria involved in caries development, but hundreds of types of bacteria have been implicated. The bacteria are transmitted from the mouth of a caregiver to the infant through saliva, a process called colonization. Once the teeth are colonized (during the first year of life), they cannot be eliminated; only the number of bacteria and their metabolic activity can be altered. Delaying colonization and minimizing bacterial load are protective against developing caries (Berkowitz, 2006).

3. Carbohydrates—Frequent ingestion of simple sugars contributes to both obesity and dental caries. The carbohydrates trigger acid production that demineralizes the tooth surface. Remineralization begins to occur 20 to 40 minutes later, when acid is buffered by saliva. The enamel is constantly undergoing demineralization and remineralization, so tooth decay can be prevented by shifting the balance toward remineralization.

Less frequent consumption of carbohydrates, not choosing sticky foods that adhere to tooth surfaces for a long time, regular brushing and flossing to remove carbohydrates, and not drinking or eating at night are all methods to minimize tooth carbohydrate exposure.

Saliva is protective against the development of tooth decay; thus, decreased saliva production promotes the development of caries. Saliva promotes enamel remineralization by buffering acid and supplying calcium, phosphate, and fluoride to strengthen enamel (Featherstone, 2004).

Risk Factors for Caries

Certain populations are at increased risk for early caries development. Risk factors for early childhood caries include (AAPD, 2011b; Centers for Disease Control and Prevention, Fluoride Recommendations Work Group, 2001):

Physical characteristics

*   Children with special health care conditions
*   Chronic conditions that weaken enamel, promote gum inflammation (gingivitis), or decrease saliva production

Social/environmental characteristics

*   Poor nutrition or feeding habits
*   Poor or impaired oral hygiene

- Families with minority or low socioeconomic status; low levels of parent education

- Limited or no dental insurance

- Limited or no access to dental care

- Inadequate fluoride exposure

- Caries in a parent or sibling (especially if caries occurred in the past 12 months) and high levels of oral bacteria in parents.

Children with special health care needs are at increased risk for early and more severe tooth decay for several reasons (AAPD, 2012):

- Oral hygiene and dental care can be challenging for young children, in particular those with motor delay or impairment, difficulty swallowing, and oral aversion.

- Children with special needs often have multiple medical issues; families may be overwhelmed with care needs, not understanding the importance of oral health.

- Modified diets with prolonged or frequent feeds may increase caries risk.

- Decreased saliva production (*xerostomia*) can result from the underlying medical condition, but more commonly is a medication side effect. Adequate saliva to buffer acid is very protective against the development of tooth decay. Common medications that inhibit saliva production include glycopyrrolate; other anticholinergics; antihistamines; stimulants; some diuretics; and some depression, anxiety, seizures, and high blood pressure medications.

- Gastroesophageal reflux disease is more common in special needs populations. Repeated enamel exposure to stomach acid can cause enamel erosion and increase caries risk.

- Gingival hyperplasia, which is commonly triggered by medications (phenytoin, cyclosporine), may interfere with hygiene, speech, and chewing. Tooth crowding also may promote decay.

Young children with special health care needs may also experience a delay in seeking or accessing dental care and definitive treatment because:

- Young children and special needs patients may not be able to communicate oral pain.

- Fear of behavioral issues in the dental office may inhibit families seeking care.

- Financial impact of multiple visits or costly restoration may force families to choose among pressing needs (Chen & Newacheck, 2006; Rouleau et al., 2011).

- Families of young children with special health care needs often encounter physical challenges in accessing dental care (Rouleau et al., 2011).

Challenges to Accessing Dental Care

In 2011, 4 million children in the United States 2 to 17 years old (6% of all children) had unmet dental need because their families could not afford dental care (U.S. Department of Health and Human Services, Centers for Disease Control and Prevention, 2012). This rate is higher among populations with special health care needs; children who are both low income and severely affected have 13.4 times the adjusted odds of having unmet dental care need than their age-matched peers (Lewis, 2009). Despite most families having high education levels, private dental insurance, and above-average incomes, 20% of children with special health care needs had an unmet dental need, with highest rates among children with craniofacial anomalies, cerebral palsy, autism, developmental delay, and Down syndrome (Nelson et al., 2011).

Many general dentists are not comfortable with the care of children less than 2 years old, or those under 3 years old, and may not feel they have the expertise in caring for populations with special health care needs or the behavioral concerns of these two populations (Casamassimo, Seale, & Ruehs, 2004). The net result is that dental care of all children who are young and have special needs defaults to pediatric dentists, a rare commodity in many communities. This disparity is further exacerbated by the paucity of dentists accepting Medicaid dental coverage, the primary dental and medical health insurer of children with special health care needs. Children with special health care needs may also require sedation, even for routine cleanings, restorative procedures, and minimal oral surgery, necessitating access to a dentist trained in these procedures. Consequently, families should work with their care providers to establish a dental home in their community starting at 1 year old (Hale & AAP Section on Pediatric Dentistry and Oral Health, 2003). All providers who work with children with special health care needs have a unique opportunity to participate in the primary prevention of dental caries by encouraging good hygiene, healthy eating and drinking, and early establishment of the dental home. Moreover, tooth decay can be prevented, reversed, or halted by focusing on six basic methods (AAPD, 2011a; Hale & AAP Section on Pediatric Dentistry and Oral Health, 2003):

1. Improve oral hygiene—Regular brushing and flossing. For young children with special health care needs, proper positioning and toothbrush adaptation can make hygiene easier.

2. Healthy feeding and nutrition practices—Less-frequent eating and fewer sticky/sugary snacks, especially in combination with eliminating the bottle and nighttime feeds as early as possible, promotes more healthy feeding and nutrition practices.

3. Delay colonization of the teeth—Delaying the transmission of bacteria from caregiver to baby can slow down tooth colonization and decrease the risk of caries. Bacteria are spread through saliva-sharing activities; families should be counseled to minimize saliva-sharing by not sharing utensils, drinks, tasting or prechewing baby's food, and not sharing toothbrushes.

4. Ensure proper fluoride exposure—Fluoride is very effective in the prevention of caries and should be provided both topically (e.g., toothpaste, mouth rinse, gel, varnish) and systemically (e.g., drinking water or fluoride supplementation) to children at increased caries risk (Featherstone, 1999).

5. Adequate saliva—Another protective factor against caries development is the presence of adequate saliva. Decreased saliva production is known to promote the development of caries and is more common in children with special health care needs. Children with known or suspected decreased saliva production should be monitored closely by a dentist.

6. Early establishment of a dental home—Oral health examinations, routine cleanings, anticipatory guidance, and treatment of existing disease all occur within a dental home. The AAP recommends that all children have their first dental visit at or around 1 year old (Hale & AAP Section on Pediatric Dentistry and Oral Health, 2003) with prioritization for children with known or suspected risk factors, including children with special health care needs.

Connections to Later Health and Well-Being

Early childhood caries are the single greatest risk factor for tooth decay in the permanent teeth, which, in turn, can result in:

- Aesthetics and self-image concerns
- Costly restoration
- Tooth loss

Good oral health is a necessary part of good overall health and well-being (U.S. Department of Health and Human Services, 2000). Many studies have demonstrated the adverse impact of poor oral health on general health conditions. For example, the inflammation of periodontitis may be associated with poorer diabetes control (Mealey, 2006), adverse pregnancy outcomes, and coronary heart disease (Demmer & Desvarieux, 2006).

Maximizing Collaborative Efforts Between Dentistry and Pediatrics

Collaborative efforts between dentistry and pediatrics can be maximized because:

- Pediatric dentists are capable of treating children of all ages and are ideal for children 3 years and younger.
- Children should be referred by 1 year old to a dentist who is willing and capable of providing a dental home: a pediatric dentist or a general dentist who is comfortable with children.
- Care providers of children with special health care needs need to know the dental resources available in their areas and local communities. Helping families navigate the oral health system will likely result in earlier

establishment of care, improved access to quality care, and improved outcomes.

- Caregivers should be encouraged to voice difficulties encountered with oral hygiene with the pediatric dentist and the occupational or speech therapist who works regularly with the child. They may be able to help the family with strategies to optimize good oral health.

Bringing Families on Board: Oral Health Literacy

Collaborative efforts between oral health care providers and families and facilitating oral health literacy are important strategies toward improving the overall oral health of young children. In the end, toward achievement of this goal:

- Caregivers should provide the appropriate oral care for young children and those with special health care needs until they acquire the fine motor ability to perform these actions independently. This is typically until 6 years old among children without special health care needs or until they can tie their own shoes.
- If a child's sensory issues cause the taste or texture of fluoridated toothpaste to be intolerable, a fluoridated mouth rinse may be applied with the toothbrush.
- Community groups that advocate for patients with special health care needs can be very valuable in helping families overcome the psychosocial, transportation, financial, physical, and structural barriers that impede access to care.
- Case management, social workers, and other health professionals (e.g., EI providers) who regularly interact with high-risk families

are important resources in helping families prioritize the need for proper oral hygiene and regular dental care.

Chapter Summary

This chapter provided an overview of the nutritional needs and proper oral health care for infants and toddlers. Oral health is directly related to overall health and tooth decay, which is a very common health concern in children in the United States, and can result in a variety of physical, psychological, and social problems. The chapter highlights the factors related to the increased risk for early and more severe dental problems in children with special needs, as well as strategies to improve their oral health.

Key Points to Remember

- Proper nutrition is important for all children and may be more challenging for families caring for young children with special health care needs.

- Children with special health care needs are at increased risk both for failure to gain appropriate weight or for becoming overweight.

- Dental disease is largely preventable, but failure to prevent early dental decay has significant consequences including pain, infection, impaired nutrition, interference with speech, poor sleep, missed school and work, poor self-esteem, and increased risk of dental caries in the adult dentition.

- Children with special health care needs are at increased risk for early and more severe tooth decay and should be referred for establishment of a dental home by 1 year old.

- Families of young children with special health care needs often encounter difficulty accessing dental care. Dental care is the most common unmet health care need within special needs populations in the United States.

- The risk of tooth decay will lessen with good oral hygiene, healthy feeding and nutrition practices, delay of colonization of the teeth, proper fluoride exposure, adequate saliva, and early establishment of a dental home.

Implications for Families and Professionals

All children should begin to receive oral health risk assessments at routine medical visits, starting at 6 months old. Children who are identified to be at high risk for the development of early childhood caries should be prioritized for early establishment of a dental home.

- Children with special health care needs should be referred for establishment of a dental home by 1 year old.

- Children with known or suspected decreased saliva production should be monitored closely by a dentist with careful consideration of medications known to inhibit saliva production.

- The presence of sugar in medications also is an important consideration. If no sugar-free preparation is available for a necessary medication, it may be important to give the medication with a meal or brush the teeth immediately following feeding/eating.

- Techniques for assisting young children with special health care needs with proper oral hygiene, including proper positioning and toothbrush adaptation, are available in many web-based teaching programs (National Maternal and Child Oral Health Resource Center, Georgetown University, 2006).

References

Al-Shalan, T. A., Erickson, P. R., & Hardie, N. A. (1997). Primary incisor decay before age 4 as a risk factor for future dental caries. *Pediatric Dentistry, 19*(1), 37–41.

American Academy of Pediatric Dentistry (AAPD). (2011a). Guideline on caries-risk assessment and management for infants, children and adolescents: Reference manual. *American Academy of Pediatric Dentistry, 34*(6), 118–125.

American Academy of Pediatric Dentistry (AAPD). (2011b). Policy on early childhood caries (ECC): Classifications, consequences, and preventive strategies. *Pediatric Dentistry, 34*(6), 50–52.

American Academy of Pediatric Dentistry (AAPD). (2012). Guideline on management of dental patients with special health care needs. *Pediatric Dentistry, 34*(6), 152–157.

American Academy of Pediatrics Section on Breastfeeding. (2012). Breastfeeding and the use of human milk. *Pediatrics, 129*(3), e827–e841.

Berkowitz, R. J. (2006). Mutans streptococci: Acquisition and transmission. *Pediatric Dentistry, 28*(2), 106–109.

Blumenshine, S. L., Vann, W. F., Gizlice, Z., & Lee, J. Y. (2008). Children's school performance: Impact of general and oral health. *Journal of Public Health Dentistry, 68*(2), 82–87.

Casamassimo, P., Seale, S., & Ruehs, K. (2004). General dentists' perceptions of educational and treatment issues affecting access to care for children with special health care needs. *Journal of Dental Education, 68*(1), 23–28.

Centers for Disease Control and Prevention, Fluoride Recommendations Work Group. (2001). Recommendations for using fluoride to prevent and control dental caries in the United States. *Morbidity and Mortality Weekly Report, 50*(RR-14), 1–42.

Chen, A. Y., & Newacheck, P. W. (2006). Insurance coverage and financial burden for families of children with special health care needs. *Ambulatory Pediatrics, 6*(4), 204–209.

Demmer, R. T., & Desvarieux, M. (2006). Periodontal infections and cardiovascular disease: The heart of the matter. *Journal of American Dental Association, 137*(Suppl. 2), 145–205.

Featherstone, J. D. (1999). Prevention and reversal of dental caries: Role of low-level fluoride. *Community Dental Oral Epidemiology, 27*(1), 31–40.

Featherstone, J. D. (2004). The continuum of dental caries: Evidence for a dynamic disease process. *Journal of Dental Research, 83*(1), 39–42.

Gift, H. C., Reisine, S. T., & Larach, D. C. (1992). The social impact of dental problems and visits. *American Journal of Public Health, 82*(12), 1663–1668.

Hale, K. J., & American Academy of Pediatrics Section on Pediatric Dentistry and Oral Health. (2003). Oral health risk assessment timing and establishment of the dental home. *Pediatrics, 111*(5), 1113–1116.

Institute of Medicine (IOM). (2011). *Advancing oral health in America.* Washington, DC: The National Academies Press.

Kanellis, M. J., Damiano, P. C., & Monamy, E. T. (2000). Medicaid costs associated with the hospitalization of young children for restorative dental treatment under general anesthesia. *Journal of Public Health Dentistry, 60*(1), 28–32.

Lewis, C. W. (2009). Dental care and children with special health care needs: A population–based perspective. *Academic Pediatrics, 9*(6), 420–426.

Mealey, B. L. (2006). Periodontal disease and diabetes: A two-way street. *Journal of the American Dental Association, 137*(Suppl. 2), 26S–31S.

National Maternal and Child Oral Health Resource Center, Georgetown University. (2006). *Special care: An oral health professional's guide to serving young children with special health care needs.* Retrieved from www.mchoralhealth.org/SpecialCare

Nelson, L. P., Getzin, A., Graham, D., Zhou, J., Wagle, E. M., McQuiston, J., . . . Huntington, N. L. (2011). Unmet dental needs and barriers to care for children with significant special health care needs. *Pediatric Dentistry, 33*(1), 29–36.

Ogden, C. L., Carroll, M. D., Kit, B. K., & Flegal, K. M. (2012). *Prevalence of obesity in the United States, 2009–2010* (NCHS Data Brief No. 82). Hyattsville, MD: National Center for Health Statistics.

Rouleau, T., Harrington, A., Brennan, M., Hammond, F., Hirsch, M., Nussbaum, M.. . . . Bockenek, W. (2011). Receipt of dental care barriers encountered by persons with disabilities. *Special Care Dentistry, 31*(2), 63–67.

Tomar, S. L., & Reeves, A. F. (2009). Changes in the oral health of U.S. children and adolescents and dental public health infrastructure since the release of the Healthy People 2010 objectives. *Academic Pediatrics, 9*(6), 388–395.

U.S. Department of Health and Human Services. (2000). *Oral health in America: A report of the Surgeon General.* Rockville, MD: National Institute of Dental and Craniofacial Research, National Institutes of Health.

U.S. Department of Health and Human Services, Centers for Disease Control and Prevention. (2012). *Summary health statistics for U.S. children: National health interview 2011 survey data* (Series 10[254]).

PART 2

*Screening and Assessment of
Infants and Young Children*

CHAPTER 5

Newborn Screening, Assessment, and Discharge Planning

David A. Clark and Susan A. Furdon

Highlights of the Chapter

At the conclusion of the chapter, the reader will:

- understand the basics of delivery room management of the newborn

- be familiar with the initial examination and resuscitation of the newborn

- be familiar with routine screening and care of the newborn prior to discharge

- be aware of decisions that families need to make when planning with medical staff for discharge of their newborns

Screening Before and at Delivery

The assessment of the fetus by obstetricians prior to birth has become important for anticipating serious problems in the newborn that may require immediate attention at birth. Use of prenatal ultrasound and fetal magnetic resonance imaging can identify anomalies of the uterus, placenta, and fetus that may be life threatening. The outcome of the fetus is dramatically improved by referring these complex pregnancies to a regional perinatal center with high-risk obstetric specialists (fetal maternal medicine) and neonatologists (newborn medicine), as well as the other supporting pediatric medical and surgical subspecialties.

Fetal Assessment

A first-trimester ultrasound allows physicians to appropriately date the timeline of the pregnancy (Jeanty, 2011), which helps to avoid the over- or underestimation of the degree of maturity of the fetus. On the basis of this assessment, doctors can project the due date to correlate and monitor fetal growth and development.

Fetal imaging can detect many of the major malformations, including neural tube defects (e.g., meningomyelocele), complex heart malformations, abdominal wall defects (e.g., omphalocele and gastroschisis), and many other abnormalities of the kidneys and the central nervous system. The severity and type of lesion may influence the timing of the delivery, as well as the mode of delivery (vaginal or cesarean section).

Biochemical screening of the mother's blood can detect potential protein markers of fetal disease (Wilkins-Haug & Heffner, 2012). If the screening detects a fetal anomaly, the physician may perform an amniocentesis to analyze the fetal karyotype (chromosomes), looking for a specific genetic etiology of the abnormality.

Newer techniques, including the detection of free fetal DNA in the mother's blood, can assess genetic abnormalities, especially of the major trisomies (e.g., Trisomy 21, Trisomy 18, and Trisomy 13). The screening can identify some conditions that are lethal and allows the medical team to counsel the families regarding various options for pregnancy management, as well as the care of the newborn (National Institute of Health and Clinical Excellence, 2014).

Delivery Room

The majority of newborns in the United States (also worldwide) are born healthy and require no intervention at birth. At delivery, the newborn is wet with amniotic fluid and will lose heat rapidly by evaporation. The baby is dried quickly and placed on a heat source, typically on the mother (skin to skin) or a radiant warmer. The newborn is stimulated to cry, and the quality of the respiratory effort is assessed. The baby requires close observation during the stabilization period.

Some infants require resuscitation to ensure adequate heart rate and respiratory effort. The components of the scoring system developed in 1953 by Virginia Apgar assess heart rate, respiratory effort, muscle tone, reflex irritability, and color (Apgar, 1953). Heart rate and

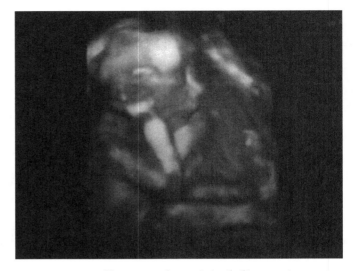

respiratory effort are the critical dimensions of the Apgar score. Reflex irritability, muscle tone, and color are less critical and are never the primary reason for initiating cardiopulmonary resuscitation. The 1-minute Apgar score is an indication of the severity of in-utero compromise and may predict how well the child may respond to resuscitation. The 5-minute Apgar score correlates more predictably with morbidity and mortality. Specifically, a 5-minute Apgar score of 3 or less is associated with up to a 5% risk of neurodevelopmental disability (Ringer & Aziz, 2012).

Neonatal resuscitation is a rapid sequence of events that is performed if the baby is in distress. The American Academy of Pediatrics and American Heart Association (2011) developed national guidelines called the Neonatal Resuscitation Program (NRP). This program is an educational effort, not a certification effort, and includes didactic lessons, workbooks, periodic tests, and skills demonstrations that train health care professionals who may be involved in the resuscitation of a newborn (Ringer & Aziz, 2012).

At each delivery in hospitals and birthing centers, there should be a skilled professional, educated in NRP, who can initiate resuscitation. If significant antepartum risk factors are identified, there should be a team of skilled health care providers who are able to properly resuscitate the newborn. The basics of resuscitation are the same initially, including drying the newborn and keeping the baby warm, followed by stimulation and clearing the airway for the baby to breathe. If these initial efforts do not produce the appropriate response, the next step is to establish effective ventilation, either by bag mask ventilation or intubation (placing a tube into the trachea) and providing positive pressure. If the heart rate remains low, the next step is cardiac (chest) compression, followed by the use of medications, if the newborn is not responding appropriately. The vast majority of resuscitations are successful, and only 3% to 5% of babies resuscitated for more than 5 minutes have long-term neurologic disabilities, either cerebral palsy or intellectual disabilities. Too often, low Apgar scores have led doctors to tell the family to expect a poor outcome. Many infants are born with some degree of distress and may not be evaluated accurately in the hectic activity of resuscitation. Despite the simplicity of Apgar scores, it remains helpful as a general description of the state of the newborn that can be shared among facilities, if the newborn requires transfer to the regional neonatal center.

There are guidelines for when resuscitation is inappropriate. Medical staff should not initiate resuscitation if the child is very preterm, less than 23 weeks gestation, or has a birth weight of less than 400 grams. It is usually technically impossible to provide the supportive care for these babies, given the immaturity of the internal organs, as well as the lack of equipment miniaturized to that degree. The severe degree of immaturity and the virtual lack of lung development at < 25 weeks gestation may preclude resuscitation. Resuscitation may be withheld if the fetus has a major anomaly, such as anencephaly (no brain) that was detected prenatally.

Assessment of Gestational Age

Once the newborn is stabilized, the assessment of gestational age is important to determine the relative growth of the child, as well as to anticipate other pathological processes. In recent years, obstetrical dating has become more accurate. Fetal growth can be followed closely, using the size of the head and the length of long bones as parameters to assess continuous fetal growth. Babies who are growth restricted are far more prone to having genetic or metabolic defects.

Several methods are available to assess gestational age of the newborn on the basis of physical and neurologic characteristics (Dubowitz & Dubowitz, 1977). The physical characteristics progress in an orderly manner through the third trimester. These include the following:

1. There is a progressive disappearance of vernix, a cream-cheese-like, fatty material that initially appears at approximately 24 weeks gestation. It covers the body of the fetus and begins to diminish at 36 weeks gestation. At term, it is found only in the creases of the body. The vernix is displaced from the skin in utero by the increasing amount of fetal pulmonary surfactant that is secreted from the maturing fetal lungs into the amniotic fluid.

2. The skin of extremely immature infants is thin and translucent, with blood vessels very prominent. As gestation increases, the vessels become less apparent as a result of the deposition of subcutaneous fat and the thickening of the skin.

3. Lanugo, fine hair that covers the entire body as early as 22 weeks gestation, vanishes from the face only 3 to 4 weeks prior to birth. Lanugo is commonly seen on the shoulders of newborns, especially those born to

mothers with diabetes. The excess of fetal hair in this situation is due to the increased secretion of fetal insulin in response to the excessive glucose that has come across the placenta from the mother.

4. The areola (nipple) and surrounding tissue are barely visible in the extremely premature infant. By 34 weeks gestation, the areola begins to rise or may be more pigmented in response to maternal hormones that are deposited in the breast tissue. By term, a 5–6-ml nodule usually can be palpated.

5. At term, the ear has a well-defined outer edge that stands erect from the head. The ear of the extremely premature infant is flat and shapeless and does not spring back when folded because little cartilage is present. Genital development is easily traced in males with descent of the testes. Testes begin as intra-abdominal organs that first appear in the upper inguinal canal at 28 weeks gestation, then descend into the scrotum and become pendulous. After this occurs, the inguinal canal should close. Failure to do so increases the risk of inguinal hernia. In response to the descent of the testes, the scrotum develops folds and becomes more pigmented, especially in darker skinned babies.

6. Genital development. In the female, deposition of fat plays a role. In a 32-week female baby, the clitoris is prominent; labia majora are small and mildly separated. As the fetus approaches term, with fatty deposition the labia minora and clitoris are typically completely covered.

7. The sole of the foot is smooth at 28 weeks gestation. As the pregnancy proceeds, there is a progressive increase of sole creases, which cover the anterior two thirds of the foot by 36 weeks gestation.

In general, these physical characteristics must be documented within the first 24 hours.

With a predictable loss of extracellular fluid, the characteristics of the skin and appearance of sole creases may be altered. Once the infant is cleaned, vernix is no longer useful as an adjunct to assess the gestational age.

Initial Neurologic Evaluation

Although determination of gestational age by physical criteria should be performed immediately after birth, the neurological evaluation becomes more accurate when the infant's condition is stable (American Academy of Pediatrics & American College of Obstetricians and Gynecologists [AAP & ACOG], 2013). Given the events of transition, this assessment is more accurate by the end of the first day. Numerous perinatal factors may affect the neurological assessment, including perinatal asphyxia, maternal anesthesia, maternal medications, birth trauma, and various illnesses and syndromes that may affect the newborn.

Chapter 3 (Fisher, 2016) provides a more comprehensive discussion of the development and functioning of the nervous system. In brief, the neurological development of the fetus during the last trimester is characterized by the increase of muscle mass and tone, as well as changes in reflexes and mobility of the extremities. Infants born before 30 weeks of gestation have very poor muscle tone (hypotonia) with a resting posture of fully extended arms and legs. Flexor tone begins at 30 weeks gestation and increases first in the lower extremities. At 35 to 36 weeks gestation, the infant has good muscle tone in the lower extremities with only partial flexion in the arms. At full term, the resting posture should include full flexion of the joints of both upper and lower extremities. The extremely preterm baby does not resist various passive maneuvers, such as movement of the heel to the ear (i.e., the *scarf sign*).

By 30 weeks gestation, the neck extensors and flexors begin to function, and by 38 weeks many infants can hold their heads for a few seconds, when pulled to a sitting position. The tone in the trunk can be measured by ventral suspension. Preterm infants prior to or at 30 weeks gestation have very poor trunk tone and will appear to be draped over an outstretched hand. By 32 to 34 weeks gestation, the back is straightened. By full term, the head rises above the straightened back.

A number of primitive reflexes such as the Moro reflex, crossed extension reflex, and rooting and sucking reflexes have been used to determine gestational age. (For specific information regarding newborn reflexes, please refer to chapter 10, Cummings & Fisher, 2016.) However, most of these reflexes are absent prior to 32 weeks gestation and are only well established by term. In the interval between 32 and 36 weeks, they are not sufficiently discriminating to assess gestational age accurately. Most of these reflexes disappear in the first year of life.

Growth and Gestational Age

Once the gestational age of the newborn has been established, the growth parameters of the newborn are measured to determine if the intrauterine growth has been appropriate. Babies born less than the 10th percentile in the major growth parameters of weight, length, and head circumference are considered small for gestational age (SGA). Babies whose weight, length, and head circumference are greater than the 90th percentile are considered large for gestational age (LGA). These indicators are based on normative curves that predict the weight, length, and head circumference for the growth of fetuses at each gestational age after 24 weeks of gestation. SGA babies, despite the degree of gestational age, are more likely to have syndromes, chromosomal abnormalities, or fetal malnutrition. LGA babies are more likely to be born to families who are genetically large or to mothers who have diabetes.

The specific and complex problems of preterm babies requiring intensive care are discussed in detail in several other chapters of this book. Of special note here are the infants born several weeks prematurely who may not require intensive care (Tomashek, Shapiro-Mendoza, Davidoff, & Petrini, 2007). The "late preterm" infants (LPI), defined as 34 0/7 to 36 6/7 weeks gestation, have been identified as being at risk for many of the same issues as the more preterm infants in the days following birth. Compared to full-term newborns, these include:

1. Hypoglycemia (low blood sugar) due to inadequate production or increased use of glucose. Frequent feedings are necessary.
2. Respiratory distress—LPI have higher incidence of transient tachypnea (i.e., abnormally rapid breathing) of the newborn, respiratory distress syndrome, pulmonary hypertension, and respiratory failure than term infants; apnea (i.e., cessation of breathing, of a temporary nature) can occur in this gestational age group.
3. Temperature instability—LPI have difficulty maintaining body temperature due to less subcutaneous fatty insulation, less flexion, and decreased ability to produce heat.
4. Nutrition—Synchronization of suck-swallow-breathe is usually complete by 36 to 38 weeks. As a result of this and immaturity in neurobehavioral organization, LPI may be unable to demonstrate sustained/coordinated feeding and may have inadequate oral intake, and difficulty breastfeeding.
5. Sleeping—These infants may sleep longer and be more difficult to arouse than full-term babies; they may have less stamina, especially as it relates to feeding.

6. Jaundice—Due to delayed physiologic maturation, the LPI is more likely to develop jaundice; decreased gastrointestinal motility and poor feeding contribute to this problem.

7. Infection—LPI have less mature immune systems, thus are at greater risk of bacterial infections.

LPI requires close assessment post-delivery. Many of these infants may require admission to a neonatal intensive care unit for management of hypoglycemia, respiratory distress, inadequate oral intake, infection, or jaundice. The rate of early neonatal mortality (death in the first week of life) for LPI is 6 times higher than that of full-term infants. During the first year of life, LPI are twice as likely to die than term infants as a result of sudden infant death syndrome, accidents, and sepsis (i.e., presence of microorganisms and/or their poisonous products in the bloodstream; Tomashek et al., 2007).

As Tomashek et al. (2007) reported, significant differences in mortality were found between late preterm and full-term singleton infants in the United States from 1995 to 2002.

Routine Newborn Care

Following resuscitation and stabilization, a number of procedures are performed, including proper identification, care of the umbilical cord, eye care prophylaxis against infection, administration of Vitamin K, and newborn screening (AAP, 2011).

Umbilical Cord Care

After delivery, the cord is clamped to prevent blood loss. It then dries within several days and in approximately 7 to 10 days is spontaneously shed. The dried cord is shed by enzymatic action of the white blood cells that have been attracted to the site in response to normal bacterial colonization. Antibacterial substances are no longer applied to the cord because they delay colonization and prolong the time until the cord is shed. A persistent cord suggests an inadequate number of white blood cells or an inability of the white blood cells to respond appropriately to colonization of the cord. A persistent blood supply to the base of the cord, as might be found with a small hemangioma or omphalocele, also delays shedding (Donlon, Furdon, & Clark, 2002).

Eye Prophylaxis

Conjunctivitis (ophthalmia neonatorm) of the newborn can be caused by a variety of infectious agents. In the early 1900s, gonorrhea was a primary cause of newborn conjunctivitis, commonly resulting in severe vision impairment. Newborn eye care, known as the Crede's method, involves instilling a prophylactic agent into the eye of the newborn. The recommended medications are erythromycin or tetracycline, which are both effective in treating gonorrhea and may be effective against chlamydia, a less serious eye infection. State law and health department regulations in virtually every state require newborn eye care. For the few infants who develop conjunctivitis, the specific infectious agent must be identified and treated to prevent vision loss.

Vitamin K

Hemorrhagic disease of the newborn was first described in 1894 as a generalized bleeding that occurred in the first week of life in otherwise healthy infants (AAP Committee on the Fetus and Newborn, 2006). It is caused by a severe deficiency of the coagulation Factors II, VII, IX, and X, all dependent on adequate Vitamin K for their synthesis in the liver. Bacteria in the intestine typically produce Vitamin K. However, the newborn intestine is sterile and would not be sufficiently colonized with Vitamin K–producing organisms until the baby reaches at least 1 week old. The administration of Vitamin K intramuscularly at birth allows improved coagulation during this very specific interval until the intestine is colonized with bacteria. A few states allow oral administration of Vitamin K.

Newborn Screening

Screening of the newborn has become much more comprehensive and sophisticated within the past 30 years. Rapid advances in technology allow for many more diseases to be detected and treated prior to any clinical symptoms. The overall goal of newborn screening is to identify, as early as possible, children who may be affected and to intervene to ensure a healthier child. Screening can detect many diseases that are difficult or impossible to treat. In general, newborn screening falls into a number of categories including metabolic, endocrine, hematologic, infection, pulmonary, and vision and hearing.

Each state determines the number of tests performed on babies born within the state, based in part on the frequency of each genetic abnormality in the state's population. States with few births and limited testing may elect to send blood samples to nearby states for more comprehensive testing. For example, Massachusetts performs some of the analyses for several other states in New England.

Metabolic Screening

This topic is covered more thoroughly in chapter 7 of this text (Adams & Clark, 2016) on genetic diseases. *Tandem mass spectrometry* is a technology that includes the pairing of one mass spectrometer with a second mass spectrometer to analyze in detail various chemicals produced within the body. The vast majority of inborn errors of protein and fat metabolism may be detected with this technology, and most of these are treatable by diet or medication. A prototype of these conditions, and the first to be screened was phenylketonuria (PKU), which is the inability to metabolize the amino acid phenylalanine. Untreated, this disease causes growth retardation and poor neurologic development. Simply minimizing phenylalanine in the diet allows these infants to develop normally.

Endocrine Disease

The common endocrine diseases that may adversely affect the newborn are hypothyroidism and adrenal hyperplasia. Hypothyroidism has an incidence of approximately 1 in 4,000 in newborns. If not treated with thyroid hormone (thyroxine), these infants are at great risk for abnormal neurologic development and delay that is irreversible.

Congenital adrenal hyperplasia is a genetic disease in which there is a defect of an enzyme in the adrenal gland that results in the failure to produce key hormones. Affected infants lose a substantial amount of sodium in the urine and may die of hyponatremia (low blood sodium). Newborn females with this condition may have genital anomalies, resembling a male phenotype.

Hematology and Infection Screening

Hematology screening is done primarily to detect abnormal hemoglobins. The prototype is sickle cell disease. Sickle cell disease does not directly affect newborns because their hemoglobin is a fetal hemoglobin. Infants with sickle cell disease are at great risk for infection in the first 6 months of life. They require special surveillance and immunizations.

Infection screening remains limited and currently includes HIV and toxoplasmosis. Screening for cytomegalovirus, an organism responsible for early hearing loss, has been added as a pilot program in several state newborn screening programs.

Cystic Fibrosis—Gene Defect Screening

Screening for cystic fibrosis is done by analyzing the blood for immune-reactive trypsin (IRT), an enzyme that would not be in the blood at high concentration, if the disease were absent. Children with a high level of immune-reactive trypsin are examined for specific gene defects. Aggressive nutrition management that promotes fat absorption in these infants may promote better growth and development.

Vision and Hearing

Neonatal vision is limited. Full-term infants can only focus approximately 10 inches, and the initial color they see is red. With continued exposure to various wavelengths of light, the retinal cones of other colors develop. Table 5.1 outlines the timing of eye development

At fewer than 34 weeks gestation, the infants do not have sufficient cone development in the retina. These infants can discriminate between dark and light but at a very limited distance.

The newborn eye examination is limited to primarily discover defects such as incomplete iris (coloboma), absent or hypopigmented (albinism), cataracts, or glaucoma. The "red reflex" is elicited by shining a light into the eye and seeing the red reflection off of the retina. Cataracts, an opacity of the lens, or an abnormal retina cause a white reflex. Abnormal retinas may be found with a neonatal tumor

TABLE 5.1 Visual development

CHARACTERISTICS	GESTATIONAL AGE
Blink/squint in response to bright light	26 weeks
Pupils constrict to light	30 weeks
Ability to fixate vision on large object in close proximity	32 weeks
Track large moving object	34 weeks
Color perception (red first)	34 weeks

Note. Sources: Graven (2011) and Moore & Persaud (2008).

(retinoblastoma) or in recovering premature babies, whose immature retinas at birth may grow improperly with scarring and detachment of the retina. This condition is termed *retinopathy of prematurity* (AAP Section on Ophthalmology & American Academy of Opthamalogy, 2013).

The most developed sense at birth is hearing. Chapter 8 (Pinheiro, 2016) provides an in-depth discussion of newborn hearing. Newborn hearing screening is performed in most birthing hospitals. The early identification of hearing difficulties in infants is critical to early social and communication development.

Discharge Planning

Planning for discharge from the hospital or birthing center involves a number of considerations about caregiving and infant health and development. Preparation for leaving the hospital includes ensuring that the baby is able to consume adequate calories for growth, is able to maintain body temperature, is free of serious medical conditions or they are well controlled, and that the parents have the knowledge to adequately care for the newborn. Social workers work closely with the nursing and medical team when there are concerns about family stressors or risk factors, such as adverse living situations, drug use, maternal depression, or domestic violence in the home. Some considerations for parents include:

Pediatric Primary Care

Parents usually choose their primary care physicians, typically pediatricians or family practice physicians, prior to birth, and schedule a check-up within the first few days of discharge. The primary care provider is one of the most important resources for new parents, due to the frequency of doctor visits and the opportunity they have to guide and support new parents. The medical professional will provide a schedule of well-baby check-ups, including recommended vaccinations. The provider should offer guidance on a wide variety of newborn caregiving topics such as eating, growth, sleeping, bathing, umbilical cord care, developmental milestones, and common health issues such as jaundice or reflux.

Feeding

Chapter 4 (Clark & Clark, 2016) provides a discussion of infant nutrition and feeding, including the well-documented benefits of breast milk. Lactation specialists, often available through the hospital or birthing center as well as pediatric practices, can help women who may experience challenges with breast feeding. If parents are formula feeding for medical or other reasons, their provider should guide them about formula choices, as well as correct preparation. The physician will also advise parents on feeding schedules, amounts, elimination issues, and any potential feeding issues or problems.

Sleeping

Infant sleep habits can be one of the most challenging aspects of newborn care. Newborns tend to sleep in short cycles throughout the day and night, allowing little sleep for parents. Physicians can help parents understand infant sleep needs and how to develop healthy habits from birth. Current recommendations are to put infants to sleep alone, on their backs, and in a crib free of blankets or toys to reduce the risk of sudden infant death syndrome. The AAP provides guidelines for creating a safe sleeping environment for infants, including sleep position and surface, ventilation, and additional factors that reduce risk (AAP, 2011).

Immunizations

Although the majority of immunizations begin at 6 months old, Hepatitis B vaccine must be given soon after birth, often prior to discharge. A child with Hepatitis B infection often develops severe hepatitis with cirrhosis. The vaccine is a viral protein, not a live virus (AAP & ACOG, 2013).

Umbilical Cord Care

The umbilical cord is composed primarily of water, three vessels, and *Wharton's jelly,* a gelatinous matrix. It dries rapidly after birth and normally falls off by 7 to 10 days. Bacterial colonization of the cord attracts white blood cells that release chemicals (lysozyme and others), which subsequently cause the dried cord to drop off. A persistent cord implies a continued blood supply or a white blood cell defect (Donlon et al., 2002).

Child Passenger Safety

A car safety seat appropriate for the maturity of the infant and any persistent medical condition must by law in nearly every state be available for travel. These must meet the Federal Motor Vehicle Safety Standard 213 (AAP & ACOG, 2013).

Circumcision

Newborn male circumcision has been a common practice in the United States, but more recently the benefits and risks have come under scrutiny, with arguments both for and against the practice. The decision to circumcise involves ethnic, religious, cultural, and medical considerations. Circumcision may be done in the hospital, or it may be done following discharge as part of a religious ceremony, such as the Jewish bris. Expectant parents are encouraged to become educated on the risks and benefits of circumcision so that they can make informed decisions in consultation with their physicians. Following circumcision, the baby should be observed for at least 2 hours to assure that there is not excessive bleeding. Circumcision of females is practiced at birth or puberty in some cultures. There is no medical indication for female circumcision, and it should not be performed at any age.

High-Risk Infants

Children who are born with special health care needs or developmental concerns may require specialized supports and services that should be initiated prior to discharge. Parents may need education on how to use medical equipment, how to care for their child's special needs in the home environment, and how to access community resources. When appropriate, discharge planning should include a referral to the local Part C Early Intervention Program for Infants and Toddlers with Disabilities (see chapter 17, Beckstrand, Pienkowski, Powers, & Scanlon, 2016, for more information about the early intervention process).

Chapter Summary

This chapter has described the typical process of delivery room management of the newborn, as well as initial evaluations of newborn functioning. The chapter highlighted basic newborn care and the various types of screening for health and developmental problems, as well as newborn discharge planning with families.

Key Points to Remember

- Fetal assessment identifies intrauterine growth pattern and reflects fetal well-being.

- When risk factors are identified prior to or at delivery, professional guidelines are available to train health care professionals on how to resuscitate the newborn.

- Gestational age can be determined by examination of physical characteristics at birth and neurologic evaluation after the newborn is stable.

- An understanding of growth, maturity, and gestational age risk factors in conjunction with newborn screening provides a framework for defining wellness or subsequent problems.

Implications for Families and Professionals

Ongoing evaluation and early developmental intervention support the optimal development of infants and are particularly important for the high-risk newborn who may require special supports and services. Professionals working with expectant parents can educate them about what to expect in the delivery room so that families are familiar with routine newborn procedures as well as prepared for emergency situations, such as resuscitation. Parents can ask medical providers to explain the screening tests and results that are performed on their infant. Prior to discharge from the hospital or birthing center, parents need support and information about infant development and caregiving practices and access to community resources to ensure they are equipped to manage the care of their newborn in the home environment.

References

Adams, D., & Clark, D. A. (2016). Genetic disorders and their impact in early infancy. In G. L. Ensher & D. A. Clark (Eds.), *The early years: Foundations for best practice with special children and their families* (pp. 157–182). Washington, DC: ZERO TO THREE.

American Academy of Pediatrics. (2011). *SIDS and other sleep-related infant deaths: Expansion of recommendations for a safe infant sleeping environment.* Retrieved from http://pediatrics.aappublications.org/content/128/5/1030.full.pdf+html

American Academy of Pediatrics & American College of Obstetricians and Gynecologists. (2013). Care of the neonate. In *Guidelines for perinatal care* (7th ed., pp. 265–320). Elk Grove Village, IL: American Academy of Pediatrics.

American Academy of Pediatrics & American Heart Association. (2011). *Textbook of neonatal resuscitation* (6th ed.). Elk Grove Village, IL: American Academy of Pediatrics.

American Academy of Pediatrics Committee on the Fetus and Newborn. (2006). Controversies concerning Vitamin K and the newborn. *Pediatrics, 112,* 191–192.

American Academy of Pediatrics, Section on Ophthalmology & American Academy of Ophthalmology. (2013). Screening examination of premature infants for retinopathy of prematurity. *Pediatrics, 131,* 189–195.

Apgar, V. (1953). A proposal for a new method of evaluation of the newborn. *Anesthesia Analgesia, 32,* 260–264.

Beckstrand, K., Pienkowski, T., Powers, S., & Scanlon, J. (2016). Early intervention at home: When, why, and how? In G. L. Ensher & D. A. Clark (Eds.), *The early years: Foundations for best practice with special children and their families* (pp. 353–365). Washington, DC: ZERO TO THREE.

Clark, M., & Clark, D. A. (2016). Nutrition and oral health of infants and toddlers. In G. L. Ensher & D. A. Clark (Eds.), *The early years: Foundations for best practice with special children and their families* (pp. 109–117). Washington, DC: ZERO TO THREE.

Cummings, J. J., & Fisher, M. A. (2016). Major physical, motor, and neurologic impairments. In G. L. Ensher & D. A. Clark (Eds.), *The early years: Foundations for best practice with special children and their families* (pp. 209–228). Washington, DC: ZERO TO THREE.

Donlon, C. R., Furdon, S. A., & Clark, D. A. (2002). Look before you clamp: Delivery room examination of the umbilical cord. *Advances in Neonatal Care, 2*(1), 19–26.

Dubowitz, L. M. S., & Dubowitz, V. (1977) *Gestational age of the newborn.* Boston, MA: Addison-Wesley.

Fisher, M. A. (2016). Neurologic development of infants and young children. In G. L. Ensher & D. A. Clark (Eds.), *The early years: Foundations for best practice with special children and their families* (pp. 73–107). Washington, DC: ZERO TO THREE.

Graven, S. N. (2011). Early visual development: Implications for the neonatal intensive care unit and care. *Clinics in Perinatology, 38,* 671–683.

Jeanty, P. (2011). Fetal biometry. In A. C. Fleischer, F. A. Manning, P. Jeanty, & R. Romero (Eds.), *Sonography in obstetrics and gynecology: Principles and practice* (7th ed., pp. 135–156). New York, NY: McGraw Hill.

Moore, L. M., & Persaud, T. V. N. (2008). *The developing human. Clinical oriented embryology* (8th ed., pp. 429–432). Philadelphia, PA: Saunders.

National Institute of Health and Clinical Excellence. (2014). *Antenatal care* (CG62). Retrieved from http://guidance.nice.uk/CG62

Pinheiro, J. M. B. (2016). Hearing: Development and disorders. In G. L. Ensher & D. A. Clark (Eds.), *The early years: Foundations for best practice with special children and their families* (pp. 183–196). Washington, DC: ZERO TO THREE.

Ringer, S. A., & Aziz, K. (2012). Neonatal stabilization and postresuscitation care. *Clinics in Perinatology, 39* (4), 901–918.

Tomashek, K. M., Shapiro-Mendoza, C., Davidoff, M. J., & Petrini, J. R. (2007). Differences in mortality between late preterm and term singleton infants in the United States, 1995–2002. *Journal of Pediatrics, 151,* 450–456.

Wilkins-Haug, L., & Heffner, L. J. (2012). Fetal assessment and prenatal diagnosis. In J. P. Cloherty, C. Eric, M. D. Eichenwald, A. R. Hansen, & A. R. Stark, *Manual of neonatal care* (7th ed., pp 1–11). Philadelphia, PA: Lippincott, Williams & Wilkins.

PART **2**

CHAPTER 6

Evaluating Infants and Young Children in the First Years

Gail L. Ensher and David A. Clark

Highlights of the Chapter

At the conclusion of the chapter, the reader will:

- understand the importance of early referral of neonates, infants, and young children when there is a suspected or known developmental delay

- understand federal mandates in evaluating infants and young children, birth to 3 years old

- be knowledgeable about ways to partner with families in developing Individual Family Service Plans (IFSPs) and determining their priorities

- be cognizant of new visions and approaches for assessing infants, toddlers, and preschool children with diverse family backgrounds

- be familiar with selected functionally meaningful measures that are appropriate for screening and evaluating infants and young children, birth to 3 years old, in natural environments

- be cognizant of strategies for linking assessment and intervention to meet the diverse needs and abilities of families, infants, and young children

The Whys and Hows of Developmental Observation and Assessment Processes

Screening, early referral, and developmental follow-up with medical or early intervention (EI) personnel, or both, are very important. Being proactive can prevent or circumvent secondary complications, and it frequently can allow for parents to receive assistance and support at critical, early stages of their child's growth and development. Surveillance and screening are two important methods for monitoring children's development. *Surveillance* is the practice of monitoring children's development as part of their regular health care visits. *Screening* refers to brief procedures that help determine whether a child needs further evaluation of a developmental or health concern.

Surveillance and screening do not provide a diagnosis. Rather, they primarily indicate whether further examination and evaluation are necessary to identify or rule out the concern that a parent, teacher, or someone who has frequent interactions with the child has expressed.

Surveillance and screening also are essential in light of the growing prevalence of developmental disorders. There have been increases in the identification of autism, co-existing pervasive developmental disabilities, and attention-deficit/hyperactive disorders. In addition, there is serious need for heightened parent and pediatrician awareness concerning the development of extremely premature newborns who are now surviving with the benefit of new technology, as well as the prevalence of "late preterm" babies who are born 1 to 3 weeks early, likely the result of a host of environmental, medical, genetic, social, and economic factors. Highlighting this point, in May 2011, the Centers for Disease Control and Prevention published a report indicating that, over the past 10 years, there has been an increase of 17% of American children, or 1 in 6 children, 3 to 17 years old, who have been diagnosed with a developmental disability (Boyle et al., 2011).

Developmental Surveillance and Screening

The importance of developmental surveillance of infants and young children by health care professionals (in particular, pediatricians) has been recognized for more than a decade. Referencing this need, in 1992, Paul Dworkin defined developmental surveillance as

a flexible, continuous process whereby knowledgeable professionals perform skilled observations of children throughout all encounters during child health care. Components of surveillance include obtaining a relevant

developmental history, making accurate and informative observations of children, and eliciting and attending to parental concerns. Emphasis is placed on monitoring development within the context of the child's overall well-being rather than viewing development in isolation during a testing session (p. 1254)

Subsequent articles published by the American Academy of Pediatrics (Committee on Children With Disabilities, 2001; Council on Children With Disabilities, Section on Developmental Behavioral Pediatrics, Bright Futures Steering Committee, Medical Home Initiatives for Children With Special Needs Project Advisory Committee, 2006) likewise have emphasized the role of developmental surveillance in light of the Individuals with Disabilities Education Act (IDEA) Amendments of 1997 that mandate early identification of infants and young children (birth to 3 years old) in order to offer opportunities for services and support to children and their families through EI. As Dworkin (1992) noted, it is important to recognize that developmental surveillance by professionals is best achieved in partnership with parents or caregivers who know their child best.

Screening, as differentiated from developmental surveillance, is the next step in the early identification process, should pediatricians or other professionals share family concerns about an infant's or young child's behavior, mental health, or overall development. Screening of neonates, infants, toddlers, and young children may be carried out within the context of at least four medical, clinical, and educational contexts. First, as described in chapter 5 (Clark & Furdon, 2016), multiple routine, mandated screens are carried out in hospitals before and at the time of delivery, or shortly thereafter, for preventative purposes, in order to rule out metabolic, endocrine, hematologic, and infectious diseases; cystic fibrosis and specific gene defects; and neurologic conditions that are known to be associated with later developmental and/ or medical conditions. These tests, somewhat variable from state to state, are essential to the well-being of young children and are increasing in number with the mounting body of new information and rapid advances in technology (Clark, 2009).

Second, with the growing number of extremely low-birth-weight, preterm infants surviving, coupled with possible hearing and visual impairments associated with severe prematurity, many neonatal intensive care nurseries across the United States now offer screening for these sensory losses shortly after birth, with periodic follow-up extending throughout the first year of life. Such services are critically important for early detection and the referral of newborns to EI and specialized services that are offered to babies and young children, at no cost to families. Moreover, if neonates meet certain criteria in terms of gestational age, birth weight, and/or other medical-neurologic conditions, they can be referred directly at the time of hospital discharge to EI, and/or are followed periodically at 9, 18, 24, or 30 months by their own private pediatricians (Centers for Disease Control and Prevention, 2011).

The third context for screening of neonates involves initial neurological evaluations, typically done within 24 hours after delivery, once newborns are stable. As Clark (2009), citing Dubowitz and Dubowitz (1977) indicated, "numerous perinatal factors may affect the neurological assessment, including perinatal asphyxia, maternal anesthesia, maternal medications, and various illnesses and syndromes that affect the newborn" (p. 34). Neurological examination constitutes part of the gestational age assessment, along with a "combination of detailed prenatal information and confirmatory physical findings" (Clark, 2009, p. 34).

Such practices also need to be extended to infants who, because of "unsafe" home environments, have been placed within the child welfare system (Dicker, 2009). Although they have been historically grossly underserved, increasing populations of vulnerable infants and young children should be screened, given a comprehensive evaluation within 30 days of foster placement, and accorded the benefit of EI services, as required by the 2003 Child Abuse Protection and Treatment Act (Cooper, Banghart, & Aratani, 2010).

A fourth context for screening, most familiar to educators, is the sampling of developmental milestones and skills within a particular group or population of young children in order to detect or identify youngsters who are at risk for later developmental delays. When infants, toddlers, and preschoolers are referred for screening by their physicians or other professionals such as child care providers because of concerns, that screening provides a quick "snapshot" of developmental milestones. It often takes place in clinical, program, or home environments and may be repeated over time to produce multiple observations prior to more in-depth evaluation and assessment.

Choosing a Screening Tool

Screening instruments appropriate for infants, toddlers, and 3-year-olds are numerous and diverse in terms of their intended purposes. Some are normed or standardized (as defined in chapter 1; Ensher & Clark, 2016); others are not—having been field-tested only, without the use of norming tables for standardized scores. Moreover, Bagnato, Neisworth, and Pretti-Frontczak (2010) noted that screening instruments entail "casting the net wide" (p. 34), usually involve merely a sampling of behavior and developmental domains, are fairly quick to administer, and never should be used as a firm basis for diagnosis. Therefore, results based on screening instruments always need to be followed up with further evaluation and "authentic assessment." An exhaustive list of screening measures is beyond the scope of this chapter; readers can find excellent reviews of available measures elsewhere (Bagnato et al., 2010; Ringwalt, 2008). Consider the following questions when making best-practice decisions about authentic screening measures:

- What are the purposes of the screening?

- What are the developmental milestones and behaviors to be sampled?

- Does the screening measure include adaptations and/or levels of assistance for the child with special needs?

- Does the screening measure include a sampling of functional behaviors and skills that can be observed within the natural environments of the child?

- Does the screening measure include information gathered from parents, caregivers, and others who interact regularly with the child?

- Are toys and materials needed for administration readily available within the

daily routines of the child at home and/or the screening site?

- Does the screening measure specify training requirements for administration by a range of qualified professionals or paraprofessionals?

Selected Screening Tools

The following are a few screening measures for development and behavior that are appropriate for infants, toddlers, and young children from birth to 36 months.

Ages and Stages Questionnaire (ASQ-3)

This measure (Squires & Bricker, with assistance from Twombly et al., 2009) samples language/communication, gross and fine motor, cognitive/problem-solving, and adaptive behavior skills from **birth to 66 months.**

Greenspan Social-Emotional Growth Chart (SEGC) A Screening Questionnaire for Infants and Young Children (Greenspan, 2004)

This developmental, social-emotional growth chart (Greenspan, 2004; Greenspan et al., 2008) is a screening measure that is appropriate for infants and young children from **birth to 42**

months old. The 35-item validated, norm-referenced instrument is used as a first step in child care, early identification, and pediatric screenings to determine the need for further assessment, for monitoring growth, and as a starting point for developing intervention plans.

Communication and Symbolic Behavior Scales Developmental Profile Infant/Toddler Checklist

This screening tool (Wetherby & Prizant, 2002) is appropriate for infants and toddlers from **6 to 24 months** old and can be used to identify children who are at risk for developing communication problems or for monitoring changes in the communication and symbolic behavior of infants and toddlers over time.

Temperament and Atypical Behavior Scale (TABS): Early Indicators of Developmental Dysfunction

The 15-item screener (Bagnato, Neisworth, Salvia, & Hunt, 1999) is a measure that is appropriate for toddlers and young children from **11 to 71 months old** at risk for later developmental delays and has been used as a first step toward identifying young children with autism.

Brief-Infant-Toddler Social-Emotional Assessment (BITSEA)

The 42-item measure (Carter & Briggs-Gowan, 2006) can be used to screen for social-emotional and behavior problems in toddlers and young children from **12 to 35 months old.**

Assessment: Purposes, Mandates, and Approaches

There are at least four primary purposes for evaluation of infants and young children beyond the screening phase: (a) to determine the child's initial eligibility for EI services, (b) to develop developmentally appropriate plans for the child and family, (c) to monitor the child's (and family's) growth and progress throughout the course of EI, and (d) to prepare for the transition to preschool programming.

Federal regulations for Part C of IDEA (Individuals With Disabilities Education Act, as amended by the Individuals With Disabilities Education Improvement Act of 2004) define *infants and toddlers with disabilities* as young children from birth through 2 years old who require EI services in light of the following conditions; that is, children who:

- are experiencing developmental delays, as measured by appropriate diagnostic instruments and procedures, in one or more of the following areas: cognitive development; physical development, including vision and hearing; communication development; social or emotional development; and/or adaptive development.

- have a diagnosed physical or mental condition that has a high probability of developmental delay. Examples of diagnosed conditions with a high probability of developmental delay as set forth in Note 1 to 34 CFR 303.16 include chromosomal abnormalities, genetic or congenital disorders, severe sensory impairment, inborn errors of metabolism, disorders reflecting a disturbance of nervous system development, disorders secondary to exposure to toxic substances, and severe attachment disorders. (Department of Education, 2011)

Moreover, both state and federal regulations specify that the five areas or domains of development—as noted previously, communication, cognition, physical development (gross and fine motor abilities), social-emotional behavior, and adaptive behavior (e.g., feeding and other self-care skills)—must be assessed as part of the process for determining eligibility for the EI program (EIP). The degree or extent of developmental delay that allows a child to qualify for EIP services varies from state to state (Shackelford, 2006), as well as the "lead agencies" under which such services are funded and provided (National Early Childhood Technical Assistance Center, September 2011). For example, New York State (where the lead agency is the Health Department) defines a *developmental delay* as:

- a 12-month delay in one functional area;

- a 33% delay in one functional area or a 25% delay in each of two functional areas;

- a score of at least 2.0 standard deviations below the mean in one area or 1.5 standard deviations in two areas; or

- a developmental diagnosis previously established such as Down syndrome.

The diagnostic team carrying out the evaluation must be multidisciplinary, including qualified professionals from at least two different disciplines (e.g., teacher, speech-language therapist, occupational therapist, physical therapist, psychologist, physician), and the evaluation must include information drawn from a variety of sources such as review of records, direct observation of the child in the natural setting of the home or day care setting, child performance as assessed with diagnostic measures, and parent and teacher interviews. In New York, as in other states per federal mandate, a parent or caregiver must be included throughout the evaluation and final decision-making process.

Approaches to Assessment

Time constraints, limited financial resources, shortages of trained professionals, and ease or lack of difficulty of administration are at least four factors that contribute to prevailing ways and means of testing young children in the first 3 years of life. Current requirements and prevalent assessment strategies with infants and young children in many states, however, contradict what professionals know to be best practices for assessing young children; parents, too, "fearing a diagnosis that suggests a limited future for their child, are frustrated when they observe professionals basing their assessment on a sampling of behavior that is not representative of what their child does with them outside the assessment context" (Miller & Robinson, 1996, p. 313).

More than a decade ago, Meisels and Fenichel (1996) addressed the challenges of appropriately assessing infants and young children:

Despite widespread awareness of the importance of a systematic, contextually based approach to the developmental assessment of infants and young children, demands for "immediate expertise" and the pressures associated with enormous service challenges present formidable barriers to best practice. Because professionals feel that they must act quickly, a fragmented, piecemeal, occasionally undermining approach to assessment has emerged, rather than one that reflects a comprehensive, integrated understanding of infants and young children and their relationships within their families and larger communities and cultures.

Under pressure to produce quick formulations or "scores," professionals have often called on their experiences with procedures and instruments developed for assessing selected competencies and skills in older children. These procedures and instruments can often yield misleading information. They are not built on a model of how the infant and young child develop within the family. . . . There has been a tendency to assess the functions of infants and young children for which there are tests or scales already in existence. (p. 15)

Current practices for assessment promote a "deficit-based" rather than a "strength-based" perspective and philosophy of infants and young children, especially those with already identified special needs or at risk for developmental delays. Using such practices is at odds with much of what is known about how infants and young children display their developmental stages: in relationship with their families and within the context of play, discovery, and exploration.

Conventional tests and high-stakes testing procedures are decontextualized from the typical daily activities and routines of young children in home, center, classroom, and community settings. Young children do not display their competencies by sitting quietly at tables, responding on demand, and pointing to pictures on flip-cards. Rather, preschool children learn and display their skills appropriately through play, both unstructured and structured. Moreover, preschoolers show problem-solving, literacy, motor, social, and self-care skills in everyday activities such as talking on the telephone, finding the right toy at the bottom of the toy box, discriminating between a box of Cheerios and a box of Fruit Loops at the grocery store, and playing computer games. In this respect, conventional tests and testing are archaic since their dated methods fail to capture the real-life skills of children in real-life activities. (Bagnato & Yeh-Ho, 2006, p. 26)

Authentic Assessment

"New visions of assessment" as described by Meisels and Fenichel (1996), the concept of "authentic assessment" (Bagnato et al., 2010), and the "routines-based" approach for gathering interview and assessment data (McWilliam,

2010a; McWilliam & Casey, 2008) represent three efforts to change the direction of thinking about evaluation and assessment, offering more developmentally appropriate, positive paradigms.

Bagnato and Yeh-Ho defined *authentic assessment* as "the systematic recording of developmental observations, over time, about the naturally occurring behavior of young children in daily routines by familiar and knowledgeable caregivers in the child's life" (2006, p. 29). Evaluations that take place within the context of natural environments determine eligibility for EI services in a needs-based rather than deficit-justified approach. Authentic assessment offers professionals and families positive, strength-based strategies for assessing infants, toddlers, and young children, and it has been advocated for some time both by national organizations in early childhood (Division for Early Childhood of the Council for Exceptional Children, 2007; National Association for the Education of Young Children, 2009; Shepard, Kagan, & Wurtz, 1998) and by noted scholars in early childhood education and pediatrics (Bagnato, 2005; Bagnato, McKeating-Esterle, Fevola, Bortolamasi, & Neisworth, 2008; Bricker et al., 2008; Bricker, Yovanoff, Capt, & Allen, 2003; Macy, Bricker, & Squires, 2005; Meisels & Fenichel, 1996; Snyder, Wixson, Talapatra,

& Roach, 2008; Waddell, Pretti-Frontczak, Johnson, & Bricker, 2007).

We have identified the following 10 characteristics as the most important qualities and dimensions of an authentic assessment:

1. The child's strengths and challenges are evaluated within the context of his family's strengths and challenges, because professionals know that ongoing development is nurtured primarily in relationship with the child's primary caregivers.

2. Strengths discerned in the assessment are as important as the needs and challenges identified for the child and family.

3. The assessment includes identification of "levels of assistance" determined to be requisite for the child's successful functioning, learning, and behavior.

4. The assessment includes tasks and activities directly related to the child's functioning and behavior that he demonstrates in current daily routines.

5. Mental health issues, temperament, and behavioral/social-emotional styles of communication of the child and family are weighed with respect to their impact on child–caregiver interactions and family relationships.

6. The assessment is based on multiple sources of data, gathered over several opportunities for observation and interaction with the child and family.

7. The assessment reflects an "inclusive" or "integrated" perspective of child development and behavior; that is, behavior and development in certain domains have overarching effects on learning and behavior in other developmental areas or domains.

8. The assessment takes place within the context of at least one of the child's familiar, natural settings in which she has daily interactions and experiences.

9. The assessment is responsive to the family's native culture, language, and ethnic background.

10. The assessment of the child takes into account that the child will at some point transition to different learning environments and daily routines.

Best Measures for Best Practices

Several measures and strategies have been developed that are more aligned with authentic assessment than are traditional norm-referenced tools. We recommend the following tools as appropriate for determining whether infants and young children qualify for EI services.

Assessment, Evaluation, and Programming System for Infants and Children, 2nd ed. (AEPS)

The AEPS (Bricker, 2002) is a criterion-referenced, curriculum-referenced, authentic alternative assessment that can be used to determine Part C eligibility of infants and young children for services. The assessment captures real-life skills and abilities of children in their daily routines and is directly connected to EI and program planning. The measure has been field validated with "empirically derived cutoff scores from Item Response Theory (IRT) analyses" (Waddell et al., 2007, p. 6). Further, the authors stated that

the AEPS test can now be used as a stand alone measure for eligibility determination for IDEA services in states and territories where teams are allowed to (1) use any valid and reliable instruments/methods (not restricted to the use of standardized norm-referenced tests); and/or (2) use informed clinical judgment as a primary method of determining eligibility" (Waddell et al., 2007, p. 6).

The measure is organized into two primary levels; the first is appropriate for infants and young children from **birth to 36 months old**, and the second extends from **36 to 72 months old.** The instrument is aligned with NAEYC and the Division for Early Childhood recommended practices and encompasses the cognitive, language/communication, social-emotional, and fine and gross motor developmental domains. The AEPS is considered to be sensitive for differentiating small increments of child variability and progress. In addition to corroborating and/or determining initial eligibility for EI services, the AEPS can be used for monitoring child progress over time in response to programming for accountability purposes. The system is available in Spanish, encourages family participation, and includes a web-based data management and electronic scoring system with the AEPSi (interactive), where scores, team notes, and comments can be entered.

Infant-Toddler Developmental Assessment (IDA)

The IDA (Provence, Erikson, Vater, & Palmeri, 1995) is an assessment that "extends beyond traditional measures by addressing health, family, and social aspects of development as well as developmental dimensions" (Meisels & Atkins-Burnett, 2000, p. 249) for infants and young children from **birth to 36 months old.** The IDA offers an integrated assessment process in which parents or caregivers participate throughout the evaluation. The measure is organized into six phases: (a) Referral & Pre-Interview Data Gathering, (b) Initial Parent Interview to discuss parent/caregiver concerns and priorities, (c) Health Review to gather and organize health information from the family, health care providers, and medical records, (d) Developmental Observations and Assessment, based on parent information and a play-based assessment in a natural environment, (e) Integration and

Synthesis to summarize findings for the parent conference, and (f) Sharing of Findings with the Family and Report Completion, where information is communicated to the family to facilitate EI services, as needed.

The Developmental Observations and Assessment phase uses the Provence Birth-to-Three Developmental Profile, a standardized developmental assessment that offers a descriptive summary of the child's developmental competencies: gross motor and fine motor; relationship to inanimate objects (cognitive); language/communication; self-help; relationship to persons, emotions, and feeling states; and coping skills. The Provence Profile does not yield percentile ranks, standard scores, or age equivalents, but it does offer important information about the specific developmental milestones the child has reached in relationship to his chronological age, which can be used to develop an initial IFSP.

Transdisciplinary Play-Based Assessment, 2nd ed. (TPBA2); Transdisciplinary Play-Based Intervention, 2nd ed. (TPBI2)

The recently revised second edition of this curriculum-embedded assessment (Linder, 2008a) affords multidisciplinary teams a wealth of play-based information, coupled with the TPBI2, a companion intervention manual (Linder, 2008b) that can be used in a variety of natural-environment home- and school-based settings. In addition, the three-set package includes a separate manual for administration.

Unlike the IDA, the TPBA2 uses toys and materials that are selected on the basis of interests of the particular child to be evaluated. The assessment is appropriate for young children from **birth to 6 years old**, and is strength focused, with a flexible design to capture the developmental skills and competencies that the child has developed across the communication, cognitive, sensorimotor, and social-emotional domains. The "play facilitator" (who is familiar with the child) is encouraged to include parents, caregivers, and siblings in the assessment process in order to maximize optimal child functioning as she engages in natural, play-based activities. In so doing, the play facilitator is able to gather important qualitative, developmental, and functionally relevant information about the child's repertoire of daily skills, information that can be readily corroborated in discussions with the parent-partners.

Finally, all necessary forms are included on a CD-ROM for synthesizing assessment information to develop an IFSP and an Individualized Education Program (IEP)—or both—with the family, in addition to a 50-minute DVD of a recorded play session. The DVD offers an excellent example of ways in which a play session can be facilitated and adapted for the complex, multiple special needs of a preschooler, Kassandra. In addition to providing information to document a child's eligibility for EI,

the transdisciplinary assessment/intervention approach provides an exceptionally creative system for planning, programming, and monitoring child progress over time.

The Ounce Scale

The Ounce [of Prevention] Scale (Meisels, Marsden, Dombro, Weston, & Jewkes, 2003), reflecting "new visions for the developmental assessment of infants and young children" (Meisels & Fenichel, 1996), is a curriculum-referenced assessment for infants and young children **up to 42 months** (3.6 years) old. The scale takes a whole-child approach and is organized around six meaningful, functional, developmental areas:

1. Personal connections: How children show they trust a person
2. Feelings about self: How young children express who they are
3. Relationships with other children: What children do around other children
4. Understanding and communicating: How children understand and communicate
5. Exploration and problem solving: How children explore and figure out things
6. Movement and coordination: How infants and young children move and use their hands

The measure is unique, with the first three areas focusing on the social-emotional behaviors, the fourth concentrating on the child's receptive and expressive language skills, the fifth area focusing on cognitive skills and abilities, and the sixth dealing with gross and fine motor development. Comprising three core components, the Ounce Scale takes a whole-child approach, with an Observation Record that offers a means for observing and documenting the child's everyday skills and behaviors in natural settings, a Family Album that provides a structure for parents and caregivers to learn about and record their child's development and behavior, and a Developmental Profile that affords team members and professionals a means for evaluating a child's development and progress over time.

The scale is culturally sensitive, available in Spanish, and includes user-friendly features for online data entry and electronic scoring. The measure is considered to be a reliable instrument that can be used by child care personnel, Early Head Start teachers, home-based EI professionals, visiting nurses, pediatricians, and, most important, family members and caregivers. Finally, the Ounce Scale is considered to be a versatile tool for meeting Early Head Start and federal assessment requirements, facilitating the gathering of information from multiple perspectives and sources.

The Functional Emotional Assessment Scale for Infancy and Early Childhood (FEAS)

The FEAS (Greenspan, DeGangi, & Wieder, 2001) is another criterion-referenced, play-based measure for assessing the development of infants and young children from **7 months through 4 years**, with a particular focus on social-emotional abilities. As indicated in the title of the instrument, the approach embeds the assessment of functional skills and behaviors within the context of structured play interactions with the child's parents or caregivers. Six primary capacities are assessed:

- primary emotional capacities that are appropriate for various developmental ages, such as responding to a parent's or caregiver's gestures, engaging in complex patterns of communication, or imitating another person's behavior

- the child's range of emotions such as using gestures, verbal communication, and touch to get his or her functional emotional needs met

- the range of affective emotional skills and behaviors used by the child to organize his or her play interactions and relationships

- associated motor, sensory, language, and cognitive abilities such as moving, feeding, imitating simple gestures

- basic child capacities to self-regulate; attend; and take pleasure in sights and sounds, touch, and movement in space, for example

- parent or caregiver patterns of facilitating and supporting the child's growth and development

Another primary goal of this approach is the development of intervention strategies that help to nurture strong, positive, and supportive relationships between the child and family members, as primary functional capacities of the child to explore and meet the challenges of relationships and interactions beyond the immediate family environment. Greenspan's approach is appropriate for infants, young children, and their parents or caregivers who are at risk for, or who have difficulties with, self-regulation and engagement; children with sensory, maturational, and pervasive developmental challenges; multirisk families who struggle with anxiety, depression, and other mental health issues; and families with attachment disorders. The FEAS is grounded in a strength-based philosophy that anchors intervention strategies to the child's and family's everyday functioning, environment, and circle of relationships.

The FEAS, which includes a number of training videos and online learning opportunities developed by the Interdisciplinary Council on Developmentand Learning (www.icdl.com), is cited by the National Early Childhood Technical Assistance Center as one of the top five measures for assessing social-emotional development of infants and young children from birth to 5 years old.

In addition to the five authentic measures appropriate for infants, young children, and their families described previously, two other instruments are worth mentioning because of their unique features:

Partners in Play: Assessing Infants and Toddlers in Natural Contexts (PIP)

The PIP (Ensher et al., 2007) evolved over many years of clinical research and development to fulfill a need for a measure to assess infants and young children from **birth to 3 years** in natural contexts of home, school, and other community-based settings. Initially, the PIP was used extensively to follow preterm and sick newborns discharged to home from a Level-3 neonatal intensive care nursery located in Central New York. Per federal mandates, the measure includes activities for assessing skills and abilities in the neuromotor, sensory-perceptual (i.e., sensory-motor/adaptive), cognitive, language/communication, and social-emotional domains. Relevant information relating to medical/health issues of the child and family, as well as family/environmental factors, is recorded in the Caregiver Interview Record form.

The measure usually involves two or three flexible sessions for gathering information during the caregiver report, a time for observing interactions between the parent or caregiver during an unstructured play session, and finally a period for administration of a series of structured play activities by a play facilitator. Accordingly, this strategy underscores the need for a team (including the parents or caregivers as partners) to use multiple sources for gathering information over several occasions of interaction. The child—never separated from a significant familiar adult—participates in play sessions with siblings and/or peers, and over the assessment period becomes familiar with the play facilitator and other team members present in the natural setting of the child's home. A variety of toys and materials are suggested for the various play sessions, although other age-appropriate items can be substituted for administration of the measure. One attractive, child-friendly feature of the instrument is the "clustering" of items that are organized around certain thematic activities so that the administration represents a more "natural" play format for the child rather than moving through a series of disconnected items. Parent report items, as well as unstructured and structured play activities, are organized by age range and are scored with a Likert-type continuum from 1 = *behavior or skill not evident* to 4 = *skill or behavior is well developed*. Scoring forms are provided for duplication in the PIP manual.

Finally, an Online Companion Supplement (which can be accessed at www.earlychilded. delmarl.com) includes helpful information to assist students in training and professionals in their use and understanding of the instrument, that is, an illustrative case study, scoring rubrics, and PowerPoint slides for each chapter of the manual, in addition to suggestions for interviewing families. A wealth of qualitative information can garnered from a PIP assessment that relates directly to the development of functional goals and strategies for EI.

Pediatric Evaluation of Disability Inventory (PEDI)

The PEDI (Haley, Coster, Ludlow, Haltiwanger, & Andelios, 1992) is an authentic, criterion-referenced measure with norms, designed for infants and young children **from 6 months to 7.5 years old**. It is a unique instrument in that it:

- was developed specifically for infants and young children with multiple and severe special needs

- was field validated with infants and young children with complex physical and neurological impairments

- includes measures of current capabilities and measures of caregiver assistance; assesses modifications needed to support functioning; and includes domains for evaluating self-care, mobility, and social function (Bagnato et al., 2010)

- emphasizes engagement in life skills of adaptive, motor, self-help, and social communication functioning, related to everyday settings, tasks, and routines

- is strength-based, with its emphasis on the assessment of needed supports and adaptations for individual infants and young children with complex neurological and physical impairments

The PEDI is a culturally sensitive assessment and has been translated into multiple languages including Dutch, Norwegian, Swedish, Spanish, Portuguese (Brazil), Japanese, and Chinese, with German translations underway (Haley et al., 2010). The measure presently is under review for planned revisions, based on "lessons" learned from worldwide use of the instrument (Haley et al., 2010), including the creation of Competencies Assessment Tool software, which would allow development of a shorter, more flexible, and more precise version of the instrument.

Essential Connections: The Interface of Assessment With Early Intervention

Writing about "The Elements of Early Childhood Assessment," Meisels and Atkins-Burnett concluded:

In short, the model for assessment that is being proposed here is one that uses assessment to inform intervention but then takes information from the intervention context to help refine the assessment. This is not a one-time event that initiates the intervention and then does not recur until it is time for reevaluation a year or more later. Rather, this model is based on a continuous, functional design that is iterative and autocatalytic. That is, every change increases the rate of change. Every assessment that contributes to intervention increases the information available for further assessment in a recurring pattern that maintains a focus on improving children's well-being and on optimally utilizing the resources available in the child's environment....Adopting a dynamic view of assessment suggests that our interventions as well as our assessment must be multidimensional. (pp. 252–253)

In years past, professionals traditionally perceived assessment and intervention as two separate entities; assessment carried out with norm-referenced instruments needing to precede intervention in order to qualify infants and young children for EI services. Professionals now know that best practice dictates otherwise! Indeed, these are complementary processes that must be "fused" from the onset of referral to the time of the child's transition to preschool, if indicated. Further, these processes should be thought about not as distinct and separate but as representing an ongoing continuum of services. It was the recognition of these interactive dimensions on behalf of children and families that spawned the development of assessments that "embedded" or "referenced" companion curricula, which in turn created essential connections to evaluation processes. Given this contemporary thinking and philosophy, assessments have become more meaningful, functional, and relevant to the routines and everyday activities of infants, young children, and families in their natural environments and settings of home and school. Moreover, curriculum-embedded-referenced measures are extraordinarily beneficial in terms of reassessment/program planning/EI processes beyond the initial stage of establishing eligibility for services. As indicated by Meisels and Atkins-Burnett (2000), "constant infusions of new assessment information, acquired in the process of intervention, are essential to maximize the relationship between the child, the child's family, and professionals" (2000b).

Best Approaches for Ongoing Assessment and Intervention

Over the past 2 decades, a number of curriculum-embedded, curriculum-referenced measures have been developed, with a strong focus on parents as partners in the assessment-intervention-reevaluation processes for infants and preschool children. The measures listed below are just a few of the well-designed, authentic assessment/intervention guides that can be used for programmatic and ongoing evaluation purposes.

The Hawaii Early Learning Profile, 3rd ed. (HELP); The Hawaii Early Learning Profile for Preschoolers, 2nd ed. (HELP for Preschoolers)

The HELP (**birth to 3 years old**; Parks, 2007) and the HELP for Preschoolers (**3 to 6 years**; Teaford, Wheat, & Baker, 2004) are curriculum-embedded tools that have been widely used by itinerant and preschool teachers and found to be extremely helpful for documenting the progress of infants and young children. The two measures cover six domains including gross and fine motor development, social and adaptive behavior skills, language and communication, and cognitive development (with regulatory and sensory organization added to the original six domains). Age ranges are provided for each developmental skill or behavior.

In addition to the assessment strands, checklists, and curriculum reference guides from birth to 6 years, the HELP includes sample family-centered interview questions (birth to 3) and HELP at Home, offering parents and caregivers ideas for developmental appropriate activities in the natural home setting. The 0-to-2-year package also features a guide for professionals with adaptations for when the parent has disabilities. The HELP promotes a cross-disciplinary, integrated approach and can be used by EI and early childhood educators, nurses, social workers, psychologists, and physical, speech, and occupational therapists. The instrument does not include manipulative materials, a feature that thus allows team members to select items that are of special interest to the child. The HELP materials have been translated into Spanish and have been field-tested in at least 35 states and seven different countries.

The Carolina Curriculum for Infants and Toddlers with Special Needs, 3rd ed. (CCITSN); The Carolina Curriculum for Preschoolers with Special Needs, 2nd ed. (CCPSN)

The Carolina Curriculum for Infants and Toddlers with Special Needs (**birth to 36 months old**; Johnson-Martin, Attermeier, & Hacker, 2004) and *The Carolina Curriculum for Preschoolers with Special Needs* (**24 to 60 months**; Johnson-Martin, Hacker, & Attermeier, 2004) constitute an authentic, curriculum-embedded system developed for infants and young children who have mild to multiple/severe disabilities. The CCITSN and CCPSN cover five developmental domains: personal-social, cognition, communication, fine motor, and gross motor. For each skill area, team members are provided a list of behaviors, guidelines to facilitate and elicit skills and behaviors, and functional activities to support development in the child's daily routines and play activities. Assessment logs are available for each of the age levels of the curriculum, as well as developmental progress charts for summarizing the child's performance on the assessment. Assessment items at both younger and older age levels are clearly linked to curriculum activities to facilitate the later development of IFSPs and IEPs that can be implemented in a variety of natural environments. Assessment and curriculum items from birth to 5 years old can be easily adapted for those infants and young children with significant developmental challenges and special learning needs. Assessment logs and progress charts are available online or on a CD-ROM for both the CCITSN and the CCPSN.

Similar to the HELP, the Carolina Curriculum materials have been translated into several different languages including Spanish, Korean, and Italian.

The Creative Curriculum for Infants, Toddlers & Twos; The Creative Curriculum for Preschool /Teaching Strategies GOLD: Birth through Kindergarten

The newly revised Creative Curriculum for infants, toddlers, and preschool children (Dodge et al., 2010) and the newly revised assessment (available online and in print), Teaching Strategies GOLD: Birth through Kindergarten (Heroman, Burts, Berke, & Bickart, 2010), offers professionals working with infants and young children a comprehensive system for evaluation, program planning, and curriculum development from birth through the kindergarten age levels. Teaching Strategies GOLD is grounded in 38 research-based objectives that are aligned with Head Start Child Development and Early Learning Framework and state early learning standards, and can be used to support children with a range of abilities, special learning needs, and

behavioral challenges. The tool is considered to be "fully bilingual" and can be used for assessing dual-language learners (e.g., English and Spanish).

Teaching Strategies GOLD online can be used to efficiently gather and organize meaningful data, create developmental profiles of individual infants and young children, determine child progress in response to EI and programming, and, finally, generate comprehensive reports. Easy-to-use tools also are available to assist teams in focusing their observations and documenting, organizing, and summarizing information. Assessment and the curricula are linked throughout all aspects of this comprehensive, authentic, research-based system.

Routines-Based Interview (RBI); Routines-Based Interview Report Form and Scale for Assessment of Family Enjoyment with Routines (RBI-SAFER Combo)

The RBI (McWilliam, 2003) and Scale for Assessment of Family Enjoyment with Routines (Scott & McWilliam, 2000) differ from the curriculum-referenced-embedded measures described previously in one significant way: They do not offer an established, correlated curriculum. On the other hand, these two measures do share three very important dimensions in that they are family-focused and designed for use in natural home and school settings during everyday routines, and they provide a basis for the formulation of functional goals of IFSPs and IEPs. Because they are grounded in observations of infants, toddlers, and preschool children in their daily activities of caregiving (e.g., waking up, feeding/mealtimes, bath time, and traveling), play, and interactions with others, the instruments offer extremely useful measures for following developmental and behavioral growth and change over time in relationship with key individuals (i.e., caregivers and EI and preschool teachers). These measures are available and have been described in detail in publications by Robin McWilliam and colleagues (McWilliam, 2010a, 2010b; McWilliam & Casey, 2008). In addition, the senior author (McWilliam, 2012) has created a measure for assisting EI professionals in "cataloging" the behaviors of infants, toddlers, and preschool children from birth to 3 years old. The unpublished tool, currently titled the Measure of Engagement, Independence, and Social Relationships, yet in a developmental stage, is organized by daily home routines that parallel those included in the RBI and SAFER instruments.

The SCERTS Model: A Comprehensive Educational Approach for Children With Autism Spectrum Disorders; SCERTS Easy-SCORE

In their article describing the SCERTS Model (Prizant, Wetherby, Rubin, & Laurent, 2010; Prizant, Wetherby, Rubin, Laurent, & Rydell, 2005), the authors wrote that it "prioritizes Social Communication, Emotional Regulation, and Transactional Support as the primary developmental dimensions that must be addressed in a comprehensive program designed to support the development of young children with ASD and their families" (Prizant et al., 2010, p. 296). With reference to the evidence-based studies using the model, the authors have written that the approach

offers a framework to directly address the core challenges of ASD, focusing on building a child's capacity to initiate communication with a conventional, symbolic system, and to develop self- and mutual-regulatory capacities to regulate attention, arousal, and emotional state. . . . It incorporates educational/treatment strategies derived from evidence-based practice of contemporary behavioral and developmental

social-pragmatic approaches. . . . Progress is measured in functional activities with a variety of partners in the SCERTS Model; thus, the broader context of a child's development is recognized, including family involvement, and the absolute necessity for supporting communication and socio-emotional development in everyday activities and routines. (pp. 313–314)

Accordingly, the SCERTS Model can be described as a curriculum-embedded system that provides for the collection of information and monitoring of progress in the key domains of social communication, emotional regulation, and transactional support. The first volume of the two-volume set offers guidance in using the system; the second provides information for program planning and intervention, setting social communication and emotional regulation goals, selecting meaningful activities to meet the respective goals, and linking transactional support goals to social communication and emotional regulation goals. A DVD offers helpful information on using the approach with children who require more intensive support and likewise information on using the model with children who need less support.

The SCERTS Easy-Score CD-ROM facilitates accuracy and the scoring process, with an automated tabulation of the SCERTS Profile and Summary and Social-Emotional Indicators. The SCERTS Model is appropriate for children at the **preschool and childhood age levels.**

High/Scope Child Observation Record (COR)

The COR (High/Scope Educational Research Foundation, 2003) is an authentic curriculum-embedded measure that is appropriate for infants and toddlers, **6 weeks to 3 years old** (COR for Infants and Toddlers) and preschool children from **2.5 to 6 years** (Preschool COR). The High/Scope assessment and curriculum materials have a long-standing history of program implementation with infants and young children. Focusing on a child's strengths, rather than deficits, the Infant-Toddler COR is based on six categories that represent broad domains of child development: Sense of self, social relations, creative representation, movement, communication and language, and exploration and early logic.

Within each category, infants and toddlers are assessed on three to eight COR items that describe developmentally important behavior. Each item has five levels that indicate a typical developmental sequence for the respective behavior, enabling COR evaluators to assign accurate ratings to their observations of children. Adults (caregivers/parents and professionals) record observations as they care for, play with, and attend to children during the natural routines of the day. Anecdotes are gathered over time and systematically rated according to the COR framework. This information is subsequently compiled and analyzed to offer a comprehensive profile of a child's growth and development over incremental periods of time. The Preschool COR includes the following areas for assessment: Initiative, social relations, creative representation, movement and music, language and literacy, mathematics, and science.

Assessment items of the Infant and Toddler COR and Preschool COR are closely aligned with key developmental indicators (key experiences) that facilitate the planning of program and intervention activities and strategies. Originally developed in 1962 by David Weikart, director of special services for the Ypsilanti Public Schools, the High/Scope Perry Preschool Project educational approach emphasized "active learning practices" for high-risk children (Hohmann & Weikart, 2002, p. 3). The curriculum for infants, toddlers, and preschool children is now deemed appropriate for all children, including those with special needs.

Similar to earlier described assessment-curriculum systems, the COR for Infants and Toddlers is available in Spanish, and the Preschool COR is available in Korean.

Chapter Summary

Pediatricians, early childhood special educators, and professionals in the clinical fields have shared a long-standing history of assessing infants, toddlers, and young children in various capacities. Such efforts have spanned the period from the beginning of Head Start in the 1960s, the initiation of several noteworthy longitudinal infant and preschool projects, and the present era of EI and preschool programs for 3-to-5-year-olds. Throughout this time, researchers and professionals have relied heavily on norm-referenced, standardized measures that could provide numerical "data" on child change, presumed to be "objective" in nature. More recently driven by the mandates of federal legislation, funding requirements, and to some extent the heartfelt desires of parents on behalf of their young children, these assessment traditions of earlier years have continued to persist into the 21st century—contrary to the strong voices of knowledgeable scholars, professionals, and national organizations in early childhood, calling for a shift in paradigms for evaluating infants and young children. In particular with the purpose of "establishing eligibility" of young children for EI and preschool services, many states still adhere to traditional "standards" of testing that are developmentally inappropriate, greatly lacking in meaningful connections to subsequent early intervention and program planning.

Key Points to Remember

In recent years, newer visions for evaluation in the earliest years have surfaced that offer promise for more authenticity, functionality, fairness, and accuracy in what professionals do on behalf of both young children and their families. The following contemporary changes are most noteworthy:

- Assessment usually is carried out within the natural environments of home and school.

- Parents or caregivers are key partners in the assessment process in terms of their presence and participation during the screening and/or evaluation of their children.

- Measures often are grounded in daily activities and natural routines of child play and interaction.

- Frequently, measures used are closely aligned with curricula for EI and program services, as well as activities for parents in home settings. Thus, assessment and intervention are intertwined, seamless processes.

- Measures are grounded in a strength-based philosophy, tapping into what children can do, rather than what they are unable to do.

- Measures used serve multiple purposes so that child and family progress and change can be seen and documented over time in response to intervention.

- Measures often include strategies for adaptation to elicit best child performance and behavior for children with special needs.

- Within their context of more natural and functional activities, measures offer flexibility in administration, a feature that is much more developmentally appropriate than many traditional, standardized assessments.

Implications for Families and Professionals

Even under the best of circumstances, assessment is never easy for families. However, pathways to communication between parents and professionals can be facilitated during this process if:

- Parents believe that professionals are on their side, that they understand and accept them.

- Parents do not feel judged by professionals.

- Parents retain control of their family and their child's education and care.

- Parents experience professionals as sensitive to their values and culture.

- Professionals say what makes sense to families.

- How professionals speak to parents and what they do are as important as what they say to families.

- Parents trust that professionals will respect and protect their privacy.

- Both parents and professionals are in a time, place, and frame of mind to listen.

- Parents know professionals as "real" persons who are willing to share similar struggles and challenges.

- Both parents and professionals choose to listen.

(A philosophy advocated by staff and professionals of the Jowonio School, Syracuse, NY, 2012.)

References

Bagnato, S. J. (2005). Authentic alternative for assessment in early intervention: An emerging evidence-based practice. *Journal of Early Intervention, 28*(1), 17–22.

Bagnato, S. J., McKeating-Esterle, E., Fevola, A., Bortolamasi, P., & Neisworth, J. T. (2008). Valid use of clinical judgment (informed opinion) for early intervention eligibility: Evidence base and practice characteristics. *Infants & Young Children, 21*(4), 334–349.

Bagnato, S. J., Neisworth, J. T., & Pretti-Frontczak, K. (2010). *LINKing authentic assessment & early childhood intervention: Best measures for best practices* (2nd ed.). Baltimore, MD: Brookes.

Bagnato, S. J., Neisworth, J. T., Salvia, J. J., & Hunt, F. M. (1999). *Temperament and Atypical Behavior Scale (TABS)*. Baltimore, MD: Brookes.

Bagnato, S. J., & Yeh-Ho, H. (2006). High stakes testing with preschool children: Violation of professional standards for evidence-based practice in early childhood intervention. *KEDI Journal of Educational Policy, 3*(1), 23–43.

Barnes, E. (2012). *Philosophy of the Jowonio School.* Syracuse, New York (Unpublished newsletter statement.)

Boyle, C. A., Boulet, S., Schieve, L. A., Cohen, R. A., Blumberg, S. J., Yeargin-Allsopp, M., . . . Kogan, M. D. (2011). Trends in the prevalence of developmental disabilities in US children, 1997–2008. *Pediatrics, 127*(6), 1034–1042. Retrieved from http://pediatrics.aappublications.org/content/early/2011/05/19/peds.2010-2989

Bricker, D. (2002). *Assessment, Evaluation, and Programming System for Infants and Chidren (AEPS)* (2nd ed.). Baltimore, MD: Brookes.

Bricker, D. D., Clifford, J., Yovanoff, P., Waddell, M., Allen, D., Pretti-Frontczak, K., & Hoselton, R. (2008). *Deriving and using the AEPS cutoff scores to determine eligibility for IDEA services (EMRG White Paper No. 3).* Eugene, OR: Early Intervention Management and Research Group (EMRG).

Bricker, D. D., Yovanoff, P., Capt, B., & Allen, D. (2003). Use of a curriculum-based measure to corroborate eligibility decisions. *Journal of Early Intervention 26*(1), 20–30.

Carter, A. S., & Briggs-Gowan, M. J. (2006). *Brief-Infant-Toddler Social-Emotional Assessment (BITSEA).* Upper Saddle River, NJ: Pearson.

Centers for Disease Control and Prevention. (2012). *Screening and diagnosis for healthcare providers.* Retrieved from www.cdc.gov/ncbddde/autism/hcp-screening.html

Clark, D. A. (2009). Evaluation and care of the neonate. In G. L. Ensher, D. A. Clark, & N. S. Songer (Eds.), *Families, infants, and young children at risk: Pathways to best practice* (pp. 29–38). Baltimore, MD: Brookes.

Clark, D. A., & Furdon, S. A. (2016). Newborn screening, assessment, and discharge planning. In G. L. Ensher & D. A. Clark (Eds.), *The early years: Foundations for best practice with special children and their families* (pp. 121–131). Washington, DC: ZERO TO THREE.

Committee on Children With Disabilities (2001). Developmental surveillance and screening of infants and young children. *Pediatrics, 108*(1), 192–195.

Cooper, J. L., Banghart, P., & Aratani, Y. (2010). *Addressing the mental health needs of young children in the child welfare system: What every policymaker should know.* National Center for Children in Poverty, Mailman School of Public Health, Columbia University.

Council on Children With Disabilities, Section on Developmental Behavioral Pediatrics, Bright Futures Steering Committee, Medical Home Initiatives for Children With Special Needs Project Advisory Committee (2006). Identifying infants and young children with developmental disorders in the medical home: An algorithm for developmental surveillance and screening. *Pediatrics, 118* (1), 405–420

Department of Education, Federal Register. (2011). *Rules and Regulations, 34 CFR Part 303, Early Intervention Program for Infants and Toddlers With Disabilities.*

Dicker, S. (2009). *Reversing the odds: Improving outcomes for babies in the child welfare system.* Baltimore, MD: Brookes.

Division for Early Childhood of the Council for Exceptional Children. (2007). *Promoting positive outcomes for children with disabilities: Recommendations for curriculum, assessment, and program evaluation.* Missoula, MT: Division for Early Childhood.

Dodge, D. T., et al. (2010). *The Creative Curriculum for Infants, Twos, and Toddlers.* Washington, DC: Teaching Strategies.

Dworkin, P. H. (1992). Developmental screening: (Still) expecting the impossible? *Pediatrics, 89*(6), 1253–1255.

Ensher, G. L., Bobish, T. P., Gardner, E. F., Reinson, C. L., Bryden, D. A., & Foertsch, D. J. (2007). *Partners in Play: Assessing Infants and Toddlers in Natural Contexts.* Clifton Park, NY: Thomson-Delmar, Cengage Learning.

Ensher, G. L., & Clark, D. A. (2016). Development in the first 3 years. In G. L. Ensher & D. A. Clark (Eds.), *The early years: Foundations for best practice with special children and their families* (pp. 11–47). Washington, DC: ZERO TO THREE.

PART **2**

Greenspan, S. I. (2004). *Greenspan Social-Emotional Growth Chart: A validated, norm-referenced screening of key social-emotional milestones in infants and young children from birth to 42 months of age.* Retrieved from www.icdl/com/dirFloortime/research/SocialEmotionalGrowthChart.shtml

Greenspan, S. I. (2004). *Greenspan Social-Emotional Growth Chart.* Upper Saddle River, NJ: Pearson.

Greenspan, S. I., Brazelton, T. B., Cordero, J., Solomon, R., Bauman, M. L., Robinson, R., … Breinbauer, C. (2008). Guidelines for early identification, screening, and clinical management of children with autism spectrum disorders. *Pediatrics, 121*(4), 828–830.

Greenspan, S. I., DeGangi, G., & Wieder, S. (2001). *The Functional Emotional Assessment Scale (FEAS) for Infancy and Early Childhood.* Bethesda, MD: The Interdisciplinary Council on Development and Learning.

Haley, S. M., Coster, W. I., Kao, Y-C, Dumas, H. M., Fragala-Pinkham, M. A., Kramer, J. M., … Moed, R. (2010). Lessons from use of the Pediatric Evaluation of Disability Inventory: Where do we go from here? *Pediatric Physical Therapy, 22,* 69–75.

Haley, S. M., Coster, W. J., Ludlow, L.H., Haltiwanger, J. T., & Andrelios, P. J. (1992). *The Pediatric Evaluation of Disability Inventory (PEDI).* Boston, MA: CREcare.

Heroman, C., Burts, D. C., Berke, K-l., & Bickart, T. S. (2010). *The Creative Curriculum GOLD: Birth through Kindergarten.* Washington, DC: Teaching Strategies.

Heroman, C., Burts, D. C., Kai-lee, B., & Bickart, T. S. (2010b). *The Creative Curriculum for Preschool.* Washington, DC.: Teaching Strategies, Inc.

High/Scope Educational Research Foundation (2003). *HighScope Child Observation Record (COR).* Ypsilanti, MI: HighScope Press.

Hohmann, M., & Weikart, D. P. (2002). *Educating young children: Active learning practices for preschool and child care programs* (2nd ed.). Ypsilanti, MI: High/Scope® Press.

Johnson-Martin, N. M., Attermeier, S. M., & Hacker, B. J. (2004). *The Carolina Curriculum for Infants and Toddlers with Special Needs* (*CCITSN*; 3rd ed.). Baltimore, MD: Brookes.

Johnson-Martin, N. M., Hacker, B. J., & Attermeier, S. M. (2004). *The Carolina Curriculum for Preschoolers with Special Needs* (*CCPSN*; 2nd ed.). Baltimore, MD: Brookes.

Linder, T. (2008a). *Transdisciplinary Play-Based Assessment* (*TPBA2*; 2nd ed.). Baltimore, MD: Brookes.

Linder, T. (2008b). *Transdisciplinary Play-Based Intervention* (*TPBI2*; 2nd ed.). Baltimore, MD: Brookes.

Macy, M. G., Bricker, D. D., & Squires, J. K. (2005). Validity and reliability of a curriculum-based assessment approach to determine eligibility for Part C services. *Journal of Early Intervention, 28*(1), 1–16. Retrieved from http://jei.sagepub.com/content28/1/1

McWilliam, R.A (2003). *RBI report form.* Nashville, TN: Vanderbilt University Medical Center.

McWilliam, R. A. (2010a). Assessing families' needs with the routines-based interview. In R. A. McWilliam (Ed.). *Working with families of young children with special needs* (pp. 27–59). New York, NY: The Guilford Press.

McWilliam, R. A. (2010b). *Routines-based early intervention.* Baltimore, MD: Brookes.

McWilliam, R. A. (2012). *The measure of engagement, independence, and social relationships.* Unpublished manuscript.

McWilliam, R. A., & Casey, A. M. (2008). *Engagement of every child in the preschool classroom.* Baltimore, MD: Brookes.

Meisels, S. J., & Atkins-Burnett, S. (2000). The elements of early childhood assessment. In J. P. Shonkoff & S. J. Meisels (Eds.), *Handbook of early childhood intervention* (2nd ed., pp. 231–257). Cambridge, UK: Cambridge University Press.

Meisels, S. J. & Fenichel, E. (Eds.). (1996). *New visions for the developmental assessment of infants and young children.* Washington, DC: ZERO TO THREE.

Meisels, S. J., Marsden, D. B., Dombro, A. L., Weston, D. R., & Jewkes, A. M. (2003). *The Ounce Scale.* Upper Saddle River, NJ: Pearson.

Miller, L. J., & Robinson, C. C. (1996). Strategies for meaningful assessment of infants and toddlers with significant physical and sensory disabilities. In S. J. Meisels & E. Fenichel (Eds.), *New visions for the developmental assessment of infants and young children* (pp. 313–328). Washington, DC: ZERO TO THREE.

National Association for the Education of Young Children. (2009). *Position statement: Developmentally appropriate practice in early childhood programs serving children from birth through age 8.* Washington, DC: Author.

National Early Childhood Technical Assistance Center. (2011). *NECTAC list of Part C Lead Agencies as of*

September 2011. Retrieved from www.nectac.org/partc/ptclead.asp

Parks, S. (2007). *The Hawaii Early Learning Profile (HELP; 0–3,* 3rd ed.). Palo Alto, CA: VORT Corporation.

Prizant, B. M., Wetherby, A. M., Rubin, E., & Laurent, A. C. (2003). The SCERTS model: A transactional, family-centered approach to enhancing communication and socioemotional abilities of children with autism spectrum disorder. *Infants and Young Children, 16*(4), 296–316.

Prizant, B. M., Wetherby, A. M., Rubin, E., & Laurent, A.C. (2010). *SCERTS Easy-Score.* Baltimore, MD: Brookes.

Prizant, B. M., Wetherby, A. M., Rubin, E., Laurent, A. C., & Rydell, P. J. (2005). *The SCERTS Model: A Comprehensive Educational Approach for Children with Autism Spectrum Disorders.* Baltimore, MD: Brookes.

Provence, S., Erikson, J., Vater, S., & Palmeri, S. (1995). *Infant-Toddler Developmental Assessment (IDA).* Austin, TX: Pro-Ed.

Ringwalt, S. (2008). *Developmental screening and assessment instruments with an emphasis on social and emotional development for young children ages birth through five.* Chapel Hill, NC: National Early Childhood Technical Assistance Center.

Scott, S., & McWilliam, R. A. (2000). *Scale for assessment of family enjoyment within routines (SAFER).* Chapel Hill: FPG Child Development Institute, University of North Carolina at Chapel Hill (available at www.siskin.org).

Shackelford, J. (2006). *State and jurisdictional eligibility definitions for infants and toddlers with disabilities under IDEA* (NECTAC Notes No. 20). Chapel Hill, NC: University of North Carolina, FPG Child Development Institute, National Early Child Technical Assistance Center.

Shepard, L., Kagan, S. L., & Wurtz, E. (Eds.). (1998). *Principles and recommendations for early childhood assessments.* Report submitted to the National Education Goals Panel.

Snyder, P. A., Wixson, C. S., Talapatra, D., & Roach, A. T. (2008). Assessment in early childhood: Instruction-focused strategies to support response-to-intervention frameworks. *Assessment for Effective Intervention, 34*(1), 25–34. Retrieved from www.sagepublications.com

Squires, J., & Bricker, D. D., with assistance from Twombly, D., Nickel, R., Clifford, J., Murphy, K., Hoselton, R., Potter, L., Mounts, L., & Farrell, J.(2009). *Ages & Stages Questionnaires, 3rd ed. (ASQ-3).* Baltimore, MD: Brookes.

Teaford, P., Wheat, J., & Baker, E. (2004). *The Hawaii Early Learning Profile for Preschoolers* (2nd ed.). Palo Alto, CA: VORT Corporation.

Waddell, M., Pretti-Frontczak, K., Johnson, J. J., & Bricker, D. D. (2007). *Using AEPS to determine eligibility for IDEA services.* Baltimore, MD: Brookes.

Wetherby, A. M., & Prizant, B. M. (2002). *Communication and Symbolic Behavior Developmental Profile Infant-Toddler Checklist.* Baltimore, MD: Brookes.

PART **2**

PART 3

Medical and Developmental Problems in Infants and Young Children

CHAPTER 7

Genetic Disorders and Their Impact in Early Infancy

Darius Adams and David A. Clark

Highlights of the Chapter

At the conclusion of the chapter, the reader will be familiar with:

- inborn errors of metabolism and evaluating hypoglycemia
- other inborn errors of metabolism
- chromosomal aneuploidies
- common genomic microdeletion syndromes
- epigenetic syndromes

Whenever impairments, developmental delays, and medical issues are suspected or detected in infants and young children, often there are genetic components that take many forms. Most of the time these etiologies are identified, given the recent and growing technologies presently available; and there are preventative medical treatments, although not always. In either case, we believe that, on behalf of the families of these children, clinical staff, and early childhood educators, being knowledgeable to the greatest extent possible is important in terms of medical and developmental expectations. It is for this reason that the following overview of genetic disorders and their impact in infancy and early childhood is included.

Inborn Errors of Metabolism

Newborns with metabolic disease are typically healthy and asymptomatic at birth (Girard, 1990). In utero, the fetus is protected by the placenta, which is responsible for removing toxic metabolites and transferring substrates to meet fetal energy needs. Once the fetal nutrient supply is withdrawn by clamping of the umbilical cord at delivery, the newborn infant must activate physiological mechanisms to support metabolism, remove all toxic metabolites, and maintain an endogenous energy supply. Clinical suspicion should be aroused when an infant who initially appears well progressively deteriorates despite appropriate therapy of the presenting clinical signs (Ward, Platt, & Deshpande, 2005).

The onset of symptoms caused by an inborn error of metabolism may range from a few hours to several weeks after birth, depending on the underlying disorder. Errors of intermediary metabolism will lead to an acute or progressive intoxication from accumulation of toxic compounds proximal to the metabolic block (e.g., phenylalanine in phenylketonuria, copper in Wilson's, ammonia in urea cycle defects).

Conditions in this group present with clinical similarities such as:

- a symptom-free interval and clinical signs of intoxication

- may be acute (e.g., vomiting, lethargy, coma, liver failure)

- may be chronic (progressive developmental delay, ectopia lentis, or cardiomyopathy)

- clinical expression may be late in onset and intermittent in mild forms

Additional findings that may be present during metabolic intoxication include:

- hypotonia

- vomiting

- failure to thrive

- movement disorders

- acidosis (due to elevated lactate)

- muscle weakness

- seizures

- myoclonic epilepsy

- cardiomyopathy

- mental retardation

- dystonia

Evaluating the Newborn for Inborn Errors of Metabolism

It is important to consider metabolic disorders in the sick newborn, especially if there is a lack of response to suspected sepsis (Owen, Reichard, Patel, & Boden, 1979).

Initial approach

A complete three-generation family history is an integral part of the initial evaluation. The initial assessment must also include a review of the pregnancy history. Maternal prenatal history can be useful in diagnosing inborn errors of metabolism. A newborn with a fatty acid oxidation disorder can predispose the mother to developing acute fatty liver of pregnancy and preeclampsia with hemolysis, elevated liver enzymes, and low platelet count (HELLP syndrome).

Physical examination

A thorough physical examination can provide helpful clues in identifying the correct diagnosis. Some disorders do not present with an acutely ill infant in the newborn period, but they may have physical findings that are present from birth, such as hypotonia in an infant with mitochondrial disease. The presence of atypical physical findings should alert the clinician to potential problems.

Glycogen metabolism-related disorders

Glycogenolysis occurs when glycogen stored in the liver is broken down after completion of intestinal carbohydrate absorption and occurs approximately 3 to 4 hours after eating. Liver glycogen stores are 50 to 75 g/kg of liver. During glycogenolysis, glucose-6-phosphate is produced, which releases glucose by the action of glucose-6-phosphatase, the enzyme involved in glycogen storage disease type I (GSD I). Insulin levels return to basal levels, and increasing glucagon and epinephrine levels augment glycogenolysis. The brain, red blood cells, and renal medulla use glucose exclusively.

Hypoglycemia occurring during this phase is suggestive of an abnormality in glycogenosis. Muscle glycogen cannot be used by other tissues during this phase because muscle cells lack glucose-6-phosphatase.

GSD I

GSD I has been classified as a disorder of gluconeogenesis because the enzyme catalyzes the final common step in glycogenolysis and gluconeogenesis. The most common abnormalities found in GSD types Ia and Ib are:

- hypoglycemia
- lactic acidosis
- hyperlipidemia
- hyperuricemia

GSD type Ia is secondary to a deficiency of glucose-6-phosphatase, whereas GSD Ib involves a defective microsomal transport of glucose-6-phosphate. The common end result of GSD types Ia and Ib is blockage of glucose release from the liver. Inheritance is autosomal recessive for both forms of GSD. These enzymatic defects result in an excessive accumulation of both glycogen and fat in the liver. These two types of GSD are not clinically discernable; the major difference is that GSD Ib is associated with a decreased number of neutrophils and defective neutrophil and monocyte function, which increases the risk for infections. This circumstance is another example of a metabolic disease with an increased susceptibility to bacterial infection, thereby potentially masking the metabolic disorder. Definitive diagnosis is achieved by performing a liver biopsy along with enzyme analysis or by DNA analysis. As encountered in all disorders of glycogenosis, hypoglycemia becomes evident when exogenous glucose sources are depleted. Glucose-6-phosphatase has the combined effect of blocking glucose release from both the glycogenolytic and gluconeogenic pathways.

The goal of treatment is to prevent hypoglycemia-induced brain damage. Therapy consists of frequent feedings initially by continuous nasogastric feedings and then by feeding uncooked cornstarch, particularly overnight. Uncooked cornstarch has the advantage of having a more protracted release of glucose than is available from cooked cornstarch; however, cornstarch use is limited to children older than 1 year. The dose of uncooked starch is 1.6 g/kg every 4 hours in patients between 1 and 2 years old. Children unresponsive to cornstarch can be given continuous nasogastric infusion of glucose to prevent hypoglycemia. Fructose and galactose are restricted from the diet. Both galactose and fructose must be converted to glucose-6-phosphate or to fructose-6-phosphate, respectively, before forming glucose. Because glucose-6-phosphatase is deficient, glucose-6-phosphate enters glycolysis, which results in a dramatic increase in lactate levels. Allopurinol is given to control the uric acid levels and prevent uric acid crystal accumulation. For patients with GSD type Ib, granulocyte colony–stimulating factor is used to prevent neutropenia and to decrease the severity of bacterial infections. Long-term outcomes in patients with GSD types Ia and Ib can be good if diagnosis occurs early and prompt treatment is started.

Glycogen storage disease type III (Debranching-enzyme deficiency)

GSD type III results from a deficiency of the debranching enzyme, amylo-1,6-glucosidase. The inheritance pattern is autosomal recessive. The gene for this debranching enzyme is located on chromosome 1p21. Debrancher enzyme deficiency results in an inability to degrade stored glycogen, thereby impairing the release of glucose from glycogen. Glucose production from gluconeogenesis remains unaffected. Some of the clinical features of GSD III are similar to those of GSD I. Hepatomegaly, present at birth, improves gradually during the course of childhood. Although this disorder usually occurs in infancy, severe hypoglycemia can occur at birth and steadily improves with advancing age; thus, GSD III differs dramatically from GSD I in this respect. Myopathy is the major chronic morbidity associated with GSD type III. Approximately 15% of patients with GSD type III have liver involvement without any associated muscle disturbance. In comparison with GSD type I, concentrations of lactate and uric acid are normal. Unlike GSD type I, no dietary restriction of fructose and glucose is required in these patients.

Gluconeogenesis-related disorders

Once hepatic glycogen stores are depleted, gluconeogenesis becomes the primary source for energy. Gluconeogenesis progressively replaces glycogen as the major source of glucose. Therefore, hypoglycemia during this phase suggests impaired gluconeogenesis (Ward et al., 2005). Gluconeogenesis typically begins after 12 to 16 hours of fasting once glycogen stores are depleted in the term infant. This process may occur more rapidly in preterm and stressed newborn infants. Gluconeogenesis uses amino acids, lactate, and glycerol to manufacture glucose. The most characteristic feature in newborn infants with defects of gluconeogenesis is hepatomegaly without evidence of liver insufficiency. Important substrates for gluconeogenesis are lactate, alanine, and oxaloacetate. A hallmark of the disorders of gluconeogenesis is elevation of alanine, pyruvate, and lactate levels. Both alanine and lactate are in equilibrium with pyruvate. Abnormalities in gluconeogenesis cause an increase in downstream metabolites such as pyruvate that causes elevations in lactate and alanine. At this stage the brain is not yet using ketone bodies significantly. Fatty acids used for lipolysis and glycerol production become essential when prolonged fasting occurs.

Fatty acid oxidation and ketogenesis

Pathophysiological features. Fatty acid oxidation (FAO) disorders include medium-chain acyl-coenzyme A (CoA) dehydrogenase deficiency (MCADD), which is the most common of these metabolic disorders. Through the β-oxidation pathway (fatty acid breakdown pathway), fatty acids provide energy-yielding substrates during periods of fasting and stress. This process is typically initiated after fasting for more than 12 hours. Normal metabolism of endogenous fats begins with lipolysis; this process, in turn, releases free fatty acids, resulting in an increase in plasma concentration. Free fatty acids are then bound to albumin and transported to other tissues. Short- and medium-chain fatty acids cross the mitochondrial membrane without esterification, unlike long-chain fatty acids. After conversion of long-chain fatty acids to their CoA esters, they react with L-carnitine to form acylcarnitine esters. The fatty acylcarnitine complex is then transported across the mitochondrial membrane to be broken down for energy. Therefore, disorders related to FAO may lead to multiorgan failure secondary to acute ATP (energy) deficiency. Clinical features of FAO disorders include:

- hypotonia
- cardiomyopathy
- coma
- hepatomegaly (fatty liver)

The clinical presentation may be confusing and misleading; for example, hyperammonemia may suggest Reye syndrome, and unexpected death may be taken as sudden infant death syndrome. Many patients have a family history of sudden death in siblings during infancy. The classic presentation is hypoketotic hypoglyce-mia, indicating impairment in FAO. Patients can exhibit vomiting and lethargy, which occurs after fasting. Intercurrent illness can induce prolonged fasting, potentially unmasking a primary underlying disorder of FAO. Diagnosis can be delayed considerably, given that some patients reach adulthood before experiencing a prolonged fasting episode that induces symptoms. Some affected individuals remain asymptomatic for life. This great variability in the clinical presentation can prevent prompt diagnosis in some patients. Pregnancies complicated by either acute liver failure of pregnancy or HELLP syndrome have been associated with fetuses affected with disorders of FAO. HELLP syndrome during pregnancy includes:

- hemolysis (h)
- elevated liver enzymes (el)
- low platelets (LP)

The clinician must be aware of these prenatal clues and consider all newborns delivered in mothers with acute liver failure of pregnancy or HELLP syndrome to be at risk for disorders of FAO.

Medium-chain acyl-CoA dehydrogenase deficiency (MCADD). MCADD is the most common disorder in the FAO pathway. The estimated frequency is 1 in 5,000 to 10,000 live-born infants. MCADD testing is currently included on newborn metabolic screening panels in many states. It is an autosomal-recessive disorder, with the A985G mutations occurring with the highest frequency. MCADD produces hypoketotic hypoglycemia after a fasting period of 8 to 12 hours in neonates or potentially earlier if an acute intercurrent illness is present. The most common time for presentation of MCADD is after 3 months old when the infants typically stop night feedings. Older children may need to be fasting for 18 to 24 hours before symptoms become evident.

Treatment. The first step in treatment is focused on avoiding prolonged fasts (Owen et al., 1979). As noted previously, avoiding prolonged fasts is not usually an issue for newborn infants because they generally feed every 2 to 3 hours. As individuals with this condition get older, they generally tolerate longer fasting intervals. In neonates and infants, going longer than 5 hours without a feeding should be avoided. At 1 year old, raw cornstarch may be instituted to supply a slow release source of glucose for up to 8 hours. This approach cannot be used in children younger than 1 year because of enzyme immaturity and inability to handle the osmotic load.

Plasma L-carnitine levels should be checked as soon as the diagnosis is suspected. Some individuals may have low plasma L-carnitine levels that require supplementation with oral carnitine. Low L-carnitine levels cause a progressive cardiomyopathy. Another function of L-carnitine is to remove short-chain and medium-chain fatty acids from the mitochondria to maintain CoA levels. These fatty acids accumulate as a result of normal and abnormal FAO. This mechanism prevents the build-up in the mitochondria of short-chain and medium-chain fatty acids that may interfere with the energy production essential to the normal function of the cell. In individuals who have normal plasma L-carnitine levels, experts have recommended that L-carnitine not be given because it may result in increased stress on the FAO pathway by its function in assisting the transport of long-chain fatty acids into the mitochondria for oxidation.

Other Inborn Errors of Metabolism

A variety of metabolic conditions exist that do not have hypoglycemia as a presenting symptom but will produce acidosis or hyperammonemia. Many of these conditions occur initially with feeding intolerance or irritability (or both) that can progress to increasing lethargy, seizures, and coma. If untreated, then the classic forms of these conditions cause severe neurologic devastation or death. Many of these metabolic conditions are now included on newborn screening programs in several states. However, screening results can take up to 7 days to return, and, in many of these conditions, onset of symptoms may begin at 3 days of life. Keeping these conditions in mind will allow the clinician to intervene and minimize the impact on an affected neonate. An important term to clarify in regard to treatment for some of these conditions is natural protein, a protein obtained from complete sources, that is, standard baby formulas or table foods.

Euglycemic Inborn Errors of Metabolism

The following disorders do not have hypoglycemia as a consistent finding. There is either a deficiency of an essential metabolite or an excess of an abnormal metabolite in these disorders that can result in clinical manifestations.

L-carnitine deficiency

Some individuals have low plasma L-carnitine levels that require supplementation with oral L-carnitine. Persistently low L-carnitine levels can cause a progressive cardiomyopathy. L-carnitine removes short-chain and medium-chain fatty acids from the mitochondria to maintain CoA levels. These fatty acids accumulate as a result of normal and abnormal FAO. This mechanism prevents the build-up in the mitochondria of short-chain and medium-chain fatty acids that may interfere with energy production essential to the normal function of the cell. In certain organic acidemias, L-carnitine will also bind the offending organic acid for removal, that is, propionic acid. As noted previously, in well individuals

who have FAO disorders and normal plasma L-carnitine levels, experts have recommended that L-carnitine not be given because it may result in increased stress on the FAO pathway by its function in assisting the transport of long-chain fatty acids into the mitochondria for oxidation.

Galactosemia

Galactosemia has a prevalence of 1 in 40,000 to 60,000 live births. Individuals with the classical form of galactosemia have a complete inability to metabolize galactose (see Figure 7.1). Galactosemia is an autosomal-recessive condition. The primary defect in the classical form of galactosemia is deficiency of galactose-1-phosphate uridyltransferase. Deficiency in this enzyme results in an accumulation of galactose-1-phosphate and galactose. In the newborn period, galactosemia can be lethal within 2 weeks. Many states test for galactosemia as part of the newborn metabolic screening program. However, clinical signs generally emerge before the newborn screening results are available. Initial clinical features and findings include:

- jaundice
- increased reducing substances in the urine
- abnormalities in prothrombin time and partial thromboplastin time
- liver dysfunction

The primary cause of death at 1 to 2 weeks old is *E coli* infection resulting from an affected infant's increased susceptibility to infection.

An important fact when considering a diagnosis of galactosemia is that urine-reducing substances will be markedly positive (four or more urine-reducing substances) in the context of a normal screening using a glucose meter, which is specific for glucose. This circumstance should alert the clinician to the fact that the infant is excreting a sugar other than glucose into the urine. Care must be taken in performing invasive procedures in a neonate, such as a lumbar puncture, because the associated hepatic dysfunction may cause a severe coagulopathy and bleeding. Despite the importance of evaluating the infant for possible meningitis, affected infants are at significant risk of intraspinal bleeding that may cause paralysis.

The risk of lethal *E coli* infection is high several days after birth because of increasing accumulation of abnormal metabolites. Once the galactose metabolites are lowered the risk of *E coli* infection is similar to the general neonatal population. In the past, authorities believed that tight control of galactose intake would prevent long-term sequelae. However, now apparent is that older patients with galactosemia are at high risk for specific medical issues despite minimizing galactose intake. Long-term medical complications include speech delays, premature ovarian failure in women, and, in some individuals, onset of tremor and ataxia. These complications have been associated with the *Q188R* mutation, which results in complete absence of the galactose-1-phosphate uridyltransferase enzyme.

The primary goal in management of neonates suspected of having or diagnosed with galactosemia is to minimize galactose intake. Because breast milk and standard cow's milk–based infant formulas contain lactose, these feedings must be stopped. Lactose is a disaccharide that consists of glucose and galactose.

Metabolism of lactose releases the galactose, resulting in elevations in galactose metabolites. Soy milk–based infant formulas do not have galactose and provide a safe alternative infant feeding. If a neonate has clinical manifestations of galactosemia, then a sepsis evaluation should be performed even after they are placed on a soy milk formula. Blood and urine cultures should be obtained, but a spinal tap should be avoided, given the risks noted previously, until results of coagulation studies confirm normal coagulation.

Long-term dietary management requires intensive nutritional counseling to avoid galactose-containing foods. The goal of the diet is to incorporate soy-based products and to avoid galactose-containing products. Individuals with galactosemia must remain on this diet for life.

Organic acidemias

The organic acidemias are a set of conditions that tend to occur in a similar way and have similar treatments. Organic acids form from the breakdown of branched-chain amino acids, methionine and threonine in most cases. In individuals with enzyme deficiencies, accumulation of intermediate metabolites can cause severe illness and death. Affected infants tend to exhibit severe acidosis within several days of life. The clinician should identify the involved organic acids because treatment includes use of specialized, amino acid–modified (free) infant formulas once the infant is stabilized after acute therapies.

FIGURE 7.1 Galactosemia

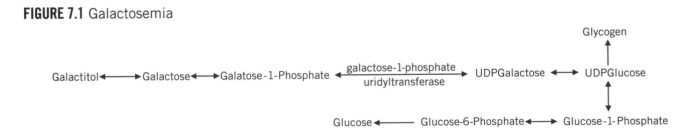

Biotinidase deficiency. Biotinidase deficiency is an autosomal-recessive condition with a prevalence of approximately 1 in 60,000. Biotinidase is an enzyme involved in the generation and maintenance of biotin (see Figure 7.2), a cofactor needed by four carboxylases: pyruvate carboxylase, 3-methylcrotonyl-CoA carboxylase, propionyl-CoA carboxylase, and acetyl-CoA carboxylase for functional activity. Infants with biotinidase deficiency may become symptomatic within several days to several months after birth. The deficiency can occur acutely with seizures, vomiting, diarrhea, feeding difficulties, tachypnea from acidosis, and apnea. Laboratory findings may include hyperammonemia, ketoacidosis, and elevations of characteristic organic acids. If biotinidase deficiency is not detected early and treatment initiated, then late manifestations of biotinidase deficiency may cause:

* hypotonia
* ataxia
* hearing loss
* optic atrophy
* alopecia
* abnormalities in cellular immunity
* basal ganglia calcification
* mental retardation
* skin rash
* seborrheic dermatitis

Treatment involves large doses of biotin; 20 mg/day is usually sufficient for life. Biotin supplementation prevents all of the disease manifestations. In some cases, with neonatal onset, seizures may begin during the first few days of life, necessitating antiepileptogenic medication in addition to supplemental biotin. Usually, as the biotin takes effect, the seizure medication can be discontinued.

FIGURE 7.2 Biotinidase deficiency

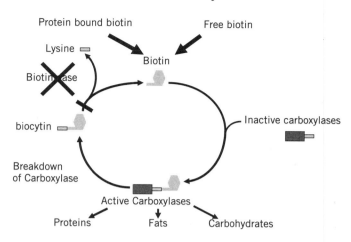

Methylmalonic acidemia, propionic academia and isovaleric acidemia. *Methylmalonic acidemia* has a prevalence of 1 in 40,000 to 50,000 live births. It is an autosomal-recessive condition that results from methylmalonyl-CoA mutase deficiency, or it may also result from a defect in cobalamin (Vitamin B12) metabolism.

Propionic acidemia has a prevalence of 1 in 50,000 to 100,000 live births. It is an autosomal-recessive condition resulting from the deficiency of propionyl-CoA carboxylase, a biotin-dependent enzyme.

Isovaleric acidemia has an unknown prevalence. It is an autosomal-recessive condition that results from isovaleryl-CoA dehydrogenase deficiency. This enzyme is involved in leucine metabolism; however, leucine is not elevated in these individuals because of an irreversible step before isovaleryl-CoA dehydrogenase.

Infants with methylmalonic acidemia and propionic acidemia usually exhibit poor feeding, irritability, respiratory difficulty with tachypnea and labored breathing, severe and repetitive vomiting, cerebral edema, and progression to coma and death over a period of days to weeks. Infants affected by isovaleric acidemia can exhibit the previously listed findings along with a very strong "sweaty sock odor."

This sign may not be noticed if the neonate has been catheterized or if the urine is dilute.

Evaluation. Laboratory findings of infants with organic acidemias include metabolic acidosis on a blood gas sampling, leukopenia, thrombocytopenia, and ketosis. Hyperammonemia can be present in methylmalonic acidemia and propionic acidemia. Hyperammonemia is thought to be the result of secondary inhibition of the urea cycle by the abnormal metabolites generated. As a consequence, affected individuals may have normal blood urea nitrogen levels despite evidence of dehydration caused by a decreased ability to generate urea.

Diagnosis of an organic acidemia requires analysis of urine organic acid patterns. Characteristic excretion patterns are identifiable for various organic acidemias. Plasma amino acid analysis is significant for a marked elevation of glycine and is the reason for the categorization of methylmalonic acidemia and propionic acidemia as ketotic hyperglycinemias. In isovaleric acidemia, glycine is not elevated, which may be the result of the conjugation of isovaleryl metabolites to form isovalerylglycine. Elevations of valine, methionine, isoleucine, and threonine can be seen in methylmalonic acidemia and propionic acidemia.

Treatment. Treatment for methylmalonic acidemia and propionic acidemia involves therapy to lower the level of the elevated plasma organic acid. Beneficial therapies in the acute management of these conditions include (a) dialysis to lower potentially elevated ammonia and the offending plasma organic acid and (b) L-carnitine in a dosage of 200 to 300 mg/kg/day to bind plasma organic acids and replenish L-carnitine. Natural protein intake should also be limited to 1.0 to 1.2 g/kg/day in the acute decompensation. In addition, although they are not routinely available, treatments such as metabolic parenteral solutions that do not contain valine, methionine, isoleucine, or threonine and administration of intravenous sodium phenylacetate–sodium benzoate (Ammonul®) to correct hyperammonemia may be helpful. Ammonul (sodium phenylacetate–sodium benzoate) is an intravenous plasma ammonia–binding solution that will lower ammonia levels.

Peritoneal dialysis has been found to be a safe, effective, and easy way to remove excess offending metabolites in neonates and infants. Some debate has occurred over hemodialysis in neonates because of reports of poor outcomes; however, it has also been used successfully and with more efficient metabolite removal. Much can depend on the experience of persons who implement the hemodialysis in the neonatal setting.

Treatment of isovaleric acidemia is as described for methylmalonic acidemia and propionic acidemia, with the following exceptions: Oral glycine is given at a dose of 500 mg/kg/day to bind isovaleryl metabolites, and parenteral solutions should not contain leucine.

Long-term treatment involves use of specialty commercial formulas to prevent build-up of the offending organic acid. Natural protein is typically maintained at 1.0 to 1.5 g/kg/day, with the remainder of protein and calories provided by the specialty formula.

Maple syrup urine disease. Maple syrup urine disease (MSUD) has an approximate prevalence of 1 in 120,000 live births. MSUD is an autosomal-recessive condition; its primary defect is in the metabolism of the branched-chain amino acids, including isoleucine, leucine, and valine. Acute clinical signs begin several days after birth when branched-chain amino acids accumulate as infants increase their feeding intake. Presenting signs include poor feeding, irritability, and stereotypical seizures characterized by bicycling motions of the arms and legs.

In addition, the infant and the infant's urine have an odor of maple syrup. Lethargic infants rapidly progress to coma and death.

Therapy. Therapy involves extracting the branched-chain amino acids from plasma, thereby reducing total body concentration of these amino acids. Dialysis is necessary to reduce the elevated amino acid levels rapidly in an affected neonate. Peritoneal dialysis has been shown to be safe and effective in lowering these amino acids; however, in severe cases, hemodialysis may be necessary. Once the leucine level is reduced to approximately 10 mg/dL, dialysis can be discontinued. Thereafter the treatment goal is to maximize caloric intake to prevent catabolic breakdown of endogenous proteins resulting in continued elevations of the branched-chain amino acids. Initially, 20% lipid solutions in a dose of 2 g/kg/day in conjunction with 12.5% to 20% dextrose are administered to prevent catabolism. Parenteral nutrition solutions without branched-chain amino acids are used to control branched-chain amino acid levels while enteral nutrition is implemented.

A thiamine (Vitamin B1)-responsive form of MSUD has been identified. Thiamine supplementation corrects the enzyme deficiency, resulting in the ability to tolerate normal protein in normal amounts. Usually, 10 mg/day of thiamine will correct the hyper-branched–chain aminoaciduria without the need for dietary intervention.

In cases in which thiamine does not have any effect, several commercial formulas are available that do not contain the branched-chain amino acids, which can be used as a protein source. Additional calories can be provided by other specialty formulas that only contain fats and carbohydrates. As the branched-chain amino acids decline into the physiological range, small amounts of natural protein are required in the form of a standard formula to prevent branched-chain amino acid deficiencies. Natural protein can be started at 1.0 to 1.25 g/kg/day and then adjusted to keep the branched-chain amino acid levels within normal range. The remainder of protein requirements, 2.5 to 3.0 g/kg/day, can be achieved with the specialty formula that lacks the branched-chain amino acids.

Long-term management of MSUD involves a low-protein diet, continued use of specialty formulas, and intensive monitoring of plasma isoleucine, valine, and leucine levels.

Urea-cycle defects

Urea-cycle defects are a category of conditions that involve primary dysfunction of the urea cycle. Several enzyme deficiencies cause these conditions, and most are autosomal recessive. One notable exception is ornithine transcarbamylase (OTC) deficiency, an inherited X-linked trait that is the most common urea-cycle disorder. This inheritance pattern results in a more severe presentation in male patients, with female patients typically minimally affected, if at all. The prevalence of OTC deficiency is approximately 1 in 80,000 live births.

Presentation. The clinical presentation of urea-cycle disorders is similar to the presentation of other metabolic conditions. However, acidosis is usually not a presenting component of these conditions. Lactic acidosis may become prominent once the patient becomes critically ill. Presenting signs frequently include anorexia, irritability, lethargy, vomiting, somnolence, asterixis (rare), obtundation, coma, cerebral edema, and combativeness and disorientation (in older individuals). Death may occur if treatment is not rapid or effective. Laboratory findings of importance are hyperammonemia (usually >150 mcmol/L; can be as high as 2,000–4,500 mcmol/L), low blood urea nitrogen, and respiratory alkalosis. Metabolic acidosis is not present unless the patient is in critical condition. Characteristic amino acid profiles can confirm the specific urea-cycle defect. Acute treatment of urea-cycle disorders involves dialysis to remove the ammonia, provision of calories by administration of 20% lipid solutions, infusions of intravenous sodium phenylacetate–sodiumbenzoate (Ammonul), and specially formulated formula once oral intake is possible. An infant with OTC deficiency requires infusions of arginine in doses of 200 mg/kg/day and intravenous glucose. In certain cases, when no response or sluggish response to pharmacologic therapy occurs, the health care professional must consider hemodialysis.

Long-term urea-cycle defects are treated by providing formulas that contain essential amino acids along with natural protein at approximately 1.0 to 1.5 g/kg/day. Typically, affected infants require treatment with oral ammonia-binding agents such as sodium benzoate or Buphenyl® to maintain plasma ammonia at an acceptable level. This treatment allows for maintenance of ammonia levels close to the normal range, in most cases, while the individual is well. However, affected patients remain susceptible to transient elevations of ammonia during illness even while on ammonia-binding agents. During episodes of illness, all protein should be stopped for 24 hours and a formula consisting of carbohydrates and fats administered. Protein is gradually reintroduced into the diet once the ammonia level declines. An important point to note is that protein must be given after 24 hours to prevent endogenous protein catabolism and further worsening of the hyperammonemia. If levels are dramatically elevated, then the acute management protocol described previously should be initiated. Depending on the severity of the condition, liver transplant should be considered, especially if the individual does not respond to

medical management or requires frequent hospitalizations.

Aminoacidopathies

Tyrosinemia type 1. Tyrosine is usually metabolized to acetoacetate; however, in classical tyrosinemia type 1, fumarylacetoacetate hydrolase deficiency will result in excess succinylacetone. Succinylacetone is toxic and leads to the clinical findings in tyrosinemia type 1. Tyrosinemia type 1 has a prevalence of 1 in 1,846 in certain regions of Quebec, Canada, and is estimated to be approximately 1 in 100,000 elsewhere. Type 1 tyrosinemia is an acute-onset disorder that initially produces diffuse liver dysfunction, which progresses to liver failure and death without intervention. The primary defect is in the fumarylacetoacetase gene. This gene encodes the enzyme fumaryl-acetoacetate hydrolase. This enzyme deficiency results in accumulation of metabolites that require metabolism via alternative pathways. An important metabolite that is formed is succinylacetone, which likely contributes to the progressive hepatic dysfunction and eventual hepatic failure in affected individuals.

Acute management of tyrosinemia type 1 has been revolutionized recently with the development of Orfadin® (2-[2-nitro-4-trifluoromethylbenzoyl] cyclohexane-1,3-dioneand). This medication inhibits enzyme function proximal to fumarylacetoacetate hydrolase, biochemically transforming tyrosinemia type 1 into tyrosinemia type 2. It also prevents the build-up of succinylacetone and the corresponding hepatotoxicity. Tyrosinemia type 2 is a milder form of tyrosinemia that results in cataract formation and skin findings without the hepatic involvement. However, even with administration of Orfadin, plasma tyrosine levels will require continued monitoring and control through dietary intervention to prevent the ocular and skin findings that are associated with tyrosinemia type 2.

Several commercial formulas are available that do not contain tyrosine. These formulas can be used to control plasma tyrosine levels. Typically, natural protein is kept at 1.0 to 1.5 g/kg/day, with the remainder of protein and calorie requirements provided by the tyrosine deficient formulas.

Phenylketonuria. Phenylketonuria (PKU) does not exhibit acutely in the neonatal period; however, given that PKU is one of the most common inborn errors of metabolism, with a prevalence of 1 in 10,000 to 12,000 live births, a brief mention is provided here. The primary defect is in reduced phenylalanine hydroxylase activity, and it results in elevations in phenylalanine. Chronic phenylalanine elevations cause brain injury that may progress to severe mental retardation if the condition is not treated.

Newborn screening for PKU does not differentiate between the classical form of PKU and rare forms that result from biopterin deficiency. The active form of biopterin, tetrahydrobiopterin, is a cofactor for phenylalanine hydroxylase. Up to 2% of affected individuals with hyperphenylalaninemia have a biopterin abnormality that disrupts neurotransmitter metabolism, in addition to phenylalanine metabolism.

PKU was one of the first conditions that was screened for on newborn screening and was the model condition for dietary management of an inborn error of metabolism. Numerous commercial formulas and low-protein products are available to aid in maintaining plasma phenylalanine concentrations at an appropriate level. Kuvan is an oral analog of tetrahydrobiopterin. In 50% of those with phenylalanine hydroxylase deficiency, at least a 20%–30% reduction in plasma phenylalanine will be noted. It is used as an adjunct therapy with dietary intervention.

In rare cases, an individual with phenylalanine hydroxylase deficiency can have normal protein intake without the need for formula while on Kuvan.

Individuals with biopterin abnormalities do not typically respond to dietary manipulations alone, given that the cofactor deficiency also adversely affects neurotransmitter production. Biopterin deficiency is treated by replacing the precursors to the affected neurotransmitters, folinic acid in some cases, and providing the active form of the cofactor, tetrahydrobiopterin. For some affected patients, treatment with tetrahydrobiopterin or Kuvan may make additional therapy unnecessary.

PKU and pregnancy. Phenylalanine is a severe teratogen. There may be severe consequences to the fetus if maternal phenylalanine levels remain high, especially during the first trimester. Microcephaly, severe mental retardation, and birth defects can be seen in an infant who has had in utero exposure to elevated levels of phenylalanine.

Homocystinuria. Homocystinuria has a prevalence of approximately 1 in 200,000. It is an autosomal-recessive condition. Most newborn screening programs test for plasma methionine concentrations to evaluate for the presence of the condition, given that methionine is elevated in individuals with homocystinuria. However, methionine can be elevated in a variety of conditions that cause liver disease, or it may occasionally be transiently elevated in the newborn. Cystathionine β-synthase is a critical enzyme in the metabolism of homocysteine. Deficiency of cystathionine β-synthase is the most common cause of homocystinuria. Cobalamin plays a critical role in the formation of cofactors for the metabolism of methylmalonic acid and homocysteine.

The acute findings in homocystinuria include thromboembolism and seizures.

Homocysteine is an endothelial irritant that that cause lesions resulting in intravascular clot formation. High concentrations of plasma homocysteine can lower seizure thresholds and may be noted as a presenting symptom. Untreated or inadequately treated patients develop mental retardation and developmental delay, psychiatric disorders, ectopia lentis, scoliosis, and osteoporosis. Fifty percent of affected individuals die before they reach 25 years old.

Approximately 50% of individuals are responsive to Vitamin B6. Vitamin B6 is a cofactor for cystathionine β-synthase. Individuals who respond to Vitamin B6 do very well and do not required further treatment. Nonresponders to Vitamin B6 therapy must be maintained on a restricted methionine and cystine diet for life. Natural protein intake at 1.0 to 1.5 g/kg/day via a low-protein diet and formula are necessary. Betaine, a trimethylglycine, is formed through the oxidation of choline and has shown promising results in the management of individuals with homocystinuria. It converts homocysteine to methionine and permits reduction of the dietary restrictions. Experts recommend that methionine levels be kept below 1000 mcmol/L to prevent cerebral edema. Studies have not yet been conducted on neonates or infants to evaluate for safety of this therapy.

Large-Scale Genomic Anomalies

Large scale genomic anomalies are anomalies that involve many genes. The trisomies are classical examples of large scale genomic anomalies, but smaller multigenic deletions and duplications fall into this category as well.

Down syndrome

Down syndrome is one of the most common large-scale genomic anomalies, with a prevalence of approximately 1 in 700 births

(Sawa, Walker, & Morris, 2016; van Gemeren-Oosterom et al., 2012). Findings include:

- low-set ears
- brachydactyly or short digits with single tansverse palmar crease (see Figure 7.3)
- up-slanting palpebral fissures (see Figure 7.4)
- Brushfield's spots

FIGURE 7.3

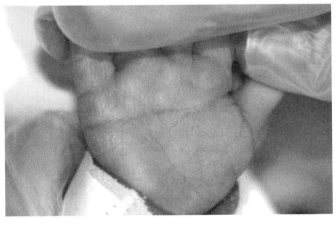

FIGURE 7.4

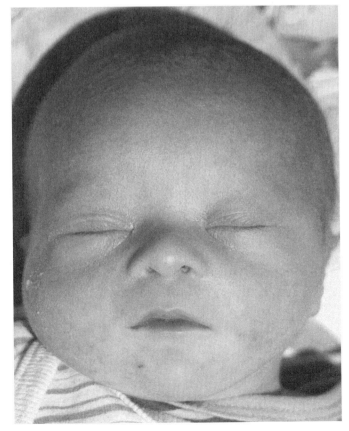

- flat facial profile
- short neck
- hypotonia/poor Moro reflex
- cardiac anomalies
- mental retardation

Early intervention services can be beneficial and can help maximize potential. An increased risk of leukemia and Alzheimer disease has been noted in older individuals.

Trisomy 13 (Patau syndrome)

Trisomy 13 has a prevalence of approximately 1 in 7,000 births (Savva et al., 2010). Findings include:

- holoprosencephaly spectrum
- cutis aplasia (usually of posterior scalp, see Figure 7.5)
- polydactyly
- microphthalmia, coloboma of iris
- cleft lip, palate, or both (See Figure 7.6)
- abnormal ears that are low-set (see Figure 7.7)
- cardiac anomalies
- severe neurological involvement

Lifespan is typically limited to weeks or months; however, there have been cases that

FIGURE 7.5

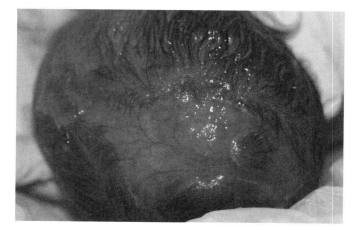

FIGURE 7.6

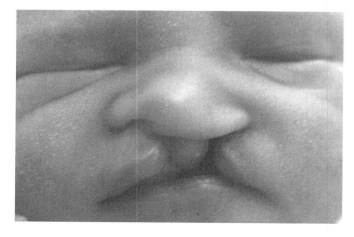

FIGURE 7.7

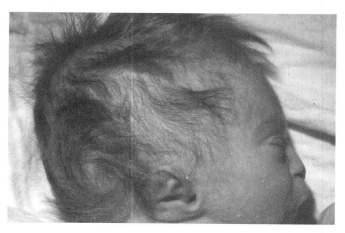

have been described with individuals living years. Individuals with mosaicism can have milder manifestations and live much longer.

Trisomy 18 (Edwards syndrome)

Trisomy 18 has a prevalence of approximately 1 in 4,500 births (Savva et al., 2010). Findings include:

- microcephaly (small head)
- low-set, malformed ears
- micrognathia
- clenched hands with overlapping fingers (see Figure 7.8)
- short sternum
- cardiac anomalies

FIGURE 7.8

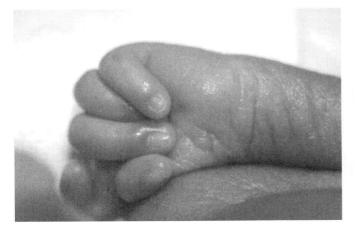

FIGURE 7.10

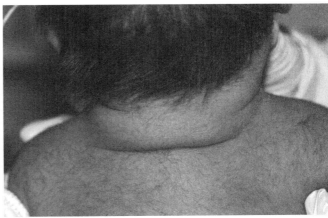

PART 3

- severe mental retardation and neurologic dysfunction

Like Trisomy 13, lifespan is typically limited to weeks or months; however, there have been cases that have been described with individuals living years. Individuals with mosaicism can have milder manifestations and live much longer.

FIGURE 7.9

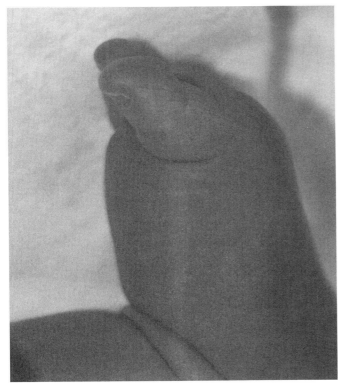

Turner syndrome

Turner syndrome has a prevalence of approximately 1 in 3,500 births (Gregor et al., 2009). Findings include:

- lymphedema in the newborn period (see Figure 7.9)
- neck webbing is common (see Figure 7.10)
- short stature
- subtle cognitive issues
- shield chest
- wide-spaced nipples
- coarctation of the aorta

Individuals with Turner syndrome can have mild difficulties in school. Many are picked up when being evaluated for delayed menarche. Lifespan is normal. If a mosaic state with a portion of 46, XY cells are noted, streak gonads may be present. This must be addressed immediately due to the high risk of gonadoblastoma formation.

Klinefelter syndrome

Individuals with Klinefelter syndrome do not have any clinical findings in the newborn period. They tend to present with infertility and gynecomastia. Typical findings include:

- hypogonadism

— small testes

— azoospermia

— oligospermia

- hyalinization and fibrosis of the seminiferous tubules
  — gynecomastia in late puberty
  — psychosocial problems

Endocrinologic findings include:

- low serum testosterone levels

- high luteinizing hormone (LH) and FSH levels

- frequently they can have elevated estradiol levels

- the decline in testosterone production is progressive over the life span, and not all men suffer from hypogonadism

Microdeletion Syndromes

Common microdeletion syndromes are shown in Figure 7.11 with their genomic locations. There can be variability in the size of these microdeletions, but they all have critical regions that need to be involved for the classical phenotype to be expressed.

FIGURE 7.11

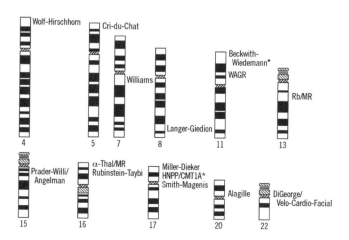

22q11.2.2 syndrome (DiGeorge/Velo-cardio-facial syndrome)

22q11.2 syndrome can present with a broad range of findings that can be primarily cardiac, which has been referred to as DiGeorge syndrome, or it can present with learning delays and velopalatal insufficiency as the only findings. Dysmorphic facial features occur in > 90% of cases; however, they can be subtle and include a long, narrow face; a tubular nose with a bulbous tip; narrow palpebral fissures; ear anomalies; and a small mouth. Developmental and learning disabilities also occur in > 90% of cases with math skills and social judgment the two areas most likely to be involved. Metal retardations can occur in 35% of cases. Hypernasal speech and velopalatal insufficiency are also seen in > 90% of cases, with cleft palate being a rare manifestation. Hypocalcemia and hypoparathyroidism occur in 65%, psychiatric disorders in 60%, recurrent seizures in 40%, and cardiac defects occur in 30%–40% of cases (Dagli & Williams, 2011; Kapadia & Bassett, 2008; Morris, 2006).

Williams syndrome

Williams syndrome is the result of a microdeleted segment on chromosome 7q. It has been noted to involve multiple systems including the cardiovascular, neurological, and endocrine systems. The cardiovascular involvement is an elastin arteriopathy that can involve any artery. Manifestations include narrowing of the arteries, but the most clinically significant and most common cardiovascular finding is supravalvular aortic stenosis. Supravalvular aortic stenosis occurs in approximately 75% of affected individuals. Peripheral pulmonic stenosis is common in infancy but is not specific to Williams syndrome.

The neurological manifestations can include cognitive deficits; however, these deficits can be masked by individuals' exceptional language skills. Some have average intelligence. Strengths also include verbal short-term memory; extreme weakness in visuospatial construction is typical. The Williams syndrome cognitive profile is independent of IQ. Individuals' personalities tend to include overfriendliness, empathy, generalized anxiety, and attention deficit disorder.

Individuals with Williams syndrome also have distinctive facial features and can include bitemporal narrowing, a broad brow, a stellate or lacy pattern to the iris, periorbital fullness, strabismus, a short nose, a full nasal tip, malar hypoplasia, long philtrum, full lips, wide mouth, malocclusion, a small jaw, and prominent earlobes, which can be observed at any age. Younger children have been noted to have transient findings that include epicanthal folds, full cheeks, and small and widely spaced teeth. Adults generally have a gaunt appearance with a long face and neck that tend to be more pronounced by sloping shoulders.

Endocrine manifestations include idiopathic hypercalcemia (15%), hypercalciuria (30%), hypothyroidism (10%), and early (but not precocious) puberty (50%). An increased frequency of subclinical hypothyroidism, abnormal oral glucose tolerance tests, and diabetes mellitus has been observed in adults with Williams syndrome.

Growth is characterized by prenatal growth deficiency, failure to thrive in infancy (70%), poor weight gain and linear growth in the first 4 years, a rate of linear growth that is 75% of normal in childhood, and a brief pubertal growth spurt. The mean adult height is below the third centile. Individuals can also have connective tissue involvement that includes a hoarse voice, inguinal/umbilical hernias, bowel/bladder diverticulae, rectal prolapse, joint limitation or laxity, and soft, lax skin.

Wolf-Hirschhorn syndrome

Wolf-Hirschhorn syndrome is associated with a microdeletion of the 4p region. The facial features tend to evolve over time. Early in life, individuals tend to have a broad nasal root that gives the appearance of a "Greek warrior helmet" appearance. As children approach puberty, this nasal root prominence tends to become less noticeable. Individuals with Wolf-Hirschhorn syndrome also have microcephaly, a high forehead, prominent glabella, ocular hypertelorism, epicanthal folds, highly arched eyebrows, a short philtrum, downturned mouth, micrognathia and unusually formed ears with tags or pits. Growth delays are typical and can be noted prenatally. The poor growth continues postnatally in all individuals.

Neurological involvement includes developmental delays and cognitive deficiency of a variable degree, but present in all. Gross motor delays are also seen and are associated with hypotonia.

Cri-du-chat syndrome

Cri-du-chat syndrome is so named because of the characteristic finding of a high-pitched catlike cry. This will lead one to strongly suspect Cri-du-chat syndrome. The condition is the result of a microdeletion in 5p. There are some individuals who also have a catlike cry without any other findings. These individuals can have a smaller deletion in the 5p region, and it tends to be confined in the 5p15.3 region. Additional clinical features include microcephaly, a round face, ocular hypertelorism, micrognathia, epicanthal folds, low-set ears, hypotonia, and severe psychomotor and mental retardation.

Langer-Giedion syndrome

Langer-Giedion syndrome is associated with a microdeletion in the chromosome region 8q. It is associated with characteristic craniofacial abnormalities that include laterally protruding ears, a broad nasal bridge, a bulbous nose, an elongated upper lip with a thin vermillion border, broad eyebrows, sparse hair, and mild microcephaly. Multiple cartilaginous exostoses are a characteristic association also. These are bony growths that project from the surface of various bones throughout the skeletal system. Cone-shaped epiphyses are also typical. Cognitive delays, short stature, increased joint flexibility, brittle nails, and excess folds of skin in infancy have also been associated with this syndrome.

Alpha-thalassemia/mental retardation syndrome

This syndrome is the result of a 16p microdeletion. These individuals can have short stature; microcephaly; a wide, flat, and broad forehead; a long philtrum; mild retrognathia; small ears; epicanthal folds; hypertelorism; downslanting palpebral fissures; ptosis; a flat, broad nasal bridge; a triangular nasal tip; anteverted nostrils; a high arched palate; a protruding tongue; tooth crowding; a short, webbed neck; asymmetric chest; abnormally positioned nipples; accessory nipples; a micropenis; hypospadias; cryptorchidism; finger clinodactyly; talipes equinovarus; and mild to moderate cognitive deficiency. The cardinal feature in alpha thalassemia is a microcytic, hypochromic anemia with hemoglobin H inclusions in red blood cells. Mild obesity and seizures are less common findings. One patient has been reported with a persistent patent ductus arteriosus.

Miller-Dieker syndrome

Miller-Dieker syndrome is associated with a microdeletion in 17p. Lissencephaly is the characteristic magnetic resonance imaging (MRI) finding. Typical features include a characteristic furrowing of the forehead and microcephaly, and the pregnancy may be complicated by polyhydramnios. Lifespan is limited, with death occurring by 2 years old in most children, with a few reaching 10 years. The oldest known individual with Miller-Dieker syndrome lived to 17 years old.

In lissencephaly, the cerebral gyri are absent or abnormally broad. The cerebral cortex is also thick, ranging from 12–20 mm with a normal cerebral cortex being 3–4 mm thick. Classic lissencephaly findings also include:

- cavum septi pellucidi et vergae

- mild hypoplasia of the corpus callosum (the anterior portion often appears flattened)

- mild vermis hypoplasia in some individuals with a normal brain stem and cerebellum

- the lateral ventricles are enlarged posteriorly

Subcortical band heterotopia can also be seen as a subcortical band of heterotopic gray matter, present just beneath the cortex. It is separated from the cortex by a thin zone of normal white matter. The subcortical bands are most often symmetric and diffuse, extending from the frontal to occipital regions; however, they may be asymmetric. Subcortical bands restricted to the frontal lobes are more typically associated with mutations of the *DCX* gene. Subcortical bands restricted to the posterior lobes are more typically associated with *LIS1* mutations. The gyral pattern is normal or demonstrates mildly simplified shallow sulci; a normal cortical ribbon is present.

Smith-Magenis syndrome

Smith-Magenis syndrome is associated with a deletion of 17p11.2. In the infantile period, mild to moderate hypotonia that can result in feeding difficulties has been noted. This may result in failure to thrive. Minor skeletal anomalies, brachydactyly, and short stature can be seen. Congenital cardiac defects and structural renal anomalies have been reported.

Hearing loss is variable, but speech delays are a more persistent finding. A peripheral neuropathy with decreased pain sensitivity, cognitive impairment (IQ 20–78), and developmental delays are also typical findings.

The most striking feature of Smith-Magenis syndrome is the distinct neurobehavioral phenotype, which includes a sleep disturbance in which individuals tend to sleep during the day and remain awake at night. Abnormal melatonin regulation appears to be the cause. Individuals also tend to engage in self-mutilation, pulling out fingernails and constant picking at the skin. Insertion of foreign bodies into body orifices and eating nonfood items can also be typical manifestations. Many of the features may not be apparent in infants and young children, so a clinical diagnosis can be difficult in those age groups. Single nucleotide polymorphism genomic microarray analysis detects 90% of cases. RAI1 gene sequencing and deletion/duplication analysis detects 5%–10% of cases.

Wilms tumor-aniridia-genital anomalies-retardation (WAGR)

Wilms tumor-aniridia-genital anomalies-retardation (WAGR) syndrome is associated with a deletion of the 11p13 region. There are two critical genes in the region, *PAX6* and *WT1*. There can be up to a 50% risk of developing a Wilms tumor with an increased incidence of bilateral involvement compared to those with isolated Wilms tumor. Those with WAGR also have an earlier age of diagnosis, but they have more favorable tumor histology and a better prognosis than those with isolated Wilms tumor.

Aniridia is almost always present in individuals with deletions encompassing the *PAX6* gene, and it is typically severe. There have been cases of deletions in the 11p13 region that do not include the *PAX6* gene and aniridia does not occur.

Up to 60% of males can have cryptorchidism. Additional genitourinary anomalies include uterine abnormalities, hypospadias, ambiguous genitalia, streak ovaries, urethral strictures, ureteral abnormalities, and gonadoblastoma.

Cognitive delays can be seen in 70% of individuals with IQ scores less than 74. Behavioral abnormalities can also be seen and include attention-deficit/hyperactivity disorder, autism spectrum disorders, anxiety, depression, and obsessive-compulsive disorder. Up to one third of individuals can have neurological involvement including hypertonia or hypotonia, epilepsy, enlarged ventricles, microcephaly, and agenesis of the corpus callosum.

End-stage renal disease risk is significant; Wilms tumor, focal segmental glomerulosclerosis, and occasional renal malformations can contribute to the increased risk. With unilateral Wilms tumor, the rate of end-stage renal disease is 36%, and it is 90% in those with bilateral Wilms tumor formation. Twenty-five percent of individuals can have variable proteinuria that can be overt nephritic syndrome in the more severe cases.

Obesity can also be a frequent manifestations of WAGR syndrome. Individuals can also have hemihypertrophy, facial dysmorphisms, growth delays, scoliosis, kyphosis, and occasionally, polydactyly and diaphragmatic hernia.

A cytogenetically visible deletion can be observed in approximately 60% of affected individuals. An additional 14% will have a microdeletion in the region with an unknown percentage having smaller contiguous gene deletions of the *PAX6* and *WT1* genes.

Rubinstein-Taybi syndrome

Rubinstein-Taybi syndrome has been associated with a microdeletion in the 16p13.3 region or, more commonly, a mutation in the *CREBBP* gene. Multiple dysmorphic features are seen in this condition and include the following: downslanting palpebral fissures, a beaked nose with the columella extending below the nares, a grimacing smile, high arched palate, and talon cusps, which are cusp-like structures on the lingual side of the maxillary incisors. However, the most characteristic features are the broad thumbs and great toes that can also be angulated. The distal phalanges may also appear broad. Almost all males have cryptorchidism, and structural anomalies of the urinary tract are typical findings also. Approximately one third of individuals with Rubinstein-Taybi syndrome have congenital cardiac anomalies. Failure to thrive is common, and adults typically have short stature. Obesity can be an issue in children or adolescents. Cognitive deficiency is also common with an average IQ of around 42, although some individuals score into the 70s. The gene that is critical for the presence of Rubinstein-Taybi syndrome is the *CREBBP* gene. Mutations can be found in this gene in approximately 30%–50% of individuals, with an additional 20% having an intragenic deletion/duplication. In only 10% of cases can one detect a microdeletion using fluorescence in situ hybridization. In an additional 3% of cases, mutations in the EP300 gene have been noted.

Alagille syndrome

Approximately 7% of individuals with Alagille syndrome have a deletion of the entire *JAG1* gene, detectable by genomic microarray analysis. Sequence analysis of *JAG1* DNA detects mutations in about 88% of individuals with Alagille syndrome. Less than 1% of individuals have been noted to have mutations in the *NOTCH2* gene. Clinical criteria have been established for the clinical diagnosis of Alagille syndrome.

The histologic finding of bile duct paucity (an increased portal tract-to-bile duct ratio) on liver biopsy has been considered to be the most important and constant feature of Alagille syndrome; however, bile duct paucity is not present in infancy in many individuals ultimately shown to have Alagille syndrome. In the newborn, a normal ratio of portal tracts to bile ducts, bile duct proliferation, or a picture suggestive of neonatal hepatitis may be observed. Overall, bile duct paucity is present in about 90% of individuals.

Three of the following five major clinical features, in addition to bile duct paucity, will establish a clinical diagnosis of Alagille syndrome:

- cardiac defect (most commonly stenosis of the peripheral pulmonary artery and its branches)
- characteristic facial features
- cholestasis
- ophthalmologic abnormalities (most commonly posterior embryotoxon)
- skeletal abnormalities (most commonly butterfly vertebrae identified in anterior-posterior chest radiographs)

In addition, abnormalities of the kidney, neurovasculature, and pancreas are important manifestations. The diagnosis of Alagille syndrome may be difficult due to the extreme range of expression of the clinical manifestations. The diagnosis of Alagille syndrome should be considered in individuals who do not meet the full clinical criteria but do have an affected first-degree relative. If an affected first-degree relative is identified, the presence of one or more features will establish a clinical diagnosis.

Retinoblastoma

Cytogenetic analysis of peripheral blood lymphocytes detects cytogenetically visible deletions or rearrangements involving 13q14.1-q14.2 in approximately 5% of individuals with unilateral retinoblastoma and approximately 7.5% of individuals with bilateral retinoblastoma. The diagnosis of retinoblastoma is usually established by examination of the fundus of the eye using indirect ophthalmoscopy. Computer tomography (CT), MRI, and ultrasonography are used to support the diagnosis and stage the tumor.

Unilateral retinoblastoma is present if only one eye is affected by retinoblastoma. Usually, in individuals with unilateral retinoblastoma, the tumor is also unifocal with only a single retinoblastoma tumor present. However, in most persons with unilateral retinoblastoma the tumor is large, and it is not possible to determine if the tumor represents only a single retinoblastoma.

Bilateral retinoblastoma is present if both eyes are affected by retinoblastoma. Usually, in individuals with bilateral retinoblastoma one or both eyes clearly show multifocal tumor growth with multiple retinoblastoma tumors present. A few individuals have multifocal tumors in one eye (unilateral multifocal retinoblastoma). Intraocular seeding (metastasizing) may mimic true multifocal tumor growth.

Trilateral retinoblastoma is present when bilateral (or, rarely, unilateral) retinoblastoma and a pinealoma co-occur.

Epigenetic/Imprinting Disorders

- Imprinting (repression): determination of the expression of a gene by its parental origin

- Results in monoallelic gene expression

- Mechanism of imprinting is unclear

- Methylation of DNA appears to play a major role in imprinting

- For some genes, imprinting is confined to certain tissues or certain stages of development

Uniparental disomy (UPD)

FIGURE 7.12 Uniparental Disomy

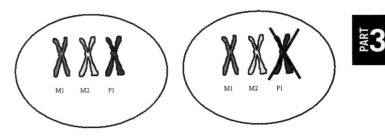

FIGURE 7.13 Normal Germline Imprinting on Chromosome 15

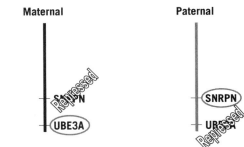

FIGURE 7.14 Angelman Syndrome: Paternal UPD 15

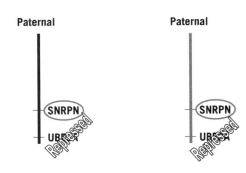

FIGURE 7.15 Angelman Syndrome: Maternal Deletion 15q11q13

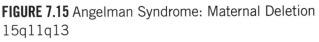
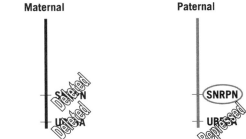

Angelman syndrome

Individuals with Angelman syndrome appear normal at birth, but begin manifesting developmental delays by 6–12 months old. This cognitive impairment progresses to severe mental retardation. One of the hallmark features of Angelman syndrome, in addition to microcephaly and seizures, is absence of speech. Individuals with Angelman syndrome do not acquire more than 6 words throughout their life. The brain is generally structurally normal on MRI or computer tomography (CT); however, individuals may have mild cortical atrophy or dysmelination. Another significant feature is ataxia and tremors of the limbs. Individuals with Angelman syndrome have a unique behavioral phenotype that includes frequent laughter and smiling, a happy demeanor, excitability with hand flapping, and other hypermotoric behaviors.

As noted, most patients have microcephaly and seizures. The microcephaly is seen by 2 years old and is acquired. Seizure is also typically present between 1 and 3 years old. Some patients also have the following:

- attraction to/fascination with water
- feeding problems during infancy
- hyperactive tendon reflexes
- hypopigmentation of the skin and eyes
- hypotonia
- increased sensitivity to heat, sleep disturbance
- strabismus
- tongue thrusting, sucking and swallowing disorders, frequent drooling, excessive chewing and mouthing
- uplifted, flexed arms during walking
- wide mouth, wide-spaced teeth, prominent mandible

In those with hypopigmentation, they typically have a deletion of the *Pigment* gene (15q11.2-q13) The *Pigment* gene encodes a tyrosine transporter (P protein) important in melanin synthesis. In rare cases, the hypopigmentation can be so severe that a form of albinism is suspected. Table 7.1 shows the various genetic anomalies that can result in Angelman syndrome.

Genetic Counseling in Angleman Syndrome

- The risk to sibs of an affected child who has a deletion or UPD, typically < 1% (see Figure 7.12). This can occur when there is a trisomy rescue in the embryo. The extra chromosome is lost, but may result in two paternal imprints of chromosome 15 and, consequently, Angelman syndrome (see Figures 7.13 and 7.14). Deletions can also result in Angelman syndrome (see Figure 7.15)

- A standard or high-resolution chromosome analysis should be offered to all to detect a chromosomal rearrangement, which will alter the recurrence risks

- An imprinting defect with deletion of IC, or a mutation of a gene: as high as 50% (i.e., *UBE3A*)

- Chromosome rearrangement depends on whether it is inherited or de novo

- Mothers of patients with deletions—tested for a possible balanced chromosomal rearrangement. Germline mosaicism for large deletions has been described

- Prenatal testing is possible when the underlying genetic mechanism is known

- Unknown etiology; undetected mutations in the regulatory region(s) of gene (UBE3A) or other unidentified mechanisms or gene(s) involved

TABLE 7.1 Risks to sibs of a proband with Angelman syndrome by genetic mechanism (Dagli & Williams, 2011)

MOLECULAR CLASS[1]	FAMILIES	GENETIC MECHANISM	RISK TO SIBS
Ia	65%–75%	5- to 7-Mb deletion	< 1%
Ib	< 1%	Unbalanced chromosome translocation or inherited small interstitial deletion	Possibly as high as 50%
IIa	3%–7%	Paternal UPD	< 1%
IIb	< 1%	Paternal UPD with predisposing parental translocation	Approaching 100% if father has a 15;15 Robertsonian translocation
IIIa	0.5%	ID with deletion in the IC	As high as 50% if mother also has IC deletion
IIIb	2.5%	ID without deletion in the IC	< 1%
IV	11%	*UBE3A* mutation	As high as 50% if mother also has a mutation
V	10%–15%	Other (no identifiable molecular abnormality)	Undetermined risk

Note. UPD = uniparental disomy; ID = imprinting defect; IC = imprinting center. From "Angelman Syndrome" by A. I. Dagli and C. A. Williams, 2011, *Gene Reviews.*

Prader-Willi syndrome

Prader-Willi syndrome has characteristic neonatal manifestations that include severe neonatal hypotonia with poor feeding. In rare cases the hypotonia may be mild and it will improve with age. Because of the feeding difficulties, failure to thrive is common in

FIGURE 7.17 Prader-Willi Syndrome: Maternal UPD 15

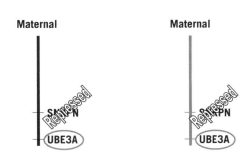

FIGURE 7.18 Prader-Willi Syndrome: Paternal Deletion 15q11q13

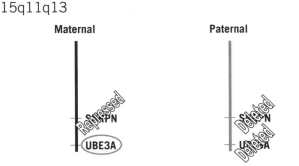

infancy. From 6 months to 6 years old there is a dramatic onset of weight gain and these individuals develop obesity. They also tend to have short stature; however, there have been cases of individuals who have been in the normal range for height. Figures 7.17 and 7.18 show the two genetic ways Prader-Willi syndrome can manifest.

The characteristic behavioral manifestation is an obsession over food. They will break into refrigerators and cabinets to eat and will wake up to eat overnight. Stealing food off the plate of other individuals is also commonly seen.

As individuals with Prader-Willi syndrome grow older, they will have noticeably small hands and feet. Major findings include:

- mild to moderate mental retardation (~90%)
- learning disabilities
- normal neuromuscular studies
- seizures

- poor gross motor coordination
- poor fine motor coordination
- global developmental delay
- behavioral problems
- sleep disturbances
- high pain threshold

Males will have:

- hypogonadotropic hypogonadism
- small penis
- scrotal hypoplasia
- cryptorchidism

Even though the SNRPN gene has been used as a marker in the critical region for Prader-Willi syndrome, it is not thought to be causative for some forms of Prader-Willi syndrome, unlike the UBE3A gene in Angelman syndrome.

Genetic counseling in Prader-Willi syndrome

- The risk to sibs of an affected child who has a deletion or UPD, typically < 1%

TABLE 7.2 Testing for Prader-Willi syndrome

TEST METHODS	MUTATIONS DETECTED	PERCENT OF INDIVIDUALS
Methylation analysis	Methylation abnormality	99%
Fluorescence in situ hybridization/ Quantitative PCR	Deletion of PWCRa	70%
Uniparental disomy studies	UPD of PWCR	25%
Sequence analysisb	Imprinting center defect	< 1%

Note. PWCR = Prader-Willi critical region.

aDeletion varies in size, but always includes the PWCR.

bSequence analysis detects small deletions that account for about 15% of imprinting center mutations. The majority of imprinting defects are epimutations (i.e., alterations in the imprint, not the DNA).

- A standard or high-resolution chromosome analysis should be offered to all, to detect a chromosomal rearrangement, which will alter the recurrence risks
- An imprinting defect with deletion of IC, as high as 50%
- Chromosome rearrangement depends on whether it is inherited or de novo
- Fathers of patients with deletions: tested for a possible balanced chromosomal rearrangement. Germline mosaicism for large deletions has been described.
- Prenatal testing is possible when the underlying genetic mechanism is known
- Unknown etiology: Unknown genes or other unidentified mechanisms or gene(s) involved

Beckwith-Wiedemann syndrome

Beckwith-Wiedemann syndrome (BWS) is another disorder that has been associated with imprinting defects. A consensus for clinical criteria has not yet been established; however, having three of the following criteria would be consistent with the diagnosis:

- positive family history (one or more family members with a clinical diagnosis of BWS or a history or features suggestive of BWS)
- macrosomia (traditionally defined as height and weight > 97th centile)
- anterior linear ear lobe creases/posterior helical ear pits
- macroglossia
- omphalocele (also called exomphalos)/ umbilical hernia
- visceromegaly involving one or more intra-abdominal organs including liver, spleen, kidneys, adrenal glands, and pancreas
- embryonal tumor (e.g., Wilms tumor, hepatoblastoma, neuroblastoma, rhabdomyosarcoma) in childhood

- hemihyperplasia (asymmetric overgrowth of one or more regions of the body)

- adrenocortical cytomegaly

- renal abnormalities including structural abnormalities, nephromegaly, and nephrocalcinosis

- cleft palate (rare)

In regard to management, up to 7.5% of individuals with BWS develop a tumor during the first 8 years of life and can include:

- Wilms tumor

- hepatoblastoma

- adrenal carcinoma

- gonadoblastoma

Tumor incidence decreases after 8 years old and is equivalent to population risk. BWS is primarily a syndrome of childhood. As affected children become older, the clinical findings disappear and they tend to "grow into" their macroglossia and macrosomia. Intelligence and development are normal. Molecular genetic testing can account for up to 75% of cases without a family history and up to 99% of cases with a family history.

Russell-Silver syndrome

Individuals with Russell-Silver syndrome can be noted to have intrauterine growth retardation. Consequently, in the neonatal period, they are small for gestational age and have persistent failure to thrive. Additional findings include:

- normal head circumference with height and weight < 5th centile

- lateral asymmetries

- fasting hypoglycemia

- occasional growth hormone deficiency

- frontal bossing and micrognathia result in triangular face

- cardiac

- hypospadias, posterior urethral valves

- Wilms and other tumors

Russell-Silver syndrome has multiple etiologies, like many conditions associated with epigenetic etiologies. The following causes have been established:

- UPD7 7%–10%

- H19 locus on chromosome 11 ~35%

- genetically heterogeneous

As noted previously, current testing is able to confirm an etiology using molecular genetic testing in less than 50% of cases.

Chapter Summary

This chapter on genetic disorders and their impact in the early years has discussed inborn errors of metabolism, chromosomal aneuploidies, common genomic microdeletion syndromes, and epigenetic syndromes. In particular, the authors have described medical and developmental components of these disorders and anomalies that professionals in the medical, clinical, and educational fields should be aware of in terms of prevention, treatment, and the need for family counseling and/or referral for early intervention services.

Key Points to Remember

- Newborns with metabolic disorders will typically appear well at birth, but will experience deterioration in days to weeks.

- Symptoms of inborn errors of metabolism can be similar to sepsis in newborns, so if initial testing does not support an infectious process, consider a metabolic disorder.

- The period of time until the onset of hypoglycemia can be helpful in determining the underlying etiology of the hypoglycemia.

- Cytogenetic anomalies should be considered in individuals with multiple congenital anomalies.

- DNA methylation analysis is the most sensitive initial test in evaluating for Prader-Willi and Angelman syndromes.

Implications for Families and Professionals

Early detection of inborn errors of metabolism is critical to implementation of life-saving therapies in the majority of cases. Even with newborn screening, results can take up to a week to return, and suspicion of an inborn error of metabolism can allow for acute management while waiting for newborn screening results. Also, the timely identification of cytogenetic anomalies allows for prompt initiation of early intervention services in order to maximize the potential of individuals as they grow older. Although many of these conditions are rare, keeping them in mind can have a profound impact on the clinical course of affected individuals.

References

Dagli, A. I., & Williams, C. A. (1998, updated 2011, June 16). Angelman syndrome. In R. S. Pagon, M. P. Adams, H. H. Ardinger, S. E. Wallace, A. Amemiya, L. J. H. Bean, … K. Stephens. (Eds), *GeneReviews* [Internet]. Seattle, WA: University of Washington. Retrieved from www.ncbi.nlm.nih.gov/books/NBK1116

Girard, J. (1990). Metabolic adaptations to change of nutrition at birth. *Biology of the Neonate, 58*(1), 3–15.

Gregor, V., Sipek, A., Sipek, A., Jr., Horacek, J., Langhammer, P., Petrzikova, L., & Calda, P. (2009). Prenatal diagnostics of chromosomal aberrations Czech Republic: 1994–2007. *Ceska Gynekologie, 74*(1), 44–54.

Kapadia, R. K., & Bassett, A. S. (2008). Recognizing a common genetic syndrome: 22q11.2 deletion syndrome. *Canadian Medical Association Journal, 178*(4), 391–393.

Morris, C. A. (2006, April 21). Williams syndrome. In R.A. Pagon, M. P. Adams, H. H. Ardinger, S. E. Wallace, A. Amemiya, L. J. H. Bean,…K. Stephens.(Eds.), *GeneReviews* [Internet]. Seattle, WA: University of Washington, Retrieved from www.ncbi.nlm.nih.gov/books/NBK1249

Owen, O. E., Reichard, G. A., Jr., Patel, M. S., & Boden, G. (1979). Energy metabolism in feasting and fasting. *Advances in Experimental Medicine and Biology, 111*, 169–188.

Savva, G. M., Walker, K., & Morris, J. K. (2010). The maternal age-specific live birth prevalence of trisomies 13 and 18 compared to trisomy 21 (Down syndrome). *Prenatal Diagnosis, 30*(1), 57–64.

van Gameren-Oosterom, H. B., Buitendijk, S. E., Bilardo, C. M., van der Pal-de Bruin, K. M., van Wouwe, J. P., & Mohango, A. D. (2012). Unchanged prevalence of Down syndrome in the Netherlands: Results from an 11-year nationwide birth cohort. *Prenatal Diagnosis*, August 6, 1–6.

Ward Platt, M., & Deshpande, S. (2005). Metabolic adaptation at birth. *Seminars in Fetal Neonatal Medicine*, 10341–10350.

CHAPTER 8

Hearing: Development and Disorders

Joaquim M. B. Pinheiro

Highlights of the Chapter

At the conclusion of this chapter, the reader will:

- understand the normal development of hearing

- understand the major causes of hearing impairment and their functional consequences

- be able to apply results of screening and diagnostic evaluations toward the development of effective interventions in infancy and early childhood

- integrate medical, surgical, and educational intervention plans to optimize outcomes of individual children in their family context

In recent decades, technological and social currents have substantially increased individual access to verbal and visual forms of communication. Consequently, the effective and efficient reception, processing, and transmission of information have assumed greater importance in modern society. Optimal hearing abilities have become critical to individual development and social functioning. Parallel with the increased demand for communication capabilities, technological advances are enabling the detection and treatment of hearing impairments in early infancy. Concomitantly, the understanding of neurosensory development and its interactions with the physical and social environment continues to evolve. This will influence the nature of therapeutic interventions and the roles of the family and the educational system in such interventions.

Normal Development of Hearing

The critical steps in the functional development of the auditory system take place during the second half of intrauterine gestation (Graven, 2011; Lasky & Williams, 2005). Infants born preterm during this period of auditory development are exposed to extrauterine physiologic instability, adverse effects of life-sustaining therapies, and extemporaneous influences of the physical environment; they are thus at particular risk for mal-development in the auditory system and for consequent deficits in hearing and speech. Among neonatal intensive care unit (NICU) graduates, the incidence of hearing impairment is at least 10-fold greater than in the population at large.

Structure and Function

The auditory system comprises three functionally related sets of structures: peripheral elements, including the outer, middle, and inner ears; the auditory nerves (cranial nerve VIII); and the auditory regions of the brain. The outer ear of the neonate features a narrow canal with thin cartilage, which is readily blocked and compressed. The middle ear reaches adult size by mid-gestation, but the ossicles remain cartilaginous until about 32 weeks gestation. Cochlear structures, including inner and outer hair cells (OHCs in Figure 8.1), are fully developed by 25 weeks gestation, by which time myelination is developing from the brainstem to the higher levels of the auditory pathways. The cochlea is more than a passive transducer of acoustic wave energy into electrical impulses, which occurs in the inner hair cells; normal outer hair cells adjust reflexively to sound input, thereby producing frequency-specific echo sounds denominated otoacoustic emissions (OAE).

Functional hearing in the human fetus appears at 25–27 weeks gestation; physiological responses to low-frequency sounds are consistently detectable beyond that age. Maturation of responses to sound frequencies and decreasing sound-pressure-level thresholds continue during the third trimester and early postnatal weeks.

The nearly complete functional maturation of hearing in the newborn infant occurs because of structural changes in the outer and middle ears, as well as increased myelination of auditory axons; the latter is manifested by increased conduction velocities and wave amplitudes on brainstem evoked response (e.g., auditory brainstem response [ABR]) tests.

FIGURE 8.1 Chronology of anatomic and functional auditory development

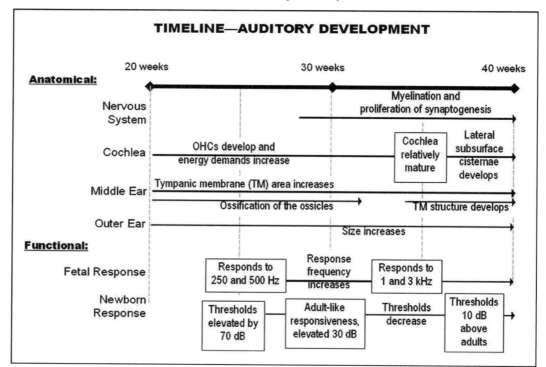

Note. Arrows denote continuing development in infancy. PMA: postmenstrual age; TM: tympanic membrane; IHCs: inner hair cells; OHCs: outer hair cells; ABR: auditory brainstem responses. Concept based on Lasky (Lasky & Williams, 2005) and Graven (Graven & Browne, 2008).

Psycho-biological research suggests that newborn hearing is conditioned by intrauterine exposure to sounds, and it is preferentially tuned to the baby's own mother's voice. Plasticity in the neuronal architecture of the auditory cortex is present during late fetal and early infant stages, so that structural development is conditioned by the acoustic environment. Research in animal models has shown that either auditory deprivation or exposure to loud noises during these periods can induce abnormalities in auditory synaptic morphology and auditory discrimination abilities (Kral & O'Donoghue, 2010). The relevance of this concept to the management of congenital hypoacusis (impaired hearing sensitivity) in humans was first demonstrated by Yoshinaga-Itano, Coulter, and Thomson (2000), who showed that early identification and treatment of infants with congenital hearing loss in the first 6 months promotes improved receptive and expressive language development.

Types and Causes of Hearing Impairment

Hearing impairment can be classified based on its anatomical substrate or according to its specific etiologic diagnosis.

Causes of Hearing Impairment

Based on the anatomical location of the hearing dysfunction, hearing loss can be classified as conductive, sensorineural, or neural. *Conductive hearing loss* is characterized by blockage of sound transmission in the outer or middle ear due to permanent conditions such as anatomical malformations or transient problems such as fluid or debris. *Sensorineural hearing loss* entails the failure of sound transduction in the inner and OHCs of the cochlea and of transmission through the auditory nerve. Neural hearing loss, also known as *auditory neuropathy* or *auditory*

dyssynchrony, is characterized by dysfunction of the inner hair cells and auditory nerve, whereas OAE from the OHCs remain intact. *Mixed hearing loss* combines conductive with sensorineural hearing deficits.

In addition to the neurophysiologic classifications, described above, hearing loss can be further categorized according to its severity (i.e., mild, moderate, severe, or profound), based on the sound pressure level of the individual's hearing threshold. Finally, hearing loss can be unilateral or bilateral.

Etiologies underlying dysfunction of the components of hearing system are varied. Current evidence implicates genetic factors as directly causing or predisposing to hearing loss in more than 50% of young children (Morton & Nance, 2006). The primary etiologies of permanent hearing loss in infants are listed as primary risk factors in the 2007 Position Statement of the American Academy of Pediatrics Joint Committee on Infant Hearing (Table 8.1; Joint Committee on Infant Hearing, 2007). These varied causes result in clinical presentations of hearing loss that can be congenital, of delayed onset, and/or progressive in nature.

The incidence of permanent hearing loss in neonates ranges between 1.4 and 3 per 1,000 births in the United States. (Dalzell et al., 2000; Gaffney, Eichwald, Grouse, & Mason, 2010; Morton & Nance, 2006). With progressive or new-onset hearing loss, the prevalence of permanent sensorineural hearing loss increases during childhood to estimated rates of about 2.7 per 1,000 in 4-year-old children and 3.5 per 1,000 in adolescents (Morton & Nance, 2006).

Approximately two thirds of congenital hypoacusis cases have underlying genetic cause (Morton & Nance, 2006). Mutations in the connexin 26 gene (*GJB2*), predominantly the 35delG point mutation, account for 20% of congenital deafness. An additional 44% of congenital deafness is due to other genetic causes, with one

TABLE 8.1 Risk factors and/or conditions associated with hearing loss

Caregiver concern* regarding hearing, speech, language, or developmental delay.
Family history* of permanent childhood hearing loss.
Neonatal intensive care of more than 5 days or any of the following regardless of length of stay: ECMO*, assisted ventilation, exposure to ototoxic medications (gentamicin and tobramycin) or loop diuretics (furosemide/Lasix), and hyperbilirubinemia that requires exchange transfusion.
In utero infections such as cytomegalovirus (CMV)*, herpes, rubella, syphilis, and toxoplasmosis.
Craniofacial anomalies, including those that involve the pinna, ear canal, ear tags, ear pits, and temporal bone anomalies.
Physical findings, such as white forelock, that are associated with a syndrome known to include a senorineural or permanent coductive hearing loss.
Syndromes associated with hearing loss or progressive or late-onset hearing loss*, such as neurofibromatosis, osteopetrosis, and Usher syndrome; other frequently identified syndromes include Waardenburg, Alport, Pendred, and Jervell and Lange-Nielson.
Neurodegenerative disorders*, such as Hunter syndrome, or sensory motor neuropathies, such as Friedreich ataxia and Carcot-Marie-Tooth syndrome.
Culture-positive postnatal infections associated with sensorineural hearing loss*, including confirmed bacterial and viral (especially herpes viruses and varicella) meningitis.
Head trauma, especially basal skull/temporal bone fracture* that requires hospitalization.
Chemotherapy*
Recurrent or persistent otitis media for at least 3 months.

Note. Asterisks (*) indicate conditions that may not be diagnosed on a neonatal hearing screen.

third of these being related to one of numerous recognizable syndromes and two thirds being nonsyndromic. Most nonsyndromic hearing loss cases follow an autosomal recessive inheritance pattern (*DFNB*), whereas a minority are autosomal dominant (*DFNA*); X-linked and mitochondrial inheritance are rare. Although numerous gene mutations have been associated

with these patterns, it is important to note that about 95% of congenitally deaf infants are born to parents with normal hearing; therefore, a negative family history of deafness does not help to exclude the possibility of hereditary hearing loss. In fact, an infant who is newly diagnosed may serve as the index case that prompts genetic counseling for the family.

However, a family history of hearing loss should trigger continued monitoring of the infant, even if the neonatal hearing screen is negative; a formal follow-up audiologic assessment should be performed by 24 to 30 months old. The rationale for this is exemplified by Pendred syndrome, an autosomal recessive condition, often due to *SLC26A4* mutation. Pendred syndrome accounts for only 3% of deafness diagnosed from birth, but it will comprise 12% of the cases of deafness in the preschool population. Although deafness occurs early, goiter, the other clinically obvious component of the syndrome, does not present until late childhood. Likewise, deafness associated with mitochondrial mutations or other neurodegenerative disorders, such as Friedrich ataxia, may first manifest beyond early infancy. Usher syndrome is another familial disorder in which progressive hearing loss occurs; it is also characterized by progressive retinitis pigmentosa leading to blindness. Clinical suspicion of other syndromes associated with hearing loss, for example, Jervell and Lange-Nielsen syndrome presenting with cardiac dysrhythmias due to a prolonged QT interval, should prompt reevaluation of hearing function. Isolated malformations of craniofacial structures derived from the first and second branchial arches, even when they are not suspected of having syndromic or genetic associations, are embryologically related to the development of the inner ear and are thus a risk factor for hearing loss.

Acute or subacute medical conditions, including infections and ototoxic exposures, account for 35% of neonatal deafness and 40% of deafness in preschoolers. In about 40% of this etiologic group, the presence of risk factors is obvious, be it prolonged neonatal intensive care, hyperbilirubinemia requiring exchange transfusion, cardiopulmonary bypass, basal skull fractures, infectious meningitis or encephalitis, or chemotherapy. On the other hand, cytomegalovirus (CMV) infection is responsible for more cases of hearing loss than all the other acute medical conditions combined. Furthermore, the majority of CMV infections are clinically unapparent, even though they cause progressive hearing loss that may not manifest until late infancy.

Overall, about half of childhood deafness is progressive or of delayed onset. Medical screening systems cannot detect many such cases in a timely manner. Consequently, caregiver concerns regarding hearing, speech, language, or developmental delay (the risk factor listed first in Table 8.1) assume an important role in the early detection of such cases. Even with contemporary health care and after having passed a hearing screen, more than two thirds of children with subsequent hearing loss were identified following parental concern and school hearing screens (Dedhia, Kitsko, Sabo, & Chi, 2013).

Conditions in which auditory impairment is combined with visual impairment are particularly disabling to communication and psychosocial functions, as illustrated by Usher and Mohr-Tranebjaerg syndromes. A more common association exists with autism spectrum disorder (ASD), which occurs in about 7% of 8-year-old children with visual or auditory impairment. It is notable that the clinical diagnosis of hearing or visual deficits has resulted in a substantial delay in the diagnosis of the co-occurring ASD (Kancherla, Van Naarden Braun, & Yeargin-Allsopp, 2013).

Functional Consequences of Impairments

Congenital or neonatally acquired permanent hearing loss adversely impacts expressive and receptive language development and, consequently, diminishes eventual academic achievement and social development. As previously noted, these sequelae can be mitigated by identification, etiologic diagnosis, and appropriate therapeutic intervention within the first 6 months of life (Yoshinaga-Itano et al., 2000). Therefore, the age of 6 months represents a critical target for initial interventions in infants with hearing loss, in order to optimize functional outcomes (Moon, 2011).

The functional consequences of hearing loss in an individual depend on the age of onset and on the specific subcategory of the hearing loss, as described previously. Although bilateral hypoacusis is most concerning, even unilateral hearing loss may affect language and educational performance (Lieu, Tye-Murray, Karzon, & Piccirillo, 2010). The effects of milder transient or reversible hearing dysfunction such as that related to external ear debris in newborns, persistent otitis media with effusion, or auditory neuropathy in severe hyperbilirubinemia, remain unknown.

Screening in Newborns and Young Children

Because the frequency, functional impact, and response to therapy of hearing impairments are greatest in early infancy, the potential benefits of screening are maximized when it is performed in the newborn period. The logistics of population screening that maximize compliance, efficiency, and cost-effectiveness are most easily applicable in the hospital setting. Screening can be based on risk factors identified from the family history, plus exposure to medical conditions occurring

PART **3**

during fetal or neonatal life, and physical findings obtained through observation or imaging. Because this approach lacks sensitivity, screening that evaluates physiologic function is desirable.

In neonatal hearing screening, neurophysiologic tests including OAE and ABR can reliably detect hearing loss. Neither test requires an active response from the infant; indeed, they perform best in sleeping infants with a quiet environment. These tests are cost-effective for universal screening, given the relatively high incidence and consequences of neonatal hypoacusis. OAE tests detect the reflex, echo-like sound responses produced by cochlear OHCs when stimulated by clicks across multiple frequencies. These test results are abnormal in conductive or sensorineural hearing loss. However, they may be normal (i.e., false negative) in cases of purely neural, retro-cochlear hearing dysfunction, such as auditory neuropathy. Because such cases are most likely to be found in the NICU setting, it is recommended that only ABR screening should be used in NICUs (Joint Committee on Infant Hearing, 2007). Because OAE testing is easy and less expensive to perform, it is often used to screen healthy newborns. Some hospitals utilize a two-stage protocol with ABR screening following OAE test failures, in order to minimize the rate of false-positive screens.

Automated auditory brainstem response (AABR) screening uses scalp electrodes to detect the VIIIth cranial nerve and auditory brainstem pathway responses to sound stimuli, applying automated algorithms to define hearing thresholds. ABR screening is sensitive to abnormalities in conductive, sensorineural, or purely neural hearing losses.

Neonatal hearing screening programs result in failure rates ranging from 0.5% to 4%. Of these screening failures, 50% to 80% are false positives for subsequently diagnosed permanent hearing loss (Morton & Nance, 2006). Although false-negative neonatal hearing screens are exceedingly uncommon, such tests cannot detect progressive or later onset hearing loss in childhood, which is as common as neonatal hearing loss. Infants at risk for such conditions require subsequent rescreening and follow-up, as discussed later.

Screening Follow-Up and Diagnosis

As previously noted, therapeutic interventions for neonatal hearing loss are most effective when instituted by 6 months old. Consequently, the Joint Committee on Infant Hearing promotes the "1-3-6" principle of screening-diagnosis-therapy for neonatal hearing loss, according to which all infants should undergo hearing screening by 1 month old, and those who fail their screens should have a diagnostic evaluation by an audiologist no later than 3 months old. Infants whose hearing loss is confirmed should receive therapy appropriate to their specific diagnosis by 6 months old (Joint Committee on Infant Hearing, 2007).

The primary obstacle to the effectiveness of neonatal hearing screening in the U.S. is the 46% loss to follow-up in infants who had failed their neonatal screen.(Gaffney et al., 2010) This represents a failure of the health care and social systems to provide necessary care to these infants, whose likelihood of having a true hearing deficit is between 15% and 50%, depending on the screening protocol used. Primary care providers in the medical home (i.e., the coordinating center for medical and health-related care) have a critical role in ensuring that these infants receive the appropriate diagnostic testing in a timely manner. Major barriers to follow-up include ineffective communication of screening results, inadequate education of families regarding the importance of screening failures (which may have been deemed "referrals"), and lack of access to hearing diagnostic services for infants.

Early Hearing Detection and Intervention (EHDI) programs, driven by professional organizations such as the American Academy of Pediatrics and supported by federal health agencies, have been implemented by many state health departments in association with EI programs. EHDI programs serve as coordinating centers for gathering data (ultimately shared with the Centers for Disease Control and Prevention), communicating with major stakeholders, and providing resources aimed at maximizing the success of the screening programs. A major focus of EHDI programs presently is the minimization of losses to follow-up in screening programs. Algorithms aimed at simplifying decision making by practitioners involved in follow-up are available through the websites of these programs and related organizations. (Some relevant resources including links to EHDI and other websites with information for practitioners and families are provided at the end of this chapter.)

Follow-up could be improved, using currently available technological solutions, including documentation of hearing screening results in electronic medical records, and automated communication of test results from hospitals to the medical homes and EHDI programs (preferably coordinated with other neonatal screening test results); also, tele-audiology could expand the availability of diagnostic testing for infants and their families (Marcin & Simon, 2014).

Diagnostic hearing tests measure age-appropriate physiological and behavioral responses to sound stimuli. The most common tests are listed in Table 8.2 below.

TABLE 8.2 Diagnostic hearing tests

TEST	PHYSIOLOGIC PRINCIPLE	TYPE OF HEARING LOSS DETECTED
Diagnostic auditory brainstem responses (DABR)	As in AABR (see section on screening, above), evoked potentials in DABR reflect the electrical activity from the entire auditory pathway, including auditory nerve and brainstem apparatus. Wave latencies and amplitudes are evaluated, rather than fit to automated algorithms.	Conductive Sensorineural Neural
Tympanometry	Immitance testing evaluates intactness and mobility of the tympanic membrane and associated middle ear and ossicles in response to changing pressure in the ear canal.	Conductive
Acoustic reflex	Measures increased middle-ear stiffness due to contraction of the stapedius and tensor tympani in response to loud sounds.	Conductive Sensorineural Neural
Vision reinforcement audiometry (VRA) (6–30 months corrected age)	VRA measures turning responses to sounds associated with visual stimuli.	Conductive Sensorineural Neural
Conditioned play audiometry (CPA) (> 2.5–4.5 years)	In CPA, the child is trained to appropriately move specific objects in response to sounds.	Conductive Sensorineural Neural
Standard audiometry (> 4.5 years)	Measures the child's behavioral responses to a variety of sounds.	Conductive Sensorineural Neural

When a diagnostic test such as diagnostic auditory brainstem responses confirms hearing loss, a battery of tests is indicated to evaluate the integrity of the full auditory pathway and to determine hearing sensitivity across the relevant frequency range. In addition to the tests listed in Table 8.2, a diagnostic battery may include full OAE testing and imaging or other evaluations necessary to define the etiology of hearing loss and appropriate therapies.

Progressive and late-onset hearing losses are not detected by neonatal screening, as discussed previously. Accordingly, the Joint Committee on Infant Hearing of the American Academy of Pediatrics has emphasized the need for a risk-factor-based rescreening (see Table 8.2), even if the infants at risk passed the universal newborn screen (Harlor, Bower, Committee on Practice and Ambulatory Medicine, & Section on Otolaryngology–Head and Neck Surgery, 2009; Joint Committee on Infant Hearing, 2007). Although the timing and number of hearing reevaluations should be individualized, infants with a risk factor should have at least one post-neonatal diagnostic audiologic evaluation by 24 to 30 months old. Children diagnosed with CMV infection or syndromes associated with progressive hearing loss may need more frequent reevaluations. Diagnostic services should be provided by audiologists with expertise and equipment appropriate for evaluating infants.

When permanent hearing loss is confirmed, the primary care physician should coordinate further diagnostic evaluation to define the etiology of the hearing loss and possible comorbidities. This should include consultation with an otolaryngologist experienced in pediatric hearing loss, and an ophthalmologist with expertise in evaluating infants. In addition, a genetics consultation should be offered to the family.

Although the logistics of universal screening for the most frequent gene mutations associated with hearing loss (e.g., *GJB2*) are still problematic, selective genetic testing for etiologic diagnosis is available. Such testing can also provide presymptomatic diagnosis in family members, and it may eventually guide therapy.

Medical and Educational Interventions

There are two main classes of intervention. Medical, including surgical, treatments usually involve hearing support devices, whereas educational interventions rely heavily on work with the family and educators.

Medical and Surgical Treatments

Following the diagnostic testing previously described, the primary care physician needs to coordinate referrals for appropriate medical and surgical therapies, as well as community-based interventions. Input from otolaryngology, audiology, and speech-language pathology, as well as awareness of local EI program (EIP) resources are needed to help the family choose communication goals and the interventions required to achieve it. Development of an Individual Family Service Plan (IFSP) is a first step in ensuring that the infant receives appropriate services no later than 6 months old (Joint Committee on Infant Hearing of the American Academy of Pediatrics et al., 2013). In addition to preventing loss to follow-up before diagnosis, the medical home must also promote timely therapeutic follow-up, given that only 39% of infants with hearing loss had been fit with hearing aids by 6 months (Spivak, Sokol, Auerbach, & Gershkovich, 2009). It is important to establish appropriate initial therapy during the sensitive period for hearing development, to take advantage of plasticity of the auditory cortex, and to optimize cross-modal (e.g., auditory and verbal) input into language acquisition.

In addition to the coordinating functions, the medical home must provide continuing surveillance for common conditions such as otitis media with effusion, which may affect hearing acuity and necessitate unanticipated audiologic reevaluation, adjustments to existing amplification, or tympanostomy tubes. Close monitoring of developmental milestones is also essential.

Modes of Communication

The choice of a preferred mode of communication is necessarily family centered, and it may change over time, depending on the child's functional hearing, development, available interventions, and social environment factors. Five options are currently available. *Auditory-verbal communication* uses only optimized listening skills. *Auditory-oral communication* uses residual hearing with amplification, supported visually by speech reading. *Cued speech* combines listening with visual cues from eight hand shapes near the face. Whereas the goal for these three communication modes is spoken language, the other two use sign language, with or without speech. *American Sign Language* can be learned by deaf children, with English as a second language. *Total communication* combines all modes of communication toward simultaneous use of speech and sign language.

Hearing Support Devices

Hearing aids consist of a miniaturized microphone and amplifier, which can be worn in or behind the ear. Ear molds can be custom-fitted, even in neonates, and changed as the infant grows. Similarly, tuning of the amplifier to the individual infant's needs is performed by the audiologist so that it provides the appropriate gain across a range of frequencies.

Frequency-modulated (FM) devices include a microphone and low-power FM radio transmitter worn by a parent or teacher, plus an FM receiver worn by the child, which relays the signal to the hearing aid or cochlear implant. These systems enable hearing selected sources in noisy environments such as classrooms, or within a 50-foot range.

Cochlear implants transduce sound waves into frequency-specific electrical signals that are delivered to residual functioning auditory nerve fibers. They can be placed in children as young as 1 year old with profound hearing loss and after 18 months in children with severe to profound bilateral sensorineural hearing loss, when amplification alone is inadequate. The device produces the greatest benefit toward speech development when inserted by 7 years old. Hearing loss due to auditory neuropathy responds particularly poorly to amplification, and early cochlear implantation may be advantageous in these conditions. Patients with cochlear implants are at increased risk for bacterial meningitis, particularly with *Streptococcus pneumoniae*, and thus they should be immunized according to a high-risk schedule and monitored for early signs of meningitis associated with otitis media or other infections.

Educational Interventions

The educational setting still has a role in helping to identify children with hearing loss. Even with contemporary health care and after having passed a hearing screen, more than two thirds of children later diagnosed with hearing loss were identified following parental concern and school hearing screens (Dedhia et al., 2013).

Students with disabilities who are qualified for special education services must receive an Individual Education Plan (IEP, or Section 504 plan) which is essential to optimize each student's achievement. Placement in an inclusive or special education setting should consider the student's

PART 3

needs and abilities as well as the resources available in each setting. Parents and educators (including an expert in education of students with hearing loss) must develop this plan, with support from the medical home. Adaptations in the learning environment may involve the student, teachers, modes of communication, and the physical design of the classroom, as well as curricular modifications, including supplemental instruction. Examples of such adaptations include an optimal amplification system, visual assistive devices (e.g., Communication Access Realtime Translation), optimal seating arrangements, and individualized communication with the student, as well as the use of an interpreter, assistance with asynchronous learning (from new vocabulary provided in advance of the session to a buddy system for note taking), and alternative testing methods. In addition, there are various options for supplemental instruction including sign language and support from deaf or hard of hearing role models. Beyond the classroom, mobile text messaging and Internet-based technologies such as e-mail are obviously useful. Continuous evaluation is essential for optimal adjustment and coordination of the educational accommodations over time. Numerous books and other resources address education of students with hearing loss, which is evolving rapidly; see Resources at the end of this chapter for links to sample useful websites (e.g., through Supporting Success for Children With Hearing Loss).

Working With Families

About 95% of deaf infants are born into families with normal hearing. Consequently, families need substantial professional guidance in developing the initial clinical, social, and home environment systems that will support optimal outcomes for their child.

Coordination of multidisciplinary referrals for evaluation and therapeutic planning will help the family access the necessary services to meet the 1-3-6 goals. Earlier diagnosis and enrollment in intervention services was associated with improved speech and language scores at 5 years old (Moeller, 2000; Yoshinaga-Itano et al., 2000), which were also positively correlated with high levels of family involvement in the intervention process (Moeller, 2000).

The family must have a predominant role in choosing the initial modes of communication, and must be able to optimally communicate with the child, using speech (with assistive strategies as needed) and sign language, if so desired. Even with cochlear implants, auditory and nonauditory cognitive processes differ from those in hearing children of the same age, and require individualized attention to learning and communication tasks. For example, treated deaf children continue to perform suboptimally in memory processes such as encoding phonologic, or written inputs, retrieving verbal information, as well as in visual-sequence learning (Kennedy et al., 2006; Kral & O'Donoghue, 2010). Assistance from the family in optimizing the school environment in close coordination with the home environment is crucial.

Because approximately 40% of infants with hearing loss are NICU graduates, they may be at risk for additional neurosensory or general health problems that can impact neurodevelopment. The increased frequency of co-occurring ASD in children who also have hearing loss or vision impairment (Kancherla et al., 2013) highlights the potential complexity of care for some affected children. In order to make the necessary diagnostic and therapeutic services as well as home, community, and educational support resources available to children with hearing and/or visual impairments and their families, referral for assistance through Medicaid or other insurance providers should occur early. Finally, diagnosing the underlying cause of hearing loss in the child may directly impact other family members, either because of genetic implications of a diagnosis that they might share (see Types and Causes section above), or the psychological burdens of having transmitted an infection such as CMV.

Beneficial Outcomes

The recent implementation of universal newborn hearing screening has dramatically changed the diagnostic and therapeutic paradigms for infants with hearing loss. With this approach, the average age at confirmation of hearing loss has decreased from 24 to 30 months to 2 to 3 months (Mehl & Thomson, 2002). Nevertheless, the potential benefits of universal newborn hearing screening have yet to be fully realized, largely due to poor compliance with follow-up after a failed in-hospital hearing screen. Although in some settings this might be improved by predischarge diagnostic testing, the most generalizable and, ultimately, essential intervention would be the implementation of reliable communication within the health care system and with the families, designed to ensure that appropriate follow-up occurs.

The currently available information on educational and other functional outcomes is difficult to interpret, given the rapidly changing diagnostic and therapeutic climate of hearing loss and the number of years needed to evaluate relevant long-term functions. Nevertheless, the demonstration that earlier diagnosis and treatment of hearing loss has been associated with improved speech and language scores at 5 years old (Moeller, 2000; Yoshinaga-Itano et al., 2000) was encouraging and consistent with expectations derived from bench research. Recent studies, designed to be less subject to biases, confirm the beneficial effects on language acquisition in middle childhood, but not in speech (Kennedy et al., 2006). It remains uncertain whether these effects will persist through adolescence and result in

higher academic achievement. It should be noted that although early treatment of deaf children with normal cognition substantially improves function, in comparison with those who were diagnosed and treated late, the literacy skills of deaf children treated early appear to remain substantially below those of age-matched children with normal hearing (Kral & O'Donoghue, 2010).

Earlier specific diagnoses may allow appropriate earlier use of cochlear implants, which may permit basic speech and language processing comparable to children with normal hearing (McConkey, Koch, Osberger, Zimmerman-Phillips, & Kishon-Rabin, 2004). This likely makes inclusive schooling a much better option for increasing proportions of deaf children.

Given the heterogeneity of hearing disorders and related co-morbidities, the outcomes of individual children are difficult to predict. Ongoing research is helping to define more precisely the benefits of available interventions for specific conditions. For example, whereas children with isolated auditory neuropathy treated by cochlear implantation performed comparably to age-matched peers with sensorineural hearing loss, those with auditory neuropathy associated with a cognitive or developmental disorder had significantly less benefit and continued to rely on nonauditory modes of communication (Budenz et al., 2013).

Ultimately, indirect benefits of care for current infants with hearing loss will result from enhanced knowledge that will allow both very early detection and prevention or mitigation of hearing loss in the highest risk infants and young children. This will underlie the design of environments optimized for developmental care of high-risk newborns (White, 2011). However, a recent report (Pineda et al., 2014) of unfavorable brain structure findings and neurodevelopmental outcomes in preterm infants cared for in NICU private rooms, compared to open nurseries, indicates that much more study is needed to fully understand the optimal combinations of environmental stimuli that will promote more desirable neonatal outcomes.

Chapter Summary

This chapter described the normal development of the auditory system and discussed the major causes of hearing impairment and their functional consequences. The chapter highlighted the importance of screening and evaluation, medical interventions, and working effectively with families in achieving timely diagnoses and implementing feasible, individualized interventions.

Key Points to Remember

- The recent implementation of universal newborn hearing screening has enabled the early identification and appropriate treatment of hearing loss in early infancy. The 1-3-6 goals for hearing screening programs aim to achieve universal screening by 1 month old, complete the audiologic diagnostics by 3 months, and implement therapy by 6 months old.

- Ineffective communication among providers and families, poor care coordination, and barriers to access are current factors that result in a 40% loss to follow-up of babies who failed the newborn screen; they also account for subsequent delays and losses to follow-up in diagnosis and treatment.

- Immediate priorities for EHDI programs include improvement in coordination within the health care system to diminish care delays and losses to follow-up, which would optimize the benefits of existing interventions.

Implications for Families and Professionals

The increasing availability of genetic testing will permit more precise etiologic diagnoses in a large proportion of individuals with hearing loss, and make pre-symptomatic genetic screening feasible, in the near future. Eventually, this information may also guide disease-specific therapies. Meanwhile, it remains the role of providers in the medical home to coordinate diagnostic efforts, help families with decisions on medical and surgical interventions, and direct families to resources available through EI and the educational systems.

As advances in diagnosis and therapy of permanent hearing loss in children continue to evolve, it is likely that timely access to specialized professional services and effective interventions such as hearing aids will continue to be restricted by limitations of public and private insurance (Limb, McManus, Fox, White, & Forsman, 2010). Legislative advocacy for appropriate coverage will remain essential.

Resources

For parents and providers:

- Centers for Disease Control and Prevention - Hearing Loss in Children Early Hearing Detection and Intervention (EHDI) Program
www.cdc.gov/ncbddd/hearingloss/index.html

- National Center for Hearing Assessment and Management (NCHAM)
www.infanthearing.org/

- New York State Department of Health (EHDI)
www.health.ny.gov/community/infants_children/early_intervention/newborn_hearing_screening

For families (some available in multiple languages):

- *Communicate With Your Child*
  http://communicatewithyourchild.org

- Hands and Voices
  http://handsandvoices.org

- My Baby's Hearing (Boys Town National Research Hospital)
  http://babyhearing.org

- American Society for Deaf Children
  http://deafchildren.org/

- Supporting Success for Children With Hearing Loss
  http://successforkidswithhearingloss.com/relationship-hl-listen-learn/accommodations

References

Budenz, C. L., Telian, S. A., Arnedt, C., Starr, K., Arts, H. A., El-Kashlan, H. K., . . . Zwolan, T. A. (2013). Outcomes of cochlear implantation in children with isolated auditory neuropathy versus cochlear hearing loss. *Otolarynglogy Neurotology, 34*, 477–483.

Dalzell, L., Orlando, M., MacDonald, M., Berg, A., Bradley, M., Cacace, A., . . . Prieve, B. (2000). The New York State universal newborn hearing screening demonstration project: Ages of hearing loss. *Ear and Hearing, 21*, 118–130.

Dedhia, K., Kitsko, D., Sabo, D., & Chi, D. H. (2013). Children with sensorineural hearing loss after passing the newborn hearing screen. *JAMA Otolaryngology–Head & Neck Surgery*, 1–5.

Gaffney, M., Eichwald, J., Grouse, S. D., & Mason, C. A. (2010). Identifying infants with hearing loss: United States, 1999–2007. *MMWR Morbidity Mortality Weekly Report, 59*, 220–223.

Graven, S. N. (2011). Early visual development: Implications for the neonatal intensive care unit and care. *Clinical Perinatology, 38*, 671–683.

Graven, S. N., & Browne, J. V. (2008). Auditory development in the fetus and infant. *Newborn and Infant Nursing Reviews, 8*, 187–193.

Harlor, A. D. B., Bower, C., Committee on Practice and Ambulatory Medicine, & Section on Otolaryngology–Head and Neck Surgery (2009). Hearing assessment in infants and children: Recommendations beyond neonatal screening. *Pediatrics, 124*, 1252–1263.

Joint Committee on Infant Hearing. (2007). Year 2007 position statement: Principles and guidelines for early hearing detection and intervention programs. *Pediatrics, 120*, 898–921.

Joint Committee on Infant Hearing of the American Academy of Pediatrics, Muse, C., Harrison, J., Yoshinaga-Itano, C., Grimes, A., Brookhouser, P. E., . . . Martin, B. (2013). Supplement to the JCIH 2007 position statement: Principles and guidelines for early intervention after confirmation that a child is deaf or hard of hearing. *Pediatrics, 131*, e1324–e1349.

Kancherla, V., Van Naarden Braun, K., & Yeargin-Allsopp, M. (2013). Childhood vision impairment, hearing loss and co-occurring autism spectrum disorder. *Disability and Health Journal, 6*, 333–342.

Kennedy, C. R., McCann, D. C., Campbell, M. J., Law, C. M., Mullee, M., Petrou, S., . . . Stevenson, J. (2006). Language ability after early detection of permanent childhood hearing impairment. *The New England Journal of Medicine, 354*, 2131–2141.

Kral, A., & O'Donoghue, G. M. (2010). Profound deafness in childhood. *The New England Journal of Medicine, 363*, 1438–1450.

Lasky, R. E., & Williams, A. L. (2005). The development of the auditory system from conception to term. *NeoReviews, 6*, e141–e152.

Lieu, J. E. C., Tye-Murray, N., Karzon, R. K., & Piccirillo, J. F. (2010). Unilateral hearing loss is associated with worse speech-language scores in children. *Pediatrics, 125*, e1348–e1355.

Limb, S. J., McManus, M. A., Fox, H. B., White, K. R., & Forsman, I. (2010). Ensuring financial access to hearing aids for infants and young children. *Pediatrics, 126*, s43–s51.

Marcin, J., & Simon, A. (2014). Tele-audiology improves access to diagnostic hearing evaluations for infants. *AAP News, 35*, 25.

McConkey, R. A., Koch, D. B., Osberger, M. J., Zimmerman-Phillips, S., & Kishon-Rabin, L. (2004). Effect of age at cochlear implantation on auditory skill development in infants and toddlers. *Archives of Otolaryngology–Head & Neck Surgery, 130*, 570–574.

Mehl, A. L., & Thomson, V. (2002). The Colorado newborn hearing screening project, 1992–1999: On the threshold of effective population-based universal newborn hearing screening. *Pediatrics, 109*, e7.

Moeller, M. P. (2000). Early intervention and language development in children who are deaf and hard of hearing. *Pediatrics, 106*, e43.

Moon, C. (2011). The role of early auditory development in attachment and communication. *Clinical Perinatology, 38,* 657–669.

Morton, C. C. & Nance, W. E. (2006). Newborn hearing screening: A silent revolution. *The New England Journal of Medicine, 354,* 2151–2164.

Pineda, R. G., Neil, J., Dierker, D., Smyser, C. D., Wallendorf, M., Kidokoro, H., . . . Inder, T. (2014). Alterations in brain structure and neurodevelopmental outcome in preterm infants hospitalized in different neonatal intensive care unit environments. *The Journal of Pediatrics, 164,* 52–60.

Spivak, L., Sokol, H., Auerbach, C., & Gershkovich, S. (2009). Newborn hearing screening follow-up: Factors affecting hearing aid fitting by 6 months of age. *American Journal of Audiology, 18,* 24–33.

White, R. D. (2011). Designing environments for developmental care. *Clinical Perinatology, 38,* 745–749.

Yoshinaga-Itano, C., Coulter, D., & Thomson, V. (2000). The Colorado newborn hearing screening project: Effects on speech and language development for children with hearing loss. *Journal of Perinatology, 20,* S132–S137.

CHAPTER 9

Respiratory Distress in Newborns and Young Children

Upender K. Munshi and David A. Clark

Highlights of the Chapter

At the conclusion of this chapter, the reader will:

- be able to enumerate various stages of fetal lung development and their relevance to lung malformations or severity of lung immaturity

- be able to define acute respiratory distress in newborn infants and its common causes and their management

- be able to describe the chronic lung disease of prematurity or bronchopulmonary dysplasia (BPD) and its implications for the long-term developmental outcomes

During normal breathing, oxygen, which is the key element in aerobic metabolism, is picked up from the inspired air, and carbon dioxide generated in the body by metabolism is exhaled. This life-sustaining exchange of gases takes place in the lungs. Disease processes affecting the lungs may impair this gas exchange, resulting in difficult breathing manifested as *respiratory distress*. Respiratory distress is a common symptom requiring medical attention during the newborn period. As the severity of respiratory distress increases, less oxygen is absorbed by the lungs, resulting in *hypoxia*, which means less oxygen carried by the blood reaches tissues and organs of the body. At the same time, there is accumulation of carbon dioxide in body tissues and blood that is called *hypercarbia*. Tissue hypoxia causes *anaerobic glycolysis* (breakdown of glucose without oxygen), resulting in production of lactic acid and accumulated carbon dioxide in the body, which is converted into carbonic acid. The net effect of hypoxia and hypercarbia is an accumulation of acid products (lactic acid and carbonic acid, respectively) called *acidosis*, which, in severe cases, may lead to multi-organ damage, including injury to the central nervous system and risk for developmental delay. Respiratory distress can occur because of several underlying problems and may affect premature as well as full-term infants. With advances in the medical technology and ventilator support, the survival rates of most premature infants have improved; however, the number of very low birth weight babies surviving with developmental disabilities and chronic

197

disease of the lungs has increased. This situation poses significant challenges to the families of these babies and their medical care providers.

Underlying causes of acute respiratory distress may vary from mild (self-resolving problems) to severe (life-threatening conditions). In broad terms, respiratory disorders affecting newborns can be divided into two categories: (a) *transition disorders,* which refer to problems that manifest at birth, in the delivery room, or within first few hours of birth and (b) *post-transition disorders,* which occur after successful transition from intrauterine to extra-uterine life, usually 12 to 24 hours after birth. The first category includes conditions such as *transient tachypnea* of the newborn; respiratory distress syndrome due to prematurity, sepsis, or meconium aspiration syndrome; and congenital malformations of the respiratory system (e.g., diaphragmatic hernia). The second category includes sepsis/pneumonia, duct-dependent congenital heart disease, inborn errors of metabolism, and aspiration pneumonia. *Chronic lung disease of prematurity* or BPD is the condition that is seen in premature infants who initially present with acute respiratory distress syndrome, then continue to require prolonged ventilatory support or oxygen therapy, or both. In order to understand the various congenital disorders leading to respiratory distress in the newborn period, it is helpful to review the normal lung development (Ballard, 2004).

Lung Development

The human fetal lung develops in five stages:

1. *Embryonic phase* (0–5 weeks gestation): An initial lung bud arises from the foregut at 23–26 days after fertilization. This bud divides into primary bronchi and forms the proximal part of the airway. Interference with development at this stage can result in conditions such as *tracheaesophageal fistula.* This congenital malformation is characterized by absence (*atresia*) of a segment of esophagus (*food pipe*) so that the upper part of the esophagus ends as a blind pouch, and the infant is unable to swallow anything down into her stomach. The malformation is invariably associated with an abnormal communication (*fistula*) between the *trachea* (windpipe) and the lower part of the esophagus, which is continuous with the stomach. Inability to swallow amniotic fluid before birth leads to an excessive accumulation of amniotic fluid around the fetus called *polyhydramnios,* which may be an initial clue on prenatal fetal ultrasound. Immediate concern after birth is the accumulation of saliva in the upper blind pouch of the esophagus that can cause choking and aspiration of secretions into the lung. Infants with this condition need to be treated in a neonatal intensive care unit with pediatric surgery service. The tracheoesophageal fistula is closed and continuity of the esophagus is established surgically. Some of these infants may be hospitalized a long time to achieve normal swallowing, and some may need gastrostomy tube (G-tube) feeding.

2. *Pseudo-glandular phase* (6–16 weeks): In this phase, the bronchial division continues to form conducting airways (bronchi and bronchioles), with epithelial or airway lining cells derived from the ectoderm layer interacting with mesenchymal or lung parenchymal cells derived from the mesoderm layer of primitive cell layers. All of these structures are nonrespiratory, and gaseous exchange is not possible. Abnormal interaction of the primitive cells during this phase of development can result in congenital cystic adenomatoid malformation (CCAM), bronchogenic cysts, congenital diaphragmatic hernia (CDH), and congenital lobar emphysema. CCAM is a cystic abnormal tissue within the lung that does not function like the lung and may be large enough to compromise the gaseous exchange

of the remaining normal lung, needing ventilator support and eventual surgical treatment. Around 8–10 weeks gestation, the diaphragm develops from the front as a septum between heart and liver and progresses backward to separate the thoracic cavity from the abdominal cavity. Failure to close this last portion of the diaphragm, known as the left *Bochdalek foramen,* results in CDH and herniation of the bowel into the left hemithorax. These infants need respiratory support to stabilize their breathing and eventual surgical repair of the CDH.

3. *Canalicular phase* (17–24 weeks): This phase comprises the continued branching of airways, forming respiratory bronchioles that represent the first gas exchange structure within the tracheobronchial tree. During this phase, there is mesenchymal thinning, achieved by apoptosis and development of pulmonary capillaries. By the end of this phase, respiration, and thus survival, is possible by gas-exchanging acini; however, the respiratory distress syndrome is severe, and adverse outcomes in terms of morbidity and mortality are very high.

4. *Terminal sac phase* (25–37 weeks): Primitive alveoli (saccules and subsaccules) develop during this phase, which increase the alveolar–blood barrier surface area and enhance the gaseous exchange capability. Severity of respiratory distress syndrome and the outcomes improve markedly by the end of this phase.

5. *Alveolar phase* (38 weeks–3 years): Subsaccules form alveoli, and their proliferation and development continue throughout the newborn period to the first 2 to 3 years of life. This may explain the ongoing lung growth and the repair processes that help to resolve the chronic lung disease or BPD in growing premature babies, unlike the adult population with chronic lung diseases.

It is important to recognize that, as the lungs are developing in structure, there are biochemical changes that take place simultaneously. Type 2 pneumocytes produce surface-tension lowering lipoproteins, which form a lining at the liquid–air interface of mature alveoli in the full-term infant. This substance is called *surfactant* and is essential to keep the alveoli open and facilitate respiration (Avery & Merrit, 1991). Surfactant production starts by the end of the canalicular phase and continues to increase as gestation advances towards the term.

Respiratory Distress in Newborns

The next sections will describe some of the types of respiratory distress.

Acute Respiratory Distress

Acute respiratory distress refers to difficulty in breathing that is manifested by faster breathing rate (> 60 breaths per minute) and increased work of breathing such as chest wall retractions; flaring of external nares; grunting noise; and, in severe cases, a pale bluish hue of skin of face, chest, and lips (*cyanosis*). Because chest wall muscles, cartilage, and the rib cage of the newborn are not as strong as those of older children or adults, the chest wall and sternum appear to be drawn in during attempts at inspiration due to negative pressure created in the chest cavity by downward movement of the diaphragm. The time of onset of respiratory distress may help in gaining a clue to its causation. Respiratory distress may be due to a problem in another organ system rather than in the lungs like acidosis, anemia, myocardial dysfunction (malfunction of heart), encephalopathy (brain injury), or infection of blood stream (sepsis).

Transition Disorders

At birth, there is a change from the intra-uterine, placenta-dependent state to an entirely different extra-uterine environment of individual existence for the baby. It is amazing to see how this transition takes place so smoothly in the majority of newborns, who adapt readily to their new outside world. However, some infants experience problems in this process of adaptation, which professionals refer to as *transition disorders*. These disorders begin to manifest at birth or within a few hours after birth and can occur as a result of various problems related to the lungs, heart and blood vessels, infections, congenital malformations, loss of blood, *anemia* (low hemoglobin), and even *polycythemia* (high hemoglobin). The common lung disorders related to transition include delayed clearance of fetal lung fluid or transient tachypnea of the newborn, lack of surfactant production in premature lungs commonly known as *respiratory distress syndrome (RDS)*, or *hyaline membrane disease*, and aspiration of material not normally present in airways such as meconium, blood, or amniotic fluid. Infection acquired before birth may become evident as respiratory distress due to pneumonia at birth and is difficult to differentiate from the previously mentioned conditions by appearance alone. Other causes for respiratory distress at birth may be air leaks into the pleural cavity, mediastinum, or pericardium. These may occur spontaneously or as a result of enthusiastic positive pressure ventilation given at the time of delivery. In addition, some congenital malformations of the respiratory system may cause respiratory distress immediately after birth (e.g., tracheoesophageal fistula, congenital diaphragmatic hernia, and cystic lung lesions). Medications given to the mother during labor, such as opiate derivatives for pain or magnesium sulfate for treatment of hypertension or preterm labor tend to cross the placenta and depress newborn respiratory effort immediately after birth. These babies require ventilatory support until they improve their own spontaneous breathing.

Transient Tachypnea of the Newborn (TTN)

While in the uterus, the fetal lung is filled with fluid that is actively secreted by the lining of potential airways and airspaces. This fluid is referred to as *fetal lung fluid* and is not same as amniotic fluid. It gradually extrudes out of the lungs by coming up the glottis and is added to the amniotic fluid pool in a one-way direction. Around the time of labor, there are certain hormonal changes in the maternal–fetal unit that result in inhibition of lung fluid secretion and rapid absorption of remaining fluid in the airways (Jain & Eaton, 2006). These mechanisms work well for most newborns. If professionals listen to a newborn baby's chest at birth, they often hear coarse crackling sounds known as râles, signifying secretions in the airways that disappear within a matter of minutes as the airways are cleared of this excessive fluid. On the other hand, a few infants, particularly after elective cesarean sections (without labor), continue to have respiratory distress beyond the first few hours of life, as a result of retained fetal lung fluid in the airways (Jain & Dudell, 2006). A chest x-ray shows normal lung volumes and fluid in the fissure between the lobes of the right lung. Most of the infants with TTN require supplemental oxygen therapy with continuous positive pressure through nasal prongs; seldom is there a need for endotracheal intubation with ventilatory support. As the name implies, the respiratory distress in TTN begins to improve as early as 6–12 hours and subsides completely by 24–48 hours after birth. Thus, a baby requiring ventilatory support beyond 24 to 48 hours suffers from problems other than TTN.

Respiratory Distress Syndrome of Prematurity

Also known as surfactant deficiency syndrome or hyaline membrane disease of prematurity, mainly seen at < 32 weeks of gestation, this can occasionally affect full-term or near-term infants as well. It is caused by a lack of surfactant production due to the immaturity of Type 2 pneumocytes and relates to the late canalicular and early-to-middle terminal sac phase of lung development. Prenatal steroids given to mothers in preterm labor seem to have a beneficial effect for the baby in terms of lung maturation and surfactant production. Because air spaces are moist, there is an inherent tendency of the fluid molecules at the fluid–air interface to attract each other and collapse the air space. These molecules need surfactant to oppose this tendency and keep the air spaces open. Lack of surfactant causes progressive collapse of air spaces and decreases the surface area for the exchange of oxygen and carbon dioxide. Respiratory distress manifests at birth or within the first few hours, then worsens over the next 1–2 days. There is injury of partially or completely collapsed air spaces and leaking of plasma proteins from the capillaries, which precipitate along the lining of air spaces, forming a hyaline membrane (thus the name hyaline membrane disease). Most newborns with surfactant deficiency syndrome will need supplemental oxygen and some form of ventilatory support. In milder cases, positive pressure is exerted by snugly fitting nasal prongs, which deliver continuous positive airway pressure. During this method of ventilatory support, breathing is done by the baby, and continuous positive airway pressure (CPAP) helps to supplement the baby's effort to keep the air spaces open and breathe comfortably. With increasing need of oxygen concentration and worsening of respiratory distress, CPAP alone may not be enough. From the oral or nasal route, an endotracheal

tube is placed in the mid-trachea (*endotracheal intubation*), and its end is connected to a ventilator. Positive pressure breaths are delivered by the ventilator to take over the work of breathing and open up the collapsed airspaces so that effective gas exchange can take place. Today, most ventilators have computer-backed sensors that can deliver synchronized ventilation, based on a baby's breathing effort.

Intubation is also critical for the administration of exogenous surfactant into the airspaces. Various surfactant preparations (Halliday, 2006; Pfister & Soll (2005), mostly derived after purification from an animal source, are available in liquid form and are delivered to the lungs via an endotracheal tube. Prenatal steroid treatment of mothers in preterm labor, postnatal surfactant treatment, and the availability of newer-generation ventilators have revolutionized the management of this condition over the last 2 decades. However, a significant number of babies with extremely low birth weight (birth weights below 1,000 g or < 2.2 lbs) still need prolonged ventilatory support and oxygen therapy, and they develop what is commonly referred to as *chronic lung disease of prematurity* or BPD There is an ongoing effort to modify the ventilatory management in order to decrease or prevent this chronic lung disease in preterm infants (Lindwall et al. 2005; Schreiber et al., 2003). Given the same degree of prematurity, there are certain factors which increase or decrease the risk of developing RDS (see Table 9.1).

TABLE 9.1 Factors for increased and decreased risk of developing respiratory distress syndrome, in addition to being born premature

INCREASED RISK	DECREASED RISK
Maternal diabetes	Prenatal corticosteroids
Multiple gestation	
Acute fetal distress	Toxemia of pregnancy
Perinatal asphyxia	

Aspiration Syndromes

Amniotic fluid stained with meconium (i.e., the passage of newborn stools before birth) occurs in about 10%–15% of all deliveries. It is uncommon in premature deliveries at less than 35 weeks but more common in postterm deliveries (41–42 weeks gestation). Only 1%–2% of neonates born with meconium-stained amniotic fluid develop *meconium aspiration syndrome*. Meconium has the mechanical effect of obstructing the airways and causing chemical irritation, with inflammation and deactivation of surfactant (Clark, Neiman, Thompson, & Bredenberg, 1987). The patho-physiology of this disorder is further complicated by associated pulmonary arterial hypertension and hypoxic/ischemic injury to multi-organ systems (Munshi & Clark, 2002). It manifests at birth or within the first few hours as progressively worsening respiratory distress, needing aggressive ventilatory management including high-frequency ventilation and novel therapies such as inhaled nitric oxide or, in severe cases, a need for invasive procedures such as extra corporeal membrane oxygenation.

Air Leak Syndromes

Following an aggressive resuscitation, or sometimes spontaneously, due to partially blocked airways acting as a ball valve, air can leak out of the distended air spaces and become trapped at various locations within the chest. This air is not available for the usual gas exchange; and if accumulated under pressure, it can compress the surrounding structures (lung tissue, heart, and blood vessels). This compression of tissues may interfere with the lung and or heart function and cause life-threatening, cardio-respiratory compromise.

There are four types of air leaks. When air collects in the pleural cavity between the chest wall and the lungs, it is called a *pneumothorax*. This is the most common type of air leak. About 5% of all newborn babies may have this type of air leak, but only 1% may develop respiratory distress. A small pneumothorax requires close monitoring, whereas large ones (particularly causing respiratory distress) require needle or chest tube drainage. When air is trapped in the center of the chest around major blood vessels and airways, the condition is called a *pnuemomediastinum*. As more air accumulates, it may tract up toward the neck or reach the pericardium around the heart, causing a serious condition called *pneumopericardium*. Under tension, pneumopericardium does not permit adequate filling of the heart with blood, thus dangerously lowering the cardiac output. Even with aggressive therapy, mortality or morbidity with this condition is very high (Carey, 1999; McIntosh, 1983).

Finally, a type of air leak that is found mainly in premature infants on ventilators with RDS, in which small amounts of air escape at multiple places and traverse around the airways and blood vessels, forming numerous tiny elongated cystic shadows on a chest x-ray, is called *pulmonary interstitial emphysema*. This condition often leads to prolonged ventilator support and development of chronic lung disease of prematurity, such as BPD.

Pulmonary Hemorrhage

Very low birth weight babies having severe respiratory distress, particularly those with *patent ductus arteriosus* causing increased blood flow to the lungs, are at a high risk of pulmonary hemorrhage (AlKharfy, 2004). The ductus arteriosus is normally open during fetal life and tends to close in term and near-term infants within the first day or so after the birth. It remains open in very premature infants, causing extra blood shunting from the aorta to the pulmonary artery. It is often treated with medications such as indomethacin or ibuprofen and, in a small number of babies who do not respond to medication, it is ligated surgically (Hermes-DeSantis & Clyman, 2006; Raval, Laughon, Bose, & Phillips, 2007). Blood loss due to pulmonary hemorrhage may cause shock and death, despite aggressive intervention. Pulmonary hemorrhage manifests as fresh bleeding, pouring out of the endotracheal tube that connects the baby to the ventilator, and sudden deterioration in the clinical status of the baby. Blood in the air spaces also deactivates surfactant, which further worsens the RDS. Survivors are at risk of chronic lung disease of prematurity and developmental delays.

Neonatal Sepsis/ Pneumonia Syndrome

Infection-causing organisms can reach the fetus along two pathways. One route is the mother's bloodstream, where infection reaches the placenta and extends to the fetus via blood supply, called the *hematogenous spread*. This spread, referred to as intrauterine infection, can occur at any time in the pregnancy, and it may pose serious threat to the developing fetus and its growth. Such babies often are growth restricted, may have stigmata of infection, and a few may manifest respiratory distress. Common organisms include toxoplasma, cytomegalovirus, rubella, herpes, HIV, and other infections, remembered by the menomonic TORCH. More commonly, infection from the maternal genital tract reaches the baby by ascending route, just before or at delivery by exposure during passage. This is referred to as *perinatal infection*. Common organisms reflect maternal genital tract flora and include E. coli, Group B streptococcus, Klebseilla, enterococcus, herpes simplex virus, and, rarely, listeria. Some organisms (e.g., herpes simplex, HIV, and hepatitis B) can infect the fetus by either route, hematogenous or ascending.

Respiratory distress or *apnea* is a frequent symptom of perinatally acquired infections and can present as early as the delivery room and, thereafter, at any time during the neonatal period. Other features of infection in a newborn include poor feeding, vomiting, lethargy, irritability, poor skin perfusion, and low blood pressure. Risk factors for infection include maternal fever, prolonged rupture of membranes, preterm labor, Group B Streptococcus colonization on the mother's screening test, maternal chorioamnionitis, and frequent urinary tract infections during pregnancy. Sepsis is an important consideration in any newborn with respiratory distress because early diagnostic work-up (Escobar et al., 2000) and empirical therapy with antibiotics can prevent morbidity and mortality related to this common problem in newborn.

Metabolic Errors

Common derangement in metabolism that may cause respiratory distress is *hypoglycemia* (low blood glucose level), often noted among the infants of diabetic mothers. Rarely, inborn errors of metabolism caused by organic acidemias or amino acid disorders, urea cycle disorders, and others can present as respiratory distress. State-run newborn screening programs have helped to identify some infants with these errors, and those not screened for them should be considered, after other common causes of respiratory distress are ruled out. Usually there is a short period of time after birth, often 1–2 days, when the baby appears to be doing well and feeding but soon afterward starts to breathe faster and heavier as a result of an accumulation of acids or toxic metabolites. Common blood tests done during the initial evaluation may point toward increased acid or ammonia accumulation, which requires specific testing and diagnosis (Enns & Packman, 2001).

Management of Acute Respiratory Distress

The main goal of management of acute respiratory distress is the maintenance of adequate blood oxygen and concurrent control of blood carbon-dioxide levels in order to prevent acidosis. Carbon dioxide diffuses more readily from blood into alveoli; thus, higher carbon dioxide content in the blood signifies a more severe lung disease. Meanwhile, the underlying and contributory causes of respiratory distress (e.g., sepsis, anemia, patent ductus arteriosus) are investigated and treated accordingly. Exogenous surfactant replacement is considered for RDS.

Supplemental oxygen is given to increase the oxygen uptake from the lungs into the blood to keep the partial pressure of oxygen in the blood from 50 to 80 mm of mercury. If an adequate oxygen level cannot be maintained by increasing oxygen concentration to > 60% in the inspired air, or the carbon dioxide level in the blood rises to > 60 mm mercury, assisted ventilation should be considered. The first step is to start CPAP by placing prongs in the nose, and the baby is made to breathe against an adjustable pressure. If this treatment fails to achieve the targeted oxygenation and elimination of carbon dioxide, mechanical ventilation is initiated after placement of a plastic tube in the airway (i.e., endotracheal tube), which is connected to a ventilator.

Two types of ventilators are commonly used today in neonatal intensive care units. One is the traditional ventilator that gives mechanical breaths over a range of normal breathing rates (20 to 60 breaths per minute) and is referred to as a *conventional ventilator*. *High-frequency ventilators* deliver very small tidal volume breaths at a very high rate (360–900 breaths per minute by oscillating the diaphragm as in a high-frequency oscillator, or 420 breaths per minute by jet stream as in a high-frequency jet ventilator). Blood gases and chest x-rays are monitored during mechanical ventilation, and as targeted lung volume and blood gases are achieved, the settings are weaned accordingly. Other supportive measures include providing adequate body warmth and temperature control, and fluid, electrolyte, and nutrition support, which is described in detail elsewhere in this book.

There are ongoing efforts for improving the management of acute respiratory distress in newborns. Newer-generation surfactants, including synthetic ones, are being developed for respiratory distress syndrome. Nitric oxide as a pulmonary vasodilator, used for term and near-term infants with pulmonary hypertension, is now being tested for antiinflammatory and lung-growth promoter (Lindwall et al., 2005) effects in preterm infants with RDS. In addition to the improved versions of conventional and high-frequency ventilators, other modes of ventilation such as liquid ventilation (Wakabayashi, Tamura, & Nakamura, 2006) are being tested for newborns with respiratory distress.

Chronic Lung Disease

As neonatal intensive care has advanced, the survival rates of very low birth weight, premature babies have improved remarkably. However, this improvement comes with the cost of an increased number of survivors who have chronic respiratory and neuro-developmental issues. Infants with mild or moderate severity of respiratory distress, with only short periods of mechanical ventilation, recover well and seldom have any chronic pulmonary or neuro-developmental issues, in the absence of other medical conditions such as infections, surgical complications, or malformations. On the other hand, very low birth weight (< 1,500g) and extremely low birth weight (< 1,000g) premature infants with severe respiratory distress may need prolonged periods of respiratory support and hospital stay (Klinger, Sirota, Lusky, & Reichman, 2006). They are at a high risk for developing chronic lung disease and adverse neuro-developmental outcomes. About one third of extremely low birth weight babies leave the hospital with a diagnosis of chronic lung disease or BPD.

Northway and colleagues (1967) first defined this condition as dependence on oxygen at 28 days of life, with chest x-ray changes. Because the population of infants surviving now is more premature than before, this definition has been broadened to include infants needing oxygen at a corrected gestational age of 36 weeks, with or without x-ray changes; and the term has been used interchangeably with chronic lung disease as well. Infants with BPD are frequently discharged on home oxygen therapy and require some form of home-monitoring equipment. They need extra care from their parents and physicians, as well as follow-up by pediatric subspecialties such as pediatric pulmonology, physical/occupational therapy, and early intervention services.

BPD, or chronic lung disease, evolves from therapeutic early lifesaving interventions such as oxygen therapy and ventilatory support for acute respiratory illnesses, such as RDS, in newborns. Pathogenesis is multifactorial; prematurity and need for ventilatory support as the most important initiating factors (Chess et al., 2006; Walsh et al., 2006). However, the life-saving interventions that occur in the initial acute phase can induce acute inflammatory changes in the lung, as a result of the mechanical effect of ventilators (e.g., barotrauma or volutrauma) or the toxic effect of high oxygen concentration; and they later turn into into chronic inflammation of the lung and interfere with lung function. These conditions typically lead to prolonged ventilator support and need for oxygen, which may hamper the target of achieving independent oral feeding and interaction of the baby with the environment. Infants with BPD show signs of respiratory distress in the form of retractions and have a tendency to retain excessive fluids. Due to increased effort of breathing, in addition to their growth, their caloric needs are higher. However, their fluid intake should be lower because of fluid retention. They frequently are treated with diuretics to get rid of retained fluid, which may cause excessive loss of minerals such as sodium, potassium, calcium, and chloride. These losses pose further challenges to their nutrition, and the majority of these infants are undernourished.

Other common problems associated with BPD include gastro-esophageal reflux, which adds another barrier to the nutritional rehabilitation of these infants. Nutritional management should be planned preferably with the help of a trained nutritionist and, in principle, involve providing high-density calorie formula with some fluid restriction; supplementation of minerals, iron, and vitamins; and management of gastro-esophageal reflux. Adequate nutrition is the cornerstone for repair and healing of chronic lung disease.

Some infants with BPD are treated with potent, anti-inflammatory drugs such as steroids; however, in recent years, serious concerns have been raised about the adverse, long-term neuro-developmental issues in steroid-treated babies (Parikh et al., 2007; Short et al., 2003). These drugs are now used very cautiously in selected infants after their parents have been informed about the risks and the benefits of such therapy (American Academy of Pediatrics, Committee on Fetus and Newborn, 2002).

Very few infants with severe BPD who remain dependent on ventilator support for prolonged periods are subjected to tracheostomy for direct access to the respiratory system through the trachea in front of the neck that allows caregivers to provide respiratory support and clearance of airway secretions and removal of respiratory devices, like nasal masks and breathing tubes, from the face. Freeing the nose and mouth further allow improvement of oral feeding attempts and facial interaction with care providers that may be considered helpful in improving developmental outcomes. Tracheostomy is an invasive procedure and has its share of complications, such as infection, and blockage of respiratory passage, and it carries a long-term (by 2–5 years old) mortality rate of 10%–20%. However, caregivers interacting with the baby and attempting to orally feed when respiratory distress gradually improves on ventilator support via tracheostomy, allow the infant to experience his surroundings, which is essential for learning and achieving developmental milestones. As respiratory status improves and ventilator support is weaned over months to the first few years, tracheostomy is discontinued (decannulation), usually by 2 to 5 years old (Overman et al., 2013).

After discharge, infants with BPD are susceptible to viral and bacterial infections. For example, *respiratory syncytial virus* (RSV) typically causes mild cold symptoms in children during the winter but may result in life-threatening bronchiolitis or pneumonia. Thus, premature babies and infants with BPD need passive immunization against RSV. One such product available commercially is a monoclonal antibody called palivizumab (synagis), which is given by injection once a month through the RSV season, from late fall to early spring (Fenton, Scott, & Plosker, 2004).

Chapter Summary

This chapter has explained the five stages of normal lung development and their relevance to lung malformations or severity of lung immaturity. The chapter describes common causes of respiratory distress in newborns and their management and defines and explains the evolution of chronic lung disease of prematurity or BPD which may have implications for infant's short-term and long-term health care needs. Their hospital stays are longer than those who do not have BPD, and often their discharge planning

is more complex, because it may involve going home on oxygen, monitors, and medications. There is a higher association of adverse neuro-developmental outcomes with severe BPD. BPD impacts the family as well; before discharge, parents need to learn how to use the equipment effectively and safely at home, and how to administer medications. They also have to keep the medical follow-up appointments with their pediatrician and other subspecialty consultants. Infants with severe BPD and with tracheostomy and G-tube or stoma care may be so difficult that they may have to be placed in rehabilitation units before making it home. Infants with BPD may show a progressive improvement in the pulmonary function and weaning of oxygen, varying from a few weeks to the first few years after discharge from the hospital. This is where BPD differs from chronic lung disease of adults: Continued growth and development of new alveoli in infants often leads to a favorable outcome, if the infants do not succumb to airway obstruction, intercurrent infections, or pulmonary hypertension. However, adverse neuro-developmental outcomes can impose a substantial burden on the family and the society.

Key Points to Remember

- Infants with BPD continue to be a very vulnerable group and may require a substantially high proportion of health care resources.

- Severe BPD is invariably associated with some degree of adverse developmental outcome; however, it is difficult to distinguish the effects of the severity of lung disease from issues related to the intensity of interventions and associated medical complications such as poor nutrition, infection, and intracranial hemorrhage, which likewise can affect neuro-development. Frequently, this population of infants has increased mortality, morbidity, and readmission to the hospital during the first 1 to 2 years of life, as compared to their counterparts without BPD.

- Follow-up of infants with BPD shows a progressive improvement in the pulmonary function and weaning of oxygen in majority of children, varying from a few weeks to the first few years of discharge from the hospital. In that respect, BPD is entirely different from the adult onset of chronic disease and has a favorable outcome most of the time; however, adverse neuro-developmental outcomes are common in infants with severe BPD.

Implications for Families and Professionals

Acute respiratory distress and associated problems in premature and term infants are managed based on neonatal intensive care unit settings. With advances in medical technology and ventilatory support, the survival rates of most premature infants have improved; however, the number of very low birth weight babies surviving with chronic lung disease and developmental disabilities has increased. Goals for discharge from intensive care units to home include complete resolution of problems or recovery to a clinically stable state in which parents and other caregivers can safely provide nutritional support, respiratory care, and other requirements such as ostomy or surgical wound care.

Infants with moderate to severe BPD are often discharged with home oxygen therapy, monitors, and medications such as diuretics, bronchodilators, and inhaled steroids. Parents and family members receive training and teaching by a neonatal intensive care discharging team, and they have to demonstrate learning before the infant leaves the unit. This situation poses significant challenges to the families of these babies and their medical care providers. Primary medical care providers (e.g., physicians, nurses, respiratory therapists, and physical, speech, and occupational therapists) must be familiar with the management of children with BPD and aware of associated problems of malnutrition and delayed developmental milestones. This population of infants tends toward increased mortality, morbidity, and readmission to the hospital during the first 1 to 2 years of life, as compared to their counterparts without BPD. Follow-up of infants with BPD is critical for progressive improvement in the pulmonary function and weaning from oxygen. Infants with BPD continue to be a very vulnerable group that requires a substantially high proportion of health care services and resources and may continue to do so.

References

AlKharfy, T. M. (2004). High frequency ventilation in the management of very low birth weight infants with pulmonary hemorrhage. *American Journal of Perinatology, 21*(1), 19–26.

American Academy of Pediatrics, Committee on Fetus and Newborn. (2002). Post-natal corticosteroids to treat or prevent chronic lung disease in preterm infants. *Pediatrics, 109*, 330–338.

Avery, M. E, & Merrit, T. A. (1991). Surfactant replacement therapy. *New England Journal of Medicine, 324*, 865–869.

Ballard, R. A. (2004). Respiratory system. In W. H. Taeusch, R. A. Ballard, & C. A. Gleason (Eds.), *Avery's diseases of the newborn* (8th ed., pp. 601–778). Philadelphia, PA: Elsevier Saunders.

Carey, B. E. (1999). Neonatal air leaks: Pneumothorax, pneumomedistinum, pulmonary interstitial emphysema, pneumopericardium. *Neonatal Network, 18*(8), 81–84.

Chess, P. R., D'Angio, C. T., Pyhuber, G. S., & Maniscalo, W. M. (2006). Pathogenesis of bronchopulmonary dysplasia. *Seminars in Perinatology, 30*, 171–178.

Clark, D. A., Neiman, G. F., Thompson, J. E., & Bredenberg, C. E. (1987). Surfactant displacement by meconium free fatty acids: An alternative explanation for atelectasis in meconium aspiration syndrome. *Journal of Pediatrics, 110,* 765–770.

Enns, G. M., & Packman, S. (2001). Diagnosing inborn errors of metabolism in the newborn: Laboratory investigations. *NeoReviews, 2*(8), e192–e200.

Escobar, E. J., Li, D. K., Armstrong, M. A., Gardener, M. N., Flock, B. F., Verdi, J. E., Xiong, B., & Bergen, R. (2000). Neonatal sepsis work-up in infants > 2000 grams at birth: A population-based study. *Pediatrics, 106,* 256–263.

Fenton, C., Scott, L. J., & Plosker, G. L. (2004). Palivizumab: A review of its use as a prophylaxis for serious respiratory syncytial virus infection. *Paediatric Drugs, 6*(3), 177–197.

Halliday, H. L. (2006). Recent clinical trials of surfactant treatment for neonates. *Biology of the Neonate, 89*(4), 323–329.

Hermes-DeSantis, E. R., & Clyman, R. I. (2006). Patent ductus arteriosus: Pathophysiology and management. *Journal of Perinatology, 26*(Supp. 1), S14–S18.

Jain, L., & Dudell, G. G. (2006). Respiratory transition in infants delivered by cesarean section. *Seminars in Perinatology, 30,* 296–304.

Jain, L., & Eaton, D. C. (2006). Physiology of fetal lung fluid clearance and effect of labor. *Seminars in Perinatology, 30,* 34–43.

Klinger, G., Sirota, L., Lusky, A., & Reichman, B. (2006). Bronchopulmonary dysplasia in very low birth weight infants is associated with prolonged hospital stay. *Journal of Perinatology, 26*(10), 640–644.

Lindwall, R., Blennow, M., Svensson, M., Jonsson, B., Berggren-Boström, E., . . . Norman, M. (2005). A pilot study of inhaled nitric oxide in preterm infants treated with nasal continuous airway pressure for respiratory distress syndrome. *Intensive Care Medicine, 31,* 959–964.

McIntosh, M. (1983). Pulmonary air leaks in newborn period. *British Journal of Hospital Medicine, 29*(6), 512–517.

Munshi, U. K., & Clark, D. A. (2002). Meconium aspiration syndrome. *Contemporary Clinical Gynecology and Obstetrics, 2,* 247–254.

Northway, W. H., Jr., Rosan, R. C., & Porter, D. Y. (1967). Pulmonary disease following therapy of hyaline membrane disease—bronchopulmonary dysplasia. *New England Journal of Medicine, 276*(7), 357–368.

Overman, A. E., Liu, M., Kurachek, S. C., Shreve, M. R., Maynard, R. C., & Moore, B. M. (2013). Tracheostomy for infants requiring prolonged mechanical ventilation: 10 years' experience. *Pediatrics, 131*(5), e1491–e1496.

Parikh, N. A., Lasky, R. E., Kennedy, K. E., Moya, F. R., Hochhauser, L., Romo, S. & Tyson, J. E. (2007). Postnatal dexamethasone therapy and cerebral tissue volumes in extremely low birth weight infants. *Pediatrics, 119,* 265–272.

Pfister, R. H., & Soll, R. F. (2005). New synthetic surfactants: The next generation? *Biology of Neonate, 87,* 338–344.

Raval, M. V., Laughon, M. M., Bose, C. L., & Phillips, J. D. (2007). Patent ductus arteriosus ligation in premature infants: Who really benefits, and at what cost? *Journal of Pediatric Surgery, 42,* 69–75.

Schreiber, M. D., Gin-Mestan, K., Marks, J. D., Huo, D., Lee, G., & Srisuparp, P. (2003). Inhaled nitric oxide in premature infants with the respiratory distress syndrome. *New England Journal of Medicine, 349,* 2099–2107.

Short, E. J., Klein, N. K., Lewis, B.A., Fulton, S., Kercsmar, C., Baley, J., & Singer, L. T. (2003). Cognitive and academic consequences of bronchopulmonary dysplasia and very low birth weight: 8-year-old outcomes. *Pediatrics, 112*(3), S52–S59.

Wakabayashi, T., Tamura, M., & Nakamura, T. (2006). Partial liquid ventilation with low dose perfluoro-chemical and high frequency oscillation improves oxygenation and lung compliance in a rabbit model of surfactant depletion. *Biology of the Neonate, 89*(3), 177–182.

Walsh, M. C., Stanley, S., Davis, J. Allen, M., Van Marter, L., Abman, S., Blackmon, L., & Jobe, A. (2006). Summary proceedings from the bronchopulmonary dysplasia group. *Pediatrics, 117*(3), S52–S59.

CHAPTER 10

Major Physical, Motor, and Neurologic Impairments

James J. Cummings and Marilyn A. Fisher

Highlights of the Chapter

At the conclusion of the chapter, the reader will:

- have a basic understanding of the physical, motor, and neurologic development of children during the first 3 years of life

- be able to identify infants and young children (under 3 years old) with motor or neurologic disorders, or both

- know the major causes of delays in motor and neurologic development in infants and young children

- be able to categorize the major types of motor and neurologic disorders seen in young children

- learn how to work with families in managing these disorders in young children

Major Components of Motor and Neurologic Development: What Are Professionals Looking at During the First 3 Years?

The first years of life are marked by rapid organ development, particularly in the brain and central nervous system (Brown & Jernigan, 2012; Hadders-Algra, 2005), however infants and young children have a limited repertoire of motor and neurologic abilities. Nevertheless, a thorough understanding of normal neuromotor development during the first 3 years is critical in order to pick up delays or regression that could point to serious underlying disorders, of not only the central or peripheral nervous system, but other areas as well.

The newborn and young infant experiences his environment in an involuntary, reflexive way. During the first years of life, as the child grows and experiences more, he learns to actively participate in his environment. Motor development can be viewed as the core of neurodevelopment, from which all other developmental skills emerge or are facilitated. As motor skills develop, the infant and young child can further explore his environment, and he creates new motor skills by linking previously acquired ones (e.g., progression from standing to walking, or from grasping to self-feeding). He also increasingly uses perceptual information to refine his motor actions, for example, adjusting his crawling in response to characteristics of the surface he is on (Joh, Adolph, Narayanan, & Dietz, 2007).

Early child development can be generally broken up into three major components: (a) motor, (b) language, and (c) social. Motor skills are further divided into gross and fine. Gross motor development requires the use of relatively larger muscles, those of the neck, trunk, arms, and legs; gross motor skills include rolling over, sitting, crawling, and walking. Fine motor development involves the use of relatively smaller muscles, those in the hands and fingers; fine motor skills include picking up and examining objects, self-feeding, and self-dressing.

Templates of Motor Development by Age During the First 3 Years

There are two basic templates of motor development during the first years of life. These include infantile reflexes and motor skills. Early motor development is associated with the extinguishing of primitive reflexes and the development of postural reflexes. Primitive reflexes are those that exist at birth but eventually disappear as the central nervous system matures; they are generally absent by a year of age. Suppression of primitive reflexes with time is not only a sign of a progressively intact nervous system; it also allows new motor skills to develop. Persistence of primitive reflexes often herald an underlying neurologic disorder, most commonly cerebral palsy (Bear, 2004; Edwards & Sarwark, 2005). Postural reflexes are specifically related to positional control. Following several months in a relatively weightless environment in utero, the newborn is faced with achieving and maintaining a stable position against the influence of gravity. Some postural reflexes are present at birth; others do not appear until several months of age. Collectively, these primitive and postural reflexes are known as *infantile reflexes.* There have been more than a dozen infantile reflexes described; examples of the more commonly referred to, and their patterns of appearance and disappearance, are shown in Table 10.1.

Motor development parallels the pattern of brain growth and development. As a result, development of motor skills progresses in two basic topographic patterns: (a) cephalo-caudal (head to toe), and (b) proximo-distal (centrifugal, i.e., from the center outward). This means that motor control progresses from head and neck to the trunk, then to the arms and legs, and finally, to the fingers and toes.

Motor development in children can also be described by the pattern of acquisition of motor skills. This progression can be characterized by four movement phases: (a) reflexive, (b) rudimentary, (c) fundamental, and (d) specialized (Gallahue, Ozmun, & Goodway, 2012). The *reflexive* movement phase is from birth through the first year; during this phase, the infant primarily engages in reflexive movements. The *rudimentary* movement phase overlaps with the reflexive phase, but extends through the second year of life; during this phase the child acquires basic motor skills such

TABLE 10.1 Some infantile reflexes

REFLEX	STIMULUS	RESPONSE	APPEARS	DISAPPEARS
Moro ("startle")	Lying supine, the infant's arms are lifted a few inches, and then dropped.	The arms move briskly back, then forward, and the infant may cry.	Prenatal (1st trimester)	2–6 months
Placing ("stepping")	Holding the infant upright, the dorsal (top) of the foot is touched to the edge of table.	The hip/knee flexes, and then the leg extends forward, as if to step onto the table.	Birth	6–8 weeks
Asymmetric tonic neck ("fencing")	Lying supine, the head is rotated to the side.	The contralateral (opposite to the side of turning) arm flexes, while the ipsilateral (same side) arm extends.	Birth	2–6 months
Propping ("righting")	With infant seated, gently tilt him/her to one side.	The head rights toward midline, the ipsilateral arm extends protectively, and the contralateral arm/leg make equilibrium movements.	6 months	Persists
Parachute	The infant is held in ventral suspension, and then suddenly lowered.	Both arms extend, as if to protect itself from a fall.	6–8 months	Persists

as reaching, grasping, sitting, standing, and walking. The *fundamental* movement phase builds on the rudimentary skills, as children gain increased control over both their gross and fine motor movements from ages 2 through 6 years old; during this phase, children first learn skills in isolation then are able to combine them as coordinated movements, for example, running, jumping, throwing, and catching. The *specialized* movement phase begins around 6–7 years old and continues through the teenage years and into young adulthood; skills acquired during this phase are primarily learned and oriented to specific tasks (e.g., writing, typing; Gallahue et al., 2012).

Motor skills are typically acquired in a relatively constant and predictable fashion during the first 3 years (see Table 10.2). The patterns of motor development, both topographic and functional, are the same for every child. However, it is important to note that there can be a wide variability in timing among normal children. Knowledge of what to expect when, as well as the normal degree of variation in timing, are important in assessing the motor development of the infant and young child. Because different

TABLE 10.2 Motor milestones

AGE	GROSS MOTOR MILESTONE	FINE MOTOR MILESTONE
1–4 months	Sits with head steady	Puts hands together
2–5 months	Rolls over from front to back	Grasps rattle
5–8 months	Sits without support	Passes block from hand to hand
7–11 months	Crawls	Thumb–finger grasps
9–14 months	Stands without support	Bangs two blocks together
11–15 months	Walks well	Dumps object from bottle
15–24 months	Walks up stairs	Builds tower of 4 blocks
2–3 years	Balances on one foot	Builds tower of 8 blocks
2.5–3.5 years	Jumps in place	Imitates bridge with blocks

Note. Adapted from the Revised Denver Developmental and AAP Clinical Reports (Noritz, Murphy, & Neuromotor Screening Expert Panel, 2013).

motor skills first manifest at different times of life, they are often referred to as *motor milestones.* There are several assessment tools that describe the normal timing of appearance of these skills. Table 10.2 illustrates a basic template of motor milestones.

Identifying Infants and Young Children With Motor and Neurologic Disorders

Motor delays are most evident during the first 18 months of life, when the infant and young child are developing rapidly, assuming new motor skills almost on a weekly basis. Early recognition of infants and young children with motor or neurologic disorders, or both, is important because it allows for prompt diagnosis and management, optimizing long-term outcomes. However, it can be difficult to differentiate between young children who are simply lagging behind their peers, but who will eventually achieve the usual developmental milestones, and those who have underlying pathology. The key components in identifying the infant or young child with motor or neurologic disorders include the standard dimensions of any clinical assessment, a good history and physical health assessment, as well as specialized developmental screening tools.

The child's medical history can provide invaluable clues that can help narrow the differential diagnosis as well as suggest which further evaluations would be most worthwhile. In the infant or young child, a thorough history should include perinatal and neonatal details, even if the child is several months old, as they can have a direct bearing on early childhood disorders. Advanced maternal age increases the risk of certain chromosomal anomalies, such as Down syndrome, which are always associated with some degree of mental and motor impairment. Conditions during pregnancy, such as infection or substance use, can increase the risk for developmental problems in her offspring. Apgar scores of 0–3 for more than 5 minutes, particularly if associated with

perinatal acidosis and hypercarbia, may suggest perinatal brain injury, which may not manifest until after the neonatal period. Prematurity or low birth weight increases the risk for later developmental problems, particularly if the infant had a complicated neonatal course.

A developmental history is clearly important in identifying motor delays. By carefully following a child's attainment of specific milestones, the provider can see whether the growing child is "on track" developmentally. The developmental history is typically organized into domains, which include gross motor skills, fine motor skills, social interaction, language, and—for older children—self-help. Developmental milestones often fall into more than one domain, so assessment of all domains is important to determine the system most likely affected (e.g., cognitive vs. motor).

A family history can provide useful information in regard to inheritable conditions that may affect motor or neurologic development, or other reasons for delayed developmental milestones (e.g., syndromes associated with hearing loss). Findings that would suggest an inheritable condition include noninfectious illnesses that have affected multiple family members, congenital anomalies, and known genetic disorders. Developmental delays in the child's parents (as children) or siblings should also be solicited.

A social history is important because the environment in which the child lives can have a direct impact on her development. Poverty, poor living conditions, single parenting, and lack of family supports can all have a negative impact on child development. Evaluating the potential impact of the environment is important in ruling out a nonorganic cause for the child's delays. Several tools have been developed and validated that can be helpful in assessing the home environment for infants and toddlers (Bradley & Caldwell, 1977; Caldwell & Bradley, 1984; Frankenburg & Coons, 1986; Rijlaarsdam et al., 2012).

The health physical assessment should include measurement of growth parameters (weight, length, and head circumference) and a comprehensive, head-to-toe exam. If the infant or young child was born prematurely, then adjusted age (subtracting weeks of prematurity from chronologic age) should be used, at least until the child is 18–24 months old. Also, when plotting growth parameters, it is particularly helpful to do so on charts that include all previous measurements, so that growth trajectories can be observed. During the physical exam, special attention should be paid to looking for possible congenital anomalies.

Perhaps the most important part of the physical assessment is the neurologic exam, and this should include not only direct interrogation (tone, reflexes, strength, symmetry, sensation, cranial nerve responses) but also quiet observation of the child's movements and responsiveness. Regarding reflexes, it is important to note not only weakness or absence but also persistence of primitive reflexes (e.g., asymmetric tonic neck reflex, or fencing pose) that should disappear in a predictable fashion.

Developmental screening tools are helpful adjuncts to the history and physical exam. Several tools are available, although some have limited motor assessment (Caputo & Accardo, 1997). Also, some involve actually testing the child, are time-consuming and must be performed by a trained evaluator (Caputo & Accardo, 1997; Frankenburg & Dodds, 1990), whereas others can be administered as simple questionnaires to care providers (Bricker & Squires, 1999; Glascoe, 1998; Ireton, 1992); in most busy clinical practices the latter are used first, followed by more sophisticated screening tools if concerns are raised. Whatever screening tools are used, it is important that they are age appropriate, easy to administer, and consistent between evaluators. As with growth parameters, developmental screens should be scored based on adjusted, not chronologic, age. Abnormal development can be identified by either failure to extinguish primitive reflexes, referred to as *abnormal persistence*, or failure to achieve postural reflexes or motor milestones, referred to as *motor delay*.

The American Academy of Pediatrics (AAP) recommends developmental surveillance at all well-child, preventive-care visits, and standardized developmental screening if any concerns arise, as well as routinely at 9, 18, and 24–30 months old (Council on Children With Disabilities, Section on Developmental Behavioral Pediatrics, Bright Futures Steering Committee, & Medical Home Initiatives for Children With Special Needs Project Advisory Committee, 2006).

The AAP Neuromotor Screening Expert Panel recommends that every child with normal or low muscle tone and suspected motor delays have serum measurements of creatine phosphokinase (a muscle enzyme) and thyroid-stimulating hormone levels (Noritz et al., 2013). Muscle enzyme measurement will screen for a variety of diseases of the lower motor neurons or muscles, and thyroid function measurement will screen for the one of the most common causes of hypotonia in early childhood.

Major Causes of Delays in Motor and Neurologic Development

Although most infants and young children with disorders such as cerebral palsy will eventually develop abnormally increased tone (resistance to passive motion) in one or more muscles (a condition termed *spasticity*), most children with delays in neuromotor development will present with abnormally decreased tone; these children are commonly referred to as "floppy." Infants and young children with hypotonia will also demonstrate hyperextensibility of joints and abnormal postures, such as increased dorsiflexion of the feet, easy apposition of the thumb against the forearm, head lag, or slipping through the examiner's arms, when being held upright with one hand under each axilla.

Acute hypotonia, or hypotonia of sudden and recent onset, in the infant or young child is generally caused by a nonneurologic disorder, such as hypoglycemia, sepsis, viral encephalopathy, inadvertent exposure to certain medications, or serious gastrointestinal disturbances, like intussusception; these can be assessed by history or laboratory evaluation, or both. Acute hypotonia may also result from a recent intracranial or spinal injury, which can be suspected by history and confirmed by imaging studies. In most cases, acute hypotonia has a specific, identifiable underlying cause, and in most cases is reversible, although it may be associated with later neuromotor delays.

Motor delays are often associated with chronic, persistent hypotonia. When this is present, the primary concern should be for an underlying, permanent neurologic condition. Dysfunction at any level of the nervous system, including the brain (cerebrum and cerebellum), spinal cord, peripheral nerves, and muscles, can result in hypotonia and subsequent motor delay(s), however, disorders of the central nervous system (brain and spinal cord) are much more common than disorders of the peripheral nervous system (anterior horn cells, peripheral nerves, neuromotor junctions) or the musculoskeletal system (muscles, bone, tendons, connective tissues). However, disorders of the central nervous system (brain and spinal cord) are much more common. These include disorders of the cerebrum (e.g., cerebral palsy), cerebellum (e.g., ataxia), and the spinal cord (e.g., spina bifida). At long-term follow-up, cerebral palsy is the most common cause of chronic hypotonia (Igarashi, 2004). Many disorders associated with the peripheral nervous or musculoskeletal system are genetic, and a family history may be present; examples

TABLE 10.3 Common causes of motor delay (chronic hypotonia) by category

CATEGORY	COMMON EXAMPLES
Endocrine	Hypothyroidism
Neurologic	
Cerebrum	Cerebral palsy
Cerebellum	Ataxia
Spinal cord	Spina bifida
Anterior horn cell	Spinal muscular atrophy
Peripheral nerve	Congenital hypomyelinating neuropathy
Neuromuscular junction	Myasthenia
Musculoskeletal	Myotonic dystrophy
Combined neuromuscular	Leukodystrophies, dysautonomia, muscular dystrophies

include the myotonic and muscular dystrophies. Chronic hypotonia may occasionally be caused by reversible, nonneurologic conditions, such as hypothyroidism; these must also be considered and ruled out. Even if the underlying cause is not reversible, early recognition and evaluation may prevent more serious deterioration and improve long-term function. Table 10.3 presents some of the more common causes of motor delay.

When dysmorphic features or a family history are suggestive, one should consider an underlying genetic condition, because many demonstrate neuromotor delay as a primary or presenting feature (see Table 10.4). When a motor delay is found in conjunction with delays in other developmental domains, such as speech or cognition, mental or visual handicaps should also be suspected.

Major Types of Motor and Neurologic Impairments

There is a wide variety of conditions leading to motor and neurologic impairments in the neonate and young child. Some of these conditions are due to abnormal formation of the embryonic

TABLE 10.4 Genetic conditions that commonly present with motor delay

CATEGORY	COMMON FEATURES
Angelman	Early hypotonia, stereotypic hand-flapping and laughing ("happy puppet"), seizures, global delay
Down	Growth restriction, mental retardation, nuchal folds, simian creases, small low-set ears, epicanthal folds, macroglossia, Brushfield spots, congenital heart disease
Klinefelter	Male condition only, microorchidism, delayed speech
Fragile X	Male condition predominantly, global delays, high-arched palate, large ears, macroorchidism, autism
Neurofibromatosis, Type 1	Neurofibromata, café-au-lait spots, axillary freckling, Lisch nodules
Noonan	Growth retardation, global delays, winged scapulae, low posterior hair line, high anterior hair line, triangular facies, webbed neck, widely spaced eyes/nipples, congenital heart defects
Prader-Willi	Infantile feeding difficulties (poor suck), small hands, tapered fingers, thin upper lip, almond-shaped eyes, cryptorchidism, mental retardation
Velo-cardio-facial	Cleft palate, congenital heart defects, elongated facies, almond-shaped eyes, wide nose, small ears, hypoparathyroidism

brain, whereas some of them are due to insults that may have been sustained by a normally formed brain or peripheral nervous system.

Hypotonia

Hypotonia (decreased muscle tone and strength) is relatively common in the neonate. Disorders causing hypotonia range from effects of prematurity to central nervous system malformations, cerebral cortex effects of asphyxia, intracranial hemorrhage, infection, toxic and metabolic effects, electrolyte abnormalities, primary muscle disorders, disorders at the level of the neuromuscular junction, and disorders at the level of the nerve (e.g., polyneuropathies, demyelinating neuropathies, motor-sensory neuropathies). Investigation as to the etiology of hypotonia is complex and may include examination of the patient's parents, acquiring a family history, electromyogram, nerve conduction velocity, muscle biopsy, imaging of the brain, and specific blood tests.

Hypothyroidism

Hypothyroidism may cause neonatal hypotonia. In addition to hypotonia, infants with hypothyroidism may exhibit temperature instability, a large tongue, poor feeding, constipation, jaundice, delayed skeletal maturation, dry skin, and a hoarse cry. Routine neonatal screening for hypothyroidism is important for early detection and treatment, even before some of these clinical findings appear. Early treatment may help to preserve neurologic function.

Hypotonia Associated With Prematurity

Although the rates of cerebral palsy and other severe sensorimotor impairments have generally decreased among preterm survivors, these children still have significantly high rates (up to 50%) of more subtle neurologic problems. These problems include mild or fine gross motor delays, persistent asymmetries in movements or tone, intellectual delay, speech problems, and learning difficulties (Ferrari et al., 2012). However, because many former preterm infants will have transient problems of tone or posture that will gradually improve with time, it is important to distinguish these normal characteristics of preterm infants from the more pathologic clinical findings.

In utero, a fetus has the boundaries of the uterine wall to help her to keep her joints generally flexed. Premature babies have relatively weak flexor muscles and are, therefore, poorly able to control their joint positioning. The laxity of their ligaments and connective tissue around their joints allows their joints to be in extreme positions for long periods of time and can cause joint damage. In addition, being relatively immobilized in the neonatal intensive care unit in order to receive mechanical ventilation and IV fluids causes abnormal pressures to be exerted on the premature neonate's developing joints. Over the long term, this immobility may lead to limited range of motion of the joints, skeletal deformation (long bones, skull, neck, and spine), and abnormal shortening of the muscles. Common skeletal malalignment consequences seen in premature infants include eversion (turning outward) of the feet, frog-leg deformity (excessive abduction and external rotation of the hips), hyperextension of the neck, retraction of the shoulders, scaphocephaly (elongation of the skull in the anterior–posterior axis), and plagiocephaly (asymmetrical occipital flattening of the skull). Positioning the premature neonate in a variety of positions that allow a variety of forces and pressures to be applied to various joints at different points in time, while still allowing the provision of life-sustaining medical technology, can promote proper development and range of motion of the joints. Positioning the premature neonate in semiflexed and midline positions will also facilitate proper development of the bones, muscles, and joints (Sweeney & Gutierrez, 2002).

Even when corrected for weeks of prematurity, infants born prematurely, particularly those born before 32 weeks gestation, will lag behind their corrected age counterparts who were born at or near term (Wilson-Costello & Hack, 2010). Both active and passive muscle tone are generally much lower in the preterm infant (Dubowitz, Dubowitz, & Mercuri, 1999). Extensor tone tends to dominate, in contrast to the predominately flexed term infant. Although tone improves with age, at 40 weeks corrected gestation the preterm infant still does not possess the same degree of flexor tone as an infant born full term (Lenke, 2003).

In addition to correcting for degree of prematurity, when conducting the neuromotor exam of the former preterm infant, one should pay special attention to the change in tone over time. The hypotonic preterm infant whose tone gradually improves toward normal with age is likely to have no significant long-term concerns, as opposed to the child whose tone either does not improve with time or who progresses from hypotonic to hypertonic.

Neural Tube Defects

Neural tube defects (NTDs) are the most common structural defects of the central nervous system and the second most common birth defect overall (Botto, Moore, Khoury, & Erickson, 1999). NTDs result from failure of the neural tube to normally close during early embryonic life. There are a variety of NTDs; spina bifida aperta is the most common type. In *spina bifida aperta*, or *open spina bifida*, there is a corresponding defect in the skin overlying the caudal neural tube, through which the meninges and spinal cord can herniate. In a *meningocele* only the meninges are herniated; in a myelomeningocele both the meninges and spinal cord are herniated. *Meningocele* is a milder form of spina bifida aperta but much less common than myelomeningocele. *Spina bifida occulta*, or "hidden" spina bifida, differs from open spina bifida in that the overlying skin is intact and the neural elements are not exposed; as a result, spina bifida occulta can be asymptomatic, whereas myelomeningocele is always associated with significant loss of sensory and motor function distal to the site of the defect. The incidence of myelomeningocele has dropped in the past 20 years due to preconceptional and periconceptional maternal dietary supplementation with folate and due to the development and availability of fetal ultrasound to detect such fetal defects, giving families the option to decide whether to terminate afflicted pregnancies.

Myelomeningocele

Management of myelomeningocele at the time of birth includes protecting the open neural tube defect from trauma, infection, and the loss of heat and fluid (see Figure 10.1). This can be accomplished by placing warm, moist, sterile pads over the open myelomeningocele, and then covering the area with a sterile plastic bag until the lesion is surgically closed. All babies with surgically closed myelomeningocele should be assessed by magnetic resonance imaging (MRI), ultrasound, or computerized tomography shortly after surgery for development of hydrocephalus, because the Arnold-Chiari malformation of the lower part of the brain stem, which increases the risk of hydrocephalus, is present in 40% of babies with myelomeningocele.

Treatment for hydrocephalus generally requires placement of a ventriculoperitoneal (VP) shunt. The VP shunt drains excess cerebrospinal fluid from the ventricles of the brain into the abdomen. If left untreated, hydrocephalus that occurs early in life, before the skull bones have fused to create a closed cranial compartment, can cause the baby's brain to expand to a very large size. If this is allowed to occur, the baby's head is so heavy that he is unable to move well on his own. If hydrocephalus occurs after the skull bones have fused, the excess fluid causes extra pressure on the brain. This can cause poor blood delivery to the brain and adds to the risk of brain damage. For cases of hydrocephalus caused by brain malformations, it is important to note

that neurosurgical placement of a VP shunt can help to control hydrocephalus, but it does not cure the developmental brain defects nor correct any underlying abnormal function of the brain.

Depending on the level at which the myelomeningocele affects the spinal nerves, affected children may have weakness or paralysis of the legs; orthopedic problems, including dislocated hips; difficulty with stooling; and urinary retention (inadequate bladder emptying) with overflow incontinence. Urinary retention may overfill the bladder, backing urine up into the ureters and kidneys, increasing the risk for urinary tract infection. Therefore, patients are often placed on daily oral antibiotic prophylaxis. In addition, the urologist often prescribes intermittent bladder catheterizations every 3–4 hours to allow the urine to fully drain out of the bladder.

A child with myelomeningocele requires a multidisciplinary approach to meet her medical, surgical, and developmental needs. This team generally includes a primary care pediatrician or family practitioner, a neurodevelopmental physician, a neurologist, a urologist, an orthopedic surgeon, a physical or occupational therapist (or both), and a social worker.

Tethered Spinal Cord Syndrome

Tethered spinal cord syndrome (TSCS) is a condition closely associated with spina bifida that may also occur following trauma to the lower back. Tethering of the spinal cord occurs as a result of tissue attaching to the spinal cord, either due to an underlying neural tube defect, such as spina bifida, or following tissue trauma, including repair of a myelomeningocele. As the spinal cord normally grows more slowly than the surrounding vertebral column, this tethering to adjacent bone or skin results in progressive stretching of the spinal cord, leading to spinal cord dysfunction. Young children with TSCS will typically present with motor and sensory disturbances in the legs, leading to weakness and difficulties with gait or running; as the condition progresses, there may be loss of urinary and eventually bowel continence, and developmental or orthopedic deformities of the foot, legs, or spine (e.g., scoliosis). Older children and adults may complain of leg and/or back pain.

When there is an obvious neural tube defect, such as myelomeningocele or lipo (myelo) meningocele, concern for a tethered cord is straightforward. However, if there is no obvious spinal dysraphism, the presentation of TSCS may be more subtle, so one must have a high index of suspicion, particularly in a young child with motor or sensory concerns restricted to the lower extremities. Careful examination of the lower back may suggest the presence of a tethered cord, because cutaneous stigmata are common; these include hypertrichosis, capillary hemangiomas, dermal sinus tracts ("sacral dimples"; see Figure 10.2), lipomas, or other skin appendages located in the midline, above the gluteal folds.

Anencephaly

Anencephaly is a fairly rare, but much more severe, type of NTD, in which major portions of the cerebrum, skull, and scalp are missing (see Figure 3.2). Disorganized nerve cells occupying the base of the skull are open to the environment, and heat, fluids, and electrolytes are lost into the environment after birth, subjecting the child's nervous system to trauma and infection. Although a brainstem may exist, it eventually becomes dysfunctional and the child stops breathing. With anencephaly, there is no significant quantity of cerebral cortex, so the baby is unable to have any thought processes. Anencephaly is considered a lethal disorder; most fetuses with anencephaly do not survive birth, and those who do usually die within a few hours or days due to apneas, the effects of the environment on the exposed nervous tissue, or both. Infants who have survived beyond this time have never attained any level of consciousness.

FIGURE 10.1 Meninges and spinal cord tissue exposed to environment

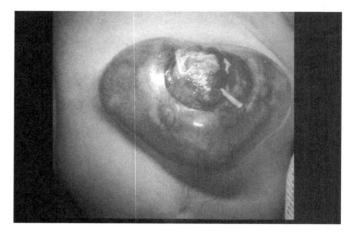

FIGURE 10.2 Sacral cleft

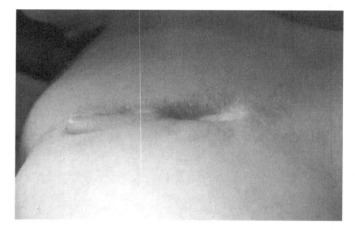

Anencephaly is not surgically correctable. Open neural tube defects, such as anencephaly and myelomeningocele, may be suspected by elevation of alpha-fetoprotein in amniotic fluid or in maternal serum.

Encephalocele

Encephalocele is another type of neural tube defect caused by faulty closure of the cranial portion of the neural tube (see Figure 3.3). Its etiologies include multifactorial inheritance, sporadic mutant genes, chromosomal abnormalities (trisomies and chromosomal duplications), syndromes, and environmental teratogens (e.g., maternal use of thalidomide, valproic acid, carbamazepine, aminopterin; maternal folate deficiency; and fetal exposure to excessively elevated serum glucose levels, as in poorly controlled maternal diabetes) during the first 28 days after fertilization, and maternal hyperthermia between 20 and 28 days gestation. Generally, encephaloceles are covered by skin, so they do not leak cerebrospinal fluid into the amniotic sac. Therefore, levels of alpha-fetoprotein in maternal serum or amniotic fluid are not elevated.

Anterior encephalocele. Rarely, encephaloceles may be anterior, protruding into the face and/or nasal cavity. Sometimes, a small nasal encephalocele may not be detected until complications ensue (nasal obstruction, breakdown of the encephalocele membrane leading to leaking of cerebrospinal fluid from the nose, or infection in the meninges, or all of these).

Posterior encephalocele. Seventy to eighty percent of encephaloceles occur in the occipital region. Brain tissue protruding from the cranium is usually derived from the occipital lobe and may be accompanied by dysraphic changes of the cerebellum and superior mesencephalon.

Surgical treatment of encephalocele is indicated for cosmetic reasons, as well as to keep the nasal passages patent (in the case of anterior encephalocele) and to prevent trauma and infection. Surgical treatment, in and of itself, cannot be expected to cure the fact that the brain developed abnormally. When the material contained in the encephalocele sac consists of brain tissue that needs to be amputated at the time of surgery, the neurodevelopmental prognosis is generally worse than when the encephalocele sac contains only cerebrospinal fluid. Neurodevelopmental abnormalities that are frequently seen in patients with encephalocele include cerebral palsy, seizures, developmental delay, ataxia, microcephaly, and vision problems. There is also an increased incidence of hydrocephalus in patients with encephalocele.

The prevalence of NTDs varies widely, ranging from 0.2 to 7 per 1,000 live births (Frey & Hauser, 2003). The highest rates are found in Great Britain, Ireland, Pakistan, India, China, and Egypt. Prevalence in the United States is approximately 0.2 per 1,000 children, with higher rates found in the East and South, and among Hispanics and Native Americans (Centers for Disease Control and Prevention, 2009). In general, NTDs are more common in girls, and recurrence rates for subsequent pregnancies are around 2.5%. Maternal dietary folate supplementation is believed to prevent approximately 60% of congenital neural tube defects because folate is important for the normal closure of the neural tube during the first 27 days of embryonic life (Wald & Sneddon, 1991).

Cerebral Palsy

Cerebral palsy (CP), as the name implies, is a motor impairment (palsy) that results from a lesion in the brain (cerebrum). What is not evident in its name, and yet is a key feature of CP, is the nonprogressive nature of the disorder. However, CP is not a specific disorder, but a syndrome that encompasses a variety of movement and postural abnormalities that first become evident during early childhood (Colver, Fairhurst, & Pharoah, 2013). Thus, the clinical presentation, as well as the site and severity of the impairments, can vary widely from case to case. In addition, CP is not a pure motor problem, but is often accompanied by difficulties in other aspects of nervous system behavior. Therefore, CP is a highly complex syndrome, and refinements in its definition and diagnosis have been made over the years. Recently, the International Executive Committee for the Definition of Cerebral Palsy proposed the following definition:

Cerebral palsy describes a group of permanent disorders of the development of the movement and posture, causing activity limitation, that are attributed to nonprogressive disturbances that occurred in the developing fetal or infant brain.

The motor disorders of cerebral palsy are often accompanied by disturbances of sensation, perception, cognition, communication, perception, and/or behavior, and/or by a seizure disorder (Rosenbaum et al., 2005, p. 572).

CP is often classified by some combination of the site of the brain lesion (cortical, pyramidal, extrapyramidal, cerebellar), the physical manifestations (spasticity, dystonia, athetosis, ataxia), and the distribution of extremities involved (diplegia, quadriplegia, hemiplegia). Some authors may also refer to the timing of the presumed insult (prepartum, intrapartum, postpartum, or postneonatal) or to the overall muscle tone (hypotonic, hypertonic).

The overall prevalence of CP is between 2.0 and 3.5 per 1,000 live births (Yeargin-Allsopp et al., 2008), but it increases with decreasing gestational age and birth weight, so that infants born less than 28 weeks gestation or weighing less than 1,000 grams have an overall prevalence of 9–10 per 1,000 neonatal survivors (Laptook, O'Shea, Shankaran, & NICHD Neonatal Network, 2005). Most cases of CP are felt to have an antenatal origin; about 10% are classified as postneonatal, and are generally a consequence of central nervous system infection or trauma. Although CP is occasionally diagnosed later in life, nearly all cases are identified during the first 3 to 5 years.

Seizures

Seizures are an important consideration in any child with suspected motor delays. Seizures may be associated with an underlying neurologic disorder, or they may present with focal or generalized weakness as a result of being postictal.

A *seizure* is an electrical event consisting of synchronous firing of groups of neurons. It is important to note that although seizures are the direct result of stimulated electrical activity in the brain, they do not always register on scalp electrodes. Therefore, a negative electroencephalogram does not rule out electrical seizure activity, and one must maintain a high degree of suspicion for clinical signs and symptoms suggestive of a seizure disorder. A *seizure disorder*, or *epilepsy*, is defined as two or more unprovoked seizures. Although 70% of epilepsy is idiopathic, a seizure disorder has prognostic significance for later neurodevelopmental outcome, even in the absence of an identified cause for the seizures.

It is helpful to consider the chronologic appearance of seizures, because this is an important factor both in terms of underlying cause(s) and long-term prognosis. Seizures during the neonatal period are usually suggestive of an underlying disturbance, such as hypoxic injury, infection, trauma, metabolic abnormality, central nervous system malformation, intracranial hemorrhage, stroke, or narcotic withdrawal. However, neonatal seizures may also be benign; these typically begin in the first days of life, are frequent but short lived, and are associated with a positive family history. These *benign neonatal familial seizures* typically resolve within 6 months and are not associated with long-term problems. In any case, it is important to verify any history of seizure activity during the neonatal period, because newborns normally have exaggerated tremors and sleep myoclonus that the inexperienced observer may mistake for a seizure.

During early infancy, several different types of seizures may present. *Febrile seizures*, as the name suggests, are associated with a high body temperature, usually as the result of a viral illness. These usually occur during the first year of life, and there is usually no other evidence of central nervous system disease; prognosis is excellent. In contrast, *infantile spasms*, or *early infantile epileptic encephalopathy*, typically present during the first year, and infantile spasms and early infantile epileptic encephalopathy carry a poor prognosis.

Other types of epilepsy usually present beyond the second year of life. Regardless of the age or type of presentation, all seizures, except perhaps for a single episode of a simple febrile seizure, should be evaluated by a pediatric neurologist. In general, a seizure disorder should be considered a potential sign of underlying brain injury (Olson, 2012); there is also the possibility that the seizures themselves could be harmful to the developing brain, although this remains a controversial point. In any case, a seizure disorder increases the risk of adverse long-term neurodevelopmental outcome (Thibeault-Eybalin, Lortie, & Carmant, 2009).

Muscular Dystrophy

Muscular dystrophy (MD) is a general term applied to a variety of inherited muscle disorders characterized clinically by progressive muscle wasting and weakness. These disorders are somewhat heterogeneous, but all MD results from a genetic defect in one or more proteins important in muscle function and development.

The best-known example, and most common type, of MD is *Duchenne muscular dystrophy* (DMD), a genetic defect resulting in dystrophin deficiency. DMD is an X-linked, recessive form of MD that affects approximately 1 in 4,000 boys. Like all MDs, Duchenne's is characterized by progressive muscle degeneration, leading to eventual cardiorespiratory failure and death—unlike the congenital muscular dystrophies, a collection of much less common conditions that present at or soon after birth (Mercuri & Longman, 2005), DMD and other childhood MD typically do not present until the third year of life, or even later, with some forms of MD not presenting until adulthood (Verma, Anziska, & Cracco, 2010).

Although children with MD typically present with weakness and delayed motor milestones,

there are exceptions. Children with *Becker MD*, which also involves a mutation of the dystrophin gene, may present without any skeletal muscle weakness; children might complain of cramps after exercise or, upon closer inspection, have evidence of isolated cardiomyopathy. In children with signs suggestive of MD, clinical suspicion can be confirmed by measuring creatine kinase, a muscle enzyme that is markedly elevated in children with MD.

Peripheral Nerve Injury

Pressure, stretching, or tearing injuries to peripheral nerves may occur in neonates and are most often associated with difficult deliveries. The two types of common peripheral nerve injuries in neonates are facial nerve and brachial plexus injuries.

Facial nerve injury

Facial nerve injury is the most common peripheral nerve injury in the neonate, with an incidence of approximately 7 per 1,000 births. The facial nerve passes under the cheekbone. It is believed that facial nerve injury is caused by pressure exerted by the maternal tailbone to the side of the fetal face during labor and delivery. Facial nerve palsy likewise may be related to a difficult, mid-forceps delivery but only rarely to low or outlet forceps application. If hemorrhage or edema (swelling) occurs in or around the facial nerve, a weakness of the muscles supplied by the nerve may result. A baby with facial nerve injury will have decreased facial expression on the affected side and will be unable to close his eye tightly on that side nor to wrinkle his eyebrow, raise the corner of his mouth, or open his mouth widely to create a crying face. While feeding, he may dribble milk from the corner of the mouth on the affected side. Fortunately, the weakness occurring with facial nerve injury is usually temporary and resolves when the hemorrhage or edema in the nerve sheath resolves. Most facial nerve palsies resolve spontaneously within 1–3 weeks. Only rarely will an affected infant have a residual deficit several months later. There is no specific treatment for facial nerve palsy. Supportive measures to protect the eye from corneal injury, if eyelid closure is ineffective, include the use of artificial tears and temporarily taping shut the eyelid on that side.

Brachial plexus injury

Brachial plexus injury occurs 0.5–2 times per 1,000 births. It is most common in full-term infants, especially large babies with broad shoulders who do not pass easily through the maternal pelvis, babies with evidence of fetal distress, and babies born to mothers with an abnormal labor and delivery. This injury generally comes about by traction being applied to the head (during head-first deliveries) or to the shoulders (during breech deliveries), so that the head and shoulder are stretched away from each other.

Stretching or tearing of the nerves in the brachial plexus causes a *Duchenne-Erb's brachial plexus palsy* and results in weakness or paralysis of the upper arm. There also may be some minor deficits in sensation, but these are difficult to evaluate in the neonate. The Moro reflex will be asymmetric, with the affected side being limp or weak. The infant will hold the affected arm close to her chest, with the elbow straight and internally rotated so that the palm of her hand points behind her. The wrist will be flexed, and the grasp reflex preserved. If the injury also involves nerves above the brachial plexus, there will be poor movement of the diaphragm on that side, which puts the baby at risk for respiratory compromise. Diaphragmatic paresis is associated with Duchenne-Erb's palsy about 6% of the time.

When the injury involves only the lower nerve roots, the forearm and hand will be affected. This is called *Klumpke palsy*. The wrist and fingers may be flexed, and the baby will not have any voluntary hand movement. The grasp reflex is absent, but the deep tendon reflexes are preserved. When thoracic nerve 1 is affected, the baby may have eyelid droop on that side and persistent constriction of the pupil of the eye (*Horner syndrome*). If the nerve injury does not heal, the iris of the affected eye eventually may have a deficit in pigment formation and remain unpigmented (blue).

More common than Klumpke's lower nerve palsy, but less common than Duchenne-Erb's upper nerve palsy, is the *total brachial plexus palsy*. In this situation, both paralysis and sensory deficit are most severe and extend from the fingers to the shoulder on the affected side. All reflexes are absent. Radiological or clinical evaluation of diaphragmatic function should be carried out in patients with Duchenne-Erb's or total brachial plexus palsy.

Long-term prognosis for peripheral nerve injury of the brachial plexus depends on the extent and severity of the lesion. Infants with initial mild weakness of only upper nerve roots have the best chance for typical outcome. Complete spontaneous recovery of most brachial plexus palsies has been reported in 50%–80% of patients. Clinical improvement within 2–4 weeks after birth is a favorable prognostic indicator. Infants destined to have complete, or nearly complete, recovery usually attain that recovery by 6 months old. Infants with total brachial plexus injury have the poorest outcome, with only about 15% of them spontaneously recovering typical function. After brachial plexus injury, x-ray studies may be indicated to look for injury to the clavicle (collar bone), upper humerus (long bone of the upper arm), shoulder joint, and cervical (neck) spine.

Treatment involves initial partial immobilization of the affected limb to avoid any additional stretching of the brachial plexus. Physical therapy should be delayed for 7–10 days after the injury due to the development of painful posttraumatic neuritis. Later, physical therapy includes gentle, passive range of motion of joints of the shoulder, elbow, wrist, and hands to prevent joint contractures. Pain may be controlled with acetaminophen and gentle massage. Occasional splinting of the wrist and hand into a position of function may be useful to prevent joint contractures. Evaluation by the orthopedic surgeon to investigate any bone or joint abnormalities may be useful, if the infant is not making much progress. When affected infants have exhibited no recovery by 3 months old, evaluation by the neurosurgeon may be helpful. Removal of scar tissue involving the nerve and surgical correction of torn nerves are some of the procedures occasionally offered by neurosurgeons for this condition (Fisher, 2009).

Other Motor and Neurologic Impairments

Many other conditions can affect normal neuromotor development in the infant and young child. Most have no cure; fortunately, they are not very common. Nevertheless, they are important to consider, because early diagnosis may be important for counseling purposes, and although they are not curable, early and directed management can lead to significant improvement in quality of life. Although there are too many conditions to detail here, some are particularly amenable to early diagnosis and management and are worth noting. These include spinal muscular atrophy, myopathies, and myasthenias.

Spinal muscular atrophy (SMA) is a genetic disorder (autosomal recessive) that results in a deficiency of a specific protein necessary for motor neuron function. Lack of this protein results in progressive loss of neuronal cells in the anterior horn of the spinal cord and subsequent generalized muscle wasting due to lack of appropriate neuronal signals. SMA is manifest by generalized weakness, loss of reflexes, and

delayed motor milestones. The muscles, although wasting, are otherwise normal, so serum levels of muscle enzymes are not elevated. SMA can present at any time of life; the most severe form, also known as Werdnig-Hoffmann disease, presents within the first months of life, usually with a quick onset and rapid deterioration resulting in death within 2 years.

Congenital myopathies are a group of genetic muscle disorders characterized by distinctive pathologic changes on muscle biopsy. These changes originate within the muscle fiber and vary widely, depending on the actual structure(s) affected within the fibers. Nevertheless, the congenital myopathies share some common clinical features, including generalized weakness, hypotonia, hyporeflexia, and decreased muscle mass. There may also be some dysmorphic features, related to the underlying myopathy, although these are more apparent as the child gets older; these include high-arched palate, elongated facies, pectus carinatum ("pigeon-chest"), foot deformities, and scoliosis. Most congenital myopathies present at or soon after birth, although a wide range of presentations exists, and some myopathies may be associated with only mild weakness that may not be appreciated for years. Muscle enzymes and electrical stimulation may be normal, and muscle biopsy remains the gold standard for diagnosis, although muscle imaging with ultrasound or MRI may be helpful. In this case, imaging may assist in selecting the best sites for biopsy, if muscle involvement is variable. Because of their overall rarity, congenital myopathies are usually considered a diagnosis of exclusion, after considering other common causes of weakness and motor delay (North, 2011).

Metabolic myopathies refer to hereditary disorders caused by specific enzyme defects that result in abnormal muscle energy metabolism. The enzyme defect interrupts normal metabolic pathways, leading to an insufficient supply of energy substrate. Different energy substrates are needed for different types of muscular activity (low intensity, brief high intensity, and sustained high intensity), so the symptoms of a given enzyme defect will depend on which substrate is affected. For example, with *glycogen storage disorder*, glucose is not readily available to the muscle, and this results in baseline weakness and hypotonia. Other types of metabolic myopathies include *lysosomal storage disorders* and *purine metabolism disorders*. In general, these conditions are progressive, and often fatal, and they first present in infancy, or much later in life, depending on the underlying disorder. Perhaps the most dramatic example is the infantile form of *Pompe disease*, a glycogen storage disorder that presents with rapidly progressive weakness and hypotonia, with death from cardiorespiratory failure within the first year of life.

Mitochondrial myopathies represent yet another class of myopathies, in which the underlying defect lies within the energy-producing structures within cells called *mitochondria*. Symptoms include weakness, hypotonia, and seizures. There are numerous types of mitochondrial disorders, and the timing and severity of presentation vary widely, depending on the type.

Myasthenia refers to weakness that is the result of dysfunction at the level of the neuromuscular junction. It is important to note that the myasthenias represent the only class of motor unit disease in which spinal reflexes may be preserved. Clinical manifestations will differ depending on the nature of the defect(s), but, in general, myasthenia can be characterized by easy fatigue; thus the diagnosis depends on a history of moderate to profound weakness after physical exertion. Most myasthenias have specific genetic defects that can be tested. One important exception is neonatal myasthenia gravis, which is a transient myasthenia caused by the transplacental passage of maternal acetylcholine receptor antibody to the fetus.

Management and Working With Families

Positive social relationships between infants and their parents are integral to forging healthy social and emotional development. Positive interactions between infants and their parents give the parents a sense of competence to care for and protect their infants. Those same positive interactions help the infant learn to trust her parents to provide for her needs, help her to develop a sense of self, and help her to regulate her own emotions. This strong infant–parent relationship promotes the thriving of the infant.

Chronic medical conditions during infancy and early childhood, such as prematurity, hypoxic-ischemic encephalopathy, and other forms of brain dysfunction and congenital anomalies interfere with the development of a positive infant–parent relationship because of prolonged hospital stays and difficulty for the parents to interpret their baby's social cues. Thus, the very babies who already have a high risk for neurodevelopmental delay because of their underlying medical conditions may have the additional risk of poor attachment to their parents.

When a newborn baby is obviously hypotonic, diagnostic evaluation and management can begin immediately, while the child is still in the hospital. In contrast, the child who initially appears well at birth but is destined to have significant neuromotor delay often presents in a much more subtle and insidious fashion during the first 2–3 years of life. The key, therefore, is close surveillance and screening, particularly in infants and young children with a history that places them at increased risk (e.g., prematurity, meningitis, family history). The primary medical provider (PMP) is in a good position to detect developmental delays that present over time, due to the frequency with which they will be seeing the infant or young child for routine pediatric preventive care during the first 3 years of life. Nevertheless, due to the normally rapid rate of neurologic and physical development during this time, the parent or primary caregiver is in even a better position, as he can see the child progress on a day-to-day basis. What primary caregivers often lack is the knowledge or expertise in assessing young child development; it is therefore important for the PMP to regularly educate them at each visit regarding what to look for and when to report concerns. Thus, although the PMP may detect a problem at a routine visit, it is often the primary caregiver who usually brings concerns regarding delayed motor development to the PMP.

When neuromotor delay is suspected, the PMP and family will work together to ensure that proper subspecialty evaluation and management are accomplished in an efficient and timely manner. Evaluation and management can involve numerous specialties, including developmental pediatrics, pediatric neurology, rehabilitation medicine, child psychology, pediatric endocrinology, genetics, metabolism, social service, pediatric orthopedics, occupational therapy, physical therapy, audiology, speech pathology, feeding and oral-motor therapy, and case management. Because the evaluation and management of developmental problems can become quite complex, the PMP can serve as the medical home for that child, to be the hub from which all selection and coordination of services emanates (Adams, Tapia, & Council on Children With Disabilities, 2013).

The following algorithm (Figure 10.3) for surveillance, screening, evaluation, and referral, has been suggested by an expert panel of the American Academy of Pediatrics.

FIGURE 10.3 An algorithm for identifying children with motor delays (Noritz et al., 2013)

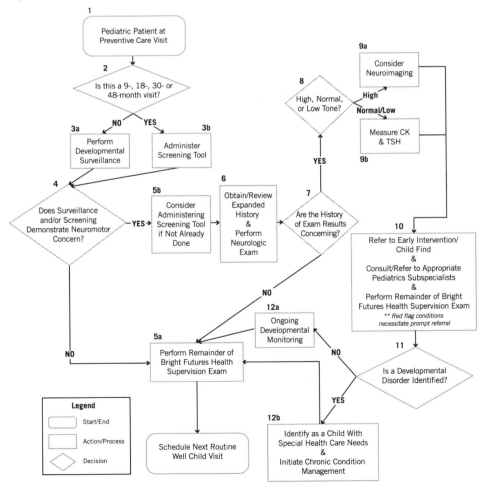

Chapter Summary

The first years of life are marked by rapid organ development, particularly in the brain and central nervous system. Motor development parallels the pattern of brain growth and development. A thorough understanding of normal neuromotor development during the first 3 years is critical in order to pick up delays or regression that could point to serious underlying disorders, not only of the central or peripheral nervous system, but of other areas as well. Whereas some disorders may be evident by history or physical examination, many can be quite subtle and require close attention to motor development. Early recognition of infants and young children with motor or neurologic disorders, or both, is important because it allows for prompt diagnosis and management, optimizing long-term outcomes.

Key Points to Remember

- Motor development is the core of neurodevelopment, from which all other developmental skills emerge or are facilitated.

- Persistence of primitive reflexes not only prevents normal motor development, but is also a hallmark of CP.

- Motor skills are acquired in a relatively constant and predictable fashion, allowing the use of "motor milestones" to assess infant and young child development over time.

- Major motor milestones are achieved in rapid succession during the first 2–3 years of life. Motor delays are therefore most evident during the first 18 months of life.

- Dysfunction at any level of the central or peripheral nervous system can lead to motor delays.

- Developmental surveillance is recommended at all well-child preventive care visits, and routinely at 9, 18, and 24–30 months old.

- Motor delays are often associated with hypotonia; when hypotonia is present, the primary concern should be for an underlying, possibly permanent, neurologic disorder.

- Timely identification of the infant or young child with significant motor delay can lead to directed therapies that will improve overall motor function and quality of life.

- Providing all children with a medical home optimizes their health and developmental outcomes.

Implications for Families and Professionals

During the first 2–3 years of life there is rapid development of motor skills. Because these skills enable the young child to explore and manipulate his environment, a delay in the acquisition of these skills will have a negative impact on his overall development, including cognition and communication. Early recognition of motor delay is not only important in diagnosing a potentially significant neurologic condition, but it can improve overall development. Even if the underlying cause cannot be cured, targeted interventions and aids can improve functional performance and optimize outcomes. The PMP and the primary caregiver have a joint responsibility for the careful monitoring and assessment of the young child's neuromotor development, in order to meet the goals of early recognition and management.

Professionals will:

- Provide surveillance and screening at regular intervals during routine well-child visits.

- Chart the young child's developmental progress over time, looking for significant deviations from normal.

- Educate the parent/caregiver regarding normal child neuromotor development, with emphasis on what to watch for and when to report concerns.

- Carefully consider and discuss parental/caregiver concerns as they are raised, offering confirmatory testing or reassuring counseling, as appropriate.

- Make appropriate subspecialty referrals as indicated.

- Facilitate evaluation, therapy, and management by establishing a medical home for the child.

- Develop a plan of care that is both child-centered and family-centered.

Parents will:

- Take a proactive role in observing and understanding their young child's neuromotor development.

- Provide a home environment that is both safe and appropriately stimulating for the young developing child.

- Recognize that each child develops at her own individual pace, and that even siblings may have very different developmental trajectories.

- Immediately bring any concerns regarding developmental progress to the attention of the child's primary medical provider.

- Ensure that their young child is seen at the recommended intervals for routine well-child medical care.

- Work with their child's primary medical provider to gain an understanding of any neurodevelopmental concerns, and follow through on the recommended plan of care for those concerns.

References

Adams, R. C., Tapia, C., & Council on Children with Disabilities. (2013). Early intervention, IDEA Part C services, and the medical home: Collaboration for best practice and best outcomes. *Pediatrics, 132*(4), e1073–1088. doi:10.1542/peds.2013–2305

Bax, M., Goldstein, M. Rosenbaum, P., Leviton, A., Paneth, N., Jacobsson, B.,…Executive Committee for the Definition of Cerebral Palsy. (2005). Proposed definition and classification of cerebral palsy, April 2005. *Developmental Medicine & Child Neurology, 47*, 571–576.

Bear, L. M. (2004). Early identification of infants at risk for developmental disabilities. *Pediatric Clinics of North America, 51*(3), 685–701. doi:10.1016/j.pcl.2004.01.015

Botto, L., Moore, C., Khoury, M., & Erickson, J. (1999). Neural-tube defects. *New England Journal of Medicine, 341*, 1509–1519.

Bradley, R., & Caldwell, B. (1977). Home observation for measurement of the environment: A validation study of screening efficiency. *American Journal of Mental Deficiency, 81*(5), 417–420.

Bricker, D., & Squires, J. (1999). *Ages and Stages Questionnaires: A parent-completed, child-monitoring system.* Baltimore, MD: Brookes.

Brown, T. T., & Jernigan, T. L. (2012). Brain development during the preschool years. *Neuropsychology Review, 22*(4), 313–333. doi:10.1007/s11065-012-9214-1

Caldwell, B., & Bradley, R. (1984). *Home observation for the measurement of the environment.* Little Rock, AR: University of Arkansas.

Capute, A., & Accardo, P. (1997). The infant neurodevelopmental assessment: A clinical interpretative manual for CAT-CLAMS. *Current Problems in Pediatrics, 26*, 238–257.

Centers for Disease Control and Prevention. (2009). Racial/ethnic differences in the birth prevalence of spina bifida: United States, 1995–2005. *MMWR Morbidity Mortality Weekly Report, 57*(53), 1409–1413.

Colver, A., Fairhurst, C., & Pharoah, P. O. D. (2013). Cerebral palsy. *The Lancet.* doi:10.1016/s0140-6736(13)61835-8

Council on Children With Disabilities, Section on Developmental Behavioral Pediatrics, Bright Futures Steering Committee, & Medical Home Initiatives for Children With Special Needs Project Advisory Committee. (2006). Identifying infants and young children with developmental disorders in the medical

PART 3

home: An algorithm for developmental surveillance and screening. *Pediatrics, 118*(1), 405–420.

Dubowitz, L. M., Dubowitz, V., & Mercuri, E. (1999). *The neurological assessment of the preterm and full-term newborn infant* (2nd ed.). London, UK: MacKeith Press.

Edwards, S. L., & Sarwark, J. F. (2005). Infant and child motor development. *Clinical Orthopaedics and Related Research, 434*, 33–39.

Ferrari, F., Gallo, C., Pugliese, M., Guidotti, I., Gavioli, S., Coccolini, E., . . . Bertoncelli, N. (2012). Preterm birth and developmental problems in the preschool age: Part I. Minor motor problems. *Journal of Maternal Fetal Neonatal Medicine, 25*(11), 2154–2159. doi:10.31 09/14767058.2012.696164

Fisher, M. A. (2009). Neonatal neurology. In G. Ensher, D. Clark, & N. Songer (Eds.), *Families, infants, and young children at risk: Pathways to best practice* (pp. 84–85). Baltimore, MD: Brookes.

Frankenburg, W., & Coons, C. (1986). Home screening questionnaire: Its validity in assessing home environment. *Journal of Pediatrics, 108*(4), 624–626.

Frankenburg, W., & Dodds, J. (1990). *The Denver Development Assessment* (Denver II). Denver, CO: University of Colorado Medical School.

Frey, L., & Hauser, W. A. (2003). Epidemiology of neural tube defects. *Epilepsia, 44*(Supp. 3), 4–13.

Gallahue, D., Ozmun, J., & Goodway, J. (2012). *Understanding motor development: Infants, children, adolescents, adults* (7th ed.). New York, NY: McGraw-Hill.

Glascoe, F. (1998). *Collaborating with parents: Using parents' evaluation of developmental status to detect and address developmental and behavioral problems.* Nashville, TN: Ellsworth and Vandermeer Press.

Hadders-Algra, M. (2005). The neuromotor examination of the preschool child and its prognostic significance. *Mental Retardation Developmental Disabilities Research Review, 11*(3), 180–188. doi:10.1002/mrdd.20069

Igarashi, M. (2004). Floppy infant syndrome. *Journal of Clinical Neuromuscular Disabilities, 6*(2), 69–90.

Ireton, H. (1992). *Child development inventory.* Minneapolis, MN: Behavior Science Systems.

Joh, A. S., Adolph, K. E., Narayanan, P. J., & Dietz, V. A. (2007). Gauging possibilities for action based on friction underfoot. *Journal of Experimental Psychology: Human Perception and Performance, 33*(5), 1145–1157. doi:10.1037/0096-1523.33.5.1145

Laptook, A., O'Shea, T., Shankaran, S., & NICHD Neonatal Network. (2005). Adverse neurodevelopmental outcomes among extremely low birth weight infants with a normal head ultrasound: Prevalence and antecedents. *Pediatrics, 115*(3), 673–680.

Lenke, M. C. (2003). Motor outcomes in premature infants. *Newborn Infant Nursing Review, 3*(3), 104–109.

Mercuri, E., & Longman, C. (2005). Congenital muscular dystrophy. *Pediatric Annals, 34*(7), 560–568.

Noritz, G. H., Murphy, N. A., & Neuromotor Screening Expert Panel. (2013). Motor delays: Early identification and evaluation. *Pediatrics, 131*(6), e2016–e2027.

North, K. N. (2011). Clinical approach to the diagnosis of congenital myopathies. *Seminars in Pediatric Neurology 18*(4), 216–220. doi:10.1016/j. spen.2011.10.002

Olson, D. (2012). Neonatal seizures. *NeoReviews, 13*, e213.

Rijlaarsdam, J., Stevens, G. W., van der Ende, J., Arends, L. R., Hofman, A., Jaddoe, V. W., . . . Tiemeier, H. (2012). A brief observational instrument for the assessment of infant home environment: Development and psychometric testing. *International Journal of Methods in Psychiatric Research, 21*(3), 195–204. doi:10.1002/mpr.1361

Sweeney, J. K., & Gutierrez, T. (2002). Musculoskeletal implications of preterm infant positioning in the NICU. *Journal of Perinatal & Neonatal Nursing, 16*(1), 58–70.

Thibeault-Eybalin, M.-P., Lortie, A., & Carmant, L. (2009). Neonatal seizures: Do they damage the brain? *Pediatric Neurology, 40*, 175–180.

Verma, S., Anziska, Y., & Cracco, J. (2010). Review of Duchenne muscular dystrophy (DMD) for the pediatricians in the community. *Clinics in Pediatrics (Phila), 49*(11), 1011–1017. doi: 10.1177/0009922810378738, Epub 2010 Aug 19

Wald, N., & Sneddon, J. (1991). Prevention of neural tube defects: Results of the Medical Research Council Vitamin Study. *Lancet, 338*(8760), 131–137.

Wilson-Costello, D., & Hack, M. (2010). Follow-up for high-risk neonates. In R. J. Martin, A. A. Fanaroff, & M. C. Walsh (Eds.), *Fanaroff and Martin's neonatal-perinatal medicine* (9th ed., pp. 1037–1048). St. Louis, MO: Elsevier Mosby.

Yeargin-Allsopp, M., Van Naarden Braun, K., Doernberg, N., Benedict, R., Kirby, R., & Durkin, M. (2008). Prevalence of cerebral palsy in 8-year-old children in three areas of the United States in 2002: A multisite collaboration. *Pediatrics, 121*, 547–554.

CHAPTER 11

Obesity in Young Children

Abigail R. Watson

Highlights of the Chapter

At the conclusion of the chapter, the reader will:

- understand the epidemiology of the current childhood obesity epidemic

- know the multifactorial causes of childhood obesity

- appreciate how obesity in young children contributes to current and future diseases

- recognize how physicians, schools, and communities can begin to work together to solve this increasing problem

The incidence of childhood obesity in the United States has increased dramatically over the last 30 years. Obesity has become the second-leading preventable cause of disease and death in the United States, second only to tobacco use (U.S. Department of Health and Human Services, 2001). For children 6–11 years old, the percentage of those classified as obese has increased from 7% in 1980 to nearly 20% in 2008. For adolescents 12–19 years old, the incidence has increased from 5% to 18% over the same period of time (Centers for Disease Control and Prevention [CDC], n.d.).

If the rates continue to increase unabated, life expectancy may begin to decrease, rather than increase as it has been doing. There are many factors contributing to this epidemic, and very few of them are *endogenous* factors, originating within the body. The vast majority of the suspected causes of this epidemic are *exogenous*, originating outside of the body, and therefore, entirely preventable if health care providers, parents, educators, and national leaders take the right steps. A glimmer of hope is arising in places that have successfully initiated childhood obesity programs (Robert Wood Johnson Foundation, 2012). Implementing more such programs would expand this glimmer of hope to become a reality, successfully reducing the incidence of childhood overweight and obesity, as well as the incidence of many of the health-related consequences of obesity, such as Type II diabetes, dyslipidemia, and hypertension.

Obesity in Young Children Defined

Obesity is a disease defined as the condition of excess body fat to the extent that health is impaired (World Health Organization [WHO], 2000). There are many ways of measuring a person's amount of body fat, but many of these methods (e.g., hydrodensitometry, dual-energy x-ray absorptiometry, and magnetic resonance imaging) are not easily conducted in most primary care offices. Therefore, weight-for-length measurements and body mass index (BMI) measurements are the most common ways of classifying overweight or obesity. BMI has been shown to correlate well with direct measures of adiposity, and with body fat, although not perfectly (Cole, Bellizzi, Flegal, & Dietz, 2000; Freedman et al., 2005; Mei et al., 2002; Pietrobelli et al., 1998).

Weight for Length

Beginning in infancy, health care providers measure babies' weights and lengths and plot these on growth curves over time. For children younger than 2 years old, health care providers look at the child's weight for length as a measure for obesity or overweight. For these children, weight-for-length percentiles above the 95th percentile are indicative of being overweight. The CDC recommends the use of the WHO's growth charts in children younger than 2 years (Grummer-Strawn, Reinold, Krebs, & CDC, 2010). This recommendation is in place partially because the WHO growth charts are based on infants who were fully breast-fed for 12 months or predominantly breast-fed for at least 4 months.

BMI

Physicians use BMI used to determine overweight or obesity in children, beginning at 2 years old (see Figure 11.1). The American Academy of Pediatrics (AAP) recommends that BMI be measured at least annually at well-child visits (Barlow, 2007). BMI is determined by dividing weight (kg) by height (m²). Alternatively, it can be calculated

FIGURE 11.1 Sample BMI curves for girls and boys, from New York State Department of Health

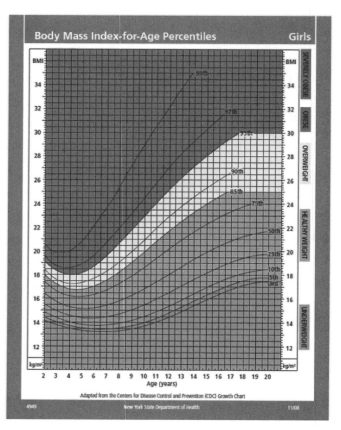

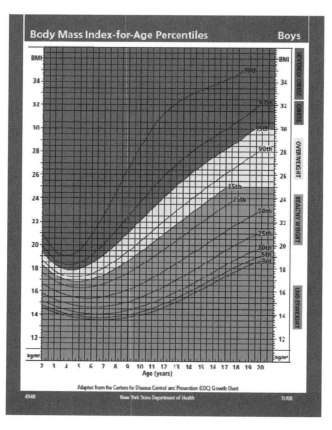

in pounds and inches as follows: [weight (lbs) / height (inches) × height (inches)] × 703. BMI is then plotted on separate curves for boys and girls, and correlated with age. BMI ≥ 85th percentile and < 95th percentile for age and sex is classified as overweight. BMI ≥ 95th percentile for age and sex is classified as obese (Ogden & Flegal, 2010). In certain cases, such as in muscular athletes, BMI may not accurately reflect a person's adiposity. In such situations, anthropometric measurements, such as skinfold thickness testing, may be more helpful.

Waist Circumference

Waist circumference is a commonly used measurement tool in adults who are overweight or obese. It helps approximate central adiposity, which is a strong predictor of some of the later health-related consequences of obesity, such as insulin resistance, Type II diabetes, and dyslipidemia (high blood triglycerides and cholesterol levels). The National Heart, Lung and Blood Institute/North American Association for the Study of Obesity Committee recommend using waist circumference cut points of 40 inches (102 cm) for adult men and 35 inches (88 cm) for adult women to define central obesity. Currently, there are no national recommendations for classification of central obesity in children and adolescents (Wang & Beydoun, 2007).

A Growing Epidemic

Data on childhood and adult obesity rates are available from many sources. The National Health and Nutrition Examination Survey (NHANES) is a cross-sectional survey including interviews conducted in people's homes and standardized physical examinations, thus presenting measured data. The National Survey of Children's Health (NSCH) is a survey of parents in each state. Although data are based on parental report,

the NSCH is the only source of comparative state-by-state data for children. The Youth Risk Behavior Surveillance System (YRBSS) includes both national and state surveys and is based on reported data by adolescents. The Behavioral Risk Factor Surveillance System (BFRSS) is an ongoing telephone health survey, begun by the CDC in 1984. It surveys a sample of adults in each state to get information on health risks and behaviors, including reported weight and height. It is likely that rates of overweight and obesity are slightly higher than these data show, as people tend to underestimate their weight and overestimate their height (Merrill & Richardson, 2009). The Pediatric Nutrition Surveillance Survey (PedNSS) examines children between 2 and 5 years old from lower income families. These data are based on actual measurements, rather than self-reports, and PedNSS is the only source of national surveillance data from the state and local level for low-income, preschool-aged children who are enrolled in federally funded health and nutrition programs, mainly Women, Infants, and Children (WIC).

Trends in Adults

It is nearly impossible to examine the obesity epidemic among American youth without looking at the epidemic among adults as well (see Figure 11.2). The prevalence of obesity in the United States has increased among adults and children over the last decades. More than two thirds of American adults are considered either overweight or obese (Flegal, Carroll, Ogden, & Curtin, 2010). According to NHANES, in 2009–2010, 35.7% (or more than 78 million) of U.S. adults were obese. There was no significant difference between men and women. This is equal to almost 41 million women and more than 37 million men, 20 years and older. There was no significant change in obesity prevalence in adults between 2007–2008 and 2009–2010 (Ogden, Carroll, Kit, & Flegal, 2012).

FIGURE 11.2 Obesity trends among U.S. adults

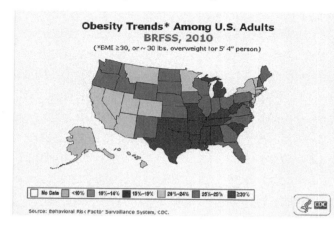

FIGURE 11.3 Obese 10- to 17-year-olds

Trends in Children

Unfortunately, the obesity epidemic among U.S. youth has paralleled that of adults, and a number of studies have shown that obesity in childhood is likely to persist into adulthood (Guo, Wu, Chumlea, & Roche, 2002; Whitaker, Wright, Pepe, Seidel, & Dietz, 1997). According to NHANES data, in 2009–2010, 16.9% of (about 12.5 million) of all U.S. children and adolescents, 2–19 years old, were obese. Of all boys, the figure was 18.6% (approximately 7 million), and of all girls, 15.0% (approximately 5 million; Ogden et al., 2012). Among boys, the prevalence of obesity increased from 1999–2000, from 14% to 18.6%. There was no significant change among girls, with a 13.8% prevalence in 1999–2000 and 15.0% in 2009–2010. As with adults, there was no significant change in obesity prevalence in children 2–10 years old from 2007–2008 to 2009–2010 (Ogden et al., 2012). Unfortunately, the most rapid increase in obesity rates among children has been seen in the highest BMI percentiles. However, in the U.S., as well as in Western Europe, Australia, and Japan, more recent studies suggest the rates may be at a plateau for the first time in 30 years (Lakshman, Elks, & Ong, 2012). According to the most recent published data from NSCH, in 2007 the lowest state childhood obesity rate was in Oregon where 9.6% of children 10–17

years old had a BMI > 95%. The highest rate, 21.9%, was in Mississippi (see Figure 11.3).

Trends in Preschool Children

Trends in overweight and obesity among U.S. preschool-age children have mirrored those seen in adolescents and adults. The WHO has estimated that the prevalence of children < 5 years old who have a BMI of more than 2 standard deviations (which is equivalent to 98%) increased from 4.2% in 1990 to 6.7% in 2010 and is expected to be at 9.1% by 2020 (Lakshman et al., 2012). This trend in preschool-age children is being seen worldwide and in some countries with even higher rates than the U.S.

Preschool-age children from lower income families have even higher rates of obesity. Of the programs that report to PedNSS, 93% reported an increase in prevalence of obesity between 1998 and 2003. However, between 2003 and 2008, only 50% reported an increase, 32% reported no change in obesity rates, and 18% reported a decrease (Sharma et al., 2009). A study (Pan, Blanck, Sherry, Dalenius, & Grummer-Stawn, 2012) conducted, using PedNSS data and reported in the *Journal of the American Medical Association*, showed that both obesity (BMI ≥ 95%) and extreme obesity (BMI ≥ 120% of the 95%, as defined by the 2000 CDC growth charts) increased between 1998 and 2003. However, this same study showed a slight downward trend in obesity and extreme obesity in this preschool population between 2003 and 2010. Pan et al. (2012) is the only national study to date to show a decrease in extreme obesity rates in this population.

Trends in Adolescents

U.S. data on adolescent overweight and obesity rates are largely derived from the YRBSS, which was most recently released in 2011. The most recent survey shows that 13% of high school students were obese, and 15.2% were overweight. Both of these show an upward trend from 1999, with the respective numbers in 1999 being 10.6% and 14.2%. Colorado had the lowest state level of obesity among high school students at 7.3%; Alabama had the highest, at 17% (Robert Wood Johnson Foundation, 2012; see Figure 11.4).

Why Is This Happening? Contributing Factors

The cause of the obesity epidemic is anything but straightforward, because there are many contributing factors. Although the biologic explanation for obesity is, simply stated, an imbalance between energy intake and energy expenditure, the factors behind this are much more complex.

FIGURE 11.4 Percent of obese high school students

PERCENT OF OBESE HIGH SCHOOL STUDENTS — Selected U.S. States, Youth Risk Behavior Survey, 2011

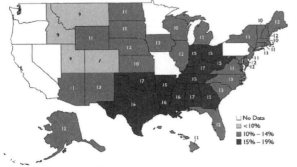

Source: YBRS. Trend maps from 2003-2011 are available at: http://www.cdc.gov/healthyyouth/obesity/obesity-youth.htm.

As was well stated by Butland et al. in the *UK Foresight Project Report* (2008), obesity is the result of a complex interplay between many societal and biological factors.

Endogenous Factors

This complex web of factors can be broken down into endogenous and exogenous factors. Endogenous factors include endocrine disorders; genetic syndromes such as Prader-Willi, Albright hereditary osteodystrophy, and Bardet-Biedl syndrome; as well as monogenic causes of obesity. Such syndromes associated with obesity should be considered whenever a child presents with severe obesity at a young age. As of 2012, more than 150 genetic loci have been conclusively linked to monogenic, syndromic, or multifactorial forms of obesity (Drong, Lindgren, & McCarthy, 2012). Although the number of these conditions being identified is increasing, syndromic and monogenic causes contribute little overall to childhood obesity (Ogden, Flegal, Carroll, & Johnson, 2002; see Table 11.1).

Heritability of obesity

Although the environmental causes of obesity cannot be ignored, the familial contributions are quite strong, with the heritability of obesity being estimated at anywhere from 40% to 70%, depending on the study (Ramachandrappa & Farooqi, 2011). Whitaker and colleagues (1997) showed that the risk of adult obesity was significantly greater if either the mother or the father was obese but that the effect of parental obesity on the risk of obesity in adulthood is the most pronounced for children younger than 10 years old. In this study, before 3 years old, the child's current weight status was not a predictor of adult obesity; the best predictor of adult obesity in children younger than 3 years was found to be parental obesity. For children 3–9 years old, the risk of adult obesity was based on both

TABLE 11.1 Obesity-related syndromes and disorders

SYNDROME/DISORDER	CLINICAL FINDINGS (WITH SEVERE OBESITY)
Single-gene mutation	
Leptin gene 7q31	Rapid weight gain in early months, hyperphagia, impaired satiety, hypogonadism, frequent infections, undetectable serum leptin levels[a]
Leptin receptor gene 1p31	Similar phenotype to Leptin gene mutation[a]
Pro-opiomelanocortin (POMC) 2p23	Similar phenotype to Leptin gene mutation[a]
Pro-hormone convertase 1 (PCSK1) 5q15-q21	Abnormal glucose homeostasis, glucocorticoid deficiency, hypogonadotropic hypogonadism, absorptive dysfunction of the small intestine in neonatal life[a]
Melanocortin 4 receptor 18q22	5%–6% of individuals with severe early-onset obesity, hyperphagia, increased lean mass, increased linear growth, hyperinsulinemia[a]
Autosomal disorders	
Albright hereditary osteodystrophy 20q13.11	Short stature, moderate obesity, mean IQ = 60, short metacarpals and meta-tarsals (especially 4th and 5th), aplasia or hypoplasia of dental enamel, areas of calcification in subcutaneous tissues, variable hypocalcemia and hyperphosphatemia[b]
Prader-Willi syndrome 15q11-13	Hypotonia, infantile failure to thrive, obesity presenting between 6 months and 6 years, mild–moderate mental retardation, small hands and feet, and small genitalia
Autosomal recessive disorders	
Alstrom syndrome 2p13	Retinal dystrophy, sensineuronal hearing loss, obesity, hyperinsulinism, Type II diabetes mellitus, hypertriglyceridemia[c]
Bardet-Biedl syndrome 11q13, 16q21, 3p13p12, 15q22.3q23 (more than 14 identified genes to date)	Retinal dystrophy, myopia, nystagmus, obesity, mental deficiency, limb abnormalities (polydactyly, syndactyly), renal abnormalities, small genitalia in males[b]
X-linked disorders	
Mehmo syndrome Xp22.13p21.1	Mitochondrial disorder with mental retardation, epileptic seizures, hypogonadism and small genitalia, microcephaly and obesity. Life expectancy < 2 years.[d]
Fragile X syndrome with Prader-Willi–like phenotype	Obesity, severe hyperphagia, variable neonatal hypotonia, small hands and feet, small testes/penis. Negative cytogenetic and methylation testing at 15q.[e]

[a] American Academy of Pediatrics & Hassink, 2007; Ramachandrappa & Farooqi, 2011. [b] Jones, 2006. [c] Joy et al., 2007. [d] Hassink, 2007; Lshinsky-Silver et al., 2002. [e] Nowicki et al., 2007.

the child's current weight status and the parental weight status, and in children older than 10 years, the best predictor of adult obesity was their current weight status. However, although some individuals certainly have a higher genetic susceptibility to weight gain, the gene pool does not change rapidly enough to fully explain the epidemic that has emerged over the last 30 years.

Prenatal influences

A growing area of interest and research over the last decade has focused on prenatal influences on later obesity. Many studies have shown a direct relationship between large-for-gestational-age birth weight and later BMI (Monasta et al., 2010). Also at the lower end of the birth-weight spectrum, lower birth weights seem to correlate with later risk for central adiposity (Oken & Gillman, 2003). Hales and Barker (1992) proposed that poor fetal and infant growth produced permanent changes in glucose and insulin metabolism and contributed to the later development of insulin resistance and Type II diabetes. This *thrifty phenotype hypothesis*, or the *Barker hypothesis*, was later confirmed; it is now understood that small-for-gestational age infants are at risk for central adiposity, insulin resistance, and Type II diabetes later in life (Hales & Barker, 1992; Vaag, Grunnet, Arora, & Brons, 2012).

Of course, many of these studies are limited by confounders such as gestational age, birth length, parental body size, maternal tobacco use, and socioeconomic factors. In studies that have been better able to control for these, the birth weight–obesity relationship still remains, which suggests that there must be some impact of the prenatal environment on later attainment of BMI. A study of sibling pairs in Pima, Indiana, in which one of the pairs was exposed to maternal gestational diabetes and the other was not, found that the offspring exposed to diabetes in utero had a higher BMI than did the unexposed sibling. This study design allowed the correlation between in utero environment and later BMI to be looked at in light of the same gene pool and the same postnatal environment (Dabelea et al., 2000). Larger birth weight has been correlated not only to obesity later in life, but also to increased risk of diabetes, hypertension, cardiovascular disease, and some forms of cancer (Poston, 2012).

Larger gestational weight gain is also correlated with higher birth weights, and therefore, increased risk for obesity later in life (Poston, 2012). The American College of Obstetricians and Gynecologists recommends pregnancy-weight gain as display in Table 11.2.

Much research has been aimed at trying to decipher the biological mechanism by which the intrauterine environment can lead to disease later in life. Many studies postulated the roles of in utero fetal hyperinsulinemia leading to larger adipocyte size or greater number, affecting pancreatic function, or causing permanent change in the structure or function of the appetite regulation centers of the brain (Oken & Gillman, 2003). These mechanisms are more recently thought to stem from epigenetics, or "changes in gene expression and cellular phenotypes that are mitotically stable but that occur without accompanying change in primary DNA sequence" (Drong et al., 2012, p. 709). However, the recent studies lack the power to conclusively define this relationship (Drong et al., 2012).

Exogenous Factors

There are many exogenous factors that affect the childhood obesity epidemic as well. Early-life nutrition and childhood dietary habits are of utmost importance, because habits learned early in life are often very persistent.

Breastfeeding

Many studies have been done looking into the effects of breastfeeding on later obesity risk in children. A recent systematic review of

TABLE 11.2 Pregnancy-weight gain

MATERNAL PREPREGNANCY BMI	RECOMMENDED WEIGHT GAIN (LBS)
< 18.5	28–40
18.5–24.9	25–35
25–29.9	15–25
≥ 30	11–20

Note. BMI = body mass index.

nine studies that adjusted for confounders of birth weight, parental weight status, parental smoking, dietary factors, physical activity, and socioeconomic status showed that breastfeeding is associated with a small but consistent protective effect against obesity risk in later childhood (Arenz, Ruckerl, Koletzko, & von Kries, 2004). Breast-fed infants may learn self-regulation of energy metabolism from a younger age, more than bottle-fed counterparts, because breast-fed infants can control the flow and the volume of milk they receive at one time, whereas an infant feeding from a bottle cannot as easily. Properties of the breast milk itself may lead to permanent metabolic changes or programming, such as protein content, which is lower in breast milk than in formula. Studies have looked at insulin levels in formula-feeding and breastfeeding infants; at approximately 1 week, formula-fed infants had significantly higher levels of insulin (Lucas et al., 1980). It is possible that the higher protein content in formula leads to this greater insulin secretion. Formula-fed infants tend to gain more weight and gain weight more rapidly than breast-fed infants. Children who gain weight more rapidly in the first year of life, crossing at least one major weight percentile band on their growth chart, have a two- to threefold increase in childhood obesity risk, as well as a stronger prediction for adult obesity (Druet et al., 2012). In these infants, the greater fat content in infancy may lead to a less-sensitive leptin feedback loop later in life (Dewey, 2003). Exogenous factors other than feeding, such as sleep duration, physical activity and sedentary behavior, and consumption of sugar-sweetened beverages, have also been linked to an increased risk for childhood obesity before 5 years old (Monasta et al., 2010).

Sleep duration

One review that summarized the results of 17 observational studies (Chen, Beydoun, & Wang, 2008) found that children with a shorter sleep duration had a 58% higher risk of overweight and obesity and that children with the shortest sleep duration had an even higher risk. There was a significant gender difference noted, with a stronger correlation found in boys. Other studies have noted that infants who sleep for fewer than 12 hours per day during infancy experienced a higher prevalence of overweight at 3 years old (Taveras, Rifas-Shiman, Oken, Gunderson, & Gillman, 2008).

Physical activity

The correlation between sedentary behavior and obesity risk seems to be even stronger. One of the first studies done on this topic by William Dietz and Steven Gortmaker found that each additional hour of television per day increased the prevalence of obesity by 2% (Dietz & Gortmaker, 1985). They purported that television watching may affect weight in many ways, including making less time in a child's day for physical activity and exposing children to media that may increase their desire to consume high-calorie foods; also, children may snack more while watching television. Many other studies have been done on this topic, most finding a small but statistically significant correlation with sedentary activities and childhood overweight and obesity, though again, many of these studies are cross-sectional in design and raise the question of reverse causality (Anderson & Butcher, 2006).

Sugar-sweetened beverages

The consumption of sugar-sweetened beverages has increased over the last 30 years (Putnam & Gerrior, 1999) and is a frequent target of anti-obesity campaigns. However, review of the scientific data to date is less convincing on the role of sugar-sweetened beverages and causality of childhood obesity. Two systematic reviews showed some of the discrepancies in the literature surrounding this issue. Gibson (2008) examined 44 studies, most cross-sectional, 17 prospective,

4 interventional, and 6 review articles on this subject. Approximately half of the cross-sectional and prospective reviews found a positive correlation between sugar-sweetened beverages and BMI, weight, or adiposity. The fact that there are relatively few interventional studies and that it is difficult to control for the many confounders make it hard to determine true causality. In another recent systematic review, Malik, Schulze, and Hu (2006) looked at large cross-sectional studies, cohort studies with long follow-up, and interventional studies and concluded that a greater consumption of sugar-sweetened beverages was associated with weight gain and obesity, but that more research is needed. Review of some experimental studies shows an effect of sugar-sweetened beverages. A 1-year intervention study (Thomas, Cavan, & Kerr, 2004) showed that school children who were randomized to participate in an educational program targeting the consumption of soft drinks had a reduction in BMI. Another randomized control trial (Ebbeling et al., 2012) showed that reducing the consumption of sugar-sweetened beverages in overweight and obese adolescents was associated with a modest reduction in BMI. As with many of the other factors linked to this obesity epidemic, it makes biological sense that increased consumption of sugar-sweetened beverages would increase a person's risk of future obesity, but it remains difficult to prove causation.

Environmental changes

No discussion on the causes of the current epidemic would be complete without touching on environmental changes including the food market, the built environment, schools and day care, and parents. None of these factors has been rigorously linked to causality of the obesity epidemic, but correlations have been found. Food markets have changed, with increased advertising of soft drinks, increased consumption of food eaten away from home, and increased portion sizes of packaged foods (Anderson & Butcher, 2006). The built environment has also changed over time, with increasing urban sprawl, more increase in daily vehicle-miles traveled, and fewer children walking or biking to school (Anderson & Butcher, 2006). The environment within schools and day care centers has also changed over time, with an increase in soft drinks and snacks sold in school vending machines, less physical education and recess time, and more children in day care. Over the past 30 years, the number of children with two parents, or their single parent, in the labor force has increased (Anderson & Butcher, 2006), which could be a driving force behind the increase in food consumed away from home and the increase in consumption of prepackaged food. More time with parents out of the home may also be related to duration of breastfeeding and increased screen time among children (Anderson & Butcher, 2006).

Health-Related Consequences

The need to prevent childhood obesity lies not only within the need to prevent complications as an adult but also to decrease the immediate comorbidities that occur during childhood (see Table 11.3). Obesity can affect the cardiovascular system with disorders such as dyslipidemia and elevated blood pressure; and it has a particular impact on the endocrine system, affecting insulin resistance and leading to Type II diabetes mellitus. Obesity carries an increased risk for asthma or worsening of preexisting asthma, and low-grade systemic inflammation (Reilly et al., 2003), and it impacts other systems as well: gastrointestinal, pulmonary, musculoskeletal, and neurologic. There are well-documented effects of childhood obesity on current and later mental health, as well as societal and economic consequences. It is important to note that obesity during childhood increases the risk of disease and premature death in adulthood, independent of obesity as an adult (Must, Philips, & Naumova, 2012). In addition, there is strong evidence, as previously mentioned, that obese children and adolescents are more likely to become obese adults (Guo et al., 2002; Whitaker et al., 1997).

Economic Consequences

The economic consequences of this epidemic are particularly staggering. It has been estimated that health care costs associated with obesity account for 27% of the growth in US health care expenditure between 1987 and 2001. Studies also estimate that obesity-related, health care costs

TABLE 11.3 Health-related consequences of obesity

CONSEQUENCE	DISEASE PROCESS
Endocrine system	
Impaired glucose tolerance	Fasting blood glucose ≥ 100 mg/dl. Insulin resistance is often a good predictor of impaired glucose tolerance, and both of these are the beginning of a pathway leading to Type II diabetes. Insulin resistance occurs when insulin is associated with a subnormal glucose response.
Type II diabetes mellitus (Type II DM)	Rates are increasing dramatically in children (Pinhas-Hamiel et al., 1996; Rosenbloom, Joe, Young, & Winter, 1999), and body mass index (BMI) during childhood is associated with Type II DM during adulthood (Tirosh et al., 2011). A \ study (Sinha et al., 2002) found that 4% of obese children had previously undiagnosed and asymptomatic Type II DM. Type II DM is characterized by insulin resistance and β cell failure.
Polycystic ovarian syndrome	Hallmarks are ovulatory dysfunction (menstrual irregularities) and hyperandrogenism. Other characteristics include acne, hirsutism (excess body hair in a male pattern of distribution), obesity, acanthosis nigricans, and +/- polycystic ovaries.
Metabolic syndrome	There is lack of consensus regarding the definition of this syndrome in both adults and children and adolescents. The most commonly used criteria are those put forth by the Adult Treatment Panel III, modified for children and adolescents. These include the presence of ≥ 3 of the following: triglycerides ≥ 95%; HDL cholesterol < 5%; blood pressure with either diastolic or systolic measurements ≥ 95%; or the presence of impaired glucose tolerance (Jolliffe & Janssen, 2007). The prevalence of metabolic syndrome in children greater than 12 years old is estimated to be about 9%, as defined by the above criteria (De Ferranti et al., 2004).
Cardiovascular system	
Hypertension	Numerous studies have shown an increased incidence of primary hypertension in children and adolescents whose BMI is ≥ 95% (Freedman, Dietz, Srinivasan, & Berenson, 1999; Rosner, Prineas, Daniels, & Loggie, 2000). Elevated blood pressure in children is defined based on age, sex, and height percentile. Blood pressure values between the 90% and 95% are considered pre-hypertensive; > 95% and < 99% + 5 mm Hg are Stage I hypertension; and > 99% + 5 mm Hg are Stage II hypertension (Kavey, Simons-Morton, de Jesus, & the National Heart, Lung and Blood Institute, National Institutes of Health, 2011). The presence of hypertension in childhood increases the risk of hypertension and metabolic syndrome in adulthood, even after adjustment for adult BMI (Sun et al., 2007).

continued

TABLE 11.3 Health-related consequences of obesity (continued)

CONSEQUENCE	DISEASE PROCESS
Dyslipidemia	The pattern most commonly seen is elevated low density lipoprotein (LDL), elevated triglycerides, and low high density lipoprotein (HDL). There are age-specific norms for children and adolescents (Kavey et al., 2011). Overweight and obese children are more likely to have dyslipidemia in both childhood and adulthood, and the pattern of elevated total cholesterol, LDL, triglycerides, and decreased HDL persists into adulthood (Srinivasan, Weihang, Wattigney, & Berenson, 1996).
Adult coronary heart disease	Elevated BMI during childhood and adolescence has been associated with increased risk for adult coronary artery disease and persisted after adjustment for adult BMI (Tirosh et al., 2011).
Gastrointestinal system	
Nonalcoholic fatty liver disease (NAFLD)	Is strongly correlated with obesity, even in children and adolescents, and is also correlated with Hispanic race, independent of BMI (Schwimmer et al., 2006). Many patients are asymptomatic, or may have right upper quadrant pain or hepatomegaly. Diagnosis remains based on biopsy, though often suspected in obese individuals with elevated transaminases. Weight loss is the first line of therapy (Chalasani et al., 2012).
Cholelithiasis (gallstones)	Obesity is the most common cause of gallstones in children without underlying predisposing conditions such as parental nutrition or hemolytic disease. Signs and symptoms include right upper quadrant pain, jaundice, nausea, vomiting and intolerance of fatty foods (Koebnick et al., 2012).
Pulmonary system	
Obstructive sleep apnea (OSA)	Intermittent complete obstruction and/or partial upper airway obstruction that disrupts ventilation during sleep and/or normal sleep patterns. Diagnosed by nocturnal polysommography. Much more common in obese individuals. Insulin resistance has been linked to OSA after controlling for BMI in adults (Fennoy, 2010).
Obesity hypoventilation syndrome	BMI > 30 kg/m^2, daytime alveolar hypoventilation (PaCO2 > 45) that cannot be attributed to another disease state. Many patients also have OSA. High mortality rate. Treatment involves nocturnal continuous positive airway pressure (CPAP), and weight loss. Many of these patients are severely obese and may benefit from bariatric surgery (Littleton & Mokhlesi, 2009).
Asthma	It is not entirely clear if obesity worsens asthma, or if asthma itself leads to decreased physical activity and worsened obesity. Many have proposed that obesity creates a state of inflammation in the body that contributes to asthma. Other postulated mechanisms involve the effect of excess weight on lung function and the effect of an inactive lifestyle on lung function (Fennoy, 2010).
Musculoskeletal system	
Slipped capital femoral epiphysis (SCFE)	Nontraumatic displacement of the proximal femoral epiphysis from the metaphysis. Very strongly linked to obesity. Suspect especially in obese adolescents during pubertal growth spurt with limp or knee, hip, or thigh pain. Diagnosed by radiographs (Fennoy, 2010).
Tibia vara (Blount's disease)	Acquired progressively bowed legs resulting from inhibited growth of the medial proximal tibial growth plate due to bearing excessive weight. Radiography is diagnostic (Fennoy, 2010).

PART **3**

continued

TABLE 11.3 Health-related consequences of obesity (continued)

CONSEQUENCE	DISEASE PROCESS
Neurological system	
Pseudotumor cerebri/ idiopathic intracranial hypertension (IIH)	Elevated intracranial pressure without evidence of radiographic, clinical, or laboratory pathology. Headache, sometimes nausea or vomiting, eye pain, and transient visual disturbances. Papilledema is often present on exam, and CSF pressure is elevated. Treatment is focused at weight loss, along with medication to reduce intracranial pressure and preserve vision (Fennoy, 2010).
Psychological system	Many studies have linked obesity in children to low self-esteem, depression, anxiety, and bullying, as well as decreased quality of life. These risks increase with age, and are more prevalent in females.

are expected to double every decade and will account for 16-18% of US health care costs by 2030 (Wang, McPherson, Marsh, Gortmaker, & Brown, 2011). The increased health care costs are not the only negative impact on society; there are also substantial indirect costs from increased mortality prior to retirement, work absenteeism, and decreased productivity (Wang et al., 2011).

Management and Prevention: Partnerships Among Families, Pediatricians, and Educators

Because the etiology of childhood obesity is not straightforward, with many factors in play, its management and prevention therefore must be multifactorial as well. The battle against this epidemic cannot be fought just on one front; rather, it must involve many levels including health care professionals, families, schools, community resources, and government. Over the last decade, the awareness of this problem has increased, and it does seem that the beginning steps have been taken in many of these arenas. Now, various professionals need to find a way to work together and continue to at least stabilize the epidemic, and eventually decrease childhood and adolescent obesity rates.

Interventions Prenatally and With Young Children

The first physicians who are uniquely positioned to help make an impact in this battle are obstetricians. Even though obstetricians will not be caring for the child after birth, maternal health during pregnancy certainly affects the risks for childhood obesity, as discussed earlier. Obstetricians should discuss appropriate maternal weight gain, diet, and exercise during pregnancy, as well as encourage breastfeeding and offer information on breastfeeding classes that can be taken during pregnancy, to ensure that women are as prepared as possible.

Physicians routinely see overweight and obese children in their offices. There are some evidence-based interventions that should be conducted consistently in any office that sees children. Physicians should encourage exclusive breastfeeding for the first 6 months of life, and longer (ideally for at least 1 year) in addition to complementary foods, if both mother and child wish, understanding that following through on this recommendation is not feasible for some women (Eidelman & Schanler, 2012). BMI should be checked at least annually, documented, and the result—as well as nutrition and exercise—discussed with the family (Barlow, 2007). Educating parents about healthy diet and lifestyle when their children are young can make a big impact. For example, at the 4-month well-child check-up, physicians can teach parents that juice is unnecessary and should be ≤ 4 oz per day of 100% fruit juice at the most; at the 9-month physical, physicians can educate parents about the importance of weaning their baby off a bottle by 12–15 months.

Screen for Elevated Blood Pressure

In an office setting, it is also important for physicians to screen for comorbidities associated with childhood obesity, of which there are many, as discussed. All children 3 years old or older should have blood pressure measured at least annually, and this needs to be done appropriately and with the correct-sized blood pressure cuff (High Blood Pressure Education Program Working Group on High Blood Pressure in Children and Adolescents, 2004). There are certain medical conditions for which children younger than 3 should have blood pressures measured including a history of prematurity, very low birth weight, or other neonatal complications requiring intensive care; congenital heart disease (repaired or unrepaired); recurrent urinary tract infections, hematuria or proteinuria, known renal disease or urologic malformations, and family history of congenital renal disease; sold-organ transplant, malignancy, or bone-marrow transplant; treatment with drugs known to raise blood pressure; and other systemic illnesses associated with hypertension (such as neurofibromatosis or tuberous sclerosis), or evidence of increased intracranial pressure (High Blood Pressure Education Program Working Group on High Blood Pressure in Children and Adolescents, 2004). Diagnosis of elevated blood pressure in children and adolescents requires comparison to norms based on age, sex, and height percentile. Children whose blood pressure falls less than

the 90th percentile for age, sex, and height are considered normotensive. BP between the 90th and 95th percentiles is considered prehypertensive. BP ≥ 95% but <99% + 5 mmHg is Stage 1 hypertension, and BP ≥ 99% + 5 mmHg is Stage 2 hypertension. Further work-up and management of pediatric hypertension can be found in the summary report of the Expert Panel on Integrated Guidelines for Cardiovascular Health and Risk Reduction in Children and Adolescents (Kavey et al., 2011).

Screen for Dyslipidemia

Physicians should also screen children at risk for dyslipidemia. The Expert Panel on Integrated Guidelines for Cardiovascular Health and Risk Reduction in Children and Adolescents (Kavey et al., 2011) recommends that lipid screening not be undertaken in children from birth to 2 years old. Thereafter, lipid screening via fasting lipid profiles is recommended, if there is a strong family history of coronary artery disease in young relatives; a parent with a total cholesterol ≥ 240 or known dyslipidemia; the child has diabetes, hypertension, BMI ≥ 95%, or smokes cigarettes; or the child has a moderate or high-risk medical condition as defined by the Expert Panel on Integrated Guidelines for Cardiovascular Health and Risk Reduction in Children and Adolescents. It is recommended that measuring fasting lipid profiles be done twice, more than 2 weeks apart but less than 3 months apart, because results can be affected by many disease states, including viral infections. In addition, universal screening of all children, regardless of health or BMI status, should be done once at 9 to 11 years old, and again once at 17 to 21 years old. Many studies have shown that non-HDL cholesterol is a significant predictor of atherosclerosis, and can be measured in the nonfasting state, so it is appropriate to provide universal screening to pediatric patients at these ages, using a nonfasting

PART 3

cholesterol measurement. BMI, blood pressure, and cholesterol results should be routinely discussed with parents beginning at 2 years and older (and weight-for-length measurements when children are younger than 2 years, if they are very elevated and there are dietary concerns).

In the Community

In the schools and community, much is being done to help combat this epidemic. Programs such as Michelle Obama's "Let's Move" campaign and the Healthy Hunger Free Kids Act of 2010, which regulates school lunches and foods provided in vending machines in schools, have pushed the obesity epidemic even more into the forefront of many communities. Studies examining school-based interventions in children 6–12 years old have found that these may be effective means of reducing BMI. In particular, the following seems to be helpful (Waters et al., 2011): school curricula including healthy eating, physical activity, and body image; increased sessions for physical activity; improvements in nutritional quality of the food supply in schools; environments and cultural practices that support healthier eating and being active throughout the day; support for teachers and staff to implement health promotion strategies and activities; and parent support and home activities that encourage children to be more active and eat more nutritious foods. Less research has been conducted on the results of intervention in younger children, although it is certainly reasonable to assume that interventions at younger ages would be more beneficial. Currently, the results of the Early Prevention of Obesity in Children (EPOCH) Collaboration (Askie et al., 2010) are still pending publication; it will be interesting to see what this meta-analysis shows on interventions in younger children. Certainly this problem cannot be fixed only at the individual level. As William Dietz reviewed in his commentary

"Reversing the Tide of Obesity" (Dietz, 2011), obesity prevention will require policy interventions and action at numerous levels of society. At the very least, providers can advocate in their communities for parks and recreation facilities, and encourage grocery stores to offer healthy, low-cost foods, as well as try to promote the accessibility of healthy foods, perhaps through local farmers markets.

Chapter Summary

This chapter has discussed the alarming increase in childhood obesity and the multifactorial causes of childhood obesity. Short-term and long-term health consequences were reviewed. Interventions by physicians and at a community level were described.

Key Points to Remember

- The incidence of childhood obesity has increased substantially over the last 30 years, but it may be beginning to plateau.

- Obesity in children is defined as a BMI ≥ 95% for age and sex.

- The etiology of this current epidemic is complex and multifactorial, and, therefore, requires a multifactorial approach to prevention and treatment.

- There are numerous health-related consequences of childhood obesity, many beginning in childhood, that often persist into adulthood including adult obesity, dyslipidemia, hypertension, and mental-health-related consequences.

- Increasing awareness through doctor's office visits, school-based interventions, and community and national interventions will hopefully project the current plateau into an eventual decline in the rates of childhood obesity.

Implications for Families and Professionals

The following are helpful implications for both parents and professionals working with infants and young children:

- Practitioners should start discussing this problem early in childhood, even at obstetrician visits before a child is born. Obstetricians can emphasize appropriate weight gain during pregnancy and stress the importance of breastfeeding, so a new mom is better prepared to take on this challenge.

- Providers must measure and discuss BMI at every preventive care visit.

- Parents should be encouraged to think about healthy weight, diet, and activity levels for their children, starting when the children are young.

- Schools should continue to increase their focus on healthy foods served at school, provide ample access to physical education classes and recess time, and educate students on nutritious eating, physical activity, and body image.

References

American Academy of Pediatrics & Hassink, S. G. (2007). *Pediatric obesity: Prevention, intervention, and treatment strategies for primary care*. Elk Grove Village, IL: American Academy of Pediatrics.

Anderson, P. M., & Butcher, K. F. (2006). Childhood obesity: Trends and potential causes. *The Future of Children, 16*(1), 19–45. Retrieved from www.futureofchildren.org

Arenz, S., Ruckerl, R., Koletzko, B., & von Kries, R. (2004). Breast-feeding and childhood obesity: A systematic review. *International Journal of Obesity, 28*, 1247–1256.

Askie, L. M., Baur, L. A., Campbell, K., Daniels, L. A., Hesketh, K., Magarey, A., . . . Wen, L. M. (2010). EPOCH collaboration: The early prevention of obesity in children (EPOCH)—An individual patient data prospective meta-analysis. *BMC Public Health, 10*, 728.

Barlow, S. E. (2007). Expert committee recommendations regarding the prevention, assessment and treatment of child and adolescent overweight and obesity: Summary report. *Pediatrics 120*(Supp. 4), S164–S192.

Butland, B., Jebb, S., Kopelman, P., McPherson, K., Thomas, S., & Mardell, J. (2008). *Tackling obesities: Future choices (Foresight Project Report)*. Retrieved from www.bis.gov.uk/assets/bispartners/foresight/docs/obesity/17.pdf

Centers for Disease Control and Prevention. (n.d.) *Childhood obesity facts*. Retrieved from www.cdc.gov/obesity/data/childhood.html

Chalasani N., Younossi Z., Lavine, J. E., Diehl, A. M., Brunt, E. M., Cusi, K., . . . Sanyal, A. J. (2012). The diagnosis and management of non-alcoholic fatty liver disease: Practice guideline by the American Gastroenterological Association, American Association for the Study of Liver Diseases, and American College of Gastroenterology. *Gastroenterology, 142*, 1592–1609.

Chen X., Beydoun, M. A., & Wang, Y. (2008). Is sleep duration associated with childhood obesity? A systematic review and meta-analysis. *Obesity, 16*, 265–274.

Cole, T. J., Bellizzi, M. C., Flegal, K. M., & Dietz, W. H. (2000). Establishing a standard definition for child overweight and obesity worldwide: International survey. *British Medical Journal, 320*, 1240–1243.

Dabelea, D., Hanson, R. L., Lindsay, R. S., Pettitt, D. J., Imperatore, G., Gabir, M. M., . . . Knowler, W. C. (2000). Intrauterine exposure to diabetes conveys risks for type 2 diabetes and obesity: A study of discordant sibships. *Diabetes, 49*, 2208–2211.

DeFerranti, S. D., Gauvreau. K., Ludwig, D. S., Neufeld, E. J., Newburger, J. W., & Rifai, N. (2004). Prevalence of the metabolic syndrome in American adolescents: Findings from the Third National Health and Nutrition Examination Survey. *Circulation, 110*(6), 2494–2497. Epub 2004 Oct 11. PubMed PMID: 15477412.

Dewey, K. G. (2003). Is breastfeeding protective against child obesity? *Journal of Human Lactation, 19*, 9–18.

Dietz, W. H. (2011). Reversing the tide of obesity. *The Lancet, 378*, 744–746.

Dietz, W. H., & Gortmaker, S. L. (1985). Do we fatten our children at the television set? Obesity and television viewing in children and adolescents. *Pediatrics, 75*, 807–812.

Drong, A. W., Lindgren, C. M., & McCarthy M. I. (2012). The genetic and epigenetic basis of type 2 diabetes and

PART **3**

obesity. *Clinical Pharmacology and Therapeutics, 92*(6), 707–715.

Druet, C., Settler, N., Sharp, S., Simmons, R. K., Cooper, C., Davey Smith, G., . . . Ong, K. K. (2012). Prediction of childhood obesity by infancy weight gain: An individual-level meta-analysis. P*aediatric Perinatal Epidemiology, 26,* 19–26.

Ebbeling, C. B., Feldman, H. A., Chomitz, V. R, Antonelli, T. A., Gortmacher, S. L., Stavroula, K. O., . . . Ludwig, D. S. (2012). A randomized trial of sugar-sweetened beverages and adolescent body weight. *New England Journal of Medicine, 367,* 1407–1416.

Eidelman, A. I., & Schanler, R. J. (2012). Policy statement: Breastfeeding and the use of human milk. *Pediatrics, 129*(3), e827–e841.

Fennoy, I. (2010). Metabolic and respiratory complications of childhood obesity. *Pediatric Annals, 39*(3), 140–146.

Flegal, K. M., Carroll, M. D., Ogden, C. L., & Curtin, L. R. (2010). Prevalence and trends in obesity among U.S. adults, 1999–2008. *Journal of the American Medical Association, 303*(3), 235–241.

Freedman, D. S., Dietz, W. H., Srinivasan, S. R., & Berenson, G. S. (1999). The relation of overweight to cardiovascular risk factors among children and adolescents: The Bogalusa heart study. *Pediatrics, 103,* 1175–1182.

Freedman, D. S., Wang, J., Maynard, L. M., Thornton, J. C., Mei, Z., Pierson, R. N., . . . Horlick, M. (2005). Relation of BMI to fat and fat-free mass among children and adolescents. *International Journal of Obesity, 29*(1), 1–8.

Gibson, S. (2008). Sugar-sweetened soft drinks and obesity: A systematic review of the evidence from observational studies and interventions. *Nutritional Research Reviews, 21*(2), 134–147.

Grummer-Strawn, L. M., Reinold, C., Krebs, N. F., & Centers for Disease Control and Prevention. (2010). Use of World Health Organization and CDC growth charts for children aged 0–59 months in the United States. *MMWR Recommendations and Reports, 59*(RR09), 1–15.

Guo, S. S., Wu, W., Chumlea, W. C., & Roche, A. F. (2002). Predicting overweight and obesity in adulthood from body mass index values in childhood and adolescence. *American Journal of Clinical Nutrition, 76,* 653–658.

Hales, C. N., & Barker, D. J. (1992). Type 2 (non-insulin-dependent) diabetes mellitus: The thrifty phenotype hypothesis. *Diabetologia, 35,* 595–601.

High Blood Pressure Education Program Working Group on High Blood Pressure in Children and Adolescents. (2004). The fourth report on the diagnosis, evaluation, and treatment of high blood pressure in children and adolescents. *Pediatrics, 114*(Supp. 2), 555–576.

Jolliffe C. J., & Janssen I. (2007). Development of age-specific adolescent metabolic syndrome criteria that are linked to the Adult Treatment Panel III and International Diabetes Federation criteria. *Journal of the American College of Cardiology, 49*(8), 891–898.

Jones, K. L. (2006). *Smith's recognizable patterns of human malformation* (6th ed.). Philadelphia, PA: Elsevier.

Joy, T., Cao, H., Black, G., Malik, R., Charlton-Menys, V., Hegele, R. A., & Durrington, P. N. (2007). Alstrom syndrome (OMIM 203800): A case report and literature review. *Orphanet Journal of Rare Diseases, 2,* 49.

Kavey, R. W., Simons-Morton, D. G., de Jesus, J. M., & the National Heart, Lung and Blood Institute, National Institutes of Health. (2011). Expert panel on integrated guidelines for cardiovascular health and risk reduction in children and adolescents: Summary report. *Pediatrics, 128*(Supp. 6), S1–S44.

Koebnick, C., Smith N., Black, M. H., Porter, A. H., Richie, B. A., Hudson, S., . . . Longstreth, G. F. (2012). Pediatric obesity and gallstone disease. *Journal of Pediatric Gastroenterology and Nutrition, 55,* 328.

Lakshman, R., Elks, C. E., & Ong, K. K. (2012). Childhood obesity. *Circulation. 126,* 1770–1779.

Littleton, S. W., & Mokhlesi, B. (2009). The Pickwickian Syndrome: Obesity hypoventilation syndrome. *Clinics in Chest Medicine, 30*(3), 467–478.

Lshinsky-Silver, E., Zinger, A., Bibi, C. N., Barash, V., Sadeh, M., Lev, D., & Sagie, T. L. (2002). MEHMO (Mental retardation, epileptic seizures, hypogenitalism, microcephaly, obesity): A new x-linked mitochondrial disorder. *European Journal of Human Genetics,10,* 226–230.

Lucas, A., Sarson, D. L., Blackburn, A. M., Adrian, T. E., Aynsley-Green, A., & Bloom, S.R. (1980) Breast vs bottle: Endocrine responses are different with formula feeding. *Lancet. 1,* 1267–1269.

Malik, V. S., Schulze, M. B., & Hu, F. B. (2006). Intake of sugar-sweetened beverages and weight gain: A systematic review. *American Journal of Clinical Nutrition, 84,* 274–288.

Mei, Z., Grummer-Strawn, L. M., Pietrobelli, A., Goulding, A., Goran, M. I., & Dietz, W. H. (2002). Validity of body mass index compared with other body composition screening indexes for the assessment of body fatness in children and adolescents. *American Journal of Clinical Nutrition, 75,* 978–998.

Merrill, R. M., & Richardson, J. S. (2009). Validity of self-reported height, weight, and body mass index: Findings from the National Health and Nutrition Examination Survey, 2001–2006. *Preventing Chronic Disease, 6*(4).

Monasta, L., Batty, G. D., Cattaneo, A., Lutje, V., Ronfani, L., Van Lenthe, F. J., & Brug, J. (2010). Early-life determinants of overweight and obesity: A review of systematic reviews. *Obesity Reviews, 11,* 695–708.

Must, A., Philips, S. M., & Naumova, E. N. (2012). Occurrence and timing of childhood overweight and mortality: Findings from the Third Harvard Growth Study. *Journal of Pediatrics, 160,* 743–750.

Nowicki, S. T., Tassone, F., Ono, M. Y., Ferranti, J., Croquette, M. F., Goodlin-Jones, B., & Hagerman, R. J. (2007). The Prader-Willi phenotype of fragile X syndrome. *Journal of Developmental and Behavioral Pediatrics, 28*(2), 133–138.

Ogden, C. L., Carroll, M. D., Kit, B. K., & Flegal, K. M. (2012). *Prevalence of obesity in the United States, 2009–2010* (NCHS Data Brief 82). Hyattsville, MD: National Center for Health Statistics.

Ogden, C. L., & Flegal, K. M. (2010). Changes in terminology for childhood overweight and obesity. *National Health Statistics Reports, 25,* 1–5.

Ogden, C. L., Flegal, K. M., Carroll, M. D., & Johnson, C. L. (2002). Prevalence and trends in overweight among U.S. children and adolescents, 1999–2000. *Journal of the American Medical Association, 288,* 1728–1732.

Oken, E., & Gillman, M. W. (2003). Fetal origins of obesity. *Obesity Research, 11*(4), 496–506.

Pan, L., Blanck, H. M., Sherry, B., Dalenius, K., & Grummer-Strawn, L. M. (2012). Trends in the prevalence of extreme obesity among U.S. preschool-aged children living in low-income families, 1998–2010. *Journal of the American Medical Association, 308*(24), 2563–2565.

Pietrobelli, A., Faith, M. S., Allison, D. B., Gallagher, D., Chiumello, G., & Hymsfield, S. B. (1998). Body mass index as a measure of adiposity among children and adolescents: A validation study. *Journal of Pediatrics, 132,* 204–210.

Pinhas-Hamiel, O., Dolan, L. M., Daniels, S. R., Standiford, D., Khoury, P. R., & Zeitler, P. (1996). Increased incidence of non-insulin dependent diabetes mellitys among adolescents. *Journal of Pediatrics, 128,* 608–615.

Poston, L. (2012). Maternal obesity, gestational weight gain, and diet as determinants of offspring long term health. *Best Practice and Research Clinical Endocrinology and Metabolism, 26,* 627–639.

Putnam, J., & Gerrior, S. (1999). "Trends in the U.S. Food Supply, 1970–1997," in America's eating habits: Changes and consequences. *USDA Agriculture Information Bulletin, 750,* 133–159.

Ramachandrappa, S., & Farooqi, I. S. (2011). Genetic approaches to understanding human obesity. *The Journal of Clinical Investigation, 121*(6), 2080–2086.

Reilly, J. J., Methven, E., McDowell, Z. C., Hacking, B., Alexander, D., Stewart, L., & Kelnar, C. J. H. (2003). Health consequences of obesity. *Archives of Disease in Childhood, 88,* 748–752.

Robert Wood Johnson Foundation. (2012). *F as in fat: How obesity threatens America's future.* Princeton, NJ: Author.

Rosenbloom, A. L., Joe, J. R., Young, R. S., & Winter, N. E. (1999). Emerging epidemic of type 2 diabetes in youth. *Diabetes Care, 22,* 345–354.

Rosner, B., Prineas, R., Daniels, S. R., & Loggie, J. (2000). Blood pressure differences between blacks and whites in relation to body size among U.S. children and adolescents. *American Journal of Epidemiology, 151,* 1007–1019.

Schwimmer, J. B., Deutsch, R., Kahen, T., Lavine, J. E., Stanley, C., & Behling, C. (2006). Prevalence of fatty liver in children and adolescents. *Pediatrics, 118,* 4, 1388–1393.

Sharma, A. J., Grummer-Strawn, L. M., Dalenius, K., Galuska, D., Anandappa, M., Borland, E., . . . Smith, R. (2009). Obesity prevalence among low-income, preschool-aged children: United States, 1998–2008. *Morbidity Mortality Weekly Reports, 58*(28), 769–773.

Sinha, R., Fisch, G., Teague, B., Tamborlane, W. V., Banyas, B., Allen, K., . . . Caprio, S. (2002). Prevalence of impaired glucose tolerance among children and adolescents with marked obesity. *New England Journal of Medicine, 346*(11), 802–810.

Srinivasan, S. R., Weihang, B., Wattigney, W. A., & Berenson, G. S. (1996). Adolescent overweight is associated with adult overweight and related multiple cardiovascular risk factors: The Bogalusa heart study. *Metabolism, 45*(2), 235–240.

Sun, S. S., Grave, G. D., Siervogel, R. M., Pickoff, A A., Arslanian, S. S., & Daniels, S. R. (2007). Systolic blood pressure in childhood predicts hypertension

PART **3**

and metabolic syndrome later in life. *Pediatrics, 119,* 237–246.

Taveras, E. M., Rifas-Shiman, S. L., Oken, E., Gunderson, E. P., & Gillman, M. W. (2008). Short sleep duration in infancy and risk of childhood overweight. *Archives of Pediatric and Adolescent Medicine, 162,* 305–311.

Thomas, J. J., Cavan, T. P., & Kerr, D. (2004). Preventing childhood obesity by reducing consumption of carbonated drinks: Cluster randomized controlled trial. *British Medical Journal, 328,* 1236.

Tirosh, A., Shai, I., Afek, A., Dubnov-Raz, G., Ayalon, N., Gordon, B., . . . Rudich, A. (2011). Adolescent BMI trajectory and risks of diabetes versus coronary disease. *New England Journal of Medicine, 364,* 1315–1325.

U.S. Department of Health and Human Services, Public Health Service. (2001). *The Surgeon General's call to action to prevent and decrease overweight and obesity.* Rockville, MD: Office of the Surgeon General. Retrieved from www.surgeongeneral.gov/topics/obesity

Vaag, A. A., Grunnet, L. G., Arora, G. P., & Brons, C. (2012). The thrifty phenotype hypothesis revisited. *Diabetologia, 55,* 2085–2088.

Wang, Y., & Beydoun, M. A. (2007). The obesity epidemic in the United States: Gender, age, socioeconomic, racial/ethnic and geographic characteristics—A systematic review and meta-regression analysis. *Epidemiologic Reviews, 29,* 6–28.

Wang, Y. C., McPherson, K., Marsh, T., Gortmaker, S. L., & Brown, M. (2011). Health and economic burden of the projected obesity trends in the USA and UK. *The Lancet, 378,* 815–825.

Waters, E., de Silva-Sanigorski, A., Hall, B. J., Brown, T., Campell, K. J., Gao, Y., Armstrong, R., Prosser, L., & Summerbell, C. D. (2011). Interventions for preventing obesity in children. *Cochrane Database of Systemic Reviews, 12,* doi:10.1002/14651858.CD00187.pub3

Whitaker, R. C., Wright, J. A., Pepe, M. S., Seidel, K. D.,& Dietz, W. H. (1997). Predicting obesity in young adulthood from childhood and parental obesity. *New England Journal of Medicine, 337*(13), 869–873.

World Health Organization. (2000). *Obesity: Preventing and managing the global epidemic: Report of a WHO consultation* (Technical report series no. 894). Geneva, Switzerland: Author.

CHAPTER 12

Common Reasons for Referral of Infants and Toddlers: Speech-Language, Feeding, and Sensory Processing Disorders

Laura A. Jenkins and Mary Beth Sullivan

Highlights of the Chapter

At the conclusion of the chapter, the reader will:

- have a basic knowledge of the many reasons children experience feeding, oral-motor, and speech-language issues

- understand components of oral-motor development

- understand components of sensory processing and regulation

- utilize a dynamic approach to assessment and treatment

- consider familial and cultural issues encountered around feeding and language development

Being able to feed and calm their own child are skills all parents expect to have; when they encounter challenges in doing so, parents tend to doubt themselves and their child. Many speech-language and occupational therapists have had the all-too-frequent experience of assessing a child's oral-motor and sensory processing/regulation skills and having a parent burst into tears, crying, "You mean it's not my fault?"

There are numerous reasons that children experience difficulties with oral-motor, feeding, and language development. A short list could include:

- Anatomical anomalies (e.g., cleft palate, displacement or interruption of function of organs of the digestive system)

- Neurologic and muscular disorders (e.g., cerebral palsy, muscular dystrophy)

- Cardiac and respiratory issues

- Diagnostic disorders (e.g., tracheostomy, gastro-esophageal reflux)

- Genetic disorders (e.g., Trisomy 21, Pierre Robin syndrome)

- Autism spectrum disorders

- Sensory integration disorders (e.g., hyper- or hypo-sensitivities to sensory input)

- Psychological issues (e.g., fears, severe bouts of choking)

- Food allergies

- Other sensory impairments such as blindness or deafness

- Practices that place children in infant seats, jumpers, standers, and walkers that limit the exploration of movement, providing inappropriate feedback to the child's movement, keeping the child in misaligned positions for proper development of the neuromuscular system—all at a time when neurons in the child's brain are making connections at a faster rate than at any other time in development.

The Development of Oral-Motor Function

Following is a description of some highlights in oral-motor development. For a good visual demonstration of what this development looks like, see Guerra and Vaughn (1994). A healthy, full-term newborn is born with *physiological flexion*. This is the term used for the typical posturing of a newborn: arms and legs drawn up toward the abdomen and chest, neck flexed downward, and hands fisted. The newborn also has fat pads in both cheeks (which develop at 34 weeks gestation and are minimal in preterm infants), and there is little space between the anatomical structures in the mouth and throat. All of these developments assist the newborn with taking in nourishment through breast or bottle. As the infant grows, physiological flexion dissipates, the fat pads dissolve, and the space between the structures in the mouth and throat grow wider. The infant has to accommodate to all of these changes in order to learn how to coordinate sucking, swallowing, and breathing. This suck, swallow, breathe synchrony

is critically important, not only for safety in swallowing liquid and moving on to solid foods, but also for many other aspects of development. For a detailed discussion of the suck/swallow/breathe synchrony, refer to Oetter, Richter, and Frick (1995). Many infants display difficulties eating right from the beginning, which can stem from conditions or problems such as prematurity (lack of physiological flexion and fat pads); genetic or neuromuscular issues impacting muscle tone; issues with hypo- or hyperresponsiveness to sensory input, impacting the infant's ability to achieve a calm, alert state for eating; and heart and respiratory issues, which can cause an infant to fatigue quickly during feedings. Most infants who eat well from the start typically experience a brief bout of sputtering and coughing at around 2 to 3 months of age, as they adapt to the changes described above. However, some infants who were eating well initially display significant difficulties managing this transition and cannot adapt to the disappearance of anatomical supports that were previously present.

The *sucking pattern* newborn infants use to draw nourishment from the breast or bottle also undergoes developmental changes. This is a pattern of forward and backward movement of the tongue that allows the infant to draw liquid into the mouth. As the changes in anatomy occur, the infant then develops a true sucking pattern in which the tongue utilizes an up-and-down, as well as stripping, movement against the nipple. As children grow, mouth objects, begin to explore solid foods from a spoon, and move on to table foods, the overall coordination of oral muscles continues and is critical for the development of sound production skills and management of a wide variety of food tastes and textures. The growing infant/toddler learns to move the tongue from side to side (related to ability to clear food that pockets in the cheeks and develop a bolus or ball of food for swallowing) and develops lip closure (assists with retention of food in the mouth and production of bilabial sounds such as "m" and "b"), as well as the ability to raise the tongue to the roof of the mouth and up and down outside of the lips (allows for removal of food from upper/lower lip and palate, as well as production of sounds such as "d", "n" and "t").

The Development of Sensory Processing in Young Children

Sensory processing is complex, involving the ability to attend to, sort through, and regulate responses to information from within (e.g., hunger, thirst, fatigue, pain) and from the world outside (e.g., sights, sounds, touch, movement). The process begins before birth and continues to develop throughout life. It is a foundational skill, meaning that growing abilities regarding sensory processing have an impact on all other areas of development. There has been much written about sensory processing, the various types of sensory dysfunction, their impact on learning and emotional responses, and strategies for treatment. This chapter will present an easy-to-understand overview of the skills, and of how difficulties with sensory processing and regulation, feeding, and communication skills are interrelated. For more detailed reading regarding sensory integration, please refer to strategies at the close of this chapter.

Most parents and professionals are familiar with what they were taught about the five senses:

- vision (what they see)

- auditory (what they hear)

- tactile (what they touch and what touches them; e.g., clothing, wind, and food)

- olfactory (what they smell)

- taste (including flavor, texture, temperature, and shape)

Children typically develop three additional senses important to understand. The *proprioceptive sense* allows children to receive sensations from their muscles and joints so that they can learn what position their bodies are in without looking at each part to do so. The *kinesthetic sense* is the sense of being aware of joint position in combination with movement, which allows children to learn to climb stairs without looking at their feet, or ride a bicycle. The development of the *vestibular sense,* which responds to the position of the head in relation to gravity (Am I right-side-up or upside down?), helps children to determine increases, decreases, and changes in direction of movement (e.g., fast, slow, forward, backward, spinning). Following are some examples of how these various senses interface with one another and impact development of various skills (adapted from Ayres, 1980):

- Hearing and vestibular input are involved in speech and language skills. The body's receptors for vestibular input are located in the inner ear; and many therapists find linking movement and working on development of speech-language skills to be beneficial.

- Touch is initially involved in sucking, eating, bonding with parents, and receiving comfort from being held and cuddled.

- Proprioceptive and vestibular systems are involved in eye movements, posture, muscle tone, balance, and gravitational security (i.e., feeling safe while exploring movement).

- When tactile, proprioceptive, and vestibular systems function together, they lead to developing a body concept, coordination of the two sides of the body, motor planning (i.e., the ability to think of and carry out a variety of motor tasks), and abilities in regulating activity level, attention span, and emotional stability.

- Add vision, proprioception, tactile, and vestibular input, and one can achieve skills such as eye–hand coordination, visual perception, and engagement in purposeful activity.

All of these components functioning well and in synchrony with each other contribute to the development of skills such as the ability to concentrate, organize, learn, engage in abstract thought and reasoning, and develop self-control, self-esteem, and self-confidence. Such skills enable children to conceptualize and execute tasks that become increasingly complex throughout development, from reaching out to grasp a cup and take a drink to driving a car.

When a child has difficulties in these higher level skills, caregivers and physicians often forget to check on how well the sensory system is functioning. This can lead to attempts to build a structure on top of an unstable foundation (i.e., trying to achieve better eye–hand coordination or attention and focus for learning reading and writing skills when there may be a problem with processing touch sensations or auditory/visual input). For additional resources regarding the sensory systems, refer to strategies at the close of this chapter.

The nervous system, especially the autonomic nervous system, plays an important role in the ability to achieve sensory processing and regulatory skills. It is easy to see the effects and control of many functions of the body, such as reaching for an object or running. However, autonomic nervous system function often goes unnoticed and is not generally under voluntary control. This includes functions such as regulation of heart and respiratory rate, blinking when something comes close to the eyes, and digesting food. It is possible to achieve some control of autonomic nervous system functions (e.g., with bio-feedback), but for the most part, neither children nor adults consciously think about such processes that allow

FIGURE 12.1 Autonomic nervous system

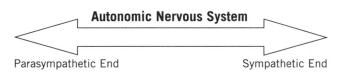

them to function more efficiently—consider having to expend energy, focus, and attention on swallowing or digesting food, or on forming every sound when speaking. Individuals also cannot stop the autonomic nervous system from functioning. A person trying to hold her breath will eventually pass out, allowing the autonomic nervous system to take control again. No one can tell her ears to stop hearing sounds or her eyes, if open, to stop seeing.

The autonomic nervous system can be visualized as a continuum with very different responses at the extremes of both ends (see Figure 12.1). This is a very simplified explanation of a complex system but serves well for the purposes of this discussion.

The parasympathetic and sympathetic nervous system are not two separate systems but rather opposite ends of a single system (see Figure 12.1). The *parasympathetic* end of the continuum is calmer, more relaxed, and moves in the direction of deep sleep. The farther a person moves in this direction on the continuum, the more difficulty he has in alerting to the sensory information around him. The *sympathetic* end of the continuum refers to more-alert states and relates to action. The further a person moves in this direction on the continuum, the greater the tendency to go into a "defend and protect" mode of operating (e.g., consider your response to being home alone and hearing a strange noise or feeling something crawling on your skin). This response is usually expressed through fight, flight, or freeze. The autonomic nervous system is a powerful force, and it is typical for children and adults to find themselves moving back and forth across the continuum throughout the day, depending on the type of activities they are engaged in. There is also wide variability in where individuals tend to fall on the continuum in specific circumstances; for example, some people bounce out of bed and others need a long time to wake up. Despite these differences, most children learn to function within a wide range of typical responses so that they can sleep, awaken, participate in a variety of activities, learn, and interact with others.

Another important concept to understand is that of *sensory thresholds*. All people have them, but again, there is wide variation within a typical range of responses to them. Sensory input builds throughout the day. A child does not start fresh with each activity. The sensory input she has already experienced, through various activities, adds to the sensory input in the next activity. This is why children and adults are often more tolerant of increased sensory input at the beginning of the day versus in the evening. For example, some children who experience hypo- or hyper-sensitivities to taste and texture may eat more at one meal of the day than other meals, based on the sensory input that has accumulated for them prior to the meal. Consider another example of a woman who drives to work with the radio on. Because this is at the beginning of the day, she tends to turn it up to assist in alerting her. When she comes back to the car at the end of the day, she may be jolted by the loud sound of the radio because now she is in a full alert state and has experienced a great deal of sensory input through the day; now she cannot tolerate the level of sound that she required to function earlier in the day. Physical health, fatigue level, stress, emotional state, motivational level, and nutritional status, as well as activity type and other people can also have an impact on children's and adults' sensory thresholds.

A child whose autonomic nervous system runs strongly toward the parasympathetic end tends to need increased sensory input in order to function; conversely, a child whose system runs strongly toward the sympathetic end tends to be overreactive to typical levels of sensory input. This can also affect how a child responds to pain. Input that is typically not painful or uncomfortable to most people may create significant discomfort or even pain for the child whose system is overresponsive to sensory input. On the other hand, a child whose system is underresponsive may not respond to painful input, thereby endangering the child's safety (e.g., touching something hot and not pulling away). The same child can also be both oversensitive to what could be considered nonpainful input and underresponsive to what should be painful. When a child (or adult) reaches his sensory threshold and cannot reduce the input or regain balance, his body may go into shut-down, tuning off most or all input in an effort to regain balance.

Development of sensory processing skills begins in utero. During pregnancy, the unborn child sees and responds to light on the mother's abdomen, hears and responds to sounds coming from both the internal (mother's heartbeat) and external environments (voices, music, other sounds the mother is hearing), receives a great deal of vestibular input as it floats and turns in the amniotic fluid, and receives proprioceptive input as the infant grows and the space within the uterus becomes more limited. During the birth process, the infant receives intense amounts of proprioceptive input through the contractions of the uterus and birth canal, and she is bombarded with a wide range of sensory input as she leaves the birth canal. During infancy, the newborn receives a great deal more visual input, which helps to develop coordinated movement of the eyes as well as accurate reach and grasp. The infant also hears a greater variety of sounds (i.e., not as muffled as in utero) and learns how to alert to and find the source of sounds. A greater variety of input to the nose (smells of food, familiar people, and other odors within the home) is present. The infant continues to receive proprioceptive input (being held and cuddled, wrapped in a blanket, massaged with lotion), a greater variety of touch input through daily routines (eating, bathing, dressing, interaction with others, play with objects), and vestibular input (being held in different positions, moved from one position to another, being gently rocked and bounced). From this point on, sensory processing continues to develop through daily routines and interactions that assist the infant to gradually adapt to a larger amount and diversity of sensory input. Sensory processing becomes a cycle of experiences requiring adaptive responses, which lead to new experiences.

Connections: Sensory Processing, Feeding, and Speech-Language Disorders

Difficulties with sensory processing can impact many areas of development. For example, over-responsiveness to sensory input may impact an infant in feeding and in the development of speech-language skills in one or more of the following ways. It may:

- Make an infant irritable and fussy and, therefore, difficult to calm and feed or engage in the early interactive games that are precursors to good communication skills.

- Create a hyperactive gag reflex, causing the baby to frequently gag on or vomit food and liquids, or both.

- Make it difficult for an infant to make the transition from bottle to solid foods or from baby food to table food.

- Cause a baby to avoid touching foods with his hands or getting food on his face, impairing the development of self-feeding skills.

- Prevent the kind of calm, alert states that promote focus on and interaction with others.

- Make it difficult to adapt to background noises, thereby causing the child to shut down in environments with sounds he finds overwhelming, and tune out all sounds.

- Cause the baby to avoid touching his tongue to other areas of his mouth.

Most people do not register the movement of the tongue in the mouth during speech as being uncomfortable. (Run your tongue lightly over the roof of your mouth. Most people experience a light ticklish sensation. To get rid of the sensation, push firmly against the roof of your mouth with your tongue.) However, if a child has hypersensitivity in the oral area, and the sensations involved in sound production are ticklish or uncomfortable, she may avoid exploring tongue movements to produce a variety of sounds. She may prefer

to continue making open vowel sounds past the typical developmental stage for doing so, or move into only using guttural sounds from the back of the throat such as "guh," labial sounds with the lips such as "m" and "b," and sounds like "d" and "n" that are created by a strong push of the tongue against the roof of the mouth. A child who avoids exploring tongue movements may also experience impaired development of mature chewing patterns for managing a variety of foods.

An infant's underresponsiveness to sensory input can adversely affect the development of speech-language and feeding skills in one or more of the following ways. It may:

- Make it difficult to arouse the infant for feedings and interactions with others.

- Cause decreased oral sensitivity in the mouth, which may make it difficult for the child to suck well, manage liquids, and manage various textures of food.

- Cause decreased taste sensation, which may create a lack of interest in food or a desire for very strong flavors.

- Cause decreased oral exploration of mouth with the tongue, due to lack of feedback or sensation.

Children with the same sensory issues can look and act very differently, and treatment must be tailored to respect the individual child's needs. One child with hypersensitivity to sensory input may hang back or withdraw to avoid unpredictable touch or touch she cannot control, or to avoid having to touch items she is unsure of, or to distance herself from noise. Another child with hypersensitivity to sensory input may plow through people and activities, pushing and shoving not to be mean but rather in an attempt to control the type of input the body receives (strong and firm versus light and ticklish). A young child with these issues can quickly be labeled as "aggressive," when the real problem lies in not understanding that his own body likes much rougher input than other children's do. If someone touches him lightly and tells him to be gentle, he may wonder why he is being asked to touch others in a way that is uncomfortable for him.

The most sensitive areas of the body are the head and face, palms of the hands, soles of the feet, and genitalia. Children experiencing sensory processing issues often show avoidance of input to these areas or seek out very strong input, creating significant issues with daily routines that can be confusing for parents and other caregivers. They may scream and cry through face and hair washing or haircuts, appear to enjoy banging their heads on the floor or against a wall, push their foreheads across the floor when crawling, avoid moving from bottle to solid foods or from bottle to cup drinking, resist holding objects in their hands or insist on carrying things around in each hand. They may also avoid putting their hands and feet in grass or sand; seem oblivious to the fact that they are crawling over or stepping on objects that should hurt; and resist or actively fight diaper changes or getting dressed and undressed, and pushing or tugging on genitalia. Car seats can be an issue due to the many points of contact, and car rides may cause dizziness and nausea in children with vestibular issues. Some parents have described a pattern of crying through local car rides but not during long-distance travel: Local travel typically involves many more starts, stops, and turns than a long-distance trip, in which the car travels for miles at the same speed on a straight stretch of road. Although many of these behaviors can also describe normal phases in early development, children with sensory processing disorders tend to demonstrate these behaviors earlier than their peers and continue them long after the typical developmental phase should be over. Such issues also impact the normal phases of tantrums. Most children have tantrums and learn through them

to adjust their responses. For instance, most toddlers will bang their heads during a tantrum but quickly learn that it hurts and adjust their tantrum behavior accordingly. Children with sensory processing disorders may continue unsafe behavior due to the alternate way they experience the input (i.e., a behavior feels good to them rather than painful).

Assessment and treatment of such issues takes time, strong observational skills, and in-depth interviews with parents and other primary caregivers across a variety of settings. Picture a cast-iron stock pot, filled with water and placed on the stove over a flame. The pot and cover represent the child's body, the water inside the pot represents the child's autonomic nervous system, and the flame represents the environment. For some children, the flame can be turned up high and the water will never boil (*hyporesponsive*). For others, the flame can be barely flickering, and the water will boil over the top (*hyperresponsive*). However, observers of these children's behavior cannot take off the "lid" and see what is happening with the autonomic nervous system. The children's behavior itself provides the clues to their difficulties.

Treatment Principles

The best treatment for children with sensory processing and oral-motor issues involves therapeutic planning between the child's primary caregivers and a therapist specifically trained in assessment and treatment of these issues (see Figure 12.2).

Trust is the essential element in any interaction between two or more people. Children know adults' attitudes from their approach to them; they know when their wants and needs are understood and respected. When children do not trust adults, when they fear they will be forced to change, they develop what adults label as "behavior problems" (e.g., ignoring, resisting, avoiding,

FIGURE 12.2 Fundamentals of treatment for children with sensory processing and oral-motor issues

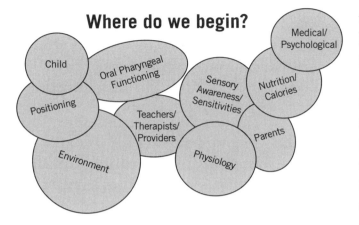

crying, screaming, pushing away, hitting, withdrawing). The fullest understanding of children comes from careful observations and input from the people who know them best, such as their parents and other close caregivers. By viewing information in sequential, global, analytical, and intuitive ways, as well as through each sensory modality, arriving at answers and insights is possible. The child knows what she wants. If adults learn to observe the messages in her body, her eyes, her face, and her voice, they too can know. What the child wants usually contains a component of what adults might want for her too. Children with sensory and motor problems find ways to respond and interact with the world that provide them with what they want and need. The challenge is to explore with the child and find additional ways of meeting these needs that allow wider opportunities for learning and development. Programs that are built upon what a child does well, and enjoys, are more likely to lead to changes and growth. When professionals work from the child's abilities and strengths, the child perceives herself as capable. When professionals refuse to judge children, parents, caregivers, other providers, and themselves, and instead concentrate on the fact that everyone in the equation is doing their very best in the given moment, it will

generate the energy and opportunity to see possibility rather than limitation.

It is evident that there is much to observe and take into account regarding treatment, and it is helpful to have a visual to organize information (see Figure 12.3).

Starting with the child and family as the center of attention, and holding a strength-based attitude regarding their competency, then a partnership between professional and parents/caregivers is possible. This partnership can be the means for great change to occur for everyone involved. Each session together becomes an opportunity for shared learning and exploration.

FIGURE 12.3 Dynamics of therapy for feeding-swallowing

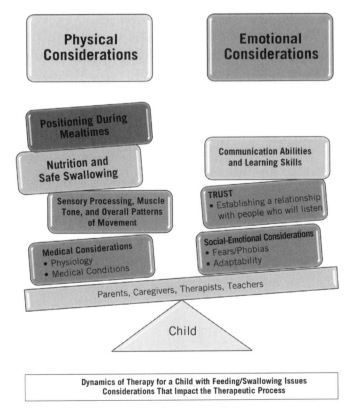

If any of these considerations is askew, the balance of the therapeutic system is thrown off and what may have been gained can be lost in an instant. Reflecting on the process of therapy is ongoing for assessment and treatment and must always take into consideration the child's abilities at each moment in time.

Next there are a number of observations to make and questions to ask regarding both physical and emotional considerations, such as the physiological, physical, sensory, communication, and social-emotional environments in which to create change. All of these environments are interconnected and overlapping, or *interactive environments*. Questions and observations that will help to assess and modify the overall environment include:

- Does the child show any indications of hunger or thirst?

- Is the child on any medications that impact appetite or alertness?

- Is the child ill?

- Is the child teething?

- Is the child tired?

- Is the child dealing with structural abnormalities, such as an enlarged tongue, cleft palate, small jaw, trachea-esophageal fistula, trachea-malasia, or other issues?

- Is the child dealing with gastro-esophageal reflux?

- Is the child in need of physical support to obtain optimal positioning for breath support and oral-motor control?

- What positions and seating options are available?

- What types of bottles, cups, plates, silverware, or other adaptations will support success?

- What else is in the room?

- What is the lighting like?

- What types, frequencies, and volumes of sounds are present?

- Are there any odors?

- What will the child be touching and what will touch the child?

- What nonverbal messages is the child communicating through body language, eye gaze, pointing, and gestures?

- What is the mood and nonverbal communication of the adults present, including the professionals?

- Does the child have oral-motor issues impacting ability to speak?

- Is the child able to communicate, using alternative/augmentative supports?

- Does the child demonstrate interest in interaction with others?

- Does the child imitate actions, sounds, or words?

- Does the child initiate interaction or respond to interaction from others?

Answers to these questions guide intervention strategies and remind professionals to consider multiple factors of behavior. In terms of treating sensory processing/integration issues in young children, several principles must be kept in mind:

- Observe, observe, observe: What does the child spontaneously accept or engage in? Are there any physical reactions to what is presented such as approach, withdrawal, going pale, flushing red (signs that the autonomic nervous system is on overload), in other words, ways to get information regarding what the water inside the pot is feeling/doing?

- Start where the child is. Join him in his interests and activities. This is where the autonomic nervous system will be in the most calm, alert state the individual child is capable of at that time.

- Be sure to evaluate other developmental issues. For instance, is she also having difficulty maintaining balance for eating?

- Provide lots of gentle, but firm pressure input through daily routines and play such as bear hugs, pushing/pulling games, games on hands and knees, throwing heavy bean bags into a laundry basket, helping to pull the sheets up on a bed, or pushing a child-size grocery cart with items in it. For activities that are difficult for the child, provide deep pressure input before and after the activity, or the child may experience a meltdown even after the activity is over, and even if he appeared to enjoy the new/difficult task.

- Listen to and respect the child's approach–avoidance patterns, as the child attempts to become more involved. This is akin to the story of the tortoise and the hare: It takes time, but there is more chance of winning in the end. Pushing the child only serves to heighten the fight, flight, or freeze reaction of the autonomic nervous system and prolong the issues.

- Change only one thing at a time. For example, if a child is sensitive to taste, temperature, and texture, choose a preferred taste and texture and gradually change the temperature (e.g., room-temperature ice cream to gradually colder ice cream) or choose a preferred temperature and taste of food and play with the texture (e.g., smooth applesauce to chunky). Be aware that the autonomic nervous system operates on survival. Therefore, some children with these issues can be very savvy to attempts to disguise change. One child refused to try any baby food if she did not see the jar and hear the "pop" of it being opened. Her parents had to resort to saving several of those empty jars, filling them with the new foods and making the "pop" sound as they removed the lid. Grinders and blenders can be an assist in changing texture and taste, and for experimenting with miniscule changes.

- Keep therapy and daily routines upbeat, motivating, and respectful through fun activities, a relaxed and playful attitude, and gentle modeling of skills.

- Vibration assists some children, but it must be approached cautiously. To explore if a child will accept vibration, be sure to have two vibrating toys/objects. Demonstrate how to turn a device on and off and what it does in a relaxed and gentle manner. Model playing with the object yourself. If the child starts to explore hers, stay relaxed, and observe her reactions. Do not try to place your object on the child; instead ,encourage the child to put hers on you. Tell her where you like it and where you don't want it. The child may then begin to explore the input on herself. If a child refuses, or avoids keeping the objects around, respect the child's timing in exploring them. If the child enjoys the play and seeks it out, she may benefit from a vibrating toothbrush or play with vibration before and after meals.

- If a child is hurting others, damaging property, or in danger of hurting himself, keep it simple. Say "no," and offer an alternative so the child knows what he can do instead. If the child continues with the injurious behavior, tell him you will help him stop until he can do it for himself. This can be achieved by placing the child in a safe place or removing the object being misused or both. Be sure to model how to play and interact in appropriate ways, as well as how to handle anger. Do not go into explanations of good boy/bad boy. Keep in mind that the child is not being aggressive because he wants to hurt himself or others but rather because he is young and does not understand why others would not enjoy the

FIGURE 12.4 Model of proprioception equalizing

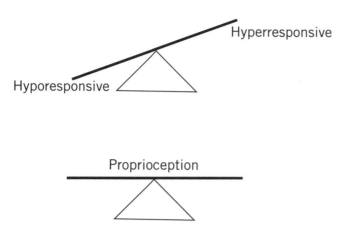

kind of roughhouse type play he does. If he is banging his head on the floor during a tantrum and not adjusting his response, it is a good indication that he is not feeling painful input the way others do.

Why is gentle but firm deep pressure input so important? Proprioception is the great equalizer, assisting those who are under- or overresponsive. Calm, focused, rhythmical, firm pressure input will assist the overresponsive child, and intermittent, changing, firm pressure assists the underresponsive child (see Figure 12.4).

For young infants, this input can be provided through swaddling (see www.mayoclinic.org/healthy-living/infant-and-toddler-health/multimedia/how-to-swaddle-a-baby/sls-20076006), cuddling, holding, hugging, giving firm kisses, and gentle but firm patting around the face and mouth. If the infant proceeds to crawling and standing, she will start to provide proprioceptive input for herself through creeping on hands and knees, crawling across various surfaces, pulling to stand, plopping back down to sitting, and eventually walking, running, and jumping, and pushing, pulling, and carrying objects. Some children avoid exploring such activities and need additional support. A child with vestibular issues may avoid rolling, getting into a hands-and-knees position, or engaging in much movement due to

feelings of disorientation, dizziness, and nausea. A child who is afraid to explore textures on the hands and feet may resist the same movements due to ticklish or painful sensations when she touches various textures to crawl or stand on her feet.

For children experiencing issues with anatomical structure, weakness, muscle tone, and fatigue, creating difficulties achieving a tight seal around a nipple and coordinating the suck, swallow, breathe synchrony, there are many strategies for positioning and techniques for supporting lip closure, jaw stability, and learning to chew. An excellent resource regarding these issues and strategies is Morris and Klein's (2000) *Pre-Feeding Skills: A Comprehensive Resource for Mealtime Development.*

Working With Families: Translating Principles Into Practice

Now let's visit two children with a combination of eating, sensory, and communication issues, and journey with them and their families on their quest for increased skill, ease of living, connection, and independence.

John

John is a timid, sweet, and intelligent toddler with a dry sense of humor. He refused to eat anything but his "shakes;" avoided deep pressure activities due to reduced strength and endurance; had a limited repertoire of sounds; gagged; and even vomited if someone offered him food in an attempt to get him to eat more; and he was overly sensitive to sounds. His parents' priorities were to get John to eat a greater variety of foods and to communicate verbally. They understood that helping John improve overall motor planning skills meant working on activities that required learning new and changing patterns of movement. At the same time, they requested some work on practicing rote skills so that he could use a ride-on toy and play with other materials appropriate for his age.

As an infant, John had been irritable, had had difficulty achieving a seal on the nipple (took in a lot of air and leaked formula from the sides of his mouth while sucking), and had been slow to explore movement. He was evaluated through early intervention (EI) and found to have delays in oral-motor and movement skills. A speech therapist assisted his parents in the use of positioning and jaw control to achieve better sucking skills and gentle-but-firm touch games around the mouth to improve oral awareness and tolerance for input. John's physical therapist demonstrated how to facilitate movement through play in a variety of positions, providing gentle-but-firm pressure input to the palms of his hands and soles of his feet, and gradually moving him through changes in position so that he could feel what the transition involved. His family practiced these techniques with John, and he gradually achieved the ability to suck well from a bottle and independently sit, crawl, stand, and walk. At this point in time, John demonstrated age-appropriate gross motor skills, and physical therapy services were discontinued. He demonstrated immature play skills, resisted transition to solid foods, had a limited sound repertoire and questionable fine motor skills. A teacher and occupational therapist were added to John's EI team. Play was encouraged regarding a variety of sensory materials and early cause–effect toys (e.g., child pushes a button and the toy plays music). It was quickly determined that John had a strong understanding of language and concepts, demonstrated through his play. However, he continued to exhibit difficulties with motor planning that were adversely impacting development of speech, fine motor skills, and his ability to physically engage in a variety of play activities. Due to his strong cognitive skills, teacher services were discontinued. John's speech and occupational

therapists worked together, often through co-visits, to address these issues. Treatment at this stage involved getting John to independently achieve deep pressure input for himself through games on hands and knees, running, activities involving several changes in position (e.g., get the puzzle piece from the floor and put it in the puzzle on the table), and exploring ride-on toys. John would gently and hesitantly explore each activity and, over several months, accomplished play with many items.

Treatment for children experiencing difficulty with development of praxis skills requires activities focused on specific skill development through both rote practice and novel movement sequences, so that they can expand play skills and participation in daily living activities as well as those focused on developing praxis for learning a variety of other skills. Another focus of treatment for John was exploring a variety of sensory materials with hands, feet, and mouth. Initially, John would only observe while the therapists and his family demonstrated play. When provided with utensils and measuring cups so that he would not have to touch the materials, he eventually began to join in the play. Gradually, he was able to put his hands and feet in a variety of textures (e.g., searching through small erasers of animal figures to find brightly colored stones or dried kidney/navy beans to find favored small figures or metal cars). To enhance suck/swallow/breathe synchrony, John explored blowing 1-inch pompoms through a pop tube, blowing on horns and whistles, and blowing bubbles. All of these activities took some time to achieve independence but taught John how to take deeper breaths for speech and physical activity, which resulted in increased strength and endurance. To address oral-motor praxis and hypersensitivity issues, a tray of food items was always placed in the play area. The same tray was used at all times; therapists and parents casually ate items off the tray, sometimes commenting on how good something tasted. They also modeled spitting out food that did not taste good onto a napkin and how to take the taste away by eating or drinking something else. If John demonstrated interest in the tray, he was gently told he was welcome to have some too, and his decision was respected.

A momentous day occurred when John asked his dad to put some bread on the tray and proceeded to take it off and eat it. During this phase of treatment, play activities revolved around oral exploration of objects such as teethers, chewy tubes, and play food, and John's family now included him in mealtime at the table. He received nutrition mainly through nutritional shakes and a few bites of foods he was beginning to eat. He was also starting to produce a greater variety of sounds and trying to form words and simple phrases. In his attempts to talk, the praxis issues were showing up again. Most children will go through phases of deleting final consonant sounds ("cah" for *car*) and making sound errors ("pisghetti" for *spaghetti*, "hopsital" for *hospital*); however, John was deleting initial consonants ("ah" for *car*), attempts to say the same word came out very differently each time ("oo," "pah," "un" for *spoon*), and he had unusual sounds for words he did use consistently ("beedlebum" for *bicycle*). At this point, therapy transitioned to the family's kitchen, where the same tray of food used in therapy and in the playroom was placed on the table, and John was encouraged to make something with real food items. This was made playful through use of aprons and chef's hats and participating in making pudding, cookies, and other hands-on activities, with no pressure to eat them, pouring water and fruits together to make "punch," and decorating food with frosting. John was encouraged to drink his shakes and eat the few foods he liked, while exploring the new textures through the activities. A tablet computer app was also used so that John could see, hear, and touch the food items on the screen without being overwhelmed by the smell, touch, and taste.

This approach resulted in getting John to taste more items. As he gradually explored more textures inside his mouth, John began to speak more clearly and put simple sentences together.

At this point in treatment (2 years, 10 months), John demonstrated age-appropriate skills across all developmental domains, making him no longer eligible for services. However, although he had increased the number of foods he would try and eat in small portions, his diet was still limited. John's family was encouraged to institute an "exploration plate" at meals. If John did not want something on his plate, he could pick it up and move it to the additional plate. This allowed him increased interaction with foods through smell and touch and, if he could, through licking or taking a taste. Not only had John improved his overall skill development dramatically, his family was also supported in the skills they already possessed and were able to continue to support their child on his journey.

Sarah

Sarah is a feisty toddler who awakens with the dawn and has trouble falling asleep at night. She takes life at full speed, with no awareness of her own safety needs. Her mother reports she is always on the move, preferring running over walking, and she will climb anything, including the bookshelf and TV stand. She is rough with her toys and with other people and seems to have no awareness of where she is, frequently stepping on and bumping into others. When Sarah wants something, she screams and throws a temper tantrum, frustrated at not being able to communicate with words; and her diet consists of crunchy and chewy snacks such as chips, cookies, chewy candy, and milkshakes. Sarah has been kicked out of two day care facilities due to biting, stepping on others, and knocking them down. Her mother has been chastised by pediatricians and WIC personnel for not providing her child with more nutritious foods, but Sarah will refuse to eat anything for 2 full days at a time unless she has the foods she favors. Sarah's mother wants her daughter to eat, talk, and interact with others safely.

Upon assessment, Sarah demonstrated interest and curiosity but was found to be very sensitive to typical touch input. She refuses most clothing, preferring those that fit her snugly; bathing, hair washing, changing clothes, brushing teeth, and fixing her hair are described as daily battles. Her communication skills were significantly delayed. Sarah began speech and occupational therapy services through EI. Initial focus was placed on teaching Sarah a variety of safe ways to obtain deep pressure input (e.g., where she could safely climb, jump, and crash) and teaching her mother ways to provide deep pressure in tasks such as fixing her hair, bathing, and dressing. As Sarah gave herself increased deep pressure input rather than be interrupted in these tasks due to safety issues, she experienced less stress and began to have some calm periods in which she could focus on speech-language activities and games to learn body awareness. Sarah began to use simple signs to indicate her needs. She had no interest in exploring foods from a tray, as John gradually did. She began to eat more by combining textures (chewy and crunchy) and tastes (sweet, sour, and spicy) with foods she had not tried in the past. Sarah began to try potatoes with ketchup, soup with crackers in it, and fries with hot sauce. Gradually, her mother could reverse the ingredients (i.e., more fries and less hot sauce, more potatoes and less ketchup). Sarah also began to dip fruits and vegetables in ranch and Catalina dressing. As she began to eat a greater variety of foods and calmly attend to activities to develop language, the vocabulary she used in attempts to communicate with others increased while frustration decreased. Sarah loved exploring vibration and started brushing her teeth with a vibrating toothbrush. Her mother began to plan play dates at the park to coincide with therapy sessions. Because Sarah had plenty of opportunity to run and climb, she was able to explore interactions with other children and find pleasure and success in doing so. Sarah was subsequently able to succeed in a day care, with caregivers open to working collaboratively with her mother on strategies that not only assisted Sarah but proved useful for the other children in the room as well.

As both John's and Sarah's parents worked closely and collaboratively with EI service providers, each child was moved toward more adaptive, age-appropriate daily routines. However, as is evident in the strategies described below, treatment scenarios are seldom simple, take time, and require much collaborative thinking on the part of both families and professionals.

Confusing Stages of Treatment

As children improve in their abilities to engage in activities that used to be difficult for them, they often reach a stage where their motivational level far exceeds their abilities to regulate themselves.

Example 1. Jacob initially presented with strong issues in eating a variety of foods. With carefully guided treatment, he was able to accept putting some things in his mouth. One night he notices the family is excited about ordering and eating pizza for dinner. To his family's delight, he decides he'll try putting that in his mouth and likes it. Jacob proceeds to eat four or five slices of pizza. Then he gags and throws up. What happened?

- Jacob's comfort level for exploring tastes has increased.

- He was now excited, just like his brothers, to "eat pizza."

- The texture of the pizza provided firm pressure to his mouth and felt really good, so he kept seeking out the input, unaware of other signals his body tried to give him.

Because Jacob cannot yet regulate the activity for himself, it is a crucial part of his treatment that adults assist him in knowing when he's had enough and redirecting him to another activity (e.g., "You really liked that pizza, and we'll have more another time. Right now you'll get a tummy ache if you eat too much. You can bite on this chewy tube if you want something more to chew on."). Another option is to redirect Jacob into a completely different activity such as outdoor play or a gentle game of roughhouse to provide his body with additional proprioceptive input, while avoiding a negative experience with food.

Example 2. Carrie presented with an inability to touch any of the play materials her teacher or speech therapist brought to entice her into engaging in play for longer periods of time. The whole team learned how to provide her with a sensory diet of firm-pressure activities throughout her day. Carrie began to show signs of enjoying play by smiling and actively participating. Her parents began to report increasing episodes of biting, which occurred for no apparent reason and after she had played with textured materials. Carrie was also having increasing difficulties settling for sleep at night. What is going on?

- Despite Carrie's outward expressions of pleasure, her autonomic nervous system is still struggling enough that once the high motivation of the activity is over, she recognizes her strong need for deep-pressure input and bites the first person or object available to assist her in self-regulating.

It is important to follow all activities involving sensory experiences that have been difficult for a child with an activity that provides deep-pressure input, until there is clear and consistent evidence that the child's system is fully integrating the experience. This strategy thus allows the child to have a positive experience with something that was previously difficult without going into sensory overload.

Example 3. Brad initially presented as very rigid regarding what he would eat, hated having his hair washed, and avoided many activities. Now he eats a variety of foods, laughs and splashes in the bath, helps to wash his hair, and likes to towel-dry himself off. The family goes camping, and Brad discovers the wonderful world of caterpillars. He is captivated by them and allows them to crawl on his arm. His mom questions whether he had any sensory difficulties, if he could tolerate this input. Suddenly, Brad starts waving his arms and stomping on the caterpillars, as they fall to the ground. Now Mom wonders if her son has a personality disorder, as he is being cruel to animals. What is going on?

- Brad was motivated to explore the insects; however, he was not in tune with what his autonomic nervous system was trying to tell him until it triggered the fight response to the light, ticklish input.

Helping children to understand how to move away from an activity when they've had enough and how to give themselves firm pressure input to make themselves feel better is an important part of treatment. Adults can teach Brad to shake off the caterpillars and then show him how to rub his arms and hands to counteract the input. This will give him strategies to use when adults aren't around to help, such as playing with other children who brush up against him. Rubbing his arm will work instead of pushing the other child.

Example 4. Nicole presented as very sensitive to light touch and almost oblivious to painful input. She would barely flinch with immunizations at the doctor's office and hardly ever cried, with even a bad fall. Temper tantrums were a real issue for Nicole and her family. Nicole would bang her head hard and bite her hand to the point of causing bruising. As services progressed, Nicole began engaging in a wider variety of activities, but began to cry when she fell and put up a big fight at the doctor's office for the next immunization. What is going on?

- As Nicole's autonomic nervous system learns to respond appropriately to all types of input, she is demonstrating more appropriate responses to pain.

- Responding to pain is actually a sign of progress and bodes well for a decrease in intensity of temper tantrums in the near future.

Information on Tickling and Spanking

No tickling or spanking allowed! Why?

Laughing is an involuntary response to being tickled. Anyone who hates to be tickled will tell you they do not enjoy it, even if they laugh. The light ticklish touch from being tickled can actually undo all the hard work of providing deep pressure input. Even if a child comes back for more, they are likely seeking continued interaction with you, rather than more tickling. If a child has sensory processing difficulties, avoid tickling at all times. Instead, play the same game by providing firm pressure input with one hand on their back and one on their tummy.

There are many reasons not to spank a child. For the purposes of this chapter, we will discuss one of them. Children with sensory processing difficulties enjoy firm pressure input. If an adult responds with spanking to behaviors they want the child to stop, they risk actually rewarding the behavior. Instead, be consistent in telling the child what she cannot do and immediately show her what she can do instead.

Strategies for Common Problems

Biting. Provide objects that are safe and acceptable to bite on. When the child goes to bite, say, "No." Immediately present him with an object that is okay to bite on and say, "Bite this."

Climbing and jumping on everything. It can be helpful to set up an area in the home that is safe for these kinds of activities. In good weather, the child can run and jump outdoors. However inclement weather or a parent's inability to go outdoors, when needed, can create difficulties. Materials for such a space could include an old mattress, pillows, bean bag chair, and something to climb on.

Screaming through baths or washing hair. When a child is upset, the adult tends to hurry through the activity, but hurrying tends to increase lighter touches. Take a deep breath, which you can encourage the child to do with you, and focus on providing gentle-but-firm pressure input to wash body and hair. Giving the child a washcloth to assist can be helpful, as is giving the child something to bite or chew on. Explore different textured washcloths or bath sponges to see if your child responds better to one over another. Acknowledge the child's feelings: "I know you are mad and upset, this will be over soon." Praise the child for getting through the activity, and provide a game of firm pressure input afterward.

Getting a haircut. Have the person cutting the child's hair place one hand firmly on the child's head, while cutting with the other. Use distraction, such as a favorite videotape to watch. Have the child chew on a chewy tube, crunchy snack, or gum.

Being rough with others. People are highly unpredictable in their movements. They often brush up against each other in unexpected ways, and groups of children do this even more than adults do. Many children with sensory processing difficulties love rougher input/play and therefore think everyone else must love it too. Simply say "No," and model appropriate interaction. Show the child how to rub out the spot where they were touched to counterbalance the uncomfortable input.

Refusing hugs and kisses from family members. It can be a painful experience for everyone when a child refuses to give relatives a kiss or wipes off a kiss received. Explain to relatives that it is not personal but rather an issue with touch that your child is working on. Teach your child that rubbing in a kiss makes it feel better, and tell relatives your child is rubbing in the kiss so they can keep it with them.

Withdrawing from interactions with others. Respect the child's need to observe activities before joining in. Respecting needs for personal space and allowing a child to explore at her own pace increases the likelihood that she will eventually join in. If a child feels she has no way out or can't change her mind, she will avoid even more.

Throwing objects. Children throw due to frustration and because throwing provides deep pressure input through the arms. Provide a place where throwing is safe and model play with heavy bean bags, pillows, balls, and boxes or laundry baskets.

Resisting dressing activities. Remember to use firm pressure input and encourage the child to actively participate in the task. The more a child can do for himself, the more he learns he can have control over how it feels. Explore clothing textures that are comfortable for the child, and begin and end the activity with firm-pressure input.

Avoiding toilet training. Proceed slowly and with patience. This task involves many skills including many language concepts, getting partially dressed and undressed, sitting on a seat with a hole in the middle of it, hearing a loud noise when flushing the toilet, washing hands, and other possibly uncomfortable or painful associations.

Falling apart in places like grocery stores, restaurants, malls, on field trips. Sounds tend to be louder in such places, and there are many unfamiliar people to deal with. Choose a time of day that is best for the child. Avoid times when the child is tired or feeling ill. Before leaving, engage in an activity that provides deep-pressure input. Choose times of the day when malls, stores, and restaurants are less crowded. Bring whatever you have found that assists the child in staying calm (e.g., sucking water from a sports bottle, chewing on a crunchy snack, carrying a favorite stuffed animal). Try to leave the place before the child becomes overwhelmed so she can learn that the experience can be a positive one. Gradually increase the amount of time you spend there.

Fighting the car seat. Really take time to assess the child's car seat. Are the straps brushing against his face or neck? Can they be adjusted to prevent this or covered with different material? Provide a drink bottle to suck on, a favorite snack, music, or songs. If the trip is a long one, take frequent breaks or travel at a time when the child is most likely to fall asleep.

Refusal to eat a variety of food tastes and textures. Be careful not to get into forcing anything—it increases resistance, rather than decreasing it. Have fun! Be playful! Be positive! Allow the child some control. Provide lots of opportunity without pressuring. Play games in the mirror around making silly faces. Exaggerate tongue and lip movements. Some children respond well to using a vibrating toothbrush, and they can apply it themselves; some like to explore flavored lip balms. Play with tastes, textures, and temperature of foods. What does the child like best? Slowly introduce other food textures with the tastes and temperatures she already likes. Be careful not to go too far, too fast. Change only one thing at a time, rather than both taste and texture. Some children like tastes you wouldn't normally think of for a young child. Play at experimenting with dipping foods into different sauces (e.g., ranch dressing, barbecue sauce, ketchup, mustard, cheese, applesauce). If you find sauces the child likes, add that flavor to other foods.

Providing Proprioceptive Input

Parents and service providers can try having children:

- Crawl on hands and knees to race to a specific target.

- Practice moving like different animals.

- Load up a box or laundry basket with toys or small canned goods, push it to another location, and unload again. Pretend you've gone to the store and are bringing things home to put away. With younger children, just the act of filling something up and dumping it out again is pleasurable and provides firm input to the body.

- Eat a crunchy or chewy snack.

- Move through an obstacle course such as crawling over a couch cushion, under a chair, and climbing up on the couch, and then do it all again.

- Play on squishy pillows.

- Push a play wheelbarrow to cart objects from one place to another.

- Pull a wagon.

- Engage in running games with specific start and stop places.

- Dance to music (i.e., play at dancing when the music starts and stopping in place when the music stops).

- Climb up and down at a playground or at a stool at the sink.

- Throw heavy bean bags into a box to make a basket; throw a ball through a hoop tied to a tree.

Additional Resources and Strategies

Books, apps, and oral-motor toys can all be additional resources for families and professionals. In addition to the strategies for common problems offered above, the following resources can be helpful:

Books and Articles:

Alexander, R., Boehme, R., & Cupps, B. (1998). *Normal development of functional motor skills: The first year of life.* San Antonio, TX: Therapy Skill Builders.

Anzalone, M. F. (1993). Sensory contributions to action: A sensory integrative approach. *Zero to Three, 14*(2), 17–20.

Aquailla, P., Yack, E., Sutton, S., & Kranowitz, C. (2015). *Building bridges through sensory integration: Theapy for children with autism and other pervasive developmental disorders* (3rd ed.). Arlington, TX: Sensory World.

DeGangi, G. (2000). *Pediatric disorders of regulation in affect and behavior: A therapist's guide to assessment and treatment.* San Diego, CA: Academic Press.

Frick, S., Frick, R., Oetter, P., & Richter, E. (1996). *Out of the mouths of babes.* Hugo, MN: PDP Press.

Kranowitz, C. (1998). *The out-of-sync child.* New York, NY: Berkley Publishing Group.

Mauro, T. (2006). *The everything parent's guide to sensory integration disorder.* Avon, MA: F & W Publications.

Mennella, J. A., & Beauchamp, G. K. (1993). Early flavor experiences: When do they start? *Zero to Three, 14*(2), 1–7.

Miller, L. (2006). *Sensational kids: Hope and help for children with sensory processing disorder.* New York, NY: Penguin.

Ostovar, R. (2009). *The ultimate guide to sensory processing disorder: Easy, everyday solutions to sensory challenges.* Arlington, TX: Sensory World.

Porges, S. W. (1993). The infant's sixth sense: Awareness and regulation of bodily processes. *Zero to Three, 14*(2), 12–16.

Saavedra, B. (2000). *Creating balance in your child's life.* Chicago, IL: Contemporary Books.

Sears, W., & Sears, M. (1996). *Parenting the fussy baby and high need child.* Boston, MA: Little, Brown.

Smith, K., & Gouze, K. (2004). *The sensory sensitive child: Practical solutions for out-of-bounds-behavior.* New York, NY: HarperCollins.

Trott, M. C., Laurel, M. K., & Windeck, S. L. (1993). *SenseAbilities: Understanding sensory integration.* San Antonio, TX: Therapy Skill Builders.

Websites:

- The Hanen Center
  www.hanen.org/Home.aspx

- American Speech-Language-Hearing Association
  www.asha.org

- American Occupational Therapy Association
  www.aota.org

- ZERO TO THREE
  www.zerotothree.org

- Chatoor, I. *Diagnosis and Treatment of Feeding Disorders in Infants, Toddlers, and Young Children.*
  www.amazon.com/Diagnosis-Treatment-Disorders-Toddlers-Children/dp/193401933X/ref=pd_bxgy_b_img_y
  This link has several feeding references at the bottom that the authors have used. Scroll down to see what is there.

- American Speech-Language-Hearing Association
  www.asha.org/public/speech/development/parent-stim-activities.htm

- Robert Owens
  http://faculty.strose.edu/owensr

- Talk Tools: Speech Therapy, Oral Placement Therapy Tools
  www.talktools.com

- ARK Therapeutic
  www.arktherapeutic.com

- New Visions
  www.new-vis.com

- Apraxia Kids
  www.apraxia-kids.org

- Ohio Speech-Language-Hearing Association
  www.ohioslha.org/pdf/Convention/2011%20Handouts/PreConv2AlexanderC.pdf

- OT's with Apps & Technology. *Apps for Regulation for Individuals With Autism or Sensory Processing Disorders*
  http://otswithapps.com/2013/04/13/apps-for-regulation-for-individuals-with-autism-or-sensory-processing-disorders/

Chapter Summary

This chapter has discussed some of the reasons that children experience feeding, oral-motor, and speech-language challenges. The chapter describes components of sensory processing and regulation and dimensions of oral-motor development. The discussion presents a visual approach to assessment and treatment and considers several family and cultural issues that may be encountered around feeding and language development. Several illustrative examples and vignettes are offered throughout the chapter as guides for the reader, as well as multiple resources such as books and websites that may be helpful to both professionals and parents.

Key Points to Remember

- Sensory processing is complex, involving children's abilities to attend to, sort through, and regulate responses to information from within themselves and from the world around them.

- A basic knowledge of the five senses (i.e., vision, auditory, tactile, olfactory, and taste), as well as of the proprioceptive, kinesthetic, and vestibular senses is important for understanding speech-language, feeding, and sensory processing disorders.

- The nervous system, especially the autonomic nervous system, plays an important role in a child's ability to achieve sensory processing and regulatory skills.

- There is wide variation within a typical range of responses to a child's sensory thresholds.

- Difficulties with sensory processing can impact many areas of a child's development.

- Assessment and treatment of sensory processing disorders takes time, strong observational skills, and in-depth conversations with primary caregivers across a variety of settings.

Implications for Families and Professionals

Facing challenges in feeding a child is a deeply emotional experience for parents and impacts all family members; therefore, it is critical for professionals to work at collaborating with families around their fears and goals for their child and to support their journey. Each session with a child and family is an opportunity for shared learning. Remembering and assisting parents in discovering that all behavior is communication, as well as encouraging parents to share their observations, lead to insights that aid in developing and modifying a treatment plan. Cultural preferences, individual temperaments, and a child's individual approach–avoidance patterns must also be taken into account. Children facing challenges in eating are also at risk for delays in development of communication skills and may be experiencing difficulties with processing sensory information; hence, comprehensive assessment, careful monitoring of development, and ongoing medical follow-up are essential. Difficulties with communication, feeding, and sensory processing can affect development across all domains.

References

Ayres, A. J. (1980). *Sensory integration and learning disorders.* Los Angeles, CA: Western Psychological Services.

Guerra, G., & Vaughn, S. (1994). *Normal oral-motor and swallowing development: Birth to 36 months.* Imaginart International.

Morris, S., & Klein, M. (2000). *Pre-feeding skills: A comprehensive resource for mealtime development* (2nd ed.). Austin, TX: Psychological Corporation.

Oetter, P., Richter, E., & Frick, S. (1995). *M.O.R.E. Integrating the mouth with sensory and postural functions* (2nd ed.). Hugo, MN: PDP Press, Inc.

PART 3

CHAPTER 13

Autism and Pervasive Developmental Disorders in Young Children

Ellen B. Barnes and Lori Saile

Highlights of the Chapter

At the end of this chapter, the reader will:

- understand behaviors commonly displayed by individuals with autism spectrum disorder (ASD)

- be familiar with recent revisions in the criteria for an individual to be diagnosed with ASD and professionals who can make the diagnosis

- understand educational interventions that represent best practices for supporting young children who are diagnosed as having autism

- be aware of some of the perspectives and challenges of families who have toddlers and preschoolers with ASD

- be familiar with components cited in evidenced-based studies that represent best practices of early intervention with young children with autism and their families

The number of children and families diagnosed with autism continues to rise. As of 2014, the Centers for Disease Control and Prevention estimated that 1 in 68 children is affected; the prior projection, in 2000, was 1 in 150 young children. It is unclear how much of this revised statistic represents heightened vigilance, improved abilities to diagnose autism, or a change and broader definition versus an actual increase in the incidence of the disorder. Regardless, there are now great incentives to carry out research that will help in understanding some of the underlying causes, as well as determining the best ways to support individuals with autism.

Diagnosing ASD in Young Children

Autism is a neurological spectrum disorder, reflecting differences related to social engagement, sensory processing, and restricted interests. Although the disorder must be diagnosed by a physician or professional within the medical field, there is no definitive medical test for autism. Rather, the diagnosis is made on the basis of evidence of a cluster of behaviors. People with autism vary widely in the nature and severity of behaviors expressed; that is, no two individuals with autism are the same. For a diagnosis of autism, a child must meet specific criteria. Whereas in the past the category of ASD included an umbrella of distinct subcategories such as *autism*, *Asperger's syndrome*, and *pervasive developmental disorder–not otherwise specified* (PDD-NOS), the newly revised *Diagnostic and Statistical Manual of Mental Disorders* (*DSM-V*; American Psychiatric Association, 2013) specified new criteria for a single diagnosis of ASD without subcategories. Thus, those previously diagnosed with Asperger's syndrome or PDD-NOS, assuming they meet the new diagnostic criteria, now would simply be diagnosed with ASD. The diagnostic criteria are broken down into three levels, to indicate severity. An individual diagnosed at a Level 1 is seen as "requiring support," at a Level 2 as "requiring substantial support," and at a Level 3 as "requiring very substantial support." The diagnostic criteria fall into two categories: (a) differences in joint attention and social engagement, and (b) differences in sensory processing and need for sameness. In order to meet the criteria for a diagnosis of ASD, the child must demonstrate challenges related to both social engagement and differences in sensory processing/restricted and repetitive interests. If the child presents only challenges with social engagement, and not the need for sameness, he may receive the new diagnosis of *social (pragmatic) communication disorder.*

In addition to the criteria noted above, for a diagnosis of ASD, the challenges must also be evident early in the child's life, although they may not rise to a level that warrants further evaluation and diagnosis until later in life, when social demands increase. Some parents have reported always knowing there was something different about their child. (Parent comments throughout this chapter are printed in italics.)

Looking back, I can see that there were signs as early as 7 weeks. I even wrote it in my son's baby book: He smiled for the first time at 6.5 weeks, "mostly at inanimate objects like the couch." Even then, I thought it was kind of strange—the books said [babies] would smile at people. Then he would fuss, even as a tiny infant, whenever we finished the book Brown Bear, Brown Bear, What Do You See? *We read it all the time, and it was always on the last page that he would become upset. Why? I had no idea, but now, after years of him having to run out of a room when a book was coming to the end, not able to bear to hear the last few words, that makes total sense. Like I said, looking back, it all makes sense now! Fortunately, we got help early.*

Others recall that their child developed normally for their first 1 to 2 years, followed by a period of rapid regression in skills. In either case, the developmental impact of autism is lifelong. Although children may develop more and more effective strategies for coping with the demands of social environments, and some may reach a point where less and less individualized support is needed, there is no "cure" for autism.

A final criterion for a diagnosis of autism specifies that the challenges a child is demonstrating are not explained by another cause, such as an intellectual disability or global developmental delay. This criterion requires skilled observation and examination by an experienced diagnostician, because the characteristics of autism often overlap with other developmental disabilities such as anxiety disorders, obsessive-compulsive disorder, attention deficit disorder, and/or an intellectual disability. Although children with ASD can demonstrate anxiety; compulsive behaviors; difficulties with determining what is relevant to attend to, maintaining focus, and shifting their attention appropriately; and cognitive challenges, their overall pattern of development also includes specific challenges with social engagement and restricted/repetitive interests (as noted previously) that point to autism as the primary underlying disability.

A pediatrician can make a diagnosis of autism, but the disorder is more commonly assessed by a developmental–behavioral pediatrician, specializing in the study and diagnosis of developmental disabilities; a clinical psychologist; or a transdisciplinary team that may include a psychologist, special education teacher, speech-language therapist, occupational therapist, and physical therapist evaluating a child along with a physician. The evaluation process generally involves gathering a medical–developmental history, as well as information about current skills and behaviors from the parents or caregivers, in addition to observation and a core developmental assessment.

Differential Diagnosis: Joint Attention, Reciprocity, Social Engagement, and Communication

Typically developing infants show social engagement with their caregivers from a very early age (about 4 months). This behavior is first demonstrated through eye contact, smiles, and/or cooing when a caregiver talks to them. Later, it is seen through joint attention, such as looking at an object their caregiver is pointing to, or pointing toward an object of interest, while vocalizing and looking at their caregiver. As language progresses, this behavior is reflected in comments, questions, and, still later, back-and-forth conversations on topics of mutual interest. Turn-taking develops naturally, first through mutual vocalizations, later through sharing and taking turns with objects, and eventually with conversational topics. Play expands through observing, imitating others, exchanging ideas and objects, and eventually expands into more complex negotiations of roles and problem solving related to carrying out shared ideas and meeting shared goals.

Persons on the autism spectrum demonstrate a variety of challenges with these areas of development. Parents may notice from an early age that their child does not seem to connect with them socially. Some describe their children as stiffening and pulling away when they were held as infants. Others say that their child appeared not to notice that they were present, with no eye contact, smiling, or engaging in the type of back-and-forth cooing and play that the parents may have enjoyed with typically developing siblings.

I was concerned from the time he was born. At 10 days old, he was hospitalized due to "failure to thrive," which we figured out was due to dairy protein intolerance. As an infant, he did not enjoy being touched and preferred to sit in a chair alone. He did not develop separation or stranger anxiety, soothed with objects instead of people, and he began hand and arm flapping, all before his first birthday.

Play of a child with autism may be self-absorbed/self-directed, rather than interactive, and present stereotypical use of objects, such as lining up or spinning toys, rather than playing

with them for their intended purpose. The child also may be less likely to imitate adult or peer models, seem not to notice peers, or even move away when peers approach, appearing fearful that peers will interrupt their play. Others may show interest in peers but have difficulty successfully initiating or maintaining interactions with peers, failing to understand and follow the unwritten rules of social interaction, demonstrating a limited range of interests, and showing difficulty with incorporating the ideas and interests of others. They also can have difficulty understanding, expressing, and responding to the facial expressions and emotions of others.

N. was our beautiful, eagerly awaited, brown-eyed beauty. She was meeting all her milestones on track. She was a difficult and challenging baby—unable to self-soothe, cried a lot, and slept horribly. Around 2 years old, we started to recognize other children her age were growing in their conversational and verbal skills, and she was still using only 1–2 words. There was really no reciprocity when she communicated. . . . Typical activities like birthday parties, walks in the mall, visiting friends were becoming painfully difficult and we started not going places and retreating to our home more and more. We also noticed she had amazing splinter skills such as knowing and recognizing the alphabet, numbers up to 20, colors, shapes, almost anything that was rote. She could hear a song from Sesame Street, *memorize it and sing it, in its entirety.*

For many children on the autism spectrum, communication skills are slow to develop or idiosyncratic, or both. Even before the development of spoken language, these children are sometimes limited in their pointing or gestural skills to convey their intent, simply crying or whining and leaving the parent to wonder what they want. In some instances, they may take the parent's hand and pull them toward the object of their desire, rather than pointing or labeling. Spoken language

sometimes does not develop at all, or may develop in unusual ways, with the child echoing whole phrases or sentences, without apparent connection to a given situation. Use of pronouns may be unusual, with the child referring to himself as he has heard others (e.g., referring to themselves by name, rather than using the pronoun "I,"; e.g., "Micah want horsie," rather than "I want the horsie"; responding affirmatively to a question, e.g., "Do you want a cookie?" by saying, "You want a cookie."). Other children seem to develop age-appropriate vocabulary, grammar, and sentence structure but have difficulty with the pragmatic aspects of language, the social rules governing how to communicate with others.

Differences in Behavior: Sensory Processing and Need for Sameness

The second set of criteria for a diagnosis of autism relates to differences in the way children process sensory information, challenges with motor planning, and the perhaps related need for consistency and sameness.

Sensory integration

The definition and impact of sensory integration challenges are described in chapter 12 of this book (Jenkins & Sullivan, 2016). Many children on the autism spectrum experience problems registering and effectively responding to sensory input from one or more "channels": Visual, auditory, taste, smell, touch/tactile, proprioceptive (information perceived through muscles and joints about the position of body parts in relation to one another), and vestibular (information received through sensors in the inner ear about the body's position in relation to gravity and movement through space). They may be overly sensitive to one or more types of input, easily distracted, sometimes experiencing input as aversive. On the other end of the continuum, they may be hyposensitive, underreactive, needing a higher degree of input for registration, sometimes seeking intensive input to help orient themselves and maintain a "just right" level of arousal to successfully engage and interact with their environment. These children may appear lethargic and non-responsive, or they may be in perpetual motion, constantly spinning, flapping their hands, staring at things that stimulate them visually, and crashing and banging into people or objects in an effort to seek the stimulation they need.

Although sensory challenges have been included in the diagnostic criteria for autism only in the 2013 release of the *DSM-V*, first-person accounts by individuals with autism have long described difficulties with sensory integration. Individuals often report extreme sensitivity to certain forms of sensory input and sometimes extreme sensory-seeking responses in one modality, at times to block out painful stimuli in other modalities. Conversely, some individuals with autism have reported hyposensitivity to a degree that they have a difficult time feeling their bodies, or demonstrate a high tolerance for pain due to limited perception of painful sensations. In either case, challenges with sensory integration may help to explain the hand flapping, spinning, or other stereotypical movements demonstrated by many people on the autism spectrum.

The first noticeable signs for us were the flapping and stimming. These came on before we noticed much speech delay.

In addition, individuals with autism have reported other sensory challenges. For example, they may be able to focus on and respond to information from only one sensory system at a time (appearing to be "mono-channeled"). Some experience sensory distortions, such as speech sounding garbled at times, or visual information sometimes wavering, blending together, or blurring. These distortions often are intermittently present, so it may be difficult to know whether the perceptions they experience are accurate.

Need for repetition and sameness

Because of sensory and motor challenges and perhaps for other reasons as well, children with autism often have a strong reliance on things staying the same. They may display repetitive patterns of movement, such as flapping their hands or twirling themselves around, or repetitive play, for example, using the same toys in the same way or lining up toys in specific patterns. They may experience extreme difficulty in shifting their attention to focus on another topic or in expanding their play to include other materials and play scenarios. They sometimes insist on certain routines, such as always using a particular bowl for their cereal or taking the same route to school in the morning. Transitions from one activity to another can be challenging, especially when activities are out of their routine. In addition, the need for sameness may impact interactions as well, with children on the spectrum insisting on rigid scripts or patterns of interaction.

Motor planning

Many individuals with autism experience problems with *motor planning*, the process of perceiving a desired action, determining the steps or sequences necessary to complete an action, initiating movement, and adjusting a plan as needed to address unexpected obstacles. Identifying challenges in this area can be deceptive for many children with autism because, although some may be clumsy and awkward in their movements in general, others may appear quite graceful and skilled with practiced movement sequences but have difficulty with novel ones.

My son was born premature so we were fortunate to have early intervention (EI) early on. When he was 13 months old and still had no verbalizations, we started to ask questions and increased his therapy schedule. He had a lot of motor challenges, we now know, due to his dyspraxia. We had him first evaluated at 2 years old. but no diagnosis was given until he was 3½ years old.

Speculations About Causes of Autism

Over the past decade, much research has been devoted to determining risks for and causes of autism. Researchers' understanding has improved, yet there still is no clear answer to that question. Autism is considered to be a neurological disorder, and autopsy studies have revealed differences in the brains of those diagnosed with autism (Bauman & Kemper, 2006). Bauman and Kemper's research on mirror neurons (a class of neurons in the premotor cortex and the inferior parietal cortex) involving abilities to copy actions and inhibit stereotyped mimicking such as echolalia, suggests a possible early dysfunction of this system that is linked to autism disorders, in light of documented impairments in social interaction and communication/language acquisition.

Identical-twin and familial studies have suggested a genetic link as well. Most recently, studies have identified particular genomes that may be affected in individuals with autism (Veltman & Brunner, 2012). Yet, although genetic links may increase the likelihood of a child having autism, they are not 100% predictive. This finding indicates perhaps a genetic predisposition with environmental/in utero factors that are still not known.

Many families have pointed to a link between the timing of their child's measles, mumps, and rubella (MMR) vaccine to the onset of symptoms of autism. However, to date, studies have failed to establish a direct causal link between autism and the MMR vaccine (Verstraeten et al., 2003). Nonetheless, for many families, the concern remains. Martha Herbert, pediatric neurologist at Harvard, proposes that particular genes interacting with environmental factors can result in autism, when there is an accumulation of "total load." For example, it has been suggested that problems with metabolism (physiology and biochemistry) may be a result of genes and the environment (e.g., toxins, prenatal health, birth complications, processed food, and other lifestyle factors). In reality, multiple risk factors possibly lay the groundwork for a "tipping point" at which, when reached, a child exhibits the symptoms of autism.

One characteristic that has been linked with autism is gastroenterological distress. This may be evident in chronic constipation, diarrhea, and gastroenterological reflux disease . These issues are still being investigated. At the same time, parents have pursued many speculations about these concerns, as reflected in the vignettes below.

We attempted some special diets, such as gluten free and dairy free, but did not experience success with them. We tried vitamins, but they had a negative effect on her; she became even more hyperactive. The one thing we did try was melatonin, in a very low dose, and it really helped her fall asleep.

The [gluten-free casein-free] diet initially helped him by regulating his digestive system. Once he was feeling healthy, he was able to attend to tasks and learn much better.

To stay abreast of current research on autism, the Autism Research Institute (www.autism. com), the Program for Early Autism Research, Leadership and Service of the Department of Allied Health Services at the University of North Carolina (www.med.unc.edu/ahs/pe), the National Institutes of Health, and the American Academy of Pediatrics are credible resources.

Early Identification of Autism

A common assumption is that autism should be identified as early as possible in order to afford an opportunity to "rewire the brain" and intervene with adapted behavioral and educational measures. However, such an assumption is probably, in the least, simplistic! It is not clear, for instance, which early symptoms (under 3 years old) might be predictive of the child who later is identified with a diagnosis of autism at 4 years or older.

My daughter was 3 when she was diagnosed as a preschooler with a disability and 4 when she was diagnosed with autism. We went through the school district for the first diagnosis. . . . I was frustrated that I knew she was smarter than what she was showing. . . . Her autism diagnosis came from a local center specializing in developmental diagnoses . . . they hit us with the A word, which I was fully expecting, and sent us on our way with some papers; it was hard. There was relief that this was what I was thinking, but the anxiety about the road ahead . . . it struck me in a profound way.

Although medical professionals disagree about the value of communitywide screenings for autism being included in the well-child assessment sequence, surveillance of development (especially with a risk factor such as a family member with ASD) is highly recommended.

Thus, delays in the following areas or "markers" warrant a physician's concern:

- By 6 months: No big smiles or other joyous expressions

- By 9 months: No back-and-forth sharing of sounds and smiles

- By 12 months: Lack of response to name, no babbling, no back-and-forth gestures (e.g., pointing, showing, reaching, waving)

- By 16 months: No spoken words

- By 24 months: No initiated meaningful two-word phrases (not imitated, repeated)

Current research focuses on the importance of a baby's eye gaze and attention to the eyes and mouth of the communication partner. Parents often report their first concerns are communication (Kozlowski, Matson, Horowitz, Worley, & Neal, 2011). Other red flags include unusual or repetitive behaviors (e.g., spinning, visual interests, preoccupation with selected topics) and extreme temperament and reactions to sensory stimuli.

When our child was just under 18 months, we noticed what we thought was a language delay. He had a pretty good labeling vocabulary but didn't seem to use language to engage others or ask for things. We had him evaluated by EI. They did not find a language delay, but rather social and adaptive delays. He began receiving services shortly after he was 18 months. As time went by, we noticed more signs of autism. These included sensory sensitivities, difficulty talking to and playing with other kids, and intense preoccupations with certain objects (clocks, elevators, computers, etc.).

Regression of any kind (in speech, gestures, and engagement in social games) is a serious warning sign. Moreover, studies using home videos of babies at 1 year old have demonstrated that infants later diagnosed with autism could be differentiated from typically developing children and children with mental retardation (Osterling, Dawson, & Munson, 2002). There is a continuity of diagnosis in that toddlers identified as having autism between 14 and 25 months tend to retain that diagnosis 1 year later (Ozonoff, Rogers, & Tuchman-Ginsberg, 2014). However, children with earlier diagnosis did not necessarily show better outcomes, even though interventions were started earlier; it did appear that those classified earlier also had other medical issues (e.g., epilepsy; Fernell, Eriksson, & Gillberg, 2012).

The American Academy of Pediatrics suggests a standardized ASD screening tool such as the Modified Checklist for Autism in Toddlers (Robins, Fein, & Barton, 1999) and a follow-up parent interview for all children at the 18-month well-child visit, and again at between 24 and 30 months. Physicians are advised to carry out further evaluation at any point at which there are concerns raised by the parent or observed by the physician and when there are risk factors such as a sibling with ASD. If the screening reveals concerns, the preschooler should be referred to the EI agency (if under 3 years old) or local school district (3–5 years old) for a full evaluation and services to meet his individualized needs. The Centers for Disease Control and Prevention has a campaign to encourage early identification (www.cdc.gov/actearly).

We went to see (a developmental pediatrician) when our son was 15 months old, and while admitting that J. showed numerous autistic tendencies, he decided to give him the benefit of the doubt because he was so young and was doing well with EI. He was 25 months when he was officially diagnosed…but this diagnosis was not at all a surprise, and we were thoroughly immersed in the EI program at this time. We were blessed with a wonderful service coordinator who enabled us to see Dr P. with a very short wait and secure numerous services for our son.

In view of this recommendation, one study (Al-Qubandi, Gorter, & Rosenbaum, 2011) raised questions about the potential negative effects of regular screening of infants and toddlers to seek early identification of children on the autism spectrum. In particular, these authors expressed concerns about the lack of quality screening tools and evidence-based programs. A false positive may change the parent–child relationship and balance in the family structure. Further, a child's

access to typical experiences may be limited as a result of early diagnosis. Alerting physicians and parents to be aware of behaviors (surveillance) is different from implementing a community-wide screening effort as part of a regular well-child check-up.

Early Intervention

Much work is being done to assess interventions that are effective in supporting growth and development of young children with autism. Each child with autism is unique, and to identify an effective range of practices one must address each child's specific strengths, challenges, and learning styles. Toward this end, Dawson and Osterling (1997) identified common key elements for effective EI programs. As described by the authors, these include:

- a curriculum focusing on skills of joint attention, imitation, language comprehension and expression, social interaction with others, and appropriate play with toys

- a highly supportive teaching environment and generalization strategies

- predictability and routines

- a functional approach to problem behavior

- plans for transition from EI to preschool and preschool to kindergarten

- an environment supporting family involvement.

Other factors include intensity of intervention (number of hours), use of a range of augmentative communication methods; occupational therapy; an emphasis on developing trusting, positive social relationships; presence of typically developing peers to promote social behavior and serve as positive role models; and a focus on developing independence, initiative, and choice making. States may have guidelines that identify components of effective EI practice. For example, in Washington State (Cowan, Mancini, & Toth, 2012), a research study summarized elements of such practices as follows:

- integrated toddler group experiences;

- intensive individualized 1:1 or small-group structured instruction;

- specialized support and parent education for families;

- communication, coordination, and collaboration across services; and

- goals that target not only core deficits of autism, but also seek skills that improve the quality of life.

Our daughter received Special Education Itinerant Teacher Services for a year as well as speech, occupational, and music therapies in our home. These people were amazing. They were phenomenal for N. in helping her, and just awesome for our family as well. They became our supports and led us in the right direction. She then went to J. for a year in their inclusive preschool program. The experience was profound. She started to grow and it was then that her love for school began to flourish.

The National Professional Development Center on Autism Spectrum Disorders (Odom & Wong, 2014) reviewed a variety of interventions for young children with autism that were supported by evidence. Evidence-based practices were defined as peer-reviewed research studies, published in scientific journals, with either randomized or quasi-experimental designs, or single-subject design studies without critical design flaws. Described next are some of the most significant approaches identified for working with young children with autism.

Understanding Characteristics of Individuals With Autism: Interventions for Support

Although every child with autism presents differently, and thus there is no clear "recipe" for intervention, understanding the challenges and learning style that lead to some of the characteristics that may be demonstrated by individuals with autism can help with determining effective strategies for support.

Communication of Children With Autism

Common communication challenges that may occur in children with autism include difficulties with language pragmatics, use of echolalia, limited functional spoken language, or a combination of these.

Pragmatics: The social rules of language

Communication abilities vary widely among young children on the autism spectrum. Some may have relatively well-developed *expressive language* (what they are able to say) and *receptive language* (what they understand of what is said to them) but have difficulty with *pragmatics* or the social rules governing how people use language to communicate. These children need to be directly taught social rules regarding, for example, getting someone's attention before speaking to them, taking turns in a conversation, maintaining a topic of conversation, asking for help, reading cues to signal a person's desire to end a conversation, and giving and accepting compliments. Because children with autism tend to be visual learners, using modeling, role play, and print cues all seem to be useful strategies for teaching pragmatic skills.

PART 3

Echolalia: Echoed speech

Some children with autism develop spoken language, but it may be delayed or idiosyncratic, or both. Children may rely on *echolalia*, or verbatim repetitions, of what they have heard to communicate. At times, these patterns make it difficult to interpret the child's intent. For example, a child relying on echolalia may say "You want juice?" to request a drink, rather than to offer one, because she is imitating the question she has heard her parent ask before juice appears in front of her. This ability to memorize and repeat whole scripts can be a useful strategy for learning, because adults can model scripts appropriate to the situation and look for the child to repeat them. On the other hand, it is important to work on expanding and varying the range of scripts available to the child, so that she is able to more effectively communicate a large range of intents. Children who use echolalia communicatively and are provided with a growing variety of scripts often are eventually able to break down those scripts and put them together in different conversations to generate more spontaneous language.

Communication of children with limited functional spoken language

Still other children may never develop, or be extremely late to develop, functional spoken communication. They may not say words at all

or may engage only in echolalia that seems unrelated to the situation at hand. Many adults with autism who develop functional augmentative communication describe their echoed speech as unintentional and beyond their control. In that circumstance, they may prefer not to have others respond to the content of their echoed speech but rather to what they are communicating in functional ways. For individuals who are nonverbal, or whose verbal language is not functional, it is important to develop an augmentative communication system. These approaches can be as simple as sign language, laminated pictures or words a child points to or hands to a communication partner to convey a message, or as complex as computerized devices with voice-output devices that speak a message once a child has composed it. These devices can be programmed with pictures, words, and keyboards that allow the child to type out a spontaneous message. It is important to note that augmentative systems can be used to support whatever spoken language the child is able to achieve. They do not get in the way of developing spoken language and, to the contrary, often cue and support language development. They also can provide a bridge to allow the child to more effectively express himself and limit frustration, while spoken language is developing. For example, Jamie Burke, a young man

with autism, originally developed the ability to communicate by typing, using facilitated communication, at about 5 years old (Biklen, 2005). Over time, the facilitator was able to fade support so that Jamie was able to type more independently. Subsequently, at about 12 years old, Jamie developed the ability to read back what he had typed. Today, although he still types to convey complex ideas, after steady practice with first reading back what he had typed and then beginning to speak without typing first, Jamie is able to communicate many thoughts and ideas verbally.

Developing augmentative communication systems

When developing an augmentative communication system for a child, it is important to consider how the child will access the device, how to make the device accessible throughout the child's day in any situation in which she might wish to communicate, and what level of symbolic representation is to be used. Although sign language is a system the child can take with her wherever she goes, she will need to rely on listeners who are able to interpret sign language and will also need to have manual dexterity to develop and use a wide range of sign language vocabulary if that is to be her primary means of communication. Conversely, computerized voice output devices can offer great flexibility and require less skilled motor control, but some are much more easily portable than others. It is important to note that even systems relying on basic pointing responses still involve some degree of motor planning and dexterity. Children with challenges with body awareness and motor planning may require thoughtful consideration of positioning, size, and complexity of the visual display, and even physical support to slow down body movements to promote more organized access to the communication device.

For many children, picture communication is first to develop. Some easily respond to line drawings or picture symbols, whereas others need to start with concrete photographs. Pairing the pictures with print helps to facilitate reading skills, prepare children to spell words, and potentially use a less cumbersome system of communication.

When my son was 15 months old, he had little to no communication ability, so my husband and I created a magnetic choice board using photographs of his favorite things. My son quickly learned to use the board to communicate, and that was the beginning of us using assistive technology. Soon after, he was given an iPad with a choice board app. This allowed us to rapidly expand his selection of choices. As his communication increased, his tantrums decreased, and his behavior became much more manageable. He was able to focus and learn for longer periods of time because he was no longer in a constant state of frustration. Around his 2nd birthday, he did become verbal, but I do not believe that he would have progressed as quickly as he did without the use of assistive technology. I believe that the iPad enabled him to understand the basic concept of communication and thus motivated him to learn more.

Our son did use some assistive technology while at school (choice boards, a Dynavox during lunchtime at Jowonio, etc.) but not much at home. We certainly learned from his teachers during parent–teacher conferences and, I hope, offered some insights back. We all discovered pretty early on that the best "technology" to help our son was a whiteboard and dry-erase marker, or a Magna Doodle, and for years we had these laying around at home, and there were always some at school. We realized that if we wrote down what was going to happen or what was different, numbering the steps that were upcoming, confusion, fear, and meltdowns were minimized.

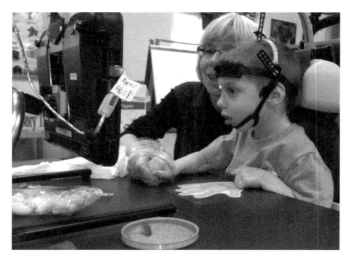

The content of the communication system is another crucial consideration. Although most systems start with pictures or symbols to allow the child to request basic wants and needs, it is important to consider the full range of things a typically developing child of his age might be communicating. This includes, for example, social commentary and the ability to ask questions, as well as the opportunity to request basic wants and needs. The long-range goal for any communication system is for the child to be able to engage in spontaneous, open-ended conversation rather than be limited to the choices an adult makes available.

Social Skills of Children With Autism

Challenges with social interaction is one of the defining characteristics of autism. However, because there are many different factors that contribute to effective engagement, and the unwritten "rules" for social interaction in a society can be abstract and ever-changing, determining how to intervene to support success in this area can be challenging.

What do social challenges look like?

Challenges with social engagement and interaction are a defining characteristic of autism, but such challenges initially may be less notable.

Infants and toddlers may be less interactive with their caregivers, may not respond when their name is called, and may not seek comfort when hurt. Nonetheless, in time these differences become more and more apparent to those closest to the children. For instances, some youngsters with hypersensitive tactile systems may resist hugs and cuddling. Others may show affection, but in unusual ways, such as backing into the caregiver for a hug or a lap, or hugging the parent from behind. Eye contact may be limited or nonexistent, perhaps because close visual contact with another person can overwhelm the sensory system, making it hard to process other input, including the person's voice. As noted previously, children may show little interest in peers, seeming to exist in their own world. Other reactions to social situations may be different from peers their age. For example, they may show anxiety when approached by peers but not demonstrate anxiety when separated from their caregiver. They may also show difficulty interpreting and responding to facial expressions and emotion, and their own affect may not match the situation.

What makes social interaction challenging?

Adults with autism have shared that their behavior in these situations often was not indicative of how they really felt. They describe desiring social connection with others but finding it extremely challenging. Social situations often, by nature, involve higher levels of sensory input such as noise or movement and frequently are highly language-based. People on the autism spectrum can have difficulty focusing and attending to what is relevant within a busy social situation, as well as processing and responding to the language. They also can have difficulty interpreting and following the unwritten rules of social interaction, as well as following the cues that others receive from facial expression or body language. In addition, social rules frequently are abstract and flexible, not following the prescribed routines and scripts that are comforting to an individual with autism. These kinds of situations can be highly anxiety producing.

We haven't always felt comfortable or felt that we could attend certain social situations, recognizing that it might be hard for him to conform to the norm at the time. . . . So we might take two cars, or divide and conquer, or not go as an entire family. . . His siblings have felt embarrassed by certain behaviors that were witnessed by their peers. . . We have been through many stages over the years . . . some of the more challenging ones have included his extreme reaction to any kind of TV or screen that was turned on in public and caused him severe anxiety, randomly lying down in public places, etc.

Simon Baron-Cohen's (1995) research led him to the conclusion that people with autism lack "theory of mind," or the ability to understand that others may have thoughts, feelings, and perceptions different from their own. He went on to connect what he termed "mind-blindness" with a lack of empathy. He saw this as the basis for the social challenges that exist for many on the autism spectrum. More recently, individuals with autism have indicated that they do understand that others have feelings and perceptions that are different but that they don't understand the social rules well enough to predict what those feelings and perceptions might be. Researcher Isabel Dziobek (2004) summed up her team's research on empathy in autism by saying, "More generally speaking, our data show that people with Asperger syndrome have a reduced ability to read other peoples' social cues (such as facial expressions or body language), but once aware of another's circumstances or feelings, they will have the same degree of compassion as anyone else." It has also been noted that neurologically typical individuals may have a hard time understanding the thoughts, feelings, and perceptions of people on the autism spectrum and thus could be considered "mind-blind" to them.

Implications for encouraging and supporting social interaction and engagement

The goal of interventions to support the development of social skills in children with autism is to help them to develop spontaneous, joyful, and reciprocal relationships and interactions—first with caregivers and then, as they move beyond infancy and toddlerhood and into the preschool years, with peers. Strategies for support are then focused on understanding their perceptions and experiences, encouraging them to become engaged with people in their environment, while offering them concrete information about the social rules that otherwise are not comprehensible to them. Potential goals include:

- helping them to become comfortable in the proximity of others

- helping them to discover pleasure in the reactions of others

- assisting with their observing and imitating the actions of others

- helping them to engage in parallel and then more interactive play

- encouraging them to initiate interactions and responses to the interactions of others

For most infants and toddlers, adult caregivers are their primary sources of interaction, and thus approaches focus on teaching parents and caregivers to prompt and reinforce meaningful engagement, imitation, and interaction. As children develop and move into preschool, the importance of access to typically developing peers to model and reinforce social interaction skills has been well documented. In this regard, some studies have found positive effects from teaching typically developing children specific strategies to engage their peers with autism.

Being exposed to typical peers is very important for him. He has difficulty initiating conversations or play. The typical peers often talk to him or ask him to play, which is good for him. Also, the typical peers give him challenges. For example, they might act in an improper way (cutting in front of him in line, taking his toys), and he has to learn to deal with these setbacks.

I have no concerns as to his exposure to his peers, only praise for how well inclusion works. Our son has always been included in school, home, family, and community. He has gained so much from peer support and peer modeling. His friends see him as a peer and not someone that has different abilities.

Along with strategies to facilitate joint engagement and imitation, approaches for teaching social skills are important, as children begin to understand and learn the "nebulous rules" of social interaction, including body orientation/eye contact, strategies for initiation, turn-taking, and topic maintenance. Ways for making these "rules" more visual include the use of modeling and role play, the use of video that allows children to watch appropriate strategies in engaging, repeated formats, and the use of written/pictured "social stories." References at the close of this chapter include resources for specific information about these approaches.

Cognitive/Learning Styles of Children With Autism

Children on the autism spectrum demonstrate a wide range of cognitive abilities. In the past, many individuals (approximately 75%) diagnosed with autism have been considered to be intellectually disabled. This assumption may be a reflection of challenges with sensory processing, motor planning, and communication that made it difficult for children to demonstrate their skills and understandings. However, with the advent of facilitated communication and the increasing use of augmentative systems of communication, it has become clear that many individuals are capable of far more than initially presumed.

Rote memory

Although every child with autism is different, some generalizations can be made about their cognitive abilities and learning styles. For example, many children diagnosed with autism have strong rote memories and quickly develop concrete skills such as color, shape, and letter identification. Some children label letters, arrange them alphabetically, or arrange them to spell familiar words, even before developing functional spoken language. Some children are hyperlexic, developing the ability to read at very early ages, although care must be taken to ensure they are comprehending what they are reading. Although they develop these strong rote skills, applying them to functional tasks and engaging in tasks that are highly language-based, requiring abstract thinking and reasoning, may be much more difficult.

Focus and attention

As mentioned earlier, attention and focus are a genuine challenge for individuals with autism. Developing joint attention is difficult. Sorting out the stream of sensory information coming in at any given point and determining what is relevant to attend to can present challenges. Further, once attention is gained, shifting attention to something new often is hard. Perhaps for this reason, many children with autism tend to be stronger visual than auditory learners. Unlike spoken language, visual stimuli are *nontransient*, meaning that they remain in place for a person to go back to, if she has momentarily lost her focus. Visual input provides concrete information that helps a child orient to what is happening. For this reason, use of props to enact a story, pictures, or print to highlight most relevant pieces of information are very useful strategies.

Holistic learning, associative learning, and generalization

In terms of processing, frequently people with autism appear to learn holistically, taking in chunks of information at once. Rote memory and memory for details can be strong but also cued through association. For instance, a particular verbal cue used when a skill was learned, a song that played in the background, or visual cue present but not necessarily relevant may prompt a skill at a later time that seems out of context. Conversely, cues an adult perceives as relevant when the skill was originally taught, used at a later time and in another situation, may fail to elicit the same skill. Thus, generalization of skills can be very tricky and illusive for children with autism. They may learn and perform a skill well in one setting but be unable to access and apply it in another situation. It is important to be thoughtful about the types of cues used when teaching a new skill and to actively work to use those same cues to teach that skill in an alternate setting. Generalization must be taught for each new skill developed.

Addressing Sensory and Motor Challenges in Children With Autism

Differences in sensory perception and movement impact all other areas of learning and development. For example, producing a wide range of speech sounds and stringing them together in sequence to form recognizable words and phrases involves very complex motor planning. Peer interaction often occurs within group social situations that require sorting out a wide variety of sensory perceptions.

Interventions to address sensory integration challenges focus on creating a "sensory diet"

that helps a child to achieve an optimal level of arousal (e.g., not painfully overstimulated and not so understimulated that he fails to take in key stimuli in his environment). One place to start is in arranging the environment and interactions to match, as closely as possible, the child's sensory processing style and challenges. For example, children who are easily overstimulated may respond well to environments in which the lights and sounds are kept low; parents' and caregivers' voices are calm and quiet; blankets, clothing, and other textures in the environment match the child's preferences; extraneous visual stimuli are removed to help the child focus on what is most relevant; and movements are slow and rhythmic. Conversely, children who are underresponsive may need a more animated approach, a higher level of stimulation, and fast or nonrhythmic movements, for instance, to engage them. Close observation can reveal what types of input are soothing to a child and which are more alerting. Occupational therapists are often trained in responding to sensory integration challenges and can be very helpful in developing sensory

diets and problem-solving strategies to address sensory needs. In addition to adjustments to the environment, children may need regular "tune-ups" of carefully planned sensory input that helps to alert or calm them, in order to prepare them to successfully engage, interact, and respond to the demands of social and learning situations. It is important to note here that children's sensory needs can vary from situation to situation, as well as change with time and maturation. Strategies may need to be adjusted frequently to respond to those changes. Many resources about strategies to address sensory integration challenges can be found in the references at the end of this chapter.

Inclusion as a Program Choice

As families are considering their child's needs and the program models available to meet those needs, they may have choices that include developmental play groups and preschool classrooms with typical peers. Inclusive programs welcome all children and adapt the classroom to meet their needs, rather than expecting the child to earn entrance, be "ready," for the classroom. (See chapter 18 [Ensher, Barnes, & Clark, 2016] for more detail about inclusive programs.) The long-term goal is for students to function within society.

My son is currently enrolled in an inclusive classroom, and he has benefitted greatly from the experience so far. . . . He needs professionals to help facilitate his peer interactions in order for him to learn appropriate social behaviors. The fact that this is happening at such a young age is going to help him gain a great deal of social competence by the time he is older and more self-aware. I think this is going to save him a great deal of frustration in the future.

Teachers should be supporting the active participation of all students in ongoing activities and routines, using adaptations and modifications to meet the unique learning styles, behavioral needs, and interests of the children. Learning opportunities are embedded in natural routines, as is planned social skills training. There are many benefits to inclusive settings for children on the autism spectrum:

- Adults have typical expectations of behavior and academic content.

- Peers initiate and model communication, social interaction and play; and children with autism have opportunities to practice communication and social skills.

- Natural settings present children with the skill demands and challenges of age-appropriate social and physical environments.

- Children are expected and supported to engage in developmentally appropriate routines, curricula, and play.

- Goals include initiation of skills, understanding of the risks and mistakes that occur for all in learning, generalization of skills, and growth toward independence and a sense of competence.

We realized very early on that N. loved peer attention and was motivated by typical peers. . . . It was a beautiful experience having her in a supportive, loving classroom at J. where they believed that all behavior was communication, each child has strengths to be built on, and that kindness, loving, and nurturing are essential. She tried new things and she copied her typical peers' behavior. It was very helpful for her and she learned so much from that exposure.

Research (Odom, 2002) tells us that children with disabilities make at least as much developmental progress in inclusive programs as they do in noninclusive programs. In fact, greater growth may occur in communication skills, social competence, and play. In particular, Harrower and Dunlap (2001) found that students with autism who are included have higher rates of social engagement and interaction, as well as developmentally having more advanced Individualized Education Plan (IEP) goals than their peers in segregated settings. Benefits occur for nondisabled peers in inclusive classrooms as well: a greater understanding of autism and its challenges, positive attitudes, and a greater willingness to interact with a wide range of peers, and practice as models and helpers of others (a "circle of friends").

J. has been in an inclusive classroom since he was 2. . . . We want him, as much as possible, to do the work that the other kids do, feel a part of a typical classroom community, not be "that different kid." . . . I know that kids have said things sometimes about him, but I have met more than one kid who has been quite understanding. . . . When I apologized to another second-grader after J. cut in front of him in line, the kid said to me, "That's OK. I know he has autism."

Koegel and Koegel (2006) have written, "Whenever possible children with autism should be included with typically developing children throughout the day" (p. 110). Strategies described earlier in this chapter also support inclusive programming: strong teacher–child relationships,

partial participation, cuing, priming, utilizing visuals and predictable routines, teaching social skills, self-management, positive behavioral supports, opportunities to make choices, activities with natural reinforcement, and a curriculum built on student interests. Parents may have mixed feelings about inclusion and many fears about their child's future, including the school supports that will be available as their son or daughter ages, potential bullying by peers, and vocational and residential options.

Benefits of inclusion are the opportunity for peer modeling, "real life" situations, and being able to participate in a general ed. setting. . . . We always want to be sure that his time is being used in a manner that is in his best interests and where he can gain the most learning . . . recognizing that he learns differently, it might not always be in the environment that is most beneficial to the majority. It seems to be a balancing act.

Biomedical Approaches: Medication and Diet

There are no medications, diets, or nutritional supplements that treat or cure autism. Although many studies are being done regarding pharmacological treatment of children with autism, many are criticized for their inadequate designs, and the interventions are not shown to be safe and effective with young children. Each child responds differently to biomedical approaches, including, over time, building up tolerances or exhibiting special sensitivities. Parents need to be informed about not only the benefits but also the potential harm, including the side effects of the approach. There should be evidence that children taking a particular medication or using special diets are monitored over time and periodically reevaluated, that there is an effective impact on targeted behaviors, and that any adverse behavioral or health effects are documented.

We experimented with a few things . . . consulting and traveling to a doctor that specializes in biomedical approaches to treating autism including vitamin B injections and chelation; we also experimented with biofeedback. Looking back, none of these experiences were too beneficial, if at all, to us and we even felt may have contributed to worsening behaviors at the time. However parents of children with autism are a very "captive audience" and are usually willing to try anything that might help their child succeed.

Most medicines prescribed for people with autism are used "off label"; that is, the medication has been FDA approved for other, sometimes-related conditions (e.g., attention-deficit/hyperactivity disorder, sleep disturbances, depression), not autism. Two drugs (Risperidone and Aripipazole) have been approved by the FDA to address irritability associated with autism and thereby reduce tantrums, aggressive outbursts, and self-injurious behaviors (Autism Speaks, 2014).

Examples of the most common medications, nutritional supplements, and special diets mentioned regarding children with autism are listed below.

- *Psychoactive medications* alter the chemical make-up of the central nervous system and have an impact on mental functioning and behavior. They are seldom used to treat young children with autism and should be used only if behaviors are severe, and other behavioral and educational interventions have been tried over time.

- *Selective serotonin reuptake inhibitors* (SSRIs; including Celexa, Proxac, and Zoloft) may be effective with anxiety, depression, and obsessive stereotypic behaviors and thereby improve behavior, language, and socialization, although side effects include warning signs of suicide.

- *Antipsychotic medications* (e.g., Risperidal) may decrease tantrums, aggression, and self-harming but have side effects of tremors, sleepiness, and weight gain.

When J. turned 7, we started Risperidal under the guidance of Dr. P. and feel that this has had a positive slightly calming effect.

- *Hormone therapies* such as the growth hormone Adrenocorticotropin (ACTH) and Secretin for children with gastrointestinal issues; these are not recommended for young children with autism.

- *Anti-yeast therapies* are based on the theory that there is an overgrowth of yeast in the intestinal tract, which is treated by oral antifungal medication; this is not recommended for young children with autism.

- *Vitamin therapies* include taking high doses of Vitamin B6 (pyridoxine) and magnesium. Research does not support this as a treatment for autism; if a child shows a trace mineral or vitamin deficiency, it should be treated appropriately by a physician.

- *Diet therapies* frequently involve the elimination of cow's milk products or gluten-free products, or both, from the diet. The theory of linking autism to food allergies is not proven; a child with autism, as any other child, may have food allergies documented by standard allergy testing methods, and appropriate dietary changes should be implemented. However, some parents report that a complete elimination of these ingredients, gluten- and-casein-free diets, was beneficial for their child with autism, improving social interaction and attention and moderating activity level.

For about 2 years, we had our son on a gluten-free, dairy-free diet, with no real changes noted. . . . Now he eats everything again, except that we give him lactose-free milk. We give him a multivitamin, but a basic one we buy at the grocery store.

The Autism Research Institute has maintained a database since 1967 of more than 27,000 parent ratings regarding the benefits and adverse effects of drugs and other interventions tried with their children. The parent ratings are not necessarily consistent with the published research findings. Parents need to collaborate with their child's physicians as they consider the wide range of interventions available to them. They may want to download and use the Medication Decision Tool Kit, published by Autism Speaks, as a structure for working through this process. There is increasing research in the area of biomedical approaches with young children with autism.

A Continuum of Approaches to Working With Children With Autism

There are a variety of approaches to working with children with autism and, although research indicates that many have shown promise, there is no one method that seems to be effective for every child. Documented and well-known approaches to working with children with autism exist along a continuum, based on the philosophical underpinnings of those approaches.

Behavioral Approaches

At one end of the continuum are behavioral approaches. These approaches focus on observable behaviors and learning through prompting and reinforcement of target behaviors. They tend to involve detailed task analysis of those behaviors and often rely on prescribed sequences of curricula. Target behaviors are carefully prescribed and reinforced, with extraneous behaviors ignored. Careful data collection helps service providers identify when to move on to the next step in the sequences. Teaching often happens in carefully controlled environments where extraneous stimuli have been removed, to increase the likelihood of students attending and focusing on what is most relevant. Once skills are mastered in that setting, attention is given to generalizing them to more natural situations, including inclusive environments.

The most well known and well researched of these approaches is *applied behavioral analysis*, or ABA, which is based on the original work of Ivar Lovaas (Warren et al., 2011) but has been significantly expanded upon by others. ABA relies heavily on *discrete trial training*, which involves first task-analyzing a skill to determine the small component parts or "steps" involved; teaching each component part through a process of prompting, waiting for the child to respond, and either reinforcing correct responses or increasing prompting to elicit a correct response; and then reinforcing, recording data, and repeating the whole process multiple times to practice. Historically, ABA programs have recommended that the child spend intensive periods of time (usually 20–40 hours per week) engaged in discrete trial training. ABA providers usually follow a set sequence of skills and rely heavily on the use of data to identify when it is time to move on to the next skill in the sequence. The focus is on discrete, observable skills, with imitation being a key focus. "Off-task" behaviors, even if communicative, are usually ignored or redirected. Skills are generally taught in isolation, and support is provided to then generalize them to natural settings, once mastered. Because so much data are maintained, this is one of the most well-researched approaches, with strong evidence of success.

If I knew then what I know now, I would have insisted on ABA with the other types of therapy. Unfortunately ABA is not well recognized in our area and it is well established that it works . . . in my opinion incorporated with other types of therapy. So I wish we had more ABA in the beginning as we do now.

Another example of a comprehensive treatment approach founded on these principles is the Treatment and Education of Autistic and Related Communication-Handicapped Children program (Corsello, 2005), which is North Carolina's statewide program model for working with children on the autism spectrum. This approach can be used in group settings such as preschool classrooms, but it relies on behavioral strategies for teaching new skills.

Social-Pragmatic Approaches

At the other end of the continuum are social-pragmatic approaches. Underlying these approaches is the belief that all learning occurs through meaningful social interactions, and children should be wooed into interactions that become self-reinforcing and create opportunities for further learning. Social pragmatists further believe that skills are best learned in the natural settings in which they will need to be applied, reducing the need for time focused on generalization. These approaches tend to be somewhat child-directed, with adults following the child's lead, incorporating their interests, manipulating the environment to elicit interaction, and interacting in a style the child will perceive as meaningful and rewarding. The child's communicative intent is responded to and rewarded, with subsequent attempts to shape the child's communication to more socially appropriate strategies. Targeted skills in these approaches follow a general developmental sequence, but the sequence is often individualized to match the strengths, needs, and preferences of the child. Meaningful relationships are a key focus of these approaches, and they often involve elements of inclusion, because inclusive environments represent the natural environments in which children will be utilizing the skills they are learning.

The most well-known, comprehensive treatment model using these approaches is the *developmental, individualized, relationship-based approach (DIR)*, based on the work of Stanley Greenspan and Serena Wieder (2006). This approach follows a general developmental sequence of engagement and interaction skills seen in all children, known as *functional developmental levels*. However, goals for each child are individualized, based on an understanding of their unique learning styles and needs. Factors such as language processing and sensory needs are considered and addressed. The R in DIR recognizes the importance of meaningful relationships as the basis for all learning. The primary component of the program is "floor time" (discussed in chapter 17, Beckstrand, Pienkowski, Powers, & Scanlon, 2016), which involves multiple, brief (20–30 minute) sessions per day of time spent with the parent or a teacher, or both, engaged in goal-oriented play with the child, following the child's lead, eliciting interaction by opening a "circle of communication" and then shaping the child's responses, verbal and nonverbal, to expand play, interaction, and sharing of ideas. The goals of floor time are generally attention, engagement, and intimacy; two-way communication; communication of feelings and ideas; and logical thinking. Floor time occurs within natural settings for the child, often at first with just the parent/provider and the child. Once the child is successfully engaged in two-way communication, a DIR program may also build in semistructured teaching situations to work on discrete skills, as well as opportunities to expand interaction to peers. Another example of this approach is the *social communication, emotional regulation, and transactional support* model developed by Prizant, Wetherby, Rubin, Laurent, and Rydell (2006).

Most service providers utilize approaches that fall more toward the middle of the continuum, utilizing components of both behavioral and social-pragmatic techniques. However, one's philosophical orientation about how children learn can promote leaning to one side of the continuum or the other. Understanding one's own belief system can be helpful in identifying which approaches to use in which situation.

Comparisons of Outcomes With Different Program Models

Dawson and Osterling (1997) conducted a study of different comprehensive treatment models, demonstrating success in outcomes for children with autism. Rather than identifying one approach as better than another, Dawson and Osterling identified common characteristics across diverse program models that seemed to promote strong outcomes. They concluded:

- The earlier the start, the better the outcome.

- High-intensity programming is better than low-intensity programming (the programs studied involved 20–40 hours of instruction per week).

- Successful programs focus on skills such as attending, imitating, communication skills, play, and social interaction.

- Successful programs use a functional approach to analyzing, preventing, and responding to problem behaviors.

- Parent involvement and support play an important role in programs with successful outcomes.

- Successful programs include thoughtful, planned transitions to next settings.

- Successful programs incorporate ongoing assessment and program adjustment.

- Inclusion components are incorporated, at some point, into successful program models.

More recently, Wong and colleagues (2014) published a study of evidence-based practices for children with autism. Their study consisted of a literature review of research studies, based on practices demonstrating effective outcomes. In order to be included in the review, the approaches reviewed had to meet defined criteria, including adhering to rigorous research design criteria as well as multiple studies by different researchers. Rather than comprehensive program models, which might incorporate a variety of practices, they chose to focus on the individual practices that have been shown to have a positive impact for children with autism. Their study identified 27 evidence-based practices. Those that have been researched with toddlers and/or preschoolers are listed below.

- *Antecedent-based intervention:* Modifications that are made to the environment or context in an attempt to change or shape a learner's behavior. These modifications are typically made after conducting a functional behavior assessment that can assist in identifying the function of an interfering behavior, along with environmental conditions that have become linked to the behavior over time and may be inadvertently reinforcing it. They may include modifying educational activities, materials, or schedule to incorporate student interests; incorporating student choice into activities and materials; preparing students ahead of time for upcoming activities; varying the format, level of difficulty, or order of instruction; enriching the environment to provide additional cues or supports (e.g., visual supports, sensory inputs); and modifying prompting and reinforcement schedules and delivery

- *Differential reinforcement of alternative, incompatible, or other behavior:* Through differential reinforcement, the learner is reinforced for desirable behaviors and inappropriate behaviors are ignored. Differential reinforcement is often used with other evidence-based practices to teach the learner behaviors that are more functional or incompatible with the interfering behavior, with the overall goal of decreasing the interfering behavior.

- *Discrete trial training:* This is a key component of ABA programs.

- *Extinction:* A strategy based on ABA that is used to reduce or eliminate a challenging behavior. The process relies on accurately identifying the function of the behavior and the responses that may be reinforcing its occurrence, in order to change that response and remove reinforcement.

- *Functional behavioral assessment:* A systematic way of determining the underlying communicative function or purpose of a behavior so that an effective intervention plan can be developed. The process consists of describing the problem behavior, identifying antecedents and consequences that impact the behavior, developing a hypothesis regarding the function of the behavior, and testing the hypothesis. Typically, functional behavioral assessments lead to the development of a comprehensive behavior intervention plan, including strategies to prevent the behavior from arising in the first place, strategies to teach more appropriate replacement behaviors to serve the same function, and strategies for responding if the behavior does occur.

- *Functional communication training:* Following a functional behavioral assessment, this involves teaching an alternative response to communicate the need currently being met through inadvertent reinforcement of less desirable behaviors.

- *Modeling:* A key component of most approaches, modeling involves demonstrating the target behavior so that the child can imitate it.

- *Naturalistic intervention:* A collection of practices including arrangement of the environment, approaches to interaction, and strategies designed to encourage specific target behaviors, based on learners' interests, by building more complex skills that are naturally reinforcing and appropriate to the interaction. Naturalistic intervention occurs within typical settings, activities, and routines in which the learner participates.

- *Parent-implemented intervention:* In recognition that parents spend the most time with their children and thus have the most frequent opportunities for instruction, this approach focuses on training parents to carry out some or all of the intervention(s) with their child.

- *Peer-mediated instruction and intervention:* Teaching typically developing peers ways to interact with and help children with autism develop new behaviors, communication, and social skills through increased social opportunities and opportunities for practice within natural environments.

- *Picture exchange communication system:* This is a means of augmentative communication designed to teach learners to communicate in a social context. Learners are initially taught to give pictures of a desired item to a communication partner in exchange for the item. Over time, children are taught to sequence pictures to create sentences, and use the system to request and comment.

- *Pivotal response training:* A naturalistic intervention developed to create a more efficient and effective intervention by enhancing the pivotal learning variables of motivation, responding to multiple cues, self-management, and self-initiation of social interactions. The theory is that these skills are pivotal because they are foundational skills upon which learners with ASD can make widespread and generalized improvements in many other areas.

- *Prompting:* Verbal, visual, or physical assistance given to help a learner demonstrate a target behavior.

- *Reinforcement:* Planned provision of an event, activity, or other circumstance occurring after a learner engages in a desired behavior that leads to the increased occurrence of the behavior in the future.

- *Response interruption/redirection:* The interruption of a prompt, comment, or other distractor designed to divert the learner's attention away from an interfering behavior.

- *Scripting:* Presenting learners with a verbal or written description (or both) about a specific skill or situation that serves as a model for the learner, helping her to anticipate what will happen and improve her ability to participate.

- *Self-management:* Approach teaching learners to discriminate between appropriate and inappropriate behaviors, monitor and record their own behaviors, and reinforce themselves for behaving appropriately.

- *Social narratives:* Written/pictured narratives or "social stories" that describe social situations in detail, offering explanations and highlighting relevant cues and appropriate ways of responding. They are individualized according to learner needs. They are usually written in first person from the perspective of the learner and include sentences describing the specific situation, as well as the potential thoughts and feelings of other people involved in the situation, and providing suggestions for appropriate learner responses.

- *Social skills training:* Group or individual instruction designed to teach basic concepts, provide role playing or practice, and offer feedback to help learners acquire and practice communication, play, or social interaction skills to promote positive interactions with peers.

- *Structured play groups:* Planned use of paired or small-group opportunities with typically developing peers, with clear delineation of themes and roles by an adult leader who provides prompting and scaffolding as needed to support the students' successful engagement in the activities and build play and social interaction skills.

PART 3

- *Task analysis:* Breaking a task or skill down into small component skills that are taught individually, then "chained" together to build mastery of the complete task.

- *Technology-aided instruction and intervention:* Use of computerized or other electronic devices to assist with communication or teaching of new skills.

- *Time delay:* Used to systematically fade the use of prompts during instructional activities. A brief delay is provided between the initial instruction and any additional instructions and prompts to encourage the student to respond without the prompt. With progressive time delay, the delay is gradually lengthened and faded out.

- *Video modeling:* Using video recording and display to provide a visual model of the targeted skill, which the learner then observes. Basic video modeling involves recording someone other than the learner engaged in the target behavior. With video self-modeling, the learner is recorded engaging in the target behavior or skill. Point-of-view video modeling involves recording the target behavior from the perspective of what the learner will see when he performs the behavior. Video prompting involves breaking the behavior into steps recorded with a pause between steps, for the learner to view and attempt a step before viewing the next step.

- *Visual supports:* Concrete, visually presented cues that provide information about an activity, routine, or expectation and support skill demonstration. Visual supports are often used to organize environments; establish expectations around activities, routines, or behaviors; provide cues or reminders; and/or provide preparation or instruction.

The Impact of a Child With Autism on the Family

There are stressors that families of young children with ASD experience, in addition to the environmental pressures that any family may have (e.g., insecure finances, lack of social supports, parental immaturity, marital differences; Guralnick, 2001). The stressors related to ASD include needs for information about the disorder; interpersonal and family distress, including stigma; needs for resources; and threats to confidence about parenting. Other factors include the need for daily care and supervision of the child, including difficulties in eating and sleeping; balancing attention to all offspring; episodic difficult behavior and the anticipation that it will reoccur; and limited social relationships as parents worry about their child's behavior in public. Koegel and LaZebnik (2004) describe the emotional roller-coaster parents may experience after their son or daughter receives an autism diagnosis: denial, blame, anger, isolation, and depression. There is the constant concern about the child's future, pursuing the right interventions, being wary of professionals who do not include you, finding ways to support a normal family life for all, and addressing the financial burden of potential interventions.

The greatest challenge has been isolation. Until recently, it was difficult, if not impossible, to have a successful family outing with our son. Over time, we began leaving the house less and less, and we found we were not connecting with our local community in any meaningful way. There are social groups within the local autism community, but they are limited and meet infrequently. When we attend social groups geared toward typical children, my son often requires constant support and attention, which makes it difficult, if not impossible, to meet the other parents.

On a personal level, the toughest thing for me has been seeing my child struggle. It is hard for any parent to watch their child go though something that they can't always fix. Seeing them get "stuck" and show such fierce frustration and be challenged by things so many of us take for granted . . . has been very hard. I have to say a big challenge for our family has been trying to navigate this journey with two parents that work full-time jobs. . . . We are blessed to have my supportive parents and a few phenomenal friends that support our family immensely.

Relationships Between Parents and Providers

It is extremely important that there be effective communication between professionals and parents, beginning with the manner in which diagnostic results are presented. The National Professional Development Center on ASD (Odom & Wong, 2014) described best practices by diagnosticians (educators, therapists, physicians) in this stage of the process.

- Be honest about your observations.

- Listen to parents' questions and concerns and show empathy.

- Check to be sure that parents understand the information you are sharing and offer repeated opportunities to talk.

- If necessary, refer for further evaluation.

- Help parents continue to see their child's strengths and remember that the child is the same child they loved prior to the diagnosis.

- Create a plan together for the next steps, to develop interventions to address the child's needs.

- Give parents contacts for additional information, services, and family supports.

I think it may have been beneficial to have an organization or a social service that walks you through steps A–Z of this journey through autism . . . a one-stop shop. . . . I have found a great parent-community support group online that enables us to get together with families that have experiences like ours.

In a qualitative study of families of children with ASD (Coogle, Guerette, & Hanline, 2013), parents felt that the personal characteristics of service providers was a positive aspect of EI. They described the following: wanting the child to succeed; being liked by the child; and being caring, easy to work with, organized, understanding, professional, personable, trustworthy, and friendly. They expressed that they wished all providers would be punctual, be effective communicators, and take family concerns seriously. Parents will respond to professionals if they believe that they are not being judged, that providers are on their side, that communication occurs in a way that makes sense to them, and that they retain control of decisions about their child and interventions.

N. received Special Education Itinerant Services for a year. She had speech, occupational, and music therapy in our home as well. These people were amazing. They were phenomenal for N. in helping her and just as awesome for our family as well. They became our supports and led us in the right direction. She then went to J. for a year in their inclusive preschool program. The experience was profound. She started to grow and it was then that her love for school began to flourish.

Autism didn't have a negative effect on us. In fact, we embraced it. I quickly learned as much as I could. . . . S. continued to learn and grow. He had wonderful therapists through EI. They became part of our family. . . . They were there for everything—the good, the bad, and the ugly. They

PART 3

gave me guidance and education, love and friendship. . . . When it was time to start thinking about S. going to preschool, . . . the thought of leaving these therapists was harder for me than for S.

Parent Involvement and Parent Training as an Intervention

When parents are involved, children on the autism spectrum demonstrate higher developmental skills (Dawson & Osterling 1997; Fernell et al., 2012). In an Indiana survey (Bellini, Hume, & Pratt, 2006) of 198 families whose children have autism, 78% of the families reported that parent training made the greatest impact on their child's growth. In a controlled effectiveness study comparing autistic preschoolers receiving Community Standard Services (CSS) with an intervention group who received CSS-plus, parents were coached to support play with their child 2 hours a day using a DIR approach; parents learned to contingently and reciprocally engage their children during 20-minute structured sessions, as well as take advantage of opportunities for learning incidental daily activities (Solomon, Necheles, Ferch, & Bruckman, 2007). Parents assess their child's profile of needs, observe a child's cues, follow her lead, and read intentions in order to increase reciprocal interactions. Even without an official diagnosis, children will benefit from work on improving the parent–child attachment bond.

In a qualitative study by Coogle et al. (2013), parents of young children on the autism spectrum reported their opinions about their experiences with EI. They valued (a) the access to resources; (b) the positive personal characteristics of service providers; (c) the opportunity to learn new skills to help their child; and (d) the convenience (location and timing) of services for their family. Stahmer, Brookman-Frazee, Lee, Searcy, and Reed (2011) used qualitative and quantitative measures from parents of preschoolers under 3 years old with ASD, and service providers, regarding the values of EI. The following themes were identified:

- Parents should be coached to provide intervention.

- Support by other parents is critical for emotional balance and stress management.

- All family members (including siblings and fathers) need training.

- Interventions should include a variety of theoretical orientations and disciplines and blend behavioral and developmental strategies.

- Each child benefits from a comprehensive program, addressing all areas of development (e.g., communication, sensory, social dimensions).

- Strategies should be fun, engaging, and play-based.

- Parents preferred interventions that were "family friendly" and used in the natural environment (incorporated into daily routines).

Create your "anyway family." This is a group of people, not necessarily blood relatives, who become your family for this journey. . . . They support our sad days, help us in our challenging days, and share our good days. Align yourself with other families going through the same things that you are. . . . Relating to someone that really knows the impact of autism can be refreshing and so very helpful. They often know what you're going to say before you say it, and they "get it."

The way you see your child in your heart is going to influence them more than any intervention you provide them. If you see them as someone who needs to be fixed, then they will grow up feeling broken. If you see them as some-one incapable, then they will live up to your low expectations. However, if you love them for who they are today and believe in them, they're going to learn to do the best they can with what they've got. Isn't that all any parent wants for their child?

Teaching parents to be primary intervention-ists is successful when parents:

- choose to participate and see that being involved themselves is a priority for their child;

- have sufficient time, energy, and logistical support;

- make a relatively long-term commitment; and

- are supported by other family members and friends.

I would have liked to have more home services; when he started preschool, our home services basically ended. We all could have benefitted from him getting additional services during these early years.

Because we did catch it so early, J. began receiving speech and OT from 13 months through EI, and we added on a special ed. teacher and a therapeutic playgroup during that time as well. He continued to receive home visits while he attended (an EI and preschool classroom). . . . All the services were helpful, but for me the long-term relationships we had with J.'s speech therapist and OT who did home visits for a few years stick out.

Approaches are effective when parents are coached to engage in enhanced milieu teaching and naturalistic intervention strategies (Kaiser & Hancock, 2003); milieu approaches involve arranging the elements of the teaching environ-ment to support specific student behaviors. When parents are included in the interventions for their sons or daughters with autism, they achieve a

greater understanding of their child's needs and insight into creating an intervention plan. There is also greater maintenance and generalization of skills. Concomitantly, there is an increase in par-ents' feelings of relatedness to their child and an increase in their sense of competence as parents, as well as a decrease in emotional stress. A study (Tonge et al., 2006) of a manual-based parent training program and a behavior management program was compared with the manual-based parent training program supplemented by non-directive counseling. Both approaches benefited the mental health and well-being of the parents of children with autism including relief of anxi-ety, insomnia, more severe somatic symptoms, and depression; family functioning also improved over time.

Chapter Summary

Autism is a complex disorder that affects each child and family differently. Although there are many challenges associated with a diagnosis of autism, there is also much to be hopeful about. Much is being learned about the causes of autism as well as effective interventions. The narratives written by adults with disabilities speak to their abilities to create meaningful and fulfilling lives, despite ongoing challenges. Professional interven-tion needs to include sensitivity to the experience that family members have in caring for a child with autism.

Key Points to Remember

- In recognizing and diagnosing autism, as well as designing interventions, professionals need to consider differences the child may be experiencing in joint attention, social engagement and reciprocity, communication, sensory processing, and need for sameness. The presentation of autism in each child is unique and therefore requires different combinations of interventions.

- Much work is currently being done to understand the causes of autism. Although it is generally considered a neurological disorder, it may have risk factors, including metabolic, genetic, and environmental contributors, that researchers are working to understand.

- Early identification of autism and EI is generally considered to lead to the most positive outcomes. Researchers have identified several common characteristics among effective EI programs, which have been described in this chapter. Philosophically, many programs fall along a continuum from behavioral approaches focused on clear task analysis, specific cuing of responses, and reinforcement to social-pragmatic approaches, focused on interventions occurring within the context of meaningful relationships and natural environments, including opportunities for social engagement with typical peers. Regardless of the philosophical approach, research has clearly linked higher intensity of programming with better outcomes.

- Although no medication, diet, or nutritional supplement has been found to cure autism, some families have found positive impact with these types of interventions. Researchers are continuing to explore these options.

- In families of young children with autism, there are stressors related to the child's need for supervision, balancing attention to all offspring, concerns about public acceptance, and parental competence to address their child's needs. Working with young children who are exhibiting signs of autism and their families presents opportunities to engage

in ways that have a strong positive impact on the child's development early, leading to better outcomes as they grow. Sensitivity to parent styles, values, and concerns, as well as strong communication, are key to the success of this collaboration.

- Much can be done to support growing community awareness of autism; through education, all can learn to respond in ways that are welcoming and supportive, minimizing stigma and negativity, and thus optimizing the potentials of young children.

Implications for Families and Professionals

Goals for supporting families include empowering parents to make choices, access community services, and become advocates to get their child's needs met. Collaboration between approaches at school and home should be supported. Families may need help in managing stress, finding joy in their child, and finding optimism in their life. And professionals need to help parents create connections with other families.

Parents of children with autism have much to tell about their challenges and wisdom to share about the supports that are effective for their children and for their families. It is critical that professionals listen to what they have to say.

At the time, after leaving with the diagnosis, I felt isolated and depressed. . . . The knowledge and availability of an immediate "support group" or activity group for others having received a recent diagnosis would have been appreciated. Over the years, we have found other parents to be an invaluable source of information and resources, and the knowledge of not being alone is also comforting.

Resources

Adams, J. B. (2013). *Summary of dietary, nutritional, and medical treatments for autism* (Publication 40). San Diego, CA: Autism Research Institute.

Cardon, T. (2007). *Initiations and interactions: Early intervention techniques for parents of children with autism spectrum disorders.* Shawnee Mission, KS: Autism Asperger Publishing Company.

Casenhiser, D., Shanker, S., & Steiben, J. (2011). Learning through interaction in children with autism: Preliminary data from a social-communication-based intervention. *Autism.* doi:10.1177/1362361311422052

Fuge, G., & Berry, R. (2004). *Pathways to play! Combining sensory integration and integrated play groups.* Shawnee Mission, KS: Autism Asperger Publishing Company.

Grandin, T., & Barron, S. (2005). *Unwritten rules of social relationships.* Arlington, TX: Future Horizons.

Gray, C., & White, A. L. (2002). *My social stories book.* Philadelphia, PA: Jessica Kingsley Publishers.

Gupta, V. B., Hyman, S., Johnson, C., Bryant, J., Byers, B., Kallen, R., . . . Yeargin-Allsopp, M. (2007). Identifying children with autism early? *Pediatrics, 119*(1), 152–153. http://pediatrics.aap-publications.org/content/119/1/152.full.html

HELPGUIDE.org. (2014). *Early symptoms and early signs: What to look for in babies, toddlers, and children.* http://helpguide.org/mental/autism_signs_symptoms.htm.

Higashida, N. (2013). *The reason I jump: The inner voice of a thirteen-year-old boy with autism.* New York, NY: Random House.

Ingersoll, B., & Schreibman, L. (2006). Teaching reciprocal imitation skills to young children with autism using a naturalistic behavioral approach: Effects on language, pretend play, and joint attention. *Journal of Autism and Developmental Disabilities, 36,* 487–505.

Kasari, C., Paparella, T., Freeman, S., & Jahromi, L. (2008). Language outcome in autism: Randomized comparison of joint attention and play interventions. *Journal of Consulting and Clinical Psychology, 76,* 125–137.

Kluth, P. (2003). *You're going to love this kid: Teaching students with autism in the inclusive classroom.* Baltimore, MD: Brookes.

Kohler, F., Anthony, L., Steighner, F., & Hoyson, M. (2001). Teaching social interaction skills in the integrated preschool: An examination of naturalistic tactics. *Topics in Early Childhood Special Education, 21,* 93–103.

Kranowitz, C. S. (2005). *The out-of-sync child: Recognizing and coping with sensory dysfunction.* (Rev. ed.). New York, NY: Perigee.

Landa, R., & Garrett-Myer, E. (2006). Development in infants with autism spectrum disorders: A prospective study. *Journal of Child Psychology and Psychiatry and Allied Disciplines, 47*(6), 629–638.

Mahoney, G., & Perales, F. (2005). Relationship-focused early intervention with children with pervasive developmental disorders and other disabilities: A comparative study. *Developmental and Behavioral Pediatrics, 26*(2), 77–85.

McGee, G., Morrier, M., & Daly, T. (1999). An incidental teaching approach to early intervention for toddlers with autism. *Journal of the Association for Persons With Severe Handicaps, 24,* 133–146.

McGinnis, E. & Goldstein, A. (1990). *Skillstreaming in early childhood: Teaching prosocial skills to the preschool and kindergarten child.* Champaign, IL: Research Press.

Mesibov, G., Shea, V., & Schopler, E. (2005). *The TEACCH approach to autism spectrum disorders.* Chapel Hill, NC: Springer.

Myers, S. M., Johnson, C. P., & Council on Children With Disabilities. (2007). American Academy of Pediatrics Clinical Report:

PART **3**

Management of children with autism spectrum disorders. *Pediatrics, 120*(5), 1162–1182.

Noonan, M. J., & McCormick, L. (2006). *Young children with disabilities in natural environments.* Baltimore, MD: Brookes.

Notbohm, E. (2007). *The autism trail guide: Postcards from the road less travelled.* Arlington, TX: Future Horizons.

Odom, S. L. (Ed.). (2002). *Widening the circle: Including children with disabilities in preschool programs.* New York, NY: Teachers College Press.

Pajareya, K., & Nopmaneejumruslers, K. (2011). A pilot randomized control trial of DIR/Floortime parent training intervention for pre-school children with autistic spectrum disorders. *Autism, 15,* 563–577.

Rao, P., Beidel, D., & Murray, M. (2008). Social skills intervention for people with Asperger's syndrome or high functioning autism: A review and recommendations. *Journal of Autism and Developmental Disabilities, 3,* 353–361.

Reichow, B., & Volkmar, F. (2010). Social skills interventions for individuals with autism: Evaluation for evidence-based practices within a best evidence synthesis framework. *Journal of Autism and Developmental Disabilities, 40,* 149–166.

Rogers, K., Dziobek, I., Hassenstab, J., Wolf, O., & Convit, A. (2007). Who cares? Revisiting empathy in Asperger's syndrome. *Journal of Autism and Developmental Disabilities, 3,* 709–715.

Schuler, A. L., & Wolfberg, P. J. (2000). Promoting peer play and socialization: The art of scaffolding. In A. M. Wetherby & B. M. Prizant (Eds.), *Communication and language intervention series: Vol. 9. Autism spectrum disorders: A transactional developmental perspective* (pp. 251–277). Baltimore, MD: Brookes.

Smukler, D. (2005). Unauthorized minds: How "theory of mind" theory misrepresents autism. *Mental Retardation, 43*(1), 11–24.

Strain, P. S., McGee, G. G., & Kohler, F. W. (2001). Inclusion of children with autism in early intervention environments: An examination of rationale, myths, and procedures. In M. J. Guralnik (Ed.), *Early childhood inclusion: Focus on change* (pp. 337–363). Baltimore, MD: Brookes.

Wilbarger, J., & Wilbarger, P. (1991). *Sensory defensiveness in children aged 2–12.* Oak Park Heights, MN: PDP Products.

Wolfberg, P. (2003). *Peer play and autism spectrum: The art of guiding children's socialization and imagination.* Shawnee Mission, KS: Autism Asperger Publishing Company.

York, E., Sutton, S., & Aquilla, P. (2002). *Building bridges through sensory integration* (2nd ed.). Las Vegas, NV: Sensory Resources.

References

Al-Qubandi, M., Gorter, J. W., & Rosenbaum, P. (2011). Early autism detection: Are we ready for routine screening? *Pediatrics, 128*(1), e211–e217.

American Psychiatric Association. (2013). *Diagnostic and statistical manual of mental disorders* (5th ed.). Arlington, VA: Author.

Autism Speaks. (2014). *Harness "cloud" for genomic breakthroughs.* Retrieved from www.autismspeaks.org/what-autism/treatment/treatment-associated-medical-conditions/gi-disorders

Baron-Cohen, S. (1995). *Mind-blindness: An essay on autism and theory of mind.* Cambridge, MA: MIT Press.

Bauman, M. L., & Kemper, T. L, (2006). *The neurobiology of autism.* Baltimore, MD: Johns Hopkins Press.

Bauman, M. L., & Kemper, T. L. (2007). *Neuropathology of autism spectrum disorders; What have we learned?* [Lecture]. New York, NY: Therapeutic Services.

Beckstrand, K., Pienkoswki, T., Powers, S., & Scanlon, J. (2016). Early intervention at home: When, why, and how? In G. L. Ensher & D. A. Clark (Eds.), *The early years: Foundations for best practice with special children and their families* (pp. 353–365). Washington, DC: ZERO TO THREE.

Bellini, S., Hume, K., & Pratt, C. (2006). Early intervention for young children on the autism spectrum: Parent's perspective. *The Reporter, 11*(2), 1–4, 18.

Biklen, D. P. (2005). *Autism and the myth of the person alone.* New York, NY: New York University Press.

Coogle, C. G., Guerette, A., & Hanline, M. F. (2013). Early intervention experiences of families of children with autism spectrum disorder: A qualitative study. *Early Childhood Research and Practice, 15*(1). Retrieved from http://ecrp.uiuc.edu/v15n1/coogle.html

Corsello, C. V. (2005). Early intervention in autism. *Infants and Young Children, 18* (2), 74–85.

Cowan, C., Mancini, J., & Toth, K. (2012). *New guidelines for birth to three services in Washington State.* Retrieved from http://theautismblog.seattlechildrens.org/new-guidelines-for-birth-to-three-services-in-washington-state

Dawson, G., & Osterling, J. (1997). Early intervention in autism: Effectiveness and common elements of current approaches. In M. J. Guralnick (Ed.), *The effectiveness of early intervention: Second generation research* (pp. 307–326). Baltimore, MD: Brookes.

Dziobek, I. (2004). *Who cares? Or: The truth about empathy in individuals of the autism spectrum.* Retrieved from www.graspflies.org/ning/media/print/whocares.pdf

Ensher, G. L., Barnes, E. B., & Clark, D. A. (2016). Inclusive preschool education: Best practices in action. In G. L. Ensher & D. A. Clark, *The early years: Foundations for best practice with special children and their families* (pp. 367–382). Washington, DC: ZERO TO THREE.

Fernell, E., Eriksson, M. A., & Gillberg, C. (2012). Early diagnosis of autism and impact on prognosis: A narrative review. *Clinical Epidemiology, 5*, 33–43.

Greenspan, S., & Wieder, S. (2006). *Engaging autism: The floortime approach to helping children relate, communicate, and think.* Cambridge, MA: Perseus.

Guralnick, M. J. (Ed.). (2001). *Early childhood inclusion: Focus on change.* Baltimore, MD: Brookes.

Harrower, J., & Dunlap, G. (2001). Including children with autism in general education classrooms: A review of effective strategies. *Behavior Modification, 25*, 762–784.

Jenkins, L. A., & Sullivan, M. B. (2016). Common reasons for referral of infants and toddlers: Speech-language, feeding, and sensory processing disorders. In G. L. Ensher & D. A. Clark (Eds.), *The early years: Foundations for best practice with special children and their families* (pp. 247–267). Washington, DC: ZERO TO THREE.

Kaiser, A., & Hancock, T. (2003). Teaching parents new skills to support their young children's development. *Infants and Young Children, 16*(1), 9–21.

Koegel, R. L. & Koegel, L. K. (2006). *Pivotal response treatments for autism: Communication, social, and academic development.* Baltimore, MD: Brookes.

Koegel, L., & LaZebnik, C. (2004) *Overcoming autism: A state of the art approach to reducing the symptoms of autism spectrum disorders.* New York, NY: Penguin.

Kozlowski, A. M., Matson, J. L., Horovitz, M., Worley, J. A., & Neal, D. (2011). Parents' first concerns of their child's development in toddlers with autism spectrum disorders. *Developmental Neurorehabilitation, 14*(2), 72–78.

National Professional Development Center on Autism Spectrum Disorders. (2014). *Early intervention professional development: Evidence-based practices.* www.autismspeak.org.

Odom, S. L. (Ed.). (2002). *Widening the circle: Including children with disabilities in preschool programs.* New York, NY: Teachers College Press.

Odom, S., & Wong, C. (2014). *Evidence-based practices for children, youth, and young adults with autism spectrum disorders.* Chapel Hill, NC: National Professional Development Center on ASD at the Frank Porter Graham Institute.

Osterling, J. A., Dawson, G., & Munson, J. A. (2002). Early recognition of 1-year-old infants with autism spectrum disorder versus mental retardation. *Developmental Psychology, 14*(2), 239–251.

Ozonoff, S., Rogers, S., & Tuchman-Ginsberg, L. (2014). *Early identification of autism spectrum disorders.* Retrieved from http://autismpdc.fpg.unc.edu/content/early-identification-asd-module

Prizant, B. M., Wetherby, A. M., Rubin, E., Laurent, A. C., & Rydell, P. J. (2006). *The SCERTS Model: A comprehensive educational approach for children with autism spectrum disorders.* Baltimore, MD: Brookes.

Robins, D., Fein, D., & Barton, M. (1999). *M-CHAT.* Retrieved from www.mchatscreen.com

Solomon, R., Necheles, J., Ferch, C., & Bruckman, D. (2007). Pilot study of a parent training program for young children with autism: The PLAY home consultation program. *Autism, 11*(3), 205–224.

Stahmer, A., Brookman-Frazee, L., Lee, E., Searcy, K., & Reed, S. (2011). Parent and multidisciplinary provider perspectives on earliest intervention for children at risk for autism spectrum disorders. *Infants and Young Children, 24*(4), 344–363.

Tonge, B., Brereton, A., Kiomall, M., MacKinnon, A., King, N., & Rinehart, N. (2006). Effects on parental mental health of an education & skills training program for parents of young children with autism.

PART **3**

Journal of American Academy of Child and Adolescent Psychiatry, 45, 561–569.

Veltman, J., & Brunner, H. (2012). De novo mutations in human genetic disease. *Nature Reviews Genetics, 13,* 565–575.

Verstraeten, T., Davis, R. L., DeStefano, F., Lieu, T. A., Rhodes, P. H., Black, S. B., . . . Chen, R. T. (2003). Safety of thimerosal-containing vaccines: A two-phased study of computerized health maintenance organization databases. *Pediatrics, 112*(5), 1039–1048.

Warren, Z., McPheeters, M. L., Sathe, N., Foss-Feig, J. H., Glasser, A. & Veenstra-VanderWeele, J. (2011). A systematic review of early intensive intervention for autism spectrum disorders. *Pediatrics, 127*(5), e1303–e1311.

Wong, C., Odom, S. L, Hume, K., Cox, A. W., Fettig, A., Kucharczyk, S., . . . Schultz, T. R. (2014). *Evidence-based practices for children, youth, and young adults with autism spectrum disorder.* Retrieved from http://autismpdc.fpg.unc.edu/sites/autismpdc.fpg.edu/files/2014-EDP-Report.pdf

PART 4

Collaborative Care, Community Networks, and Early Intervention

CHAPTER 14

Families of Young Children in a Contemporary World

Gail L. Ensher and David A. Clark

Highlights of the Chapter

At the conclusion of the chapter, the reader will understand:

- ways in which different cultures shape the perceptions, child-rearing practices, interactions, and relationships with children, lifestyles, languages spoken at home, and receptivity to professional services

- ways in which the dynamics of contemporary neighborhoods and communities affect families and their young children

- the impact of economic resources on families raising young children in the United States

- ways that diverse family membership can affect patterns of interaction; roles assumed by parents/caregivers; siblings; lifestyles; child and family resources; challenges

- the impact of disabilities and special needs of infants and young children on families

- strategies that professionals providing services can use to support families and strengthen resilience

American Families in the 21st Century

A hallmark of the American family is diversity. Families are not unitary, nor can they be narrowly defined. Across the nation, in every community—and within the heart, mind, and experience of each individual—family is personal. Our families help to define who we are and who we are not, how we view the world, how we live, and how we share our lives with others. Like the individuals within them, families change over time. In the United States and elsewhere throughout the world, families share many characteristics but differ dramatically in others. (Lynch, 2013, p. 1)

Diversity of Families in the United States

Whereas most scholars today would agree that the increasing diversity of cultures, ethnicity, languages spoken, religions, beliefs, and family membership is a strength and asset in contemporary American life (Lynch, 2013; Lynch & Hanson, 2011), many would likewise agree that difference is not always equal in the United States. In the least, diversity of families, their infants, and young children continues to greatly influence education, health care systems, and services, with a growing need for the development of competence across all professionals who interact with families.

Changing demographics of the past decade in the U.S. underscore this pressing need. Here are just a few important considerations relating to contemporary American families:

- In some large urban school districts, families for whom English is a second language speak more than 100 different languages (Umstead, 2013).

- It is estimated that by the year 2050, the white population in the United States will be in the minority (47%), and the Hispanic/Latino population (the nation's most rapidly increasing minority group) will represent a majority of the U.S. population (Passel & Cohn, 2008; Shrestha & Heisler, 2009). The distribution of diverse ethnic, cultural, and racial groups, however, varies greatly from state to state, a significant factor in planning educational, pediatric, and service-related programs (Trail, 2000).

- In the United States, the likelihood of living in a single-mother-headed family varies greatly across racial and ethnic groups; approximately 16% of white children live in single-mother families, while one fourth (27%) of Latino children and one half (52%) of African American children live in single-mother-headed families. Although some single-mother families represent cohabitating relationships with access to higher levels of income, over time such relationships may reflect less stable family relationships (Mather, 2010). Mather stated that 7 in 10 children living in single-mother families are "poor or low income." Further, "for younger children ages 0 to 8, results are even more striking. In 2008, over three quarters (77%) of young children in single-mother families were poor or low income" (Mather, 2010).

- The combination of single mothers (i.e., never married, less educated, unemployed, working in low-wage jobs, and poverty) places their young children at higher risk of less advantageous outcomes.

- Ethnicity, socioeconomic status, gender, race, and family membership influence child health and well-being via "social mechanisms" (American Academy of Pediatrics, Committee on Pediatric Research, 2000, p. 1349).

- American families over the past decade have changed dramatically, and those shifting patterns have had profound influences on the development of infants and young children (incurring both challenges and greater opportunities). For example, many mothers today are waiting until later to start their families. Although this change may afford more economic resources, advanced ages also may increase the risks of child bearing and may heighten the challenges of keeping up with active infants and young children.

- Young children of color are more likely to be the victims of experiences and events that place them at increased social, emotional, developmental, and behavioral risks (i.e., toxic stress). For example, these children are significantly over-represented in the child welfare system, are more likely to have a parent who has been incarcerated, demonstrate higher levels of aggression, are more likely to be expelled from day care and preschool programs (Aratani, 2009), and live in families without health insurance (Minority Health Initiatives, 2009).

Educators, pediatricians, and other professionals who work and interact with families and their young children know very well that such factors are not mutually exclusive. They interact, one dimension often affecting another. And thus the called-for changes in our respective service-related fields likewise need to be multidimensional, requiring comprehensive approaches.

Born Into a New World

All considered, what does it mean to be born in the United States in the 21st century? According to data reported in 2011 by the Centers for Disease Control and Prevention, National Center for Health Statistics, there have

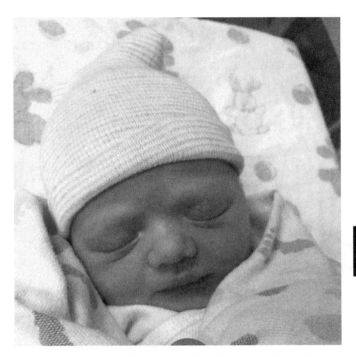

been a number of noteworthy changes (Martin et al., 2013) that reflect social and economic influences, as well as technological advances in our country relating to women, pregnancies, newborns, the incidence of low birth weight, and other important factors affecting developmental outcomes and well-being of infants and young children. For instance, in 2011, there was a decline in birth rate of 1%, to 3,953,590; the teenage birth rate fell by 8% to 31.3 per 1,000; the rate of prematurity (< 37 weeks) declined for the fifth year to 11.3%; low birth weight (2,500 grams) declined slightly to 8.10%; the rate of very low birth weight newborns (1,500 grams) was 1.4%; and the rate of twin births rose 76% from 1980 to 2009–2011. The number of births to unmarried women remained stable at 40.7%. As reported by Lazara, Danaher, and Goode (2012), in 2011, 343,000 infants and toddlers in the United States received early intervention (EI) services in accordance with Part C of the reauthorized Individuals With Disabilities Education Act legislation—likely an underestimation of the number of infants and young children who actually needed services (e.g., infants and young children in the child welfare system who were not referred to EI).

Over the past decade, there have been multiple advances in the early detection and treatment of diseases and conditions of newborns in the United States that have had an important positive impact on their health and development. One example is the recent finding that research and detection have now made possible a marked reduction in the vertical transmission rate of HIV from mother to newborn from approximately 25% to current estimates of less than 1%, thus saving numerous infants from eventual progression of the pediatric infection to AIDS (Bell, 2007). A decade ago this infection was considered to be one of the major causes of death among infants and toddlers in the United States, with hospitals inundated with "boarder babies" whose parents had succumbed to the ravages of compromised immune systems.

On the horizon now are major scientific visions for the next decade relating to pregnancy and pregnancy outcomes, reproduction, epigenetics, the prevention of disabilities and treatment of disease, and the improvement of developmental outcomes of young children (Eunice Kennedy Shriver National Institute of Child Health and Human Development [NICHD], 2012). For example, with a look toward the future when scientific data and research have the potential to ameliorate "developmental conditions or help individuals interact with the world in ways that can sustain or improve their health and well-being" (p. 10), the *Scientific Vision* report stated that:

Many research disciplines will need to work together to characterize the full range of typical and atypical behavioral and cognitive trajectories across the lifespan. First steps will involve identifying the mechanisms underlying behavioral and cognitive development at the molecular, cellular, and brain system levels; detailing how these mechanisms interact with complex environmental factors; and pinpointing sensitive periods of perception, learning, memory, language, reasoning, and executive function. . . . Identifying specific genetic variants that influence the development of behaviors or cognitive traits will . . . be important to unraveling the origins and mechanisms underlying normative behavior and cognitive development . . . this critical genetic information will provide the foundation for developing more personalized interventions to improve health outcomes. . . . For specific conditions such as autism spectrum disorders, Down syndrome, for which a stream of multidisciplinary advances is emerging, researchers should be able to identify the key mechanisms and primary causal factors leading to these conditions. This, in turn, should provide the cornerstone for developing a broad range of more timely and effective interventions. . . . It is also important to identify how . . . technologies can be used to prevent, remediate, or treat a range of learning and developmental conditions. Another research frontier lies in fully uncovering and understanding how specific physical (whether natural or engineered) and social environmental exposures shape behaviors or alter developmental trajectories and influence health outcomes. These exposures may be as direct as the use of neonatal incubators or as complex as growing up in poverty, surviving early traumatic events or injuries, being exposed to violence, or coping with incarceration as a youth. Projecting the impact of these exposures and identifying which individual, family, or community factors are most likely to promote positive outcomes, such as resilience, are essential for developing protective interventions. (NICHD, 2012, pp. 11–13)

In sum, future research holds great promise—beyond professionals' comprehension—of improving the neurological, developmental, and behavioral outcomes of infants born in the 21st century. At the same time, achieving this vision will require closer alliances across the multidisciplinary fields of medicine, education, and other clinical disciplines serving infants, young children, and their families prior to and following conception, in addition to directly addressing and resolving some of the most troubling socioeconomic-political issues that continue to plague so many young American families.

Education and Economics: Impact on Families

For many families, infants, and young children living in today's world in the United States, income level is closely aligned with multiple issues of diversity including culture, ethnicity, neighborhoods where families live, the quality of schools attended, as well as a host of other factors that may place parents and children at increased risk. This claim is supported by a number of reliable sources, such as the National Center for Children in Poverty. For example in January 2013, the Center reported that children represent 24% of the population, but they comprise 34% of all people in poverty. Among all children, 45% live in low-income families and approximately one in every five (22%) live in poor families. Young children under 6 years old appear to be particularly vulnerable, with 49% living in low-income families and 25% living in poor families. Being a child in a low-income or poor family does not happen by chance. There is a range of factors associated with children's experiences of economic insecurity, including race/ethnicity and parents' education and employment (Addy, Engelhardt, & Skinner, 2013).

In addition to understanding the economic, educational, and cultural patterns, and other unique qualities that characterize individual families, it is important to recognize that these variables also exist in context—with respect to certain communities, neighborhoods, circles of friends and relatives, and educational systems.

All of these elements interact with and influence what happens to families as a "unit" and to individual family members, determining accessibility to everyday services such as pediatric and mental health care, day care, early-morning and after-school programs, recreational activities for children, and educational supports; that is, microsystems are influenced by macrosystems (Bronfenbrenner, 1979). Neighborhoods and communities too are key determinants of the values, beliefs, and perceptions held by individual family members, as well as the challenges that they face in their daily lives. As we have discussed earlier in this book, these stresses can be greatly enhanced or diminished, depending upon the needs of particular family members; for example, raising an infant or young children with a chronic illness that requires ongoing medical attention or a son or daughter with multiple and severe disabilities.

Finally, teachers and administrative staff in public schools often mirror the income levels and perspectives of those residing within neighborhoods where they are situated (and these perspectives frequently are long-lasting). For example, in their book, *The Transition to Kindergarten* (1999), Pianta and Cox commented about the negative perceptions of public school teachers regarding 5-year-old kindergarten children who were followed in a longitudinal study. It was noteworthy that, by the time these students had reached middle and high school, years later, teacher perspectives had remained remarkably unchanged. This finding should not obscure that multiple factors are likely responsible for these results. Nonetheless, teachers' attitudes remain one of the most pressing challenges confronting school administrators, teachers, policymakers, and families in today's educational world. It is improbable that "scripted" curricula now being adopted in many public schools across the United States will resolve these disparities that continue to plague American educational systems. At the

PART 4

heart of the matter are families, relationships, and opportunities afforded to many young children, and the so-frequently-seen opportunities denied to others. At the same time, given the "transactional" nature of human development and the possibilities of resilience in the face of adversity, researchers and scholars across our multiple fields of inquiry need to focus on visions of the next decade—realizing the yet-to-be-discovered potentials, adaptations, and well-being of families and their young children. Summarizing this point, contributors to the report *Scientific Vision: The Next Decade* wrote:

> *A key challenge in population dynamics starts with understanding the rapid and profound changes shaping families in the United States and around the world. This includes understanding how biological, social, and other environmental factors, in concert with population dynamics, influence the health and well-being of mothers, fathers, children, families, communities, and societies. . . .Researchers must also examine how family structures and the intergenerational transmission of such factors as knowledge and economic security affect child health and developmental outcomes. Innovative, multidisciplinary approaches are needed to unravel how complex patterns of migration and urbanization influence health over generations by altering social, economic, and educational dynamics, including the ethnic and cultural characteristics of neighborhoods, communities, and societies.* (NICHD, 2012, p.19)

The Changing Landscape of American Families

Families of the 21st century in the United States vary a great deal from those of a decade ago. This evolving landscape of families has compelling implications for the ways in which families live their lives, interact with one another, and raise and educate their children. It has also introduced new contexts for working with young children and offering professional services to their families. For example, if there are two parents in a family, frequently both are working in order to "make ends meet" financially. These circumstances necessarily mean that many infants and young children, from their earliest months of life, spend long hours every day in home- or center-based day care (Kagan & Neuman, 2000) or are taken care of by family relatives such as grandparents. If they are in good and safe day care situations, children thrive (American Academy of Pediatrics, Committee on Early Child, Adoption, and Dependent Care, 2005)! If not, their development may be compromised (Kreader, Ferguson, & Lawrence, 2005)! Further, no longer can teachers automatically assume that when young children come to their toddler and preschool classrooms they understand English, which may be a second language for a given family. Moreover, professionals can no longer assume that family members view situations or problems with a singular or uniform set of lenses. There are multiple shades of light for perceiving and understanding that are shaped by family backgrounds, cultures, ethnicity, and environments where they live. Indeed, the diversity of contemporary communities in the United States adds a vital richness to interacting with families of infants and young children. At the same time, such differences contribute a dimension of complexity that always needs to be considered in developing and carrying out professional work and relationships with family members. The three scenarios briefly described in the next section are examples of just a few important considerations that affect family life in major ways. To be sure, they are not the only special situations, issues, and circumstances that might affect the trajectories of family lives, but these are significant variables that often emerge.

Different Cultures/Different Languages: What Do They Mean?

In 2008, the Center for Law and Social Policy (CLASP) solutions on behalf of low-income people reported:

There are more than 12 million babies and toddlers in the United States. Nationwide, 12% of households have a child under age 3. These households are racially and culturally diverse. Approximately 18% of Hispanic families, 13% of Asian families, 13% of black 11% of white non-Hispanic families include a child under age 3. In recent years, immigration has accelerated diversity among the infant/toddler population. One in four children under age 3 live in an immigrant family (i.e., one comprised of one or more foreign-born parents). Approximately 62% of immigrant families with children under 3 have origins in Latin America and the Caribbean, representing many countries and many distinct languages. Approximately one of seven babies and toddlers in the U.S. have a parent who speaks limited English, indicating that a language other than English is likely to be spoken in the house. The extent to which infants and toddlers in these households are exposed also to English— for example, through sibling interactions or in child care or other settings—varies considerably. (Matthews, 2008)

Given the changing demographics of peoples living in the United States today, scholars, educators, clinicians, and policymakers are increasingly recognizing the need for greater sensitivity and competence for working with families across different ethnic and cultural groups. "Typical" American families simply no longer exist (if they ever really did)! At the same time, it is more than a little challenging to understand exactly what

it means to be "culturally competent" in light of the tremendous range of diversity of families in the United States. Often, there is no clear pathway that is either "right" or "wrong." Decisions and best practices reside with "best judgments," with final outcomes that are difficult to anticipate. Such was the case with the three families described here:

Family scenario 1

Lai was a 3-year-old who was enrolled in an exemplary, inclusive preschool program. His mother was a graduate student in a nearby university, who was very proficient in English; however, Lai, who had recently traveled from Taiwan to the United States with his mother, did not speak a word of English. At issue were ways that Lai's classroom teachers might begin to communicate and interact with him to discern whether he had a delay or language disorder. In addition, how might other young children in the preschool class play and talk with Lai in ways that were meaningful?

Family scenario 2

A 3-year-old was enrolled in a local urban, inclusive preschool program. His family had traveled recently from the Middle East to New York and lived in an urban neighborhood. Hassan had been a very even-tempered, compliant child until the final 4 weeks of school prior to summer vacation, at which time he began to have daily "meltdowns," with inappropriate behavior such as kicking, swearing, spitting, and throwing chairs and desks. At best, staff were able to determine that these behaviors were more related to home situations than school. The teachers were concerned about their own safety and that of other children. With little to no improvement in his behavior, the social worker, teachers, and psychologist made two visits to Hassan's home to speak with his dad and other family members, who indicated that something "eventful" had occurred. However, even with the assistance of an interpreter, the school staff was unable to determine with certainty the reasons for Hassan's behavior, which continued to escalate until the close of school.

Family scenario 3

In a third scenario, the son of a Native American Indian family was born at full term with a congenital defect of spina bifida. His parents understood the immediate need for medical treatment in the neonatal intensive care nursery, for surgery to close the lesion in his back and insertion of a ventriculo-peritoneal shunt to treat hydrocephalus. After several weeks in the nursery, Aja was ready to go home. Upon his discharge, the hospital staff recommended that the baby be referred to EI for physical and occupational therapy.

Aja's family lived on an Iroquois nation reservation. The concept of *disability*, however, was not well understood by people living on the reservation, and thus Aja's family initially was reluctant to follow through with special education services. Their preference was to first seek the advice of tribal leaders before

agreeing to home visits from professionals outside of nation, using instead other "means of healing."

Each of these family scenarios poses a different set of issues, considerations, and pathways toward resolution. In the instance of Lai, he was an extremely bright little boy who developed his own styles of communication with both the teachers and other children in his class. Further, it was apparent within the first few weeks of school that he was adding English words to his expressive language vocabulary and, before long, communicating in full sentences. Because he was attending an inclusive preschool setting with other children providing verbal models, his acquisition of the English language was regularly being reinforced by his peer classmates. It also was clear that Lai had no difficulty with his receptive language and readily understood almost everything said to him in English. Lai was able to demonstrate his knowledge and capabilities in multiple ways (Tabors, 2008), and, remarkably, by the end of his first year his spoken English language, with few exceptions, appeared to be on par with that of his same-age classmates. After Lai's mother's completed 2 years of graduate school in higher education, the family returned to their native country, Taiwan, as planned.

Hassan's situation in school (Scenario 2) had a very different outcome. The head teacher of his pre-k class of 17 other children had stressed the urgency of Hassan's being observed and referred for an immediate evaluation, despite the end of the school year. However, this plea was not heeded, and the school year ended with no further action to address these issues.

The summer passed and another school year began with Hassan's enrollment in kindergarten at a different school where teachers and administrators were unfamiliar with the incidents of the prior school year. The new school year started and, within less than a week of attendance, the principal of Hassan's new school called the former teacher, asking about his behavior. As best she could, the former teacher recounted the events that had taken place in her classroom and during visits to Hassan's home with his family. The outcome of this scenario is yet to be determined, but in the least, had the responsible school authorities responded more proactively, perhaps both the family and child would have started the new school year with a better chance for success and understanding.

Finally, with respect to Scenario 3 and Aja's family's decision to decline EI services for their son, professionals always are free to recommend, but not mandate or require, that families comply with their advice. In the case of Aja's family, he was well taken care of and eventually was enrolled in a local preschool program on the reservation. Although he did not have the recommended benefits of occupational and physical therapy, he interacted well with his same-age classmates, learned to socialize and communicate, and fully participated in all of the cultural events that the family deemed important for him to learn with his brothers, sisters, and other members of the extended family. Their belief of living in harmony with nature, and their spirituality, were very different from the "mainstream concept and belief in individualism" (Applequist & Bailey, 2000; Pewewardy & Fitzpatrick, 2009, p. 91) and competition that so heavily dominate the philosophy of many public and private schools in the United States.

Recapping from the family scenarios described above, multiple factors affected the course of events, decisions that parents made, and outcomes regarding their children. Among these, professionals working with these families might have considered the following: religion, proximity to other members of their culture, community of residence, language abilities and proficiencies in communicating as non-English speakers, living arrangements of members of their immediate family, perceptions of disability, educational backgrounds, perceptions of EI and special education services, length of time living in the United States, age of the children, and levels of trust of individuals outside of their ethnic or cultural background. One caution, however, that always needs to be at the forefront of a professional's thinking when working with families of diverse cultures, ethnic backgrounds, and who speak different languages is the reality that they do not all represent uniform values, lifestyles, or approaches to raising their children. There may be commonalities represented by peoples of respective populations, but professionals always need to remember that there is as much diversity within as there is across certain cultural and ethnic groups.

Who's Living at Home: Other Family Contexts

Another dimension that needs to be considered in families with a child with a disability or special need is family membership and the backgrounds and education of those individuals who might care for the respective child.

When a family has a child with special needs

WD's birth was an occasion anticipated with much joy and excitement. He was the first grandchild to join the family, and was to be named after his granddad who had devoted years of his life to saving and treating newborns with special needs, many delivered long before their expected due dates! In the past, Dr. Dave had experienced the challenging, unenviable task of breaking news to families that their cherished, long-awaited infants were sick, might not survive, or had a disability or serious medical problem. That was a painful responsibility in his position as the director of the Department of Pediatrics and a practicing neonatologist in his regional intensive care nursery.

PART **4**

However, that pain paled in comparison with his sorrow and sadness over the unexpected news that his own first grandson, the son of one of his three daughters, was born with a small piece of a chromosome missing, a condition that resulted in a severe disability that made countless simple tasks so difficult over the course of his 4 short years. WD ultimately lost his battle with life when he died on September 1st, 2005, during the ravages of Hurricane Katrina in Jackson, Mississippi (when he and his family were displaced from their home in Metarie, Louisiana). WD was dearly loved and always will be remembered by his parents, grandparents, and other family members, whose lives he had changed forever.

While WD's short life was surely special and unique, the experiences, thoughts, feelings, grief, and joy that members of his family shared with him are echoed by numerous other families who have an infant or young child with special health care needs or a disability, or both, because:

- Most of the time, no one expects to have a baby with special needs.

- Most of the time, no one knows what the future holds.

- If newborns are admitted to neonatal intensive care nurseries, parents are ushered into a world of unknowns and unpredictability, often feeling isolated and alone.

- Depending upon the nature of the infant's care at home, parents may lose their sense of privacy with ongoing visits from multiple professionals and to multiple specialists.

- If there are other children in the family, it may be challenging to find special time for them or adequate time for relaxation and rest for the parents themselves. Depending upon the nature of the special health care need or disabilities, families may be extremely limited in their opportunities

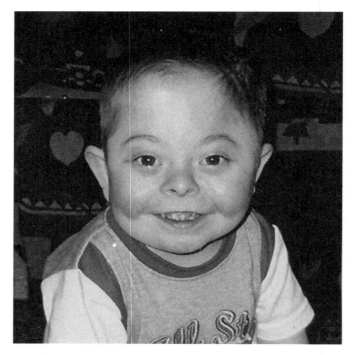

for vacations, especially if they do not have extended families to provide relief and safe child care.

- Depending upon the nature of the child's special health care needs or disabilities, parents may be unable to find appropriate, regular child care and/or not be able to return to work, thus adding to already strained financial resources.

Given all of the unknowns, responsibilities, and common stressors, it is not unusual to find that parents with infants and young children with special needs often separate, with marriages ending in divorce (Shudy et al., 2006; Stabile & Allin, 2012; Swaminathan, Alexander, & Boulet, 2006), circumstances often accompanied with a notable impact on siblings as well (Cox, Marshall, Mandleco, & Olsen, 2003; Mandleco, Olsen, Dyches, & Marshall, 2003).

Families have been quick to remind professionals also that "there are disabilities, and there are disabilities!" Some special needs may require almost constant medical treatment and special education and related services. As a result of prematurity, childhood illnesses, child abuse, accidents, and congenital conditions, most severe and multiple disabilities occur within the first 3 years of life (Ensher & Clark, 2011a).

Whenever such disabilities or special needs are first identified, factors such as resources and supports available to families, numbers of siblings, parent needs to work, the disabled child's needs for nursing or medical care, and the capabilities of the parents themselves affect the nature of interactions and relationships within any given family—and these are considerations that necessarily change over time. As professionals work with families, these considerations should serve as guideposts for determining most beneficial and accessible services.

When a parent has a disability

In the best of circumstances, when the parent of an infant or young child has a significant disability, the situation is complex! Depending upon the nature of the disability, there may be legal ramifications where the rights of the child and the caregiver with a disability need to be protected. Personal assistance programs, peer supports, accessible housing, transportation, education along with caregiver monitoring, and support services on behalf of both the child and the parents with the disability may be needed (National Rehabilitation Information Center [NARIC], 2012. Moreover, as several authorities (Kleinmann & Songer, 2009; Through the Looking Glass, 2013) have pointed out, pregnancy and birthing preparation specialized for women with intellectual disabilities may need to begin long before a baby is born.

Historically, parents with a disability have not been viewed positively, often "facing ignorance and discrimination" (NARIC, 2012). Those perceptions and attitudes are still prevalent today, largely because of concerns over the welfare of the children. In light of economic resource shortages,

such perspectives certainly are realistic and reflect a valid point of view. On the other hand, as we have noted previously, not all disabilities are equal. Some parents have more family help than others. Some families reside in resource-rich communities with greater accessibility to day care, medical homes, WIC, educational facilities, and other essential services. And some parents are more "abled" than others! Moreover, intervention services sponsored by Through the Looking Glass, a resource developed specifically for parents with intellectual and cognitive disabilities, have demonstrated notable success with out-of-home placement rates of infants and young children of parents with intellectual disabilities at 2% to 7%, as compared to national placement rates of 40% to 60% (Through the Looking Glass, 2013).

Finally, as we have indicated earlier in this chapter and text, parents who reside in communities plagued with poverty often are marginalized in several ways. They may be struggling with increased bouts of stress and depression, social isolation, poor educational opportunities, unemployment, and violence—all factors that can have a negative effect on developmental outcomes and the well-being of parents and their infants. On the positive side, however, longitudinal research of the Carolina Abecedarian Project, directed by Frances Campbell and Craig Ramey at the Frank Porter Graham Child Development Institute in North Carolina (Ramey & Ramey, 2004), demonstrated that, given appropriate community and educational services, interventions can have long-lasting, beneficial effects in the face of impoverished, adverse parenting environments. Describing the goals, design, and effects of the Carolina Abecedarian Project, a randomized trial of educational day care project Martin and colleagues (1990) wrote:

The positive impact of educational day care was especially pronounced for the children of

PART **4**

mentally retarded mothers. At 6 months of age, all experimental and control children of retarded mothers had IQ scores within the normal range; however, by 54 months, all experimental group children of retarded mothers, but only 14% of the control children of retarded mothers, had normal range IQ scores. Although the number of children with retarded mothers in this sample is small (n = *13), the strong beneficial impact of this intervention merits attention because these children are at extreme risk for intellectual impairment.*

Given the beneficial effect of early educational day care in this sample of children with retarded mothers, the question arises as to whether families such as these typically receive day care services for their children. . . .the children who may be in most need of educational day care do not tend to receive these services. Given the positive findings of the Carolina Abecedarian Project, the children of low-functioning mothers appear to be a group which public health policies should target to receive high-quality educational day care interventions. (p. 846)

Other longitudinal research projects (e.g., The High/Scope Perry Preschool Study; Schweinhart et al., 2005) have yielded similar findings that demonstrate both short- and long-term positive effects of high-quality preschool education programs for young children living in poverty, with results lasting into adulthood. Given the advantages of preventive EI and stable living arrangements, young, at-risk children of low-income families can gain lifetime benefits and opportunities to "get a fair chance to achieve their potential and contribute meaningfully to their families and to society" (Schweinart et al., 2005, p. 6), despite apparent adversities.

When parents are single or divorced

Whether by personal choice, separation, divorce, death, cultural or ethnic diversity, teenage pregnancy, or other lifetime circumstances,

being a single parent dramatically changes a family's financial, child care, educational, employment, and psychosocial situation and well-being. Single parenthood alone usually is not the sole contributing factor that increases risks and leads to less advantageous family circumstances. Variables such as poverty, housing and food insecurities, child abuse and neglect, increased bouts of illness, poorer child care arrangements, and greater levels of stress (among others) often accompany a young mother's or father's parenting a child or children alone. Such circumstances are further aggravated if the parent or caregiver has no close-by relatives or neighborhood friends who can provide support for the family. Families of infants and young children—with or without disabilities—fare less well when or if they are isolated and do not have a strong network of others to call upon on a day-to-day basis. Evidence of this reality has been documented among families where fathers or mothers have been deployed into military service; mental health issues, depression, feelings of abandonment, and the frequency of child abuse and neglect tend to increase (Lester et al., 2010; Mansfield et al., 2010). The importance of "optimizing" supportive, community networks for families of children with disabilities is echoed by Murphy, Carbone, and the American Academy of Pediatrics Council on Children with Disabilities (2011). The need for attention to this kind of networking and linking for families cannot be understated in view of the fact that over the past 4 decades the numbers of children living in single-mother families have risen dramatically, a statistic that is especially troubling because this increase aligns with the recent significant growth in child poverty in the United States (Mather, 2010).

In the field of early childhood special education, one of the most hopeful signatures of EI federal legislation is the mandated focus on the provision of services for infants and toddlers within the context of the family. If this mandate is genuinely translated into practice by professionals across disciplines who are responsible for services for the population of young children from birth to 3 years old, the potential for formal and informal networking within communities can offer tremendous, accessible, natural supports for families and their young children. In view of the changing landscape of families in America, with infants and young children, with and without disabilities, this is an imperative of this century!

When families are homeless

Rising rates of poverty and recent economic turmoil, the lack of affordable-accessible housing, and the frequency of weather-related natural disasters (Ensher & Clark, 2011a; Kronenberg et al., 2010) are just three major conditions that have contributed to the escalation of food insecurity (Cutts et al., 2011) and homelessness among U.S. families (Samuels, Shinn, & Buckner, 2010; Streever, Ensher, & Clark, 2011a) over the past decade. Recent estimates are that more than 1.5 million children live in families without a home, and that, among those, 42% or 1 in 50 children are under 6 years old. Children of color (particularly African American) are disproportionately represented within this group of homeless families (Aratani, 2009).

Definitions of *homelessness* with regard to families vary, depending upon government agency, because criteria differ between, for example, the Department of Housing and Urban Development (HUD) and the Department of Education McKinney-Vento (i.e., the McKinney-Vento Homeless Assistance Act, which was authorized as Title X, Part C of the "No Child Left Behind Act", P.L. 107-110 in 2001; Aratani, 2009). The Department of Education definition is more inclusive than the HUD definition, indicating that the term *homeless children and youths:*

1. Means individuals who lack a regular, adequate nighttime residence, and
2. Includes—
   A. children and youths who share the housing of other persons due to loss of housing, economic hardship, or a similar reason; are living in motels, hotels, trailer parks, or camping rounds due to the lack of alternative adequate accommodations; are living in emergency or transitional shelters; are abandoned in hospitals, or are awaiting foster care placement;
   B. children and youths with a primary nighttime residence that consists of a public or private place not designed for or ordinarily used as a regular sleeping accommodation for human beings;
   C. children and youths who live in cars, parks, public spaces, abandoned buildings, substandard housing, bus or train stations, or similar settings;
   D. children subjected to the conditions caused by frequent parent moves and displacements.

As indicated by several authorities writing about children and homelessness (Aratani, 2009; Streever et al., 2011), such conditions understandably have dire consequences for families including poor medical and mental health, serious developmental and educational delays, and risks of violence, abuse, and neglect of their children. The McKinney-Vento Homeless Assistance Act noted previously offers families, infants, and young children a number of assurances and accommodations including equal access to a free, appropriate public education accorded to other children such as local preschool programs, Even Start, or Head Start, as well as transportation to and from these programs and settings.

Working with homeless families continues to be particularly challenging in light of the migratory nature of the population. Medical, dental, and educational records of families frequently are difficult to track as families move from community to community, even state to state, as in the case of families displaced by natural disasters. On the other hand, there are selected federal programs that can assist homeless children and families. As professionals reach out to homeless families, they need to become acquainted with the services provided by these programs and ways for connecting parents and caregivers with these resources, responsible accessible agencies, and eligibility criteria. In addition to the McKinney-Vento Education for Homeless Children and Youth Program, other programs include the National School Lunch and Breakfast Program, Supplementary Nutrition Assistance Program, Temporary Assistance Program, Medicaid & Children's Insurance Program, Child Care Assistance Program through the Child Care and Development Fund (Samuels et al., 2010), the Continuum of Care Program developed to offer funding by nonprofit providers and state and local governments to rehouse homeless families and promote access to "mainstream" community resources "to optimize self-sufficiency among families experiencing homelessness" (Homeless Assistance, U.S. Department of Housing and Urban Development, 2013). Being knowledgeable about local, federal, and state programs is vital for beginning to address the issues, concerns, and needs of this rapidly growing population of families, in particular mothers with infants and young children.

Strengthening Resilience of Families

Professionals who work with families who have infants and young children with medical, developmental, behavioral, or mental health needs have just a small window of time to offer the information, support, education,

medical treatment, services, and resources that families—each with its unique strengths and challenges—require. Although they have much in common, like the infants and young children born into their membership, each family also reflects a unique pattern of strengths and challenges. Always, the task is to leave families in a better place than at the outset of a relationship and to empower them to continue to develop the building blocks of nurturing relationships with their infants and young children beyond the time of service provision. Families will continue to master these tasks as best as they can and refine their renewed resilience.

Working with and understanding families are mutual processes. Both parents or caregivers and professionals must do their part. In *Relationship-Centered Practices in Early Childhood*, Ensher and Clark (2011b) wrote:

> *Many professionals in pediatrics, teaching, and clinical practices ventured into their respective disciplines because of a desire to help children. . . . On the other hand, they soon discover that they must also understand how to relate to and interact with other adults. . . . The following are skills and abilities essential to achieving effective partnerships with families:*

- *Understand one's role and responsibilities as a team member.*

- *Know how to acknowledge and highlight the expertise of others (especially family members).*

- *Know how to separate one's own values, perspectives, and biases from those of others . . . Partnerships require safe boundaries to maintain respect and confidentiality.*

- *Understand how to make accommodations and modify interactions. . . Preplanned agendas often do not work out. . . change is often necessary.*

- *Know when to respond, when to listen, and when to wait.*

- *Know when to ask questions, and when to offer advice and suggestions. . . .Silence can be challenging, but sometimes is the best course of action.*

- *Know how to discern and reinforce the positives.*

- *Understand which battles to pursue and those to let go.*

- *Understand how to suspend judgment.* (p. 16)

Some skills are easier to acquire than others; some are easier to teach than others. Some people acquire these skills naturally; for others, mastery may entail a lifelong journey.

Working with and understanding families takes many different forms and translates into multiple outcomes. However, a central thread through all of these interactions invariably is that they require trust and respect for what families bring to relationships and for what professionals can share in terms of their knowledge and experiences. Rarely is there just one way of doing things, and as families and professionals plan and problem-solve together, they are more likely to learn from each other on behalf of the children involved. Inherent in relationship-building processes are a willingness to "ask" for advice and guidance toward understanding, and most especially a willingness to "give up control." Neither parents nor professionals alone understand the "whole picture."

As partners in the process, both parents and professionals will need to jointly think about what works, what does not work, and if something is not working, why! Modeling is a great strategy—for the child, for the parents, and yes, for professionals as well (Powers & Pienkowski, 2013). Those who work with families have much to learn from each other, and they need to embrace diversity as a place and space to learn.

In the words of a very astute and wise educator, Ellen Barnes (2013), the director of the Jowonio, an inclusive preschool located in Syracuse, New York:

We can help young children learn to take the perspective of others by the example we set and how we talk with them about what happens at home and at school. Adults, who express concern about people in distress and take the initiative to help, set a powerful example in promoting caring. We can direct children to pay attention to body language and words of others. Conversation is an important strategy. We can ask, "What do you think the little girl is feeling right now?" "Tell me what happened; now pretend you are your brother and tell me how he might feel." We want to teach strategies of cooperation, where one's own needs can be expressed but also take into account the needs of others. We want, as Alfie Kohn says, to "promote a disposition of wanting to know how others are feeling," to develop the habit of seeing more deeply into others.

In our classrooms children build relationships, work together as a group, learn from each other, and make decisions through discussion and consensus. In this process there is time to express one's own feelings and ideas, listen to others, and offer suggestions. As adults we can gently acknowledge the social skills and kindnesses we see. We can also express our own failings. . . . All through our daily routines we have a chance to practice caring. The range of ages and needs of the diverse students in our groups provide opportunities to take turns being helpers as well as asking for help. We operate on the assumption that everyone belongs and we will work out a way for all to be part of the group. A caring community of children and adults is a living organism, changing and growing as are the individuals who are part of it.

As it is with children entrusted to professionals' care for teaching and learning, so it is with parents, families, and professionals who can bring home the lessons of relationships for the future and the families and children who follow.

Chapter Summary

This chapter embraced "diversity" within a very broad context and described some of the ways in which "difference" affects daily life. The authors examined culture, languages, and ethnicity; changes in family membership; the effects of poverty and economic hardship and their relationship to caring for an infant or young child with a disability. In addition, the chapter offers some strategies and approaches for developing and maintaining beneficial relationships within service-related contexts.

Key Points to Remember

- Sensitivity to diversity is central to the core of what professionals across disciplines do every day, as they interact in partnership with families and their young children.

- Different cultures shape the perceptions, child-rearing practices, interactions, and relationships with children; family perspectives of special needs and disability; lifestyles; languages spoken at home; and family receptivity to professional services.

- The dynamics of contemporary neighborhoods and communities greatly influence families, school programs, and the well-being of infants and young children.

- The demographics of families in the United States have changed markedly over the past decade and will continue to do so. These changing patterns have an enormous impact on the design and implementation of educational programs for infants, toddlers, and preschool children.

- Young children of color are more likely to be the victims of experiences and events that place them at increased social, emotional, developmental, and behavioral risks. Multiple ethnic, social, racial, economic, mental health, and educational factors coexist that may result in the "disabling" of families and their young children.

- Potentially "reversing the odds," major scientific visions and research relating to pregnancy and pregnancy outcomes, reproduction, epigenetics, the prevention of disabilities, and treatment of disease hold great promise for the improvement of developmental outcomes of infants and young children, and the well-being of families.

Implications for Families and Professionals

Like the caring parent, professionals sometimes strive to bear the burdens and responsibilities of others because they see the hurt and pain and wish to help. In doing so, the task becomes heavy and, at best, unrealistic! Professionals cannot prevent those they serve from learning from the invaluable "lessons" of life, because when they are no longer present, the parent and family will find it challenging, if not impossible, to move forward on their own!

Parent–professional partnerships are mutual relationships. Professionals can support, and often they may need to tip the balance toward offering more suggestions, help, information and assistance. On the other hand, eventually, that partnership must "right itself," like the relationship between parent and child, so that the caregiver is empowered and enabled and discovers resilience and strength perhaps never fully realized. Valuable "tools of the trade" for families may include:

- learning how to problem solve
- learning how to ask questions

- learning how to find resources
- learning how to ask for support, as needed

"Tools of the trade" helpful for professionals might be:

- learning how to scaffold learning for parents and young children
- learning how to pull back so that parents can move forward
- learning how to discover families' strengths
- learning how to suspend judgment in the face of difference from themselves
- learning how to celebrate difference and use diversity for benefit of the child and family

References

Addy, S., Engelhardt, W., & Skinner, C. (2013). *Basic facts about low-income children: Children under 6 years, 2011.* National Center for Children in Poverty. Retrieved from www.nccp.org

American Academy of Pediatrics Committee on Early Childhood, Adoption, and Dependent Care. (2005). Quality early education and child care from birth to kindergarten. *Pediatrics, 115*(1), 187–191.

American Academy of Pediatrics Committee on Pediatric Research. (2000). Race/ethnicity, gender, socioeconomic status—Research exploring their effects on child health: A subject review. *Pediatrics, 105*(6), 1349–1351.

Applequist, K. L., & Bailey, D. B., Jr. (2000). Navajo caregivers' perceptions of early intervention services. *Journal of Early Intervention, 23*(1), 47–61.

Aratani, Y. (2009). *Homeless children and youth: Causes and consequences.* New York, NY: National Center for Children in Poverty, Mailman School of Public Health, Columbia University.

Barnes, E. (2013). Director's report, Jowonio: *School News, 17*(2), 1–19.

Bell, M. J. (2007). Infections and the fetus. In M. L. Batshaw, L. Pellegrino, & N. J. Roizen (Eds.), *Children with disabilities* (6th ed., pp. 71–82). Baltimore, MD: Brookes.

Bronfenbrenner, U. (1979). *The ecology of human development: Experiments by nature and design.* Cambridge, MA: Harvard University Press.

Cox, A. H., Marshall, E. S., Mandleco, M., & Olsen, S. F. (2003). Coping responses to daily life stressors of children who have a sibling with a disability. *Journal of Family Nursing, 9*(4), 397–413.

Cutts, D. B., Meyers, A. F., Black, M. M., Casey, P. H., Chilton, M., Cook, J. T., . . . Frank, D. A. (2011). U.S. housing insecurity and the health of very young children. *American Journal of Public Health, 101*(8), 1508–1514.

Ensher, G. L., & Clark, D. A. (2011a). Family loss, disasters, and young children. In G. L. Ensher & D. A. Clark (Eds.), *Relationship-centered practices in early childhood: Working with families, infants, and young children at risk* (pp.151–163). Baltimore, MD: Brookes.

Ensher, G. L., & Clark, D. A. (2011b). Teamwork and a system that helps. In G. L. Ensher & D. A. Clark (Eds.), *Relationship-centered practices in early childhood: Working with families, infants, & young children at risk* (pp. 15–30). Baltimore, MD: Brookes.

Eunice Kennedy Shriver National Institute of Child Health and Human Development. (2012). *Scientific vision: The next decade.* Washington, DC: U.S. Department of Health and Human Services, National Institutes of Health. Retrieved from ww.nichd.nih.gov/vision/Pages/index.aspx

Homeless Assistance, U.S. Department of Housing and Urban Development. (2013). *Homeless assistance.* Retrieved from http://portal.hud.gov/hudportal/HUD?src=/program_offices/comm_planning/homeless

Kagan, S. L., & Neuman, M. J. (2000). Early care and education: Current issues and future strategies. In J. P. Shonkoff & S. J. Meisels (Eds.), *Handbook of early childhood intervention* (2nd ed., pp. 339–360). Cambridge, UK: Cambridge University Press.

Kleinmann, A. E., & Songer, N. S. (2009). Parents with developmental disabilities caring for infants and young children. In G. L. Ensher, D. A. Clark, & N. S. Songer (Eds.), *Families, infants, & young children at risk: Pathways to best practice* (pp. 287–296). Baltimore, MD: Brookes.

Kreader, L., Ferguson, D., & Lawrence, S. (2005). *Infant and toddler child care arrangements.* New York, NY: National Center for Children in Poverty, Mailman School of Public Health, Columbia University. Retrieved from www.nccp.org/publications/pub_628.html

Kronenberg, M. F., Cross, T. H., Brennan, A. M., Osofsky, H. J., Osofsky, J. D., & Lawrason, B. (2010). Children of Katrina: Lessons learned about

PART **4**

post-disaster symptoms and recovery patterns. *Child Development, 81*(4), 1241–1259.

Lazara, A., Danaher, J., & Goode, S. (2012). *Part C infant and toddler program federal appropriations and national child count 1987–2012.* Chapel Hill, NC: University of North Carolina Child Development Institute, National Early Childhood Technical Assistance Center. Retrieved from www.nectac.org/~pdfs/grothcomppartc.pdf

Lester, P., Peterson, K., Reeves, M., Knauss, L., Glover, K., Mogil, C., . . . Beardslee, W. (2010). The long war and parental combat deployment: Effects on military children and at-home spouses. *Journal of the American Academy of Child & Adolescent Psychiatry, 49*(4), 310–320.

Lynch, E. W. (2013). Families in the 21st century. In M. J. Hanson & E. W. Lynch, (Eds.), *Understanding families: Supportive approaches to diversity, disability, and risk* (2nd ed., pp. 1–22). Baltimore, MD: Brookes.

Lynch, E. W., & Hanson, M. J. (Eds.). (2011). *Developing cross-cultural competence: Guide for working with children and their families* (4th ed.). Baltimore, MD: Brookes.

Mandleco, B., Olsen, S. F., Dyches, T., & Marshall, E., (2003). The relationship between family and sibling functioning in families raising a child with a disability. *Journal of Family Nursing, 9*(4), 365–396.

Mansfield, A. J., Kaufman, J. S., Marshall, S. W., Gaynes, B. N., Morrissey, J. P., & Engel, C. C. (2010). Deployment and the use of mental health services among U.S. army wives. *New England Journal of Medicine, 362*(2), 101–109.

Martin, J. A., Hamilton, B. E., Ventura, S. J., Michelle, J. K., Osterman, M. J. K., Mathews, J.J., & Division of Vital Statistics. (2013, June 28). *Births: Final data for 2011. National Vital Statistics Reports, 62*(1), U.S. Department of Health and Human Services, Centers for Disease Control and Prevention, National Center for Health Statistics, National Vital Statistics System.

Martin, S. L., Ramey, C. T., & Ramey, S. (1990). The prevention of intellectual impairment in children of impoverished families: Findings of a randomized trial of educational day care. *American Journal of Public Health, 80*(7), 844–847.

Mather, M. (2010). *U.S. children in single-mother families.* Retrieved from Population Reference Bureau www.prb.org/Publications/Reports/2010/singlemotherfamilies.aspx

Mathews, J. J., & Division of Vital Statistics. (2013). Births: Final data for 2011. *National Vital Statistics Reports, 62*(1), 1–70.

Matthews, H. (2008). *Charting progress for babies in child care project: Support a diverse and culturally competent workforce.* Washington, DC: Center for Law and Social Policy. Retrieved from www.clasp.org

Minority Health Initiatives. (2009). *Health coverage in communities of color: Talking about the new census numbers.* Retrieved from www.familiesusa.org/assets/pdfs/minority-census-sept-2009.pdf

Murphy, N. A., Carbone, P. S., & Council on Children With Disabilities. (2011). Parent-provider-community partnerships: Optimizing outcomes for children with disabilities. *Pediatrics, 128*(4), 795–802.

National Rehabilitation Information Center. (2012). *Parenting with a disability.* Retrieved from www.naric.com/?q=en/publications/volume-7-issue-2-

Passel, J., & Cohn, D. (2008). *U.S. population projections: 2005-2050.* Retrieved from www.pewsocialtrends.org/2008/02/11/us-population-projections-2005-2050

Pewewardy, C., & Fitzpatrick, M. (2009). Working with American Indian students and families: Disabilities, issues, and interventions. *Intervention in School and Clinic, 45*(2), 91–98.

Pianta, R. C., & Cox, M. J. (1999). *The transition to kindergarten.* Baltimore, MD: Brookes.

Powers, S., & Pienkowski, T. (2013, October). *Early Intervention. . .when, why, and how? More about the "how": Play-based therapy.* PowerPoint presentation, Syracuse University, Syracuse, NY.

Ramey, C. T., & Ramey, S. L. (2004). Early learning and school readiness: Can early intervention make a difference? *Merrill-Palmer Quarterly, 50*(4), 471–491.

Samuels, J., Shinn, M., & Buckner, J. C. (2010). *Homeless children: Update on research, policy, programs, and opportunities.* Washington, DC: Office of the Assistant Secretary for Planning and Evaluation, U.S. Department of Health and Human Services. Retrieved from http://aspe.hhs.gov/hep/10/HomelessChildrenRoundtable/index.shtml

Schweinhart, L. J., Montie, J., Xiang, Z., Barnett, W. S., Belfield, C. R., & Nores, M. (2005). *The High/Scope Perry Preschool Study through age 40: Summary, conclusions, and frequently asked questions.* Ypsilanti, MI: High/Scope Press, Educational Research Foundation.

Shrestha, L. B., & Heisler, E. J. (2009). *The changing demographic profile of the United States.* Congressional Research Service. Retrieved from www.crs.gov

Shudy, M., de Almeida, M. L., Ly, S., Landon, C., Groft, S., Jenkins, T., & Nicholson, C. (2006). Impact of pediatric critical illness and injury on families:

Systematic literature review. *Pediatrics, 118*(Supp. 3), S203–S218.

Stabile, M., & Allin, S. (2012). The economic costs of childhood disability. *The Future of Children, 22*(1), 65–96. Retrieved from www.futureofchildren.org

Streever, R. J., Ensher, G. L., & Clark, D. A. (2011). Homelessness and young children. In G. L. Ensher & D. A. Clark (Eds.), *Relationship-centered practices in early childhood: Working with families, infants, and young children at risk* (pp. 165–181). Baltimore, MD: Brookes.

Swaminathan, S., Alexander, G. R., & Boulet, S. (2006). Delivering a very low birth weight infant and the subsequent risk of divorce or separation. *Maternal Child Health Journal, 10,* 473–479.

Tabors, P. O. (2008). *One child, two languages: A guide for early childhood educators of children learning English as a second language* (2nd ed.). Baltimore, MD: Brookes.

Through the Looking Glass. (2013). *Parents with intellectual disabilities.* Retrieved from http://lookingglass.org/services/local-services/services-for-parents-with-disabilities

Trail, K. (2000). A changing nation: The impact of linguistic and cultural diversity on education. *SEDL Letter, 12*(2). Retrieved from www.sedl.org/pubs/sed;etter/v12n02/2.html

Umstead, R. S. (2013). *Assessing young children of families for whom English is a second language.* [PowerPoint presentation]. Syracuse University, Syracuse, NY.

PART **4**

CHAPTER 15

Mental Health Issues of Children in Military Families

Colleen M. Guthrie, Gail L. Ensher, and David A. Clark

Highlights of the Chapter

At the conclusion of this chapter, the reader will:

- understand some of the mental health issues that affect infants, toddlers, and preschool children of military families

- understand some of the social and academic challenges that confront young children in families where one or both parents are deployed into military service

- understand the joys and mental health challenges that families face when the deployed family member returns home from military service

- be aware of some of the protective and supportive strategies that professionals including physicians and educators can use to help infants, young children, and their family members with deployment, homecoming, and loss of relatives and friends

Who Are the Military Children?

Thirty-seven percent of U.S. military personnel have children, totaling approximately 2 million children of personnel in the Army, Navy, Coast Guard, Air Force, and Marine Corps, and of Reservists and Active Duty members. In a 2011 demographics study provided by the Department of Defense (DOD), most of these children were between the ages of 0 and 5 (37.4%), followed by children ages 6 to 11 (30.3%) and 12 to 18 (25.1%). More than half (54.0%), or 674,167, of the 1,247,607 children of active duty members are 7 years old or younger. Military children may live almost anywhere. There are more than 210 military installations in the continental United States alone, and the total of America's military bases in other countries in 2005, according to some sources, was 737; however, these numbers are difficult to pinpoint because official data are not released to the public.

The Military Child Education Coalition has found that more than 80% of military children and youth (preschool and school age)—1,105,267 students—attend U.S. public schools. Less than 8% attend DOD schools, which may be located within military installations in the United States or in the eight international districts of the DOD. An estimate by the Military Child Education Coalition indicated that up to 9% of military children are schooled at home (Hefling, 2013). Some military families choose to homeschool because of the flexibility it offers and for the stability it provides to their children during repeated deployments and constant moves.

Issues Military Children Face

Children of families with deployed parents and caregivers are challenged with a number of issues, depending on their ages, family membership, numbers of relocations, length of time of deployments, as well as family-specific concerns. The following discussion highlights a few considerations.

The Youngest and Most Vulnerable Groups: Infants, Toddlers, and Preschoolers

Chapter 2 of this book (Ensher & Clark, 2016), which focuses on mental health issues and families of infants, toddlers, and preschool children, is directly relevant in many respects to the challenges that confront military families with infants, toddlers, and preschoolers. In their article "The Young Military Child: Our Modern Telemachus," Cozza and Lieberman (2007) have written:

For thousands of years military children been faced with many challenges that result from the combat deployment of their parents. These challenges are likely to be particularly burdensome to infants, toddlers, and preschoolers because of their emotional and cognitive immaturity, their reliance on magical thinking, and their dependence upon their parents' healthy development. Frequent or lengthy parental absences, particularly during the early years of child development, are more likely to contribute to disruptions in parental attachment, elevation in early child childhood anxiety, or both. Families are likely to be affected by worries within the community about injuries or deaths, concern that can filter down to the youngest children in the families. Some recent reports [McCarroll, Fan, Newby, & Ursano, in press; Rentz et al., 2007] suggest that the increased deployment and operational tempo may be contributing to rising child maltreatment rates in military families. Child neglect in younger children of lower enlisted rank appears to be the greatest contributor to these elevated rates of maltreatment. (p. 3)

Circumstances such as grief, depression, and instability are not unique to children in military families; however, the combination of antecedents has been seen to add additional strain to their mental health, as compared to children in civilian families. Major issues in terms of military children are relocation, deployment of a parent, grief/loss of parent, matters surrounding homecoming and post-deployment, and the overall mental health of the entire military family. These issues may affect the child's development, her learning and development prior to and later at school, as well as her relationships with others. Such disruptions, for many families, may even be evident prenatally, thus affecting both mother and child before birth. Noteworthy symptoms seen among infants, toddlers, and preschoolers include changes in sleep patterns, increased irritability and difficulties in self-calming, trouble feeding, overall changes in affect, regression in behavioral patterns (e.g., after toilet training), and trouble separating from the nondeployed parent

(Sheppard, Malatras, & Israel, 2010)—all indicators of stress, an increased sense of insecurity, and a decreased sense of trust. It is important that caregivers and educators are aware of these issues and are familiar with ways to support infants and young children during difficult times.

Permanent Changes of Station and Relocation

The reality of the military child is that his home life will be continuously in flux. At an average of every 3 years, a military family may face an order for a Permanent Change of Station. Moving the entire family and its belongings every few years to new places is, alone, stressful for children of all ages. In addition, the relocation of friends, life in neighborhoods that are in a constant state of change from incoming and outgoing families, and parental absences create stressful instability. This creates a lack of long-term permanence for the entire household. These frequent changes have been found to affect the mental health and development of military children.

Social and Emotional Effects of Relocation

Robert Blum, professor of the Johns Hopkins Bloomberg School of Public Health, explains in an interview from the American Association of School Administrators:

Military families and military children are amongst the most transient of populations. It is not uncommon to see kids who have grown up in military families who have been in 5, 7 or 9 different schools by the end of their high school career. There is very high mobility. With high mobility come issues of engagement, disengagement and reengagement. (Canon, 2011, n. p.)

There are numerous ways that high mobility can impact children. Using Erik Erikson's Stages of Psychosocial Development, professionals can view childhood's social-emotional development as reliant on the attachment and relationships that a child develops during the earliest years of life.

As indicated in Table 15.1, during ages 4 and 5 (the preschool years), children begin to assert control over themselves and their world; they primarily do so during play and social interactions. Successfully making connections and having a sense of ownership of their direction at this stage allows them to feel capable and even develop leadership skills. Kendra Cherry (2013) stated, "When an ideal balance of individual initiative and a willingness to work with others is achieved, the ego quality known as purpose emerges." A sense of guilt, self-doubt, and lack of initiative may be felt by those who do not acquire these skills during this phase of development—a phase that might be interrupted by frequent transitions.

Through social interactions at ages 5–12, children begin to develop a sense of pride in their accomplishments and their abilities. Children who experience encouragement and have positive relationships with parents and teachers will develop a feeling of

TABLE 15.1 Erikson's stages of psychosocial development

AGE	VIRTUES	PSYCHOSOCIAL CRISIS	SIGNIFICANT RELATIONSHIP
4–5 years	Purpose	Initiative vs. Guilt	Family
5–12 years	Competence	Initiative vs. Guilt	Neighbors, School
13–19 years	Fidelity	Identity vs. Role Confusion	Social Relationships

competence and belief in their skills. Those who lack such relationships or do not receive encouragement from parents, teachers, or peers may doubt their abilities to be successful. Finding a balance at this stage of psychosocial development leads to the development of self-assurance and competence, and a belief in one's abilities to master tasks, even in toddlerhood and in the preschool years (Cherry, 2013). With the likelihood of broken relationships as a result of frequent transitions, it is possible that children at this phase will struggle.

During adolescence, children explore their independence and develop a sense of self and their roles in social relationships. Cherry (2013) described Erikson's adolescent stage:

Those who receive proper encouragement and reinforcement through personal exploration will emerge from this stage with a strong sense of self and a feeling of independence and control. Those who remain unsure of their beliefs and desires will feel insecure and confused about themselves and the future. Completing this stage successfully leads to fidelity, which Erikson described as an ability to live by society's standards and expectations. (n. p.)

We find that children's relationships in general—with family, peers, school, and within their community—are integral to the development of children's egos, their self-worth, and their mental health. When there is instability in these relationships due to frequent transitions, children are highly vulnerable to disengagement, low confidence, and poor self-esteem. These concerns can be major antecedents in creating negative mental health issues such as anxiety and depression. Children may become at least temporarily hindered in their ability to connect with others and to discuss their feelings, which can bring about feelings of isolation and helplessness.

Relocation: Social, Emotional, and Academic Effects

The needs of infants and young children of parents in the military deserve special attention because the first years of life are pivotal in establishing trusting attachment relationships, which are based on the developmental expectation that parents will be reliably available and protective both physically and emotionally [Bowlby 1969/1982]. For young children in military families, this expectation of parental availability and protectiveness can be strained and derailed by extended absences of mothers and/or fathers as a the result of deployment abroad, recurrent separations and reunions resulting from repeated deployments, parents struggling with the emotional sequelae of their experiences, and parental injury and death. In addition, the young child must cope with the caregiving parent's preoccupation with the deployed military parent's safety and the challenges of single-handedly managing household. (Lieberman & Van Horn, 2013, p. 282)

There is a direct educational impact on military children of all ages who frequently transition to new homes, caregiving situations, and school districts. They may face delayed enrollment, inappropriate grade-level placement, exclusion from educational programs and extracurricular activities, and delayed graduation. These types of educational issues may affect a child's self-esteem, as well as his levels of stress and anxiety. Immediately following relocation, a child's academic performance tends to decline. According to Ingersoll, Scamman, and Eckerling, "the most negative effects of geographic mobility were found at earlier grade levels" (1989, p. 143). Often, school curricula are dramatically different from region to region, leaving children who are entering new districts, or moving during the school year, to find they are behind their peers. Wood, Halton, Scarlata, Newacheck, and Nessim (1993) found that 35% of frequent movers were more likely to fail a grade than were those who never or infrequently moved. Families that moved frequently were 50%–100% more likely to suffer growth or developmental delays or have a learning disorder (Wood et al., 1993)

Deployment

Military deployment is defined as a time when a soldier is transferred to another place in the world to fulfill a contract of service. Wartime parental deployment can be the most stressful events of a child's life.

In recent years, more than 2 million American children have had a parent deployed to Iraq or Afghanistan. As cited in a clinical report from the American Academy of Pediatrics (Siegel, Davis, Committee on Psychosocial Aspects of Child and Family Health, & Section on Uniformed Services, 2013):

The wars in Afghanistan and Iraq have been challenging for U.S. uniformed service families and their children. Almost 60% of the U.S. service members have family responsibilities. Approximately 2.3 million active duty, National Guard, and Reserve service members have been deployed since the beginning of the wars in Afghanistan and Iraq (2001 and 2003, respectively), and almost half have deployed more than once, some for up to 18 months' duration. Up to 2 million U.S. children have been exposed to a wartime deployment of a loved one in the past 10 years. (p. e2002)

A number of factors influences a child's adaptation to deployment. In fact, each member of a family of a deployed service member must make adjustments to create new roles and responsibilities, in addition to dealing with the separation of their parent. Disorganized families with multiple preexisting problems or troubled family members tend to be at higher risk for poor adjustments during deployments and separations, especially if children are very young or have special health care needs, disabilities, or both.

Children in military families as a group suffer from more emotional and behavioral difficulties, as compared to other American youths, with older children and girls struggling the most when a parent is deployed overseas. More than one third of school-age military children show psychosocial behaviors such as being anxious, worrying often, and crying more frequently. (Flake, Davis, Johnson, & Middleton, 2009)

Changes During Deployment

Children's personality changes during deployment include variations in school performance, lashing out in anger, worrying, hiding emotions, disrespecting parents and authority figures, feeling a sense of loss, and experiencing symptoms consistent with depression (Huebner, Mancini, Wilcox, Grass, & Grass, 2007). "Today, many families describe deployment as a 'spiral.' This image captures the experience of having no time to get back to where they started before facing the next separation" (ZERO TO THREE, n. d., p. 15). Such stressors within families of infants and young children may be especially challenging as they experience: The transition from warrior to parent and being born while service members/parents are away. Children under 3 years old change dramatically during the length of a deployment.

Children react differently to adults they haven't seen for a while, depending on their developmental stage (e.g., with stranger anxiety and separation anxiety). A 2005 study by Orthner and Rose examined the adjustment of Army children to deployment separations and revealed some key findings:

- High levels of sadness were seen in children in all age groups.

PART **4**

- Depression was seen in about one in four children.

- Academic problems occurred in one in five children.

- Thirty-seven percent of children with a deployed parent reported that they seriously worry about what could happen to their deployed caregiver.

- Parents reported that one in five children coped poorly or very poorly to deployment separation.

- Media coverage of the war posed a significant source of stress for children and made it much more difficult for children to cope with a parent's deployment.

- Length of deployment was associated with mental health problems including depression, acting out, and externalizing behaviors

Public schools in North Carolina (Public Schools of North Carolina, State Board of Education, 2013) have an extremely high number of students in military families, as a result of several major Army and Marine Corps installations within the state, and offer some information about serious stress indicators for their educators on their website. Findings of recent studies about the effects of deployment on students provide important information for school districts. Educators who are aware of early "warning signs" for their military family students may help to prevent serious health or mental health issues before they surface. Some of the stress indicators that have been noted and that may be observed in the classroom include the following:

- inability to resume normal classroom assignments and activities

- high levels of emotions; continued crying and intense sadness

- depressed, withdrawn, and noncommunicative behaviors

- violent or depressed feelings expressed in "dark" drawings or writings

Other indicators of stress reactions include children causing intentional harm to themselves or others, significant weight gain or loss in a short period of time, a lack of care about personal appearance, and evidence of drug or alcohol abuse.

Media Coverage During Deployment

With the dawn of new technology has come the reality of war through the Internet and digital media. Images and video can be uploaded to be viewed by the world in a blink of an eye. Never before has a generation of American children experienced their parents' wars alongside of them via 24-hour news channels and websites. It is estimated that during the Persian Gulf War of 1991, 98% of households with televisions experienced viewing images of the conflict.

In a 1994 study by Hoffner and Haefner, children were found to have difficulty interpreting events televised during the Persian Gulf War. Behavior problems seen among some military children during this time might be attributed to acting out things that they were unable to talk about, or understand—but had witnessed through video. Increased stress was noted in children whose parents had been deployed, and the more media coverage children witnessed, the harder it became to cope.

Within conflicts of war, often there is a wide spectrum of reactions by those who remain at home. There are often vocal opponents on any military conflict. When children see these voices of opposition in the media, it may cause confusion, anger, fear, and concern about the situation and their parent's role within it.

Increased Anxiety During Deployment

More than 37% of military children with a deployed parent have expressed anxiety through severe worry. Often children who are too young to be able to express their anxiety verbally will manifest their feelings in their behavior.

Specific to younger populations of children, infants and toddlers may (as noted previously) have difficulties sleeping, evidence feeding problems, and be difficult to calm, as well as reflect other changes in their typical behavioral patterns.

Among preschool or kindergarten-age children, some common behaviors related to anxiety may be:

- clinging to people or to a favorite toy or blanket
- unexplained crying or tearfulness
- changes in relationship with same-age friends
- choosing adults over same-age friends
- increased acts of aggression toward people or things
- withdrawing from people or things
- sleep difficulties (e.g., nightmares, frequent waking)
- behavior regressions such as having toileting accidents, thumb sucking, and others
- eating difficulties

School-age children, although they may have a better grasp or ability to use language for expression, may exhibit other signs of anxiety. In addition to the symptoms noted above, children may complain about stomach aches, headaches, or other illnesses when nothing seems to be wrong. They may also exhibit increased irritability and more problems in school, such as a drop in grades, an unwillingness to attend school, or odd complaints about school and/or teachers. They may also experiment with drugs, alcohol, or sex at an earlier age.

Cumulative Deployment

A RAND study (Chandra et al., 2010), published in the journal *Pediatrics*, explored the impact of modern wars on children across social, emotional, and academic domains. The study found that as the months of parental deployment increased, so did the child's challenges regarding behavior, school performance, mental health, and general health and well-being. The total number of months away mattered more than the number of deployments.

The study also found that the impact of cumulative deployments was more pronounced among girls, particularly during the reintegration period, once a parent returned home. Researchers say this finding may be linked to girls' taking on additional household duties when a parent is deployed and issues related to connecting emotionally with an absent parent, who is usually a father.

Homecoming

After an initial "honeymoon" period following deployment and the reunification of the family, often each family member experiences an emotional adjustment period. This last stage, the post-deployment stage, ends an emotional trifecta that surrounds the event and includes predeployment and deployment.

War experiences have changed the person who was deployed. Perceptions of what constitutes a stressful or emotional situation may have shifted, making it hard to relate to those at home. The everyday stress of family life can feel overwhelming for the service member; he may become more irritated or react more strongly to common family issues.

Returning service members need to relearn how to feel safe, comfortable, and trusting again with family members—they may even feel a stronger bond with members of their units rather than their family. Some even develop a longing or depression when they have left their unit behind. Anger and aggression are common combat stress reactions, but these reactions may frighten spouses and children, and even the service member herself.

Spouses and family members may have taken on more responsibilities and control in the family to fulfill the space the service member once held. Many soldiers express feelings of worthlessness upon their return because they believe that their families have been able to successfully exist without them. Children have grown and developed new skills during their parent's absence. Often a child has gone through an emotional spectrum of resentment, sorrow, and anger when the parent left, and these emotions may resurface once the parent returns. With a parent who is returning from combat and suffering through posttraumatic stress disorder (PTSD) and readjustment issues, a child may feel insecure, anxious, and depressed because the parent is different than the one who left.

Grief

Since 2003, more than 6,750 American military personnel have been killed on deployment, and many of these deaths were under extremely sudden and traumatic circumstances. More than 2,600 have died from hostile actions, and more than 2,500 from improvised explosive devices. More than 800 have died in helicopter, automobile, or airplane accidents while overseas (Washington Post, 2013).

As may any person who has lost a loved one, a child may feel intense sadness and grief. Each individual copes with loss in his own way, and there are no right or wrong ways to grieve.

However, when young children experience grief, it often can cut across developmental levels, which may appear through a regression of earlier skills. In children, grief will often manifest as a physical problem: loss of appetite, difficulty sleeping, or general body pain such as headaches or stomach aches. Children may also manifest their grief by exhibiting changes in their behaviors; some will become isolated and withdrawn, while others may express anger and irritability. Uncharacteristic behaviors that may be as simple as a heightened number of temper tantrums in a toddler or riskier behavior from a teenager may be ways that children who are not able to discuss or express their despair demonstrate grief. Sometimes a child who has lost one parent will feel the need to take on more responsibility or to try to comfort the surviving parent. This stress and anxiety may be exacerbated if the surviving parent is also a member of the armed forces. For children in the military whose parents have died while on a wartime deployment, their death may have been sudden or happened under especially harrowing circumstances.

In *childhood traumatic grief,* children themselves may develop symptoms associated with PTSD. Children with childhood traumatic grief may have trouble recalling comforting memories of the loved one they have lost. It may be difficult to spend time with friends and families, and the grief may interfere with their everyday life. Some children try to avoid reminders of their deceased parent and refuse to talk about him. They may feel emotionally numb. Intrusive thoughts, such as details of their parent's death, may be difficult to escape. Children may even fixate on how their loved one may have suffered, in an especially traumatic death. Many children, 5–12 years old, will show signs of PTSD in their play. They may continue repeating a part of the trauma they've experienced, or think their parent experienced.

Sleep issues arise because of nightmares, which may lead children to avoid sleep, or emotional numbness may draw children to sleeping as frequently as they are able to do so. Some children may become fearful or develop new fears during these times of grief. Older children, 12–18 years old, are more likely than younger children or adults to show impulsive and aggressive behaviors. Many military service parents may have been deployed for extended periods of time before dying. Because of this, children who may already have been dealing with their parent's physical absence for some time may not experience any immediate changes in their day-to-day life when they learn of the death. Their past experience with the person's absence may make it hard for some children to accept the permanence of their loss or to take part in their family's grieving (National Child Traumatic Stress Network, 2008).

Military deaths during periods of wartime are public events and often involve the media and other military rituals. When a family is unable to have the privacy to grieve together, it may make it difficult for children to cope with the loss. These stressors might be additionally compounded by having to relocate from the military base at which they had lived before the parent's death.

Mental Health of the Entire Family

The military child is one who is not just simply dealing with his own stressful issues; the entire family dynamic is at play. The positive mental health of the family unit is in jeopardy during these difficult emotional times, especially during deployments in combat zones. The American Psychological Association Presidential Task Force on Military Deployment's 2007 study, which is in agreement with findings of the 2010 RAND study on the psychological needs of military families, found that the emotional health of a *nondeployed* parent is closely linked with the difficulties their children have during deployment. Caregiver well-being is linked to general well-being of the child,

emotional difficulties, peer and family function, and academic engagement. Parents who coped well are twice as likely as those who coped poorly to believe their children coped well (Orthner & Rose, 2005). One of the strongest predictors of a child's functioning during a war deployment was parental stress (Flake et al., 2009).

The Military Spouse

Many military spouses carry the weight of running a single-parent household during the other parent's deployment. The military spouse may be living hundreds or thousands of miles away from her extended family, and possibly in a foreign country. This means that their options for familial support may be limited. About 44% of military spouses are between 19 and 22 years old (Williams, 2009), which means they are a group of young people who may have very little knowledge of mental health issues or of coping skills during high-stress times. In 2008, there were 2 million visits by military family members for mental health care services, which is twice the figure prior to the start of the Iraq war (Hefling, 2009). Overall, the total number of children and spouses of active duty, National Guard, and Reserve members seeking mental health care has been increasing steadily.

The Returning Service Member

Once the parent who is a service member has returned from combat deployment, and the post-deployment homecoming "honeymoon period" is over, the reality of her experiences may set in. Returning veterans face extensively high levels of PTSD, depression, traumatic brain injury, and other conditions affecting mental health. Of the soldiers who return from combat in Afghanistan and Iraq, approximately one in three suffers from PTSD (Tanielian & Jaycox, 2008). These rates become higher for each additional tour of duty.

More than 70% of service personnel who remain in active duty after returning do not seek treatment for mental health issues, and only 56% of veterans seek treatment after leaving active duty. Unresolved mental health problems in a parent who has few to no coping skills can affect their children. Gibbs, Martin, Kupper, and Johnson's (2007) study revealed that:

> Among families of enlisted U.S. Army personnel with substantiated reports of child maltreatment (physical, emotional or sexual abuse), rates of maltreatment are greater when the soldiers are on combat-related deployments. In fact, the rate of child maltreatment in families of enlisted Army soldiers was 42% higher during combat deployment than during non-deployment. (Sogomonyan, & Cooper, 2010, p. 6)

An estimated 20% of returning soldiers turn to heavy drinking or drugs (Alvarez, 2008), which creates additional layers of mental health issues that may affect their children.

Protective and Supportive Strategies for Educators, Physicians, and Other Professionals

The 210 military installations across the United States employ the parents of nearly 2 million children, of whom 80% attend public schools or will soon be school age (Militarychild.org, 2015). Schools, medical facilities, physicians, and teachers need to be attentive to all of the issues that military children may face, so they can best support them. Although most children can cope with these issues, a greater-than-typical number (one in four) face serious mental health issues that include depression, suicidal thoughts, debilitating anxiety, and extreme stress. Educators and those in the health care professions should be able to help children and their families develop coping strategies to deal with the extensive and prolonged stress, anxiety, and worry during their parent's combat deployment. A supportive and predictable environment can help to reduce the risk of lasting emotional consequences and poor mental health.

A military child's child care or school setting may have much to do with how well he adjusts to a parent's deployment. For example, a child in a military-impacted school (a school that has a high concentration of military children) may know many friends and peers who are experiencing similar anxiety or stress. Relationships among these children can offer a sense of normalcy and community, because children know that they are not isolated in their experience. However, a child whose parent is in the Reserves and lives within the civilian community may be the only child in school with a deployed parent. This may create solitude within the experience, which may add a tier of despair; if this information is not shared with the school district, the child's teacher will be unaware and unable to help.

By establishing a relationship with a family at the onset, educators can create a dialog that is helpful for both the family and the school. Teachers can ask questions about planned deployments, if the parent is in combat zones, when there might be times of furlough, any recent changes of station, or any other pertinent information that a family chooses to share. This information will help a teacher support the child through any changes or transitions that the family is experiencing.

Specific to helping new parents cope with the challenges and ensure that the crucial developmental years are as smooth as possible, the military has developed the New Parent Support Program which helps parents—including expectant parents—develop the skills they need to provide a nurturing environment for their children" (Military OneSource, n.d.).

The program, staffed by nurses, social workers, and home visitation specialists, offers a number of benefits including home visits, referrals to other resources, prenatal classes, parenting classes, and play groups.

Among other strategies that can help children and their deployed parents remain connected are the following (eXtension.org, 2012):

- having both parents speak with a professional before deployment

- recording favorite children's stories, bedtime prayers, or other familiar routines

- having the child create items to share with the deployed parent such as photos, monthly calendars, and stories about field trips

Most important, friends, caregivers, non-deployed parents, and others connected with the family need to focus on the following:

Remembering the child's relationship with the deployed parent and allowing it to continue despite separation. It's often valuable to remind a child about the relationship she has with her parent, and the positive aspects of the relationship. Helping a child correspond with her deployed parent, making a time capsule or scrapbook of daily events to share upon their parent's return, and having comforting reminders of their parent available are important to many children. These strategies keep the humanity and the relationship at the forefront, during a time when it might be easy to fixate on the often-traumatizing circumstances of their separation.

Honesty—one of the more important aspects of having any type of supportive relationship with a child who is experiencing combat deployment. Unrealistic promises like "your dad will be home soon," or "life will be back to normal" should not be made. It's important to be positive,

and reassuring, but remember that their parent is in a potentially dangerous situation for an extended amount of time. Avoid discussing scary, painful, or detailed aspects of deployment, because they can only fuel the anxiety that a child may have. If a child asks questions, provide factual age-appropriate information about a deployment. If a teacher doesn't know the answer, they can make contacts within the military to find out who can answer their questions.

Predictability—another critical necessity. For a military child, change and transition are a fact of life. Whenever possible, maintain regular routines, especially for students who are stressed or going through transitional phases like deployment or post-deployment. Structure gives children a sense of continuity, stability, and safety. The military child needs to know that the supportive adults in his life, both parents and teachers, will follow through with what they say and do. A daily schedule or events should be consistent, and adults should use caution when discussing a special event like a phone call from a deployed parent, or even a potential furlough.

Support from other peers and military families who are experiencing deployment is valuable to all involved. Among older children and teenagers, sometimes the support of a peer is more meaningful, because they feel that they can relate better with their peers than with adults. Teachers can help seek out programs, groups, or events where a military child can connect with a community of support of peers as well as adults.

Understanding the behavioral and academic challenges that military children face. From the high mobility to the anxiety and stress of having a deployed parent, life can be hectic and unpredictable. Often, children's behavior is communicating that a child is struggling with these issues. For younger children, themes of guilt, fear, anxiety, or aggression in their play may reveal that they are struggling. Be patient and calm when a child has increased anger, irritability, and withdrawal. By developing a rapport and relationship with the child, a teacher can be a major emotional as well as academic support. Monitoring for physical symptoms including headaches and stomach aches is important because many children express anxiety through physical aches and pains. An increase in symptoms that appear to be without medical cause may be a sign that a child is having trouble coping.

Encouraging limitations of screen time to help decrease anxiety. The realities of war can be overwhelming for a child whose parent is involved in combat situations. Personal critiques of these situations by a teacher also have no place in the classroom, and may even be detrimental to the mental health of military students. Dr. Robert Blum of the Johns Hopkins Bloomberg School of Public Health (2013) recommended:

Be sensitive to how current events are taught. Most of us discuss current events, such as the wars in Afghanistan and Iraq, as relative abstractions. But children talk and think about it in terms of their father or their mother. It is at a very different personal level. This isn't to say we don't discuss it, but it is to say we need to be sensitive to those kinds of issues.

Validating military children's feelings and helping them to express themselves. Educators can help guide children who appear to be having a difficult time by offering them healthy ways to cope with their anxiety or grief. Respond empathically when a child is showing the need for more attention. It is important for adults to take cues from the child, and to not force them to talk about things that they are not ready to discuss. A child's frame of reference is different from the experience of an adult; children may take more time to sort out their feelings or to feel comfortable enough to ask questions. Children who are preoccupied with questions about war, fighting, or terrorism should be evaluated by a

qualified mental health professional. It is most important to reassure children that their feelings of loss, anger, frustration, and grief are natural. Normalizing common reactions to separation may help the child realize that she is responding appropriately to this major event.

Inspiring children to just "be kids"! Many military children experience anxiety and stress at extreme levels in ways that most civilian children don't, worrying about the safety of a parent on deployment or the trauma that has changed the parent post-deployment. Military kids might feel like they need permission to take a break from worrying. Encourage them to join into activities that might allow them to forget about their family's situations and enjoy themselves. Normal activities like grocery shopping and doing homework and household chores can help to bring a calming sense of predictability to their day. Extracurricular activities are great ways to stay active. Teachers can introduce parents to resources that help pay for after-school activities for military kids. Staying busy and active is helpful and healthy for children who are coping with their parent's deployment, as it allows for more distraction and less time to perseverate on the potential for traumatic events.

Help the child cope with a non-deployed parent who may be suffering from a type of secondary PTSD or may be emotionally unavailable to the child. The transition of the household once the deployed parent returns may not be how children (or the adults) expect it to be; it likely won't return immediately to how "things once were." Some of the following can help a child whose *parent* is struggling with a common post-deployment mental health issue like PTSD or depression:

- knowledge that the parent(s) is ill and the child is not to blame

- help and support from other family members

- a stable or predictable home environment

- psychotherapy for the child or the parent(s), or both

- a sense of being loved by the ill parent

- building positive self-esteem

- teaching healthy coping skills

- friendships, positive peer relationships

- finding areas of interest and success at school

- healthy interests outside the home for the child

- help from outside the family to improve the family environment (e.g., marital psychotherapy or parenting classes)

National Organizations That Offer Support

With the broadening knowledge of the need for supporting military families, programs are being developed on national, state, and local levels. The resource guide from Military Pathways (militarymentalhealth.org) provides a variety of options to support children and family members through whatever phase of life they are in.

Some other national programs of importance to note are as follows:

Military Kids Connect: Educators (www. militarykidsconnect.org/educators) offers a wealth of information and support for teachers, administrators, and counselors. This illuminating site offers insights on the military culture and ways to help children and students cope with issues in their lives in their own words and from professionals. The site also includes a number of lesson plans for all age levels to integrate aspects of their lives with current classroom curriculum.

The home base for **Military Kids Connect** (www.militarykidsconnect.org) is full of information that is geared directly to military kids of all ages in age-appropriate sections (Kids, 'Tweens, and Teens). This website features blogs, activities, and videos that allow military children to become part of a larger national community of kids who are experiencing similar issues. This type of connection should be encouraged because it may help to eliminate the sense of solitude and isolation that a child might feel. Military kids can relate best with one another, and this website allows them to be part of an interactive experience. Teachers and other professionals might find this especially useful for the older, more independent, and more technically savvy children.

Since 2005, **Operation: Military Kids** has been an effort by the U.S. Army to reach out to and collaborate with local communities to help support their children. The program works with local 4-H Clubs and the Boys and Girls Clubs to create opportunities for military children to meet other kids like them. These clubs arrange recreational, social, and educational clinics and camps that foster connections among communities and military children, but also help them develop leadership and organizational skills.

The **National Military Family Association** has developed three programs under **Operation Purple** that help to support military families through different phases of life. Operation Purple Camp is a summer camp for all military children to create a memorable and unique experience in a supportive environment. Operation Purple Family Retreats support the military family in post-deployment by offering an opportunity to reconnect as a family unit. Operation Purple: Healing Adventures is a retreat program for families with a service member who has suffered a traumatic injury. These retreats offer family-focused activities and use specially adapted communication programs to help heal connections in fun ways.

The YMCA of America offers a program called **Y: Military Outreach** that helps to provide memberships to military families. Getting involved and active in programs offered by the Y can help children maintain a sense of normalcy and predictability and, of course, enjoy what is great about childhood. The Military Outreach program also offers respite care for the remaining spouse during a deployment. This is helpful to the mental health for this parent who may use the time to go to appointments, run errands, or just take a much-needed break.

For younger children, *Sesame Street* has developed a program called **Talk, Listen, Connect!**, a series of videos, workbooks, and storybooks for young children who have a parent in the military. The program guides children through tough transitions like deployments, combat-related injuries, and even death by showing how real families (and monster families) deal with these types of issues. Studying children following the program, Russell Research (2006) found that "preschoolers exhibited fewer negative behaviors, such as being demanding and impatient, as a result of the materials, and parents themselves felt significantly less 'down, depressed, or hopeless.'" Approximately 71% of caregivers indicated that the *Sesame Street* materials helped their child cope with an injured family member (Russell Research, 2006). The Center for the Study of Traumatic Stress (2011) found that 83% of caregivers using the *Sesame Street* "When Families Grieve" materials feel they now "have more appropriate language to better discuss death with my child."

For child care providers, the following resources may be helpful:

- Honoring Our Babies and Toddlers: Guidebook for Care Professionals (www.zerotothree.org/about-us/funded-projects/military-families/hbt-2.pdf)
- Community-Based Child Care for Military Families (www.naccrra.org/)

For families:

- Deployment: Keeping Relationships Strong (focused on infants and toddlers; http://main.zerotothree.org/site/DocServer/DEPLOYMENT__OPE_2_.pdf?docID+5822)
- Deployment and Children (www.healthychildren.org/English/healthy-living/emotional-wellness/Pages/Deployment-and-Children.aspx)
- Babies on the Homefront (for families with infants and toddlers; http://babiesonthehomefront.org)

Chapter Summary

This chapter has focused on understanding some key issues and challenges that affect infants and toddlers and preschool-aged and older children of military families; understanding some of the joys and mental health challenges that families face when the deployed family members return home from military service; and understanding some protective and supportive strategies that physicians, child caregivers, nurses, educators, and other professionals can use to help these children; and their families with deployment, homecoming, and the loss of relatives and friends (in the event of death). Resources and websites are included at the conclusion of the chapter. Resources and websites are included at the end of this chapter in the References.

Key Points to Remember

- Recent studies increasingly indicate not only that service members need higher levels of support, but also that their spouses and children are at risk for mental health issues such as depression and anxiety.

- The culture of the military is one of transition, with frequent potential for trauma. A military career affects the entire family, often creating circumstances of high stress, depression, and anxiety for both adults and children. Sometimes the realities of adulthood may encroach on the joys of childhood.

- Strategies for supporting families and children need to vary by age and need to be accessible to non-deployed family members. At the same time, efforts need to be available to maintain connections between deployed family members and their partners and spouses and their children.

- The reentry and "homecoming" phase for the deployed family member requires as much attention and support for the entire family as does the phase of deployment(s).

- Infants, toddlers, and preschool children in military families experience mental health problems. More research needs to be focused on these younger populations and their families

Implications for Families and Professionals

The emotional health of the remaining-at-home parent during a deployment is closely linked to the mental health of the child. Fortunately for future military families, more services and supports are being developed in an effort to decrease the number of mental health issues before they arise.

Professionals must understand the issues that military children face and the ways that problems may manifest in the lives of children. Teachers and often other school-based professionals are adults who spend much of a child's day with them; a trusting relationship is important to establish with any student, but is especially needed with a military child. A child who has a deployed parent may require additional effort, attention, empathy, and understanding. Teachers may be some of the only adults with whom a child comes into contact regularly during their day, and children will find comfort knowing that their teachers hear and support them. Going the extra mile to help a child write a letter to a deployed parent or simply just asking "How are things going?" *may be beyond meaningful.* The outreach programs that are now being created for military children help to address and cope with the many related issues and can be extremely helpful toward additional support a child or older and their family.

By creating an open, honest, supportive and predictable environment, we can help address a child's fears and concerns, and reduce the risk of lasting emotional consequences (Fassler, 2013).

References

Alvarez, L. (2008, July 8). *Home from the war, many veterans battle substance abuse.* Retrieved from www.nytimes.com/2008/07/08/world/americas/08iht-vets.1.14322423.html?pagewanted=all&_r=0

American Psychological Association Presidential Task Force on Military Deployment Services for Youth Families and Service Members. (2007). *The psychological needs of U.S. military service members and their families: A preliminary report.* Washington, DC: Author.

Blum, R. (2013). *Q and A: Meeting the military child's needs.* Retrieved from www.aasa.org/content.aspx?id=9554

Canon, G. (2011). Military children face greater academic challenges due to relocation and emotional stress. *Huffington Post.* Retrieved from www.huffingtonpost.com/2011/04/12/military-children-education_n_847537.html

Center for the Study of Traumatic Stress. (2011). *Preliminary findings from the Talk, Listen, Connect III: When families grieve kit evaluation.* Uniformed Services University.

Chandra, A., Lara-Cinisomo, S., Jaycox, L. H., Tanielian, T., Burns, R. M., Ruder, T., & Han, B. (2010). Children on the homefront: The experience of children from military families. *Pediatrics, 125*(1), 16–25.

PART **4**

Cherry, K. (2013). *Erikson's theory of psychosocial development: Psychosocial development in infancy and early childhood.* Retrieved from http://psychology.about.com/od/psychosocialtheories/a/psychosocial.htm

Cozza, S. J., & Lieberman, A. F. (2007). The young military child: Our modern Telemachus. *Zero to Three, 27,* 27–33. Retrieved from http://main.zerotothree.org/org/site/PageServer?pagename=ter_key_military_journal_ article

Ensher, G. L., & Clark, D. A. (2016). Social-emotional development, families, and mental health needs in the earliest years. In G. L. Ensher & D. A. Clark (Eds.), *The early years: Foundations for best practice with special children and their families* (pp. 49–71). Washington, DC: ZERO TO THREE.

eXtention.org. (2012, May 1). *How child care providers can help deployed parents and their children stay connected.* Retrieved from www.extension.org/pages/61674/how-child-care-providers-can-help-deployed-parents-and-their-children-stay-connected#.VfQtIJc6yh5

Fassler, D. (2013). *Children in military families: Tips for parents and teachers.* Retrieved from www.incharge.org/military-money/story/children-in-military-families-tips-for-parents-and-teachers

Flake, E. M., Davis, B. E., Johnson, P. L., & Middleton, L. S. (2009). The psychosocial effects of deployment on military children. *Journal of Developmental & Behavioral Pediatrics. 30*(4), 271–278.

Gibbs, D. A., Martin, S. L., Kupper, L. L., & Johnson, R. E. (2007). Child maltreatment in enlisted soldiers' families during combat-related deployments. *Journal of the American Medical Association, 298*(5), 528–535.

Hefling, K. (2009). More military children seeking mental care. *Marine Corps Times.* Springfield, VA: Army Times Publishing Company.

Hefling, K. (2013). Military parents embrace homeschooling. *The Washington Times.* Retrieved from www.washingtontimes.com/news/2013/oct/26/military-parents-embrace-homeschooling

Hoffner, C., & Haefner, M. J., (1994). Children's news interest during the Gulf War: The role of negative effects. *Journal of Broadcasting & Electronic Media 38*(2), 193–204.

Huebner, A., Mancini, J., Wilcox, R., Grass, S., & Grass, G. (2007). Parental deployment and youth in military families: Exploring uncertainty and ambiguous loss. *Family Relations, 56*(2), 112–122.

Ingersoll, G. M., Scamman, J. P., & Eckerling, W. D. (1989). Geographic mobility and student achievement in an urban setting. *Educational Evaluation and Policy Analysis, 11*(2), 143–149.

Lieberman, A. F., & Van Horn, P. (2013). Infants and young children in military families: A conceptual model for intervention. *Clinical Child Family Psychology Review, 16,* 282–293.

Militarychild.org. (2015). *Student identifier: Military child attending school? And how are they doing?* Retrieved from www.militarychild.org/student-identifier

Military OneSource. (n.d.). *The New Parent Support Program.* Retrieved from www.militaryonesource.mil/parenting?content_id=266691

National Child Traumatic Stress Network. (2008). *Traumatic grief in military children: Information for educators.* Los Angeles, CA: National Center for Child Traumatic Stress.

Orthner, D. K., & Rose, R. (2005). *SAF V Survey report: Adjustment of army children to deployment separations.* Chapel Hill, NC: University of North Carolina at Chapel Hill. Retrieved from www.afrmy.mil/fmwrc/docs/saf5childreportoct05.pdf

Public Schools of North Carolina, State Board of Education. (2013). *How deployment affects families.* Retrieved from www.dpi.state.nc.us/militarysupport/deployment/affect

Ruff, S. B., & Keim, M. A. (2014, April). Revolving doors: The impact of multiple school transitions on military children. *The Professional Counselor.* Retrieved from http://tpcjournal.nbcc.org/revolving-doors-the-impact-of-multiple-school-transitions-on-military-children

Russell Research. (2006). *Findings from the* Talk, Listen, Connect *kit evaluation.* East Rutherford, NJ: Author.

Siegel, B. S., Davis, B. E., Committee on Psychosocial Aspects of Child, & Family Health and Section on Uniformed Services. (2013). Health and mental health needs of children in U.S. military families. *Pediatrics, 131*(6), e2002–e2015.

Sheppard, S. C., Malatras, J. W., & Israel, A. C. (2010). The impact of deployment on U.S. military families. *American Psychologist, 65*(6) 599–609.

Sogomonyan, F., & Cooper J. L. (2010). *Trauma faced by children of military families: What every policymaker should know.* Retrieved from Columbia University Academic Commons, http://hdl.handle.net/10022/AC:P:8857

Tanielian, T., & Jaycox, L. (Eds.). (2008). *Invisible wounds of war: Psychological and cognitive injuries, their consequences, and services to assist recovery.* Santa Monica, CA: RAND Corporation.

Washington Post. (2013). *Faces of the fallen.* Retrieved from http://apps.washingtonpost.com/national/fallen

Williams, R. F. (2009). War's silent stress: Healing the military family. *SitRep.* Retrieved from GlobalSecurity. org

Wood, D., Halton, N., Scarlata, D., Newacheck, P., & Nessim, S. (1993). Impact of family relocation on children's growth, development, school function, and behavior. *Journal of the American Medical Association, 270,* 1334 –1338.

ZERO TO THREE. (n.d.). *Honoring our babies and toddlers: A guide for caring professionals—coming together around military families.* Retrieved from www.zerotothree.org/military-families/docs/veteran-families-resources.html

CHAPTER 16

Working With Families in Hospital Settings

Melissa M. Doyle

Highlights of the Chapter

At the conclusion of the chapter, the reader will:

- recognize the stress and strain a hospitalization places on both the child and the family

- understand the implications of hospitalization for the development of parenting identity

- identify strategies hospital staff and community providers can utilize to bridge the gaps in services

- Identify how effective discharge planning and community support services including early intervention (EI) and the pediatric medical home can be implemented effectively

Kelly hesitates at the doorway of the nursery, appearing uncertain about what to do, anxiously looking around the room. Her eyes are drawn to the infant somewhat concealed behind equipment, but then dart around to the various pieces of equipment in the room. She hears the low hum of the motor of a nearby machine, sees numbers

that flash on different screens, the staff members who move in and out of the room. She is unable to hear what they murmur to each other, then sees them check a machine, pause in front of her baby, now writing on some paper at the end of the machine, but also clicking furiously through a laptop also in the room. Thoughts rapidly progress through Kelly's mind: "Is that about my baby? . . . What do those machines mean? . . . Are those numbers good or bad?" she wonders, as she hesitates in the doorway. It's unclear where she can stand or how she can be here out of the way of the staff, the machines, yet be near enough to see her baby's face.

Meanwhile, in another part of the nursery, another mom, Sarah, walks quickly into the room with her infant, standing right in front of the isolette. Her presence also appears to go unnoticed by the staff, who are engaged in similar activities such as quiet talking, checking machines, writing, and adjusting the machines. Sarah looks around when yet another staff member enters, and asks "What is that and what does it do," pointing to some wiring attached to the baby. The staff member indicates they will be over in a moment to talk with her. Sarah, frustrated, narrows her eyes, but turns back to the baby, placing her hands on the clear container. Her two hands cover the entire expanse of the infant's body, almost as though Sarah were seeking a way of holding, connecting with, and protecting her child.

The experience of having a child in the neonatal intensive care unit (NICU) has universal implications for parents—the sense of uncertainty and helplessness—that supersedes cultural, economic, and educational boundaries. In the above vignette, both women are united in their experience of sadness, frustration, and angst yet could not be more different in every other way. Kelly, a 39-year-old married attorney with a thriving downtown practice who has a nursery already prepared in her home, is across the hall from Sarah, an unmarried 15-year-old girl, whose high school education has been paused while she and her infant will share her childhood bedroom and learn how to grow up together. Despite age, background, and cultural differences, all parents will have similar emotions as they navigate the uncertainty of the NICU experience.

Parenting poses new challenges for a family system as it grows and adapts when a child is added to an already established system. Regardless of the family configuration, people have embedded cultural views of how the "ideal parent" behaves, despite any stress that they may be experiencing. In a supportive and nurturing environment, it is possible to have a parallel developmental process; as the newborn begins to grow, adapt, and change, so too do parents as they develop this new identity for themselves. However, medical complications at birth leading to extensive or repeated hospitalizations can hinder or even interrupt this process.

Cleveland's 2008 review of the literature identified six primary needs for families of infants hospitalized in a NICU: accurate information and involvement in care and decision making, the ability to watch over and

protect the infant, parent–child physical contact, feeling positively perceived by the nursing staff, believing their child received individualized care and reassurance, and partnership with the nursing staff. The need for accurate information and a desire to be involved in the child's care may best be understood in the context of what parents anticipate should happen after a child is born. They likely expect the arrival of a healthy infant, a short hospitalization, and a discharge to their home with the comfort and support of a network of extended family and friends. Hospitalization in a NICU is often overwhelming for new parents and requires the acquisition of new information and development of new skills. Here, both the parent and child are placed in an unfamiliar environment, severely restricting the parents' roles as caregivers and providers for their child and inundating them with information and decisions that they often have no background or training to understand. All of these challenges occur in a very public setting, frequently leaving parents feeling vulnerable and inadequate. Wigert, Johansson, Berg, and Hellstrom (2006) noted mothers' perceptions that they were intruding in the care of their infants in the NICU, often feeling excluded from decision making. These feelings were noted in some cases to persist for several years following discharge, impacting a parent's sense of autonomy and efficacy, and the parent–child relationship (Wigert et al., 2006). The need for vigilance may best be understood in the context of trauma; admission to the NICU is not the normal course postdelivery, and it may be rightly viewed as an attack on the parent and family unit. Physical contact, which is impeded by extensive medical care and hospitalization (Cleveland, 2008), is a critical mechanism for a parent to bond with her infant immediately after birth and in the days following. In most cultures, families and friends surround a new mother and the family, providing education and support in an environment of love and care. In contrast, the primary support network for parents of hospitalized infants are the nursing staff, who may be perceived as having more knowledge than the parent, and control access and information about the infant. Cleveland's 2008 comprehensive literature review reported parental perception of an adversarial relationship with the nursing staff who were viewed as withholding access to the child, holding information about medical care, and supervising all contact between mother and child. This behavior—whether real or imagined—diminishes the parent's confidence with developing both their parental skills and the bond between them and their child.

Developmentally Appropriate Practices With Families

Ideally, the NICU staff recognizes the challenge that the environment and medical complications place on the development of a parent–child bond and on a parent's sense of competence. Cleveland (2008) identified four staff behaviors positively viewed by parents. These include emotional support, parent empowerment, welcoming environment in the NICU with inclusive policies, and parent education with opportunities to practice parenting skills. Staff response can promote a critical, parallel developmental process; as the nursing staff welcome, engage, educate, and include the parent as a partner in their child's care, the parent is then able to welcome, engage, and connect with his child. The nursing and other hospital staff can function in a role typically assigned to close family and friends, and assist with the development of a parent's sense of competence. Positive parent–child interactions and, specifically, parent responsiveness to their child that develop early in the infant's life have been correlated with

the parent's ability to adjust to the individual needs and characteristics of the child over time (Guralnick, 2013). These interactive moments may consist of simple encounters, moments of teaching new skills, and opportunities to emotionally connect that reinforce, for both adult and child, that this is a "mutually responsive" relationship where each can have expectations for meeting emotional needs (Guralnick, 2013). In particular, Guralnick noted that "high quality parental-sensitive responsiveness occurring during parent–child interactions represents an awareness of their child's interest, skills and abilities as well as their emotional and motivation state" (p. 354). Although this is important for all children, a parent's ability to recognize the specific needs of his preterm infant has a critical impact on the child's ability to achieve developmental milestones. Other interventions associated with increasing parental empowerment noted by Cleveland (2008) include increasing the parent's familiarity with the NICU through a prenatal visit, one-on-one orientation shortly after admission, high levels of parental involvement in care and decision making, implementing discharge planning procedures that involve parental training and ongoing contact with the infant, and emphasizing the role of the parent as primary caregiver and the nurse and other staff as facilitating that process.

Issues can emerge when infants and young children are hospitalized at any point in development. Although these families may have already established groundwork toward developing a parenting identity, a hospitalization—whether for an urgent need or as part of management of a chronic medical condition—strips parents of their role. Parents have reported feelings of fear and helplessness, increased stress, and difficulty establishing their role as the decision makers (Jackson, et al., 2007).

PART 4

Developing Parental Identity

The literature suggests that parental identity is highly influenced by role congruence, or the ability to act in accordance with the expectations of that role. Parents of hospitalized children are unable to fully complete tasks that are considered typical for their caregiving roles, and the NICU environment that provides alternative caregivers for a child whose needs cannot be met by the parent does not support or validate their importance to the child (Cast, 2004). *Maternal role attainment* (MRA) describes the process through which mothers develop a maternal identity which is aided by an internal belief that she is acting in a motherly role and by engaging in tasks and activities that are culturally consistent with "mothering" (Shandor Miles, Holditch-Davis, Burchinal, & Brunssen, 2011). MRA in the context of a medically fragile or hospitalized child may be delayed because of the mother's inability to provide care and comfort or to gain physical proximity, either due to medical equipment surrounding the infant, the fragility of the infant's condition, or the struggle the parent may have to be in the hospital at the bedside. Shandor Miles and colleagues (2011) have explored the impact that a chronically ill or medically fragile infant may have on the development of MRA. These authors suggest that the identity of "mothering" includes three factors: *maternal identity*, or the internal sense or perception of one as a mother; *maternal competence,* the quality of the mother's interactions with her child; and *maternal presence*, defined by the amount of care or ability to be physically close to her child. Mothers recalled that their worrying about their fragile and hospitalized infants and challenges to their parental role had a much greater impact on their development of MRA than did the severity of the infant's condition or length of time children were hospitalized (Shandor Miles et al., 2011). Mothers of critically ill infants were noted to have lower reports of maternal identity, which could be related to their inability to provide care or be physically close to their infants, in addition to the parent potentially guarding against the possibility the infant may not survive the hospitalization. Mothers' sense of their competence also was correlated with infant alertness, suggesting that infants who were more medically fragile were allowed to have less "hands-on" care.

The use of role models during pregnancy and after birth was a factor cited by Singer et al. (2003) as a component of the development of maternal identity. Mothers learn the behaviors associated with their role and cultural expectations for performing that role, and they received support from other new moms when they felt overwhelmed and incompetent. Although there are many new moms in the neonatal ICU and inpatient floors, often parents are unable to connect due to differences in treatment and outcome as well as to the overwhelming stress that impedes reliance on connecting and communicating with others as a support. It is critical for health care providers to understand the correlation between a mother developing a maternal identity and engaging in the care of her child. Hospitalization can derail this process, and efforts must be made by the health care staff to support the role of mothering and provide opportunities to develop this identity (Nelson, 2003).

The impact of hospitalization on the father's role is less well understood and has received less focus in the literature. This may be because, culturally, mothers are more frequently responsible for the primary care of an infant. The role of fathers, even accounting for cultural variability, tends to focus less on direct care for the child and less time at the bedside and more on outside responsibilities such as returning to work or handling paperwork. It is possible that a less direct role is protective in some way for fathers, because it distracts them from the day-to-day bedside routine yet they may still feel that they are offering a concrete contribution to the family function and well-being. Regardless, understanding the impact hospitalization has on fathers is an area for further study.

An Ecological View of Development

To accurately understand the various factors that complicate development of a parenting identity in the NICU environment, it is useful to take an ecological view. Urie Bronfenbrenner conceptualized a model that reflects the individual interacting within a multilayered, dynamic system that promotes growth and learning, leading to identity development (Swick & Williams, 2006). This view connects the most immediate physical, social, and psychological interactions of the individual with the extended system surrounding the individual and her family, all of which exist under the umbrella of cultural beliefs, social mores, and community norms. Bronfenbrenner (1979) further suggested the need to recognize the characteristics of the individual, the time in development, and the environment in which each had a significant impact on an individual's reaction and adaptation to certain events. This particular view is helpful in considering how new parents, needing to develop an identity consistent with their new role, are significantly impacted by the hospital environment during the stress of their child's diagnosis or illness.

The anticipated developmental course for new parents likely involves elements of the following fantasy: Following the quick and painless birth of their child, the family spends a restful interlude in a peaceful obstetrics unit, greeting family members and opening gifts, and eventually returns to their home with a new family to begin their lives. This fantasy rarely exists when a child has an uneventful birth and hospital course, but it is very different when an infant requires extended hospitalization or needs to be hospitalized for medical care. An ecological lens first looks to the immediate connections, or microsystem, to aid in the process of growth. The microsystem for a new family consists of support from friends and family in their own home as they learn about infant care, adjust to the needs of a newborn and adapt their home to provide for an infant. In these instances, the exosystem also serves as a support, with time off from work, neighbors bringing over meals, and the community offering signs of welcome. It is within this supportive cocoon that new parents develop a sense of competence and an ability to engage in physical and emotional tasks required as part of parenting. Mistakes will be made by a new parent, but these can quickly and quietly be modified without significant shame or public exposure for the parent or lasting injury to the child.

A parent whose child is ill or hospitalized does not have the benefit of the care of an extended family network, privacy for growing and learning, and a known and comforting environment within which to develop their identity as a parent. For these parents, their new physical environment now includes an ICU, a vocabulary filled with complicated terms or confusing acronyms, busy and rapidly changing staff, and beeping and unfamiliar machines. The most consistent interpersonal relationship may be with the bedside nurse, whose connection with the parent will be the most decisive factor in how the parent develops and connects with their child. In this case, the exosystem is the extended system that the parents are engaged with, such as the employer who may offer extended time off for an extensive hospitalization. The hospitalized infant and their parent will have to adapt to an exosystem of other care providers, hospital staff, policies for health insurance, and other less personal systems. The macrosystem in a typical new parent's world may be the roles and values suggested by their religious faith, their culture, and extended community supports. The macrosystem of

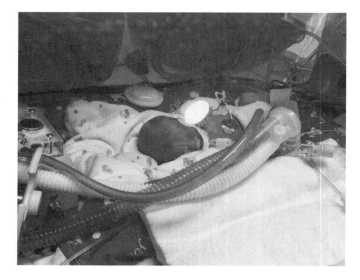

the hospital has its own culture, hierarchy, and norms, and presents very clear views about parenting ideals and behavior, which are fairly rigid irrespective of cultural values and norms.

A bio-ecological view strongly suggests the critical influence of relationships and supports within the hospitalized setting that function in place of the normative ecological system the parent with a hospitalized infant is isolated from. Socioeconomic stresses and limited financial resources, factors associated with pre-term birth, contribute to a significantly strained exosystem. The hospital can become a macrosystem of needed resources for these families (Guralnick, 2013).

Strategies Used by Hospitals

Hospitalized care that is more developmentally based can be traced to the implementation of the Newborn Individualized Developmental Care and Assessment Program. This evidence-based approach provides formal training for NICU staff and guidelines for the entire multidisciplinary team on the provision of care that will enhance the infant's neurodevelopmental growth. The program recognized the need for the premature brain to have a more sensory-friendly and less stimulating environment in which to promote growth and development of critical

skills including self-regulation. These guidelines also recognize the important role played by the parents and the need to incorporate them as full partners in the care team.

The recognition of the significant impact of hospitalization on the family has led to the addition of several support roles in the NICU. Most hospitals have social work staff assigned to the NICU. Social workers are trained to conduct clinical assessments of family members to determine the impact of stress and provide support to improve coping. In addition, social workers are able to assist families with understanding the hospital system, facilitating communication with various medical providers, and providing information about resources available in the hospital and community. A *child life specialist*, a role that is unique to inpatient hospitals, is trained to recognize the impact of hospitalization on growth and development. In the NICU, the child life specialist is able to work with parents on interventions for their infants as well as assist siblings with understanding the infant's medical complications and needs.

There are also many community groups on local, regional, and national levels that have developed programs to assist and support families with children hospitalized in the NICU. One well-known example is the March of Dimes, an organization that for several decades has been working to raise awareness of factors that contribute to healthy pregnancies and provide support for mothers who have infants born preterm or with complications. The March of Dimes also funds the NICU family support program in many hospitals, which provides information and assistance to families who have children hospitalized in the NICU. These programs vary in level of service; in some hospitals there may be literature and community support available, others may have a mom of a preterm infant available to visit or call new families, and still other programs have a March of Dimes support staff member who may be on staff and available as another professional resource.

Discharge to home for all patients is a process that ideally begins on the day of admission and continues with varying attention and energy throughout the course of the hospital stay. Many families eagerly anticipate the return to a more comfortable and familiar environment, underestimating the stress of having a preterm child who may have extensive care needs for which they are now exclusively responsible. This stress may result in earlier risk factors or vulnerabilities in the individual parents or in the family system that emerge later (Guralnick, 2013). Although practices and procedures vary among programs, most include a combination of bedside teaching, handouts, and videos or demonstrations. Discharge teaching is a greater priority when the patient is a young child who, due to age or medical condition, is more medically fragile and may require more care and oversight once home. The parent's ability to engage in teaching must first be ascertained; the shock of the hospitalization and ongoing fears and concerns about the child's status may compromise the parent's ability to engage in the teaching process or understand the teaching that is being offered. Discharge teaching is often completed by bedside nurses in the days leading up to discharge or may be done in larger groups prior to discharge, but it does require that parents are available, which may be complicated by work schedules, care of other young children, poor transportation, and other factors. Bedside teaching by the nursing staff has been noted as the most effective preparation for discharge, particularly when the nursing staff can be empathic, good listeners, promote confidence, and choose a time to teach when the parents feel ready (Sneath, 2009). Often when parents are not as available, the staff may assume that they are not interested or have emotionally distanced themselves from the child. However, some parents, particularly teens and older mothers, tend to skip discharge teaching, believing that hospitals view them as nontraditional parents and are not as supportive of them (Schlittenhart, Smart, Miller, & Severtson, 2011). In response, some programs have developed more flexible discharge-teaching strategies, such as the use of DVDs or other electronic media that can be accessed in a more flexible manner, and in a modality with which teens are quite familiar. This approach may allow the parent to feel less dependent on the nursing staff as the source of information, thus resulting in a decreased sense of dependence and increased sense of efficacy. Incorporating discharge teaching as an ongoing process, starting at the time of admission, further emphasizes the importance the family plays in the child's life and provides the parents with knowledge and skill they will need when dealing with their child. Despite all the teaching, discussion, and planning that is involved in discharge, Sneath (2009) found that most parents were surprised when the day arrived, because they continued to be concerned that their infant might die, and they feared bringing home a medically fragile child. In a review of the literature on discharge teaching for NICU families, parental preparedness was increased when a focus was placed on building parent confidence, increasing coping skills, setting realistic expectations for the parent and child, and facilitating connections with community resources, while providing direct teaching and experiential learning (Sneath, 2009).

Shandor Miles and colleagues (2011) strongly urged the involvement of mothers in caregiving at the bedside and the development of strategies to connect those mothers to their infant when they cannot be at the bedside, such as phone calls with the nursing staff to be updated on progress, taping their voice telling a story to be played for the child, and pictures at the bedside.

Swick and Williams (2006) suggested three approaches hospital staff should take when working with families undergoing significant stress.

These include viewing the stress from the family perspective, or ensuring that hospital staff continue to gain insight concerning the family perception of the hospitalization. Second, it is important to partner with the parent and family in "exploring" ways to help them address these stressors. This approach emphasizes the need to individualize care and interventions. Finally, staff need to implement interventions that empower the family. Examples may include encouraging the parent to participate in care and discussions regarding medical treatment, connecting the family with other support services in the hospital and other families experiencing a hospitalization, and identifying discharge needs and supports early in the hospitalization.

Early Intervention Services

One of the major components of any discharge plan are the community-based services for which the infant and family qualify. Many infants who are discharged from the NICU are eligible for services, either as a result of a disability or medical condition or because of the impact that extreme prematurity has on the development of all physical systems, neurobehavioral concerns, and other developmental impingements. Research has shown that the infant brain is still growing and developing, and exposure to therapeutic interventions, particularly those conducted in the natural environment of the child's home, incorporating "experientially based environmental influences" can facilitate neural development and lead to improvements in social, cognitive, and motor functioning (Guralnick, 2013). Further, Guralnick (2013) noted that developmental research has supported programs with a coregulatory model, according to which direct services are aimed at improving a child's cognitive, social, and motor deficits while staff assist

parents and other caregivers to learn and adjust to the developmental needs of the infant.

The discharge process of preterm infants requires a significant amount of coordination between the inpatient hospital staff and community providers to ensure that the family and child have the resources and services they need. Although this process varies across institutions, there has been considerable recent interest in determining a "best practice" approach to the NICU discharge process. Sims, Jacob, Mills, Fett, and Novak (2006) suggested several strategies and approaches to enhance support for the child and family after discharge, including planned follow-up appointments to assure that all durable medical equipment are ordered and available in the home. One of the most well known of these programs is Early Intervention (EI), which was established by Congress in 1986 to offer therapeutic services for infants and children who have been diagnosed with a developmental delay or disability. Based on diagnosis, the infant or child may be eligible for a range of therapies and programs, including physical, occupational, speech, special education (teacher) services or other adaptive or communication resources. EI services are coordinated by the local counties. Each family is assigned a family service coordinator who provides a written plan for services with specific goals and objectives that are addressed by the therapists and itinerant teachers. EI services can remain in place for as long as the infant demonstrates a developmental delay, or until the child transitions to a preschool program. When the child is approaching her third birthday, county providers coordinate with the local school district to take over all assessment and service provision. Parameters for services are more defined for the school system; that is, the child's disability must impact her ability to learn in the classroom, which can limit some of the services for which the young child is eligible.

Family-Centered Medical Home

Recognizing that gaps in the health care system have left vulnerable populations at risk, the American Academy of Family Physicians, the American Academy of Pediatrics, and the American College of Physicians and the American Osteopathic Association developed the Joint Principles of the Patient-Centered Medical Home (PCMH; Green, Wendland, Carver, Hughes, & Seong, 2012). PCMH was conceptualized as team-based health care, intended to provide cost-effective and coordinated health care primarily focused on serving all patients with chronic health care conditions—a population that is steadily rising and increasingly living in their own homes in the community. Successful medical home programs should consist of family-oriented, comprehensive, coordinated, compassionate, and culturally sensitive care that is accessible to the family (Guralnick, 2013). Regulation of standards for PCMH are governed by the National Committee for Quality Assurance, which is moving primary care providers away from the concept of volume-driven care, where primary care providers are reimbursed for the quantity of patients evaluated and treated face-to-face by the medical provider. Under PCMH, the care team includes everyone in the office from the receptionist who initially speaks with the family to the nursing team who evaluates the patient's need, care coordinators who assess the family system and the community supports available, and the physician who directs the care process. Patients with chronic health conditions are identified by the practice, with both acute as well as long-term goals, to improve overall compliance with health maintenance tasks and provide education about disease conditions and follow-up (Green et al., 2012). The National Committee for Quality Assurance requires implementation of an "electronic medical record" to enhance tracking of patients with chronic conditions, to increase communication between primary and specialty care providers, and to document efforts to promote education and health care behaviors.

Initial parental reaction has largely been positive, qualitative reports indicating that parents are willing to wait longer for preventative care in order to have services such as same-day sick appointments and 24-hour phone support (Zickafoose, DeCamp, Sambuco, & Prosser, 2013). At the same time, it is important to educate parents about the costs of the medical home and what services or resources are not available. PCMH has a number of challenges in that developing a large-scale coordinated and integrated system of care historically has been a struggle. Outcome studies have yet to be conducted, and further research will need to determine if this approach can provide a better system of care, be sensitive to individual family needs, and lead to cost-effective health care outcomes.

Chapter Summary

Parental identity can be viewed as a developmental process that parallels infant growth. Absent the expected resources provided by extended family, religious institutions, and community programs, hospitals must provide these supports to new parents of babies in the NICU. Promoting parental involvement in care and decision making requires a cultural shift for hospitals. Many programs, influenced by the Newborn Individualized Developmental Care and Assessment Program and community programs such as the March of Dimes, have developed a growing awareness of the struggle for parents of hospitalized children. As a result, hospitals have added training for medical staff and team members such as social workers and child life specialists and challenged them to incorporate parents as members of the care team. This shift has supported the development of parental identity, a critical role for parents as they move toward the discharge process and engage in various EI and other community supports to continue to facilitate optimal development of their child.

Key Points to Remember

- Extended or repeated hospitalizations may impede both the child's achievement of developmental milestones and the parent's development of an identity as primary caregiver.

- Viewing staff and parent interactions as a partnership establishes the most ideal circumstances to promote successful care for the infant.

- Extended hospitalizations remove parents from known and established familial and community supports and parental role models. The NICU staff and environment can function as a substitute community and support network for parents.

- Extended hospitalizations place significant economic and emotional burdens on families that often impact their ability to remain at the child's bedside frequently or consistently.

- Community supports and services such as EI play critical roles in facilitating a smooth transition from hospital to home.

- The patient-centered medical home (PCMH) holds promise as a bridge for families when transitioning between the hospital and community.

Implications for Families and Professionals

The NICU environment can be overwhelming, even for experienced parents. Parents and caregivers need to be patient with themselves as they adjust.

- The NICU staff is available and interested in providing families with information and education about their child, their diagnosis, and care.

- Parents will be given a lot of information from many different sources. It can be helpful to write down as much as possible, ask lots of questions, and remember that parents play a critical, essential role in their child's health. There are members of the health care team who can assist parents with any difficulties or challenges with obtaining resources and with preparing for the transition to home.

- Each member of the medical team in the nursery should be challenged to recognize his unique role with assisting moms and dads with gaining confidence and skills as parents.

- Parents may need the staff to remind them of the importance they play in their child's care, even when their baby or young child is hospitalized. Parents should be encouraged to visit their child as often as they can, ask questions about unfamiliar terms and procedures, and participate in care.

- Even experienced parents are likely to struggle when their child is hospitalized. Involving parents in providing physical care for their child, being included in medical decisions, and providing reassurance and support are strategies that result in a partnership between staff and parents that is critical, in both the short and long terms. This partnership between parents and NICU staff aids the discharge planning process and is the best indicator of a successful transition to home for the new family.

- NICU staff must reach out to parents who visit sporadically, because they may be struggling with socioeconomic or adjustment issues that may need to be further investigated or addressed.

References

Bronfenbrenner, U. (1979). *The ecology of human development: Experiments by nature and design.* Cambridge, MA: Harvard University Press.

Cast, A. D. (2004). Well-being and the transition to parenthood: An identity theory approach. *Sociological Perspectives, 47*(1), 55–78.

Cleveland, L. M. (2008). Parenting in the neonatal intensive care unit. *Journal of Obstetric, Gynecologic & Neonatal Nursing, 37*(6), 666–691.

Green, E. P., Wendland, J., Carver, M. C., Hughes R. C., & Seong, K. M. (2012). Lessons learned from implementing the patient-centered medical home. *International Journal of Telemedicine and Applications.* Retrieved from www.ncbi.nlm.higgov/PMC3437280

Guralnick, M. J. (2013). Preventive interventions for preterm children: Effectiveness and developmental mechanisms. *Journal Developmental and Behavioral Pediatrics, 33*(4), 352–364.

Jackson, A. C., Stewart, H., O'Toole, M., Tokatlian, N., Enderby, K., Miller, J., & Ashley, D. (2007). Pediatric brain tumor patients: Their parents' perceptions of the hospital experience. J*ournal of Pediatric Oncology Nursing, 24*(2), 95–105.

Nelson, A. M. (2003). Transition to motherhood. *Journal of Obstetric, Gynecological & Neonatal Nursing, 32,* 465–477.

Schlittenhart, J. M., Smart, D., Miller, K., & Severtson, B. (2011). Preparing parents for NICU discharge. *Nursing for Women's Health, 15*(6), 484–494.

Shandor Miles, M., Holditch-Davis, D., Burchinal, M. R., & Brunssen, S. (2011). Maternal role attainment with medically fragile infants: Part 1 measurement and correlates during the first year of life. *Research in Nursing & Health, 34,* 20–34.

Sims, D. C., Jacob, J., Mills, M. M., Fett, P. A., & Novak, G. (2006). Evaluation and development of potentially better practices to improve the discharge process in the neonatal intensive care unit. *Pediatrics, 118* (Supp. 2), S115–S123.

Singer, L. T., Fulton, S., Davillier, M., Koshy, D., Salvator A., & Baley, J. E. (2003). Effects of infant risk status and maternal psychological distress on maternal-infant interactions during the first year of life. *Journal of Developmental and Behavioral Pediatrics, 24*(4), 233–241.

Sneath, N. (2009). Discharge teaching in the NICU: Are parents prepared? An integrative review of parent's perceptions. *Neonatal Network, 28*(4), 237–246.

Swick, K. J., & Williams, R. D. (2006). An analysis of Bronfenbrenner's bio-ecological perspective for early childhood educators: Implications for working with experiencing stress. *Early Childhood Education Journal, 33*(5), 371–378.

Wigert, H., Johansson, R., Berg, M., & Hellstrom, H. (2006). Mothers' experiences having their newborn child in a neonatal intensive care unit. *Scandinavian Journal of Caring Sciences, 20,* 35–41.

Zickafoose, J. S., DeCamp, L. R., Sambuco, D. J. &, Prosser, L. A. (2013). Parents' preferences for enhanced access to the pediatric medical home: A qualitative study. *Journal of Ambulatory Care Management, 36*(1), 2–12.

PART 4

CHAPTER 17

Early Intervention at Home: When, Why, and How?

Katherine Beckstrand, Tara Pienkowski, Sandra Powers, and Jillian Scanlon

Highlights of the Chapter

At the conclusion of this chapter, the reader will be able to:

- explain the early intervention (EI) process from initial referral through the initiation of services including connections to State Child Find activities and the referral of infants and toddlers in the child welfare system

- identify people and professionals in EI

- identify how a family participates in EI

- describe strategies and techniques for best practice in EI programming

I dreamed of a daughter. My husband and I had a busy household with two boys. My husband had recently been promoted and found less and less time to spend with us. I was hopeful that a new baby girl would bring my family closer and complete our family picture. I had suffered from depression following the birth of my second son, but had grown confident in my skills as a mother and was eager to expand our family. During my

second pregnancy, I had been hoping for a daughter; however, I learned to love my two boys and all the things that make them unique. My pregnancy with my third child was uneventful, other than my intense longing for a girl. In my mind, I called her Samantha. When the stressful delivery was over, my heart sank when I realized that Samantha was Samuel.

After a typical hospital stay, Samuel and I went home. We quickly settled in to our new routine with the older boys being helpful and loving with their new baby brother. By the time Sam had his 3-month check up with the pediatrician, we had concerns with the positioning of his neck. We could tell it was difficult for him to turn his head. He seemed interested in his older brothers, but he wasn't consistently turning his head toward them. When I breastfed him, he seemed to only want to turn one way. I had so many questions: Was I doing something wrong? Why couldn't he move his head? Was he hearing okay? While his pediatrician was not overly concerned, he recommended we call EI services to have Samuel evaluated. And so our journey began.

The Mission of EI

The preceding mother's narrative tells of one family's journey leading up to their first encounter with EI. Every family goes through their own personal experience—the family members, the service providers involved, the age of the child, and the particular needs of all individuals—which varies greatly with each case. The best EI programs take all these circumstances into account in order to provide the most appropriate services for each family. This chapter will revisit this one family and what EI looked like for them from referral to provided services to transition to preschool. However, before exploring their journey, it is necessary to first understand the history, purpose, and definition of EI. (See Figure 17.1 and Table 17.1 for EI timeline, mission, and goals.)

The Education of All Handicapped Children Act was originally passed by Congress in 1975 in order to ensure free and appropriate public education to school-age children with disabilities in the United States. The EI program for infants and toddlers with disabilities became

FIGURE 17.1 Early intervention (EI) timeline

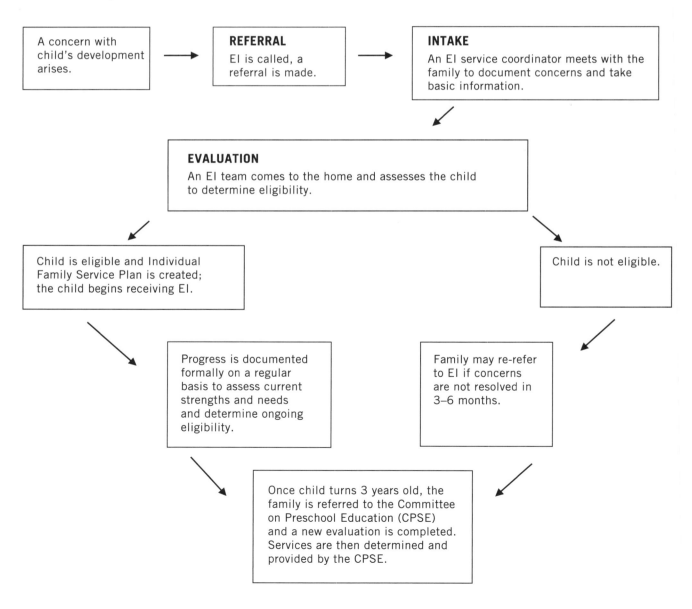

TABLE 17.1 Early Intervention (EI) program mission and goals

Family-centered:	Support parents in meeting their responsibilities to nurture and enhance their children's development.
Community-based:	Create opportunities for full participation of children with disabilities and their families in their communities by ensuring services are delivered in natural environments to the maximum extent appropriate.
Coordinated services:	Ensure EI services are coordinated with the full array of early childhood, health and mental health, educational, social, and other community-based services needed by and provided to children and their families.
Measurable outcomes for children and families:	Enhance child development and functional outcomes and improve family life through delivery of effective, outcome-based, high-quality EI services.
EI and the medical home:	Ensure EI services complement the child's medical home by involving primary and specialty health care providers in supporting family participation in EI services.
Local control, fiscal reform, and programmatic accountability:	Ensure equity of access, quality, consistency, and accountability in the service system by ensuring clear lines of public supervision, responsibility, and authority for the provision of EI services to eligible children and their families.

Note. The mission of the EI program is to identify and evaluate as early as possible those infants and toddlers whose healthy development is compromised, and provide for appropriate intervention to improve child and family development (New York State Department of Health, Division of Family Health, Bureau of Early Intervention, 2011.

part of the law with its reauthorization in 1986 (Public Law 99-457). In 1990, the Education of All Handicapped Children Act was renamed the Individuals with Disabilities Education Act (IDEA; PL 101-476). Since 1975, IDEA has been revised several times, most recently in 2004 (PL 108-446).

The current IDEA is comprised of four parts that delineate the regulations for providing free and appropriate public education. Part A describes the general provisions for the legislation. Part B explains services for school-age children; this includes children ages 3 to 5 years (preschool age) and children in grades K–12 (ages 5–21). Part C focuses on infants and toddlers with disabilities (birth to 2 years old, up to 3 years old), which often is referred to as "Early Intervention." Part D describes national activities to improve the education of children with disabilities.

EI, as outlined in Part C, states that:

. . . it is the policy of the United Stated to provide financial assistance to states—

(1) to develop and implement a statewide, comprehensive, coordinated, multidisciplinary, interagency system that provides early intervention services for infants and toddlers with disabilities and their families;

(2) to facilitate the coordination of payment for early intervention services from Federal, State, local, and private sources (including public and private insurance coverage);

(3) to enhance State capacity to provide quality early intervention services and expand and improve existing early intervention services being provided to infants and toddlers with disabilities and their families; and

(4) to encourage States to expand opportunities for children under 3 years old who would be at risk of having substantial developmental delay if they did not receive early intervention services. (PL 108-446)

The EI Process

Each state is responsible for developing an EI program that meets the minimum requirements established by IDEA 2004 Part C. For example, each state must designate a lead agency to receive the grant and administer the program and must ensure that services will be available to every child who is eligible. However, states also have discretion in many areas such as determining eligibility criteria, the evaluation process, and frequency of plan reviews. For example, preterm newborns who meet certain specifications in terms of gestational age or birth weight, or both, who are considered to be "at risk" for later developmental delays can also qualify for EI and be followed up to such time that they no longer meet EI eligibility criteria or age out of EI. In addition, infants and toddlers who are in the child welfare system are entitled to EI services, a benefit often not sought on their behalf. Specifically, per a statement by the Child Welfare Information Gateway (2013),

Enactment of the Part C referral provisions in the 2003 reauthorization of the Child Abuse Prevention and Treatment ACT (CAPTA) and in the Individuals with Disabilities Education Improvement Act of 2004 (IDEA) opened the door to a powerful partnership with great potential benefits for children under 3 years old involved in substantiated cases of abuse or neglect and their families. For child welfare administrators, these provisions offer tools to enhance a policy and practice and ensure compliance with Federal child welfare requirements that focus on child well-being. The provisions also connect child welfare staff to early intervention service providers, which can help child welfare staff in assessment, service delivery, and permanency planning. (http://www.childwelfare.gov)

In addition to the above, IDEA 2004 also details specific requirements for state EI programs with respect to establishing provisions for Child Find services as follows:

[To] implement a comprehensive Child Find system to identify, locate, and evaluate children needing early intervention services and to raise public awareness about what EI services are available. The lead [State] agency must coordinate Child Find activities with other programs, including child protection and foster care. (www.childwelfare.gov) For more information about Child Find, visit http://www. ectacenter.org/topics/earlyidoverview.asp.).

Counties within each state may differ as to how they apply the regulations in practice. The basic framework for the EI process typically includes a referral, evaluation, eligibility determination, and creation of a service plan, initiation of services, and a periodic review of the service plan. The following steps outline New York State's implementation of Part C: (New York State Department of Health, Division of Family Health, Bureau of Early Intervention, 2011).

Referral

Referrals often come from parents concerned about a particular area of development with their child (e.g., walking, talking). Referrals for EI evaluations may also come from pediatricians, an infant's neonatal intensive care unit team, or other professionals. Ultimately, parents have the final decision to move forward with the EI process or to decline an evaluation. Parents can refer their child by contacting the respective county department of health or local school district, depending on the state. At that point, the county assigns a family service coordinator to the family. The service coordinator meets with the family before the evaluation to gather intake information such as family concerns, developmental history of the child, and basic medical information, as well as continuing to work with the family and assist in managing services as long as the child is in EI.

Evaluation

Evaluations can take place in a clinic, at the child's school, in the child's home, or wherever the family requests that the evaluation take place. Evaluations are carried out by licensed professionals with experience in pediatrics, child development, and discipline-specific areas of expertise. The evaluation team consists of a special education teacher as a generalist and specialists relevant to the child's needs (e.g., physical therapist, occupational therapist, speech-language pathologist). The developmental areas assessed during the evaluation are:

- *Cognition.* Skills assessed in this domain include memory, problem solving, pretend play, object exploration and manipulation, object relatedness, concept formation, and sensorimotor development.

- *Social-Emotional.* This domain includes skills such as the ability to display, express, and discuss emotions; the ability to respond, initiate, and maintain interactions; interest in and awareness of both adults and peers; daily transitioning skills; attention to task and following directions; frustration tolerance and capacity to self-soothe; and the ability to communicate (verbally and nonverbally) to make needs and wants known to others.

- *Self-Help (Adaptive Skills).* Tasks in this domain consist of participation in dressing/undressing, toilet readiness and training, basic hygiene, feeding skills, and other activities of simple self-care.

- *Motor.* Motor skills include both gross/large motor (e.g., crawling, walking, running, jumping) and fine motor (e.g., use of utensils, cutting, object manipulation). This also includes motor planning and sensory processing skills.

- *Communication.* Language skills are divided into receptive (how a child understands and responds to language) and expressive (how a child uses language with sounds, words, and gestures) development.

Eligibility Determination

As indicated in chapter 6 of this text (Ensher & Clark, 2016), there remains much controversy about how eligibility for EI services are (or should) be established from state to state, with many authorities contending that current practices such as the use of norm-referenced tests are developmentally inappropriate for infants, toddlers, and preschoolers. Nonetheless, in many states, as in New York, professionals administer standardized tests during the evaluation specific to the areas of concern. A screening of all other developmental areas is carried out with subsequent evaluations completed, as needed. Eligibility is then determined based on set standard deviations from the mean score or percent delay. Should a child not meet the requisite criteria for delay but developmental concerns yet remain, a team-related professional may recommend services, based on informed clinician opinion or judgment.

Individual Family Service Plan (IFSP)

If a child is deemed eligible for EI, an Individual Family Service Plan (IFSP) is then drafted (in all states) by the team of professionals at a meeting, with the family in attendance and driven by the family's needs and input. This plan establishes goals and desired outcomes for therapy. It is a fluid document that is effective for 6 months but can be altered at any time to better meet the child's needs. A service team is then put in place to administer the requisite therapy or therapies, as determined by the IFSP and approved by the county. The IFSP should always be responsive to and supportive of the family's routines, values, language, challenges, and culture. In particular, it should always include:

- the child's present levels of functioning and need in the key domains noted previously (i.e., physical, cognitive, communication, social-emotional, and adaptive development)

- family information including resources, priorities, and concerns

- major results or outcomes expected to be achieved for both the child and the family

- specific EI services that the child will be receiving

- identification of where in the natural environment (e.g., home or community) the services will be provided. If such services are not to be offered in the natural environment, the IFSP must include a statement that justifies the reason for an alternative setting

- when the services will be provided (i.e., the number of days and times that each service will be offered)

- a statement as to who will be paying for the services

- the name of the service coordinator overseeing implementation of the IFSP

- finally, steps to be taken to support the child's transition out of EI to another program, as deemed appropriate

Although IFSPs may vary from state to state and county to county, the working part of the document includes the goals put forth by the family and evaluation team. There is typically a broad overall goal created by the family such as, "My child will talk/walk/improve overall development." The evaluation team then creates more

specific objectives, or steps along the way, to help achieve the broad overall goal. Steps along the way may include milestones such as, "will imitate sounds and actions," "will make choices," or "will respond to name." The evaluation team also provides ideas for implementation, or ways to make it happen, by listing various activities that will support a child's progress toward the overall goal. These strategies may include activities such as, "provide choices," "music, songs, finger plays," "give extra wait time," or "use of silly environmental sound play."

Developmental Progress Reports

Every 6 months, providers review the child's progress to determine if the child continues to be eligible for EI services. If the child remains eligible, the family, family service coordinator, and service providers come together to discuss the child's progress, set new goals, and write a new IFSP for the next 6 months.

Looking at the Whole Child

A service coordinator came to take some basic information and set up an evaluation date. The day of the evaluation arrived. The evaluation team included a physical therapist and a special education teacher, and my service coordinator was also there. I couldn't begin to imagine how they would test Sam, and I didn't understand why a special education teacher would be involved. My only concern was that he wasn't turning his head the way I thought he should. What would the evaluation look like? What do I have to do? How do you test a child this small? What if he fails?

Well, sometimes your worst fear comes true. Sam failed. They called it "delayed" but it is not what I heard. All I knew was that I was right. Sam needed help. The evaluators talked to me at length about Sam's everyday life. They played with him, talked to him, watched how he moved, and even put him in a variety of positions. They continually asked about Sam recognizing me, showing affection, and responding to us. I didn't understand what these things had to do with Sam's neck. The teacher explained that she was a "generalist" and it was her job to assess everything but gross motor skills because the physical therapist specialized in that. She was able to point out things about Sam that I hadn't considered—things that I had taken for granted with my older boys. At that point, physical therapy was recommended for Sam to address what they called torticollis. I was somewhat relieved that he would get the help he needed for his neck. I could not stop thinking about those questions that the teacher had asked me. What does it mean that sometimes Sam does not look at me? What does it mean when I can't always calm him? How do you teach a baby to do those things? What would therapy for his neck look like?

Sam's case highlights how the family's main concern was with one area, physical development. It also suggests that the special education teacher, as the generalist, was looking at the whole child, as is required by IDEA. In this section, we will discuss why it is necessary to assess all the developmental domains and how they are integrated and interrelated.

As mentioned previously, the five domains assessed in an evaluation are cognition, adaptive, social-emotional, physical, and communication development. Regardless of the provider's area of expertise, all domains are assessed. Both in the initial evaluation and in continued progress reports, all domains are assessed to ensure that the child is meeting age-appropriate developmental milestones. Clinicians also look at all domains because of the interconnected nature of development. Best practice in early childhood education, as put forth by the National Association for the Education of Young Children, indicated that:

. . . all domains of children's development and learning interrelate. For example, because social factors strongly influence cognitive development and academic competence—and the cognitive domain influences the social domain—teachers must foster learning and development in both, as well as in the emotional and physical domains. (Copple & Bredekamp, 2009, p. 2)

The same can be said for physical therapists, occupational therapists, and other professionals. All clinicians need to consider and address all areas to best understand the child as a whole rather than the subset of a specific domain. As seen in Sam's case, the physical concerns prompted his family to initiate the evaluation. The evaluation revealed other skills and behaviors that were indicating concern due to the overlapping of all the domains. Sam's torticollis impacted his ability to turn his head and be soothed by his mother; his physical development was connected to his social-emotional development.

Service: Accessible and Available

The EI program offers a variety of therapeutic and support services to eligible infants and toddlers with disabilities and their families. These services (as indicated in Figure 17.2) can be provided in tandem or separately and at the discretion of the family. These include family education; counseling; home visits; parent support groups; special instruction; speech and hearing services; occupational therapy; physical therapy; service coordination; and psychological, nursing, nutrition, social work, vision, and assistive technology services. These services can be provided in tandem or separately and at the discretion of the family. EI is a voluntary program that is designed to meet a family's individual needs and circumstances. It is offered at zero cost to participating families, and no financial

PART 4

FIGURE 17.2 The Intervention Pyramid for Children With Special Needs

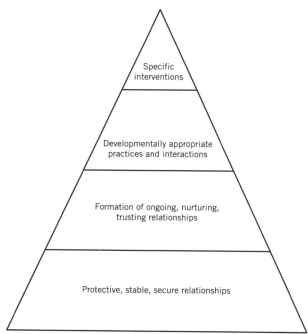

Adapted from Interdisciplinary Council on Developmental and Learning Disorders *Clinical Practice Guidelines* (2000), p. 67, Bethesda, MD: ICDL. Reprinted with permission.

requirement is used to determine eligibility for the program or administration of program services (New York State Department of Health, Division of Family Health, Bureau of Early Intervention, 2011).

Qualified providers are certified and licensed in accordance with the New York State Department of Health, Department of Education, and Department of Labor standards. They must meet a variety of criteria and maintain professional development to ensure that they are qualified to work with this specialized population according to the New York State Department of Health, Division of Family Health, Bureau of Early Intervention. Turning back to the family in our example:

We received the evaluation report, and it seemed that the evaluators understood my concerns about Sam. The goals and strategies written for the IFSP at the evaluation reflected what I wanted to happen for Sam. It also included additional goals the therapists had in mind and shared with me. A routine of scheduled sessions was established, and we began to see progress with the support of the physical therapist. Despite progress, new challenges seemed to keep popping up. Sam was struggling to sleep through the night, having difficulty with eating, and screaming at bath time. Even though the therapist said his torticollis was improving, I was starting to wonder about his vision because he still tilted his head and brought things close to his eyes.

After 6 months, the physical therapist said it was time for a progress report to look at Sam's progress in physical therapy, as well as his skills in all other areas. Sam's physical therapist was pleased with his progress—he was sitting, crawling, and pulling up to stand. She acknowledged our concerns with his sleeping, eating, and bathing, and recommended occupational and speech-language therapy evaluations. I was familiar with the evaluation process, but I was still anxious. Would they find my new concerns valid and give Sam the support he needed?

Coordinating Services With the Whole Team

As noted previously, Sam's challenges related to torticollis were indeed impacting other areas of development. This condition resulted in his need for additional services. As Sam's therapeutic team grew, his family remained the key to the intervention process. When coordinating services, it is important to consider the dynamics of the whole team. The team consists of providers and is led by the family. The family drives the therapeutic process from goals to implementation (see Figure 17.3). As the child's needs change, so too will the goals and methods of intervention. A family's needs vary over time and from family to family. Cultural differences, socioeconomic status, religious beliefs, and family structure all play a role in the strengths and needs of a family. Providers must take into consideration how best to support the family's individual differences.

Following the second evaluation, they recommended speech therapy for eating and occupational therapy to help with finding ways to calm Sam down. That meant that I would have three people coming into my home every week. We worked out a schedule that felt overwhelming at first, but soon became a natural rhythm. Even though each therapist had specialized areas of knowledge, they all worked on their goals through play. Once in a while we had opportunities for everyone to meet as a whole group. It seemed as soon as Sam achieved one goal, something else would come up. It was starting to feel like a never-ending cycle. How could I help Sam? When would he begin to talk? I remember when his brothers were babies they would light up when I walked in the room. When would Sam start to do that?

Sam's mother is feeling overwhelmed due to her concerns with Sam's new challenges, the intimate nature of providers in her home, and the growing team. The providers need to recognize and value the family's complex emotional response to the EI process. This is the primary reason that the relationship with the family and their needs drive therapy (Brazelton & Sparrow, 2006). The family determines where, when, and how therapy takes place (New York State Department of Health, Division of Family Health, Bureau of Early Intervention, 2011).

The child's natural environment is the ideal setting for working with families and children. This environment may include the home, day care, or community setting, as deemed most appropriate by the family. The child's natural environment allows for a familiar safe space in which to explore new concepts and to refine existing skills. This becomes increasingly important as professionals want to create scenarios that can be reproduced and practiced frequently, following models and education introduced by the providers. Providers have a limited amount of time with families and can empower them to work toward goals, even when providers are not present. This can only be done by building a partnership between families and providers (Brazelton & Sparrow, 2006). Thus, skills can be carried over and repeated in a functional manner to achieve mastery.

Both the family and providers can offer unique perspectives and feedback regarding a child's individual development (Greenspan, Wieder, & Simons, 1998). Providers must develop a reciprocal relationship that fosters open and constructive dialogue. These conversations supply information to all parties regarding the child's strengths and needs. Parents and caregivers intimately know their children and can offer providers insight into various aspects of their child's day. Children display different abilities in different contexts; and different materials, environments, persons present, and relationships all affect how a child may demonstrate skill (Greenspan & Lewis, 1999). When providers and caregivers share information, they can enable children's greater successes in any environment. By assuming a family's competence and coming from a strength-based perspective, providers promote a family's confidence in moving forward with their child (Brazelton & Sparrow, 2006). Real-life opportunities practiced in the child's natural environment and reinforced by families consistently make therapy practical and applicable.

The relationship developed between the provider and the family is critical. This relationship fosters success by integrating the parents' intimate understanding of their child and the provider's experience and knowledge. Providers empower families to move towards self-advocacy by:

1. supporting families in navigating the EI system and finding available community resources

2. listening to and discussing the family's and child's ongoing and ever-changing needs

3. providing education regarding developmental milestones, next steps, and strategies for increasing various skills, and modeling interactions

4. coaching families through play interactions, stressful situations, and behavioral challenges

Observing and Looking Beyond the Obvious

After a full year of service, another progress report was completed. At that time, my concerns had shifted again. It seemed that I could never soothe Sam. He was cranky all the time. No matter what I did, I couldn't connect with Sam the way I had with his older brothers. He still wasn't lighting up when he saw me or laughing with me in play. Sometimes the therapists seemed to get more joy from him than I could. He continued to get services and when he was around 2 years old a special education teacher was added to our team. Her role was to focus on Sam's social skills. She began to provide ideas for how we could play with Sam, expand his communication, and help him engage with our family. I just wanted to feel that connection with Sam. Why was Sam so hard to connect with? How is a teacher going to help me connect with my own son? Why couldn't I do this on my own?

Sam's mother still had many concerns around her interactions with him. Many parents may need support around understanding the differences between typical and atypical play. Play has different purposes and evolves from exploration to complex problem solving and pretend-play schemes. So what is play, and what does it look like?

Play is a way for a child to explore the environment and learn about the world around her. It is a way to act out and explore emotions, a way to cope with reality through imaginary play, and a way to discover her role in her family and the world. Play is the foundation for learning. Play follows a developmental sequence (Interdisciplinary Council on Developmental and Learning Disorders, 2000). For example, in infancy a child is in the exploration phase. Examples of exploratory play include mouthing, banging, and looking at and listening to any object that the child can get her hands on. As a toddler, a child begins to experiment with cause-and-effect relationships. This phase includes testing limits to get a reaction, pushing buttons to activate toys or objects, and dumping and filling containers. As the child turns 3 years old, she begins to experiment with role playing and acting out her emotions through play (Linder, 2008). Table 17.2 follows a typical developmental sequence of play. It also offers examples of the differences between typical and atypical play.

Approaches to Intervention: It's Time to Play

This time, therapy was focused on my interactions with Sam. Although I had received strategies along the way that supported me to work on

TABLE 17.2 Development and behaviors of concern

TYPICAL PLAY	ATYPICAL PLAY
Exploratory/sensory-ased	Primary sensory-focused
Imitative	Lack of imitation
Reciprocal-engaged	Solitary-fleeting
Self-regulating	Hyper- or hyporesponsive
"Checks in"-feedback	Inconsistent checking
Range of interest/repertoire	Restricted repertoire
Flexibility of object use (functional)	Adheres to sameness
Watches peers	Less attentive to peers
Integrates eye contact/gestures	Minimal nonverbal
Initiates play interactions	Passive participant

specific skills like fixing his neck, getting him to eat different foods, and getting him to say more words, this was different. The teacher was asking me to get down on the floor and show her my play with Sam. The focus was now on my biggest concern—feeling that connection. Would it work; would I ever be able to connect with Sam?

There are a variety of approaches to providing direct EI therapy. Some of these therapies may require providers to receive additional training or certification. These methodologies include, but are not limited to, applied behavioral analysis, skill streaming, the Treatment and Education of Autistic and Related Communication-Handicapped Children model (Mesibov & Shea, 2005), the Miller method (Miller & Tien, 2007), and DIR Floortime (Greenspan et al., 1998).

A methodology that focuses on play and social-emotional development as the driving force behind learning is the DIR Floortime model. The DIR Floortime approach centers around a child's social-emotional development (D), individual differences (I), and relationships (R) through the use of play and interactions (Greenspan et al., 1998). Sam's social-emotional development includes his inability to "light up" when his mother walks into the room. His individual differences include his biological challenges with eating, sleeping, and calming. His relationships include how he interacts with his mother, other family members, and providers. The DIR philosophy is applied through Floortime play (Interdisciplinary Council on Developmental and Learning Disorders, 2000).

Sam's mother was surprised at the new direction of her son's therapy sessions. A goal of therapy became understanding Sam's intentions through his play. This shift in therapy allowed the focus to be on Sam's capacity to generate creative ideas, develop his ability to relate joyfully with warmth, express a range of feelings, and communicate meaningfully. His therapists were changing the focus of sessions from specific tasks to social-emotional connections. Initially the focus of therapy was on physical skills such as on learning to turn his head, and on increasing his range of foods. Sam's success in developing social-emotional connections was measured by his taking more initiative, using communication purposefully and with intent, becoming more flexible, and tolerating frustration. With these skills in place, he would have the foundation for acquiring traditional pre-academic skills.

Here are some Floortime strategies:

- follow the child's lead
- treat what the child does as intentional and purposeful
- use a calm voice and gentle looks
- use encouraging gestures
- demonstrate supportive listening
- be aware of the child's rhythms and gestures
- be able to help the child identify play themes
- join in perseverative play
- do not treat avoidance or "no" as rejection (Greenspan et al., 1998)

What Comes Next: Transitioning to Preschool

I could never have imagined how complex the journey from Sam's first evaluation at 3 months to beginning preschool at 3 years would be. He has made so much progress, and we are happy that he is ready for preschool. We know he will continue to need support in preschool and can't help but feel disappointed and anxious about this transition. Even with the uncertainty of the future, I remain hopeful about the connections we have developed with Sam. We have come so far.

As previously discussed, the transition from EI to preschool-level services varies by state and local school district. For the purpose of this chapter, we discuss the transition as it applies to New York State. The transition period is often a confusing time for families, because preschool does not mean that a child is going to school, but rather to services provided to children in the 3-to-5-year old group. As a child approaches 3 years old, another evaluation is necessary to determine eligibility (New York State Department of Health, Division of Family Health, Bureau of Early Intervention, 2011). Services are then provided through the local school district. Similar to EI, services can be carried out at home or within a school-based program.

When we first met Sam and his family, the primary concern was his physical development. Over time, and with the collaboration of his team, the focus of intervention changed to best meet Sam's changing needs. Throughout the entire process, the team considered all areas of his development to ensure an approach that looked at the whole child. In doing so, the team supported Sam's family in understanding his development, thus growing in their independence and advocacy for their child.

Chapter Summary

This chapter has covered a number of topics related to EI for infants and toddlers, up to 3 years old. Among the topics discussed are federal regulations for the Part C legislation approved in 2004, defining eligibility criteria for EI services; regulations specific to New York State; the referral, evaluation, and IFSP process in partnership with families, and the relationships between Part C legislation, Child Find, and provisions of service earmarked for infants and toddlers in the child welfare system.

Key Points to Remember

- *Explain the EI process from initial referral through the initiation of services:* The EI process begins with a referral, followed by an evaluation specific to areas of concern. The evaluation results in eligibility determination and the creation of a service plan, at which time the most appropriate services to meet the child's current needs can be initiated. While receiving EI services, a child's service plan is reviewed periodically and adjusted as needed.

- *Identify people and professionals in EI:* Services provided by EI may include those of one or a combination of the following specialists: a special instruction teacher, speech-language pathologist, audiologist, occupational therapist, physical therapist, psychologist, service coordinator, nurse, nutritionist, social worker, teacher of the visually impaired, teacher of the hearing impaired.

- *Identify how a family may participate in EI:* Families can participate in EI in a number of ways. The family is always encouraged to participate in sessions by being on the floor and engaged in play with the child. The family is in constant conversation with the service team to discuss the child's ongoing and ever-changing needs. The family is given the opportunity to receive education regarding developmental milestones, next steps. and strategies for increasing various skills, as well as modeling interactions. In addition, the family may receive coaching through play interactions, as they encounter stressful situations and behavioral challenges that may arise from the EI and treatment processes.

Implications for Families and Professionals

The following are a few suggestions that may be helpful to parents or caregivers and professionals, as they engage together as partners in the EI process:

For Parents:

- Ask questions and inquire about concerns and unclear practices.

- You are the real expert on your child; you know your child best.

- You are your child's advocate.

- You will be the one to make the difference in your child's development through the collaborative partnership you have with your provider(s).

- The way a provider plays and interacts is done intentionally to facilitate your child's development.

For Professionals:

- Listen to families.

- Accept that it is truly families that determine the effectiveness of any interventions and recommendations made.

- Include the entire family in the EI processes, and use materials, toys, and items that you find within the home.

- Go beyond being just "good with kids." Play with them with purpose and intention.

- Strive for spontaneity and joy, keep therapy natural.

References

Brazelton, T. B., & Sparrow, J. D. (2006). *Touchpoints birth to 3: Your child's emotional and behavioral development* (2nd ed.). Cambridge, MA: Da Capo Press.

Child Welfare Information Gateway. (2013). *Addressing the needs of young children in Child Welfare: Part C—Early Intervention services.* Washington, DC, Children's Bureau, Administration on Children, Youth, & Families; Administration for Children & Families; Health & Human Services. Retrieved from https://www.childwelfare.gov/pubs/partc/

Copple, C., & Bredekamp, S. (2009). *Developmentally appropriate practice in early childhood programs serving children from birth to age 8 (3rd ed.).* Washington, DC: National Association for the Education of Young Children.

Department of Education, Federal Register. (2011). *Rules and Regulations, 34* CFR Part 303, Early Intervention Program for Infants and Toddlers with Disabilities.

Ensher, G. L., & Clark, D. A. (2016). Evaluating infants and young children in the first years. In G. L. Ensher & D. A. Clark (Eds.), *The early years: Foundations for best practice with special children and their families* (pp. 133–153). Washington, DC: ZERO TO THREE.

Greenspan, S. I., & Lewis, N. B. (1999). *Building healthy minds: The six experiences that create intelligence and emotional growth in babies and young children.* Cambridge, MA: Perseus.

Greenspan, S. I., Wieder, S., & Simons, R. (1998). *The child with special needs: Encouraging intellectual and emotional growth.* Reading, MA: Addison Wesley.

Interdisciplinary Council on Developmental and Learning Disorders. (2000). *Clinical practice guidelines: Redefining the standards of care for infants, children, and families with special needs.* Bethesda, MD: Author.

Linder, T. (2008). *Transdisciplinary play-based assessment: A functional approach to working with young children* (2nd ed.). Baltimore, MD: Brookes.

Mesibov, G., & Shea, V. (2005). *The TEACCH approach to autism spectrum disorders.* New York: Kluwer Academic/Plenum.

Miller, A., & Tien, K. (2007). *The Miller Method developing capacities of children on the autism spectrum.* London, UK: J. Kingsley.

New York State Department of Health, Division of Family Health, Bureau of Early Intervention. (2011). *Early Intervention program regulations, laws, and reimbursement rates.* Retrieved from www.health.ny.gov/community/infants_children/early_intervention/regulations.htm

PART 4

CHAPTER 18

Inclusive Preschool Education: Best Practices in Action

Gail L. Ensher, Ellen B. Barnes, and David A. Clark

Highlights of the Chapter

At the conclusion of this chapter, the reader will:

- understand that inclusive education is not a place but a different way of thinking about teaching and working with young children and their families

- understand ways that inclusive education offers support and optimal learning for young children and their families

- understand that inclusive education facilitates adapting to the strengths and special needs of all children and families

- understand ways that inclusive education changes the perspectives and practices of teachers, clinical and support staff, and students in training who participate in such environments

- understand ways that authentic inclusive education facilitates realizing the full potential of young children and their families.

Essential Opportunities for All Children and Families

Reflecting the authentic inclusive philosophy of the Jowonio School, a nationally known inclusive preschool in Syracuse, New York, more than 2 decades ago, Kunc (1992) wrote:

When inclusive practice is fully embraced, we abandon the idea that children have to become "normal" in order to contribute to the world. Instead we search for and nourish the gifts that are inherent in all people. We begin to look beyond typical ways of becoming valued members of the community and, in doing so, begin to realize the achievable goal of providing all children an authentic sense of belonging.

One of the most far-reaching pieces of legislation that affected the quality of education for toddlers and preschoolers, with and without disabilities, was the passage of PL 99-457 in 1986, which amended PL 94-142 and its regulations. This legislation required states to provide free public education services to young children

between the 3 and 5 years old. Part H was later added to the legislation and subsequently developed incentives for states to offer early intervention (EI) services to infants and toddlers with special needs. In 1990, the Education of All Handicapped Children Act was renamed the Individuals with Disabilities Education Act (IDEA; PL 101-476), and in 1991 it reauthorized and amended both Part H and Part B, Section 619, of the legislation (i.e., PL 102-119). Following in 1997, PL 105-17 reauthorized IDEA, and Part H was changed to Part C. This legislation ensured the access of all young children with disabilities to the regular, general curriculum; strengthened and highlighted the role of parents in the educational decision-making process; and increased the accountability of educational staff for young children with disabilities. Further changes to the legislation on behalf of infants and toddlers were ushered in with the passage of the Individuals with Disabilities Education Improvement Act (IDEA) of 2004 (PL 108-446). In particular, the Improvement Act of 2004 stipulated that states were required to establish programs for finding and identifying infants and toddlers who might qualify for EI services (e.g., Child Find), programs that were best coordinated with primary care providers who served in key positions to identify infants and toddlers with developmental and behavioral disabilities (as

described in chapter 17, Beckstrand, Pienkowski, Powers, & Scanlon, 2016). These were the legislative mandates that provided the "framework for change in early childhood inclusion" (Guralnick, 2001, p. 3). Foundational principles undergirding these changes were:

- recognizing the critical importance of environments for the neurological and developmental progress of infants and young children during the first 5 years of life

- maximizing the potential and celebrating the diversity of all infants and young children

- focusing on parent partnerships with professionals; providing educational services within the most natural environments

- highlighting and enhancing the strengths of families and their young children

- enhancing collaborations and coordination of services for families and young children across disciplines

- making available resources that would be accessible to families within their immediate neighborhoods and communities

Underscoring these mandates, a joint position statement of the Division for Early Childhood

(DEC) and the National Association for the Education of Young Children (NAEYC) offered the following definition of early childhood inclusion:

Early childhood inclusion embodies the values, policies, and practices that support the right of every infant and young child and his or her family, regardless of abilities, to participate in a broad range of activities and contexts as full members of families, communities, and society. The desired results of inclusive experiences for children with and without disabilities and their families include a sense of belonging and membership, positive social relationships and friendships, and development and learning to reach their full potential. The defining features of inclusion that can be used to identify high quality early childhood programs and services are access, participation, and supports. (Division for Early Childhood & National Association for the Education of Young Children, 2009, p. 9)

With the extensive body of research that followed the passage of these well-known pieces of legislation, translations of "inclusive" practices have been as diverse as the children and families who have been enrolled and who have participated, from one community to the next. For instance, some programs have interpreted inclusive education to mean that the majority group of children would consist mainly of "typical" or non-identified children into which a few, select toddlers and preschoolers with IEPs would be included, with push-in and/or pull-out special education services taking place within these classes. Other programs have defined the model with offering services to identified children entirely outside of the general education classroom context. Still other options have been interpreted to mean programming basically for groups of identified children, with a few non-identified children serving as "token" typical classroom models, with special services

embedded into classroom routines. In all of these "models" of inclusive education, it is safe to say that the emphasis has been placed largely on the setting or context of numbers and ratios of typical to identified children, with specialized services being offered either outside of the classrooms or within the context of typical routines and activities of the preschool day. Best practices and authentic inclusive education, however, extend far beyond the physical presence of identified children and setting.

Including All Children: Foundations of Best Practices

For more than 3 decades, the Jowonio School (meaning to "set free"), a small school of approximately 165 children located in Syracuse, New York, has exemplified—in philosophy and practice—the best "ingredients" of inclusive education for all children—with no exceptions! Jowonio was founded in 1980 (Barnes & Jowonio

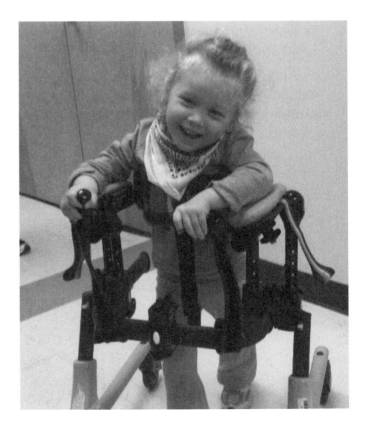

staff, 2013) with classes that placed a wide range of children in classrooms together. The school staff of administrators, teachers, clinicians, and families daily welcomed all children (representing diverse ethnic and cultural backgrounds, speaking multiple languages, reflecting diverse ranges of learning, abilities, and behavioral challenges) and worked to create effective teaching strategies and practices. Most important, everyone learned, contrary to commonly held beliefs about presumed limited developmental potentials of youngsters with significant physical, learning, and behavioral needs. Further, as children graduated from Jowonio, their parents subsequently advocated within their home schools to continue "inclusive programming." As a result, many school districts in central New York persisted with these efforts toward "least restrictive" approaches and models, thus promoting within communities a wider and changed vision of what education might and should be for all children.

The "big ideas" at Jowonio that have informed and served as the foundation of best practices include the following:

- All children belong and are welcomed into the learning community. Young children with many learning styles, needs, and gifts have a right to a high-quality, developmentally appropriate education with individual accommodations.

- The "least dangerous assumption" is that all children can be competent with the right supports; these supports should be responsive to each person's needs and strengths, aim for children's independence, and be "only as special as necessary."

- Children learn through warm and nurturing relationships with adults and peers. We want students to become caring human beings. When they understand and value themselves as well as understand and value the differences in others, they

become comfortable and confident in their interactions, and are not constrained by stereotypes.

- Staff understand children's behavior as communication, and the primary intervention is prevention. Children develop appropriate social skills through consistent and warm responses from adults, positive redirection, and an environment that meets the needs of each child rather than through striving to adapt to a standard teaching approach.

- A partnership with parents and families is critical in appropriately supporting individual children and creating an effective school.

- Inclusive programming is best achieved with a team approach in which everyone—administrators, teachers, support staff, and parents—solves problems together.

When a school exemplifies these principles and is genuinely inclusive, sensitive to the needs of each child and making accommodations to meet these needs, it makes all the difference for young children. At the Jowonio School, supports in and out of classrooms, in gymnastic and therapeutic settings, on playgrounds, and on field trips come in all forms. Sometimes these supports are people; sometimes they are special visual schedules; sometimes they are adapted equipment; sometimes they are alternative forms of communication such as sign language or technologies (e.g., iPad); at times, these involve different accommodations for seating or a child's focusing at circle time. Being a part of social interactions that take place with other children is a vital part of learning and play for young children. Facilitating this kind of involvement for toddlers or preschoolers who may be limited in terms of their motor abilities or have sensory issues is critical for their full participation; for instance, on playgrounds and other open areas for physical activity (e.g., providing adaptations such as hand controls or special foot supports on tricycles).

A supportive community for families is another theme of the Jowonio School philosophy that is embedded in day-to-day interactions, relationships, and activities with parents and siblings. The following are the thoughts and words of a mother of a young preschooler who entered Jowonio at just a little over 5 years ago:

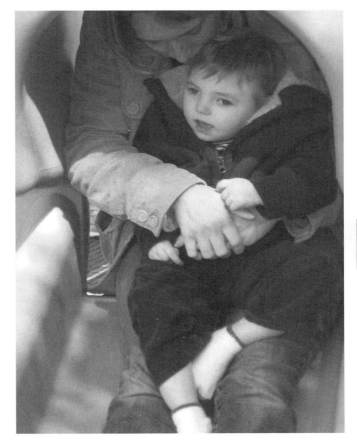

In June of 2008, our lives changed forever with the birth of our first son Ryan and the devastating diagnosis of Hypoxic Ischemic Encephalopathy, CP, seizures, etc. In the chaos that followed Ryan's birth, we spent time grasping the concept that our child was going to be severely handicapped in every way from vision impairment to his wheelchair and adaptive equipment. However, there was a solemn peace that came over us as we both looked at one another in the NICU and talked with hope and faith that we wanted our son to attend Jowonio as soon as he could. Ryan began Early Intervention services immediately upon NICU discharge, started the Jowonio program when he was 2, and enjoyed 3 years of pre-K there.

Jowonio provided Ryan superior inclusive education, speech, occupational therapy, and physical therapy services. Jowonio's social work and support staff connected us with family resources and a community network we now enjoy and

rely upon. Jowonio's staff saw no educational or physical boundaries with the endless possibilities for Ryan; other professionals saw only restrictions and limitations. Jowonio provided him with adaptive equipment to allow Ryan the ability to communicate and move independently and support to sit and interact with classmates.

Ryan's sister, Molly, was born in 2010 and was naturally immersed in the "Jowonio family" as well. When she turned 2, she became a Jowonio student. Up until her start in a Jowonio classroom, Molly's experience with peers was with the disabled population where playing with her brother and his friends with similar needs was all normal for her. Sitting through countless therapy sessions and doctor appointments don't phase her, and she's learned a lot through her experience as a sister of a severely disabled brother. Jowonio allowed her to play and interact with "typical peers" like herself. Jowonio provided the social opportunities that our immediate family unit could not. Molly is also bonding with other siblings of students with special needs in a unique experience that Jowonio can provide, a peer network that will become essential for her social-emotional development in the future.

Jowonio is more than a preschool. It has become an extension of our family living-room. The wonderful teachers, therapists, and other professionals at Jowonio that work diligently to enhance the lives of families like ours are truly appreciated and will never be forgotten in the years that follow pre-K. (J. MacMaster, personal communication, December 2, 2013)

Jowonio: It's Not Just a Preschool!

The cornerstone of state and federal mandates at the infant, toddler, and preschool levels is that families must be centrally involved in EI and preschool services. Further, at the core of referral, assessment, planning, and intervention processes is the mandate that family relationships and parent partnerships are the essential foundation for best practices (Ensher & Clark, 2011; Ensher, Clark, & Songer, 2009; Hanson & Lynch, 2013). In this regard, compliance with federal regulations is vital. On the other hand, as most professionals well understand, genuine partnerships with families extend far beyond mere compliance with federal and state requirements.

Implementation of authentic partnerships with families involves creating an environment of genuine collaboration and community. This philosophy and sense of community is captured in the following excerpt from the Fall 2014 Jowonio newsletter:

Since school began you may have noticed that there is more to Jowonio than classroom teaching and hard-core playing going on. Jowonio has always been, and continues to evolve, not just as a preschool but as a community school. We serve a large and diverse group of children but our community of family and friends is just as important to the mission of Jowonio as are the kids. While the building is bustling with child-centered activities every day, it also serves as a meeting spot for parents, local nonprofit and advocacy groups, college classes, seminars, and recreational classes. We collaborate on workshops, resource distribution, student training and community planning with countless local agencies, and our school community keeps getting bigger and stronger as a result. . . .Thanks to generous grants from the CNY DDSO/OPWDD, the Family Support Team is able to offer supportive and educational programs and services throughout the year for parents. These could include joining us for occasional school-wide events such as Pot Luck or March Follies, while others might enjoy a day of gardening, helping with a playground improvement project or writing an article for our newsletter. Bring the whole crew to a family-fun event on an evening or weekend or during a school vacation, or join us at an evening event such as a workshop for parents offered by Jowonio staff, or a CNY Autism Society of America meeting. (Hyman & Vercelloni, 2013)

However, just as Jowonio is "not just a preschool," it also is not just a collection of activities and events. Some of the special qualities that differentiate authentic inclusive programming for families of young children, in particular at the Jowonio School, reside in the unique perspectives of the administrative, clinical, social work, and teaching staff. These perspectives are reflected in some of the following attitudes, philosophies, approaches, and assumptions:

- Although families represent great diversity of educational, cultural, linguistic, social, and economic backgrounds, all universally bring their own unique strengths to raising their young children. Such strengths need to be highlighted and confirmed by professionals in their day-to-day interactions with family members and their young children.

- Discern and reaffirm the positives and joy, even in the face of what appear to be adverse situations (Ensher & Clark, 2011). This perspective does not imply naïveté on the part of either staff or family members. The attitude is grounded in the belief that good solutions can emerge from very challenging events and that these are most likely to surface with partnerships in problem solving. Dwelling on negative situations can leave families devoid of energy and resilience to move beyond immediate difficult encounters and developments.

- Listen and suspend judgment! Elsewhere in our writing relative to families (Ensher & Clark, 2011), we have written:

Learning when to respond to families and when to simply listen is not an exact science. Such lessons are garnered largely from experience. Professionals, especially when faced with the uncomfortable silence following delivery of sad or difficult news, may tend to rush in with advice in hope that words will help minimize the pain. . . . However, providers need to be mindful of the simple truth that situations are what they are. They must be compassionate and deliver news with understanding and hopefulness, but they should not deny or devalue the salience of a given situation for families. Families need time to grieve, to recover, and to regain hope—especially when first learning that their child may have a disability or special needs. (p. 17)

Above all, the Jowonio staff is masterful in helping families to get back on their feet and to feel supported with the often-hard responsibilities of raising young children with disabilities,

especially those with severe disabilities. Moreover, although professionals may have many years of experience in working with families of infants and young children with disabilities and special needs, few have shared these kinds of experiences. As one mother of a now 27-year-old who attended Jowonio as a preschooler commented, "There are disabilities, and there are disabilities!" Since the birth of her daughter more than 2 decades ago, this mom has been able to sleep through the night uninterrupted perhaps 10 times.

Being flexible, accommodating, and accessible is essential for working with families of infants and young children with disabilities and special health care needs. Given busy agendas, it is not always possible for professionals to respond and adapt to the requests and needs of families. On the other hand, just as the behavior of families and young children should be seen as communication, likewise the behavior of professionals "speaks volumes" when professionals display willingness to "meet" families where they are in their lives. This is a skill and ability greatly exemplified, almost without exception, by members of the Jowonio staff, who sincerely appreciate diversity in values and perspectives of others. In short, staff members of the Jowonio School display an overwhelming sense of acceptance and caring for other people—colleagues, parents, children, and other professionals in community schools and help-giving agencies—that draw people together.In the face of extraordinarily challenging impairments and disabilities, professionals must make a commitment toward realizing the "potentials" and abilities of children and families that subsequently empowers parents. As reflected in Julie MacMaster's vignette, whereas others viewed her son, Ryan, as having limitations, the Jowonio staff believed in his potential and possibilities to grow and learn within a wonderfully nurturing family.

Miracles on Ordinary Days

"Cannot" is not a part of the vocabulary of professionals at Jowonio! Genuine inclusive education enables all children—those who do and those who do not have disabilities and special needs. Within the wonderfully supportive environment of Jowonio, we have met:

- Nonverbal children who, given augmentative systems of communication, begin to speak and are fully engaged in every aspect of daily classroom activities

- Nonambulatory children who, given the benefit of adaptive equipment, become mobile, walk, and enjoy outdoor and playground activities with their peers

- Nonverbal children who learn how to initiate interactions with their peers and wait their turn

- Children who are unusually bothered by sensory input who learn to adapt to loud and unexpected sounds and noises

- Children who are greatly challenged by transitions who learn how to accommodate to changes in classroom schedules and routines

- Children who eat only five foods such as rice, cheese, vanilla yogurt, and white bread, who learn to explore other foods with different textures, temperatures, and colors

- Young children who were never invited to a birthday party before they entered school who develop close relationships with peers in their classrooms and are invited to out-of-school family-fun activities.

Individuals alone are not responsible for such accomplishments; together, a welcoming inclusive community environment goes a long way toward facilitating ordinary miracles that can make all the difference in the daily lives of families and their young children. Moreover, teachers, administrators, and others at Jowonio share the beliefs of Deborah Labovitz, an occupational therapist at the Steinhardt School of Education, New York University, who edited the book *Ordinary Miracles: True Stories about Overcoming Obstacles and Surviving Catastrophes* (2003). She wrote:

I believe that every problem has a solution, and we just have not discovered the best one yet for those problems still unresolved; that not only is the glass half full, but refills are on the way. When people tell me that "those who can keep their heads when all about them are losing theirs just don't understand the gravity of the situation," my response is that only those who can keep their heads—and find a ray of hope—can ultimately fix the grave situation. I believe that even if we cannot control the circumstances we are in, we can control our reaction to those circumstances and can turn tragedy into triumph with our own strength and with the help of others. (p. xiii)

It is indeed those small miracles that emerge so unexpectedly that reaffirm parents' beliefs and faith in possibilities for their children—for example, when Sean wondered who had moved his son Ryan, when it was Ryan himself who had moved unseen across the living-room floor in his walker. Sean subsequently returned his son to his original position and then, in disbelief, watched Ryan slowly move his usually immobile feet to touch the floor, inching closer and closer in his walker toward his father. With perseverance, hope, much practice, and sustained support, ordinary miracles do happen—a reflection of many hours of occupational and physical therapy, teaching, affection, and encouragement from school staff and parents.

Adapt, Adapt, Adapt: Assuming Strength and Potential

Within an educational preschool setting, the starting point for adaptation is an assumption of building from strength and potential! Adaptations also are best nurtured within the natural environment of home, school, and communities. These include providing a range of accommodations in terms of behavior, communication, gross and fine motor development, adaptive skills, and abilities such as dressing, feeding, washing, and other aspects of self-care and development, as well as facilitating participation in daily play routines and activities. All of these accommodations are an important part of best practices in an authentic inclusive preschool environment and are an integral dimension of the Jowonio School curriculum, teaching, and programming.

Inherent in the terms *adaptation* and *accommodation* is an underlying tenet of needing to make a change or difference in a task in order to assist with accomplishing a task or activity. On the other hand, within best practices of inclusive education for young children, we believe that the following also are essential qualities and dimensions of adaptations, whatever the need. Adaptations must:

- take place within the context of positive relationships (with family members, teachers, therapists, physicians, peers and other children, and individuals with whom the child is familiar)

- be flexible in terms of diverse natural environments (e.g., home, school, and community settings, those most frequented by the child and family)

- be least restrictive in making the child "appear to be different" or "setting the child apart" from his or her peers (i.e., be as normalizing as possible)

- foster the child's participation in a variety of program and daily activities

- grow with the child as she transitions to kindergarten and the primary elementary grades

- be functional with several different people with whom the child interacts at home, in school, and in the community

- facilitate the child's feeling valued and positive about himself and gaining a sense of accomplishment

- have dimensions that can be "scaffolded" and broken into smaller steps relative to intensity and demands

- facilitate the family's feeling positive and joy about the child's steps toward progress and accomplishment

The impact of being a part of a classroom and school "community" cannot be underestimated in helping to develop positive self-esteem—for young children and their families. Most scholars and educators would agree that a positive sense of self is most readily nurtured within the first 5 years of life!

Celebrating Progress With Every Step

Tasks that come so readily to most children often are a major challenge for infants, toddlers, and preschool children with special health care needs and disabilities. These tasks include a multitude of skills and accomplishments such as:

- rolling over from stomach to back
- sitting up independently
- taking a first step
- imitating sounds or saying a first word
- holding a crayon for the first time
- inserting a puzzle piece in an appropriate spot
- taking a turn with rolling a ball back and forth to a peer or an adult on cue
- singing a song with peers and teachers in circle
- finger-feeding Cheerios or Goldfish crackers
- holding a spoon and bringing to mouth without spilling
- drinking from a cup
- using the toilet for the first time during the day

These are just a few of the tasks that emerge during the first 3 years that parents, caregivers, and teachers may take so much for granted. For many children, accomplishing of these developmental steps and milestones requires expertise and experience of qualified teachers and highly skilled therapists, as well as knowledgeable and compassionate physicians and specialists, depending upon the special needs of the child.

Knowing how and when to offer encouragement and praise to young preschool children is a vital part of genuine inclusive programming. Moreover, this support needs to come from multiple key individuals with whom children have significant relationships—parents or caregivers, siblings, peers in school, teachers, and other professionals. Many scholars and educators have written about the power of positive reinforcement and modeling for toddlers and preschool children (Bovey & Strain, 2013; Hollingsworth & Buysse, 2009; Landy, 2009). In particular, Landy indicated that in order to develop "growth-promoting" environments, teachers and parents can do the following:

- Let children know that they are valued and accepted.
- Acknowledge the successes, behaviors, and abilities of children.

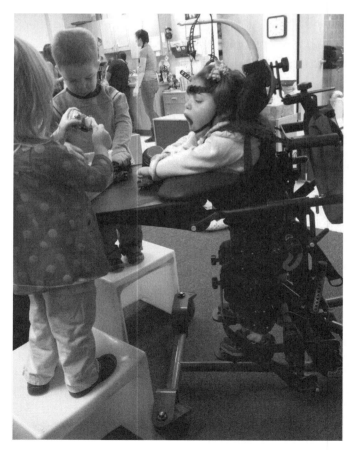

- Structure situations that are likely to help children experience success.

- Give children reasonable control over specific tasks, decisions, and activities, and set effective limits.

- Value the special uniqueness and qualities of children.

- Praise children for attempting difficult or challenging tasks.

- Intervene when children seem to experience failure and appear to be putting themselves down.

- Communicate acceptance, even when children need to be redirected in their behavior.

- Model a sense of optimism and positive sense of self in interactions with other persons in the environment (e.g., family members, classroom peers, other colleagues and adults).

- Be clear about positive expectations.

- Be proactive so that conflicts and adverse situations can be averted as much as possible. (pp. 347–348)

Demonstrating these positive attitudes and behaviors can be extremely powerful in enhancing young children's self-esteem and enabling children to try "the next step." At the same time, parents and teachers can be helpful with supporting peers and siblings to develop and interact in more positive ways within inclusive environments (Guralnick, 2010) by modeling ways for sharing toys, using words to resolve conflicts, modeling strategies for entering play groups, modeling ways to offer praise and encouragement to others, role playing with puppets, having toys and materials that foster collaboration and interactive play, modeling ways to help one another, and encouraging children to observe situations and ask

questions rather than react impulsively. All of these strategies are commonly observed in the Jowonio School.

"It Takes a Village": Learning From Each Other

In her book *Do You Hear What I Hear? Parents and Professionals Working Together for Children With Special Needs*, Janice Fialka (1999) wrote:

Collaboration is the cornerstone to effective inclusive programs. . . . Forming partnerships between professionals and parents of children with special needs is like learning a new dance… The real dance of partnership occurs when all listen to each other's music, try out each other's dance steps, and work toward a new dance that involves the contributions of partners. (Fialka, 1999, quoted in Cate, Diefendorf, McCullough, Peters, & Whaley, 2010, p. 27)

Collaboration, partnerships, and listening are all essential elements of effective, authentic inclusive programs that require a "village" of contributors. As the related fields of neonatology, pediatrics, and other health care professionals advance in terms of technology and improving the survival rates of newborns at earlier gestations (Batshaw, Roizen, & Lotrecchiano, 2011; Ensher et al., 2009) and as professionals learn more about research in epigenetics, it is clear that the incidence of more complex special needs of newborns and young children is rising. This reality is evident in inclusive programs such as the Jowonio School, which serves increasingly diverse populations of toddlers and preschoolers with special health care needs and disabilities. These complexities require that administrative staff, teachers, therapists, other professionals, and families collaborate in planning and implementing developmentally appropriate, effective, programs that meet the needs of all of the children enrolled in inclusive preschool programs. No one discipline has the expertise and experience to develop and carry out the necessary methods, curricula, and strategies. In addition, there is an enormous educational benefit for teachers who integrate speech, language, occupational, and physical therapies into the course of their young children's daily classroom routines and activities. Important questions concerning feeding, positioning, communication, and ways to facilitate interactions with other children can thus be much more readily addressed within the ecology of the natural classroom environment as they arise. Such programming offers a much more powerful intervention for children than individual pull-out services and a much more empowering curriculum for teachers who are able to add to their knowledge base and repertoire of information across disciplines and developmental domains (Buysse, Wesley, & Able-Boone, 2001; Scherak, Kirkpatrick, Nelson, & Propes, 2003). At Jowonio, staff also benefit from weekly opportunities to learn from each other in in-service sessions and training from professionals across disciplines, from within and outside of the school program. Odom and Bailey (2001) highlighted the importance of such professional development:

To plan a high quality inclusive program for children with disabilities, early child education teachers often require the support of and collaboration with specialized staff (e.g., itinerant special education teachers, speech pathologists). (p. 269)

A School for All Learners: Pathways Toward Achievement

Over the years as a result of extensive research, there has been much written about the benefits of inclusive programming for all learners—those who have identified special needs and those who do not. From these findings, researchers and professionals have learned that, for example:

- **All children—those who do and those do not have disabilities—do at least as well in inclusive programs as do other children** who attend more specialized or "select" programs, especially with regard to their social and emotional development (Guralnick, 2001; Rafferty, Piscitelli, & Boettcher, 2003). The presence and quality of early preschool friendships have been found to have long-lasting effects, predicting "aspects of social understanding in the school years such as understanding friends and moral sensitivity . . . and that children who are rejected and who do not form friendships are more likely to have poor social outcomes and to be depressed and maladjusted later" (Landy, 2009, p. 567).

- As is evident in the parent vignette at the beginning of this chapter, **authentic inclusive programs can have enormous positive influences on families of both children with disabilities and those without special needs.** Over many years of working in the fields of pediatrics, neonatology, and early childhood special education with families, we have consistently noted that many parents of children with special needs feel isolated and alone—even those with extended family nearby. Often when infants and very young children are identified as having disabilities, especially with severe and multiple needs, friends separate themselves and drift away. Older siblings, perhaps embarrassed by having a brother or sister with severe special needs, often do not feel comfortable with inviting friends into their homes. If these kinds of situations persist, family members lose one of their most valuable sources of support and strength that is vital to their well-being.

The best authentic inclusive preschool programs focus on working with parents and developing activities in which families can connect with one another and form strong relationships. These connections have been a signature dimension of the Jowonio School, and, for the most part, the friendships that have developed over the years among families with and without disabilities have been a tremendous resource for many. Such supports are essential in view of high stress levels (especially among mothers), depression, social isolation, and separation and divorce that professionals frequently see and which have been noted in research about families of children with disabilities (Cox, Marshall, Mandleco, & Olsen, 2003; Martin & Baker, 2001; Singer & Farkas, 1989; Wang et al., 2004). According to Martin and Baker, most factors that contribute to severe and multiple disabilities occur during the first 3 years of life—a time when supportive inclusive programs can offer invaluable resources to families.

- **Genuine inclusive programs change everyone in significant positive ways— including administrative staff, teachers, and clinical staff.**

  While elusive and often intangible to quantify and document, the power of self-fulfilling prophecies and a commitment to growth and change can be strong determinants of the realization of potential for all people. These are all essential qualities that touch one's sense of self-esteem, confidence, and positive attitudes, among others. These are perhaps the qualities that are most challenging for educators to teach, because they are translated

and communicated in myriad ways and styles among professionals who work with families and young children with special needs. Some of these qualities may include faith, compassion, understanding, ability to empathize with others, ability to listen, and a reflective and caring attitude. These are essential characteristics for developing strong and lasting relationships and resilience in response to adverse situations and events in our lives and assisting others in persevering through difficult times and in sharing the small joys of everyday life. However, in the end, professionals can sense immediately whether the individuals with whom they interact do or do not project and "own" such qualities. From our perspective, these are the very special qualities that are the foundation of authentic and quality inclusive programs for families and for young children with and without disabilities. They are some of the very special qualities that differentiate the Jowonio School and its staff, recognized for almost 50 years of best practices in the field of early childhood education, from many other preschool settings.

Beyond School Walls: Reaching Into the Community

The inclusive program of the Jowonio School has been remarkable in its success in bringing about change within local school districts at the kindergarten and elementary-childhood age levels. As we noted in the opening introductory remarks of this chapter about defining ingredients of quality inclusive schooling, parents and children who have graduated from Jowonio have become advocates for implementation of some of the philosophical principles and features of educational opportunities that they were afforded to their children. This advocacy on behalf of all children with special needs has not been without challenges, including those of developing and monitoring appropriate inclusive programs, maintaining the safety of children with special needs, developing partnerships with teachers and public school staff, facilitating friendships among student classmates, and maintaining resources for families of students with special needs. In reality, many families of children, with and without disabilities, have commented about the marked differences with entering public school systems, feeling alone and much less supported than they had while at the Jowonio School—despite the carefully crafted transitions that the Jowonio staff attempt to establish as children move on to kindergarten. On the other hand, many families, strengthened with their prior experiences of advocacy and commitment to inclusive best practices, have persevered until successfully gaining the services that they deemed essential to the well-being and progress of their sons and daughters.

Many families of children and students with special needs would agree that much remains to be done in the name of best practices of inclusive education in the public schools today, especially with the recent ongoing emphasis on the Common Core curriculum, the stresses on teachers of performance-based assessment, the use of scripted curricula driven by state-mandated requirements, extended hours of the school day in many schools, and the heavy emphasis on academics to the neglect of the development of social-emotional skills among primary and elementary age children. Nonetheless, however challenged, parents who have experienced best practices of inclusive education understand the lifelong benefits for themselves and their children, and their voices continue to be heard!

Chapter Summary

This chapter has focused on the advantages, philosophical basis, and strategies for implementation of authentic inclusive education. In particular, best practices of the Jowonio School, a preschool nationally recognized for its inclusion of a diverse group of 2½- to 5-year-old young children, are described in detail, highlighting signature features of partnerships with families, augmentative systems and adaptations for children with significant disabilities, teamwork among members of the school staff, and extensions of the philosophical base into local public school districts. The benefits and importance of authentic inclusive education for all families and young children in the early years are discussed in detail.

Key Points to Remember

- Genuine inclusive education for preschool children starts with a belief in the strengths and potential of young children and their families of all dispositions, cultures, languages, racial and ethnic groups, and abilities.

- All challenges have solutions; in partnerships with families, professionals just need to find them!

- Genuine inclusive preschool education extends far beyond the classroom, into family living rooms, local community gatherings, local public schools, and other "natural" environments and contexts.

- Genuine inclusive preschool education incorporates the daily routines of families of young children with and without special needs.

- Genuine inclusive preschool education changes perspectives not only of children and families, but also of administrators, teachers, clinical staff, and others who participate in the inclusive environment.

Implications for Families and Professionals

Both the NAEYC and the DEC recommend quality inclusive educational programs for young children. However, determining what that means and what parents are searching for and what professionals are seeking to develop require consideration of several dimensions and variables. Here are a few important factors and elements that contribute to the foundation for best practices in inclusive preschool education:

- administrators who are experienced in working with families and young children with and without special needs, who are knowledgeable about community resources and who have extensive experience in working with diverse teaching and clinical staff
- teaching staff who are trained and who have experience in working with families and young children with and without special needs
- clinical staff (i.e., speech, occupational, physical therapists, social workers, nurses, physicians, and psychologists) who are trained in working with families and diverse groups of young children with a range of special behavioral, learning, sensory, physical, and special health care needs, and who are experienced in supporting and collaborating with teaching staff
- an accessible, bright, and clean physical setting
- a vibrant and ongoing in-service training program
- team meetings during the school program for brainstorming and planning programs for children with and without special needs

- adequate financial resources to address special needs, as necessary
- contemporary, culturally relevant toys and teaching materials for clinical and teaching staff
- clearly written and understood staff responsibilities
- a clearly defined, positive approach for guiding the challenging behavior of all children
- defined developmentally appropriate curricula and evaluation processes for children to determine evidence of learning, and for guiding all teaching and clinical staff in program planning and implementation
- clinical and teaching staff who are knowledgeable about strategies for adaptation and augmentative systems, who genuinely enjoy working with young children and their families
- space for gross motor indoor and outdoor play activities
- an established system for collecting child and program data for monitoring child progress and making program decisions and improvements

In the end, as Schwartz, Odom, and Sandall (quoted in Cate et al., 2010, p. 5) wrote, in order to ensure positive outcomes for all children, "programs, not children, have to be 'ready for inclusion,'" because their future is in our hands!

References

Barnes, E., & Jowonio staff. (2013). Ingredients for quality inclusive schooling. *School News, 17*(2), 10.

Batshaw, M. L., Roizen, N. J., & Lotrecchiano, G. R. (Eds.). (2011). *Children with disabilities* (7th ed.). Baltimore, MD: Brookes.

Beckstrand, K., Pienkowski, T., Powers, S., & Scanlon, J. (2016). Early intervention at home: When, why, and how? In G. L. Ensher & D. A. Clark (Eds.), *The early years: Foundations for best practice with special children and their families* (pp. 353–365). Washington, DC: ZERO TO THREE.

Bovey, T., & Strain, P. (2013). *Promoting positive peer social interactions.* Champaign, IL: Center on the Social and Emotional Foundations for Early Learning.

Buysse, V., Wesley, P. W., & Able-Boone, H. (2001). Innovations in professional development: Creating communities of practice to support inclusion. In M. J. Guralnick (Ed.), *Early childhood inclusion: Focus on change* (pp. 179–200). Baltimore, MD: Brookes.

Cate, D., Diefendorf, M., McCullough, K., Peters, M., & Whaley, K. (2010). *Quality indicators of inclusive programs/practices.* National Early Childhood Technical Assistance Center. Retrieved from www.nectac.org/~pdfs/pubs/qualityindicatorsinclusion.pdf

Cox, A. M., Marshall, E. S., Mandleco, B., & Olsen, S. F. (2003). Coping responses to daily life stressors of children who have a sibling with a disability. *Journal of Family Nursing, 9*(4), 397–413.

Division of Early Childhood & National Association for the Education of Young Children. (2009). *Early childhood inclusion: A joint position statement of the Division for Early Childhood (DEC) and the National Association for the Education of Young Children (NAEYC).* Washington, DC: Author.

Ensher, G. L., & Clark, D. A. (2011). *Relationship-centered practices in early childhood: Working with families, infants, and young children at risk.* Baltimore, MD: Brookes.

Ensher, G. L., Clark, D. A., & Songer, N. S. (2009). *Families, infants, and young children at risk: Pathways to best practice.* Baltimore, MD: Brookes.

Fialka, J. (1999). *Do you hear what I hear? Parents and professionals working together for children with special needs.* Ann Arbor, MI: Proctor Publications.

Guralnick, M. J. (2001). A framework for change in early childhood inclusion. In M. J. Guralnick (Ed.), *Early childhood inclusion: Focus on change* (pp. 3–35). Baltimore, MD: Brookes.

Guralnick, M. J. (2010). Early intervention approaches to enhance the peer related social competence of young children with developmental delays: A historical perspective. *Infants & Young Children, 23*(2), 75–83.

Hanson, M. J., & Lynch, E. W. (2013). *Understanding FAMILIES: Supportive approaches to diversity, disability, and risk* (2nd ed.). Baltimore, MD: Brookes.

Hollingsworth, H. L., & Buysse, V. (2009). Establishing friendships in early childhood inclusive settings: What roles do parents and teachers play? *Journal of Early Intervention, 31*(4), 287–307.

Hyman, M., & Vercelloni, E. (2013). Family corner: Jowonio . . . It's not just a preschool! *School News, 17*(2), 18.

Kunc, N. (1992). *The need to belong: Rediscovering Maslow's hierarchy of needs.* Retrieved from http://broadreachtraining.com/articles/armaslow.htm

Labovitz, D. R. (2003). *Ordinary miracles: True stories about overcoming obstacles and surviving catastrophes.* Thorofare, NJ: SLACK Incorporated.

Landy, S. (2009). *Pathways to competence: Encouraging healthy social and emotional development in young children* (2nd ed.). Baltimore, MD: Brookes.

Martin, S. S., & Baker, D. C. (2001, January 31–February 2). *Families and children with severe disabilities: Daily lives, systems, and concerns.* Paper presented at the meeting of the American Association of Behavioral and Social Sciences, Las Vegas, NV.

Odom, S. L., & Bailey, D. (2001). Inclusive preschool programs: Classroom ecology and child outcomes. In M. J. Guralnick (Ed.), *Early childhood education: A focus for change* (pp. 253–276). Baltimore, MD: Brookes.

Rafferty, Y., Piscitelli, V., & Boettcher, C. (2003). The impact of inclusion on language development and social competence among preschoolers with disabilities. *Exceptional Children, 69*(4), 467–479.

Scherak, K. M., Kirkpatrick, D. B., Nelson, K. C., & Propes, J. H. (2003). Physical therapy in preschool classrooms: Successful integration of therapy into classroom routines. *Pediatric Physical Therapy, 15*(2), 93–104.

Singer, L., & Farkas, K. J. (1989). The impact of infant disabilities on maternal perception of stress. *Family Relations, 38*(4), 444–449.

Wang, M., Turnbull, A. P., Summers, J. A., Little, T. D., Poston, D. J., Mannan, H., . . . Turnbull, R. (2004). Severity of disability and income as predictors of parent satisfaction with their family quality of life during early childhood years. *Research & Practice for Persons With Severe Disabilities, 29*(2), 82–94.

AFTERWORD

Foundations for Best Practices

Gail L. Ensher and David A. Clark

In closing and as we think about foundations for best practice in our respective fields on behalf of families, infants, and young children with special needs, we have taken the reader along four key pathways in this book:

- Development and Well-Being of Infants and Young Children (Part 1)

- Screening and Assessment of Infants and Young Children (Part 2)

- Medical and Developmental Problems in Infants and Young Children (Part 3)

- Collaborative Care, Community Networks, and Early Intervention (Part 4)

We would like the reader to keep in mind several key points:

- **Maintain a strength-based perspective.** In working with families, infants, and young children, all learn best when given the foundation of a strength-based perspective. Such a philosophy does not deny the realities and challenges that many families, young children, and service providers face in today's world; however, it acknowledges and validates the competence and abilities that all bring to the table and moves beyond deficit approaches that have so long pervaded the educational, medical, and clinical professions of service provision in the United States.

- **Use relationship-based practices.** Research in our respective educational, medical, and clinical fields has provided us with an amazing fund of information and technology (and will continue to do so in the future), but such knowledge and science must be firmly grounded in the rich resources of relationship-based practices as we work and interact with young children and their families.

- **Address bias and socioeconomic disparities.** Someone once said that "the more things change, the more they stay the same." Although we live in a fast-paced, ever-changing world with diverse cultures, ethnic groups, languages, income and educational levels, and numerous other differences, some needs and issues continue to remain "the same." Mental health illness, bias, violence, child abuse and neglect, and widespread disparities between those who have and those who do not persist, and they are perhaps the most challenging concerns to be moved to new visions with new possibilities. The continuing negative, disempowering impact of these issues on the lives of infants, young children, and families is utterly unacceptable in a country of such wealth and opportunity. We linger with the misconception that these challenges affect only the "poor and less affluent." Such could not be further from existing realities in this country. They may be more hidden or initially less evident; however, serious concerns of mental health and mental illness, for example, in the United States cut across all age, educational, and income levels of all families and young children from infants to toddlers to preschool on up.

We have the knowledge and technology in this country to bring about truly meaningful change

in the lives of young children and their families. The question for all of our readers and ourselves is: Will we?

In their seminal book, *From Neurons to Neighborhoods: The Science of Early Childhood Development*, Shonkoff and Phillips (National Research Council & Institute of Medicine, 2000) wrote:

State-of-the-art knowledge about early childhood development is multidimensional and cross-disciplinary. It extends from painstaking efforts to understand the evolving circuitry and biochemistry of the immature brain to large-scale investigations of how family characteristics, neighborhood influences, and cultural values affect the well-being of children as they grow up. It includes studies of infants, toddlers, and preschoolers with a broad range of typical and atypical behavioral patterns, as well as young children with diagnosed developmental disabilities. It is derived from a variety of quantitative and qualitative research methods that have been used to understand the process of development as it unfolds, as well as from evaluation of efforts to alter its course.

[Across the years], four overarching themes . . .have guided scientific inquiry and have important implications for the design and implementation of the nation's early childhood policies: (1) all children are born wired for feelings and ready to learn, (2) early environments matter and nurturing relationships are essential, (3) society is changing and the needs of young children are not being addressed, and (4) interactions among early childhood science, policy, and practice are problematic and demand dramatic rethinking. (p. 285)

The time has come to stop blaming parents, communities, business, and government—and to shape a shared agenda to ensure both a rewarding childhood and a promising future for all children—matching needs and capabilities;

supporting families in their efforts toward creating safe and nurturing environments that promise healthy physical, cognitive, linguistic, social, emotional, and moral development of young children, as well drawing upon the wealth of community resources to support family well-being (National Research Council & Institute of Medicine, 2000, p. 414).

This is the challenge for families, service providers, policymakers, and researchers alike on behalf of infants and young children in this country. The task is well within our reach! Moving the vision to reality in the 21st century is the yet-to-be fulfilled charge and goal for all of us. We hold the future of all children with special needs in our hands!

Reference

National Research Council & Institute of Medicine. (2000). J. P. Shonkoff & D. A. Phillips (Eds.), *From neurons to neighborhoods: The science of early childhood development.* Washington, DC: National Academy Press.

About the Authors

Gail L. Ensher, EdD

Professor of Education, Teaching and
Leadership Programs, School of Education,
  Syracuse University
  155 Huntington Hall
  Syracuse, NY 13244

In addition to her work as professor of education for more than 40 years at Syracuse University, Dr. Ensher is the coordinator of two master's degree programs in the School of Education at Syracuse University: Early Childhood Special Education, and the Inclusive Program in Severe and Multiple Disabilities. She received her doctorate in special education from Boston University in 1971, and prior to that time taught for 3 years in Hanover, New Hampshire, and in Quincy, Massachusetts. Prior to coming to Syracuse University, she held a position as assistant professor at the Pennsylvania State University in State College.

For many years, Dr. Ensher has been and continues to be actively involved in teaching, writing, research, and community service related to families and young children who are at risk for or who have developmental disabilities. She works in close partnership with the Jowonio School, a nationally known inclusive educational setting for preschool children.

At Syracuse, she teaches graduate-level courses about methods and curricula in early childhood special education, families of young children with special needs, assessment and early intervention, and the theoretical foundations of early childhood special education. She also supervises graduate students in their clinical and field placements as they prepare to work with infants, young children, and their families.

Dr. Ensher has authored or coauthored several books about families, infants, and young children with special needs. These include *Partners in Play: Assessing Infants and Toddlers in Natural Contexts* (Delmar-Thompson/Cengage Learning); *Newborns at Risk: Medical Care and Psycho-Educational Intervention* (Aspen Publishers, two editions); *Families, Infants, and Young Children at Risk: Pathways to Best Practice* (Brookes); and *Relationship-Centered Practices in Early Childhood: Working With Families, Infants, and Young Children at Risk* (Brookes).

Dr. Ensher is the proud mother of two daughters adopted from Calcutta, India—Kimberly and Lindsey—both teachers of young children, and she became a first-time grandmother in early February 2015.

David A. Clark, MD

Professor and Martha Lepow Chairman
of Pediatrics, Professor of Obstetrics and
Gynecology, Albany Medical College; Director,
Children's Hospital at Albany Medical Center
  43 New Scotland Avenue
  Albany, NY 12208

Dr. Clark is a pediatrician and neonatologist who trained at North Carolina Memorial Hospital, University of North Carolina at Chapel Hill, and completed a neonatology fellowship at Rainbow Babies and Children's Hospital, Case Western Reserve University in Cleveland, Ohio, and State University of New York, Upstate Medical Center, in Syracuse. Dr. Clark's certifications include Diplomate, American Board of Pediatrics; the American Board of Pediatrics, Sub-Board of Neonatal-Perinatal Medicine; and the Neonatal Resuscitation Program, Regional Instructor.

Dr. Clark is a member of more than 25 professional societies including the American Academy of Pediatrics—Fellow, Section on Perinatal Pediatrics, Section on Gastroenterology and Nutrition, Section on Transport Medicine, and Critical Care Section; the Society of Pediatric Research; American College of Nutrition; American Pediatric Society; and the New York Academy of Sciences.

Dr. Clark's curriculum vita includes more than 150 peer-reviewed publications; five books, more than 300 abstracts, and numerous invited chapters, reviews, and national and international presentations.

Dr. Clark is the father of three daughters and the grandfather of six, including William David (WD), who tragically died during Hurricane Katrina at 4 years old.

Contributing Authors

Darius Adams, MD
Associate Professor of Pediatrics
Albany Medical College
Albany, NY
Director, Personalized Genomic Medicine
Atlantic Health System
Morristown, NJ 07960

Ellen Barnes, MS, PhD
Director
Jowonio School
3049 East Genesee Street
Syracuse, NY 13224

Katherine Beckstrand, MS
Itinerant Early Childhood Special Education
Teacher/Evaluator
Liberty Resources—Post
1045 James Street, Suite 100
Syracuse, NY 13203

Melinda Clark, MD
Associate Professor of Pediatrics
Albany Medical College
Children's Hospital at Albany Medical Center
43 New Scotland Avenue
Albany, NY 12208

James J. Cummings, MD
Professor of Pediatrics
Albany Medical College
Children's Hospital at Albany Medical Center
43 New Scotland Avenue
Albany, NY 12208

Melissa M. Doyle, PhD, LCSW-R
Associate Professor of Pediatrics
Co-Director of Developmental Behavioral
Pediatrics
Children's Hospital at Albany Medical Center
Albany Medical College
Albany, NY 12208

Marilyn A. Fisher, MD, MS
Associate Professor of Pediatrics
Albany Medical College
Children's Hospital at Albany Medical Center
43 New Scotland Avenue
Albany, NY 12208

Susan A. Furdon, MS, RN, CNS, NNP-BC
Instructor in Pediatrics
Albany Medical College
Albany, NY 12208

Colleen Guthrie, MS
Teacher/Early Childhood Special Education
Jowonio School
3049 East Genesee Street
Syracuse, NY 13224

Laura A. Jenkins, MS
OTR-L Coordinator of Center-Based Toddler
Early Intervention Program
Liberty Resources—Post
1045 James Street, Suite 100
Syacuse, NY 13203

Upender K. Munshi, MBBS, MD
Professor of Pediatrics
Albany Medical College
Albany, NY 12208

Tara Pienkowski, MS
Itinerant Teacher in Early Childhood Special
Education, Certified DIR Expert, Teacher Team
Trainer and Supervisor
Liberty Resources—Post
1045 James Street, Suite 100
Syracuse, NY 13203

Joaquim M. B. Pinheiro, MD, MPH
Professor of Pediatrics
Director, Neonatal-Perinatal Medicine Fellowship
Program
Albany Medical College
Children's Hospital at Albany Medical Center
43 New Scotland Avenue
Albany, NY 12208

Sandy Powers, MS
Itinerant Early Childhood Special Education
Teacher, DIR Team Leader, ICDL, DIR Certified
Expert
Liberty Resources—Post
1045 James Street, Suite 100
Syracuse, NY 13203

Lori Saile, MS, CAS
Associate Director
Jowonio School
3049 East Genesee Street
Syracuse, NY 13224

Jillian T. Scanlon, MS
Early Childhood Mental Health Consultant
School of Science and Education
Penn State Harrisburg Capital Area Early
Childhood Training Institute
2001 N. Front Street
Building 1, Suite 314
Harrisburg, PA 17102

Mary Beth Sullivan, MS
Speech-Language Pathologist and Feeding
Specialist
Margaret L. Williams Developmental Evaluation
Center
215 Bassett Street
Syracuse, NY 13210

Abigail R. Watson, MD
Assistant Professor of Pediatrics
Albany Medical Center
Children's Hospital at Albany Medical Center
43 New Scotland Avenue
Albany, NY 12208

Photo Credits

Part 1
p. 9: Courtesy of Lindsey Kurak and Mary Jo Champlin

Chapter 1
pp. 13, 16 (top), 22: David Clark
p. 14: Marc and Emily Manuel
pp. 15, 16 (bottom): Jeanne Schmidt
p. 17: Wendy Harbour and Tracey Villiinski
pp. 18, 19: Michelle and Jerome Garciano

Chapter 2
p. 50: Jeanne Schmidt
p. 51: Michelle and Jerome Garciano
p. 65: Lindsey Kurak and Kimberly Ensher

Chapter 3
pp. 77, 90, 91: David Clark

Chapter 4
p. 110: David Clark

Part 2
p. 119: Kimberly Ensher and BrandiLee Schafran

Chapter 5
p. 122: Lindsey Kurak

Chapter 6
pp. 134, 141: David Clark
pp. 136, 139: Michelle and Jerome Garciano

Part 3
p. 155: Kimberly Ensher and Michele Provo

Chapter 7
pp. 169, 170, 171: David Clark

Chapter 10
p. 218: David Clark

Chapter 12
pp. 252, 253: Laura Jenkins and Mary-Beth Sullivan

Chapter 13
pp. 271, 278, 280, 283, 284, 285: Jowonio School staff

Part 4
p. 301: Jowonio School staff

Chapter 14
pp. 304, 309: Staci and Kelly Toia
p. 305: Marc and Emily Manuel
p. 312: David Clark

Chapter 16
p. 346: David Clark

Chapter 18
pp. 368, 369, 370, 371, 375, 376: Jowonio School staff
p. 374: Michele Provo

Afterword
p. 384: David Clark
p. 385: (left) Staci and Kelly Toia, (right) David Clark

Index

Note: Page numbers in *italics* indicate figures and tables.

A